Teaching Inclusively

Resources for Course, Department & Institutional Change in Higher Education

Edited by Mathew L. Ouellett

NEW FORUMS PRESS INC.

Published in the United States of America
by New Forums Press, Inc.1018 S. Lewis St.
Stillwater, OK 74074
www.newforums.com

Library of Congress Cataloging-in-Publication Data

Teaching inclusively : resources for course, department and institutional change in higher education / edited by Mathew L. Ouellett.
p. cm. — (New Forums faculty development series)
Includes bibliographical references.
ISBN 1-58107-113-2
1. Multicultural education—United States. 2. College teaching—Social aspects—United States. 3. Education, Higher—United States—Curricula. I. Ouellett, Mathew L., 1957- II. Series.
LC1099.3.T436 2005
378.1'2—dc22

2005025136

This book may be ordered in bulk quantities at discount from New Forums Press, Inc., P.O. Box 876, Stillwater, OK 74076 [Federal I.D. No. 73 1123239]. Printed in the United States of America.

International Standard Book Number: 1-58107-113-2

About the Cover

"The Color of Words VI," 2002, 50-by-$46^{1/4}$-inch Acrylic on Linen, by Wosene Worke Kosrof. Photographed by Black Cat Studio, San Rafael, CA.

For over 25 years, Ethiopian-born Wosene Worke Kosrof has explored the esthetic potential of language using the written symbols of his native Amharic as the major compositional element in his work. His work is represented in the permanent collections of museums in Africa, the United States and Europe including the National Museum of African Art, Smithsonian Institution and the Library of Congress. He currently maintains a studio in Oakland, California and resides in Berkeley, California.

The New Forums Faculty Development Series

New Forums Press presents another fine work in the Faculty Development Series. The titles in the series, including *The Journal of Faculty Development* currently being published in volume 20, offer faculty development practitioners a wealth of valuable information and guidance for enhancing professional development in higher education.

Series Senior Editor

Dr. Christine A. Stanley, Texas A&M University

Series Board Members

Dr. Edward Neal, University of North Carolina–Chapel Hill
Dr. Douglas Dollar, New Forums Press

Other Titles in the Faculty Development Series

Developing Practitioners: A Handbook of Contextual Supervision, by Edwin G. Ralph

Practically Speaking: A Sourcebook for Instructional Consultants in Higher Education, edited by Kathleen Brinko and Robert Menges

Face to Face: A Sourcebook of Individual Consultation Techniques for Faculty/Instructional Developers, edited by Karron G. Lewis and Joyce T. Povlacs Lunde

Professors as Writers: A Self-help Guide to Productive Writing, by Robert Boice

Writing Your Way to Success: Finding Your Own Voice in Academic Publishing, by Susan Drake and Glen Jones

Making Time, Making Change: Avoiding Overload in College Teaching, by Douglas Reimondo Robertson

Chalk Talk: E-advice from Jonas Chalk, Legendary College Teacher, by Donna M. Qualters and Miriam Rosalyn Diamond

Contexts for Learning: Institutional Strategies for Managing Curricular Change Through Assessment, edited by Bruce Keith

New Faculty Professional Development: Planning an Ideal Program, by Henryk Marcinkiewicz and Terrence Doyle

Cases for Community College Teachers: Thought-Provoking and Practical Solutions for Community College Educators, by Rebecca Kamm

Contents

Introduction

Creating multicultural classroom environments has been one of the most challenging endeavors to face college and university campuses over the past several decades. To help instructors address individual course innovation and teaching development goals related to diversity, teachers, faculty and instructional developers, and academic administrators have developed and shared useful classroom-based strategies and resources. More recently, however, teaching centers, faculty, and instructional developers have been called upon to structure similar opportunities (e.g., consultation support, programming) to foster the collegiality and collaboration necessary for multicultural change goals at the department, college, and university-wide levels.

Our contemporary challenge is to align faculty and organizational development for diversity initiatives within the context of campus cultures. Understandably, many individual faculty members who witnessed and/or participated in social justice and diversity programs during the '70s, '80s, and '90s can be susceptible to a "been there, done that" attitude about such initiatives. However, the lack of substantive progress on these issues points to our collective need for open, ongoing dialogues that introduce new tools of analysis and fresh strategies for sustaining such change efforts.

Teaching Inclusively brings together a broad array of current "best practices" in the design, implementation, and assessment of faculty development opportunities oriented toward more inclusive teaching and learning environments. This volume advocates for more transparent connections between change initiatives at individual, departmental, and college-wide levels by highlighting the ways in which such practices and change goals can relate to and support each other, thus addressing a noticeable absence in the current available literature. The contributors to this volume present readers with a balance between theoretical models and demonstration projects that address change processes at three levels: individual courses, programs and departments, and across schools and institutions. In addition, there are descriptions of current, multi-year or multi-phase efforts at both departmental and organizational levels. Whenever possible, the contributors include their perspectives on important lessons learned from their efforts. Finally, we offer resource materials that promise concrete support for applications.

Part I addresses models and perspectives that help to conceptualize, implement and assess diversity-related instructional and faculty development programs at the systemic level. Contributors offer models and descriptions of practices aimed at making transparent the values, beliefs, and goals that shape institutional and classroom climates. Note that in the context of this volume, "diversity" is deliberately defined broadly to encourage a more systemic approach to the analyses of and response to diversity-related issues. For many readers, this may offer new dimensions and greater texture to their current conceptualization of diversity. This section reflects the contributors' interests in analytical tools and organizational frameworks useful in addressing individual, departmental, and institutional changes. Whenever appropriate, authors in this section identify a range of practical applications, such as course-based efforts in the major to courses that fulfill general education requirements.

In Part II, contributors describe change initiatives that use departments (or programs) as the unit of analysis for diversity-related change efforts. In this section, readers will benefit from the descriptions and assessments of programs designed specifically to bring faculty and academic administrators together in cohorts to address diversity and teaching development goals within the disciplines in a sustained dialogue on diversity. Assessment of current efforts indicate that such initiatives illuminate the content, skills, and values necessary for sustained change and that such experiences can become important models for broader institutional change efforts.

In Part III, the contributors discuss multicultural change efforts at the college or institutional level directed at creating and sustaining more inclusive teaching and learning communities. Additionally, contributors describe programs and practices useful in addressing diversity issues across the disciplines as well as within discipline-specific contexts. Particular emphasis is placed on understanding how systematic multicultural organizational change can support a departmental or campus-wide emphasis on teaching inclusively. These chapters offer rich descriptions of efforts at institutions learning how to address diversity-related initiatives in a sustainable, comprehensive manner. Such efforts can help others determine how best to assess their organization's needs and strengths, and to determine what is needed in the larger environment to initiate and sustain successful pro-equity organizational change and innovations.

Finally, Part IV pays particular attention to resources and program models particularly useful for faculty developers and centers. Contributors to this section provide a rich set of tools for self- and course-assessment, planning for new or revised programs, and suggesting well-proven strategies for approaches to diversity-related teaching development and organizational change initiatives. These include descriptions of specific, "hands on" consultation practices, workshop exercises, resource materials, and design elements (e.g., use of writing prompts) proven effective across the disciplines in engaging faculty in reflection, analysis, dialogue and innovation related to diversity-related teaching development goals.

In conclusion, this volume seeks to respond to the challenge of initiating fresh, results-oriented, and context-specific dialogues on teaching inclusively by providing an overview of effective faculty, instructional, and organizational development programs that address a wide range of diversity-related goals. By highlighting the "best practices" of change on the individual, departmental, and institutional levels in the same volume, the editors hope that readers will more clearly see the possibilities and intersectionality of diversity initiatives on their campuses, and beyond.

A project of this scope is necessarily a collective effort. I begin by thanking all of the contributing authors for their generosity and spirit of collaboration. Colleagues from the University of Massachusetts Amherst that offered enormous support and guidance to this project include Heather Bourne, Sean Robins, and Sarah Bramley; Mary Deane Sorcinelli, Bailey Jackson, Pat Griffin, Maurianne Adams, and Barbara Love; Laura Wright, and Jung Yun (editors extraordinaire). I thank Anne Miller who understands how to lead organizational change better than anyone else I know. More broadly, I also thank Nancy Ramsay, Christine Stanley, Thomas S. Edwards, Lisa Kornetsky and Rebecca Leonard who all helped to keep this project on the right theoretical and practical tracks. My long-standing partner in teaching, Edith Fraser, and our Smith College colleagues, Kathryn Basham, Mary Hall, Mary Gannon, Alex Deschamps, Josh Miller, Ann Marie Garran, Victor Mealy and Lois Bass, contributed invaluably by their ongoing friendships and willingness to share their personal and collective insights and strategies. And finally, but most importantly, I thank Ronald G. Parent.

Mathew L. Ouellett,
University of Massachusetts Amherst
April 14, 2005

About the Editor

Mathew L. Ouellett is the Associate Director of the Center for Teaching at the University of Massachusetts Amherst. In this capacity, he works closely with faculty members, department chairs, and deans to implement a broad range of teaching development and diversity-related programs for faculty and graduate students across the disciplines, including the year-long teaching development fellowship, *Teaching and Learning in the Diverse Classroom Faculty and Teaching Assistant Development Program*. In addition to his responsibilities at the Center for Teaching, Dr. Ouellett serves as an adjunct faculty member in the School of Education, University of Massachusetts Amherst, where he regularly teaches EDUC 595K: Introduction to College Teaching. Additionally, he is a summer lecturer in the Smith College School for Social Work where he team teaches both required and elective courses on the implications of race and racism for social work practice in the United States.

Dr. Ouellett is past president of the New England Faculty Development Consortium and served as a member of the executive board of the Professional and Organizational Development Network in Higher Education (POD). He has published a number of articles and book chapters on a broad range of research and teaching interests including: teaching inclusively, multicultural education, and organization development. He is also regularly invited to present at regional and national faculty development institutes. Dr. Ouellett has most recently been the recipient of research support from the Ford Foundation, Annie E. Casey Foundation, and the Richard Nathan Trusts through the Institute for Gay and Lesbian Studies, Amherst, Massachusetts.

I. Theoretical Frameworks and Useful Models

Chapter 1
The Theory and Practice of Multicultural Organization Development in Education

Bailey W. Jackson

This chapter begins with an overview of the development and evolution of multicultural organization development (MCOD) in the private corporate sector. Next, this chapter explores how MCOD is currently being transformed and adopted as a tool for supporting social justice and social diversity in both K-12 and higher education systems. Finally, the chapter reviews the core assumptions behind the theory and practice of MCOD with particular emphasis placed on those modifications beyond the corporate application that must be considered for this model to be most effective in K-12 schools, school districts and higher education systems.

Historical Overview

The pursuit of what is currently termed social justice and diversity, whether for moral reasons, legal reasons, or in the service of a system's mission, has been a priority for both corporate and educational organizations for several decades. While corporate and educational sectors often emphasize these priorities for different reasons, and tend to favor strategies that are most consistent with their individual missions and goals, they also share in common a number of objectives and tactics in their effort to become multicultural organizations (MCO).

Over twenty years ago, researchers and practitioners in various applied behavioral sciences interested in understanding organization development (OD), came together with those concentrating on issues related to "social diversity" in the workplace. The result of this fusion, multicultural organization development (MCOD), has developed and evolved into a model and set of practices that continues to show promise as an approach for change agents working with systems seeking to become fully multicultural organizations

This union between OD and diversity, while perhaps obvious today, was slow to develop. Prior to the interconnection of OD with diversity, internal and external change agents working to develop effective high performing businesses with techniques that would enhance their competitive advantage generally addressed diversity issues in the workplace only as a module in a large systems change initiative. In actuality, even that module only focused on what is now referred to as "social justice" rather than "social diversity," terms that are often used interchangeably. In MCOD terminology, these terms are meant to describe different aspects of the social or organizational change agenda. Organizational change interventions focused on social diversity tend to address issues related to "social group inclusion". The goals of this type of intervention focus on building an organizational culture that includes people from various social identity groups based on differences in race, ethnicity, gender, sexual orientation, social/economic class, religion, nationality, age, and other socially defined group identities. A change effort with a social justice focus would concentrate on the elimination of racism, sexism, heterosexism, classism, anti-Semitism, and other manifestations of social oppression or social injustice. While MCOD acknowledges the difference between the justice and diversity agenda, many practitioners use the term *diversity* to refer to both social justice and social diversity concerns.

Much of the literature on the theory and practice of OD was originally intended to speak to, and about, the business community. OD was rarely seen to have much widespread consequence or value for education systems and its values were seen as "too corporate." On the occasions when practitioners were given the chance to introduce OD concepts and strategies into an education system, it was often seen as missing the mark. Often this lack of fit resulted from the OD practitioner's failure to consider the unique attributes of education systems (e.g., organizational structures, accepted cultural norms, decision-making processes, and use of language). This failure of OD to reflect the values and "speak the language" of education organizations could be especially apparent in the context of large research campuses, which are often quite different from business environments.

In the education community, social justice has primarily been sought through a focus on divisions of student affairs, the creation of curricular interventions, focused student and faculty recruitment efforts, and the institution of campus policies and procedures. These efforts often attempted to create a civil and diverse community through policy legislation. The most popular change strategies were often intended to persuade individuals in the education system that to be supportive of social justice and diversity was to be a good citizen of the academic community.

In large part, OD and the strategies for pursuing diversity are still separate enterprises in education. However, recently OD practitioners have begun to recognize those parts of OD theory and practice that can be modified to be of service to educational organizations and have begun to adapt their theories and practices and to better communicate how their field can support change efforts in education systems. On the same note, diversity practitioners and theorists are now better able to understand how OD models can help them address holistically the needs of education organizations to make them healthier systems and, therefore, better able to achieve and sustain their goals of diversity and social justice.

Bringing OD, Social Justice and Social Diversity Together

Applied behavioral scientists that were grounded in both OD and diversity were the first to recognize or consider the integration of these two change agendas (Miller & Katz, 2002; Cox, 2001; Thomas, 1996; Thomas, 1992; Jackson, Foster, Jackson, Cross, & Hardiman, 1988; Jamison, 1987). Kaleel Jamison (1987) was one of the first to write about the possibility of justice, or affirmative action work in systems as having a positive effect on systems health in other areas and that the reverse was also true. Jackson and Hardiman were among the first theorists and practitioners to bring OD, social justice, and diversity together as MCOD and it was Jackson and Holvino who first contributed this work to the literatures

Jackson and Hardiman recognized that their work in systems to address the behaviors and attitudes related to various forms of discrimination manifested by individual managers and workers, was indeed necessary, but not sufficient, to produce the kind of systemic change that would result in an increasingly socially just system, much less to move the system to become a multicultural organization (MCO). Based on their work in both OD and diversity, or social justice in the workplace, race relations, and social identity development, they theorized that to achieve the vision of a MCO it would be necessary to view *the system* as the target of change, or the client, rather than the individuals in the system. This perspective was based on their conceptualization of organizations as organic or "open." By this, they meant that systems, like individuals, can grow, adapt, and change and could therefore be systematically influenced to become MCOs.

The education community has traveled a different road to get to the point of recognizing that the entire system was the key unit of change for becoming a MCO. They have come to recognize that individual consciousness-raising, education, and behavior change in support of social justice and social diversity must be approached in the context of a set of change goals for the whole campus (or system). Currently, there are a number of educational systems and campuses pursuing change in their core elements (mission, management practices, teaching and learning approaches and content, personnel profile and the general learning/working environment) using forms of MCOD theory and practice.

By presenting the theoretical tenants of MCOD and the practice of MCOD, this chapter presents the essence of what MCOD has become over time as it has been applied to educational systems.

Assumptions Behind the Theory and Practice of MCOD

The assumption that "consciousness raising and training activities for individuals in systems may be necessary but not sufficient" to produce systems change is one of the assumptions that is embedded in MCOD theory and practice. Others include the assumption that:

- *Systems are not simply good, "multicultural," or bad, "monocultural."* Organizations exist on a developmental continuum with monocultural and multicultural on opposite ends. It is important to understand where the campus (or system) is located on this continuum when the intervention begins. Then, and only then, can we operate from an accurate diagnosis when developing change goals and intervention plans for the educational system.
- *The change process needs to be pursued with a clear vision of the "ideal" end state, or MCO vision, in mind.* A well-articulated vision is a manifestation of the ideal MCO and needs to inform all aspects of the change process. Only with a clear sense of the "ideal" can the data help to describe the current or "real" situation with any meaning. In addition, it is only when one juxtaposes the ideal with the real and acknowledges the resulting discrepancies will the most important issues and problems emerge.
- *The picture of the "real" should be derived from an internal assessment process.* A structured assessment that can be used to identify and describe the current state of diversity and social justice in the system should be used to establish the baseline or current state of what "is," in the system.
- *Ownership of the assessment process is a key to success.* A significant majority of the members of the educational system must feel ownership of data that describe what "*is,*" the vision that describes the ideal or the *"ought,"* and the problems that have emerged from the comparing of the real to the ideal. They must also "own" the identification of the change goals and any sense of priority in working to remove those problems for an MCOD initiative to be a success.
- *Significant systemic change in social justice and diversity will only occur when there is someone monitoring and facilitating the process.* In any

change process, there is a natural pull back towards the status quo. Change occurs when there is a commitment to stay with the change effort over time and there is significant support for the organization as it learns to be a MCO. Like individual change efforts, education systems benefit from regular feedback and support to recalibrate their efforts.

- *It must be clear that the pursuit of the goal of becoming a MCO is in the best interests of those who live, learn and work in the system.* The education system must see the MCOD change goals as integral to and serving the overarching health and well being of the system. Only when the change goals link to and facilitate the achievement of the system's overall mission, will efforts to become a MCO be successful and sustainable.

Three Major Elements of MCOD

With these assumptions in mind, the theory and practice of MCOD in both business and education was further developed around three major elements: 1) The MCOD Goal; 2) The MCOD Developmental Stages; and 3) the MCOD Change Processes.

The MCOD Goal

The first element of an MCO systems change effort focuses on the goal of the MCOD effort. Typically, systems enter into an MCOD process because they understand or believe that a system that manages its human resources well has a greater chance of achieving its overall mission. A system that is invested in its human resources also recognizes that to develop and maintain a strong, productive and high performing human resource system, there must be an effective management of social justice and social diversity in that education system. *An MCO is thought of as a system that seeks to improve itself and/or enhance its ability to reach its mission by advocating and practicing social justice and social diversity internally and external to the educational system.*

- The MCO is a system that has explicit policies and practices that prohibit anyone from being excluded or unjustly treated because of their social identity or status. This system not only supports social justice within the system and on the campus, it advocates these values in its interactions within its local, regional, national and global communities.
- The MCO is a system that has explicit policies and practices that are intended to ensure that all members of the diverse workforce feel fully included and have every opportunity to contribute to the goal of achieving the mission of the educational system or campus. This system also advocates for the appreciation of all forms of social diversity and a realization of the

strengths that social diversity brings to the local, regional, national and global community.

When applying this goal to an MCOD effort, it is important to recognize that a level of social justice must be achieved before social diversity can be pursued. Many have tried to move directly to social diversity objectives by building a climate of inclusion in the workplace without adequately attending to the absence of social justice (e.g. the existence of sexism, racism, classism, anti-Semitism, heterosexism, and other manifestations of social injustice). The goal of becoming a MCO involves the achievement of both social justice, or an anti-exclusionary objective, and social diversity or an inclusion objective.

When there is evidence that there is a significant investment in becoming an MCO, or at least in exploring the possible benefits of becoming such a system, the MCOD process can begin. Often the first steps are to engage the leadership and as many of the workforce at-large to become more familiar with, and hopefully begin to "own" the MCO goal, or at least to develop a goal of this type in their own words.

MCOD Development Stages

One of the core assumptions of MCOD is that most systems are neither all good nor all bad. In the language of multicultural organization development, systems are neither wholly "multicultural systems," nor are they wholly "mono-cultural systems," it can be assumed that they are on various places on the continuum. In fact, in most large systems, it is typical to find divisions, departments, groups, or other single units in different places from each other and/or from the larger system with respect to the strength of their affinity for, or against, MCO goals for the educational system or campus.

The MCOD Developmental Stage model is a significant element of MCOD theory and practice because it allows us to assess the current developmental issues, opportunities, and challenges unique to a specific system as it attempts to move toward becoming an MCO. It is also provides the change process with an essential conceptual organizer to guide the identification of change strategies that are consistent with the developmental readiness of the educational system. Together Rita Hardiman and I developed the MCOD Developmental Stage Model based on our work in Social Identity Development theory (Jackson & Hardiman, 1994) and Racial Identity Development theory (Jackson & Wijeyesinghe, 2001). We coupled our research and writing on individual development with our work with/and observations of organization development practitioners. This model identifies six points on a developmental continuum, each describing the consciousness and culture of a system with regard to issues of social justice and diversity, or relative to becoming a MCO.

Stage One: The Exclusionary System. The Exclusionary System is openly devoted to maintaining the majority group's dominance and privilege, and these values are typically manifested in the system's mission and membership criteria. Such a system is usually openly hostile to anything that might be seen as a concern for social justice or social diversity in the system. A system that is rooted in this stage of development is unlikely to entertain anything like a MCOD process; however, most large systems can identify a department, group, or some other systemic unit that does embrace this developmental perspective.

Stage Two: "The Club". The system or systemic unit that is at the Club stage can be thought of as a system that stops short of explicitly advocating the "majority" group's supremacy, but does seek to maintain the privileges for those who have traditionally held social power within the social system. This is done by developing and maintaining missions, policies, norms, and procedures seen as "correct" from their perspective. The Club allows a limited number of people from "minority" social identity groups into the system if they have the "right" perspective and credentials. The Club is seen as more "liberal" with regard to social justice issues, when compared to the Exclusionary system; however, when we look closely we find that its interest in and commitment to issues of social justice tend to be "soft" when convenient, at best. The club only engages with social justice issues when it can be approached on the club member's terms, therefore not disturbing its "comfort zone."

Stage Three: The Compliance System. The Compliance System is committed to removing some of the discrimination inherent in the "club" by providing access to members of social identity groups that were previously excluded. It seeks to accomplish this objective, however, without disturbing the structure, mission, and culture of the system. The system is careful not to create too many waves or to offend or challenge its "majority" employees' or customers' bigoted attitudes or behaviors.

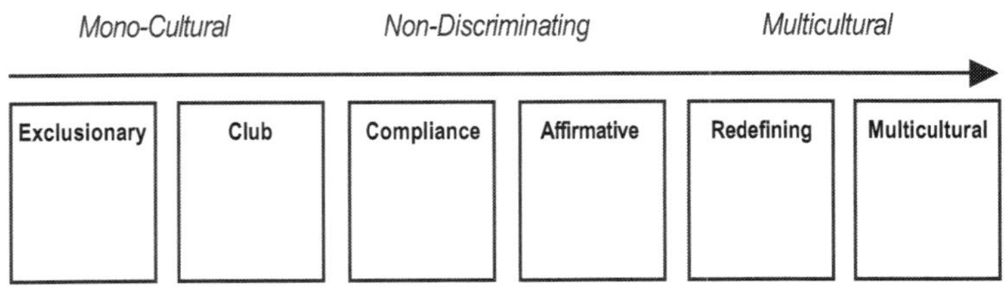

Figure 1. Multicultural system development: Stages in the development of a multicultural system.

The Compliance System typically attempts to change its social diversity profile by actively recruiting and hiring more "non-majority" people. On occasion, such organizations will hire or promote "token" non-majority people into management positions, but most often, they are brought in at the bottom of the system, usually staff positions. When the exception is made to place a "non-majority" person in a line (senior staff) position it is important that this person be a *"team player"* and that s/he be a *"qualified"* applicant. A "qualified team player" does not openly challenge the system's mission and practices and is usually 150% competent to do the job.

Stage Four: The Affirming System. The Affirming System is committed to eliminating the discriminatory practices and inherent advantage given members of the "majority" group in the Club by actively recruiting and promoting members of those social groups typically denied access to the system. The Affirming System, moreover, takes an active role in supporting the growth and development of these new employees and initiating programs that increase their chances of success and upward mobility. All employees are encouraged to think and behave in a non-oppressive manner and the system may conduct awareness programs toward that end.

Stage Five: The Redefining System. The Redefining System is a system in transition. This system is not satisfied with being only socially just or "non-oppressive." It is committed to working toward an environment that goes beyond managing diversity, to one that values and capitalizes on diversity. This system is committed to finding ways to ensure the full growth of all social identity group perspectives as a method of enhancing growth and the potential success of the system.

The Redefining System begins to question the limitations of relying solely on one cultural perspective as a basis for the system's mission, operations, and product development. It seeks to explore the significance and potential of a multicultural workforce. This system actively engages in visioning; planning and problem solving activities directed toward the realization of a multicultural system.

The Redefining System is committed to developing and implementing polices and practices that distribute power among all of the diverse groups in the system. In summary, the Redefining System searches for alternative modes of organizing that guarantee the inclusion, participation, and empowerment of all its members.

Stage Six: The Multicultural System. The Multicultural System reflects the contributions and interests of diverse cultural and social groups in its mission, operations and products or services. It acts on a commitment to eradicate social oppression in all forms within the system; includes the members of diverse cultural and social groups as full participants, especially in decisions that shape the system. Finally, it follows through on broader external social responsibilities, including support of efforts to eliminate all forms of social oppression and to educate others in multicultural perspectives. This is the description of the Vision of a MCO. As there are no known MCOs, this must remain a vision, a statement of the ideal. When we see aspects of this vision manifest in a system or systemic unit, it is important that they be recognized and celebrated, even if it is not a perfect representation of the vision. It is important to believe that we can "get there."

As already mentioned the developmental stages of MCOD are most useful in the assessment and planning phases of the MCOD change process. The stage model offered by Jackson and Hardiman (1994) provides a framework for selecting and designing assessment instruments and techniques for identifying the developmental stage and for ascertaining a developmental benchmark for the system. A range of MCOD assessment instruments have been developed by many of the MCOD practitioners mentioned in this chapter. However, it is important to note that assessment instruments are often tied to a particular version of MCOD theory that it is ascribed to by the developer of the instrument. Additionally, there are related instruments that while not specifically designed to assess MCOD stages do address some of the aspects of each stage and can be suitable for benchmarking a system or unit.

Once it has been determined where the system currently is on the MCOD continuum, or benchmarked, the next task is to develop a change plan that will address the specific manifestations of that stage as demonstrated by this system and implement strategies that will help the system move to the next stage on the developmental continuum. It is important here to present the overall MCOD process so that the assessment and change planning processes are understood in context.

The MCOD Process

The MCOD change process has four components with a number of subcomponents. Once the decision is made to pursue the goal of becoming an MCO, the process has begun. The process involves four steps: 1) Identification of the *change agents*; 2) determination of the *readiness* of the system for an initiative of this type; 3) *assessment or benchmarking* of the system as it currently exists; and 4) *change planning and implementation.*

The Change Agents

There are three primary actors or change agents in this process: the internal change team, external consultants, and the leadership team. The internal change team is a group of people from within the system who agree to take on the responsibility of managing the MCOD process for the system. Managing the process can take a number of forms. For some change teams, managing the process may mean hiring an outside consultant who will come into the system and run the process for that change team. The team's role at this level of involvement would be to hire the consultant, monitor the consultant's activities, provide input where necessary to the consultant regarding the best way to negotiate the system's culture, and report on the progress of the initiative to the leadership. In other systems, the change team may itself take on a more involved or higher level of responsibility for the MCOD change process. In that case, the team may internally have the competence to assess the system, develop change plans, and implement those change plans with only minimal technical assistance or guidance from outside sources. Therefore, once the team is formed one of its first tasks is to determine how involved it wants to be or feels that it is capable of being. The level of involvement of the change team should also influence the level of involvement of the offsite resources or consultant team. Regardless, the internal change team should:

a. Be a manageable size: usually no more than 12 members. The group members should understand that it is expected that every member will come to every meeting (except in the case of emergencies).
b. Understand that this is now part of their job. This is "regular" work and they should be released from some other assignment or task so that this work is not an overload. In many systems, because it is part of their regular job, they can and should be evaluated on their performance and rewarded

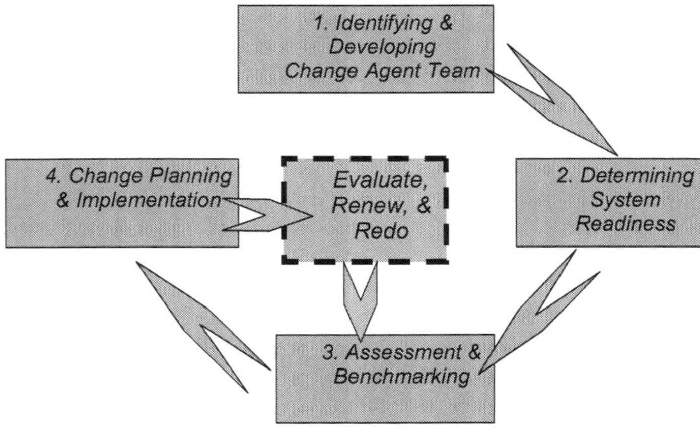

consistent with the regular merit and recognition system for efforts related to this initiative.

c. Have good connections with as many constituencies as possible within the system. As the size of the group is limited, it will not be possible to have all specific constituencies represented on the team, but it is possible to have the voices of all constituencies heard through those who are chosen to serve on the team. There should also include a representative sampling of organization members from across the system both horizontally and vertically. For example, an Academic Affairs team in higher education might include: exempt and nonexempt staff members, undergraduate and graduate students, tenure-track and tenured faculty members, and academic administrators like deans or department chairs.

d. Be comprised of people who are thought of as opinion leaders in the system. Such individuals are not always those in formal positions of authority. Often, their legitimacy comes from the trust that their peers have in them.

e. Understand that committee membership should be thought of as at least a two-year commitment from each member. This should be made clear to each member's supervisor as well.

f. Be supportive of the system's intention to engage in this process and become a MCO. The voices of those who are opposed to this effort need to be heard and their concerns addressed, but it will not help the process if they are on this team.

Once assembled, the change team and the external consultant will meet to review the MCOD process. The external consultant can also be very helpful in facilitating team building within the change team. It is often helpful if the leadership announces the formation of the team, expresses gratitude for their contribution, and uses this moment to also announce the beginning of the MCOD initiative.

An external consultant team provides important support to such a change committee. For example, it provides the outside or objective perspective to this process. It is also imperative that the external consultants have a familiarity with MCOD or MCOD type change processes. In addition to providing guidance on the best way to conduct an MCOD change effort, the external consultant can:

1. *Assist with the identification or construction of appropriate assessment instruments*. For the assessment phase itself, the consultant can be helpful in the collection of sensitive data that might be difficult for members on the change team to collect such as individual interviews or focus groups.
2. *Stay clear of internal politics*. The apolitical perspective of the external consultant can be both an asset and a limitation. As the external consultant is not a part of the power politics that exists in any system, in many ways

their credibility is not in question in the same way that an internal change team members will be. It is also important to recognize that the external consultant's lack of an understanding of all of the history and internal politics can cause blind spots that can hurt the effort if not recognized. It is therefore imperative that there be both an internal perspective and an external perspective available to this effort at all times.

3. *Provide a buffer between the leadership of the system and members of the change team.* The external consultant is often better able to deal with the leadership of the system than are members of the change team, who more than likely report to members of the leadership team, have a "history," or are seen as allied with specific outcomes.
4. *Help facilitate team building among change team members.* The external consultant should be able to help the change team with its own team building and group dynamics. MCOD change teams typically have need for help with their own group process. Social justice and social diversity issues bring their own tension to any group. It is very difficult for a group to manage these issues for itself. Having an external consultant/resource that can help the group work through these issues as they arise will benefit the team and the effort.
5. *Understand that part of their charge is to "build internal capacity" for the system.* This means that the internal consultant understands that the MCOD process will need to go on for a long time and it is not the intention of the system to have the consultant become part of the system. The role of the consultant is to guide the change team through the process the first time, and in so doing build, the skills and knowledge necessary to the team so that on the next round, the capacity to manage the process will exist in the system and therefore only require limited external resources.

The third primary agent in the MCOD change process is the leadership team. The term 'leadership team' is used rather than 'leader' because in most systems, especially larger systems, leadership functions are typically diffused across a group of individuals. These system leaders, (Presidents, CEOs, CFOs, Chancellors, Vice-presidents, Provosts, Deans, Superintendent, Principals, etc.), usually have primary responsibility for, and authority over, all internal policies and procedures involving broad areas. These individuals are responsible for their own area and collectively responsible for leading the system. For an intervention like MCOD, it is important that this leadership team knows what is going on and has direct involvement in the manner in which the initiative is carried out.

The leadership team must be involved in the initial decision to engage in an MCOD initiative. While one key officer often brings a process like MCOD to the system, to ultimately be successful that person must receive the approval of the entire leadership team before going too far with the process. This process of getting such approval is one of those places where an outside consultant can be a significant player. The leadership team must have some understanding of the process and its role, must decide what level of involvement it will want to have in the process. Like the change team, the leadership team can decide to be very involved or it can decide to bless the process and charge the team with moving forward and reporting to the leadership team from time to time. The more that the leadership team has direct involvement in the initiative, the faster the MCOD process will move and the greater its chances of success.

System Readiness

The question of how ready a system is for a change initiative, especially one that focuses on an area as volatile as social justice and diversity, must be considered before the effort shifts into full gear. It is important to know whether the system has the kind of leadership support and awareness in the workforce that will allow the effort to have a chance of succeeding; therefore, a critical component of the MCOD process is a test of system readiness. A test of this type should ask some critical questions about the level of support or awareness in the workforce for an initiative whose goal it is to make this an MCO, and how ready the leadership is to do what must be done to support and engage in this process. A MCOD readiness test should be developed when it is determined that an assessment at the very beginning of the process is essential in determining how best to enter into a system with an intervention of this type, one that ultimately calls for a rather intensive data collection phase.

The MCOD Readiness Test is usually given to a sampling of the system and all of the Change Team and Leadership team. The inventory asks six basic questions:

1. How racial and sexual harassment are handled
2. Whether diversity is valued in the system
3. If there is a commitment to social justice
4. If the leadership has made it known that social justice is supported in the system
5. How well the leadership models a value for diversity and social justice
6. Whether a commitment to diversity and social justice is clearly stated in the mission and values of the system

These and other questions have been shown to help the change agents get a sense of the system's general readiness to move forward. While no system at this point is going to score very high on a test of this type, a minimum score equivalent to fifty percent should be attained. This readiness inventory can also serve to provide some preliminary data on the nature of issues in the system. On rare occasions it has been determined that some work is needed to bring the leadership and/or workforce up to another level of awareness before trying to fully engage in the MCOD process. This might involve more pronouncements from the leadership about the commitment and intent to be more like an MCO; it might involve addressing some long standing social justice issues in the system that when addressed will send a message throughout the system that something serious is happening; or it might involve conducting some harassment training sessions for the workforce. There are a number of introductory interventions that can be implemented without waiting for the MCOD assessment process to begin. These interventions are intended to address some key issues that need to be addressed, while also letting everyone in the system know that "this is serious".

Assessment and Benchmarking

MCOD is a data driven process. The identification of the benchmark where the system begins its journey to become a MCO is critical to the process. Establishing this benchmark is essential to understanding how far the system has to move to become an MCO, and how it is progressing as it implements the action or change plans.

The initial assessment is set to accomplish a number of objectives. First, it is intended to engage the system in naming and owning the current developmental stage of the system – establishing the benchmark. Collecting data that allow the system to provide the detailed description of how it manifests the stage of development that it is in on the MCOD Developmental continuum is critical to this process. Once this detailed description of the system's way of acting out its MCOD stage of development is established, it is easier to focus on issues and problems that need to be addressed, determine the priority that the various issues and problems have, and develop a focused set of strategies with criteria for measuring success.

The assessment strategy that is used in MCOD initiatives is based on survey feedback methodology. The MCOD Assessment calls for the collection of three types of data: 1) Survey data; 2) Interview data; 3) and Audit data.

Survey Data. A range of MCOD or MCOD type assessment questionnaires can be useful as survey instruments designed to be administered to everyone in the system. In some cases, systems construct their own instrument. In these cases, it is critical that the survey instrument provide the kind of data that will give the change agents information that can effectively inform the development of a change plan. Surveys are best at providing data that allow an overview of trends across the entire system. The MCOD Assessment Survey is keyed to the Continuum of MCOD developmental stages, therefore makes the task of organizing the data less difficult, and makes it easier to develop change plans.

Interview Data. While surveys can provide useful quantitative data, interviews help to flesh out nuances and provide a context for data that can be confusing or initially appear to be contradictory. Though desirable, there is rarely, if ever, enough time or resources allocated to MCOD change processes to collect interviews of every individual; therefore, focus groups are typically employed at this stage. Focus groups are pulled together from the various social groupings in the system (e.g. gender, race/ethnic, sexual orientation, class, as well as systemic grouping e.g. secretarial staff, managers, engineers, part-time workers, instructors, students, counselors, etc.). Within these focus groups, two types of data are usually collected. First, the group is asked to talk about their perceptions of the system relative to social justice and diversity. The data that is collected from these discussions helps to flesh out, or fill in, some of what is known via the survey instrument. Second, the focus groups are presented with some of the survey data, particularly survey data that is not giving a clear message, or seems to contradict other data, and asked to provide a perspective on those apparent contradictions.

Audit Data. MCOD audit data is information that is gleaned from a review of the system's records. There is a specific set of questions that are often asked of the system records. These questions focus on information that tends to be in the system's personnel office and in the budget office. The audit asks for information on hires, terminations, resignations, grievances, and promotions. Data is aggregated by race, gender, physical/developmental ability, sexual orientation (when available), religion, (when available), and other social identity groups as requested and available. Data is further aggregated by systemic unit (e.g. division, department, or work group, and by job grade or classification). As the data from the survey and from the focus groups is impressionistic, it is important to have the facts from the records to support those impressions, or to highlight where there are serious misunderstandings about the system's record on certain social justice and diversity issues.

Once the assessment data is collected, the change agents, or those managing the data for the change agents, "sanitize" and compile the data for presentation back to the system. By sanitize, we mean clean the data up without changing the data. Cleaning the data involves removing language or names that will cause the anonymity of the respondent to be compromised. In some cases this can eliminate a group from the data set for example, if there is only one

African American woman in a unit, this person's identity cannot be protected and therefore may need to be included in responses from "People of Color," or removed altogether.

It is important that the change agents understand that at this stage their responsibility is to compile, rather than analyze, data. Data should be organized in a format that any audience can understand. The primary purpose for the presentation of the data is to allow those who work in the system to hear what was said in the assessment stage, offer any major adjustments or corrections, and ultimately to "own" the data. Once the data is owned, or the group has indicated that, "Yes, the data represent our system", the next step is to identify those things that must be changed so that the system can become an MCO. These are key steps to ensuring that the MCOD process results in an initiative that most members of the system both understand and embrace. This process of inviting members of the organization to confirm the accuracy and to make sense of the data differentiates this approach to systems change from others that tend to be either top-down or bottom-up. This process is intended to be all-inclusive.

Change Planning and Implementation

Once the assessment phase is completed and the data has been presented to and vetted by members of the system, then the members of the change team will assist (or have the consultants assist) each unit within the system with identification of the issues and problems that they want to address first. In MCOD, these individual units are encouraged to identify goals related to those issues and problems that, when addressed successfully, will affect the issues or problems in an observable and measurable way. This is the first step in building a change plan for the systemic unit. In most cases, the units determine change goals based on the identified issues and problems, and prioritize them by isolating those that can be addressed within 18 months to two years and will significantly affect the identified issue or problem. As previously mentioned, it is critical that results can be seen and measured. To be successful, the MCOD change process generally, and all those who work on it, must have clear strategies for such accountability.

When the change plan has been implemented, and the results evaluated, it is time to redo the assessment, renew the commitment to becoming an MCO, and to develop and implement the next change plan. With the completion of each of cycle of this process, it is expected that the MCOD process will become even more internalized within the system and its culture. It is also expected that the internal capacity of the system to run and monitor its own MCOD process will continue to develop and take root ever more deeply.

Concluding Comments

This chapter describes how Multicultural Organization Development emerged from the work of organization development and diversity practitioners who shared a common commitment to creating organizations in the corporate sector that were socially just, diverse, and high performing systems. While MCOD has been in practice in the corporate environment for more than two decades now, the way it is practiced, and the theory behind the practice, continues to grow and evolve.

The latest evidence of this evolution is the current movement to adapt MCOD practices and models developed for corporate organizations to environments in K12 and higher education. Future directions for the theory and practice of MCOD offer many interesting lines of inquiry. What are the long-term uses and effects of MCOD as an organization change model? Do systems that use this model indeed become MCO's? And, if so, does being an MCO bring such organizations significantly closer to enacting both their social justice and diversity visions and also significantly enhance their ability to realize the overall missions unique to their system?

As new applications of this model unfold, we should also pay attention to the ways that the practice of MCOD in these different environments changes the theory of MCOD and the theory and practice of OD, as well. In a corporate environment, judging the usefulness of a model like MCOD may be as straight forward as discerning the impact of the MCOD change process on the organizations' bottom-line (whatever that measurement of success is in the context that organization). How will higher education organizations construct equally compelling measurements suited to their particular needs?

MCOD by its very nature is a commitment to the holistic health of human beings in systems. Bringing together the values, practices, and perspectives of both organization development and diversity offers a model to help fulfill the promise of organizations and society to be both successful and socially just. MCOD was in part an invention intended to fill a perceived gap in the contemporary theory and practice of organization development however, it seems now that as MCOD continues to evolve, not only will that gap be filled but the theory and practice of OD and MCOD will be thought of as one, rather than two separate or overlapping fields.

References

Cox, T. (2001). *Creating the multicultural organization: A strategy for capturing the power of diversity*. San Francisco: Jossey-Bass.

Jackson, B.W., & Wijeyesinghe, C.L. (Eds.). (2001). *New perspectives on racial identity development: A theoretical and practical anthology.* New York: New York University Press.

Jackson, B.W. (1994). Coming to a vision of a multicultural system. In E.Y. Cross, J.H. Katz, F.A. Miller, & E.W. Seashore (Eds.), *The promise of diversity: Over 40 voices discuss strategies for eliminating discrimination in organizations* (pp. 116-117). Arlington, VA: NTL Institute.,

Jackson, B.W., & Hardiman, R. (1994). Multicultural organization development. In E.Y. Cross, J.H. Katz, F.A. Miller, & E.W. Seashore (Eds.), *The promise of diversity diversity: Over 40 voices discuss strategies for eliminating discrimination in organizations* (pp.231-239). Arlington, VA: NTL Institute.

Jackson, B.W. (1993). Multicultural organization development: A model for the human resources professional. *Resources.* Wellesley, MA: The Human Resources Association of the Northeast.

Jackson, B.W., Foster, B., Jackson, G., Cross, W., & Hardiman, R. (1988). Workforce diversity and business. *Training and Development Journal, 42*(4), 38-41.

Jackson, B.W, & Holvino, E. (1988). Developing multicultural organizations. *Creative Change: Journal of Religion and Applied Behavioral Sciences, 9*(2), 14-19.

Jackson, B.W. (1983). Racial identity development: Implications for managing the multi-racial workforce. In A.G. Sargent & R. Ritvo (Eds.), *NTL manager's handbook.* Arlington, VA: NTL Institute.

Jamison, K. (1987). Affirmative action program: Springboard for a total organizational change effort. *OD Practitioner, 10*(4).

Miller, F. A., & Katz, J.H. (2002). *The inclusion breakthrough: Unleashing the real power of diversity.* San Francisco: Berrett-Koehler.

Thomas, R. (1992). *Beyond Race and Gender: Unleashing the power of your total work force by managing diversity.* New York: AMACOM.

Thomas, R. (1996). *Redefining diversity.* New York: AMACOM.

Bailey W. Jackson teaches at the University of Massachusetts Amherst.

Chapter 2

Letting the Hydra Roam: Attending to Diverse Forms of Diversity in Liberal Arts Education

Sammy Basu

This chapter offers a Hydra-like heuristic framework consisting of nine distinct conceptions of diversity. For each conception it notes the attendant vision of liberal arts education, the curriculum and pedagogy entailed, and the main weaknesses identified by critics. Rather than privilege any single conception, it is argued that for institution-wide diversity initiatives to be successful, they must allow participants to span the various conceptions.

Diversity in education remains controversial, needless to say, between those who identify themselves as broadly 'for' multiculturalism and monoculturalists who see themselves as 'against.' But there is also considerable confusion and disagreement within the 'for' camp, particularly once it

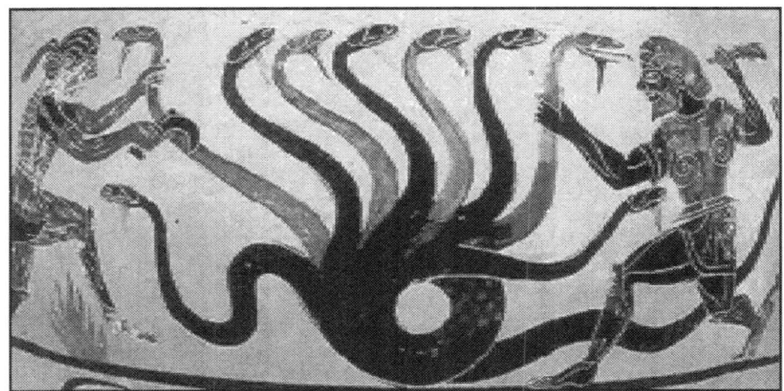

Figure 1. Herakles and Iolaos slaying the Lernean Hydra, attributed to the Eagle Painter Date: 525 BCE (Malibu, The J. Paul Getty Museum; http://www.theoi.com/Illustration.htm).

moves beyond salutary affirmations. It is, more specifically, widely agreed that 'diversity' centers upon the 'holy trinity' of 'race, class, and gender,' and extends to encompass ethnicity, religion, age, and sexual orientation, and generally acknowledged that while this is an arbitrary and heterogeneous list it reflects the arbitrariness of historically patterned political, economic, and social exclusion on the basis of various ascribed physiological and behavioral criteria. There is, by contrast, less consensus about the implications of diversity in education for curricular content and pedagogical practices. Whence, notwithstanding their assumed solidarity, proponents of diversity sometimes talk past one another and work at cross-purposes. Indeed, and all too ironically given the centrality of multiplicity as an organizing concept, one of the obstacles to the institution-wide incorporation of diversity in undergraduate college instruction is a failure to adopt a sufficiently pluralistic conception of the purview of diversity and otherness.

Among the notable archetypes of resistance to otherness, the labors of Heracles loom large. Heracles never met a creature he didn't find strange, regard as monstrous, and undertake to vanquish. His second labor was to slay the huge and formidable Hydra, apparently concocted and sent by Hera to kill him. The Hydra consisted of nine serpentine heads affixed to the body of a hound. Heracles pursued the Hydra to its lair, in the marshes of Lernia in the Argolid, drew it out with flaming arrows, and eventually slew it, burying its final severed head under a rock.

In what follows I distinguish nine distinct conceptions or headings of diversity, which are, if I may be permitted the device of alliteration: criticism, celebration, cosmopolitanism, connection, curiosity, confidence, citizenship, correction, and conservation. These conceptions are arranged and discussed in terms of their political relationship to the status quo: from social justice through neutrality to social conservatism (otherwise known as the radical-left, liberal-center, and conservative-right); and of the intensity of this affect: from disinterested neutrality to transformative advocacy.

For each conception of educational diversity, I specify the attendant vision of liberal arts education. I also discuss briefly the appropriate curricular content and pedagogical practices, and very briefly what radical, liberal, and/or conservative critics find most problematic (Sleeter, 2001).

To be sure the 'culture wars' or 'school wars' have been sustained by the acrimonious exchange of controversy-mongering and polarizing monographs by some otherwise highly esteemed scholars. There is, however, a quite different body of scholarship, preoccupied less with ideological demolition than with specifying the theoretical and pedagogical foundations upon which to build a legitimately multicultural form of education. Contributors to the latter tend to be teachers rather than polemicists, and for all their differences as we shall

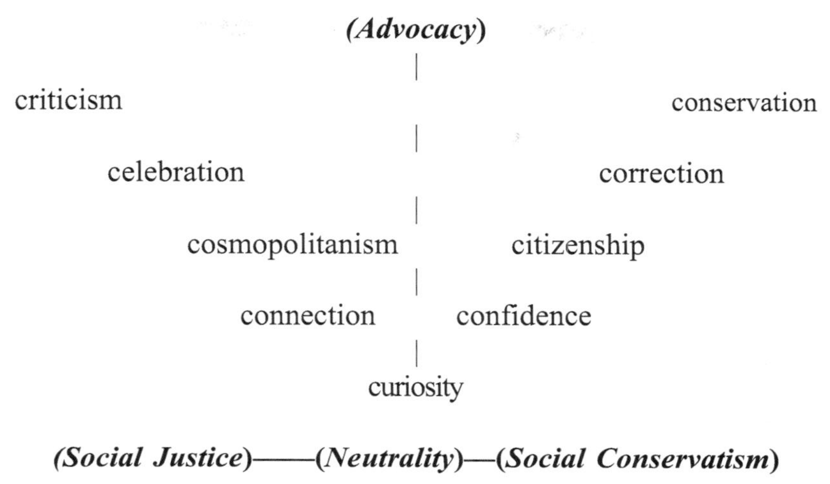

Figure 2. The Hydra of Diversity

see, they share the sense that attending to diversity is part of their responsibility as educators. The conceptual map developed here is intended as a contribution to the latter. While it converges with the schemas of others (Gibson, 1976; Sleeter & Grant, 1988; Olguin and Schmitz, 1997; Banks, 2001; Gay, 2001), and will be illustrated with occasional examples from the theoretical literature, it is borne of personal observation.[1] I would be remiss not to admit that I can picture former teachers and faculty colleagues who occupy each of the delineated positions. My aim in offering an admittedly starkly rendered and ahistorical heuristic schema is precisely to acknowledge something of this variegated range of sincere faculty commitments to diversity. Moreover and crucially, it is my contention that for a college or university to make institution-wide progress in the deeper incorporation of diversity or multicultural education, one that might encompass new interdisciplinary diversity programs and involve traditional disciplinary departments themselves, and prompt not just elective course credits but core general education requirements, this range of legitimate faculty positions must be taken seriously. Diversity is not a fearful monster to be vanquished and buried under a rock, nor for that matter to be relegated to a swamp. Instead, its Hydra-like multiplicity ought to be embraced.

Criticism

Educators committed to Criticism, many informed by Freire (1970), conceive of diversity education as a transgressive and transformative process of raising collective 'critical consciousness,' in order to advance 'social justice' (Kanpol & McLaren, 1995; Adams, Bell, & Griffin, 1997; Tai & Kenyatta, 1999). What unites these conceptions is the analysis of the status quo as a pervasive, complex, hierarchical, cross-cutting, restrictive, and self-perpetuating system of material and cultural stratification and oppression yielding racism, sexism, classism, heterosexism and sometimes also antisemitism and ableism. This approach to diversity sponsors courses explicitly about social justice which focus either on one or more of the malign 'isms,' or on one or more current controversies which are examined from a critical, holistic, and historical perspective in terms of power and oppression. Since this oppression is internalized by both the targets (or victims) and agents (or conscious and unconscious perpetrators), the cognitive and affective aspects of the social relations between all of the students in a given classroom are themselves a necessary part of the content of the course. That is, pedagogically, such courses are student-centered, drawing upon students' own experiences of oppression and privilege. Anti-oppression content connects this personal level to the larger social system and ultimately to activist coalition strategies for achieving social transformation. Crucially, however, students are not forced to give an account of themselves in individual terms but rather to represent and relate in terms of their social group status (Adams et al., 1997). Practicing small group and intergroup discussions and simulations builds social action skills and models democratic practice. However, the teacher may also need to make use of the authority of his or her role to provide relevant historical information about political and socioeconomic oppression and to direct students towards the more

---

[1]The immediate impetus for this paper was the author's attendance (as part of a college team) at a 10-day curriculum and faculty development project of The Association of American Colleges and Universities, entitled Boundaries and Borderlands III: The Search for Recognition and Community in America, in 2000. What was both enlightening and frustrating about the conference was the extent to which faculty, student activities professionals, and college administrators hailing from a wide range of institutions around the country but brought together by their shared commitment to 'diversity' were unable over the course of sustained small group discussions to reach a consensus about concrete curricular goals and pedagogical practices. The analysis of the paper also draws on the author's decade of experience as one of a handful of visible minority faculty members at a Carnegie 1 West coast private liberal arts college in the *US News and World Report* top 50 that is ostensibly committed to diversity. Finally, the author is also currently a member of the Advisory Board for the Multicultural Center of a local Community College.

critical, complex and personally challenging modes of thinking (Giroux, 1985).

The problem with Criticism for liberal (Gutmann, 1994) and conservative (Higham, 1993) multiculturalists alike is that it risks throwing out the baby with the dirty bath water. That is, it leaves proponents of diversity without access to what remain important revolutionary– albeit unfinished – universalist, egalitarian, liberal democratic moral resources, principles and concepts (such as consent of the governed, or rule of law) not only for internal social criticism of the status quo but also for moral reflection *in toto*. In brief, it is self-defeatingly antagonistic.

Celebration

Celebration involves education 'for' cultural pluralism. It cultivates social selves because the unencumbered life is not worth living. In the name of educational equality, moreover, it consists in valuing and affirming the rich cultural specificities of non-dominant groups. Since the hegemonic culture demoralizes those excluded, multicultural education provides a vitally necessary means of protecting and revitalizing the minds and hearts of these populations. It offers an empowering politics of identity so that separate and distinctive identities are recognized and validated free from invidious comparisons to the dominant culture. It also anticipates the future of America as a multi-centered culture. In curricular terms, Celebration calls for separate courses and indeed entire ethnic studies or group-specific studies and programs with ennobling role-models and affirmative narratives that center minority students within their own distinctive cultures and enable outsiders to develop a fuller appreciation for the distinctive cultural and historical perspective and contributions under study. It may also sponsor facilitated intergroup dialogue programs as a prelude to more vigorous cross-group work (Young, 1990; Hurtado et al., 1999).

For radicals, this is 'diversity without oppression' that misses the material-structural dimension because of its focus on particularistic culture (Tai & Kenyatta, 1999). Liberals worry that identity politics may cause "ethnosclerosis: the hardening of the walls between the races" (Liu, 1998, p. 65), reserving group membership for those who are 'queer enough' or 'black enough' and so on. Conservatives charge that some group differences are over-dramatized and that not all recognized differences are worth valuing, nor certainly worth valuing equally (Taylor, 1994).

Cosmopolitanism

Cosmopolitanism, literally to think of the world as one's salient polity, pursues diversity in education in order to enlarge students' appreciation for humanity. It cultivates "worldliness," the recognition that we occupy and can move about in "the large, many-windowed house of human culture as a whole" (Said, 1993, p. 312). It includes the local, and yet by locating and contextualizing it within an universal experience of multiple cultures, transcends romanticizing parochialism and the essentialization of culture (Hollinger, 1992; Nussbaum, 1997). It supplements domestic ethnic and area studies with non-Western area studies, international studies, and global education by linking all domestic groups to their origins in world cultures, and relating domestic diversity challenges to migration and diaspora issues elsewhere in the world (Mahalingam & McCarthy, 2000). Pedagogically, adherents emphasize the merits of comparative methodologies, cross-cultural social competencies, and exchange and study abroad programs.

The radical worry with Cosmopolitanism is that the global village is easily co-opted by a predatory consumerist globalization in which differences are commodified (Kanpol & McLaren, 1995). For both radicals and conservatives (Barber, 1993), moreover, the possibilities of an America beyond recognition, of solidarity with ethnonational strangers, are seen as undesirable, too psychologically demanding, and hence unrealistic.

Connection

In the Connection approach to diversity a Liberal Arts education is thought of "as entailing arts of translation and connection on all levels" (Minnich, 1995, p. 13). Given that students from low status groups have likely either internalized negative exclusionary self-images or adopted reactionary aggressive ones, their academic performance will be distorted by resignation or resentment. Nevertheless, diverse learners are resources and not merely problems (Murray, 1992). Accordingly, diversity in education should manifest both a compensating sensitivity to what negatively affects the self-esteem of such alienated students and a positive appreciation for their "cultural learning styles, perspectives, experiences, contributions, and heritages" (Gay, 2001, p. 33), even though they may be notably field-sensitive, and people- as opposed to text-, object-, or visually-oriented, and relatively affectively and physically rather than verbally communicative. Connection justifies empowerment strategies that call for student reflection upon their own concrete, everyday, real-life experiences. The cultural and linguistic empowerment of students in turn requires that teachers relinquish the authoritarian role in favor of that of the participant or co-learner. Finally, students' personal growth and change in bicultural and bidialectal terms (i.e., within both their sub-culture and the dominant culture) becomes the central measure of learning success.

For radicals, this liberal approach amounts to a soft form of assimilation.

For conservatives, by capitulating on standards, this approach does minority students a disservice by expecting too little of them.

Curiosity

On this view diversity in education serves primarily instrumental epistemological purposes. It calls attention to the partial (i.e. sociological and political) nature of the processes of both social and natural scientific knowledge construction about the very categories of diversity, self, race, class, gender, and so on. Courses focus on the ways in which universalist and relativist paradigms alike obscure even as they reveal and shift for reasons both empirical and political. They are structured so that students find themselves experimenting with multiple perspectives, rival historiographies, and theories of difference. The pedagogy of Curiosity leans towards "cultural detachment" (Fuller, 2000, p.35) and defamiliarization a'la Montaigne. Learning occurs as students come to see the familiar in the strange and the strange in the familiar, as they begin to disaggregate categories, and ultimately as they develop a disinterested delight in nominalist knowledge for its own sake (Kogler, 1999).

The problem with this approach for radical (Kanpol & McLaren, 1995) and conservative (Barber, 1993; Gomes, 1999) multiculturalists alike is that general skepticism and neutral agnosticism can give way to cynicism and a paralyzing apathy towards the dichotomy of social justice versus the status quo.

Confidence

As a matter of basic effectiveness, faculty must make themselves understood, must convey their lessons in ways that make sense to their students, and as a matter of equity they should strive to reach all of their students. According to the Confidence view, diversity in education is of instrumental value insofar as it improves academic outcomes and thereby the likelihood of social adjustment and productive success in the work world. In order to motivate otherwise under-prepared and 'at-risk' students, faculty have to instill confidence in them. Culturally deprived or disadvantaged minority and low-income students, many of the them first-generation college-goers, lacking in early familial and community experiences supportive of learning, reading, and formal language need socially relevant *entrées* into the college world of scholarly skills and disciplines. In Kolbian terms, they may need instructional activities that dwell upon concrete experience and reflective observation before even attempting abstract conceptualization and active experimentation (Kolb and Smith, 1986).

Radical critics (Murray, 1992) point out that this approach assumes that minority students are deprived of culture, or suffer from cultural illiteracy, when in fact they practice different cultural literacies and that the real problems are cultural conflict and structural obstructions. Conservatives worry that this liberal form of starting-point egalitarianism coddles students and delays learning.

Citizenship

In the Citizenship conception diversity in education is 'about' cultural pluralism. It maintains, drawing on Dewey, that diverse sources of value and commitments can motivate liberal-democratic national citizenship even while enriching the core cultural values of freedom, equality, and the individual, the associational pursuit of happiness and the enlarging of civic competencies (Jacobsohn & Dunn, 1996; Reeher & Cammarano, 1997). Since the logic of democratic egalitarianism dictates that the different are equally deserving of and hence eligible for citizenship, multicultural education achieves prejudice reduction by disseminating more democratically just attitudes towards minority races and groups (Barber 1993; Macedo 2000). Course content might study the contributions of long-standing and recent non-dominant groups to the vector sum of America, study not only Ellis Island but Angel Island (Takaki, 1993), reminding us that the demographic challenges posed by surges of difference are nothing new in American history (Higham, 1993). This approach also favors relational pedagogies of collaborative as well as of community-based instruction and service-learning.

To radicals, this sort of approach blunts the critical edge of democratic participation and risks co-opting it entirely "in the lie of democratic ubiquity" (McLaren, 1995, p. 13). Basic political participation obscures social and economic inequalities. Liberals, on the other hand, might worry that this approach is not only politically assimilationist but acculturating and mobilizing too, that is, not just politically liberal but comprehensively statist.

Correction

According to the Correction conception of diversity, there are some necessary changes that must be made incrementally to the existing educational system. To correct past omissions as well as miseducation on the margins there must be some content revision and content integration, especially in the social sciences and humanities. Gaps and errors should be addressed with the addition of special units, supplemental readings, and so on. In addition, however, canonical works can and should be read in ways that open them up, sometimes dramatically, to new kinds of readers and questions (Euben, 1997; Sterba, 1995). Indeed, such complexity and richness is part of what makes them great. Ultimately, all students should be called to the eternal questions and perennial problems addressed by the shared curriculum of great works within the Western tradition. Correction offers students a benignly hierarchical classroom in which the teacher guides his or her students with lectures and prompted discussions.

To radicals, the inherent conservative limitations of prevailing academic discourse and cultural literacy preclude critical engagement with diversity issues (Bizzell, 1992). Liberals regard this form of multiculturalism as cultural inertia (Musil, 1997). For both it is a superficial accommodation that does not penetrate to the deeper layers of the controversies and issues at stake.

Conservation

For proponents of Conservation diversity is not an institutional or societal goal in itself but rather "a means to include a diversified population in shaping shared goals to enhance the quality of our common life both in college and in the wider world" (Gomes, 1999, p.116). The contemporary challenges of diversity are best understood as additional residual forms of ethnicity. Hence, just as previous generations of immigrants of diverse ethnicities, with some passing pains, have flavored the American multicultural melting pot, so too can the remaining and new self-ascribed groups. Conservation offers an inclusionary model of color-blind assimilation to anyone and everyone prepared to embrace the few essential values of the American creed: individual rights, freedoms, and responsibilities, and to achieve a modicum of cultural literacy (Ravitch, 1990). The appropriate pedagogy is one that observes the time-tested conception of the teacher-student relationship as a benevolent hierarchy. The teacher as a guardian and initiate of the received wisdom of Western civilization utilizes formal, presentational pedagogies while enabling advanced students to practice collaboratively and independently the established research techniques. Learning is seen not only as a personally transformative process of maturation or enlightenment in the Kantian sense then, but also as the acquisition of knowledge. To deny minority students access to this latter cultural capital is to disable them unfairly from functioning and indeed flourishing in the modern world.

Although Freire (1993, p.135) himself stressed "the need to master the dominant language," contemporary radical and liberal multiculturalists alike note the presence in justifications of Conservation of telling phrases such as 'shedding one's skin' to describe the process of cultural assimilation. They argue to the contrary that the new (Hispanic, Caribbean, and Asian immigrant) forms of diversity together with those that remain historically unassimilated (Native and African Americans) are unlike the old assimilated European ethnicities in their conspicuousness. The dominant culture is not a monoculture but is rather a

Eurocentric collusion of cultures that ill-serves and misrepresents members of America's other minority cultures.

Conclusion

Diversity is not a monster to be destroyed or domesticated. On the contrary, in all of its multiplicity, it must be given institutional room to roam. Drawing on Heracles's experience, I close with three more specific lessons intended primarily for the sort of advocates of diversity, illustrated on my reading by Olguin and Schmitz (1997), who favor a particular conception of diversity over others and who are made impatient by the noisy process of institutional transformation.

First, in his encounter with the Hydra Heracles discovered that when he attempted with his hooked blade to lop off one of its heads, two grew back in its place. Try as he might, that is, the assault on the Hydra's multiplicity served only to further agitate it. I would venture a similar observation about diversity. The effort to eliminate some among the panoply of conceptions of diversity, be it by those critical of diversity or by those who adhere to competing conceptions, may serve only to generate the "considerable strife" bemoaned by Olguin and Schmitz (1997, p. 437) that further splinters and diffuses the positive educational potential of diversity.

Second, Heracles eventually stifled and slew the Hydra but to do so he had to enlist the aid of his friend and charioteer, Iolaos, who, firebrand in hand, cauterized each stump as Heracles severed the head. Again, I would suggest a parallel. Olguin and Schmitz warn that a general education diversity

> requirement can become diluted during faculty deliberations about which courses will be included in the list of courses fulfilling the requirement. Disparate courses are often added to a multicultural menu when political compromises rather than student learning goals dictate curricular choices. (1997, p. 450)

However, proponents of diversity can disagree markedly at the concrete curricular and pedagogical levels because there are multiple legitimate conceptions of the goals of affirming diversity. Far from achieving some sort of purity or coherence, then, searing shut some of these conceptions to privilege others may leave callouses that actually undermine the institutional viability of diversity *in toto* by excluding and undermining some faculty sympathizers.

Third, because Heracles needed the aid of Iolaus he was not credited with completing the second labor. Now, according to Olguin and Schmitz,

> while faculty are the ultimate arbiters of educational practice, the diversity of faculty members by discipline and background is so great that clear and

> sustained commitment and support from the administration helps overcome sometimes overwhelming divisions in faculty preferences for content and approach. (1997, p. 454)

To the contrary then, I would argue that faculty favorably disposed towards diversity likewise should be wary of enlisting the administration to settle their differences by fiat lest they too be discredited in the eyes of students, their colleagues, and the general public. Faculty must practice what they preach and model effective deliberation, norm mediation, and accommodation on the intellectual middle ground and the borderlands of their discrepancies. They must demonstrate that they can co-exist (Musil, 1997; Smelser & Alexander, 1999).

In sum, institution-wide diversity programming should accommodate faculty who differ on their reasons for commitment to the program. Unanimity is not to be expected. Indeed, the most robust institutional program may be precisely one in which these various reasons are kept in generative and hybrid tension.

References

Adams, M., Bell, L.E., & Griffin, P. (Eds.). (1997). *Teaching for diversity and social justice: A sourcebook.* New York: Routledge.

Banks, J.A., & Banks, C.A.M. (Eds.). (2001). *Handbook of research on multicultural education.* San Francisco: Jossey-Bass.

Banks, J.A. (2001). Multicultural education: Historical development, dimensions, and practice. In J.A. Banks & C.A.M. Banks (Eds.), *Handbook of research on multicultural education* (pp. 3-24). San Francisco: Jossey-Bass.

Barber, B. (1993). The civic mission of the university. In R. Battistoni & B. Barber (Eds.), *Education for democracy* (pp. 456-455). Dubuque: Kendall/Hunt.

Bizzell, P. (1992). *Academic discourse and critical consciousness.* Pittsburgh: University of Pittsburgh Press.

Euben, J.P. (1997). *Corrupting youth: Political education, democratic culture, and political theory.* Princeton: Princeton University Press.

Fitzgerald, A.K, & Lauter, P. (2001). Multiculturalism and core curricula. In J.A. Banks & C.A.M. Banks (Eds.), *Handbook of research on multicultural education* (pp. 729-746). San Francisco: Jossey-Bass.

Freire, P. (1970). *Pedagogy of the oppressed.* (M.B. Ramos, Trans.). New York: Herder & Herder.

Freire, P. (1993). *Pedagogy of the city.* New York: Continuum.

Fuller, S. (2000). Social epistemology as a critical philosophy of multiculturalism. In R.

Mahalingam & C. McCarthy (Eds.), *Multicultural curriculum: New directions for social theory, practice, and policy* (pp. 15-35). New York: Routledge.

Jacobsohn, G. J., & Dunn, S. (Eds.). (1996). *Diversity and citizenship: Rediscovering American nationhood.* Lanham, MD: Rowman & Littlefield.

Gay, G. (2001). Curriculum theory and multicultural education. In J.A. Banks & C.A.M. Banks (Eds.), *Handbook of research on multicultural education* (pp. 25-43). San Francisco: Jossey-Bass.

Gibson, M.A. (1976). Approaches to multicultural education in the United States: Some concepts and assumptions. *Anthropology and Education, 7*, 7-18.

Giroux, H. (1985). Critical pedagogy, cultural politics and the discourse of experience. *Journal of Education, 167*, 22-41.

Gomes, P.J. (1999). Values and the elite residential college. *Daedalus, 128*, 101-119.

Gutmann, A. (1994). Introduction. In A. Gutmann (Ed.), *Multiculturalism* (pp. 3-24). Princeton, NJ: Princeton University Press.

Higham, J. (1993). Multiculturalism and universalism: A history and critique. *American Quarterly, 45*, 195-219.

Hollinger, D.A. (1992). Postethnic America. *Contention, 2*, 79-96.

Hu-DeHart, E. (2001). Ethnic studies in U.S. higher education: History, development, and goals. In J.A. Banks & C.A.M. Banks (Eds.), *Handbook of research on multicultural education* (pp. 696-707). San Francisco: Jossey-Bass.

Hurtado, S., Milem, J., Clayton-Pedersen, A. & Allen, W. (1999). *Enacting diverse learning environments: Improving the climate for racial/ethnic diversity in higher education.* Washington, DC: George Washington University Press.

Jacobsohn, G., & Dunn, S. (Eds.). (1996). *Diversity and citizenship: Rediscovering American nationhood.* Lanham, MD: Rowman & Littlefield.

Kanpol, B., & McLaren, P. (Eds.). (1995). *Critical multiculturalism: Uncommon voices in a common struggle.* Westport, CT: Bergin & Garvey.

Kogler, H.H. (1999). New arguments for diversifying the curriculum: Advancing students' cognitive development. *Diversity Digest, 3*, n.p.

Kolb, D., & Smith, D.A. (1986). *The user's guide for the learning-style inventory: A manual for teachers and trainers.* Boston: McBer & Co.

Liu, E. (1998). *The Accidental Asian: Notes of a native speaker.* New York: Random House.

Macedo, S. (2000). *Diversity and distrust: Civic education in a multicultural democracy.* Cambridge, MA: Harvard University Press.

Mahalingam, R., & McCarthy, C. (Eds.). (2000). *Multicultural curriculum: New directions for social theory, practice, and policy.* New York: Routledge.

McLaren, P. (1995). *Critical pedagogy and predatory culture: Oppositional politics in a postmodern era.* New York: Routledge.

Minnich, E. (1995). *Liberal learning and the arts of connection for the new academy*. Washington, DC: Association of American Colleges and Universities.

Murray, D.E. (Ed.). (1992). *Diversity as resource: Redefining cultural literacy*. Alexandria, VA: Teachers of English to Speakers of Other Languages.

Musil, C. M. (1997). Diversity and educational integrity. In J.G. Gaff & J.L. Ratcliff (Eds.), *Handbook of the undergraduate curriculum: A comprehensive guide to purposes, structures, practices, and change* (pp. 190-211). San Francisco: Jossey-Bass.

Nussbaum, M.C. (1997). *Cultivating humanity: A classical defense of reform in liberal education*. Cambridge, MA: Harvard University Press.

Olguin E., & Schmitz, B. (1997). Transforming the curriculum through diversity. In J.G. Gaff & J.L. Ratcliff (Eds.), *Handbook of the undergraduate curriculum: A comprehensive guide to purposes, structures, practices, and change* (pp. 436-456). San Francisco: Jossey-Bass.

Ravitch, D. (1990). Multiculturalism: E pluribus plures. *The American Scholar*, *59*, 337-354.

Reeher, G., & Cammarano, J. (Eds.). (1997). *Education for citizenship: Ideas and innovations in political learning*. Lanham, MD: Rowman & Littlefield.

Said, E. (1993). The politics of knowledge. In C. McCarthy & W. Crichlow (Eds.), *Race, identity, and representation in education* (pp. 306-314). New York: Routledge.

Sleeter, C.E., & Grant, C.A. (1988). *Making choices for multicultural education: Five approaches to race, class, and gender.* Columbus, OH: Merrill.

Sleeter, C.E. (2001). An analysis of the critiques of multicultural education. In J.A. Banks & C.A.M. Banks (Eds.), *Handbook of research on multicultural education* (pp. 81-94). San Francisco: Jossey-Bass.

Smelser, N.J., & Alexander, J.C. (Eds.). (1999). *Diversity and its discontents: Cultural conflict and common ground in contemporary American society*. Princeton, NJ: Princeton University Press.

Sterba, J.P. (Ed.). (1995). *Social and political philosophy: Classical western texts in feminist and multicultural perspectives*. Belmont, CA.: Wadsworth.

Tai, R.H. & Kenyatta, M.L. (Eds.). (1999). *Critical ethnicity: Countering the waves of identity politics*. Lanham, MD: Rowman & Littlefield.

Takaki, R. (1993). *A different mirror: A history of multicultural America*. New York: Little, Brown, Co.

Taylor, C. (1994). The politics of recognition. In A. Gutmann (Ed.), *Multiculturalism: Examining the politics of recognition* (pp. 25-74). Princeton, NJ: Princeton University Press.

Young, I.M. (1990). *Justice and the politics of difference*. Princeton, NJ: Princeton University Press.

Sammy Basu is an associate professor in the Department of Politics at Willamette University.

Chapter 3

It Takes a Campus: Situating Professional Development Efforts Within a Campus Diversity Program

Nancy Chism and Karen Whitney

This chapter focuses on the organizational dimension of efforts to promote inclusiveness. It draws upon the case of Indiana University Purdue University Indianapolis (IUPUI) and the ways that the university models a comprehensive approach toward diversity efforts. The chapter describes the special kind of leadership that unifies the campus approach, the ways that both support units and grass roots groups are brought together in conversation and joint programming, and above all, the unique system of public indicators that have been developed to gauge and display progress and promote more targeted and intensive activities in areas of poor performance.

The Issue and Its Components

If, as Barr and Tagg (1995) and many others have suggested, higher education should situate its teaching mission around the learner, we can think of student diversity efforts on campus as encompassing all those activities that support the success of underrepresented learners as well as those that help majority learners to enlarge their understanding and valuing of diversity. While the ways that faculty structure learning opportunities and interact with students are central activities, other activities are also critical. These include advising and academic support services, as well as activities focused on student campus life, such as the work of supporting the co-curriculum, student leadership development, residential environments, financial aid, and counseling. Also related are activities that indirectly affect student success, such as the recruitment and retention of diverse faculty and staff, the promotion of scholarship on diversity, staff multicultural development, and community outreach and engagement. All of these activities are informed by the work of institutional research and guided by administrative leadership and resource allocation.

The professional developer, then, works within a context of interdependence that must be acknowledged and taken into account. Promoting the awareness and behavior change of individual faculty members with respect to inclusive teaching is a worthy goal, but one that can easily be undermined if students lack sufficient funds to pay the upcoming semester's tuition or encounter hostility from roommates or the academic support center's receptionist. As several scholars have pointed out (Chang, 2002; Hurtado, 1999; Smith et al, 1997), diversity involves institutional transformation, rather than individual change.

Classic descriptions of the work of professional development, such as those found in Gaff (1975) and now embraced in the mission statement of the Professional and Organizational Development Network in Higher Education (2002), the main faculty development association in the United States, distinguish between faculty, instructional, and organizational development. Faculty development focuses on the faculty member as a person and as a teacher, scholar, and professional; instructional development on courses, curriculum, and student learning; and organizational development on the organizational structure of an institution and its subcomponents. Although the POD group began with a strong emphasis on organizational development, the need for pedagogical change quickly shifted the attention of most of its members to faculty and instructional development. From time to time, as indicated by the title of a 1992 POD conference session, "Building community through organizational development: Where is the OD in POD?" (Nichols, Chism, & Wheeler) and more recently, the writings of Brew and Boud (1996), Chism (1998), James (1997), and Lieberman and Guskin (2003), developers have questioned the lack of emphasis on organizational development. Given the recent pace of educational change and the need for organizational direction, development centers have been increasingly asked to work at the institutional level and are of necessity embracing a more holistic view of their work.

The work of improving the success of students of color and expanding the horizons of majority students with respect to diversity requires all three development approaches. It entails faculty development by supporting faculty in thinking differently about their teaching approaches and classroom practices. This work requires instructional development through assistance in redesigning curricula and broadening course content. In addition, it requires organizational development by working with other units on campus to understand the issues more broadly, collaborate on changes, and thus affect institutional transformation. (The broader term "professional development" is being used in this chapter to accommodate all three types of development efforts. An alternative name, "academic development," proposed by Anderson (1996), is perhaps more apt, but is not widely used in this country.) In the following campus portrait, the ways in which the professional development unit works at the organizational level are described along four dimensions: working with top leadership, mounting programs and collaborating with others' initiatives, fostering exchange among other units, and contributing to assessment efforts.

Working with top leadership

As a campus of Indiana University, IUPUI's diversity efforts stem from the central administration of the University as well as the Indianapolis campus. One main way that the University exercised leadership occurred in 1998 when the President of Indiana University established the Office of the Vice President for Institutional Development and Student Affairs to advance diversity throughout all eight campuses. This office provides university-wide coordination for programs and services that enhance academic excellence, diversity, and student retention. Since 1998, university-wide initiatives have included securing ten million dollars in grants for retention and outreach; promoting teaching and curriculum efforts to infuse diversity into the curriculum; sponsoring conferences focusing on enhancing minority attainment; setting aside tuition dollars to support student retention; distributing mini-grants to improve the campus climate; collaborating with university development; and supporting multicultural admissions outreach.

Inspired by university efforts, in 1999, the IUPUI Chancellor established the Office of the Vice Chancellor for Student Life and Diversity to focus and enhance the campus diversity efforts. Since that time, campus-wide initiatives have included the creation of the Chancellor's Diversity Cabinet, the annual publication of a state of diversity at IUPUI report; presentation of the report to the campus and metropolitan community; development and institutional adoption of an IUPUI Vision for Diversity Statement; development of an annual award and recognition for outstanding efforts in achieving diversity; regular dialogues and discussion with the deans of the 19 schools that comprise IUPUI regarding each school's advancement of the vision for diversity; establishment of campus-wide or school specific programs and services with a core purpose of advancing the vision for diversity at IUPUI; and institutionalization of the assessment of diversity efforts.

Diversity efforts have been prominent in highly visible institution-wide planning efforts. For example, in December 2003, IUPUI's new chancellor charged four task forces to consider how to advance the institution's mission by 2010. Three of the task forces focused on the specific mission areas of teaching and learning, research, and civic engagement, but a fourth task force was entrusted with diversity. Each task force was asked to make recommendations for how IUPUI could "double" accomplishments in the task force's respective area. Based upon the previously established vision, actions, and indicators of diversity, it was imperative to tightly coordinate the Doubling Diversity report recommendations with those of the other task forces. To achieve the goal of infusing diversity considerations across all task forces, the Doubling Diversity Task Force included the chairs of the other task forces as part of its group, and appointed remaining members from the Chancellor's Diversity Cabinet, including a representative from the campus's professional development unit, the Office for Professional Development (OPD). Each of the Doubling Task Force reports included a section responding to advancing diversity within each of their charges. In this way, the Doubling Diversity Task Force and the Chancellor's Diversity Cabinet served as resources and dialogue groups working in partnership with the other task forces in order to infuse vision and action items for diversity across the areas of teaching and learning, research, and civic engagement.

The professional development unit worked closely with all of these central leadership initiatives. The Office for Professional Development at IUPUI is a comprehensive center that includes the Center for Teaching and Learning, but also other units, such as the Office for Women, the Center for Service and Learning, and the Office for Multicultural Professional Development, designed to foster the professional development of faculty and academic staff. OPD has worked consistently with Indiana University's efforts. In response to the first call to form a team for the initial Leadership Institute on Multicultural Curriculum Transformation, OPD identified a group of faculty and academic staff for the Chancellor to invite to participate. Their discussions led to the formation of the Diversity Inquiry Group (DIG), described in a separate chapter of this volume. The directors of OPD and DIG became members of the Diversity Cabinet and participated in the development of future Indiana University Leadership Institutes and the all-campus conference each year, as well as serving as presenters. They contributed to Retention Forums held in subsequent years. This representation allows OPD opportunities for understanding other dimensions of the diversity issue and knowing what other units are doing. It also allows OPD to shape university policy and approaches, through pointing out ways in which existing practices need to change and suggesting alternatives. Those entrusted with planning the activities have come to rely on OPD for print resources, suggestions for speakers, and advice on logistics.

Developing programs within academic and administrative units

At the IUPUI campus, central administrative units have been deeply involved in the diversity considerations of their work. The most extensive campus-wide effort was the reorganization of the department that is currently called Student Life and Diversity Programs. Historically, this department housed the typical set of student activities programs. Student Life and Diversity Programs strives to "help students connect to each other and the campus in meaningful ways; i.e., promote a sense of belonging for students; provide programming to cultivate leadership development; and promote diversity as a value for the campus and campus community. Programs are developed by students for students and or by various faculty, staff, and student groups with extensive collaborations throughout the campus and the university" (2002, Mission Statement).

Specific outcomes from Student Life and Diversity Programs include the administration and leadership of a Cultural Arts Gallery and Cultural Enrichment Programming Committee. The campus-wide Cultural Enrichment Programming Committee is responsible for the coordination of an annual calendar of cultural programs for the campus community. The committee, which is comprised of students, faculty, and staff from across the campus, coordinates and generates collaborations that produce culturally stimulating programs in support of the Principles of Undergraduate Learning and other learning objectives of academic programs across campus. Student Life and Diversity has brought national programs, such as programming for the creation of a Diversity Awareness Resources Team and Study Circles on Diversity, to the IUPUI campus.

Other campus administrative units with major involvement in diversity issues include Human Resources Administration, which presents frequent diversity awareness workshops in administrative and academic units on units; Enrollment Services and the Graduate School, which continually expand efforts to identify and recruit a diverse student body; Financial Aid, which works to identify sources of funding to support diversity and to adjust restrictive policies; and University College, which infuses diversity through its orientation and academic support programs as well as ensures that the curriculum of its first-year courses is infused with multicultural considerations.

Within OPD, four major activities toward promoting diversity occurred. The first was initial and continuing support for the creation and programming of the DIG, which is described in Chapter 8. Secondly, efforts to ensure that a multicultural perspective infuses the general approach of the Center for Teaching and Learning were escalated. Such efforts involved the creation of an online faculty development module on inclusive teaching, but also involved integrating material on multicultural teaching throughout modules and programs devoted to more generic topics, such as classroom management. Thirdly, a full-time director was engaged for the Office for Multicultural Professional Development, with a mission to support the recruitment and success of faculty of color as well as to work with the DIG to help individuals and academic units to assess the climate for diversity and implement programs to make it more inclusive. Fourth, all OPD staff were involved in professional development of their own through workshops within the unit, readings, and conference attendance.

In addition, the DIG, CTL, OMPD, and another related unit within OPD, the Office for Women, have collaborated extensively with the efforts of other units on campus. Examples include jointly-offered programs, such as the reception for staff of color each year, co-sponsorship of sessions on accommodations for students with disabilities, and the awards program for women leaders on campus. Additional efforts include consultation to other units, such as help to Human Resources Administration in designing workshops on diversity for staff. Conversely, collaboration has often involved OPD's invitations to other units to advise the OPD programs through membership on its advisory committees or task groups.

A new initiative just getting underway is the establishment of a Diversity Corps, a group of volunteer faculty and staff with expertise in various diversity issues, such as recruitment, inclusive teaching, and sexual harassment. Through the offering of a three-day Diversity Institute facilitated by professional consultants, Diversity Corps members received preparation experiences designed to help them do organizational consultation. They now exist as a trained cadre of consultants available to assist campus units with needs analysis or climate assessment, intervention of programs, changes in policies or practices, and assessment of their efforts with respect to diversity. This initiative is jointly sponsored by the Offices for Professional Development, Affirmative Action, Student Life and Diversity, and Human Resources.

Given IUPUI's organizational culture and program-based budgeting approach that promotes strong school infrastructures, efforts to advance diversity occur as much within individual schools as throughout the entire campus. The School of Nursing houses one of the first school based programs recognized for advancing diversity (Stokes, 2002). The school organizes diversity efforts into three categories: educational, social, and celebratory. According to Stokes:

> The intent of educational programs has been to inform individuals about varied aspects of diversity using a variety of approaches. The social component has allowed for informal interaction through culinary experiences. These have served to inform as well as provide a medium for fellowship and dialogue. Celebrations serve to recognize the contributions of pioneers in the school and nurse leaders, as well as the contributions faculty make to enhance diversity in our environment. (p.2)

Other schools, such as the School of Dentistry and the School of Business, have also made significant investments in staff and support programs in order to increase minority student admissions and retention.

OPD has worked closely with units such as Nursing in organizing workshops on diversity and helping to promote inclusive pedagogy and curriculum. OPD has also worked on issues of faculty recruitment and retention with particular units such as Dentistry, by consulting with search committees, talking with candidates, and helping to promote community among faculty of color. It celebrates the scholarship of all units through an annual symposium on the scholarship of students, staff, and faculty of color.

Mechanisms for exchange among the units involved

While the Diversity Cabinet involves leaders of units throughout campus, a forum for those program leaders who do the frontline work of development was needed. The DIG has taken the lead over the past three years in holding town halls for this purpose. These full-day events have gathered not only students and central administrative staff, but also the leaders and staff of those units who are working on student life or academic support issues, and faculty or administrators working within schools and departments. The purpose of these meetings is to communicate across organizational lines and generate ideas for collaboration or future work.

The director of the DIG is supported in convening these town halls by OPD, which provides communications and logistics support in organizing the meetings. He is assisted by the OPD staff and others, whose role is to analyze needs, promote critical and creative thinking, and record ideas on courses of action. In many cases, issues or ideas are generated across organizational units, leading to plans for joint activities. Sometimes, structural constraints or policies at the central level are identified as impediments to action, and the appropriate people to deal with these concerns are present. Holding the forums is one way that the faculty development staff can further organizational development through establishing a community of practice across reporting lines, engaging those who are involved in the actual work of promoting multiculturalism.

Assessing Progress: The Diversity Indicators

IUPUI has developed a comprehensive system for assessing its mission. An essential part of the campus planning process, the system relies on a "culture of evidence" that is pursued through articulating assessable outcomes aligned with the campus mission, developing instrumentation, collecting and analyzing data, and applying findings. Within this system is a mechanism for tracking diversity efforts. As with other performance indicators, the assessment activity in this domain began with broad performance objectives derived from the campus mission and vision and the specific vision statement developed pertaining to diversity, as well as with dialogue among deans and review of relevant past assessment reports. The Office of Information Management and Institutional Research (IMIR) has provided leadership by engaging units it terms "champion groups," composed of those whose interests or jobs are related to diversity initiatives. These groups meet in brainstorming sessions aimed at identifying indicators for performance objectives related to the campus mission activities on diversity: recruit and enroll a diverse student body; retain and graduate a diverse student body; engage students, through the curriculum and co-curriculum, in learning about their own and other cultures and belief systems; support diversity in research, scholarship, and creative activity; contribute to the climate for diversity in Indianapolis, Central Indiana, and the entire state; recruit, develop, and support diverse faculty and staff; engage the campus community in global issues and perspectives; and improve student, faculty, and staff perceptions of the campus climate for diversity. Measures suggested by the champion groups range from examining institutional data on student enrollment and progress to looking at specific items from nationally-administered instruments such as the National Survey of Student Engagement to analyzing the results of campus surveys of student opinion. A list of diversity performance objectives and data assembled for judging them is available at http://www.iport.iupui.edu/performance/perf_diversity.htm.

IMIR assembles the data from these sources and then presents the resulting documentation to a panel of the champion group members (in the case of diversity, the Diversity Cabinet) to make judgments on the level of performance obtained. A simple rubric for scoring performance and communicating it to the campus and surrounding community uses red, yellow, and green lights as follows:

- Red light: Our current status or direction of change is unacceptable. Immediate, high priority actions should be taken to address this area.
- Yellow light: Not at an acceptable level; either improving, but not as quickly as desired, or declining slightly. Strategies and approaches should be reviewed and appropriate adjustments taken to reach an acceptable level or desired rate of improvement.
- Green light: Either at an acceptable level or clearly heading in the right direction and not requiring any immediate change in course of action. Continuing support should be provided to sustain momentum in these areas.

Individuals within the group first rate the performance using an electronic balloting process, then meet to look at the range of responses and hear arguments when there is difference of opinion, and finally arrive at a common rating for each indicator. Once the indicators have been rated, they are communicated through such vehicles as the State of Diversity speech and report (http://www.iupui.edu/administration/chancellorsnews/state_of_diversity_04.pdf) and the campus institutional portfolio, a web-based vehicle for demonstrating outcomes (http://www. iport.iupui.edu). To promote planning, results are also sent to academic and administrative units from central administration with an annual request for information on how the indicators will be used to improve performance in each unit.

The Office for Professional Development has assisted with the indicators on diversity by helping to identify indicators and criteria, in collaboration with others brought to this task by the Office for Information Management and Institutional Research. It has also collected information that helps to assess the state of diversity at IUPUI. One of the more notable ways in which the DIG attempted to collect information from students on the climate for learning was the "Pizza Surveys." Disappointed with student attendance at focus groups called for this purpose, the DIG staff took the survey on the road, setting up a room close to the lunch area where students of color gather. They used table tents to invite students to come and talk about their experience in exchange for free pizza. Although the sample was not scientific, it was plentiful, and the survey generated an immediate portrait of the experiences of students of color at IUPUI. It was repeated a second time two years later and is being used to inform our efforts on changes made and the continuing need for intervention. Through representation on the Diversity Cabinet, OPD was part of the panel that assessed campus performance on the diversity indicators and is engaged in helping academic and support units develop plans for improving performance on the indicators relating to diversity.

Implications for Faculty Development Centers

One of the reasons for why professional development centers may be slow to engage in organizational development is uncertainty about what this work entails. From the work of such founding members of the professional development movement as Bergquist and Philips (1995) to that of recent organizational theorists who speak of promoting learning organizations (Senge, 1990) and communities of practice (Wenger, 1998), those advocating an organizational development approach suggest a variety of strategies. All emphasize changes that are larger than the individual and involve organizational structure, policies, knowledge management, rewards or sanctions, or even the culture itself. These changes are promoted through providing information, stimulating conversation and inquiry, changing organizational arrangements such as space or assignments, or supplying resources such as consultation or incentives. Applying these to the work of institutional diversity efforts suggests the following courses of action for professional development units in using an organizational development approach.

Being a part of the conversation. Indicating an interest in multicultural initiatives is important. In addition to making comments at meetings, faculty developers can send key leaders copies of good print resources or names of experts or conferences that are helpful in guiding these undertakings, thereby making their interest and knowledge visible. Raising the profile of the professional development unit with respect to diversity increases the chances that it will be part of the conversation.

Creating strong programs. There is no better way to create a high profile than implementing successful programs. When a professional development center initiates workshops, consultations, and print or web resources supporting inclusive teaching and multicultural curriculum transformation, it is not only doing its work well, but it is also situating itself for work with organizational development.

Collaborating with other programs. Making efforts to learn of related diversity programs in other academic and administrative units inspires joint work. Sharing information resources or the cost of a speaker, co-hosting a program, and consulting with another program on how efforts can be complementary are all ways that professional development centers can establish a community of practice.

Serving as the hub of activities. Through taking collaboration to the next level and hosting meetings of staff from other initiatives, organizing a common publication, coordinating a diversity calendar of events, or implementing other activities that make it the hub of networking, the professional development center can serve an important organizational development function.

Assisting with the assessment. The professional development unit can further support organizational growth through helping faculty to assess the impact of their diversity efforts, assisting programs or academic units with climate surveys or program evaluation activities, and working with the campus institutional research office to collect and organize data.

Finally, the professional development center can help to tell the institution's story, reporting in print and at conferences on the discoveries that have been made. Once again, these presentations are likely to be joint ones, reflecting the comprehensive approach that needs to be made in addressing diversity issues. It takes a campus.

References

Anderson, L. (1996). The work of academic development: Occupational identity, standards of practice, and the virtues of association. *International Journal of Academic Development, 1*(1), 38-49.

Barr, R. B., & Tagg, J. (1995). From teaching to learning: A new paradigm for undergraduate education. *Change, 27*(6), 12-25.

Bergquist, W., & Phillips, S. (1995). *Developing human and organizational resources: A comprehensive manual.* Point Arena: Peter Magnusson Press.

Candy, P. C. (1995). Promoting lifelong learning: Academic developers and the university as a learning organization. *The International Journal of Academic Development, 1*(1), 7-11.

Chang, M. (2002). Preservation or transformation: Where's the real educational discourse on diversity? *The Review of Higher Education, 25*(2), 125-140.

Chism, N. (1998). The role of educational developers in institutional change: From the basement office to the front office. In D. Lieberman (Ed.), *To improve the academy, 16*, 141-143. Stillwater, OK: New Forums Press.

Gaff, J. G. (1975). *Toward faculty renewal: Advances in faculty, instructional, and organizational development.* San Francisco: Jossey-Bass.

Hurtado, S. (1996). How diversity affects teaching and learning: A climate of inclusion has a powerful effect on learning outcomes. *Educational Record, 77*(4), 27-29.

James, R. (November, 1997). An organizational learning perspective on academic development: A strategy for an uncertain future. *International Journal for Academic Development, 2*(2), 35-41.

Lieberman, D. A., & Guskin, A. E. (2003). The essential role of faculty development in new higher education models. In C. M. Wehlburg, (Ed.), *To improve the academy, 21,* 257-272. Bolton, MA: Anker.

Nichols, R., Chism, N.V.N., & Wheeler, D. (October, 1992). Building community through organizational development: Where is the OD in POD? Paper presented at the 17th annual conference of the Professional and Organizational Development Network in Higher Education, Tampa, FL.

Office of Student Life & Diversity (2002). Mission statement for student life & diversity programs. Retrieved June 8, 2003, from http://www.life.iupui.edu/docs/SLDVisionWord.pdf

Professional and Organizational Development Network in Higher Education. (2002). *What is faculty development?* Retrieved June 6, 2003, from http://www.podnetwork.org/development/definitions.htm

Senge, P. (1990). *The fifth discipline: The art and practice of the learning organization.* New York: Doubleday.

Smith, D. G., Gerbick, G. L., Figueroa, M. A., Watkins, G. H., Levitan, T., Leeshawn, C. M., Merchant, P. A., Beliak, H. D., & Figueroa, B. (1997). *Diversity works: The emerging picture of how students benefit.* Washington, D C: The American Association of Colleges and Universities.

Stokes, L. (2002) *A progress report of diversity and enrichment initiatives.* Indianapolis, IN: Indiana University School of Nursing.

Wenger, E. (1998). *Communities of practice: Learning, meaning and identity*. Cambridge: Cambridge University Press.

Nancy Chism is the Associate Dean of the Faculties and Associate Vice Chancellor for Academic Affairs at Indiana University Purdue University Indianapolis.
Karen Whitney is the Vice Chancellor for Student Life and Diversity Indiana University Purdue University Indianapolis.

Gratitude is expressed to Victor Borden, Associate Vice Chancellor for Information Management and Institutional Research at IUPUI, who has provided leadership for the diversity indicators and was involved in the generation of ideas for this chapter.

Chapter 4
Defining the Shape of Diversity Pedagogy

Lynn Leonard, Sue Akersten, Stephen Adkison and Edward Nuhfer

Drawing on a broad range of theories about learning and diversity, this chapter describes how the Center for Teaching and Learning at Idaho State University combines student academic services with faculty services to help faculty and students go beyond knowledge about differences to real engagement with the meanings of differences.

I. Synergy and Diversity Pedagogy

In her remarkable book, *Listening to the World: Cultural Issues in Academic Writing,*University of Michigan Professor of English Helen Fox provides a valuable resource for university professionals working with diverse students. Whereas academia has improved since the 1960s and 1970s in terms of representation from the world's cultures,

> multiculturalism has been limited for the most part to theoretical understanding, a mastery of facts and theories, and major ideas, *knowledge about differences* rather than a *real feeling for* what it is to make sense of the world and communicate in totally different ways (p. x).

She wants all instructors to dig deep and understand empathetically, not simply intellectually, what cultural "differences" are:

> Differences, learned from early childhood, affect the way students interact with their professors and classmates, their attitudes toward the books they read, and the problems they are called upon to solve. They affect how students give oral presentations, from short critiques of articles they've

> read to dissertation defenses. They affect how students understand assignments, how they study and how they comment on their classmates' papers. But most of all, these differences affect the way they write, for writing touches the heart of a student's identify, drawing its voice and strength and meaning from the way the student understands the world. (p. xiii)

Understanding differences and developing real feelings for them, then, can be said to be the goals of diversity pedagogy in the Center for Teaching and Learning (CeTL—see http://www.isu.edu/ctl/) at Idaho State University (ISU). Engagement, with all its contradictions, dilemmas, risks, dangers, confusions and discomforts, is at the heart of changes in our brains and of the encounters with complexity that nurtures them along.

The CeTL at ISU combines student academic services with faculty services and bringing together faculty development, content area tutoring, a writing center, a math learning center, management of freshman seminars, the university honors program, clustered learning, college learning strategies, and, of importance to this chapter, the programs in English for speakers of other languages (ESOL) for domestic and international students enrolled in academic and professional programs. This structure permits a mutual contact point for faculty development, research, management, assessment, and a central haven for student support. It has the potential to respond to Fox's challenge to help faculty and students go beyond knowledge about differences to real feeling for the differences.

Comparatively speaking, our ethnic and racial diversity at ISU is modest (700 in a total enrollment of 13,300). This includes representatives of 62 nations, six American Indian tribes, African Americans and students of Mexican heritage. Many of these will visit CeTL for support, along with "majority" undergraduate and graduate students from all disciplines.

Our academic community at ISU may also be unusual in that it constitutes a minority that serves a significantly different majority. Pocatello, the adjoining region, and the vast majority of students that attend ISU are from the nearby area, conservative, very dominantly Latter Day Saint, and generally isolated from the influence of diverse ideological systems. In contrast, the university professorate is not conservative, not particularly bound to a particular religion, and comes mostly from states outside Idaho. Coming to this region of Idaho gives many professors a first experience in being a member of a community as an ideological minority. Recognizing this feeling is probably one of the better ways to confront one's own biases about minorities and to develop compassion for the status of being a minority member. To produce high quality education, both professors and students must transcend ideological boundaries.

Our Center works with development of both faculty and students in helping them achieve this.

Our good fortune in being a central "hub of synergy" enables us to hold the kinds of conversations that could not occur without this convergent structure. While the ESOL staff has a range of academic support expertise at its door to draw upon, conversely, Writing Center tutors can also walk a few feet to the offices of the ESOL staff with questions about cultural or language differences facing a non-native speaker who has made a writing appointment. A College Learning Strategies coordinator can pop her head into the office for suggestions on how to draw a new student from Kenya into discussions; the Math Lab director, upon receiving complaints that students cannot understand a tutor from China, can immediately arrange an assessment, get support for the tutor, and explore attitudes of the tutees themselves. A freshman seminar instructor notices a student from Mexico struggling with reading comprehension, and we can work immediately with the student to build skills and confidence. More importantly, the instructor can learn about the needs of this ever-increasing 1.5 generation population (37% over the last two years, reflecting the one in 10 Idaho Hispanics). The CeTL offers tutor training and faculty development that draws from these richly diverse experiences to better align outcomes with pedagogy. The intellectual growth, and the enhancement of sensitivity and "feeling for" that occurs in all of us results from a cooperative synergy in learning diversity. Development practiced in the CeTL is holistic, with emphasis on teaching, learning, and thinking, and grounded in an understanding that specific neural networks develop as brain changes occur from particular kinds of educational experiences. Neural networks grow in branching fractal patterns, and we model our faculty development in accord with that awareness so that the developmental experiences draw on a diversity of characteristics that goes beyond content learning and pedagogical techniques (Nuhfer, 2003).

II. Educating the Brain: Biology and Diversity

When we speak of diversity as an educational strength rather than as an obstacle to overcome, it is consistent with how we support and develop educators by providing opportunities through which they can choose to grow in many dimensions. In this endeavor, we echo the foundational early work of L. S. Vygotsky (1986) and his Zone of Proximal Development (ZPD). Vygotsky's concept of the ZPD posits that for a given cognitive task, any individual occupies a zone of proximal development that represents his learning potential in that context. Vygotsky found that individuals working alone tend to operate in the lower reaches of their ZPD, while rich and structured social interaction with peers and instructors pushed individuals higher into their zones. Thus, the more individuals interact with others in learning situations, the more effectively they learn. Vygotsky's findings and related work by A. R. Luria (1976) and Jerome Bruner (1986, 1990) form the cognitive foundation upon which much of our knowledge of collaborative learning rests.

Additionally, social interaction by its very nature is language-based, symbolic behavior (Deacon, 1997) through which we do not just communicate but also create and shape meaning. Since the symbolic aspects of this behavior are founded in social interaction between members of a given group or community, it is easy to understand learning, in one sense, as a series of acts of making meaning both to and between ourselves. Our most effective approaches to learning, particularly in language and writing contexts, see learning not as a set of discrete activities, but rather as an integrated activity in which we engage the fullest possible range of cognitive processes such as speaking, reading, listening, seeing, and writing. Deacon's work in comparative neuroscience led him to theorize that symbolic language behavior and exchange between brains through language favored survival and thereby evolved. This led to who we are — language-using social animals — in a literal sense, both cognitively and biologically.

This realization is crucial to understanding why the process of learning is fundamentally neural in nature, not just metaphorically but literally. Robert Leamnson (1999) notes that the human brain is composed of roughly a hundred billion neurons connected by axons that form synapses between neurons, and that the brain's capacity to perceive and make sense of the world is a function of these neuronal connections. And Leamnson further notes the number of connected neurons (synapses) increases several-fold with increased age as particular experiences lead to development and stabilization of synapses. Two points here are of particular significance: it is the multiple connections between neurons that allow perception and thought – not just the number of neurons, and it is experience and sensory interaction with the environment that promote and stabilize neural connections. Learning occurs in all normal adults, regardless of race, color, creed, income, age, religion, ethnicity, or language background in exactly the same neurological way. Thus, the conceptualization of diversity is also largely the result of reinforced experiences. This information tells us that teaching practices likely to be most effective employ and develop the widest range of neural functions and structures. Promoting an understanding of how suitable brain development occurs and how the laying down of diverse neural pathways relates to appreciating diversity is a top priority in the work we do.

III. Faculty and Fractals

Assume three students, a vegetarian, a vegan, and a meat lover discuss the nutritional and moral merits of food and perceive the others' different affective responses to their claims; synaptic growth occurs in all three brains. This simple case involving differing viewpoints enables intellectual development and awareness. If only two held the discussion, it would not be as rich, and neural growth would be more constrained. Just as views of food are limited through respective gastronomic or ethnic experience, so are views in every conceivable discipline and branch of learning. This simple case also starkly highlights the outright necessity—not just desirability—of diversity in terms of teaching and learning. The wider the range of multiple perspectives that learners encounter and engage, the more effective and meaningful the learning that results. Likewise, faculty development that incorporates a rich approach of both introspection and interaction with others is more likely to promote the neural growth needed for faculty to become increasingly competent professional practitioners. In our summer program, Boot Camp for Profs®,[1] our faculty interact in a prolonged retreat setting with faculty from diverse institutions and from diverse cultural backgrounds. When faculty members return and use similar approaches to coach students so as to enrich their own reflective learning processes, incredible beneficence results from such development. The fractal model promotes a richness of development that, in turn, promotes a personal evolving identity of self-awareness at intellectual, ethical, and emotional levels. It can inform practice through the spectrum of work that ranges from individual tutoring sessions through classes, courses, academic curricula, and support of institutional missions. This model allows us to build a comprehensive diversity pedagogy that is an integral part of producing educational quality. The inclusion of "shape" in our chapter title is an important word choice. Readers can learn more about the fractal model by examining the Developers' Diary columns we furnished for the National Teaching and Learning Forum between 2001 and 2005. Readers can also see the fractal basis for design of our summer faculty development retreat, Boot Camp for Profs (http://www.isu.edu/ctl/nutshells/old_nutshells/6_604.htm).

Our approach to development integrates assessment and employs some unique, sophisticated tools: formative surveys (see http://www.isu.edu/ctl/facultydev/extras/60%20pt.htm) that validate good practices as informed by the research; knowledge surveys (see http://www.isu.edu/ctl/facultydev/KnowS_files/KnowS.htm) that promote organization and planning, and disclose

[1]Boot Camp for Profs is a registered term.

content, levels of thinking and the learning changes imparted through a course; and student management teams (see http://www.isu.edu/ctl/facultydev/webhandbook/smt.htm) that insure face to face discussions between faculty and students about the teaching, learning, and thinking process. These all involve mutual engagement by both students and faculty. This differs greatly from development that emphasizes sequestering faculty into their own workshops and evaluating "success" through evaluation forms completed by students at the end of a course when any chance for mutual engagement is gone.

We advocate for active learning techniques, for moving students progressively toward higher levels of thinking, and for assessment of learning outcomes. We believe meaningful engagement of diversity requires these things. Yet, in an institution where student satisfaction ratings take precedence in importance for faculty over assessment of student learning, a faculty member in a class of students not motivated or not enthusiastic about moving past assumptions may engage initially in such activities at some personal peril. Weimer (2002) was refreshingly candid about the fact that effective learner-centered approaches in any subject will be unappreciated by students unaccustomed to them and that the faculty member who introduces these will meet resistance. Thorn (2003) also noted lower student evaluations of faculty who strove initially to move their students toward higher levels of thinking instead of merely conveying low-level content. Resistance to moving undergraduates out of their comfort zones through alternative pedagogies or toward higher levels of thinking in a classroom appears to result, at least initially, in lowered student evaluations, even in subjects that have no particular political or emotional weight. While Fox wants instructors and students to dig deep and have real feelings for one another and for the ways cultures perceive and communicate about the world, this does not mean that the process is comfortable or free of risks. Laying down and strengthening synapses is hard work for both faculty and students.

IV. Practical Applications of the CeTL Approach

No intellectual development, increased instructional competence, or appreciation of diversity, happens by mystical transformation. One on one tutoring, small group interaction, self assessments, journaling, and the stimulation of engagement and introspection are tools that teachers can use to foster the multicultural understanding that Fox seeks.

Preachy approaches or misguided political agendas that educate by force of guilt or punishment are not rooted in either an ethical framework or much awareness of how people learn and internalize meaning. In contrast, brains change by choice when learning happens through meaningful inquiry and cooperation within a diverse environment. Personal introspection is probably one of the dominant characteristics of a master teacher (and master learner). We believe that the role of introspection that leads to constant adaptation, innovation, and student-centered philosophy in the successful teacher is also at the heart of the pedagogy we seek. The best practices in general contain common recognizable qualities that lead to responsive teaching that benefits all students, not simply "minorities," or "different," especially if this includes "different from the instructor."

It is through personal introspection that we can determine where our focus is relative to where it needs to be. When one perceives educational outcomes as the assessable results of collaboration between faculty and students to better achieve and to visualize mutual interests, that realization produces an advantage in intellectual creativity and exploration. This is no trivial matter; rich exploration in a brief time is not possible in a monoculture. Diversity pedagogy makes use of the differences among us to perceive our assumptions, which in turn develops the brain in ways that can value newly discovered complex areas of human endeavor. This pedagogy strengthens self-awareness and optimizes chances for the "Aha!" moments. Successful teachers allow for introspection and feedback at every stage of the journey and maintain a good balance between self-awareness and engagement. In diversity pedagogy, progress occurs during self-assessment as students realize the complexity of the world, make better sense of it, and are more comfortable with differences, ambiguities, and unsolved problems. To get to this point, they must be able to withhold judgment long enough to analyze what is really happening. Here we see the balance needed between knowledge about something and a real feeling for it.

Another emphasis of the CeTL is the efficacy of one-on-one interaction between teacher and student and between developer and faculty consultant. Tutoring is the primary mode of support in our ESL/ESOL programs, Writing Center, Math Center, and Content Area Program. Although it may be true that tutoring done badly breeds dependence, tutoring done well does not, and to date, Bloom's (1984) report that nothing produces better learning outcomes than tutoring still stands. Our approach focuses on students identifying areas where things did not go as expected and coming up with reasons why. The tutor acts as a facilitator to help explore the hidden assumptions.

The mandated mission of ISU is the training of health professionals for the state. Most future health practitioners here are "mono" cultural, representative of the ISU student majority mentioned earlier: local, conservative, dominantly Latter Day Saint, and generally isolated from the influence of diverse ideological and linguistic systems. They must be taught to think and serve diverse clients responsively and inclusively in much the same way as future "mono" teachers should be trained (Villagos & Lucas, 2002). In this spirit, self-assessment through peer and small group discussion, journaling, and one on one dialogue with supervisors and consultants, are effective diversity pedagogies used in the Accent Modification Evaluation (AME) at ISU, sponsored by the ESOL program and the ISU Department of Communication Sciences and Disorders. "Mono" graduate speech clinicians and "multi" ESOL clients complete a highly collaborative, inclusive practicum. To date 80 therapists and 240 students from 37 language backgrounds have participated in this cooperative project that responds to participant feedback and changing circumstances. When one compares the evolution of thinking in clinician and client self-descriptions to the well-established, sophisticated student assessment framework based on the findings of Perry (1999), developed at Alverno College (Loacker, 2000), and used in the AME process, one sees immediate parallels in the patterns of higher level critical thinking skills that emerge.

Before the AME experience, ESOL students' self-rankings in various communication situations, the examples they give, and their explanations for misunderstandings with native speaking Americans, are often supremely different from the perceptions of the native speaking instructor who referred the student to the program or from those of the native speaking Americans with whom the student works on class projects. The clinicians marvel at the distance between their perception of the client after the first meeting and the self portrait painted in the intake questionnaire. Later, after the reflection process, both clinicians and clients realize how cultural values and perceptions contribute to the answers on the questionnaire. Some students rank themselves modestly because to do otherwise is "boasting." On the other hand, some students rank themselves highly, especially students from countries where the *lingua franca* is English, such as India, many African and Caribbean nations, and Australia. These speakers often attribute misunderstandings to American listeners' bias, racism, or cultural and linguistic imperialism. Their descriptions of when and why a breakdown occurs are often vague ("They said I didn't pronounce it right") or imply that the listener is at fault ("Even when I repeated it louder, she couldn't understand, so I hung up;" "They don't understand British"). When the speakers understand on a conscious level how first language and American English differ and how culture unconsciously informs all behavior of everyone involved, they become less defensive about making changes to open up the native speaking American listeners to their ideas.

Not all learning results in healthful or optimal pathways that best serve the needs of an individual or a modern society. As Oscar Hammerstein (1949) in *South Pacific* warned, "You've got to be taught to hate and fear/...It's got to be drummed in your dear little ear." If prejudice and snobbery are learned, then they become rooted in synaptic pathways just as surely as do acceptance and respect. One AME example stands out. A Mexican client, age 22, was "introduced" by audiotape and self-survey at the weekly staffing. She reported that she had dropped out of high school to take care of her siblings when her mother suffered a catastrophic stroke working in the fields. She completed her GED during her mother's recuperation. Four years later, the young woman was taking her first course at ISU and was worried about her spoken English intelligibility. An AME clinician wrote in her journal, "Why are we wasting time with this one? How do we know she is motivated? She will just drop out again." Later, that same clinician wrote, "I was so wrong. I only noticed that she had dropped out; I spaced out that she had cared enough to get the GED. When I met her, I saw her resolve and intelligence. I reread the questionnaire and relistened to the intake tape. How could I have missed 'hearing' what she said?" Fox would be proud of this clinician who was now listening in an informed way.

In our Center, much of our coaching and tutoring involves rubrics that other professors have given to students for assignments in their courses. Sometimes, the rubrics we see are badly constructed or are not really rubrics at all, and a student is unclear about what it is that is in a paper that makes it successful or why. As rubrics reflect the cultural experiences and assumptions of their creators, those that rely narrowly and exclusively on the culture of the writer place major hurdles in front of the student from a different cultural background that must be negotiated before he or she can successfully use the rubric. The research on thinking and rubrics has serious implications for diversity pedagogy. Every discipline from hard sciences to fine arts uses an established framework of reasoning to make evaluations and decisions. In order to reach high-level thinking, students need to understand the process for using the framework of reasoning. Further, open-ended assignments must involve evaluation based on the thinking process rather than arriving at pat right or wrong (or worse, the professor's!) conclusions. This framework requires the discipline of diversity to likewise disclose its frameworks of reasoning, to stress the process of reasoning, and to write rubrics that disclose what constitutes high quality reasoning. For these reasons, faculty development at ISU includes the principles for constructing rubrics, especially for writing. If students or other faculty perceive diversity education as indoctrination rather than education, it is likely because the faculty involved in diversity pedagogy have not conveyed the framework of reasoning or clarified the rubrics employed in evaluation.

A case of broad interest is the understanding of plagiarism (see http://www.isu.edu/ctl/nutshells/nutshell11-3.html). We frequently address the related issues in both our Writing Center and in our ESOL programs. Our experiences of helping students to "think plagiarism through" via the tutoring format confirms that this form of pedagogy is effective. Typically, a student from another culture brings in a paper that fails to follow the acceptable rules to properly attribute ideas to their sources. Undoubtedly, the student's syllabus states that plagiarism will result in failure, yet in her culture, intellectual property is communal. The student frequently has trouble recognizing that in the American academic culture, intellectual property is an individual property right and that the professor is interested in her personal viewpoint. The idea that she is to read what others have said, think critically, and come to her own conclusions that she then expresses in her paper is a new concept. Once students have internalized the concept, they may still be unskilled in the integration of material and attribution of sources, ideas, and facts. These processes range from distinguishing what is common knowledge in a culture from what requires attribution, to ascertaining which choice of synonym in a paraphrase will best reflect the author's intention and tone.

One on one tutoring intensely fosters the laying down and strengthening of synapses, but note that when students plagiarize once and succeed in obtaining their desired grade, this also establishes a neural network. Stabilizing inappropriate connections precludes better choices for dealing with academic expectations. One challenge of diversity pedagogy, as in all disciplines, is to bring components of the tutoring relationship into the classroom itself. Culture-bound thinking, absent or poorly constructed rubrics, and the dozens of steps needed to avoid plagiarism are both student support and faculty development issues.

Summary

Students request services because they are not satisfied with their own efforts and want counseling in order to know what they can do differently to be more successful. The idea that "education" is merely content learning – most of it low-level — is prevalent across most cultures. By modeling our efforts to produce education as a fractal form, we use content as an entry connection for students and faculty, but we also do not lose sight of other essential components. A major goal, therefore, is to provide students with opportunities to obtain an appropriate command of the language of disciplinary content, because meaningful discussion of ideas requires a certain breadth and depth of language including syntax. But another major goal is to provide students with opportunities to gain understanding of the assumptions underlying the academic community as well as the broader culture as a whole. The structure of our particular center allows us to promote the same messages to students and faculty, and to better support our institution's goals and objectives. We begin at the current level of the individual and go as far as he or she deems desirable. It is important to note that common problems found in ESL/ESOL students are also shared by native speakers of American English—problems that arise from being unaware of effects of assumptions. To the extent that students and faculty have limited or no experience in dealing with other cultures, they face real challenges in being able to gain perspectives on their own cultures in the larger context.

Fractal shapes and patterns provide excellent models through which to develop a holistic, comprehensive view of teaching, learning, thinking, and education as it occurs at the level of the individual, through the institution, and over time. Teachers need a more comprehensive view than their disciplines usually provide, and students need a similar comprehensive view to develop a philosophy of learning. There are good reasons that "thinking in fractals" can improve practice based on research from a variety of disciplines.

The word "diversity" is politically charged, and biases and preconceptions will precede students' (and some faculty members') acceptance of diversity as a legitimate area of scholarship. Diversity content, at the heart of changes in our brains and of the encounters with complexity that nurtures them along, simply adds one more degree of risk to the faculty member if his or her career depends too much on receiving high ratings of satisfaction from students. The assessment movement, which values documentation of actual learning outcomes over satisfaction ratings of professors, is a positive step forward, in particular for diversity pedagogy. But if we as a culture wish to go beyond emotional responses that flare into divisions and strife, we must protect the trained faculty member who is coaching our students into the knowledge and sensitivities needed to live creatively and productively together.

References

Bloom, B. S. (1984). The 2 sigma problem: The search for methods of group instruction as effective as one-to-one tutoring. *Educational Researcher, 4*(6), 4-16.

Bruner, J. (1986). *Actual minds, possible worlds*. Cambridge, MA: Harvard University Press.

Bruner, J. (1990). *Acts of meaning*. Cambridge, MA: Harvard University Press.

Davis, B. G. (1993). *Tools for teaching*. San Francisco: Jossey-Bass.

Deacon, T. (1997). *The symbolic species: The coevolution of language and the brain*. New York: Norton.

Fox, H. (1994). *Listening to the world: Cultural issues in academic writing*. Urbana, IL: National Council of Teachers.

Leamnson, R. (1999). *Thinking about teaching and learning: Developing habits of learning with first year college and university students*. Sterling, VA: Stylus.

Loacker, G. (Ed.). (2000). *Self assessment at Alverno College*. Milwaukee, WI: Alverno College.

Luria, A. R. (1976). *Cognitive development: Its cultural and social foundations*. Cambridge, MA: Harvard University Press.

Nuhfer, E. B. (2003). Developing in fractal patterns I: Moving beyond diagnoses, evaluations and fixes. *National Teaching and Learning Forum, 12*(2), 7-9.

Perry, W. G., Jr. (1999). *Forms of ethical and intellectual development in the college years: A scheme*. San Francisco: Jossey-Bass.

Villegas, A. M., & Lucas, T. (2002). *Educating culturally responsive teachers: A coherent approach*. Albany: State of New York Press.

Vygotsky, L. S. (1986). *Thought and language*. Cambridge, MA: MIT Press.

Weimer, M. (2002) *Learner-centered teaching: Five key changes to practice*. San Francisco: Jossey-Bass.

Lynn Leonard, **Sue Akersten**, **Steve Adkison** and **Edward Nuhfer** are colleagues in the Center for Teaching and Learning, Idaho State University, Campus Box 8010, Pocatello, ID, 83209.

Chapter 5
Transcultural Issues in Teaching and Learning

Bland Tomkinson

University-level teaching often features a student body from a wide range of backgrounds. In a university with an international reputation, this body may well include a number of students from a range of other countries, as well as lecturers from a similarly diverse background. This chapter introduces some of the issues that this confluence of cultures raises and describes part of the modules that are designed to deal with them. In a sense it is a "double-whammy," not only dealing with the issues of teaching a many-cultural group of teachers but also teaching them how to teach diverse groups of students.

Why Transcultural?

We often use the word multicultural or even intercultural but *transcultural* might seem a little unusual. The obvious difference is between multicultural, where we are looking at the effects of different cultural backgrounds within a nation, and inter-cultural, where we are looking at differences in culture between nations. Sometimes the phrase cross-cultural is also used and embraces the other concepts. The term transcultural will be used here to reflect both of the previous terms to some measure, although primarily in the intercultural sense.

Bob Garratt (1994) makes references to the terms "micro-culture" and "macro-culture" to distinguish between the cultural differences at a local level (for example, between subject specialisms and work groups) and at a national level. He also uses the terms "mini-culture" as a variant on micro-culture when talking specifically about the organization and its social structures and "meta-culture," which he sees as transcending other aspects of culture in the sense of giving direction to an organization. I find these latter two distinctions less helpful than the others.

The Context

In a university with an international reputation, there may be both a number of students from a variety of other countries and also teaching staff from a wide range of international backgrounds. This can pose special problems for the lecturer who needs to be aware not only of language difficulties but also of the effects of different cultural backgrounds on how students learn. Even within a single country, there can often be a great diversity of cultures both from regional differences and also from major immigrant groups.

The temptation is to try to list all the possible groups that might be met and to list their cultural attributes. This can easily lead to stereotyping – viewing a person as having a set of qualities thought to be typical of their country – and the overlooking of individual differences, as well as perpetuating wrong ideas about other people's cultures. What we are looking for in the university setting is an approach to understanding how students differ and how their cultural backgrounds may influence these differences.

This chapter is written largely from a British university background of teaching lecturers, who in turn may be teaching students from a diverse mix of national and ethnic backgrounds. The same principles can apply to teachers of any cultural background who are teaching to mixed groups of students in any country. Indeed, we have applied the same approach to a group of Chinese lecturers learning to teach in English to students who were not necessarily British. Some of the material described here has also been used with other groups – for example a mixed group of teaching and administrative staff following a program in Student Support, and the induction of students following an international program at the masters level.

The Approach

The approach is both didactic and experiential: with an international group, it is possible to draw on their own experiences to help themselves as well as their colleagues. In a specific session on transcultural aspects of teaching and learning, first we look at some of the problems that students from overseas might face, some of which may be held in common with indigenous students. Some of these may also be faced by students moving within a country, for example, from a small rural community to a large city university, or from a region with a strong regional identity to a more metropolitan one. We then move on to concepts that we associate with "culture" and some of the ideas of Edward T. Hall (1966) on different aspects of culture. Then we look at some of the problems that students from one country may face when studying in another country. The next sections deal with strategies for helping those who teach students from other countries, including ways of helping cross cultural communication, and finally we look at the processes involved in adjusting to another culture. Participants are invited to compare these experiences with how they feel (or would feel, for indigenous participants) about settling down in another culture.

Depending upon the context, we might start the specific session, or a series of sessions, with an international "warmer" (the phrase "ice-breaker" was thought to convey the wrong sense by some of our international participants. The word "warmer" was suggested by a Norwegian student). Much of the material that we use for sessions dealing explicitly with transcultural issues is drawn from Lago (1990), later revised by Lago and Barty (2003).

Transcultural aspects are also embedded in other sessions in our key programs so that, for example, a session on learning theories and learning styles picks up on studies showing cultural impact on learning styles (for example, Edwards,1994; Mohamed, 1997); a session on teaching and learning in groups looks at cultural influences on group work, and a session on personal tutoring looks at aspects of cross-cultural communication.

Getting Started

Games with a cultural spin can be very useful "warmers'" for sessions looking at transcultural issues, but they need to be used with care. Lago and Barty (2003) give an example called "Cultural Greetings" that we adapted for use in our programs. Our version comprises sets of colored cards and a set of greetings printed on the cards of each color. The cards are shuffled and dealt out one to each participant, and the object of the exercise is to find players with matching cards by greeting the other participants in the manner shown on the card. An example of this idea is shown in Figure 1. Those of you who are experienced may spot some of the danger signs instantly, and we allowed an exchange of cards for those who would face difficulty in using a specific form of greeting. For example, it was no surprise, for example, that "Rub noses" was the one most often traded greeting. But the danger here is that merely using a particular form of greeting might give offence – any form of physical contact, including shaking hands, is anathema to some. However, the exercise can be useful in prompting a discussion of fears, prejudices, and stereotypes that arise when different greetings or body language are used.

A more successful, but often time-consuming, starter has been to divide the class up into groups of eight to12 (smaller groups detract from the richness, and larger groups become unmanageable) and ask each individual for a five minute presentation to their group about their name. Participants are allowed to talk about all or part of their given name or nickname. This works for monocultural groups when the objective is simply to help individuals learn a little more about one another, but with groups of different ethnic or national background, the activity can also provide a trigger for insight into different naming systems and can enrich the cultural understanding of participants.

Setting the Transcultural Scene

Having warmed up the audience, the next stage is to set the scene. We do this in two ways: first there is an interactive session that explores the requirements or goals of this particular group, and second, we explore our conceptions of culture. For example, often a group of faculty or support staff need to look at the student perspective, so our initial exploration will focus on that territory. Table 1 gives an example of the ideas that would arise – this table would be issued later as a "here is one that I prepared earlier" handout.

Different groups of staff have different needs, and it is important both to be flexible and also to discuss with the group the direction that the rest of the session might take. I do consider it important, at this stage, to identify what we understand by the term "culture," particularly when I am dealing with groups that have significant representation from other cultures. Some groups – largely academic teaching staff – then prefer to have more background theory, and we will focus on first Hall and then Hofstede (1980). Other groups, for example support staff, prefer a more pragmatic approach, and we will perhaps start with Hall and then move on to discussion of case studies. Perhaps surprisingly, the approach varies less with the macro-cultural mix of the participants than with the micro-cultural mix and is illustrative of the fact that ethnic back-

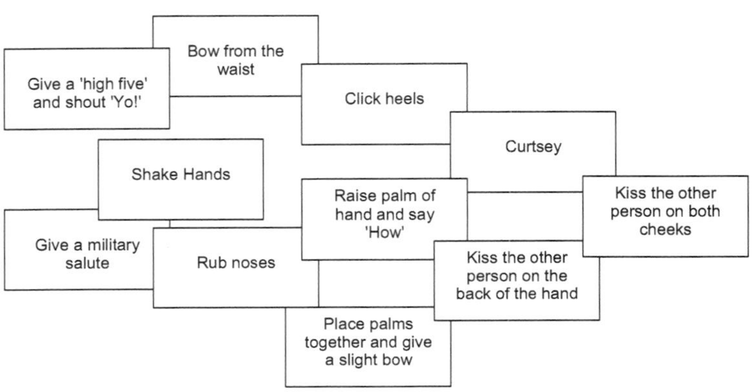

Figure 1. Cultural Greetings

Table 1. Problems that students from other cultures may experience

In lectures

- lecturer may speak too quickly
- lecturer may speak with an unfamiliar accent
- lecturer may use colloquial expressions
- student may have lack of confidence in contributing
- lecturer may perceive student interjections as ill-mannered
- lecturer may use unfamiliar examples and analogies

In seminars and tutorials

- time taken to translate statements into own language and formulate a response in English
- lack of confidence in own spoken English
- lack of confidence in delivering and engaging
- lack of ability in planning and producing an input
- lack of experience with discussion methods
- unwillingness to debate with the teacher and other students
- difficulty understanding what is expected in terms of ideas
- difficulty in writing case study reports

In project work

- difficulty in thinking of appropriate ideas
- lack of experience in working independently
- problems with planning and organising the work
- difficulties with writing reports
- may perceive quantity as a substitute for quality
- may be highly motivated but lacking confidence

In practical work

- not good at working alone
- communication difficulties, especially in fieldwork
- practical work is perceived as demeaning
- difficulties with writing practical reports
- use of equipment

In role-play

- lack of confidence in spoken English
- difficulty with an unusual method
- worry about 'loss of face'
- tense and withdrawn approach

In independent learning

- lack of experience with these methods
- difficulty in planning and organising own work
- may prefer to be directed and helped by teacher
- may be a tendency to rote learning ie surface, rather than deep, learning style

ground has less bearing on the approach than subject background and, more particularly, role. The other key factor in applying what is essentially the same pack of materials to different audiences is the embeddedness of this section. In teaching new faculty, whether British or overseas (and remember that U.S. culture is often very different from U.K. culture), transcultural issues will come in the immediate context of other sessions on the ethics of teaching; on teaching those with physical disabilities; on the hegemony of equality and diversity; and on teaching and learning styles. Staff concerned with the support of students, on the other hand, will attend a session in a diffuse (one session every two weeks or so) program covering issues relating to the psychological, physical, emotional, and financial needs of students and the problems that they face in their studies.

Exploring the conceptions of culture is undertaken in a similar way to the exploration of student needs, starting with a blank flip-chart or white board. The model that we are aiming for here is the "iceberg" model devised by American Field Service (AFS) Intercultural/International Programs (1990) that seeks to distinguish between the aspects of culture of which we are consciously aware (the tip of the iceberg) and those of which we are less aware. In the former group are aspects such as customs, dress, folklore, food, history, language, and literature. Examples of the latter (the nine-tenths that lies beneath the surface) include attitude towards authority, communication style, ethics, learning styles, management styles, motivation, pace of work, patterns of thought and speech, patterns of working, ways of establishing rapport, and ways of reaching agreement. These attributes can be illustrated by inviting contributions from participants and writing them up in such a fashion that the iceberg can afterwards be superimposed. The iceberg serves to illustrate the complexity and diversity of culture while also pointing to the subtlety of some cultural differences.

In the field of learning, Martin Cortazzi and LiXian Jin (1997) make a distinction between "academic culture," which they see as the cultural norms and expectations of academic activity, "culture of communication," which refers to ways of dealing with dialogue and communication, and "culture of learning," which refers to beliefs and values about education. Both Cortazzi and Lin, as well as Tobias Specker and Johann Engelhard (2004) make use of Johan Galtung's (1981) intellectual styles, although Cortazzi and Lin make the point that the typology is fundamentally incomplete and introduce a fifth, "Sinic," style to Galtung's four of "Saxonic," "Nipponic," "Teutonic," and "Gallic." One might also question whether the intellectual cultures of Africa and South America have been simplified in Galtung's typology, and, hence, I find it better not to use it.

The Work of Hall and Others

For the main part of the session, I draw largely on Hall (1959, 1966), with additional material from Lago (1990) and Serpell (1976). With some audiences I also use material from Hofstede (1980) *(vide infra)*. Hall proposes five major categories of difference between cultures, based on much research literature (Lago & Barty, 2003). The five categories are space, time, verbal behavior, nonverbal behavior and context.

Space. Hall considers space under five headings: interpersonal space,

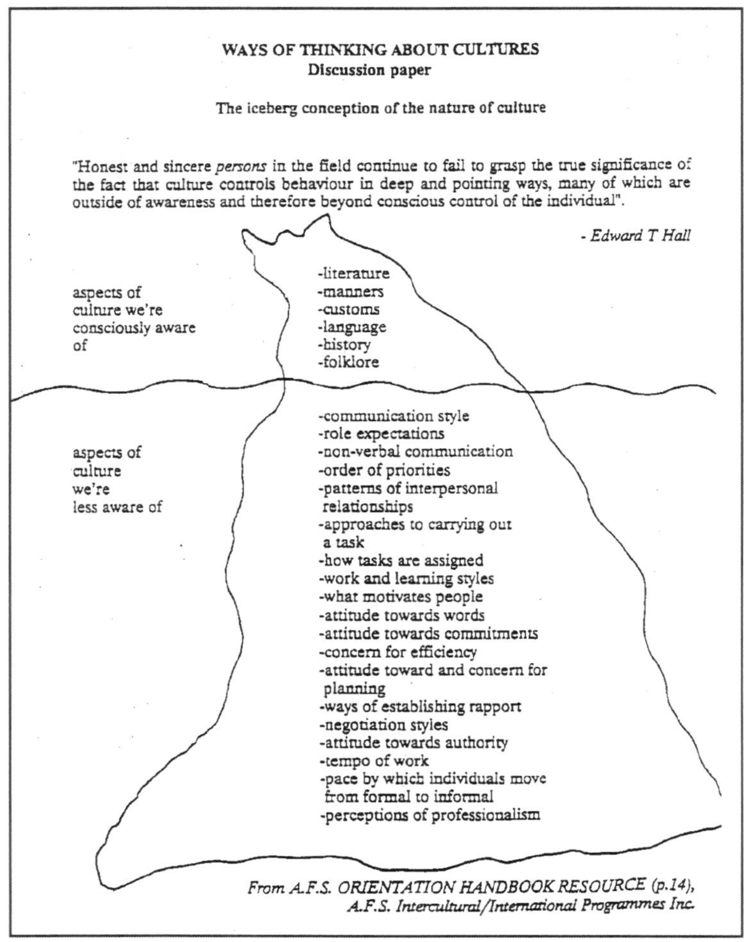

Figure 2. The 'Iceberg' model of the nature of Culture

olfactory space (a way of sensing the other person), thermal space (for example, going "red in the face" when angry or blushing), visual space, and social space (for example, arrangements that either enhance or inhibit interactions between people). Cultures have different conventions about the space between individuals in social situations. For example, people from certain cultures stand and converse at much closer distances than those from other cultures. Feelings of discomfort can be generated in such circumstances by the person who feels her or his space is being "intruded." This discomfort can lead to the "Embassy shuffle" (supposedly arising from diplomatic functions where people of many cultures are gathered together), where one individual moves closer to someone else only for that person to move back as the first person encroaches on their personal space, and so on.

We use visual space to gather and convey information. Serpell (1976) looks at some of the cultural cues in pictorial depiction, for example three-dimensional representation and conceptualisation and perception of depth. He also suggests varying degrees of field dependence or independence between different cultures. Some part of this variation may be environmentally determined, and some he attributes to nurture. Field dependence relates to an individual's tendency to identify objects or concepts within a frame of reference, whereas field-independence suggests that the individual is able to perceive objects or concepts independently of their frame of reference.

Time. Hall divides time into two broad categories, monochronic and polychronic. In general terms, monochronic time refers to the western dominated view of the 24 hour day in which only that time system for measurement exists(The train leaves at . . ., Come to dinner at . . .'). Polychronic time is a much less well-known view of time, but is practised by certain cultures. Hall (based on earlier work by Whorf) cites the example of the Hopi Indians in the United States who have a belief in each thing and each person having their own time. At this stage, I often find it a useful discussion point to get a show of hands as to how many people turn up early, exactly on time, and "fashionably late" for a dinner engagement.

Verbal behaviour. This is a much more obvious division between cultures, especially where languages differ. However, even in the case of both participants using the same language, the use of similar words may have different meanings, and there are different conventions for expressing opinions and so forth. The capacity to which empathy may be extended to culturally different others may therefore be quite limited.

Nonverbal behavior. Cultural differences in nonverbal behaviour can include: movements of the body (head, arms, legs, and so forth), the use of or avoidance of eye-to-eye contact, and where, how, and how often people can touch each other while conversing. The differences of role, class, and status are also arenas for considerable confusion between cultures as the various signals and cues to infer these positions are often quite invisible to "outsiders."

Context. Hall draws broad distinctions between what he terms "high context" and "low context" cultures. In low context cultures, words are presumed to carry all meaning. In some cultures, words and meaning do not have such a direct connection. Notions of truth, consequently, are relative and culturally based. By contrast, high context cultures tend to be more conservative structures where individual needs are sacrificed for group goals. However, these are cultures in which "a person's word is his or her bond," and there is less reliance on formal, written contracts.

All of this information has to be set in the teaching and learning context, using examples relevant to the particular group. I can almost count on one or more students turning up late, just as I am talking about cultural attitudes to time. This situation provides the perfect opportunity to apply real-life experience to the material that is being taught.

The Work of Geert Hofstede

I tend to use Geert Hofstede's work (1980, 1988) only with groups who have expressed a preference for a deeper theoretical underpinning, where this approach may be of more benefit. Hofstede is best known for his four dimensions of cultural variability, to which he added a fifth in 1988. These dimensions are Individualism/Collectivism, Masculinity/Femininity, Power Distance, and Uncertainty Avoidance, with the fifth known either as Confucian Dynamism or Long-term Orientation.

Individualism-Collectivism. This focuses on the degree the society reinforces individual or collective achievement and interpersonal relationships, and is similar to Hall's concept of context. A high Individualism ranking indicates that individuality is dominant within the society; individuals in these societies may tend to form a larger number of looser relationships. A high Collectivism ranking is found in societies with closer ties between individuals. These cultures reinforce extended families, clans, and other groups where everyone takes responsibility for their fellows.

Masculinity-Femininity. This focuses on expected gender roles. A high Masculinity ranking indicates that the country experiences a high degree of gender differentiation. In such cultures, males dominate a significant portion of the society and power structure, with females being controlled by male domination. A high Femininity ranking indicates the country has a low level of differentiation and discrimination between genders. In these cultures, females are treated as equal to males in all aspects of the society.

Power Distance. This focuses on the degree of equality or inequality between people. People in high Power Distance countries are likely to be more at ease with large status differentials within society. These societies are more likely to follow a caste or class system that does not allow significant upward mobility of its citizens. A low Power Distance ranking indicates that the society places less value on differences between citizens' power and wealth, and that opportunity for everyone is stressed.

Uncertainty Avoidance. This focuses on people's level of tolerance for ambiguity in uncertain and unstructured situations. A high Uncertainty Avoidance rating shows that citizens have a low tolerance for uncertainty and ambiguity. This often leads to a rule-oriented society that decrees rules and regulations in order to reduce the ambiguity. A low Uncertainty Avoidance rating indicates that the country has more tolerance for ambiguity and for a variety of opinions. This is reflected in a society that is less rule-bound and is more willing to accept change.

Long-term Orientation. This focuses on the extent to which a society embraces long-term attachment to traditional, forward thinking values. High Long-Term Orientation indicates that the country subscribes to the values of long-term commitment and respect for tradition. A low Long-Term Orientation ranking indicates that society does not attach importance to long-term, traditional orientation. In this type of culture, change can occur more rapidly.

These concepts can aid a better understanding of the underlying psychology that underpins cultural differences, but I find it more difficult to relate the analysis to classroom teaching. It is worth stressing the importance of avoiding stereotypes: it is easy to look up an analysis for any given country according to Hofstede's approach and assume that all its citizens will behave in exactly the same way. In practice, the diversity within any culture is very likely to have considerable overlaps with people from very different societies. A recent example of this reality occurred when I was preparing to teach a Chinese group and consulted a website that offered me an analysis for any country according to Hofstede's approach. I had thought that it would be interesting for my class to compare the analyses for China and the U.K.; the analyses were useful for discussion, but were accompanied by some less scientific anecdotes about both countries that I found derisory if not insulting. This example underlines the need for caution in using material from the world-wide web: make sure that you know the academic *bona fides* of the provider before giving material too much credence. Hofstede's underpinning ideas are often more difficult to get over than may first seem the case, and some authors have a tendency to reduce them for easy digestion. Therefore, I tend to be cautious about delving into his work unless the group shows a keen interest in methodology.

Table 2. Twelve Hints for Teaching Overseas Students (after Crowther)

i. Lecture structure and delivery must be clear and logical (to the recipient as opposed to the specialist).

ii. Key words - an OHP, chalkboard, flip chart can be used as reference points, chances to summarise. They must be written clearly and in order. Students can use these subsequently as a basis for research, cross referencing- using books to illuminate your erudite words (to help their understanding!).

iii. Use signposting to their understanding- make clear where the discussion is going.

iv. Visual material has impact - it often enhances words. It can also replace words most effectively. Allow time for students to make notes from or copy diagrams etc. Illustrative material, even if not a specific diagram, extends the senses in use, creates ambience. (This can be used to great effect in literature but also in scientific courses.) Any visual material must be well executed and all must be able to see it.

v. Cross reference information and sources and make this clear. Relate one part of a lecture/discussion to another. Make a clear reference to other relevant lectures or materials.

vi. Encourage questions - ensure that overseas students have time to formulate their question and ask it- Encourage other non-overseas students to help them gain confidence in asking questions.

For example.

- pair a native and non-native English speaker
- tell them to ask each other a question
- they can then each answer a question
- each ask the other's question of you
- ask what their answer was
- clarify/extend as necessary

Such exercises may be time-consuming at first but the skills, confidence and hence understanding that is obtained outweigh this and in time the questions come more effectively and directly to you - long term 'efficiency' is gained.

vii. Explain what behaviour is acceptable eg can questions be asked at any time in a lecture, will you stop at set points to review and allow questions?

viii. Clarify - is there a right or wrong answer, or is it a matter of opinion - in which case what supporting evidence should be included?

(continued)

Table 2. Twelve Hints for Teaching Overseas Students (after Crowther) (continued)

ix.	Speak clearly, find more than one way of saying something. Present one short piece of information then pause - allow this to 'sink in', notes to be taken, questions asked, or simply observe (with your knowledge of non-verbal cues) - do you receive any clues of understanding or confusion? Act accordingly, use clear, unambiguous language.
x.	Encourage the students to write as soon as possible - for your consumption. The first lecture, seminar, tutorial is an excellent opportunity to begin to assess what can be a major problem - writing in English. Ensure all students give you something written on the first occasion - if they don't (after you have asked for it of course) or you have any concern about it, call in the experts - contact the ESL specialists, who can arrange proper diagnostic assessment and English classes where needed. Always present this positively to students - it is about ensuring you reach the standards set, not saying you are a failure.
xi.	Assessment - say exactly what is being marked and how. If clear layout is relevant; if spelling is important, say so. Be honest - what am I really assessing ? It is amazing what this question reveals, especially if the subsequent 'why' is asked.
xii.	Use any opportunity possible for pair and group work which has to be presented orally and in written format to the rest of the group. In this situation it is often useful to place people in pairs/groups which combine native and non-native speakers. Do have confidence in the authority of your role which means you can do this.

Application to Teaching International Students

For some groups, a more direct approach of giving a series of tips is of greater value. In this case, I use Penni Crowther, (in Morris and Christopoulos, 1988). Table 2 gives a list of helpful hints based on her ideas.

Of course, what is good practice for international students is also likely to be good practice for all students. Reflection on the personal experience of teaching classes made up entirely of Chinese students (including teaching them about transcultural issues in teaching) has certainly made me think more keenly about teaching mixed groups of students.

Putting Pastoral Roles into Practice

Most of the groups to whom I deliver sessions on transcultural aspects have some pastoral duties, and we try to pick up these issues through case studies and sometimes through role-play. Newly formed mixed groups are often wary of role-play, and I use the approach with caution. However, the presence of international students in such a group can often add poignancy to role-playing activities. The sorts of scenarios that we use may be concerned with academic or personal issues. In the former category, we often try to deal with issues around dissertation and thesis writing, such as differences in expectations of and from supervisors. Personal problems can sometimes be the source of academic problems, and we tend to use case studies involving family, housing, or interpersonal problems. Some of these are derived from real-life cases exemplified by Andrew Jackson (in Wisker, 2000). I find the role-plays valuable in challenging pre-conceptions, even in fairly homogeneous groups.

Moving on, we are looking at a game, produced by staff at the CHN (Christelijke Hogeschool Nederland) as an aid to improving students' intercultural understanding. The game, designed in English, involves progression across a playing board by answering factual points about other countries or discussing issues where there might be different cultural perspectives. The approach is enjoyable, as well as challenging and informative, and provides a different way of tackling the issues, particularly with students. At the time of writing, the game has not yet been put on the market, but this line of attack could readily be adapted to our situation and to other scenarios in order to add further to the flexibility of approach.

Does It Work?

It is difficult to say just how much impact a focused session on transcultural issues has. And in many cases the work described above has been preceded by considerable groundwork on styles of learning and teaching, approaches to teaching, the ethics of teaching, and so forth. The feedback that we get from our participants (remember that most of our students are staff) is that they have found it helpful, or even enlightening, to look at issues in this way. We still have problems with teachers trying an inappropriate approach with a group of students because they have failed to take account of cultural sensibilities, but having the groundwork already in place makes it easier to discuss remedies.

The approach recounted here has been developed over a dozen years and is the result of a couple of stand-alone sessions that we had developed in conjunction with the British Council, the United Kingdom Council on Overseas Student Affairs, and AFS in the U.K. The initial, more didactic, approach has given way to a more flexible, collaborative one that enables us to tailor it more closely to the needs of a particular group of participants. Much of this development has been the result of student feedback, both direct and indirect. Participants in our two postgraduate programs have to complete a reflective portfolio, and the process of reflection on their own development has also fed into ours, giving us an insight into how the ideas discussed here have been implemented in classroom practice.

At the end of the day, we have to remember two things: we are all different, and culture is one aspect of our differences; what is good practice for international students is likely to be good for all students.

Acknowledgement

I am grateful for the help given with this chapter by United Kingdom Council for Overseas Student Affairs, particularly in allowing me to use material from Lago and Barty's book.

Related Resources

Adler, P.S. (1975). The transitional experience: Alternative view of culture shock. *Journal of Humanistic Psychology, 15*(4), 13-23.

Furnham, A. & Blochner, S. (1986). *Culture shock: Psychological reactions tounfamiliar environments.* London: Methuen,

Harris, P. R., & Moran, R. T. (1989). *Managing cultural differences.* London: Gulf Publishing.

Jarvis, P., Holford, J., & Griffin, C. (1998). *The theory andpractice oflearning.* London: Kogan Page.

Matters, H., Winter, J., & Nowson, C. (2004). Enhancing learning for culturally and linguistically diverse (CALD) students. *Focus on Health Professional Education, 6*(1), 26-36.

Othick, J. (1992). The world: Post-compulsory education and the international community. In I. McNay (Ed.), *Visions ofpost-compulsory education* (pp. 161-167). Buckingham, UK: Open University Press.

Ryan, J. (1999). *A guide to teaching international students.* Oxford, UK: Oxford Brookes University, Oxford Centre for Staff Development.

Sudweeks, F. & Ess, C. (Eds.), (2001). *Cultural attitudes towards technology and communication.* Murdoch, Western Australia: Murdoch University School of Information Technology.

Todd, E.S. (1996). Supervising overseas post-graduate students: Problem or opportunity? In D. McNamara & R. Harris (Eds.), *Quality teaching in higher education for overseas students* (pp. 173-186). London: Routledge.

Triandis, H. C. (1975). Culture training, cognitive complexity and interpersonal attitudes. In R. W. Brislin, S. Bochner, & W. J. Lonner (Eds.), *Cross-cultural perspectives on learning.* London: Wiley.

References

American Field Service (1990). Ways of thinking about cultures. *AFS Orientation Handbook.* New York: Author.

Cortazzi, M., & Jin, L. (1997). Communication for learning across cultures. In D. McNamara & R. Harris (Eds.), *Quality teaching in higher education for overseas students* (pp. 76-90). London: Routledge.

Crowther, P. (1988). The Lecturer's Perspective. In R. Morris & M. Christopoulos (Eds.), *Helping overseas students succeed* (pp. 17-25). Nottingham, UK: Nottingham Area Council for Overseas Students' Affairs.

Edwards, R. (1994). *The influence of national culture upon individual learning styles.* Unpublished MEd dissertation, University of Sheffield, UK.

Galtung, J. (1981). Structure, culture and intellectual style: An essay comparing Saxonic, Teutonic, Gallic and Nipponic approaches. *Social Science Information, 20*(6), 817-856.

Garratt, B. (1994). The cultural contexts. In A. Mumford (Ed.), *Handbook of management development* (4th ed., pp. 317-331). Aldershot, UK: Gower.

Hall, E. T. (1959). *The silent language.* New York: Anchor Press.

Hall, E. T. (1966). *The hidden dimension.* New York: Doubleday.

Hofstede, G. (1980). *Cultures consequences: International differences in work-related values.* London: Sage.

Hofstede, G., & Bond, M. H. (1988). Confucius and economic growth: New trends in culture's consequences. *Organizational Dynamics, 16*(4), 4-21.

Jackson, A. (2000). Support services for overseas students at Plateglass University: Highlighting needs and influencing practice. In G. Wisker (Ed.), *Good practice working with international students: SEDA paper 110* (pp. 21-32). Birmingham, UK: Staff and Educational Development Association.

Lago, C. (1990). *Working with overseas students: A staff development training manual.* London: British Council.

Lago, C., & Barty, A. (2003). *Working with international students: A cross-cultural training manual.* London: United Kingdom Council for Overseas Affairs.

Mohamed, O. (1997). Counselling for excellence: Adjustment development of South-East Asian students. In D. McNamara & R. Harris (Eds.), *Quality Teaching in Higher Education for Overseas Students* (pp. 156-172). London: Routledge.

Morris, R., & Christopoulos, M. (Eds.). (1988). *Helping overseas students succeed.* Nottingham, UK: Nottingham Area Council for Overseas Student Affairs.

Serpell, R. (1976). *Culture's influence on behaviour*. London: Methuen.

Specker, T., & Engelhard, J. (2004, June). *Academic ethnocentrism in theorizing global knowledge management and practical misfits: The concept of learning styles as a missing link.* Paper presented at the 11th EDiNEB Conference, Maastricht, Holland.

Wisker, G. (Ed.). (2000). *Good practice working with international students: SEDA paper 110*, Birmingham, UK: Staff and Educational Development Association.

Bland Tomkinson is the University Adviser on Pedagogic Development at the University of Manchester.

Chapter 6

Building Multiculturalism into Teaching Development Programs

Constance Ewing Cook and Mary Deane Sorcinelli

This chapter addresses the role that faculty development centers can play in preparing instructors to teach a diverse student body. Using examples of programs and services from the Center for Research on Learning at the University of Michigan Ann Arbor and the Center for Learning and Teaching at the University of Massachusetts Amherst, the authors discuss the challenges, benefits, and lessons learned from building multiculturalism into their respective faculty development programs.

In its 2003 opinions regarding admissions to the University of Michigan (*Grutter v. Bollinger* and *Gratz v. Bollinger*), the U.S. Supreme Court agreed that diversity in colleges and universities is a compelling national interest. The Court ruled that higher education institutions can assemble a diverse student body in order to gain the educational benefits such diversity provides. As Justice Sandra Day O'Connor wrote for the majority in the *Grutter* case, "The Law School's educational judgment that such diversity is essential to its educational mission is one to which we defer." The Court cited the research for the defense which demonstrates that learning in a diverse environment enhances the learning of all students, regardless of race (*Grutter v. Bollinger*, 539 U.S. 245, 2003).

The teaching and learning centers on our campuses, the University of Massachusetts Amherst (UMass), and the University of Michigan, Ann Arbor (U-M), regularly explore how diversity is linked with teaching and learning. As the directors of these centers, we have often been asked, "How should centers play a role in preparing instructors to teach a diverse student body?" In seeking answers, we have conducted interviews with numerous campus constituents, sought the advice of colleagues around the country, piloted innovative multicultural programs on our campuses, and reviewed the many multicultural resources that our centers provide to improve teaching and learning.

We have discovered that many campuses have been slow to incorporate multiculturalism into their faculty development programs for several reasons. First, institutions have tended to focus such efforts on students, suggesting that diversity concerns are a student-development rather than a teaching-development issue. Second, many faculty and graduate student teaching assistants (TAs) are reticent about addressing issues of diversity in the classroom due to lack of training. Finally, initiating diversity programming is risky; discussions on many campuses have been clouded by unskilled or inadequate prior efforts (Ouellett and Sorcinelli, 1998). Despite these challenges, our campuses have long treated multiculturalism as a critical component of our teaching-development programs. In doing so, we have learned lessons which we share not as final answers but as suggestions, with the hope of improving teaching and learning, not just at UMass and U-M, but at colleges across the country.

The aforementioned Supreme Court cases generated a record number of amicus curiae briefs in support of the University of Michigan position. Leaders in higher education, business, and the armed forces endorsed the University's stand on the value of diversity in higher education. Equally important, undergraduate students also express broad support for the type of learning outcomes our centers are trying to help teachers achieve. For example, the Diverse Democracy Project, a major study funded by the U.S. Department of Education and led by Dr. Sylvia Hurtado of the University of Michigan, found that 79% of entering first-year students at the 10 participating institutions, which included the University of Massachusetts Amherst and the University of Michigan, believe that "it [is] essential or very important to promote racial tolerance and respect" (U-M News Release, April 5, 2000).

In spite of this level of public support among students, educators, business, and military leaders for the goals of our centers' multicultural teaching development programs, those of us responsible for programs sometimes face charges of political correctness. We counter that our work is responding to the changing demographics within and beyond our campuses by exploring the genuine diversity of ideas, beliefs, and world views; encouraging academic excellence; and promoting community and mutual respect, both in and outside the classroom.

We believe that a good education is one that incorporates and honors diversity, fosters critical thinking, and creates a more inclusive student learning environment. At our centers, we seek to demonstrate the range of possibilities for multicultural teaching and learning, rather than prescribing a single perspective. We work with instructors to help them prepare students to live and work in a diverse democracy and global economy – and we do so in myriad ways.

Our purpose is to explain how such an agenda operates in our respective teaching centers, the Center for Teaching (CFT) and the Center for Research on Learning and Teaching (CRLT). We also wish to share the lessons we have learned with Center colleagues and others eager to initiate similar programming, or to evaluate current diversity-related programming.

Embedding Multiculturalism in Teaching Development Activities

While our centers maintain balance so that multiculturalism is only one emphasis in our teaching-development work, we do try to infuse diversity awareness into all programs and services. For example:

Consultations for individual instructors. As we at CFT and CRLT consult with instructors, we may discuss how to teach students who have a variety of learning preferences and needs, or we may strategize about ways to handle sensitive topics and emotional discussions in the classroom. We urge instructors to reflect on the balance of student participation and performance in class. We often suggest classroom assessment techniques and mid-semester student feedback so that instructors can get a better understanding of their students' learning processes and the impact their teaching has on all students.

University-wide orientations. In our orientation programs for new faculty and, separately, for new TAs, our centers typically include sessions in which a panel of students with diverse backgrounds and characteristics talks about how instructors can help students learn. Not only does this session provide tips for new teachers, it also serves as a reminder in our large institutions that the sea of student faces is composed of individuals with a myriad of perspectives and needs. We sometimes have panels of faculty who facilitate a session about the excitement of teaching a diverse student population, such as "Teaching and Learning in the Diverse Classroom." We also ask faculty with various backgrounds to share the ways in which their own identities have an impact on their students' learning, including "International TAs and Cross Cultural Issues."

University-wide workshops and programs. Our teaching centers present workshops and other programs for faculty and TAs each term, and topics vary, ranging from interactive lecturing to building web pages. To infuse multiculturalism into the workshop series, we now include subjects such as "Moving Toward an Inclusive Classroom," "Gender and Authority in the Classroom," and "Difficult Dialogues in the Classroom." We also provide occasions for international instructors to meet colleagues in order to feel more of a sense of community around campus teaching issues. Individual academic departments and schools often request customized programs, some of which directly focus on issues of diversity. For example, CRLT collaborated with the School of Social Work on its Intensive Focus on Privilege, Oppression, Diversity and Social Justice, a faculty development and curricular reform initiative involving 20 key courses. The CFT facilitated a syllabi review by faculty in the Clinical Psychology program directed toward the identification of desired multicultural competencies for graduate students. Both of our centers are working with professional schools whose accrediting bodies emphasize multicultural education to prepare students to serve an increasingly diverse client base.

Intensive seminars. At both centers, we have initiated intensive seminars that bring diversity issues to the forefront. The CFT sponsors "From Graduate Student to Faculty Member," a yearlong mentoring program designed to prepare graduate students of color for the challenges of an academic career by addressing teaching and faculty development issues specific to instructors of color. In the "Teaching and Learning in a Diverse Classroom Program" (TLDC), faculty and TAs from a selected department or college engage in a yearlong program to improve understanding of the connection between diversity and teaching issues, and to develop practical pedagogical skills for creating learning environments that serve the needs and interests of an increasingly diverse student population (Ouellett & Sorcinelli, 1995). At CRLT, the seminar takes the form of a two or three day retreat on multicultural teaching and learning, which is hosted by the provost and attended by teams of faculty members from the schools and colleges. Additionally, each spring, CRLT runs a Preparing Future Faculty Seminar for 50 doctoral candidates about to enter the job market. Multicultural content is infused in most aspects of the Seminar – from information about today's undergraduates to pedagogical techniques designed to promote active learning in the classroom.

Theatre productions. CRLT has a theatre program that performs for faculty and TAs on matters related to multicultural teaching and learning. The CRLT Players is an interactive theatre troupe of local professionals and student actors who use research on the experiences of instructors and students in the classroom to develop and present provocative vignettes on pedagogy, diversity, and inclusion. Players have performed sketches on gender, disability, and conflict in the classroom as well as a traditional theatre production, *Voices and Visions of Diversity*. A trained facilitator supplements the theatre productions by engaging audience members in dialogue about the complexities of everyday classroom situations.

Evaluation research. At both centers, evaluation of multicultural teaching and learning projects is part of the overall effort to determine the best use of resources and improve both pedagogy and curriculum. At the request of a dean or department chair, staff collect student data through surveys, focus groups, and interviews in order to provide empirical information to faculty and administrators who want to bring student voices into the curricular decision-making process. When faculty are concerned about learning outcomes for specific groups of students, CRLT does climate studies that often lead to curricular reforms (Cook, 2001).

Grants for individuals and departments. CRLT offers several grant competitions in which multicultural projects are one of the foci. Some grants go to groups of faculty or to academic units, such as the grant to the medical school for a program that prepares students to communicate effectively with culturally diverse patients. CFT funds "Faculty Grants for Teaching" to encourage exploration of new and improved instructional approaches, including projects such as a video on the dynamics of intercultural groups, and faculty training in techniques for creating and facilitating dialogue on issues of race.

Resources and publications. The CFT has developed an annotated bibliography of stimulating and practical works on the linkage between diversity and teaching and learning issues, called "Stepping into Teaching and Learning in the Diverse Classroom." "Two Thumbs Up: A Selection of Teaching and Learning Videos" annotates videos on diversity issues. A handbook entitled *Disability Resources for Teaching Inclusively* (2000) helps faculty understand the disabilities that affect students and offers effective strategies for teaching students with disabilities. CRLT publishes *Occasional Papers* on various teaching-related topics, including "Students of Color and Their Perceptions of Faculty Behavior," and "Providing Support for Women Students in Science and Engineering." Additionally, CRLT has disseminated *Resources for Instructors Concerning Class Discussions About Affirmative Action*; the resources include "Guidelines for Class Discussions." All of these resources, as well as multicultural education bibliographies and additional teaching strategies and program examples, are available to instructors on our websites: http://www.umass.edu/cft/ and http://www.crlt.umich.edu.

Challenges and Lessons Learned

Successfully implementing a multicultural agenda presents challenges and carries an element of risk. Academic administrators on campuses without teaching centers may experience personal criticism if they infuse multiculturalism into teaching-development programs. For those in teaching centers, the centers themselves may be criticized, even when, as at our universities, there is strong central support for their efforts. Teaching centers, like most central administration offices, are not entirely secure entities. Their fortunes can rise and fall as key administrators, faculty opinion leaders, and campus funds come and go. For some centers and individuals, tackling the volatile multicultural agenda may only add to the sense of vulnerability they feel.

Furthermore, some individuals may feel unprepared both personally and professionally for the multicultural education they are trying to do. Like the faculty on our campuses, most center directors and instructional consultants are white, and their understanding and sensitivity to diversity issues can be questioned. They often have expertise in a specific discipline and bring to their work more experience with issues of teaching development and student learning than with social and cultural diversity. Since they have been trained in consultative, developmental, and supportive models, they might be unprepared to respond to the emotion that some faculty and TAs bring to this topic. For this reason, both centers, at the urging of concerned faculty, hired faculty developers with expertise in multicultural teaching and learning, to serve as campus consultants as well as internal consultants to our centers.

Finally, many of our campuses have had complex histories of social activism and multicultural education. Initiatives have occurred in disparate quarters, and there has been little cohesion among the variety of diversity agendas. For example, on both our campuses, training has been done by student affairs professionals and by human relations or affirmative action offices, as well as by committees or offices within the schools and colleges. Trying to collaborate and sort out agendas with all who share an interest in multicultural education may seem overwhelming.

Because of these and other challenges, we considered the potential repercussions of multicultural programs as our centers began to undertake them. We wanted to provide inclusive programming that would be sensitive to the needs and responses of faculty, administrators, and students, rather than polarizing them. We wanted to involve all segments of our campuses and encourage them to share ownership of our initiatives. Here we suggest five general lessons and offer concrete ideas that might be of value to those doing or wishing to do similar work.

1. Build an Inclusive Framework for Multicultural Teaching

- From the outset, define diversity and multiculturalism broadly to include any difference that makes one teacher or learner unlike another. A broad definition typically encompasses gender, race/ethnicity, age, socioeconomic status, sexual orientation, disability, geographical region, religion, and other characteristics that might affect teaching and learning.
- Include international faculty and TAs in the multicultural programming. Their numbers are growing on many campuses, so it is becoming more important to serve their needs and help them understand the students in their class-

rooms. At the same time, it is helpful to find ways to educate and inform students about the value of international instructors and how to learn most effectively from them.

- While defining diversity and multiculturalism broadly, focus especially on the issues the campus community considers very important. The CFT participates in a campus-wide Community Diversity and Social Justice (CDSJ) Initiative; each administrative division is working to create a more inclusive and equitable learning and working environment.
- Interview various stakeholders to assure understanding, encourage their involvement, and profit from their suggestions and insights. For example, both centers have interviewed undergraduate and graduate students of color in several departments to gather perspectives and feedback on their experiences.
- Use representativeness across race, gender, rank, and discipline as a criterion for program facilitators. There may be special roles for campus activists, especially faculty who worked on the diversity agenda long before multiculturalism was specifically incorporated into teaching-development programs.
- Use similar representativeness as a criterion for program participant selection. Especially seek out individuals not necessarily "in the choir."
- Create a network or forum to encourage faculty to share ideas being implemented in the classroom, for example, electronic message groups or a brown bag luncheon series over time.
- Reach out and support – formally and informally – the diverse faculty across campus, paying attention to new constituents and underserved units.
- Focus on modeling collaboration (for example, cosponsoring events with other diversity units on campus). Since other campus offices are already engaged in multicultural work, a teaching-development program should complement their work and avoid superseding or duplicating it.

2. Move Multicultural (and Undergraduate) Education in From the Margins

- Focus the conversation on good teaching and learning rather than just "diversity," emphasizing that *all* students benefit from improvements such as more collaborative teaching techniques.
- Start with faculty who are committed and genuinely interested in diversity issues.
- Recruit and highlight respected faculty "stars," both teachers and scholars, who do good work or have special expertise in multicultural issues. After creating a critical mass, gradually reach out to more and more faculty over time.

- Build alliances with department chairs and deans and discuss with them how to support multicultural education at all levels: program, department, college, and whole campus. Encourage both disciplinary and multidisciplinary discussions.
- Use grants and other incentives to encourage multicultural course and teaching development, and provide resources for initiatives taken by academic units.
- Encourage faculty to document multicultural work to increase the likelihood that it will be recognized in the formal reward system. For example, through the CFT's Teaching Documentation Program (TDP), graduate students are guided in various methods of including their multicultural work in their formal teaching portfolios. Similarly, CRLT assists faculty in the development of "multicultural course portfolios" so that those who teach courses focusing on multicultural issues can document their curricular and pedagogical innovations, as well as student learning outcomes.

3. Plan Carefully in Order to Offer High-Quality Programming

- Refer to the extant literature and research on multicultural teaching and learning.
- Investigate successful programs and strategies used on similar campuses.
- Provide professional development and team-building for those who will be engaged in this work, and expect the process to move slowly.
- When possible, provide co-facilitators for programs. Two heads really are better than one.
- Connect with national initiatives, such as the Diversity Web project of the Association of American Colleges and Universities (www.aacu.org).

4. Address Faculty Concerns About Multicultural Programs

- Define multiculturalism to focus on its core tenets of inclusion, attention to multiple perspectives, and mutual respect.
- Ask faculty what they think the problems and solutions are. There are always more questions than answers, but faculty discussion sometimes yields ideas that work for faculty members individually.
- Make the connection between multicultural objectives (for example, inclusivity, active learning) and discipline-based priorities, particularly when there is no obvious multicultural content (for example , in the natural sciences and mathematics). Recognize the need for *all* students to attain higher levels of competency.
- Create multiple points of entry for faculty and TAs, from readings on diversity, to webpages, to workshops, to intensive seminars.

- Make sure multicultural education does not become the only emphasis in teaching development work; maintain balance in programs and services.
- Avoid responding to all campus multicultural issues; focus multicultural program goals only on teaching and learning.
- Anticipate criticism because working on diversity issues is difficult and emotional. Be willing to listen to and engage with critics.

5. Demonstrate that Multicultural Programs Bring about Improvement

- Multicultural programs may not draw the large attendance of technology workshops. Collect and show evidence that individual instructors and units request consultation and support for the challenges they face.
- Evaluate all workshops and programs to determine faculty satisfaction and track the development of new skills in teaching and learning in the diverse classroom. Anticipate that workshops on multiculturalism and diversity might get a more mixed response than those on traditional topics (for example , lecturing, teaching technologies).
- Try to assess affective as well as cognitive dimensions of change that result from these programs and services. The aim is to cultivate not only new knowledge but also an appreciation of differences and interpersonal understanding that will build community within our classrooms and support lasting change on campus and beyond.
- Gather evidence to demonstrate that the world outside the institution, especially employers, seeks students who have global competency and multicultural awareness.

Spanish essayist Jose Gasset remarked that "effort is only effort when it begins to hurt." Building multiculturalism into teaching-development programs is never easy, but we have had much less "hurt" than could be the case at other institutions. On both our campuses, a high-level commitment to multiculturalism has been sustained steadily over time. We regularly receive support from academic administrators and involvement from faculty leaders. They share our belief that teaching-development programs are incomplete without a multicultural perspective. Programs that ignore diversity are ignoring some of the most pressing issues of our time, to the detriment of both instructors and student learners. Programs that promote diversity can help to increase the multicultural fluency of our instructors and enhance democratic values and practices in and outside of our diverse classrooms.

References

Cook, C.E. (2001). The role of a teaching center in curricular reform. In D. Lieberman (Ed.), *To improve the academy, 19* (pp. 217-231). Stillwater, OK: New Forums Press.

Gratz v. Bollinger, 539 U.S. 244 (2003).

Grutter v. Bollinger, 539 U.S. 245 (2003).

Ouellett, M. L. (2000). *Disabilities resources for teaching inclusively: A university-based resource guide on teaching students with disabilities.* Amherst: Center for Teaching, University of Massachusetts Amherst.

Ouellett, M.L., & Sorcinelli, M.D. (1998). TA training strategies for responding to diversity in the classroom. In M. Marincovich, J. Prostko, & F. Stout (Eds.), *The professional development of graduate teaching assistants* (pp. 105-120). Bolton, MA: Anker.

Ouellett, M.L., & Sorcinelli, M.D. (1995). Teaching and learning in the diverse classroom: A faculty and TA partnership program. In E. Neal (Ed.), *To improve the academy*, *14*, (pp. 205-217). Stillwater, OK: New Forums Press.

The authors wish to acknowledge their center colleagues who have contributed greatly in developing and implementing the diversity agenda, and who have made important contributions to the ideas presented in this chapter.

Constance Ewing Cook, Director, Center for Research on Learning and Teaching (CRLT), and Associate Professor, Center for the Study of Higher and Postsecondary Education (CSHPE), School of Education, University of Michigan, Ann Arbor; **Mary Deane Sorcinelli**, Associate Provost and Director, Center For Teaching (CFT), and Associate Professor, Department of Educational Policy, Research, and Administration, University of Massachusetts Amherst.

Chapter 7
Warming up the Chill: Teaching Against the Structures

Audrey Kleinsasser and Jane Nelson

"Warming up the Chill," an initiative of the University of Wyoming's Ellbogen Center for Teaching and Learning, links a commitment to improve the campus climate for diversity with the scholarship of teaching and learning. "Warming up the Chill" produced a series of events culminating in the publication of a book that celebrates and institutionalizes a public conversation on teaching and diversity. The initiative shows the potential of engaging the broader university community in open dialogues on diversity and teaching effectiveness while promoting the scholarship of teaching and learning.

Gold name plates on three expensive-looking wooden plaques dominate a wall in the University of Wyoming's Ellbogen Center for Teaching and Learning, a faculty development center. The plaques register the names of the winners of the John P. "Jack" Ellbogen Meritorious Classroom Teaching award created in 1979 by the benefactor after whom the faculty development center is also named. In May 2005, seven more names were added, bringing the total to 156.

The Ellbogen teaching award, commonly viewed as the university's highest teaching prize, is conferred in a manner common to many institutions. A campus committee invites nominators to construct a packet documenting teaching. This packet includes teaching evaluations over a three-year duration, a list of titles and enrollment figures of all courses taught, nomination and support letters from students and colleagues, and a curriculum vitae. For the selection committee designated by Faculty Senate, the materials are inspiring. Details in the support materials illustrate faculty and lecturers who care deeply about learning, seem to go the extra mile in their commitment to students, and demonstrate characteristics of exceptional teaching. Faculty winners are touched and delighted by the recognition.

Too often the effect stops with that simple recognition. The teaching award does not reveal hard choices about curriculum and instruction: what to teach or what not to teach and what is the best approach. These teachers surely have learned much about themselves and their students, though packet materials do not detail that journey. The list of winners fails to reveal what awardees know about the deep structures of their disciplines. Nor does the list inform how students uncomfortable in a university environment, perhaps first generation college or older students, learn to think like mathematicians or musicians. The list does not show what it takes to be successful in formal school environments. There is no way to know what students have learned or how they changed. Perhaps most importantly, there is little or no evidence that a teaching award and its recipients have an influence on a community, whether that community is a department, college, university, or discipline. Moreover, the list of award winners illuminates two troubling statistics:

1. Almost three times more men than women hold Ellbogen Meritorious Classroom Teaching awards (74%).
2. One of the seven UW colleges is hardly represented (3%).

How might we understand the institutional practices behind these striking percentages?

Though a superb individual accolade, a teaching award fails to influence deeply entrenched departmental or institutional cultures, especially in the context of a changing student population. Such awards might do the opposite, especially if they reify disciplinary based practices. One such practice, lecturing in large enrollment, first year general education courses, disadvantages increasing numbers of students, especially those who struggle most with postsecondary study. Individual teaching awards reveal nothing about teaching practices or how we might better understand them in order to help students learn more. Having identified exemplary teachers, how might a wide audience learn from their practices?

The inquiry methods practiced by scholarship of teaching and learning advocates offer some answers. The scholarship of teaching and learning aims to better understand teaching and learning issues and to disseminate those results. Two of the movement's leaders, Lee Shulman (1998, 1993) and Pat Hutchings (1996), argue that curiosity, methodical documentation, and conversation within a community of scholars –habits of mind that scholars honor and prize –apply to questions about teaching and learning. For questions about teaching and learning to be scholarly, teaching must be viewed as public property. Scholarship of teaching and learning advocates maintain that the problems of teaching are public property and, therefore, the subject of inquiry. The inquiry process demands methodical documentation, disseminates the resulting findings through books, articles, conferences, and the Internet, and enables centers for faculty development to engage in a different kind of work.

As a center, we want to be a proponent of the scholarship of teaching and learning. The Ellbogen Center has supported faculty inquiry and sponsored UW faculty at national meetings including the Carnegie Academy for the Scholarship of Teaching and Learning (CASTL). As a center, it seemed both smart and potentially effective to address diversity issues through this approach. We called the project "Warming up the Chill" and created a series of events over two years in two phases. The University of Wyoming's "Warming up the Chill" initiative is aimed at exposing the teaching issues surrounding diversity and inclusion and celebrating those teachers who do address these issues effectively.

Warming up the Chill: Two Phases of a Funded Project

At the University of Wyoming, significant momentum to improve the climate for minority and women students, faculty, and staff can be credited to a diversity committee called the President's Advisory Council on Minorities and Women's Affairs (PACMWA). Annually, the university president allocates $70,000 to the group's mission, and much of the money is dispersed through an incentive grants program open to students, faculty, and staff. Go to http://www.uwyo.edu/pacmwa/ for more information about the committee's charge and work.

The funding for "Warming up the Chill" began with $5000, the result of a successful PACMWA incentive grant proposal. We were able to supplement this internal support with a $5000 Going Public grant from the American Association of Higher Education, and another $3000 from the Northern Rockies' Consortium for Higher Education. The combination of internal and external funding plus in-cash support from the Ellbogen Center for Teaching and Learning brought the total project costs to roughly $20,000. In addition, the Ellbogen Center provided considerable in-kind support through staff time devoted to the project.

Phase I: Nominations and celebrations. The "Warming up the Chill" initiative began in the fall of 2001 with student nominations. We were interested in learning from students the names of classroom teachers who value diversity as defined by age, disability, ethnicity, gender, national origin, religion, sexual orientation, or socioeconomic background. On the nomination form, we asked students to describe the organization of the class, the kind of discussion the teacher encourages, the office visits, the assignments, the lectures, and/or the readings. We asked for details about ways the teacher is skillful in teaching students from a variety of backgrounds and with different ways of knowing and learning.

Aware that the conventional channels of advertisements in the student newspaper or announcements on the student listserve would limit the range of nominations, we met with the vice president for student affairs to seek advice and brainstorm strategies. Well acquainted with the work of Bernice Sandler (Sandler, Silverberg, & Hall, 1996) who coined the term "warming up the chill," the vice president alerted us to key faculty, staff, and students who could help us gain entrance to student groups. We arranged to attend and talk about "Warming up the Chill" at a regular meeting of student groups, including the Movimiento Estudiantil Chicano de Aztlan (MEChA), the Minority Engineering Program/Society of Professional Hispanic Engineers, the Association of Black Student Leaders (ABSL), the Asian American Pacific Islander Student Association, Keepers of the Fire (KOF), the Lesbian, Gay, Bisexual, Transgendered population (LGBT), the Women's Center, International Student Life, the United Multicultural Council, and the Associated Students of the University of Wyoming (ASUW). We also contacted academic support offices to meet with formally recognized student groups in each of the seven UW colleges. By way of the Outreach School, we invited students enrolled in distance learning courses (through such formats as interactive compressed video, audio-conference, and the Internet) to nominate a teacher. If we could not attend a meeting of the group, we emailed or telephoned the faculty or staff sponsor so students would be alerted.

We received 52 nominations, some carefully detailed and formal and others short email transmissions. Approximately 13% of the nominators sought anonymity, an option we included on the nomination form. The seven anonymous nominations reminded us that our campus was chilly in ways most teaching personnel would not anticipate. In one anonymous nomination letter, a UW student self-identified as transgendered explained that on a university sponsored trip away from Laramie, the teacher made special accommodations for the student to share a room with trustworthy friends. This teacher, wrote the student, "has been more than willing to cultivate an environment of acceptance for me."

Phase I of the project and the nomination activities culminated with an awards ceremony and celebration in December 2001 to congratulate the 52 UW teachers and the students who nominated them. In addition to these teachers and their nominators, we invited deans, department heads, and colleagues in student affairs and other key academic offices. We invited the president of the university and the vice president for student affairs to address those assembled.

Following the ceremony, the 52 awardees were named in a paid advertisement appearing in the university newspaper and three Wyoming daily newspapers, including the statewide paper. Each awardee received a congratulation letter, with copies to the respective department chairs and deans, and also an invitation to participate in the second phase of the project, which involved inquiry into teaching.

Phase II: Inquiry into teaching inclusively. Eleven of the 52 nominees completed an application to participate in the second phase, an inquiry based project on the scholarship of teaching. Participants were asked to write one to two pages delineating aspects of their teaching about which they wanted to learn more. They were also asked to identify what they hoped to learn from participating in the project and from the other teachers selected.

A selection committee invited six of the 11 teachers who completed applications to participate in the case study project. Each participant signed an informed consent that enabled the research team to interview him or her individually and as part of a group and to examine his or her course materials. The consent spelled out risks and benefits, including a $500 stipend for participating. As a group, we talked about the timeline of the study as well as the three-pronged dissemination approach.

Also important to the spirit of this inquiry into teaching was their collaboration in identifying the list of interview topics. Through this process, each of the teachers responded to the same list of questions in a semi-structured interview format that they helped to create. Each participant then received a draft of a written version of the interview to edit and rewrite. Through a process involving several more drafts, the written interviews were eventually published as chapters in a book that are also available on a CD-ROM and a website.

Project Findings

Examining the case studies as a set, we have identified two significant themes: taking risks and leadership development. In the context of their disciplines (art, engineering, adult learning and technology, counselor education, and Spanish), each teacher described specific practices that encourage students to take risks. All six teachers in "Warming up the Chill" emphasized the importance for students to learn each other's names in the context of group and cooperative learning strategies. If students do not know or come to trust one another, collaborations of any kind are destined to fail. Art students, for example, have to be able to participate in a critiquing process that is central to being successful in the discipline, but that is also risky. Similarly, students in a language class or in an engineering class must be willing to make many mistakes in public conversation and group study. While pressing students to continually take risks, the teachers also gave them individual support, classroom practice, and frequent feedback that showed the students how to be more self-determining and successful.

The second broad theme in the cases was learning to be a leader through collaboration. The structure of schooling, especially its grading systems and its emphasis on individual achievement, often becomes a barrier to one of the fundamental goals of a student: to grow into and think of oneself as a learner for life rather than as a good student in a one semester course. These teachers ask students to imagine a future and to grapple with questions about the future. What will it be like to be a civil engineer? A dual language teacher? A counselor? Just as important, what will it be like to work in an office or organization that values teamwork and collaboration? At the same time, it is evident that the teachers were asking questions of their own. What kind of preparation in a classroom setting must students experience in order to become confident, self-determined leaders? How might collaborations develop into leadership roles? The case studies reveal a remarkable commitment to create leadership opportunities for students outside of class meetings in research projects, international travel, and student productions such as art shows and senior student engineering design exhibitions. Through such assignments and projects, the teachers modeled the collegiality, collaboration, and leadership they asked students to rehearse in the classroom.

Challenges and Limitations of the Inquiry Methodology

The most challenging aspect of "Warming up the Chill" was replicating interview and write-up methods created by Pat Hutchings in *Opening Lines: Approaches to the Scholarship of Teaching and Learning* (2000) and *Ethics of Inquiry: Issues in the Scholarship of Teaching and Learning* (2002). We continue to be impressed by these books because they tell the teachers' narratives, honoring their voices and language cadences, even though the narratives were not written by the contributors. Hutchings' interview and write-up methods were attractive because they reduced the writing and editing burden for the six case study participants. Our lead editor, Laurie Milford, had worked as a copy editor for *Opening Lines* and had observed Hutchings' methodology on several projects. Using this experience, Milford organized the cases around a set of themes identified by the six participants early in Phase II. Through a process of audiotaping, listening to tapes, transcribing, and editing, Milford crafted the oral language of the six cases into engaging narratives told in a scholar teacher's voice, not the stylized, sometimes stilted written language of research accounts.

Perhaps more important than saving time for the teachers and organizing the set of cases to be interdependent, the interview and write-up methods created a reflective distance for the six teachers from their practices. The strategy was both risky and uncomfortable. As we finalized the book project and the teachers read and reread their cases for accuracy and clarity, we acknowledged their discomfort with the readability of the accounts even as we held to our purpose. One participant wanted to insure that the uniqueness of his oral language would be preserved in the written account. Conversely, another of the participants told us that the tone and voice of her narrative was far too informal for the way she would have written a manuscript in her discipline. Until the book was published and she talked with readers who were enthusiastic about the details in her case study and how the case read, she was wary of our methods. For another participant, talking in depth about teaching was uncomfortable and her responses were brief. She explained, "Engineers just don't talk about teaching." And, in fact, her case study is the shortest in the collection. Several of the authors worried that their teaching methods would be misunderstood or even ridiculed, and *all* expressed anxiety about going public in this kind of project.

Summary and Implications

We are not surprised that the two year "Warming up the Chill" initiative produced both intended and unintended effects on the six teachers, the campus community, and the Ellbogen Center. There is little question that the power of the president's office and a standing diversity committee like PACMWA can create momentum. When a high profile committee collaborates with a teaching and learning center, resources can be particularly well-spent. We have learned, too, about the importance of celebratory events. It is anything but trivial to send attractive invitations, serve festive beverages and food, advertise the events, and put a vase of flowers on the reception table. The book *Warming up the Chill: Teaching Against the Structures*, the CD-ROM, and the website were designed to be completed in time for the culminating celebration, a book signing in conjunction with the University of Wyoming's Shepard Symposium on Social Justice in March 2003, an important closure to which the university community was invited and during which nearly 300 books were distributed and signed. The authors were uneasy about the signing; one brought office work so the hour would not be wasted. Each was astounded and thrilled to sign books for a full hour. As planners, we were reminded again that celebrations play an important role in improving climates and making small changes in institutional cultures. Creating institutionally recognized opportunities to celebrate teaching is neither automatic nor easy. Envisioning celebrations so that they lead into the scholarship of teaching and learning projects requires multiple levels of support and funding. Faculty development centers for teaching and learning are well-poised to take on the challenge.

The effects on the six "Warming up the Chill" authors are still becoming evident. Thus far, they report that they highly value becoming acquainted with a group of faculty across the campus in ways that are impossible through committee assignments or other professional interaction. They have learned much about their own teaching and students by hearing about the issues that are important to those in other disciplines and other demographic groups. The six are grateful for the opportunity to examine their own teaching, to discover what is working and what is not, what they are proud of and what they want to change. Finally, they report that they are challenged to actively seek change in their classrooms, their departments, their colleges, and in the university. They feel less passive about the issue of teaching inclusively and more confident about taking leadership roles. The engineering case in this project is valuable to consider in this context in that the author, like one other participant in "Warming up the Chill," had been honored several years ago with the Ellbogen Meritorious Classroom Teaching award. The engineer's participation in "Warming up the Chill" asked that she re-examine her leadership role in the engineering college and in the university as she became more articulate about teaching and more confident in her statements. She has become a credible advocate for teaching principles and strategies that enable women and minority engineering students to be more successful in courses where they are greatly outnumbered and where the bank of problem sets does not account for their interests or experiences.

As planners, we were pleased and surprised at the energy generated by the public awards ceremony and book signing. We have been asked frequently since those events if the Ellbogen Center is going to repeat the call for nominations, which reflects a common desire to institutionalize this kind of ceremony and celebration. By connecting the project to institutional events such as the January Martin Luther King "Days of Dialogue" and the annual Shepard Symposium on Social Justice in early spring, we have come to view Ellbogen Center participation in both as important.

"Warming up the Chill" links a commitment to improve the climate for diversity with the national scholarship of teaching and learning initiative. The book, CD-ROM, and website provide a set of multi-format documents that forced us to learn a lot about new technologies. They help to take teaching public and make it community property, as described by Shulman and Hutchings.

The accounts provide powerful counter forces to the apocrypha of teaching that enjoys an oral tradition. This project also confirms the value of interviewing as a persuasive way for faculty to articulate how they teach inclusively and how we all might teach better. In fact, the two year project became a recursive series of events as we talked, conjectured, wrote, and talked some more about teaching. Our talking was mostly public, with the Ellbogen Center as the backdrop. The book signing event was followed by three brown bag noontime book discussions during which most of the chapter authors and editors participated. We were disappointed that more faculty did not attend. The sessions had an average attendance of about 15 to 20 people and included more student affairs personnel than tenured faculty. Many more women attended than men. We recognize that these troubling observations create the context for another Ellbogen Center scholarship of teaching and learning project. That, we believe, is the real power of a faculty development center committed to a scholarship of teaching and learning philosophy and principles of inclusive teaching.

Authors' Note

Information about the Ellbogen Center for Teaching and Learning and *Warming up the Chill: Teaching Against the Structures* with its CD-ROM can be accessed online at www.uwyo.edu/ctl as well as in book and CD-ROM version.

References

Huber, M. T., & Morreale, S. P. (Eds.). (2002). *Disciplinary styles in the scholarship of teaching and learning: Exploring common ground.* Washington, DC: The American Association of Higher Education.

Hutchings, P. (1996). *Making teaching community property: A menu for peer collaboration and peer review.* Washington, DC: The American Association for Higher Education.

Hutchings, P. (Ed.). (2000). *Opening lines: Approaches to the scholarship of teaching and learning.* Menlo Park, CA: The Carnegie Foundation for the Advancement of Teaching.

Hutchings, P. (Ed.). (2002). *Ethics of inquiry: Issues in the scholarship of teaching and learning.* Menlo Park, CA: The Carnegie Foundation for the Advancement of Teaching.

Sandler, B. R., Silverberg, L. A., & Hall, R. M. (1996). *The chilly classroom climate: A guide to improve the education of women.* Washington, DC: National Association of Women in Education.

Shulman, L. S. (1993). Teaching as community property: Putting an end to pedagogical solitude. *Change, 25*, 6-7.

Shulman, L. S. (1998). Course anatomy: The dissection and analysis of knowledge through teaching. In P. Hutchings (Ed.), *The course portfolio: How faculty can examine their teaching to advance practice and improve student learning* (pp. 5-12). Washington, DC: American Association for Higher Education.

Audrey Kleinsasser directs the Wyoming School-University Partnership and is a professor of educational studies in the College of Education at the University of Wyoming. **Jane Nelson** directs the Ellbogen Center for Teaching and Learning at the University of Wyoming.

Chapter 8
Enhancing the Climate for Diversity in the Classroom: An Experiment in Campus Transformation

Richard C. Turner, Gina Sanchez Gibau, Monica M. Medina, and Sherree A. Wilson

This chapter describes the work of the Diversity Inquiry Group (DIG), part of a University wide initiative to address issues of inclusion for minority students at Indiana University campuses. As Indiana University-Purdue University Indianapolis is primarily a commuter school, most of these efforts were focused on the classroom environment.

Pursuing activities to enhance the climate for diversity at Indiana University-Purdue University Indianapolis (IUPUI) took a distinct turn when a group of faculty and professional staff chose to define the task as a scholarly enterprise. (See "Appendix A" for a profile of IUPUI.) Rather than approach colleagues about enhancing diversity in their classes as the right thing to do (although we believed that it was), the Diversity Inquiry Group (DIG) suggested that working on a more welcoming climate was a professional responsibility because currently some students were encountering barriers to learning in some classrooms and because all students learn better in an open and welcoming environment. These climate barriers are especially daunting to African American and Latino/a students who stay and succeed in far fewer numbers than their majority peers. Thus, working on diversity and teaching inclusively, the DIG argued, were professional responsibilities and therefore central to faculty work. This experiment in campus change began as a focus on changing classroom practices and has evolved into collaboration with other IUPUI diversity activities to create a coherent and positive sense of the value and success of diversity at IUPUI.

The DIG took shape in response to a call from IUPUI's then chancellor, Gerald Bepko, to form a group to work on enhancing diversity on campus in tandem with groups at the other seven campuses of Indiana University. Charles Nelms, Indiana University's Vice-President for Student Development and Diversity, had initiated this call as part of a three-year project to create a dramatic increase in the work on diversity at Indiana University. In conjunction with an annual IU faculty leadership institute, teams from all eight IU campuses gathered to develop plans for enhancing diversity at their respective campuses. The IUPUI group, recognizing that students at this urban, commuter school spend most of their time on campus in the classroom, decided to work on the IUPUI classroom environment. Choosing this focus meant that the group's first task would be to get the attention and the support of faculty. Getting that attention meant competing with the many other research, teaching, and service responsibilities that have most faculty members thinking that they are already overloaded and barely able to keep up with the changing academic environment and the increasing burdens of academic life in American universities. Any suggestion about working on diversity that appeared as an "add on" to their work might be rejected out of hand as impossible.

Thus, the DIG decided to frame its work as a scholarly enterprise so that the work would be recognizable to faculty as inherently valuable and as something congruent with the central nature of their other responsibilities. The DIG thought that a request to consider the scholarly and professional dimensions of diversity in the classroom might catch the attention and support of faculty colleagues. The DIG also concluded that it should develop connections and/or collaborations with other groups working on important university priorities such as retention of first-year students, increased contact between faculty and students, and stronger ties with IUPUI's constituents and communities so that doing what the DIG asked would as much as possible dovetail with other, already-established activities. Like some other grassroots faculty/staff initiatives, the DIG had no clear organizational ties, except that it would report its activities to the chancellor through the Chancellor's Diversity Cabinet, a group of community and campus leaders who gather monthly to advise the Chancellor on diversity initiatives at IUPUI. The DIG also had no budget, but received generous support for specific activities and some salary and programming support from the Office for Multicultural Professional Development, part of the IUPUI Office for Professional Development.

The first task in developing this scholarly project was to gain the knowledge and expertise necessary to be a credible voice in matters of diversity in the classroom. The members of the DIG sought this expertise first in the literature available on enhancing diversity in the classroom. Initially, DIG members found and shared relevant and important articles, and these were gathered in a common database. Other pertinent bibliographies were included so that DIG members would have a sense of the field and would be prepared to speak with authority when the time came to ask colleagues to undertake an inquiry into the advantages and benefits of inclusive teaching. Constructing an accessible database also looked forward to the time when DIG would be able to provide faculty with some resources at hand rather than expecting each to navigate an unfamiliar field. The IUPUI University Library had introduced an electronic format for reference materials that proved very user friendly for the DIG's dissemination of its materials. The DIG also met every other week in a brown-bag lunch format to discuss relevant articles and sort through their implications for classroom climate work at IUPUI.

The other decision the DIG made about getting faculty attention was that faculty, who might not listen very long or hard to colleagues, might listen to the voices of their students on how classroom climate, and especially faculty actions and remarks, affect their learning. The DIG planned to capture those voices in two ways: carefully constituted focus groups and anecdotal stories gathered through open-ended, informal surveys. The focus groups never attained the participation needed to create an authoritative case, but the informal surveys have yielded a rich and interesting take on how minority students experience diversity in the classroom at IUPUI. The DIG expected the informal surveys to capture a set of horror stories that would make a dramatic impact on faculty. With a few exceptions, the horror stories never materialized, but the student responses did suggest that teaching inclusively makes a difference to minority students. (The literature is clear on the point that teaching inclusively improves the environment and hence the learning for all students. See Kitano, 1997.)

The first informal survey offered pizza to minority students in exchange for completing an open-ended, single-question instrument on their experiences in IUPUI classrooms. The surveys were taken during a two-hour period over the lunch hour on two consecutive days toward the end of the spring 2001 semester. The 89 completed surveys indicated that half of the respondents felt that they had been treated fairly in IUPUI classrooms and felt comfortable with their experiences. A quarter of the students reported being generally comfortable, but had one or two difficult experiences to report. A final quarter reported that they had experienced unfair and/or disrespectful treatment in a significant number of their classes at IUPUI.

A second informal survey was taken toward the end of the following spring semester and followed the same procedure (pizza at lunch time over two days), but the survey this time consisted of seven more specifically focused questions and looked for open-end short answers. Although these reports lacked the dramatic impact that we had initially thought we needed, they established the need to look carefully at how a class is taught. The DIG has shared these results in a number of formats and with some faculty groups, perhaps the most engaging being a reader's theater presentation of student comments at a university-wide meeting on diversity.

Once the DIG had created its claim to authority by pursuing what is known about the area and by capturing the voices of students, it began addressing faculty about the nature of its mission and its work. The group hosted an opening reception to announce its presence on campus and its aspirations to engage faculty in addressing the needs of a diverse campus.

During the previous summer the DIG had solicited presentations about best practices from faculty already working successfully at teaching inclusively. The group offered two workshops that semester – one on curriculum change and one on pedagogical change; both were reasonably well-attended. At about the same time, Chancellor Bepko and Vice-President Nelms made $10,000 available for grants to faculty to encourage work on classroom transformation. The DIG awarded funding for five projects and asked that the recipients report back and then offer presentations during the next year at best-practices sessions. The reports of those grant recipients and the presentations by others on best practices demonstrated to other IUPUI faculty that course transformation was possible and that its effectiveness rewarded the time and energy invested.

The DIG pursued its commitment to create connections and collaborations with other IUPUI groups by seeking conversations with others as occasions presented themselves and by welcoming members from those groups as they came forward. The chair of DIG was asked to sit on the Chancellor's Diversity Cabinet. The DIG's organizational support was brought under the Office for Multicultural Professional Development, enabling an extensive and productive collaboration. The DIG volunteered to take responsibility for a Gateway Forum, a faculty development series focused on enhancing the teaching and retention of students in introductory courses with large enrollments. The DIG coordinated the Chairs' Fall Symposium, part of a program of development for chairs, to focus on taking a leadership role in introducing diversity into programs and curricula and assessing achievements in diversity efforts. The DIG also devoted one of its presentations in the 2003 – 2004 academic year to helping chairs develop useful and appropriate responses to the IUPUI Diversity Indicators, a new set of measures of success in diversity introduced at the campus this past year. (The Campus has identified eight measures of success in meeting its diversity goals and a set of measures for establishing from year to year how well the University is doing in meeting its goals. This effort will make clear from one end of the campus to the other, and to the University's various communities, that IUPUI is serious about reaching its diversity goals and is willing to be measured regularly and publicly as to its successes and failures in those eight areas. The IUPUI Diversity Indicators are listed in "Appendix B;" see www.iport.iupui.edu/performance/perf_diversity.htm for a complete view of how IUPUI uses the Indicators.) The DIG and the Office for Multicultural Professional Development organized the campus's representation at an annual conference of all IU campuses, the Enhancing Minority Attainment (EMA) Conference, and provided follow-up after the event. Taking the lead in keeping various campus groups in conversation helps the DIG's goals by increasing the visibility and cohesion of diversity efforts and so moves them closer to the center of faculty life.

The DIG got a special opportunity when IUPUI received two grants, a FIPSE dissemination grant and a retention grant from the Lumina Foundation, to create faculty learning communities (FLCs). The DIG suggested that one of the FIPSE faculty learning communities be devoted to multicultural course transformation; four of the seven participants were DIG members. The Lumina grant created two FLCs, each focused on generating conversation and classroom research on diversity in block-course formats. The participants in these FLCs have created formidable course projects on their own and have presented on their findings to various campus audiences. Some of the projects have reached national audiences at conferences and in publications. The FIPSE group has continued beyond its supported year to become a cohesive and important force for course transformation and discovery about enhancing diversity on its own. Through initiatives such as this one the DIG has begun to move work on diversity into the fabric of campus life.

The DIG expanded its function at IUPUI as it started planning to work beyond its original three-year plan. The DIG saw a need to engage with others working on diversity at IUPUI in order to clarify its role and the best use of its resources. In April 2002 it invited groups from across campus to an informal retreat to discuss what people were doing and where they saw a role for wider and sustained conversations about diversity. The retreat generated a number of suggestions about future directions and possible collaborations, ranging from increased training in diversity concerns for faculty and staff to the founding of a center focused on excellence in diversity. Perhaps the most unanimous call was for an annual meeting to have the kind of conversation that occurred at the meeting itself.

The proposal that took shape called for a meeting of individuals, groups, schools, and offices at IUPUI working on diversity to come together annually to report to each other what they had accomplished and what they planned to do with an eye toward eliminating overlapping efforts and of being of greater service to each other and to their various constituencies. The reporting was to take the form of presentations and poster sessions, the poster sessions used to present information and plans and the presentations to foreground work that might be recognized as best practices in the field. The meeting would provide an occasion for gathering information for the Chancellor as he looks forward to his annual message on diversity and prepares a Campus-wide report to the other IU campuses at the EMA conference. Perhaps even more importantly, the meeting would serve to highlight diversity efforts at IUPUI and to create a higher profile for those efforts. A higher profile was sought to emphasize that working on diversity is a central and regular part of campus life rather than a marginalized activity as it has sometimes seemed in the past. The profile should also work to assure our community partners that our work on diversity is deep, sustained, and effective.

The DIG organized the first "Excellence in Diversity" conference in Spring 2003 as a pilot conference to see how the process might work. It worked well and there was general support for organizing the conference in Spring 2004 on a larger scale. Building on the experience gained in the first conference, the DIG organized the "IUPUI Diversity Fair" in Fall 2003 and attracted 70 members of the IUPUI community to view presentations by 22 individuals and groups working on diversity at IUPUI. The second "Excellence in Diversity" conference in spring 2004 focused on issues and concerns central to establishing best practices in pursuing diversity. The conference got its directions from three experts on diversity programs and assessment– James Anderson (Texas A&M), Nancy Chism (IUPUI), and Orlando Taylor (Howard). The conference asked its participants to think about capturing, representing, and assessing work in pursuing diversity. Future conferences will encourage presentations on achievements recognized and measured by common and authoritative sets of expectations and practices. The DIG currently plans to continue this program of surveying the work that's being done in the fall and the demonstrable achievements of that work in the spring.

Having developed its expertise and a record of encouraging and recognizing faculty work in enhancing the climate for diversity in the classroom, the DIG prepared to ask faculty to look seriously at its initiatives and begin the process of reflecting on how their own courses welcome students and create an inclusive environment. The first step in that process was to transform the database of relevant literature on class transformation to a web-based format that would make the material not only accessible, but also coherent and suggestive about how to proceed with an inquiry about classroom research on climate. The "Multicultural Classroom Resource Guide" (www.opd.iupui.edu/ompd/guide/index.htm) took shape through collaboration among the DIG, the Office for Multicultural Professional Development, and the Center for Teaching and Learning. That group organized the material in the DIG database along the lines of current educational models of classroom transformation and wrote introductions to the various sections. The "Guide" took a number of suggestions from related materials at other universities, but shaped itself finally to the special needs of IUPUI. IUPUI has invited other Indiana University campuses and other Indiana Universities to collaborate in developing the "Guide," expecting that each campus or university will use what it needs from the IUPUI material and add or shape it to fit local needs and aspirations.

With these tools in hand, the DIG is ready to move its work out into the schools and departments where the policies and practices that create classroom environments take shape. At IUPUI, however, moving out into the greater academic community is a special problem because of the various and complex nature of the university itself. The name itself (the longest name of any American university) begins to suggest the complexity of this institution, but it cannot capture just how many cultures and traditions constitute the teaching environment at IUPUI. This is not to say that these are all or even dominantly hostile environments, just that they are different and so each requires a specialized and distinct approach.

The DIG has collaborated with the Office of Professional Development and the IUPUI Human Resources Administration to develop a corps of "consultants" out of its membership and from various interested faculty and staff across the campus. The planning team for the Diversity Institute brought together 35 members of the IUPUI community for a three-day intensive experience to orient the consultants regarding diversity issues and best practices. The consultants will be available to schools and departments that want to begin working on diversity initiatives. The DIG fully expects that the responses to this initiative will be as varied and idiosyncratic as the campus community, but the move toward such a conversation is a necessary next step. The Office for Multicultural Professional Development has assigned an intern to begin the conversations across campus and develop a model for how diversity consultants will operate. This work laid the groundwork for the 2004 Diversity Institute.

The DIG has asked a subgroup of its members to create an assessment plan for the DIG. The assessment task requires that the group look at its success in meeting its overall goals. The DIG has carried out most of its original plan and has pursued some later additions to its plan, but it has not established the impact of that work or the connection between its previous successes and its designation of resources for its future plans. In a tight economic environment the DIG will need to argue for the effectiveness of its work in order to capture the resources it will need to support and encourage transformation on a campus-wide scale. There is no lack of good intentions at IUPUI to advance the DIG goals, but effective change will require a convincing case for adequate resources to pursue those goals.

The primary problem the DIG has encountered in its work has been the difficulty in keeping very many faculty engaged in the work in a sustained way. Faculty tend to come to the DIG with strong convictions about the value of the work, but find it hard to sustain that commitment in the face of their other professional responsibilities such as continuing their research success both in terms of their disciplinary as well as their departmental demands. The time and energy required of a successful research program and serious teaching commitments often leave little available for further commitments to campus transformation. Many faculty face mixed responses to their research and teaching associated with diversity when their departments and/or schools have yet to make curricular or pedagogical change for the sake of inclusive teaching a priority or even an activity that deserves a place in the area of professional recognition. Until all campus officials line up behind a commitment toward nurturing and sustaining diversity work and until peers share these aspirations, faculty will continue to face this obstacle. The DIG had developed a document that counseled faculty on steps to take to ensure that their DIG activities became a positive and energizing force in their lives. This advice, alas like so much other very good advice, has yet to change the lives of faculty enough to keep many of them engaged over the long haul.

Related to the problem of keeping faculty engaged is the frustration of getting a uniform and consistent institutionalization of the policies and practices that will enhance the climate for diversity at IUPUI. As suggested earlier, this problem is entwined with the complex structure and climate of the university. But even partial success in meeting the DIG aspirations requires some critical mass of the university community committing itself and its programs to teaching inclusively. The Diversity Indicators promise to enhance some of the efforts to institutionalize diversity work. The DIG is likely to gain from this initiative because the Chancellor's office has announced that it will expect all segments of the University to use the indicators as a central part of their annual reporting requirements. Furthermore, IUPUI's new chancellor, Charles Bantz, has made increasing diversity one of the central elements of his goals for IUPUI. These initiatives may suggest to many departments and schools that what the DIG has to offer may serve them very well in meeting the Chancellor's mandate.

The DIG is ready to help and is positioned well to assist in creating the kind of atmosphere that the Campus aspires to in its commitment to enhancing the climate for diversity. It will continue reflecting on its mission and its goals as the opportunities and the needs of the campus develop. It remains centrally concerned with enhancing the climate for diversity in IUPUI classrooms and is encouraged by its increased experience and impact that the learning for all IUPUI students will improve as more classrooms teach inclusively.

Reference

Kitano, M. (1997). A rationale and framework for course change. In A. Morey, & M. Kitano (Eds.), *Multicultural course transformation in higher education: A broader truth* (pp. 1-17). Needham Height, MA: Allyn & Bacon.

Richard Turner is a professor in the English department at Indiana University-Purdue University Indianapolis. **Gina Sanchez Gibau** is an assistant professor in the Anthropology department at Indiana University-Purdue University Indianapolis. **Monica M. Medina** a lecturer in Teacher Education at Indiana University-Purdue University Indianapolis, and **Sherree Wilson** is Special Assistant to IUPUI Chancellor Charles Bantz and Clinical Assistant Professor of Education in the Indiana University School of Education.

Appendix A

About IUPUI

IUPUI is an urban research university created in 1969 as a partnership by and between Indiana and Purdue Universities, with IU as the managing partner. Thus IUPUI is a campus of Indiana University that grants degrees over 180 programs from both Indiana University and Purdue University. IUPUI offers the broadest range of academic programs of any campus in Indiana and is the state's principal site for first professional degrees. This campus ranks among the top 15 in the country in the number of first professional degrees it confers and among the top five in the number of health-related degrees. IUPUI is the home campus for state-wide programs in medicine, dentistry, nursing, allied health, and social work and extends its program offerings through IUPU Columbus. IUPUI currently enrolls just under 30,000 students.

Appendix B

The IUPUI Diversity Indicators

- Recruitment and enrollment of a diverse student body
- Retention and graduation of a diverse student body
- Engagement of students, through the curriculum and co-curriculum, in learning about their own and other cultures and belief systems
- Diversity in research, scholarship, and creative activity
- Contributions to the climate for diversity in Indianapolis, Central Indiana, and the entire state
- Recruitment, development, and support of diverse faculty and staff
- Engagement of the campus community in global issues and perspectives
- Student, faculty, and staff perceptions of the campus climate for diversity.

Chapter 9

Positionality and Authority in Curriculum Transformation: Faculty/Student Collaboration in Course Design

Betty Schmitz and Anupama Taranath[1]

—Teaching is also learning. Teach what you need to learn.

Audre Lorde

The Center for Curriculum Transformation at the University of Washington has been working with the University community since 1992 to promote and support curriculum development aimed at critical thinking, teaching, and learning about cultural diversity. This chapter reports on lessons learned from 10 years of experience in faculty/student collaboration. We investigate the dynamics of collaborative work, such as positionality and authority, different formats and their effectiveness, and the benefits and results of these efforts.

Seminar Structure

Curriculum transformation brings new scholarship, conceptual frameworks, and pedagogies from the fields of women's studies, American ethnic studies, and other comparative cultural studies to faculty members interested in changing courses to reflect the diversity of human experiences. It also focuses on the development of inclusive frameworks in women's studies, American ethnic studies, and area studies. Butler (1991) argues that ethnic studies and women's studies provide the transformative content and pedagogy for the study and definition of the experiences and aesthetics of neglected groups of people,

[1]The authors wish to acknowledge and thank Rekha Kuver and Fatema Karim for their research assistance in analyzing student evaluations of seminars between 1992 and 1999.

studied not in comparison to the dominant group and not as problematic to the dominant group, but in and of themselves and in relation to one another. These studies help correct distortions in the study of all groups, and further the development of a curriculum that through its content and pedagogy affirms the interconnectedness of human life, experience, and creativity.

Between 1992 and 2002, the Center for Curriculum Transformation at the University of Washington has sponsored an annual seminar or summer institute for faculty members and students interested in curriculum transformation. The primary venue for this student/faculty collaboration has been an annual seminar of one or two academic quarters in length. During the seminar UW faculty members and students examine new theory and pedagogy, participate in lively and often contentious discussions, and rethink courses with the help of colleagues.

The format of the seminar has varied from year to year, but there are several constants. The seminar always includes a common set of readings that students and faculty members explore together to develop an understanding of the need, methods and desired results of curriculum transformation. It always includes meetings of the group as a whole and research time outside of these meetings. It provides time for individual faculty members and research teams to present results of their course revision activities. Finally, and most importantly, the seminar method allows participants to frame the issues for discussion. There is no mandate for faculty members to change courses in specific ways, only to engage with new ideas, new experiences, new theories, and new subject matter in order to reevaluate the bases upon which they have constructed teaching approaches.

The core seminar readings vary from year to year, but usually include these topics:

- Conceptual frameworks and approaches of interdisciplinary fields that focus on cultures, such as American ethnic studies, area studies, disability studies, queer studies and women's studies.
- History and contested meanings of multiculturalism and multicultural education. How do we relate U.S. pluralism to global pluralism?
- Historical perspectives on U.S. groups of color, literary and creative production, and contemporary issues. How does one apply a comparative, relational approach to history and contemporary issues?
- Critiques of theories, paradigms, approaches in the disciplines – for example, what does the American past look like? How does one effectively describe and critique U. S. core values (notions of equality, freedom, individualism, democracy, expansionism)?
- Analyses of race, gender, and so forth, and their intersections. How do we describe the fluidity and multiple nature of identities, personal and cultural?

How are identities socially constructed? Defined by power and privilege?
- Distinctions among bias, discrimination, and structural inequities. How do we teach about these issues while avoiding focusing on "victims" and "disadvantaged" people?
- Course and curriculum design methods.

In addition, a range of pedagogical issues are covered in the seminar discussions: How to establish one's own positionality in the classroom; how to deal with tensions that arise from guilt, defensiveness, anger, pain; how to deal with student resistance to new world views and perspectives; and how to deal with an incident of bias or prejudice in the classroom. As an example, the goals, list of readings, and seminar schedule for the 1999 curriculum transformation seminar appear in the Appendix.

While the earliest seminars tended to organize material along a single analytic framework such as race or gender, more recent seminars have emphasized the important scholarship on intersectionality, that is, the teaching and research on issues of diversity as interconnected and inseparable from one another. One analytical framework is no longer sufficient for critical scholarly work; analyzing an issue, social problem, or history through the multiple lenses of gender, race, class, sexuality, nation, disability, power, and privilege has set the standard for many academics in the humanities and social sciences. For example, the 2003-2004 seminar focused on transnational perspectives that challenge the local/global and U.S./international paradigms. Seminar discussions focused on:
- reformulations of "area" studies influenced by transnational flows of ideas, capital, people and images;
- phenomena such as transnationalism, diaspora, hybridity, and global culture in a variety of settings; and
- efforts to develop new pedagogies that address the complexities of multiple and competing theories of race, gender, ethnicity, and nationality and how they shape and are shaped by concrete details of social and cultural life in U.S. institutions.

The new courses will help students rethink ways of looking at identity in relation to globalization, changes in processes of racialization, formations of community, the nature of work, the meaning of citizenship, nationality, and place in settings transformed by globalization and the shifting subjectivities of race, class, gender, sexuality and disability.

Profile of Faculty Participants

> I am an expert on American Indian history, but before this Institute, I never had a Native teacher.—Faculty participant, 1993

Since 1992, 94 University of Washington faculty and staff members and 80 undergraduate students have participated in annual curriculum transformation seminars or other activities, such as summer institutes sponsored with external grants. The faculty members represent nine schools and colleges and 34 departments, the majority of the latter in social sciences and humanities. In the earlier years, participants tended to be faculty members with keen interest, but little experience, in teaching the new scholarship on race, gender, and ethnicity, although there has always been a mix of scholars from American ethnic studies and women's studies in the seminars. Those scholars with backgrounds and experience in the fields of American ethnic studies and women's studies tended to be concentrated in the junior ranks, while those from traditional disciplines included faculty members from all ranks.

Interviews with participating faculty members over the years have yielded information about their motives for joining the seminar. Most have been interested in keeping up with the advances in their disciplines. These faculty, for the most part, were not the scholars creating the new knowledge and epistemic paradigms in ethnic and women's studies, but were interested nevertheless in integrating new perspectives into their courses. In some cases, faculty realized that they themselves would not have initiated curricular change, but were highly encouraged to do so because of considerable shifts in the diversity of their students. More students of color in their classrooms compelled some faculty to reconsider their class materials, textbooks, and pedagogical styles. Many faculty members joined the seminar because they wanted to make their courses more relevant to the newer materials being generated in their fields or because they realized they were teaching homogeneous materials to a heterogeneous class. Some faculty explicitly stated that their participation in the seminar was motivated by a desire to become better skilled at handling sensitive topics in classrooms, such as racial identity, racist thinking, gender, patriarchy, and so forth. In short, faculty wanted students to learn critical thinking skills, to ask important questions that are relevant outside of the classroom environment, and to reflectively consider their thinking and behaviors.

While these goals were generally true for faculty in the first several years of the seminars, the changing nature of the seminar itself has attracted a changing faculty composition as well. More recently, designing the seminar around the interdisciplinary notion of "intersections" makes obsolete a singular category of analysis such as only race, only gender, and so forth. Changes to the focus of the seminar were met with enthusiasm and attracted a different kind of scholar, one who was already engaged in scholarly work on diversity. Therefore, the Center for Curriculum Transformation now works closely with faculty members who are also experts on issues of intersectionality as well as deeply committed to teaching issues. We believe this is an important constituency to support within the academy, not only to build collective spaces of collaboration, but also to validate the work such scholars have been doing for many years.

Profile of Student Participants

Most of the student participants over the past decade have been junior and senior undergraduates majoring in the humanities and social sciences, with heavy representation from American Ethnic Studies, Comparative History of Ideas, and Women Studies departments. Most had research experience, whether paid or unpaid, and were involved with student organizations or volunteered with groups that dealt with issues of diversity. Over half the students who participated attributed their interest in cultural pluralism to Ethnic Studies courses they had taken over the years, and mentioned racism as the motivating factor for their desire to improve curriculum in one way or another. Undergraduate student participants expressed a desire to engage in curriculum transformation as, as one student said, "a positive step toward exposing students to peoples and diverse histories that will equip students to better and more effectively deal with cultural diversity as it exists in the U.S." An interesting point to note is that all applicants expressed a desire to learn more about issues related to diversity, not simply through the development of one particular class, but to have those issues integrated into their respective disciplines. Students were attracted to the opportunities of the Center for Curriculum Transformation because they hoped the seminars would address the structural inequities in the university, not merely classroom dynamics. Students expressed a belief in the power of education and their hopes in being a part of that process by working collaboratively with faculty.

As faculty participants have changed, so have students. In recent years, they have joined the project in order to work with faculty members engaged in development of new things theoretical perspectives related to diversity.

Positionality and Authority in Faculty/Student Collaboration

> I think it is essential for undergraduates to work on projects like this along with faculty.... We are, after all, directly affected by what is taught and how it is taught.—JD Leza, undergraduate, 1993

Curriculum transformation asks faculty members to take a critical stance on issues of power and difference in the classroom, interweave multiple perspectives, and integrate student voices and knowledge into the learning process. In order to learn how to employ new pedagogies and adopt a different relationship of expertise and power with students, the Center's seminar has an explicit goal of creating mutuality in the collaborative faculty/student research project. This experimentation was possible because the students brought knowledge and information to the seminar that the faculty members needed in order for their courses to be successful for a diverse group of undergraduates.

The 1999 seminar cited above provides an excellent example of this process and how it played out differently across small groups depending upon participants. There were 10 faculty members and 20 students in the seminar. The group met as a whole for lecture and discussion of key topics. Faculty members and students formed triads – one faculty member and two undergraduates – based on student interests and expertise. There were biweekly meetings of these teams so that faculty members and students could share course development strategies.

After initially being introduced to the faculty members and the types of research they were looking for, the students submitted preferences as to faculty with whom they would like to work. After people were grouped in their triads, each triad was arranged entirely at the discretion of each group. According to the seminar evaluations, half of the triads ended up being straightforward research assistance situations, where the faculty member instructed the students to find specific information (always related to the content of the specific course); the students carried out the requested research and remitted the information back to the faculty member. The level of dialogue within these types of triads was limited. One example of a straightforward research relationship between students and faculty is expressed in the seminar final evaluations written by a faculty member: "the student contributions of this seminar are a direct result of their attempt to find current music that would be considered representative of Latin (Mexican) and African American cultures." Attached to this statement is a long bibliography of songs that the undergraduates had researched to aid in the content of the course.

However, there were also groups that arranged their triads a little differently, by combining direct bibliographic research with some critical discussions about course content, pedagogy, classroom climate, larger political and societal issues, and curriculum transformation. The students and faculty in these types of discussions evaluated the entire process of the seminar much higher than did students and faculty that only engaged in bibliographic research. The participants who had a combination of bibliographic research and critical dialogue reported that they had grown in their understanding of curriculum change, had broken down uncomfortable hierarchical barriers that placed faculty as knowledge-holders and students as knowledge-receptacles, and had created an evolving microcosm of curriculum change within their triad. Conversely, the students who only engaged in bibliographic research had more critical things to say about their seminar experience. In his report on participant interviews that he conducted at the end of the seminar, one teacher states, "[students] felt that they mostly served the roles of researchers and were not allowed to tap their own knowledge." Yet the students in these more traditional triads still reported gaining important insights into course development and the constraints many faculty members experience due to departmental norms and expectations.

This issue is related to another one that comes up repeatedly in the evaluations (especially students' evaluations of faculty). Many of the students had a preconceived broad definition of what curriculum transformation is and should be, and often felt their definition was in conflict with what the faculty envisioned. Students generally saw the seminar as a place to address changes in course content and (sometimes more importantly) a place to address larger issues of pedagogy, critical education theory, the politics of academia, and other related issues. Many of the evaluations show that faculty members were perhaps more or solely interested in course content issues alone, thereby widening the disconnect between the issues with which many students expected the seminar to engage, and faculty members' recalcitrance to push the discussion outside the boundaries of their coursework. This point is also related to the fact that there were different expectations about what exactly the role of the undergraduate student participants was. Because of the way that the triads were often structured (and the way that the students objected to that structure while the faculty members thought everything was going well), it seems obvious that the students saw themselves in a more collaborative role than did the faculty members.

There is a third type of research triad that was employed by a few members of the seminar. This type was engaged in by only a few research teams and was characterized by a total departure from the traditional "research assistant" model. One team in particular stood out for creating a truly collaborative process and was the most careful about engagement of important pedagogic principles. The team was also the most enthusiastic about what its members accomplished in their group.

This last type of group departed from the research assistant model and replaced that model with one of open dialogue between all participants. As faculty member Donna H. Kerr from the College of Education put it: "My goal was to listen carefully to [students], to try and get a sense of who they are and how they experience their education." In her triad, participants read and discussed several literary texts: Wole Soyinka's *Ake: Years of Childhood*, Maxine Hong Kingston's *Woman Warrior*, Dorothy Allison's *Bastard Out of Carolina*, and they screened Todd Solonz's *Welcome to the Dollhouse*. Having a common basis of texts allowed participants to reflect upon their own educational formation as individuals, and the formal and informal curricula that have shaped all of us. Using the characters of the novels as imaginary students, triad participants anticipated possible curricula for all the Woles, Bones, Dawns, and Brandons that are in our classrooms.

The often commented upon feature that singled out this triad from other student-faculty collaborations was the self-reflexivity demonstrated by all participants. We understand self-reflexivity to encompass critical thinking about power, privilege, and diversity within the context of the course materials, as well as how material is taught, how we learn, how we know. Questions engaged by the triad may provide a starting point for others reconsidering their pedagogy and course materials in a holistic manner: how does the educator situate her/himself historically, politically, racially, and so forth? With what context does he/she come to the process, and how does this context affect the educational process? How do we know what we know, and how does this process affect our teaching and learning? Self-reflexivity seemed crucial to the participants' success with their group, and was elaborated upon by both faculty and students:

> My principal, and I would argue, crucial formal learning is this: I have over the course of the project come to understand better the importance of resisting my inclination to offer my interpretation of the text and to over-guide the discussion—to engage in the very domination that I would counsel others to resist in the shaping the curriculum for others. —Donna H. Kerr, faculty member

Students echoed this focus on educator self-reflexivity:

> Our task was interesting and perhaps unique in that instead of asking what are these values and how can Donna's course or any course exhibit them, we asked: what are we? How have we been constructed to act in dominating or oppressive ways? How do we invent new ways of being that could interrupt this domination or oppression?—Aaron Montoya, undergraduate

> I have learned…that the curriculum in our classrooms can be influenced by the teacher's personality more than we would like to admit. —Tyler Fox, undergraduate

> One aspect of curriculum transformation is changing the way in which one interacts with one's peers, colleagues, and students. In order to do this there needs to be intensive self-inquiry into how one is already interacting with others and a critical analysis into how society reinforces certain dominating tendencies. For me, the autobiographies we read and the discussions that ensued played a critical role in facilitating the self-inquiry and critical analysis but also they provided a platform from which to imagine different patterns of human interaction. –Aaron Montoya, undergraduate.

This self-reflexive quality was always directly related to pedagogy and content and mindful of relating self-inquiry back to student needs and curriculum change.

Kerr states, "curriculum transformation and formation for ourselves and others requires that we have a sense of what would contribute to our own flourishing and to that of another." As in evidenced in the preceding quotes, triad participants were actively engaged in locating their inquiries within a larger social, political, and multicultural context. In other words, the straightforward "research assistant model" tended to garner student criticism because it was too narrow, with a focus on course content, and divorced from a deeper conversation about the broader context within which the content sits:

> The purpose of this [curriculum transformation] was, in my mind, to look at a curriculum not as just an event that takes place only in the classroom, nor to think of the events in the classroom as purely academic. –Tyler Fox, undergraduate

> I saw these questions leading us to address broader moral and ethical questions about the nature of human relationships and the challenges of maintaining human interaction that is humanizing and democratic. Why do people relate to or interact with others in a certain fashion and what implications does this have for an increasingly...multicultural society? This later question is really interesting in the context of curriculum transformation because it strives to further understand how we can practice multicultural values like democracy, equality, inclusiveness, critical consciousness, power sharing, dialogue, and so forth. I take these values or ideas to be at the heart of curriculum transformation. –Aaron Montoya, undergraduate.

These types of statements were generally missing from the groups that worked within a more traditional paradigm.

Results

In terms of how faculty revised their courses and transformed curricula, all mentioned adding new materials and expanding their range of pedagogical strategies. All faculty insisted on the importance of how one chose to frame the discussions, point out what was missing, and make links between seemingly disparate issues. "The most important change," one faculty stated, "was the subtle ways of framing the issue. I was more confident of the big issues, had a sense of critical insight. It was very encouraging to me. It changed the way I think about diversity." Many felt that they had been exploring issues of race and ethnicity in their courses, but were seeking an institutionalized space for learning and reflection. The directed readings of the seminar proved to be most effective, for faculty continuously stated that they read essays and documents from a wider interdisciplinary reach than they would have had time or energy to do on their own. While most faculty involved in the early project had experience with issues of race, gender, and other social differences, some faculty required assistance in infusing their syllabus with this sensitivity. Attending the seminar allowed faculty to actively interrupt the university structure in which they are framed as "experts" in their field and reconstruct their identities as "students" in a larger conversation on social differences and pedagogy. The seminar provided participants with opportunities to practice and rehearse the skills and behaviors they sought. Faculty continually mentioned how important it was for them to learn from other faculty, read materials for which they had no time to search themselves, and critically converse with a group of interdisciplinary colleagues and with the undergraduate students in the seminar. All faculty insisted on the importance of how one chose to frame the discussions, point out what was missing, and make links between seemingly disparate issues. They noted increased agility and confidence in navigating often sensitive discussions with students.

Student inclusion in curriculum transformation projects results in a powerful process of students participating in constructing their own learning. Students represent new complexities of race, gender, and intersectionality through their voices and experiences. It is apparent that the students who participated learned valuable lessons. For those interested in teaching, participation offered them a glimpse of the challenges faculty face, as well as how the academic bureaucracy might work.

Students who participated in the earlier seminars expressed a critical urgency for this kind of curriculum transformation in both their departments and course offerings. In the past few years, student participants believed that improvements were certainly required in their departments and course offerings, but did not articulate the raw urgency expressed in the earlier cohorts. Undoubtedly this is because many of the changes that students and faculty have been working for have been partially implemented. More classes that explicitly emphasize diversity are available now, and classes incorporate diversity on some level more than 10 years ago. While progress definitely has been made, students warn that these classes are often marginal to their major or are offered as electives, thereby not challenging the underlying premise of their disciplinary rationale. The Center for Curriculum Transformation sees the future grounded in the ongoing challenge of working with new generations of students and their different experiences and engagements with social difference. Our undergraduates present new and changing challenges. To be successful, we must answer their call with new pedagogical strategies.

References

Butler, J.E. (1991). Transforming the curriculum: Teaching about women of color. In J.E. Butler & J.C. Walter (Eds.), *Transforming the curriculum: Ethnic studies and women's studies* (pp. 67-87). Albany: State University of New York Press.

Chan, S. (2004). You're short, besides. In M.L. Andersen & P.H. Collins (Eds.), *Race, class, and gender: An anthology* (5th ed., pp. 296-302). Belmont, CA: Wadsworth.

Cooper, R.S., Rotimi, C.N., & Ward, R. (1999, February). The puzzle of hypertension in African-Americans. *Scientific American, 281*, 56-62.

Durham, J. (1992). Cowboys and ... notes on art, literature, and American Indians in the modern American mind. In M. A. Jaimes (Ed.), *The state of Native America: Genocide, colonization and resistance* (pp. 423-438). Boston: South End Press.

Fox, R.E. (1997). Becoming post-white. In I. Reed (Ed.), *MultiAmerica: Essays on cultural wars and cultural peace* (pp. 6-21). New York: Viking.

hooks, b. (1997). Keeping close to home: Class and education. In A. Lunsford & J.J. Ruszkiewicz (Eds.), *The presence of others* (2nd ed., pp. 85-950). New York: St. Martin's Press.

Lugones, M. (1994). Purity, impurity and separation. *Signs 19*(2), 458-479.

Root, M.P.P. (Ed.). (1996). A bill of rights for racially mixed people. *The multiracial experience: Racial borders as the new frontier* (pp. 3-14). Thousand Oaks, CA: Sage.

Takaki, R. (1993). *A different mirror: A history of multicultural America*. Boston: Little, Brown.

Betty Schmitz is Director of the Center for Curriculum Transformation at the University of Washington Seattle. **Anupama Taranath** is a lecturer in the English department at the University of Washington Seattle.

Appendix A

Curriculum Transformation Seminar, Spring 1999

The College of Arts and Sciences
The University of Washington

Seminar Directors:
Dr. Ana Mari Cauce, Psychology
Dr. Betty Schmitz, College of Arts & Sciences

Seminar Goals

1. To provide faculty members with support for creating or redesigning courses to incorporate the study of cultural diversity
2. To provide undergraduate students with opportunities for research experiences in cultural diversity and curriculum development
3. To develop effective collaborative research strategies for faculty and students
4. To develop curriculum transformation resources to share with other faculty and students
5. To augment the number of courses in the undergraduate curriculum that teach critical thinking about diversity

Seminar Schedule

April 1 Welcome and Introductions: Overview of faculty projects and student interests—getting to know one another. What does it mean to transform the curriculum?—Case Studies. What are the challenges of teaching in multicultural classrooms? Organizing ourselves into work groups. Assigned Reading: Case study "It's My Experience"

April 8 Topics: Identity development; social construction of race, gender, ethnicity, class, sexuality.

Readings: Please read in depth the article assigned to you below and peruse as many of the others as time permits. We will spend

(continued)

the first part of April 8th's meeting in small groups to prepare a summary of key concepts in each article.

1. Butler, Johnnella E., T**ransforming the Curriculum: Teaching About Women of Color**
2. Cooper, Richard S. et al., **The Puzzle of Hypertension in African-Americans**
3. Chan, Sucheng, **You're Short, Besides!**
4. Durham, Jimmie, **Cowboys and ... Notes on Art, Literature, and American Indians in the Modern American Mind**
5. Fox, Robert Eliot, **Becoming Post-White** and Waters, Mary C. **Optional Identities: For Whites Only**
6. hooks, bell, **Keeping Close to Home: Class and Education**
7. Lugones, Maria, **Purity, Impurity, and Separation**
8. Root, Maria P.P., **A Bill of Rights for Racially Mixed People**
9. Takaki, Ronald T., Excerpt from **A Different Mirror**

April 9 Meet in working groups to discuss application of Thursday topics to course development; assign student work.

April 29 Topics: Relationship between "culture," art, spatial design, etc.; does race, ethnicity, gender, etc. influence art and science? If so, how? Readings:

April 30 Meet in working groups to discuss application of Thursday topics to course development; assign student work

May 13 Topics: Teaching "multicultural" histories; new frameworks and paradigms

May 20 -21 **Symposium**: Black Identity in Theory and Practice

June 11 Final reports due

Chapter 10
Teaching and Diversity: Collaborative Lessons Learned

Pamela Ashmore, Kathleen Sullivan Brown, G. O. Akura, and Carole Murphy

The Center for Human Origin and Cultural Diversity (CHOCD) at the University of Missouri St. Louis prepares people of all ages for positive roles in our global society by empowering them with knowledge regarding their common biological and anthropological heritage. The Center also provides educators with the tools that are necessary to incorporate these skills into the educational process. This chapter describes the Center's creation through faculty collaboration and then provides reflections on the experience as a form of faculty development.

An Innovative Approach to Teaching about Diversity

In 1994, several faculty members from the Department of Anthropology and the Division of Teaching and Learning in the College of Education began a dialogue about the need for an innovative approach to diversity education that would be based on contemporary scientific knowledge. Their vision was to introduce the inclusive possibilities of science, as well as the potential for utilizing science to help us to understand our collective humanity (Kim, Clarke-Ekong, & Ashmore, 1999). As educators, we needed to give science a human face, especially for the underrepresented learning communities that have been traditionally underserved in the sciences. All children and their teachers need a basic knowledge of the African origin of the human family, as well as experience with a variety of human cultures in order to develop an informed understanding and identity of ourselves and how each of us represents an important facet of human diversity. However, problems of racism, educational access, community development, human values, and the place of our children within the global community act as barriers to this development.

Although the educational community has been addressing the challenges of diversity for decades, we have not been very successful at developing programs that make a difference (Apple, 1996; Banks, 1995; Banks, 1996; Bennett, 1988; D'Souza, 1995; Fass, 1989; Glazer, 1997; Jones, 1992). Thus, novel and constructive strategies are needed to prepare teachers and students for a global community. An "outside the box" approach using science-based content enables participants to identify commonalities that all human beings share. This approach provides an initial level playing field upon which to then frame discussions of human diversity, biological and cultural adaptations, and the implications for us as members of a human family.

Many teachers and students in the United States have grown up in communities that do not understand our global heritage and its effects on our daily lives. The St. Louis region is the 17th largest U.S. metropolitan area, with a population of 2.4 million, and the region faces the same challenges as many urban areas. The inner city of the region can be characterized as one of the most troubled cities in the nation in terms of family poverty, racial polarization, and high school drop out rates. St. Louis is one of the poorest cities in the nation, with one in four city residents and approximately 60% of the children living in poverty. Since 1950, the inner city has experienced a decline in population, and the suburbs that surround it are older, showing signs of decline in desirable housing stock and an increase in poverty (Mannie, 2001). Thus, like many urban communities, the St. Louis metropolitan area suffers from a lack of understanding of its own diversity. People isolate themselves into homogeneous communities. Often, this translates into a mindset of intolerance and a misunderstanding of others not like themselves. Faculty of our urban university felt a need to be engaged in finding a remedy to "bridge the racial divide" (Wilson, 1999).

Because many teachers are not prepared to teach about the science of humankind, and because St. Louis is made up of people who can also be culturally isolated, the faculty of the University of Missouri St. Louis approached the Deans of the College of Education and College of Arts and Sciences about forming an alliance to create an interdisciplinary program. In the past, these two Colleges had worked through joint faculty appointments in the preparation of teacher educators. The new program was to be housed in the Department of Anthropology and would utilize the pedagogical expertise of the faculty and students of the Division of Teaching and Learning. This unique affiliation would afford pre-service teachers an in-depth knowledge of the science of humankind that would help to make them better teachers. An initial obstacle in the collaboration was that of translating the highly specialized and complex scientific terminology into a language that was appropriate for lesson plans intended for the initial audience of K-12 students. In 1995, a team of faculty and students from both Teaching and Learning and Anthropology was formed. Using a "learning-to-learn" model (Loacker & Mentkowski, 1993; Mentkowski & Doherty, 1984), this team developed four integrated, hands-on learning stations. Learning stations are stand-alone, theme-based, intensive investigations in which participants experience a particular aspect of human origin and diversity.

The curriculum at the Center was developed around these learning stations that focus on human origin and biological diversity, and the continent of Africa is presented as a model for explorations into cultural diversity. Upon entering the new human origin laboratory, students were placed in equally sized groups in each of the learning stations. Each station was a 30-minute experience. Students rotated through each of the learning stations that were integrated to form a coherent program. Generally, stations contained the following content:

Station 1 — Human Fossil Record:

Participants examine fossil casts of the human family and verbalize their observations. Participants place these casts into chronological order using informational cards that provide clues about the time frame for each of these humans. They then examine how human beings have changed over time. In addition, participants map the geographical sites where these fossils were discovered.

Station 2 — Archaeological Dating and Functional Morphology:

In order to understand the interpretative process, participants analyze fossils and artifacts that come from archaeological sites. To accomplish this, participants must measure their own body dimensions and make comparisons. They analyze the relationships between teeth and diet to understand the functional connection between the two.

Station 3 — Skin Color Variation:

Using the scientific method of hypothesis testing, participants investigate how melanin (skin pigment) production is related to the geographic distribution of early modern humans. On a wall-sized map, participants place pictures of humans, using latitude to plot the location and gradation of different skin colors.

Station 4 — Geological Time Scale:

Participants use deductive reasoning to develop a timeline of life forms and events.

These lab activities stress the positive adaptive aspects of diversity and underscore the importance of the African continent to the story of humankind's existence on earth. To date, more than 17,000 participants have experienced the CHOCD learning program. Armed with this knowledge, teachers and students can more appropriately address issues of human diversity. As one sixth grade student commented, "I think the most important thing I learned today was the way melanin and environment affects your skin. I already knew this, but now I can emphasize it. It is this – DARKER PEOPLE ARE NOT LESSER PEOPLE AND I HAVE PROOF." [Emphasis in original]

By promoting an understanding of the scientific story of human beings on earth, CHOCD hopes to provide a framework upon which to build a new perspective of understanding among diverse people.

Lessons Learned During CHOCD's Development

At CHOCD, we have learned that our curriculum fits a wide variety of learners. Types of participants have included students and their teachers from private and public schools, mainstream and alternative schools, accelerated and gifted schools. Students have included those with physical and behavioral disabilities, English as a second language students, and students who are incarcerated in local jails. In addition, the Center has worked with intergenerational programs that have included individuals from 5 to 86 years of age.

Most participants come away from the lab experience with a new appreciation of how they fit within the human family. There are two important lessons learned, the first is that everyone can claim full and equal membership within the human family; the second is that biological diversity (for example, skin color, height, facial structure) is to be celebrated, rather than feared or condemned. As one student wrote, "I would tell a friend that I learned that all humans have a common ancestry and that we are more alike than different." Participants also come away from the experience with increased content knowledge pertaining to each of the four learning stations, and their attitudes about human diversity show positive changes.

Emerging Use for Faculty Development

As mentioned previously, the primary focus for CHOCD was K-12 students and, secondarily, their teachers. The Center has increasingly become a site of learning for university faculty who hope to become better able to address diversity issues in their own classrooms. The Center has become a vehicle where faculty can explore their own life experiences and reflect on the concepts of race and culture. In the Center we confront issues and misconceptions about race and diversity to which we all have been acculturated. The emerging use of CHOCD specifically for the purposes of faculty development for the College shows that this unique program has potential for helping faculty to understand diversity challenges within their own classrooms and to confront misconceptions that they may have about human diversity.

The education student interns refined the lessons within the learning stations after seeing what worked to help learners of differing ages and abilities work out the final lessons. The lessons emphasized hands-on, inquiry-based learning procedures that are steeped in constructivist pedagogy because these strategies have been shown to promote and enhance the learning of science content (Willis, 1995). Thus, content specialists in anthropology and archaeology collaborated with teacher-educators and education students on the best pedagogical approaches to learning these in-depth lessons about human development. Not only did this lab achieve a multidimensional pedagogy for carrying out objectives, it proved that an interdisciplinary collaboration could work between anthropologists, biologists, mathematicians and educators from other disciplines (Linn, 1992). The collaboration itself became a form of professional development, with a focus on ways to teach diverse learners using a hands-on, inquiry-based approach.

A second stage of development, The African Cultures Lab, was intended to demonstrate the important African cultural aspect of *ujaama*, cooperation among people with diverse skills and abilities to create successful communities (Nyrere, 1973). These additional new stations evolved as more and more diverse visitors (including some with disabilities) used the materials and asked additional questions, for which answers needed to be researched. Combining the cultural aspects with CHOCD's science-based program helped to incorporate social and cultural practices in teaching which, according to Vygotsky (1978; & Kim, Clarke-Ekong, & Ashmore, 1999) helps reinforce intellectual work that individual learners accomplish in the disciplinary-based content.

In January 2001, although CHOCD was still thought of as a program for K-12 students, Dr. Brown encouraged Dr. Murphy, the chairperson of Educational Leadership and Policy Studies Division (ELAPS), to schedule a visit of the entire Education Leadership faculty to the Center. One of four divisions within the College, this group is itself a small but diverse unit of 20 faculty members, combining three different program emphasis areas: K-12 educational administration, adult education, and higher education. Members of the newly constituted division were looking for ways to share individual research interests, reduce isolation, and explore innovative approaches to teaching. The visit to CHOCD provided the focus for a stimulating faculty development session. The regularly scheduled faculty meeting was held in the Center. Fifteen faculty members participated in this meeting. Our major purpose was to acquaint the faculty with this new resource on our campus. Second, faculty were asked to take on the role of learners with regard to new developments in the field of anthropology. As learners, faculty had the opportunity to manipulate fossils, measure bones, and map out regional variations in skin color. After visiting several of the CHOCD stations, individual faculty members reexamined their own concepts of race and culture and held a dialogue about how this thinking impacts the teaching of diverse students in a metropolitan university.

Since that initial visit, specific lessons about diversity have been incorporated into the course content and pedagogy in the division of Educational Leadership and Policy Studies. For example, Dr. Brown uses the interactive experience of the melanin station to work with aspiring school administrators in her classes. In these classes, she and her students discuss the biological and cultural meanings attributed to skin color and the effects of racism, racial stereotypes, and cultural differences, and how these factors may impact student and teacher expectations for classroom learning.

The next step in our college's use of CHOCD for faculty development is planned for this year. As part of an upcoming accreditation visit, the College faculty has formed a "Diversity Committee" as a pre-visit preparation activity. The entire College of Education faculty will be asked to visit the Center and to experience the science behind diversity. It is anticipated that rich conversations, innovative research and collaboration ideas, and even some personal epiphanies may result from this planned experience. Already, the Center has been imbedded in the teacher preparation program with approximately 100 pre-service teachers experiencing the Center each semester. The faculty is considering making the CHOCD experience a required element of the teacher preparation program.

Another group of 20 faculty has formed a social justice study group to examine personal and institutional issues to:

- develop awareness of individual and collective belief systems regarding race and class
- promote a culture of change in the college that supports diversity and advocates for social justice
- develop a position paper on the recruitment and retention of students, faculty and staff of color
- strengthen the College's preparation for the NCATE diversity standards for the upcoming accreditation visit.

Because of overlapping goals and membership, the "Diversity" committee and the "Social Justice Study Group" are combining and coming up with action steps as part of the college's long-range strategic planning process. All of this is a work in progress and assessment is ongoing. In these ways, the faculty have begun to address the issues of diversity, racism, and racial stereotypes in our very segregated urban community (Focus St. Louis, 2001).

As teachers interested in promoting the teaching of diversity, we believe the most important lesson learned during this project was a new way of thinking about teaching. Frequently, university faculty use a didactic "chalk and talk" type of approach, relying on a textbook and a syllabus, with the content being simply passed on to students. However, the lessons that could be problematized in the Center can help faculty to become more culturally aware and responsive teachers. Working with students and colleagues from all ability levels, and with subject matter from a variety of disciplines requires one to think critically about the actual teaching and learning process. Young students are not the only people who need "hands-on learning." Faculty also can benefit from a more experiential and constructivist approach to professional development, especially when exploring and challenging perceptions of cultural diversity.

References

Apple, M. W. (1996). *Cultural politics and education.* Buckingham, England: Open University Press.

Banks, C. A. M. (1996). The intergroup education movement. In J. A. Banks (Ed.), *Multicultural education, transformative knowledge, and action* (pp. 251-277). New York: Teachers College Press.

Banks, J. A. (1995). Multicultural education: Historical development, dimensions, and practices. In J.A. Banks & C.A.M. Banks (Eds.), *Handbook of research on multicultural education* (pp. 3-14). New York: Macmillan.

Bennett, D. H. (1988). *The party of fear: From nativist movements to the new right in American history.* Chapel Hill: The University of North Carolina Press.

D'Souza, D. (1995). *The end of racism: Principles for a multicultural society.* New York: The Free Press.

Fass, P. S. (1989). *Outside in: Minorities and the transformation of American education.* New York: Oxford University Press.

Focus St. Louis (2001). *Racial equality in the St. Louis region: A community call to action.* St. Louis, MO: Author.

Glazer, N. (1997). *We are all multiculturalists now.* Cambridge, MA: Harvard University Press.

Jones, M. A. (1992). *American immigration* (2nd ed.). The University of Chicago Press.

Kim, S., Clarke-Ekong, S., & Ashmore, P. (1999). Effects of a hands-on multicultural education program: A model for student learning. *The Social Studies, 90*(5), 225-229.

Linn, M.C. (1992). Science education reform: Building on the research base. *Journal of Research in Science Teaching, 29*(8), 821-840.

Loacker, G., & Mentkowski, M. (1993). Creating a culture where assessment improves learning. In T. W. Banta (Ed.), *Making a difference: Outcomes of a decade of assessment in higher education.* San Francisco: Jossey-Bass.

Mentkowski, M., & Doherty, A. (1984). Abilities that last a lifetime: Outcomes of the Alverno experience. *AAHE Bulletin 36*(6), 5-6, 11-14.

Nyerere, J. K. (1973). *Uhuru na ujamaa (freedom and socialism): Selections from writings and speeches.* London & Nairobi: Oxford University Press.

Mannie, J. (2001, March 16). St. Louis officials find some relief in census figures they say they thought population decline would be worse [Editorial]. *St. Louis Post Dispatch*, p. A10.

Vygotsky, L. S. (1978). *Mind and society: The development of higher psychological expectations.* Cambridge, MA: Harvard University Press.

Willis, S. (1995). Reinventing science education: Reformers promote hands-on, inquiry-based learning. *Curriculum update.* Alexandria, VA: Association for Supervision and Curriculum Development.

Wilson, W. J. (1999). *The Bridge over the racial divide: Rising inequality and coalition politics.* Berkeley, CA: University of California Press.

Dr. Pamela Ashmore is Assistant Professor of Anthropology, College of Arts and Sciences at the University of Missouri St. Louis. She is Associate Director of the Center for Human Origin and Cultural Diversity.

Dr. Kathleen Sullivan Brown is Associate Professor of Educational Leadership and Policy Studies in the College of Education at the University of Missouri St. Louis. She served as an external grant evaluator during the development of the Center and is an advocate for using the Center specifically for faculty development purposes.

G. O. Akura, a native of Kenya, received a Master's degree in Secondary Education at the University of Missouri St. Louis and then entered the doctoral program in the College of Education. He is currently writing his dissertation in science education. He served as an intern during the formative stages of the development of the two labs in the Center for Human Origin and Cultural Diversity.

Dr. Carole Murphy is Associate Professor of Education and Division Chair in Educational Leadership and Policy Studies at the University's College of Education. Dr. Murphy is one of the four founders of the Center.

Chapter 11

Teaching Inclusively: The Whole Is Greater Than the Sum of Its Parts

Christine Martin

Professional development for academics is often a solitary activity and may have little systemic impact. The Multicultural Learning Institute at Pierce College creates a bi-yearly, two-quarter-long opportunity that provides a supportive learning community. Within this collegial context, participants achieve two learning outcomes: link a multicultural skill-building activity or assignment to an existing classroom assignment or activity and plan for how one's own cultural identity will influence the teaching and learning process.

Pierce College is a two-year community college with over 1350 employees who serve more than 30,000 students a year throughout much of Pierce County in Washington State. As the state's third largest community college district that includes two colleges and 13 contracted sites, we find ourselves in classrooms and offices on military bases and in community buildings, correctional institutions, hospitals, and residential centers. In any given class or group, one is likely to find students who are "Running Start" students, (students who receive high school and college credit concurrently), dislocated workers, recent high school graduates, adults, international students, first-generation college students, military personnel and veterans, people from different sexual or religious orientations, and displaced homemakers. And each of these groups is made up of students with distinct ethnic and racial identities.

In our commitment to multiculturalism, we agree to work effectively with all who enter our doors to learn in our various professional technical, continuing education, transfer, and basic skills programs. Our common purpose is to learn and grow, and we have found we often do that best together. The Multicultural Learning Institute is guided by Pierce College's mission statement and statement of values and goals. For example, the Pierce College mission statement asserts that, "we are a community of learners open to all. Together, we strive to meet the needs of our diverse community and to develop each member's abilities." Likewise, in our statement of values and goals, we find three indicators of how multiculturalism is manifested: (a) Recruit, retain, and involve a diverse faculty, staff, and student population; (b) value the dignity, strength, and contribution of each individual in our community; and (c) celebrate our diversity (Pierce College, 1997). This commitment to multiculturalism is articulated again in the Pierce College Strategic Plan (2000) where we promise to "increase the number of faculty, staff, and administrators who teach and model the five core abilities," one of which is multiculturalism.

Assessment of the college mission and strategic plan is an ongoing process that informs us of how we are doing. We learned from our spring 1999 student survey that in spite of our stated value of and commitment to multiculturalism, we were not doing enough:

> Although Pierce College students make progress in adopting a multicultural perspective over time, they do not significantly increase the frequency of their serious discussions with students whose ethnic or cultural background is different or who are from a different country.
>
> (Pierce College Student Survey, Spring 1999 –Stamoulis, 1999)

It was clear we needed to get students talking to each other, not just appreciating each other's perspectives.

Institute Design

The "Multicultural Learning Institute: Making Multiculturalism Come Alive at Pierce College" was originally designed as a pilot project in response to the results of the 1999 student survey. It is a two-quarter-long, professional-development learning community for college exempt and classified staff, faculty, and administrators (and more recently, student leaders as well) from across the college district. Embodying an underlying assumption that all college employees affect student learning and success, each person comes to the institute with a desire to develop multicultural competence in practical ways that promote student success regardless of her or his role in the district. The Multicultural Learning Institute is intentional in its design and directed in its dual purpose: (a) link a multicultural skill-building activity or assignment to an existing classroom assignment or activity, and in doing so, (b) articulate and plan for how one's cultural identity will influence the learning process or the educational setting.

The institute design is based on five principles. It is important that the "Making Multiculturalism Come Alive at Pierce College" instructional design and process precisely model what we want the participants to do in their work environments. Therefore, the institute strives to model the following five principles:

1. Learning does not happen in isolation. The institute is a functional learning community that provides collegiality during and after completion of the institute (Cox, 2001).
2. Multiculturalism includes more than race. The Pierce College definition of multiculturalism is deliberately broad, acknowledging multiple ways of knowing, being, and thinking as well as multiple social identity attributes such as ability, age, ethnicity, gender, gender identity, religion, sexual orientation, and socioeconomic status. Participants in the Multicultural Institute have the opportunity to engage with many types of diversity in many different settings across the district.
3. Practice what you preach. The institute intentionally strives to mirror the curriculum development model we want participants to learn and use in their teaching and work.
4. Cultural sensitivity and competence develop with time and practice. The institute curriculum and group process must be flexible enough to respond to the different developmental levels or stages of participants (Bennett, 2000). This is really no different from what we expect to offer those under our own guidance or in our classrooms, but we often do not think that we need to demonstrate such empathy towards peers and colleagues.
5. There is an inseparable bond between instruction and student services. Students' experiences are informed by interactions with a range of people and offices on campus such as advising, registration, veterans' affairs, men's and women's programs, student programs, and other co-curricular services. These encounters have an indelible impact on student learning and success. The institute makes our "student learning and success" model come alive by recognizing the systemic and interdependent nature of our efforts to successfully achieve the college's mission.

To implement these five principles, the institute's pedagogical design addresses the unique needs of adult learners (The Washington Center, 1998). This is accomplished by addressing the following six elements: (a) *manageability* is accomplished by conducting six two-hour workshops held over two quarters; (b) sessions are *co-facilitated,* and facilitators are drawn from both instructional and student services; (c) *relevancy* is crucial so the content is both practical and applicable to participants' current work; (d) *variety* in instructional design and delivery is emphasized (for example, cooperative learning, independent study activities, off-campus learning opportunities, web-enhanced curriculum using Blackboard Virtual Classroom software, one-on-one consultations, individualized coaching, and classroom/office/workshop visits);

(e) resources must be *accessible* and readily available; and (f) *recognition* (such as salary credits for tenured faculty or $200 for part-time faculty or staff) for participation is linked directly to the completion of assigned activities by assigned due dates.

Participants are selected by specific criteria. Potential members must be available to attend all institute workshops and activities; be willing to work toward the two learning outcomes; contribute to the learning of other participants; and add to the demographic representation of their cohort (by being representative of instructional or student services, coming from diverse fields of study, or being affiliated with different service areas). Additionally, exempt and classified staff members need written authorization from a supervisor in order to participate.

Prior to each institute, marketing and publicity are intense. Our goal is that every potentially eligible person in the district see something about the institute at least three times before the registration deadline. Over time, however, the institute has come to "sell itself." This has come about through the quality of its design and, more importantly, by the need it fills: people are hungry to engage in this learning, and they tell each other about it.

Because instructional types of professional development opportunities designed to impact learning are usually viewed as "faculty only" events, we do a lot of personal, one-on-one outreach to administrators and exempt and classified staff to achieve our goal of modeling inclusiveness and to fulfill our mission of being "a community of learners open to all." The success of this outreach produces a mixture of participants who consistently cite this mix as one of the most beneficial and richest aspects of the institute experience. Tying institute outcomes to the results of the 1999 student survey is also a powerful draw.

District-wide support for the institute has been given without reservation from all levels of administration. We have been fortunate that the financial support of International Education, the Assessment Team, and Multicultural Services has continued far beyond the initial commitment to fund our first institute. Total expenditures equal roughly $3000 for a group of 12. The largest expenditure is to send the institute's participants to the Washington Center annual conferences. (http://www.evergreen.edu/washcenter).

Curriculum Design

Within the institute's pedagogical parameter, the five principles address inclusion issues while adult learning theory addresses the participants' specific needs. We used Ruth Stiehl's outcomes assessment model to develop the institute's curriculum (Stiehl, 2000). Example 1 (below) is the completed Content/Curriculum Outcome Guide (CCOG) developed for the institute. Since curriculum development starts with the two learning outcomes, begin reading at the right side of the chart and work your way to the left. Note that the learning outcomes, assessment tasks, skills, and content are all broad and relevant enough to be incorporated into the work of student services personnel, faculty, and administrators.

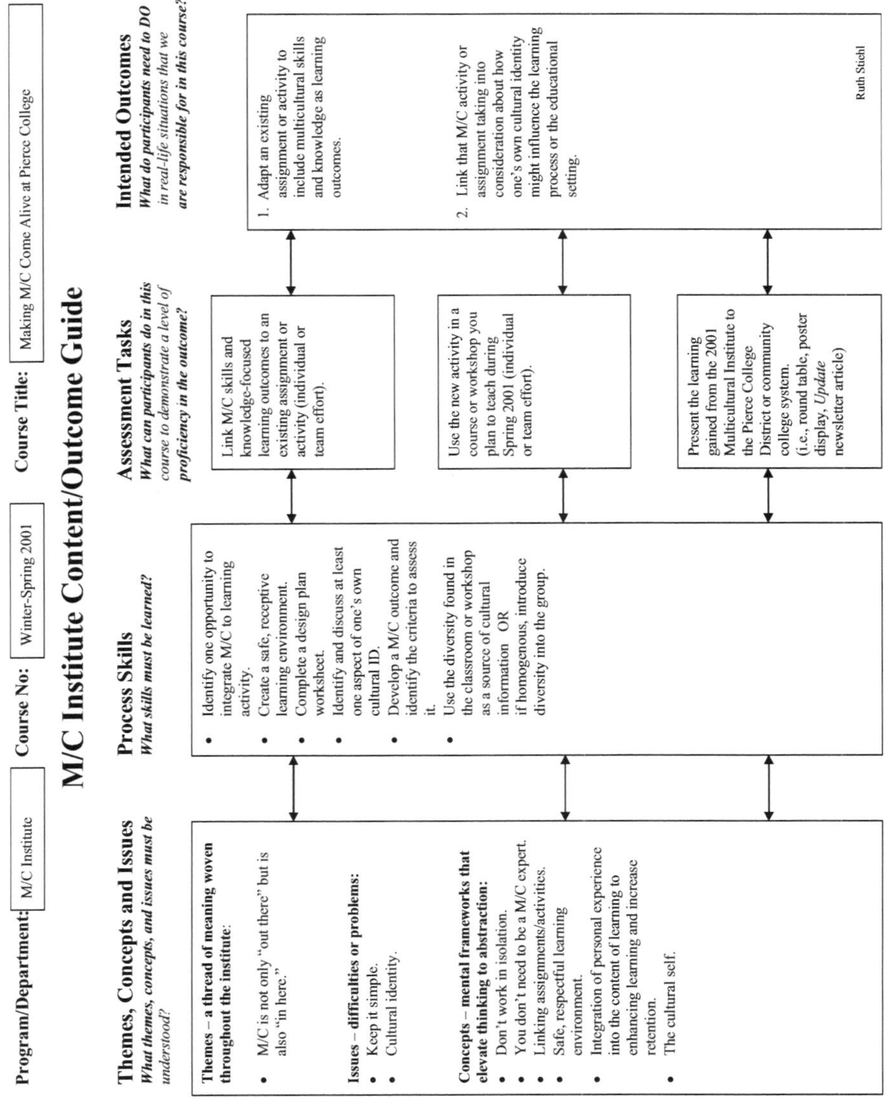

Program/Department: M/C Institute **Course No:** Winter-Spring 2001 **Course Title:** Making M/C Come Alive at Pierce College

M/C Institute Content/Outcome Guide

Themes, Concepts and Issues *What themes, concepts, and issues must be understood?*	Process Skills *What skills must be learned?*	Assessment Tasks *What can participants do in this course to demonstrate a level of proficiency in the outcome?*	Intended Outcomes *What do participants need to DO in real-life situations that we are responsible for in this course?*
Themes – a thread of meaning woven throughout the institute: • M/C is not only "out there" but is also "in here." **Issues – difficulties or problems:** • Keep it simple. • Cultural identity. **Concepts – mental frameworks that elevate thinking to abstraction:** • Don't work in isolation. • You don't need to be a M/C expert. • Linking assignments/activities. • Safe, respectful learning environment. • Integration of personal experience into the content of learning to enhancing learning and increase retention. • The cultural self.	• Identify one opportunity to integrate M/C to learning activity. • Create a safe, receptive learning environment. • Complete a design plan worksheet. • Identify and discuss at least one aspect of one's own cultural ID. • Develop a M/C outcome and identify the criteria to assess it. • Use the diversity found in the classroom or workshop as a source of cultural information OR if homogenous, introduce diversity into the group.	Link M/C skills and knowledge-focused learning outcomes to an existing assignment or activity (individual or team effort). Use the new activity in a course or workshop you plan to teach during Spring 2001 (individual or team effort). Present the learning gained from the 2001 Multicultural Institute to the Pierce College District or community college system. (i.e., round table, poster display, *Update* newsletter article)	1. Adapt an existing assignment or activity to include multicultural skills and knowledge as learning outcomes. 2. Link that M/C activity or assignment taking into consideration about how one's own cultural identity might influence the learning process or the educational setting. Ruth Stiehl

There is a tendency to believe that adult learners have the self-directedness and self-discipline to follow an individualized, somewhat open form of instruction. In fact, in spite of their independent natures, adult learners often benefit from some structure, found here through the framework of a learning community, routine check-ins by the facilitators (not to be underestimated!), and flexible instructional content and processes that address their needs.

These three elements cannot be ignored for at least two reasons. First, when multiculturalism discussions start to move from theory to practice (in the institute and in the classroom), attrition can occur as people begin to face difficult issues, potential conflict, and perhaps guilt. And second, it is easy for busy faculty and staff to put their own learning aside when the institute's demands are high, when their students are knocking on the door, or when they are feeling somewhat nervous or incompetent. A major part of the instructional design of the institute is the need for participants to experience inclusive acceptance, as well as feel the liberty to take the risks ultimately expected of them as instructors and college employees.

Up to this point, this chapter has addressed much of the process of the institute. Now, I wish to address the content that comes from a variety of sources and is accessed in a variety of different ways.

Pierce College faculty, staff, and administrators are often their own best resources, and the cultural and institutional identities they bring to the institute are not only valued but also help to direct the content and process of our work as a community. People enjoy working with their colleagues, and the degree to which they engage in discussing pertinent content and practical materials is often cited as the most meaningful part of any workshop. For example, when the human resources director works on a supervisor training, when a student advisor develops ways to improve her intercultural communication skills, or when a faculty member develops diverse work teams in a chemistry lab, they see how they each have something valuable to contribute to student learning and success.

There are varying levels of experience and skill with multiculturalism among participants. Some participants have a relatively high level of multicultural awareness and sensitivity since many participated in past diversity training offered at the college and elsewhere; others are culturally competent, and yet others are new to these ideas and skills. The curriculum needs to be flexible enough so that everyone feels included, can take the risks they need in order to learn, and can see themselves as contributors of knowledge and community.

All the materials are selected and presented in a global or broad enough way so that individuals and departments can adapt the materials and concepts to meet their particular needs. People learn how a single resource may be used in different contexts. A notebook containing institute materials and resources considered necessary for achieving the institute learning outcomes and serving as a repository for future handouts and hard-copy resources is prepared for each participant . Such materials may include, for example, a variety of different multicultural educational learning theories that help people to reflect on and internalize their ideas, experiences, and values. Principles of inclusive teaching, such as the following, are often included as well:

1. When teaching multicultural skills and cultural sensitivity, it is safe to assume that participants are at different stages in the development of their intercultural sensitivity. Bennett and Bennett offer a paradigm for the design of curriculum from both the content and process points of view (Bennett, 2000).

2. Equitable access to learning is often difficult to comprehend for many folks, especially those who enjoy a place of privilege (in terms of economic status, age, race, gender, and so forth) in a given country (Johnson, 2001). Readings are explicit in naming the assumptions and practices that create the barriers to equity in educational settings and provide concrete standards for promoting excellence in learning (CREDE, 2000).

3. Viable examples of learning outcomes address intercultural knowledge, skills and attitudes so that people better understand the differences between them and how those differences link to student success in the world of work, family, and society (Stanley, 1997).

4. Teaching and assessing multicultural learning outcomes are new skills for many educators, so we use a template to assist people in developing multicultural outcomes and linking those to an existing assignment or activity (see Appendix A).

Written materials are also intended to address participants' immediate experiences and needs. Readings about cultural identity, intercultural communication, creating a safe, receptive learning environment, and so forth are selected to provide theoretical understanding and practical support for the learning process in the institute and in the participant's own classrooms and workplace settings. Readings may also present and address the needs of different cultural groups (in terms of age, gender, and sexual orientation, for example) that we assume are present in any given institute and for major groups in the student population that may not represented by a particular cohort – fundamental religious groups, for example – but may be part of the larger student body (Burkholder, 1999; Dougharty, 2000; Laird, 2000; Zemke, 2000). Other models that have practical uses in a classroom or workshop may also be included, such as the Cultural Venn Diagram (Wlodkowski, 1995) and the Guide for Setting Ground Rules (Gorski, 2000).

Blackboard virtual classroom materials help to introduce many people to our Blackboard online classroom and help us reach a broader range of learning preferences. On the first day of the institute, we spend about 45 minutes in the computer lab working on the computers. Participants in the institute are usually reluctant to use the online classroom, so this initial hands-on orientation has proven to be very valuable. Crib sheets are provided with step-by-step instructions on how to access and maneuver in this virtual classroom. One strategy to assure that people will go to the classroom is to post information there, such as templates and online resources, which they cannot get in the face-to-face setting.

Additionally, we provide exemplary materials such as examples of learning outcomes written in everyday language that demonstrate cultural competencies (Stanley, 1997). We start with the outcomes because this is the point at which participants begin to develop their own linked activities. For many, developing multicultural skills and assessing the degree of cultural competence in themselves or others is an illusive and slippery task.

The "Designing a Linked Assignment or Activity" template (Whalley, 1999), guides participants through a process of identifying the best place(s) in the curriculum to "link" a multicultural activity in a classroom or work setting (for example, advising, HR workshop, psychology class, and so forth). They are then asked to determine "Where is there room within my regular course or work assignments to integrate multicultural skills, knowledge and/or attitudes?" The idea is that participants are *not* expected to start from scratch and invent something new, but to build on what they currently do.

The following are some of the outcomes and activities people in the institute developed to guide their curriculum development:

1. Chemistry Faculty – Students will work in diverse work groups to analyze various chemical aspects of Lake Waughop bordering the Pierce College campus. "Prior to beginning work, each student completed a values inventory designed to encourage them to think about what they bring, and don't bring, to the group experience" (Martin & Steward, 2000).
2. Displaced Homemakers Coordinator – Students will describe a workplace situation from two different cultural frames of reference. "The activity consisted of identifying the stereotypes associated with age that exist in our country, especially as they relate to entering the workforce and to one's own self-presentation" (Martin & Steward, 2000).
3. Human Resources Director – Supervisors will identify contrasting cultural values and examine how individual cultural values may impact perceptions of job elements. "The activity will occur within the training of supervisors and other employees about using a new [state] performance evaluation form" (Martin & Steward, 2000).
4. International Education Faculty – Students will produce a culturally sensitive business report. "International students will incorporate what they have

learned about cultural sensitivity into their analysis of opening a new factory in a given city" (Martin & Steward, 2000).

5. Tutoring Center Coordinator – Tutors will resolve a student/staff issue using three different approaches in order to serve a diverse population. (Martin & Steward, 2000.)

As demonstrated in the above examples, the "link" is intended to tap into the cultural richness students and employees bring to our classrooms and workplace settings. Starting with the outcome and following the template, participants embark on a guided process, in the workshops and individually, to develop a linked assignment that meets the needs of a given class or group of students.

Multiculturalism at its Best

Attending events off campus exposes participants to other ways of thinking, being, and doing. One example is how two groups, using ideas garnered at the Washington Center Annual Conference, came together after the institute was over and created several programs that continue to be attended by employees throughout the district. These programs are the Pierce College "Safe Zone" project for people who are lesbian, gay, bisexual, or transgender, and a district-wide book group on white privilege.

Learning Outcomes Assessment

The institute has been offered three times, twice by request, over the last three years. A total of 35 faculty, staff, and administrators have participated, along with one student leader. We use a formative assessment rubric to determine the degree to which a participant is achieving the two learning outcomes two or three times throughout the institute so that participants have ongoing feedback (see Appendix B). The assessments also give the facilitators feedback throughout the institute in order to best meet learning needs. The results have also been used to influence future institutes' curriculum and design. For example, in the first institute we expected people to implement their linked activities by the end of spring quarter. This was an ambitious outcome for a variety of reasons. First, some classes for which the activity was designed were scheduled for the upcoming academic year. So it was impossible to achieve the "Integrating" level of skill on the rubric (Appendix B). Second, the desire to integrate multiculturalism in one's work was at times higher than the level of personal awareness and skill permitted, meaning the person was at an "Emerging" level of skill development as opposed to "Developing" or higher. As a result, future institutes eliminated the immediate application of the new linked assignments, and we strove instead to work more effectively with what could be defined as movement for a given individual. For example, one person had never before considered her own cultural identity or how that identity impacted her interactions with people from other cultures. Her need was to use the institute as a resource and support to do some introspective work. She was far from being ready to incorporate multiculturalism into her work with students.

The Whole is Greater than the Sum of its Parts

I have often been asked, "Why an institute [as opposed to a single workshop]?"

To quote our associate dean for planning and assessment:

> What we really do well at Pierce is team around goals. Professional development is often a solitary activity, and has little real systemic impact. But as a team and in community, we can extend our learning multifold.
>
> (J. Kvinsland, conversation, 2001)

And that is exactly why we create institutes – to build on our strengths and to deepen our learning, not only as individuals but collectively as employees of a complex district. As groups we create a community of scholarship where members from different constituencies of our college district can learn from and teach each other. Teaching students may be a responsibility for faculty, but creating an environment of learning and success is the responsibility of all who are involved. By placing Pierce College employees in a cohort, the institute helps them to develop their learning in a context of a new community, giving them more perspectives, more support, and more tools to extend their learning into their classrooms, offices, and workshops.

"Making Multiculturalism Come Alive at Pierce College" applies not only to our students, but includes tapping into and developing the differences our employees bring to the work of the college in a systemic and intentional way. By supporting learning communities that are in line with our mission, we become an example of Stephen Covey's "Learning Organization" in which everyone benefits:

> Once you get information, you tend to use it. When you get enough people with information, you raise the consciousness and unleash energies. The higher the consciousness, the more the social, national, and political will

develops ... information then becomes power, the power of a collective will to accomplish the mission of the organization.

(Covey, 1992)

Teaching inclusively demands us to provide training models where participants literally experience that they need the skills and knowledge of others in order to be inclusive, and that the whole is, indeed, greater than the sum of its parts.

References

Bennett, J. M., & Bennett, M. J. (2000, February 24). *Culture and the process of learning.* Handbook prepared for the 13th Annual Conference of the Washington Center for Improving the Quality of Undergraduate Education, Seattle: WA.

Burkholder, B. G. (1999). *To know and be known: Honoring and valuing the men in our midst.* Unpublished manuscript, Pierce College Puyallup: WA.

Covey, S.R. (1992). *Principle centered leadership.* New York: Simon & Schuster.

Cox, M. D. (2001). Faculty learning communities: Change agents for transforming institutions into learning organizations. In D. Lieberman, & C. Wehlburg (Eds.), *To improve the academy, 19* (pp.75-100). Bolton, MA: Anker.

Center for Research on Education, Diversity and Excellence. (2002). *Five Standards.* Retrieved on September 21, 2004, from http://www.crede.ucsc.edu/

Dougharty, W. H., & Greene, T. (2000, Fall). Supporting and celebrating our LGBT students and colleagues. *The Washington Center News* (pp.19-20). Olympia, WA: The Washington Center for Improving the Quality of Undergraduate Education.

Gorski, P. (2000). *A guide for setting ground rules. Multicultural Supersite: Multicultural Activities online.* Retrieved on September 24, 2004 from http://www.mhhe.com/socscience/education/multi/

Johnson, A.G. (2001). *Privilege, power, and difference.* Mountain View, CA: Mayfield.

Laird, L. (2000, Fall). Encountering religious commitments in the classroom. *The Washington Center News* (pp.25-28). Olympia, WA: The Washington Center for Improving the Quality of Undergraduate Education.

Martin, C., & Steward, A. (2000, Fall). Making multiculturalism come alive at Pierce College: A learning institute. *The Washington Center News* (pp.10-13). Olympia, WA: The Washington Center for Improving the Quality of Undergraduate Education.

Pierce College mission. (1997). Retrieved September 21, 2004, from Pierce College Web site http://www.pierce.ctc.edu/whatis/mission.php3

Saunders, S., & Kardia, D. (2004). Creating inclusive classrooms [Electronic Chapter 3]. *Guidebook for University of Michigan graduate student instructors.* Retrieved September 24, 2004, from University of Michigan, Center for Research on Learning and Teaching Web site: www.umich.edu/~crltmich/F6.html

Stamoulis, L. (1999). *Pierce College student survey: Spring 1999.* Lakewood, WA: Pierce College District, Office of Institutional Research.

Stanley, D., & Mason, J. (1997). *Preparing graduates for the future: International learning outcomes* (Final Report). Victoria, BC: Centre for International Education.

Stiehl, R. (with Lewchuk, L.) (2000). *The outcomes primer: Reconstructing the college curriculum.* Corvallis, OR: The Learning Organization.

Whalley, T. (1999, June). *Internationalizing learning through linked assignments.* Paper presented at the meeting of B.C. Centre for International Education (BCCIE), Victoria, British Columbia, Canada.

Principles of Faculty Development. (1998, Fall). *The Washington Center News, 12*(1), 31.

Wlodkowski, R. J., & Ginsberg, M. B. (1995). *Diversity and motivation: Culturally responsive teaching.* San Francisco: Jossey-Bass.

Zemke, R., Raines, C., & Filipczak, B. *Generations at work: Managing the clash of veterans, boomers, xers, and nexters in your workplace.* New York: AMACOM.

Christine Martin is the Curriculum Development Specialist and Interim Assessment Team Coordinator for the Pierce College district in Washington State.

Appendix A

Making Multiculturalism Come alive at Pierce College

Pierce College Learning Institute: January – May 2001
(Adapted from Tom Whalley's work at Douglas College in British Columbia, as part of a project directed by the British Columbia Centre for International Education)

Designing a Linked Assignment or Activity

Use this worksheet to ask yourself: Where is there room within my regular instruction or advising to integrate multicultural skills, knowledge, and attitudes?

1. Identify the course or activity:
   (for example, Chemistry, English 98, Study Skills, Literacy Skills, Speech, orientations, and so forth)

2. Identify or write a multicultural outcome:
   (Refer to the International Learning Outcome article in notebook for examples.)

3. Inventory the diversity offered by the students enrolled:
   (consider age, race, socioeconomic status, gender, sexual orientation, physical ability, and so forth)

4. Decide if you want and/or need to involve students from other courses.
   (for example, ESL, class from another country or content area)

5. Identify a commonly used assignment or learning activity or situation that you feel has possibilities to be a linked assignment to achieve your outcome stated in number 2 above. (such as working in teams, interview skills, social services, cooperative learning, presentations or research)

6. Brainstorm a list of multicultural skills, knowledge, and attitudes related to the outcome in the context of number 2. List a few below. (See reference sheets in your notebook for examples.)

Multicultural knowledge:

Multicultural skills:

Multicultural attitudes:

7. Identify one or two of the above abilities that most easily fit into the context of your usual assignment or activity. (Consider the outcomes you want!)

8. Identify how you are going to "link" the above abilities to your existing assignment or activity and how you are going to "link" learners engaged in the assignment.

9. Sketch out the background content knowledge that learners would need to have to engage in the learning activity.

10. Sketch out the background knowledge that learners bring to the activity.

11. Identify activities learners would need to do to prepare for the linked assignment.

12. Outline the instructions for the learners.

13. Describe the product you expect from the assignment.

14. Identify the criteria you will use to teach and assess the ability (ies) you have identified. (What will learners need to DO to demonstrate their knowledge, skills, or attitudes?)

15. Create a rubric or assessment tool that contains the above criteria that you and learners will use to assess the multicultural learning outcomes that you integrated into the linked assignment.

Appendix B

2001 Multicultural Institute

Circle the date of this assessment: 3/5 4/15 6/15

Consider the M/C Institute Content/Outcome Guide.
Use the standards at the bottom of the page to determine the degree to which you have moved towards achieving the two intended outcomes for the institute. Please explain why you placed yourself where you did and what you or the facilitators can do to help you take your next step.

1. Adapt an existing assignment or activity to include multicultural skills and as learning outcomes (or develop a new activity).

2. Develop a linked M/C activity or assignment taking into consideration how your own cultural identity might influence the learning process or the educational settings that you facilitate.

Unobserved:	**Enacting:**	**Developing:**	**Integrating:**	**Emerging:**
You have no detectible movement towards the attainment of this outcome nor are related skills present	You are designing and implementing linked M/C activities that demonstrate incorporation of the institute's themes, concepts, issues, and skills to attain the intended outcomes.	You are attempting to incorporate new M/C knowledge, skills, and/or attitudes into your daily work settings AND/OR you are using new M/C knowledge, skills, and/or attitudes in starting the development of the Linked Assignment Design Plan.	You design, integrate, and collaborate in activities that demonstrate the skillful integration of the intended outcomes.	You have started to grapple with the themes, concepts, issues, and skills of the Institute but have yet to put these thoughts and feelings into any concrete action or plan.

Chapter 12
Renewing Diversity Initiatives Within an English Department

Anne J. Herrington

This chapter describes how one English Department, by participating in the Teaching and Learning in the Diverse Classroom Fellowship Program, renewed ongoing commitment to diversity by creating forums for discussion of values related to diversity, assessment of current needs, and the generation of strategies related to curriculum and pedagogy, faculty and student representation, and overall climate.

In 2002-03, ten of us (six faculty and four graduate students) received a Departmental Forum Fellowship from the University of Massachusetts Amherst's Center for Teaching's (CFT) Teaching and Learning in the Diverse Classroom (TLDC)[1] Fellowship Program. We initiated the project out of a feeling that it was time for us, as a Department, to take stock and renew our commitment to diversity in our curriculum and amongst the faculty and students. Our primary goal for the year was to create forums for discussion among our group and the Department overall as to what we mean by diversity, why we value it, and how we should act on those values. Specifically, our aims were to assess needs and solicit suggestions related to 1) curriculum and pedagogy, 2) faculty and student representation, and 3) overall climate. My goal for this

[1]The TLDC program, first introduced in 1994-1995, has included 126 participants (faculty and teaching assistants) from 32 departments, across nine schools and colleges. Former fellows of the program include awardees of the Distinguished Teaching Award, the College Outstanding Teaching Award, the Conte Research Award, Chancellor's Community Service Award and a recipient of the McArthur "Genius" Grant. Since 1999, the TLDC program has involved a broad array of department and school based teams including teams from: Student Development and Pupil Personnel Services, psychology, English, nutrition and sports management. The program provides consultations for instructors and entire departments, University-wide orientations, departmental and campus-wide workshops, grants for individuals, resources such as bibliographies and videotapes, and two year-long seminars that form the centerpiece of TLDC and the Career Development Seminar for Graduate Students of Color.

chapter is threefold: to report on what we did during the year of the fellowship, to reflect on whether we achieved our goal of having some effect on future actions, and to do so in ways that others with similar interests might learn something from our work that would inform their own efforts.

Context

Our Department has a historical commitment to a racially diverse graduate population and faculty and to multi-ethnic studies of literature. Beginning in the mid-1960's, then under the leadership of the late Professor Sidney Kaplan, who was dedicated to African-American studies and to building a more diverse graduate student population, our department has attracted distinguished African American graduate students, most all pursuing studies in African-American studies. Since that time, our department has committed resources and personnel to rebuilding this tradition and population of graduate students.

With the help of the Graduate School Office of Graduate Student Recruitment and Retention, we have had some modest success: we have had one of the higher percentages of ALANA admissions in the University and have been able to maintain our ALANA graduate population of about 15% of the graduate student body. In this same period, we have hired in the fields of Native, Latino, and Asian American studies as well as Post-colonial and transnational studies; furthermore, a number of faculty have been involved in mentoring graduate students teaching introductory literature courses that fulfill our University's General Education "diversity" requirement. Our efforts in graduate recruitment have now reached something of a plateau, and we have no similar departmental recruitment effort at the undergraduate level. Indeed, while we are aware of the numbers of ALANA students in our graduate population, we do not know the number of ALANA students who are undergraduate English majors, except to know that there are very few. As far as faculty, according to official calculations from our Office of Equal Opportunity and Diversity, in 2002, 29% of our faculty were women and 13% were minority: when compared with national availability estimates, we were designated as officially underrepresented for women, but not so for minorities. Still, many of us in the Department feel that we are underrepresented in both areas.

An important institutional context for our Fellowship Year was the University-wide Community, Diversity, and Social Justice (CDSJ) Project. This multi-year project represents a substantial commitment by the University to create a more inclusive and equitable learning, working and living environment and develop proactive practices regarding matters of community, diversity and social justice. During our Fellowship year of 2002-03, the CDSJ project was in its assessment phase, with comprehensive assessments being carried out within each major executive area of the University, including Academic Affairs (2004). Both Matt Ouellett and I were members of the Academic Affairs Team. This on-going effort, now in planning and implementation stages, provided and continues to provide broader institutional support for our departmental efforts.

It was in this context that we initiated our project.

Getting Started

As Department Chair, I worked with others to constitute a group that included both faculty and graduate students in order to include student perspectives in our ongoing discussions and planning. We also consciously aimed for ethnic diversity within the group and gender diversity (although the group was predominantly women). We did not have much diversity in terms of scholarly interest, as most all participants were in American literature/studies.

As we discussed whether to even submit a proposal for the project, a number of us expressed skepticism about proceeding: would this just be more meetings and talk with no action? Still, individually and collectively, we felt the project was important enough to take the risk and proceed, believing that we could and would accomplish something.

Essential to our work was establishing a trust within the group in working with one another and keeping all of our conversations confidential. The trust-building activities that Matt Ouellett, Associate Director of the Center for Teaching, led us through at our initial meeting were instrumental in establishing this trust and his informed guidance throughout helped us frame our work in terms of models of multi-culturalism.

Assessment and Programming

We began with intensive discussions amongst ourselves: what did we mean by "diversity"? Some in our group found the term itself offensive, connoting a kind of paternalism where the problem is one only for people of color who are not admitted to our ranks in sufficient numbers. We also knew that some colleagues equated the term with political correctness. We agreed that we valued a nuanced view of diversity, needing to consider, as another colleague wrote in assessment, "interactions and complications that arise between/in race and class and when they interact with gender, with sexuality, with cultural positions." Critically examining the concept in this way was important for us in beginning to delineate what was involved and understanding this complexity through our multiple perspectives. It also helped us shape our own agendas for the year.

In our proposal, we identified assessment of faculty and student experiences and perspectives as a primary objective. In retrospect, and now having learned more about Multicultural Models for Organizational Change, I understand more fully the value of beginning with assessment (Jackson and Hardmian, 1994). Not only does it elicit information that informs planning, but it represents an intervention in itself as it brings attention to issues and values and prompts discussion. Our assessment activities included the following:

1) a faculty survey asking what they considered the most pressing issue "under the rubric of diversity" and for an anecdote or short narrative that illustrates one of their concerns (responses to this second question were used in a subsequent departmental colloquium).

2) a focus group with ALANA undergraduate English majors led by Tracy Vaughn, a PhD student in the Department and member of our TLDC project group. We felt that for students to feel comfortable speaking candidly, faculty should not be present, and that the session should be led by a person with whom some of the students had already had positive contact. To invite students to the meeting, we posted announcements, promising pizza, and issued specific invitations to students some of us knew.

3) a meeting of the TLDC Fellows with ALANA graduate students, who were more of an established group. We also had reason to believe that they would speak candidly to us, and indeed, that they wanted the opportunity to speak directly to the entire group. While we recognized the importance of seeking feedback from all students, that was more than we could take on and we reasoned that the ALANA students were our priority.

At each of the student meetings, those attending were also asked to complete a survey asking them when they felt most included in the English major/Department, and when they felt most excluded? Matt also posed these same questions to us at the initial meeting of our TLDC group. Some of the responses from the student and TLDC session follow. I present them without identifying whether a faculty member or student made them because I believe it is interesting that in many cases you cannot tell who made the comment. The feeling of wanting to be represented, in our human presence and in the curriculum, and validated as people and as learners and scholars, is shared by students and faculty.

When do you feel included?

When in the classroom teaching

When my scholarship is accepted

Taking classes that deal with social issues and questions of culture and identity

When my opinion seems welcomed, which is usually

When a professor opens a forum amongst the students and keeps literature at the center

When staff and faculty members greet students with respect

When do you feel excluded?

In the classroom as a graduate student

When homophobic or racist remarks are made and not challenged

When not being welcomed in a social way

When I am put in the position of being a spokesperson for a "people"

Having professors who don't seem to care

Not being represented in the curriculum or in speakers' and visiting writers series

When diversity issues are marginalized, a feeling of being "sectionalized" results

Having so few models for a "faculty of color"

Clearly, some comments can be identified as coming from a student or teacher. The first statements on the lists—feeling included: "when in the classroom teaching"; feeling excluded: "when in the classroom as a graduate student"—reported by two of us in the TLDC group at our initial meeting, underscore how differently we may perceive the same situation. Further, that first statement of exclusion, "in the classroom as a graduate student," when considered in light of the other items on the list, underscores how feelings of exclusion are experienced in relation to the heart of our academic enterprise: in scholarship, curriculum, and classroom interactions. These remarks also reaffirmed our initial decision to focus on 1) curriculum and pedagogy, 2) faculty and student representation, and 3) overall climate, as that relates to 1 and 2.

Curriculum

Curriculum was one of the pressing issues that faculty identified in relation to diversity. In these responses, diversity was seen as a curriculum that studies a range of texts and that considers the interaction between cultures and identities. Some called for a broader notion of diversity to include a wider global perspective, aesthetic diversity, and historical diversity and range. Reflecting the specter of political correctness, one cautioned against "supposing that identity politics is a fundamental structure of 'diversity'." Others' comments suggested curricular goals that went beyond identity politics: e.g.., "to promote dialog among different histories and different backgrounds," "problematize what it means to be 'American" and "international" at the same time, " consider "how does difference inform form? In what ways does it, can it, make itself felt, experienced?"

Another professor commented that any effort to "diversify" our curricula needs to be fully integrated into a course and not be an "add-on." This comment was echoed by a graduate student who argued that "diversity discussions should not be treated like a nicety or like a special favor, but rather as integral to academic thought, as enriching and central to academic discourse for everyone, not just persons of color."

To follow-up on this feedback, we sponsored a Department colloquium on "Designing Courses: How to Get Issues of Difference on the Table," with a panel of three faculty and one graduate student, chosen to represent a range of scholarly areas in the Department, from English Medieval literature to contemporary American Studies. (Supplemented with articles by Stanley, 2000-01, and Stanley & Ouellett, 1998.)

Pedagogy and Classroom Interactions

In a comment referring to classroom interactions as well as the overall climate, one faculty member identified as a pressing issue that many ALANA students felt "isolated and sometimes insulted" because of the insufficient numbers of faculty and students of color, and by curriculum and classroom interactions. We also heard from students about feeling isolated in the classroom. One undergraduate wrote: "When race or issues regarding people of color arise I feel somewhat excluded because I know that my experiences and responses may not be understood by the other students. It is also a matter of not creating a situation where I am defensive or defending an opposing view or opinion all by myself." Another student echoed this feeling of not being understand or heard: "I also feel excluded when I have had an experience, mention it in class (relating to the text), and no one can really relate." What we did not hear explicitly, perhaps because of the nature of the assessment approach, was explicit mention of the value of discussions where a range of perspectives are included.

The feedback from these sources became the focus for another departmental colloquium on "Teaching and Learning in the Diverse Classroom," convened by Matt Ouellett, a professor, and one graduate student from our group. They used specific anecdotes mentioned by faculty in their assessment to prompt discussion of how we might understand and address the underlying concerns the anecdotes expressed. Two of those anecdotes follow:

> In a class on modern literature, two students of color brought up the issue of how an African American character was being used by the author in socially abhorrent ways. The rest of the class quickly jumped in to "defend" the author in question (a woman), saying primarily that these socially loaded issues were not what the work "was about." The two students felt dismissed and silenced. Privately, they let me know how angered they were, both by the other students' responses, and my own inept handling of the issue.
>
> Just this week, an African-American English major told me that students of color are routinely advised—often by family as well as advisors in minority program offices—to choose majors in the professional schools, especially management and engineering, rather than in English and humanities, in general.

As you might guess, these anecdotes prompted discussion, which I will not try to represent here, about classroom interactions, literary interpretation, and perceptions of career options for English majors. In addition to these two departmental colloquia, we also sponsored a one-day workshop for approximately twenty faculty and graduate students on developing inclusive syllabi and teaching approaches for the general education literature diversity courses.

Faculty and Student Representation

The assessment reports from all three groups underscored that all perceive a need to increase diversity amongst the faculty and students and undergraduate students in particular. Many faculty identified the need for "greater numbers of professors of color and of women" as a pressing concern. A few, explicitly made the connection between having a greater proportion of faculty of color and attracting students of color, another pressing issue identified by faculty.

ALANA graduate students pointed to the difficulty of finding faculty mentoring or advising around ALANA issues and explicitly wanting to have more faculty of color available for advising and as models for their future. One spoke of needing more models "aside from the over-taxed, over-committed model of minority faculty." Others pointed to range of scholarly perspectives gained by having a faculty that is diverse in terms of race, culture and gender.

The comments from ALANA undergraduate students pointed to the problem of having few undergraduate English majors of color. One commented, "The most obvious feeling of exclusion comes from not seeing other minorities in the classroom. Since I have become an English major, I can estimate that there have been about 6 total minority students from all the classes I've taken." Another wrote, "I want to feel comfortable enough to speak out, but when it is only me in a class of 20 other white students, I get intimidated and sometimes uncomfortable." In this comment, the link between having a greater proportion of ALANA students and feeling comfortable to contribute to the intellectual life of a classroom is evident. In contrast, another student commented that "What I enjoyed the most [about my English classes] was open class discussions. What made me feel extremely included was the acceptance of my opinion from peers and facilitators." While these two students have different views of their classroom experience, both point to the importance of feeling that a teacher invites all views and that they are "accepted" equally.

Overall Climate

The assessment of the overall climate is evident in comments about curriculum and pedagogy and representation. It includes comments ALANA graduate students made about wanting more minority faculty role models, calls for advising support outside the classroom, comments about the value, either in its absence of presence, of people being friendly and welcoming, and calls for including a range of ethnicities in our annual Visiting Writers Series and invited lectures. Others pointed to the importance of welcoming comments in department documents, including handbooks for graduate and undergraduate students and on our website.

During the year of our project, we engaged in the kind of activities that students and faculty said they would like to see. They included the gatherings for ALANA graduate and undergraduate students and a roundtable discussion with recent graduates for undergraduate ALANA English majors. In addition, the graduate students, with participation from ones involved in our project, broadened their annual Graduate English conference to include the departments of African American Studies and Comparative Literature.

Final Report

At the end of our project year, we prepared a final report with recommendations which we issued to the faculty, asking the Directors of Undergraduate and Graduate Studies and the Chairs of those committees to consider the recommendations relative to their areas. Because of the rush of end of the year activities, we did not have time to call a meeting to report on these recommendations. In preparing the report, we chose to be inclusive in our list, leaving it to a next stage for decisions about priorities and feasibility. Here, I highlight a few key recommendations and note what progress, or lack thereof, we have made.

Curriculum and pedagogy. One key recommendation was to "continue to revisit undergraduate and graduate offerings, including the design of the undergraduate major." What we did not do was address what this might mean in practice. While we believe the majority of faculty, as well as students, value diversity in our scholarship, creative work, and curriculum, it is not clear how we aim to achieve this goal. While a multi-ethnic approach is integral to a couple required courses (e.g., American Identities), do we also try to build it more fully into the structure of the curriculum in some way? Do we address it through hiring and collegial persuasion, say, with periodic colloquia such as were held during the project year? These questions point to the need for a follow-up stage that focuses on implementation.

Faculty and student representation. We recommended "hiring more faculty of color (and women), in addition to faculty who teach in areas that can diversify the curriculum." Coupled with this was the recommendation that "in planning, the department should prioritize approaches that diversify the curriculum (e.g., multiethnic approaches) and design position descriptions accordingly." We have made some steps toward realizing this objective: As Chair, I have exercised my authority in constituting search committees that would accept recruitment of minority faculty as one priority and making certain that each search committee selects a diverse group of finalists from the available qualified applicants. In developing hiring priorities and position descriptions, we are also aiming to diversify the curriculum by envisioning new possibilities that build from our existing sense of ourselves. For instance, recognizing an present strength in post-colonial studies and transnational literature in English, we designed a position in 19th century British literature as "19th Century British Literature/Empire Studies." The description succeeded in attracting qualified candidates who were interested in transnational questions and who were racially diverse. We also designed a position in Composition and Rhetoric to focus on "American Ethnic Rhetorics/Literacies," a position should link as well with our American Studies program. To continue to move in this direction will require sustained commitment by the Department, and we are only just beginning.

We did not develop any specific initiatives for recruiting more ALANA undergraduates. As with efforts to revise curriculum and develop hiring priorities, following up on this recommendation requires a good deal of planning and time and resources for implementation. It is more challenging than working with our graduate students given the large number of undergraduate majors (approximately 850); and the fact that undergraduate students are not admitted directly through a departmental office.

Overall Climate. Our recommendations focused on making visible our values related to diversity in our curriculum, scholarly and creative work, and in our people. One recommendation that we implemented was to draft a statement of welcome to students that conveys the message to all students that we welcome them and that we value an array of scholarly and creative approaches. (See Appendix A.) It is now included in documents from both the graduate and undergraduate offices, including the undergraduate Guide to the English major. We are also making sure that our Visiting Writers Series and invited lectures include a racially diverse group.

We have incorporated our goal of making the Department more welcoming to undergraduate ALANA students with the more inclusive goal of making it welcoming to all students. To that end, the Undergraduate Studies Office has created a Student Advisory Board to consult with the Director and Chief Advisor on advising and other programs for majors. By design, we include ALANA students on the Board. On their own initiative, they have developed a volunteer mentoring program, linking upper class majors with new majors who indicate a desire to participate in the program. In its first year, approximately 75 students participated. They also sponsored an ice cream social and advised the Undergraduate Office on alumni and career forums offered for English majors. With the exception of a job search forum for ALANA graduate students, we chose not to convene specific meetings or open forums for graduate and undergraduate ALANA students, although we are open to doing so for specific purposes. This choice points to the question of considering the trade-off between what one respondent called "sectionalized" events and more inclusive ones.

What did we learn? What did we accomplish?

Dedicating a year for a group of us, faculty and students, to focus on values and issues of difference, diversity, and multiculturalism, was invaluable. It was also helpful to do this work under the auspices of the TLDC grant from our Center for Teaching. Having a defined project and a group, each of us felt committed to make the project a priority. The grant also provided some modest financial support for programming. It was also helpful to have someone from outside the Department with expertise in multicultural models of faculty and pedagogical development.

The activities of the year provided many, much needed, occasions for frank and searching discussions. We learned from each other about the exclusions some of us have experienced, and we learned from other colleagues and ALANA graduate and undergraduate students. The value of such occasions should not be underestimated.

As far as what we accomplished beyond the year's activities, the critical part of me says that perhaps all we accomplished was to have those discussions. Still, we do have some carry-over, and it is valuable to have a document such as our final report with recommendations. It gives all of us something to look back to and to consider what we still want to do. What I see now is the limitation of having no formal mechanism for carrying forward a second year. Specifically, we might have been better to think of a two stage model, ending our first year with an assessment report and then launching a second stage effort to develop action plans. That planning effort would have to involve not only our group but key department officers and committees (Personnel, Graduate, and Undergraduate) and ultimately a critical mass of the faculty. The recommendations we did pose provide a viable starting point for that planning.

The challenge remains to persuade sufficient ones of us that the status quo is insufficient—that as a predominantly Anglo/Euro-American and male faculty and Anglo/Euro-American student body, the overall climate for learning and intellectual and creative work is not sufficiently supportive for non Anglo/ Euro-American and non-male faculty and students; furthermore, the intellectual and creative work we all do is limited without the variety of perspectives and textual practices that diversity makes possible. But more than persuasion is needed. Our assessment showed us that many agree with this claim. We need to "walk the talk," to do the hard work of deciding on specific actions and carrying them out. In a time of huge budget pressures, declining faculty numbers, and in turn, increased pressure on all of us, doing so is not easy. Yet, if we believe that who we are as faculty, and students, and who we are in terms of our curricular, scholarly, and creative work is at stake, we need to persist.

References

Academic Affairs, Community, Diversity and Social Justice Assessment Report. (2004). Retrieved June 18, 2004, from University of Massachusetts, Amherst, Provost's Office Web site: http://www.umass.edu/provost

Center for Teaching. (2004). *Teaching and Learning in the Diverse Classroom Fellowship Program.* Retrieved June 18, 2004, from University of Massachusetts, Amherst, Web site: http://www.umass.edu/cft/teaching_development/tldc_grants.htm

Jackson, B., & Hardiman, R. (1994). Multicultural organizational development. In E.Y. Cross et al. (Eds.), *The promise of diversity* (pp. 231-239). New York: Irwin.

Stanley, C. (2000-01). Teaching in action: Multicultural education as the highest form of learning. *Teaching Excellence, 12*(2).

Stanley, C., & Ouellett. M. (1998). The diverse classroom. *NEA Higher Education Advocate, 1*(2), 5-8.

Anne Herrington is professor of English and Chair of the department of English at the University of Massachusetts Amherst.

Acknowledgments

I thank the other TLDC Fellows, who included Professors Margo Culley, Sunaina Maira, Joseph Skerrett, Jr., Jenny Spencer, Ron Welburn, and PhD candidates Karen Cardoza-Kane, Justine Diamond, Robert Hayashi, and Tracy Vaughn for their commitment to this project and their sensitivity, wisdom, and good spirits. I hope this manuscript does justice to their efforts. All of us of are appreciative of Matt Ouellett of the Center for Teaching for his expertise, good council, and support throughout our Fellowship year. Special thanks to Margo Culley, Tracy Vaughn, and Matt Ouellett for their helpful feedback on earlier drafts of this manuscript.

Appendix A

Statement of welcome.

Welcome to the English Department. As a group of faculty, staff, and students, we are a diverse group, representing a range of life experiences, cultures, and social identities. As a Department, we strive to meet the social justice goal stated in the University's 1990 Mission Statement: "to achieve a multicultural campus where men and women of diverse racial, social, and economic groups play major roles and, in a spirit of mutual respect, come to understand and appreciate the variety of perspectives that diversity makes possible." That variety of perspectives spurs intellectual and creative work and, more specifically, learning in our classrooms. A spirit of mutual respect is key to fostering such a community by enabling open give and take in discussion and supporting individual students as they seek to pursue a wide range of inquiries. This goal places a responsibility on each of us to recognize and respect one another's social identities, to invite perspectives other than our own, to listen well and honor one another's views, to strive not to ignore, distort, or dismiss those views.

As a Department, we are committed to treating everyone with respect. Should you feel that you are being discriminated against or treated disrespectfully, we invite you to speak with your advisor or the Director of Undergraduate or Graduate Studies. We affirm as a value the University's Affirmative Action and Non-Discrimination Policy Statement: "The University of Massachusetts Amherst prohibits discrimination on the basis of race, color, religion, creed, sex, age, marital status, national origin, mental or physical disability, veteran status, or sexual orientation."

Chapter 13

Teaching Diversity and Fostering Inclusivity at the University: A Collaborative Approach

Abby L. Ferber and Andrea O'Reilly Herrera

In many institutions, diversity related programs are forced to compete for limited resources, fostering antagonistic, competitive relationships. In contrast, we discuss the collaborative model we have pioneered between Ethnic Studies (EST) and Women's Studies (WMST) on our campus, and the tremendous benefits to the EST/WMST faculty, faculty across the campus, and the institution as a whole. We tie our experiences into the larger literature regarding successful models for creating inclusive Universities, and discuss our campus experience as one model that may be learned from and replicated.

The Educational Testing Service revealed that minority student enrollment will rise dramatically, reaching 37% of undergraduate enrollment by 2015 (Association of American Colleges and Universities, 2000). And yet, while our student bodies are becoming increasingly diverse, most colleges and universities have yet to create an inclusive and welcoming learning environment. In addition to being far from achieving a diverse faculty and administration, most campuses, moreover, are plagued by persistent discrimination and have not yet achieved a fully inclusive curriculum.

Nevertheless, a growing body of research documents that multiculturalism is overwhelmingly supported by most faculty *and* has positive effects. For example, a majority of faculty claim that they value racial and/or ethnic diversity on campus and support the creation of multiracial classes. In general, faculty and students in these classes believe that the new range of perspectives and experiences offered generates more critical and complex thinking skills among *all* students, and has a positive effect on their cognitive and personal growth. In the same vein, the completion of a diversity course requirement toward graduation significantly reduces prejudice; and it has been proven that a diverse student population has a direct and beneficial effect on white students' educational experience. Socializing across race and/or ethnic lines and engaging in constructive, open discussions about race helps erode prejudicial attitudes, which are often based on stereotypes that are perpetuated at home and through the media; produces widespread positive effects on *all* students' academic and personal development; and ultimately helps to eradicate discrimination (*Diversity Digest,* 2000).

Clearly, the complexion of our nation's colleges and universities has changed over the past 50 years. If one examines the national context, there are tremendous accomplishments we can applaud, such as the growing numbers of Ethnic Studies and Women's Studies programs and departments. There has also been an increased presence of research institutes that expand the focus of academic research on and off campus to include diversity issues. Many campuses have also begun to focus upon recruitment and/or hiring policies and processes aimed at attracting and retaining faculty and students of color; establishing mentoring networks, as well as faculty development programs; and institutionalizing faculty committees on the status of women and racial/ethnic minorities. There has also been an increase in diversity training workshops for students, faculty and staff, which have provided models of curriculum transformation as well as concrete strategies for improving campus climate. Finally, expanded national/regional networks promote diversity initiatives and serve as resources to other institutions, thus improving methods of gathering data to assess diversity efforts on campus and identify needs (Lesage, Ferber, Storrs, & Wong, 2002).

Nevertheless, serious obstacles and barriers to developing diversity programming and integrating diversity into the curriculum persist. For example, many institutions across the country are currently facing dramatic budget cuts. As a result, diversity related programs are oftentimes collapsed or merged — thereby threatening their disciplinary integrity as well as their impact on campus — or these programs are forced to compete for limited resources, thus fostering antagonistic, competitive relationships. In the same vein, higher education administrators and state boards of education fail to be accountable for long-range planning, implementation, and assessment of diversity planning. In such climates, diversity plans and mission statements can quickly become reduced to largely empty rhetoric that erodes clarity and levels the significant differences that distinguish individuals and groups. Also, diversity initiatives can be become marginalized as issues that concern (and benefit) only women and minorities. At the institutional level, this collapsing of diversity initiatives can lead to such efforts being ghettoized in Women's Studies and Ethnic Studies programs or in offices of multicultural affairs. At many colleges and universities, the curriculum is based upon largely traditional standards that focus on, and forefront, the perspective(s) of privileged groups. For example, senior administrators and faculty tend to be overwhelmingly White and male (especially at the higher ranks), and their perspectives are the ones most often reflected in the curriculum. Typically, in such university settings the greatest deterrent to change is often not outright hostility to diversity, but instead acquiescence to the long established "paths of least resistance."

As Allan G. Johnson observes, systems of privilege and oppression operate through these "paths of least resistance," which are reinforced by the dominant culture we are all a part of. "Because systems are identified with privileged groups, the path of least resistance is to focus on them—who they are, what they do and say, and how they do it" (2001, 107). To create real change, we must establish new paths of least resistance. Not only is a comprehensive approach imperative to achieving and maintaining diversity, a strategic initiative that has concrete goals, which are subject to assessment as part of the evaluation and renewal process, must be defined and reinforced at every level of the hierarchy (from the vice president or provost's office to the deans, chairs, and individual faculty). Moreover, the highest level of advocacy for these goals must be prioritized and advocated at the highest levels of the administration and must include a widely diffused mission statement for creating an inclusive and equitable institution that upholds its democratic ideals. In other words, diversity must be integrated into higher education at all levels, both horizontally and vertically.

In our case, as directors of our respective programs and as former Co-Assistant Vice Chancellors of Academic Diversity and Development, we have discovered that leadership from the president and/or chancellor's office is fundamental. Such leadership is demonstrated by including and responding to faculty and staff who represent diversity issues on cabinets at the upper-administrative level. We have also seen the benefits of the formation of a cross-campus task force that has worked together with senior administrators to prioritize funding and to lay out an appropriate reward system for faculty. In particular, this task force has worked to recognize the efforts of those faculty members that increase the diversification of the curriculum through their research and/or instructional methods, participate in diversity initiatives inside and outside of the classroom, and increase student-faculty interaction by mentoring students of color.

In addition to the obstacles and barriers mentioned above, ongoing anti-diversity sentiment also characterizes many campuses. This sentiment often springs from a small, persistent, and vocal minority, which may even regard itself as progressive and anti-discriminatory. Often this minority promotes a seemingly egalitarian, "color-blind" position based upon the assertion that race and ethnicity do not, or should not, matter. Following the same logic, they argue that diversity initiatives actually cause resentment, stigmatize minorities and/or people of color, and promote balkanization. Some take up a "reverse-racism" argument, which asserts that diversity initiatives are racist, anti-American (anti-assimilationist), and fly in the face of the American ideal of meritocracy.

Positions such as those described above are not only founded on privilege, but they suggest also the tenacity of racial stereotyping, which remains so common in our country. Interviews conducted with students of color reveal that they are frequently accused by their instructors and peers of being underprepared and thus unqualified for admission and scholarships (Lesage, Ferber, Storrs, & Wong, 2002). Likewise, minority faculty often report that they are regarded as tokens or as intellectually inferior by their colleagues. When students or minority faculty do not succeed, we must understand this within the larger context of racism and inequality. Students, faculty and staff of color face the additional threat of hate groups and hate speech on campuses and on Internet sites; email is frequently used to deliver anonymous racially based or homophobic insults as well as rape threats. In general, people of color are grossly underrepresented in faculty and administrative leadership positions. When they are recruited, retention rates for faculty of color remain poor nation-wide—a fact that is due in part to the lack of critical mass of faculty and administrators of color, as well as to what many perceive to be generally unsupportive or even hostile social and academic environments.

Although we have much to learn, what follows is a discussion of our own positive experiences in collaboratively developing and implementing minors and diversity programming at the University of Colorado at Colorado Springs, where we currently serve as the directors of Ethnic Studies and Women's Studies. We will also briefly discuss the programs we developed in our former roles as Co-Assistant Vice Chancellors for Academic Diversity and Development. This collaboration has not only increased our visibility on campus and contributed to the growth of our academic programs, but it has also encouraged diversity programming and curriculum across campus and consequently inspired college- and institution-wide change.

A Collaborative Climate

The collaborative relationship we have established between the Ethnic Studies and Women's Studies programs at UCCS has been recognized as ground-breaking and unique. We have found that collaborating makes good sense for a variety of reasons. First, there is a tremendous overlap among most of the faculty involved in the two programs. Recent waves of faculty are coming out of graduate school with some measure of training in both race and gender studies. Because women of color have forcefully criticized traditional women's studies literature, which narrowly focused on the experiences of white women, as well as the narrow models of Ethnic Studies limited to the experiences of men of color, gender has been more fully integrated into ethnic studies courses, and race and/or ethnicity into gender courses and research. Indeed the leading theories in the fields today emphasize that race, gender, class and sexuality are interlocking, interacting systems, which shape everyone's lives (Hill Collins, 1990; Johnson, 2001; Kimmel & Ferber, 2003). Each one of us possesses a race and a gender identity, and they work together in shaping our life opportunities. Looking at our own lives, for example, Abby's experiences as a white woman have been very different than Andrea's experiences as a Latina, and our experiences of what is means to be a woman are shaped by our racial and/or ethnic backgrounds. Race and/or ethnicity are central to understanding gender, and gender to understanding race. It is, therefore, essential that we examine the ways these categories interact at both the experiential and theoretical levels.

As faculty members, each of us integrates both race and gender into our research as well as our teaching, and we are dedicated to advancing the study of both topics on our campus. Additionally, because we are a relatively small campus, we need to draw upon the expertise and resources of our entire faculty conducting work in these areas. Due to this tremendous overlap in the faculty involved in each of these programs, it makes sense for us to minimize the time commitment of our colleagues by holding joint meetings, organizing and sponsoring joint events, and working together to build both programs simultaneously. Furthermore, these collaborative efforts — coupled with a series of social events, which we jointly host and sponsor (such as a bi-annual pot luck dinner) — provide an increased base of support, networking, and nurturing for faculty and students, and thereby contribute positively to recruitment and retention efforts.

Pooling our resources and efforts during tough economic times has also enabled us to capitalize on our resources and thus strengthen and enlarge our programs. For example, we initiated an Ethnic Studies and Women's Studies newsletter, which features a campus-wide calendar of diversity-related events and is published and featured on our web pages each semester. We also offer a number of cross-listed courses, including an internship course, a course on women of color, and a new, innovative, joint Introduction to Ethnic Studies and Women's Studies course, which meet the needs of so many students interested in the intersections of race and gender. As mentioned previously, we also jointly organize and sponsor a film series as well as a visiting speaker series, both of which focus on race and gender issues. We also host or sponsor a number of additional extracurricular events on campus, such as a K-12 outreach program, which includes a creative writing partnership with a local elementary school that is composed of low income minority families; and we are currently working together to develop a diversity outreach training program for local schools and businesses.

Emphasizing the celebratory aspects of diversity, our programs also co-sponsor the annual Rosa Parks Scholarship Competition and Awards Ceremony and Mother's Day Card Fundraiser, an event that provides four one-time scholarships to students selected from those submitting research or creative works that address the ideals of social justice and equality exemplified by Parks. The ceremony has expanded to include a community non-profit organization fair, and we sponsor joint fundraising activities for the scholarships. Additionally, a group of students in the Ethnic Studies Program has established an annual conference and scholarship competition which will feature undergraduate research on diversity issues (The Cesar E. Chavez Student Conference and Scholarship Competition).

The success of our collaboration as directors of Women's Studies and Ethnic Studies can be attributed to several factors. Capitalizing on the assumption that most faculty regard diversity as a desirable and positive goal in and of itself, we go to great lengths to be simultaneously inclusive and supportive of our colleagues. Simply put, we welcome and attempt to assist all faculty and staff who wish to join us in our efforts to increase diversity on our campus with the firm belief that the process of change, as Valverde and Castenell, Jr. argue in *The Multicultural Campus: Strategies for Transforming Higher Education*, must involve many participants from all areas of the campus (2000). By promoting what one might refer to as "large-scale buy-in," we have prevented the marginalization of diversity efforts on our campus. Such collaborative efforts of course raise unique pitfalls. We have had to tackle a number of difficult issues, including making clear which programs and departments receive the student credit hours for cross-listed courses; dividing FTE among programs and departments; and securing faculty to teach courses for the programs. We have found that with time, effort, and much discussion, we can usually find win-win solutions to most obstacles we have faced. Finally, it has been imperative to us to maintain the integrity of each program and the separate minors in Ethnic Studies and Women's Studies in the midst of this climate of collaboration.

In our view, creating a multicultural, inclusive environment demands that universities overcome the kind of compartmentalized thinking and planning that occurs on most campuses. Positioning ourselves as cooperative players in our academic community, we are mindful also of the oftentimes competing needs of other departments and programs both inside and outside of our college. As a result, we make our best effort to work collaboratively with our colleagues and to assist them whenever possible by offering cross-listed courses, which form the cores of their majors and minors, and by co-sponsoring speakers or diversity programming. We have also developed a one credit course that is offered as a pre-professional course for students majoring in course intensive programs such as Education, Psychology, and Business. In addition, we regularly showcase various courses and instructors by inviting our colleagues to participate in our WMST/EST Film Series (oftentimes we feature films that they have already integrated into their courses). Equally important is the positive emphasis we place on integrating diversity into the curriculum and campus programming. Rather than dwelling on the lack of diversity on our campus, we keep faculty abreast of grant opportunities and conferences that focus on diversity, and we seek out ways to reward, recognize, and celebrate the successes of faculty who actively contribute to our programs and events by distributing small research and travel grants (in collaboration with the Office of Academic Diversity and Development, the Women's Faculty Committee, and the Faculty Minority Affairs Committee, the latter two of which are permanent branches of our faculty governance structure).

Faculty Development

Perhaps the single most important event that we host is an annual Curriculum Transformation Workshop. As directors of EST and WMST, we strive to provide faculty who teach in our programs the proper tools to transform the curriculum, as well as the professional and personal support which is critical to their success. A growing body of research demonstrates that women and faculty of color, as well as anyone teaching such sensitive subject matter, regularly receive lower student evaluations, face more student resistance, and deal more often with emotionally charged classroom situations (Ferber & Storrs, 1995). As a result, faculty need to learn methods for dealing with students who have powerful responses to our courses, such as hostility, anger, sorrow, depression, and/or guilt. According to Bohmer and Briggs, "students from privileged ... backgrounds are frequently hostile, or at best neutral, to presentations on race, class, and gender stratification; often they respond with guilt, anger, or resistance" (Ferber & Storrs, 1995, p. 33). While such responses may be open, we also want teachers to be sensitive and responsive to students who are internalizing such feelings, as well. Faculty must manage these complex emotions in the classroom, enfranchising all students to explore these feelings in order to move towards a more critical understanding of their own views and assumptions. On the other end of the spectrum, the sensitive subject matter that WMST and EST faculty treat in their classrooms also raises new issues for students of color and female students, who often have first-hand experience with the histories and perspectives of oppressed groups. This experience often creates additional emotional work for these students and serves to increase their sense of vulnerability in the classroom (Ferber & Storrs, 1995).

The goal of our Curriculum Transformation Workshop is three-fold: to assist faculty with revising and/or generating their course subject matter; to encourage faculty to focus on pedagogy and methodology; and to explore and develop concrete strategies for dealing with the diversity of experience, background, emotion, and preparation students bring to the classroom. Each spring, we invite applications for a summer workshop, and we usually accept approximately twelve faculty members from across the campus. We make a special effort to encourage faculty applications from disciplines that do not traditionally participate in our programs. We recognize the need to reward the efforts of our faculty, and participants receive a summer stipend of $1000 and a packet of reading materials. They then spend the summer revising and retooling an existing course or developing a new course that focuses on both race and gender, and they attend a facilitated workshopretreat at the end of the summer.

In the workshop, we focus on some of the specific tools and strategies we have found useful for creating a classroom climate that engages all students while also preempting insensitivity and hostility. For example, we focus on the development and use of ground-rules; the importance of journaling; the stages of racial identity development; and the significance of presenting a theoretical framework, rather than focusing on specific information. Our curriculum workshops present what we call an "Integrative Oppression/Privilege Framework," which also models the kind of inclusive approach we implement throughout our program structure. The perspective integrates gender, race, class, and sexuality, and other potential axes of inequality, including age, ability, religious orientation, and so forth. It is our firm belief that although these categories are distinct, they can be separated neither in terms of how they impact our lives, nor in terms of how they operate in society. This perspective also integrates a special focus on privilege and oppression. While "the concept of oppression points to social forces that tend to 'press' upon people and hold them down, to hem them in and block their pursuit of a good life," Johnson observes, "privilege exists when one group has something of value that is denied to others simply because of the groups they belong to" (2001, 13, 23). Privilege and oppression operate hand in hand; one cannot exist without the other.

Traditionally, inequality has been explored and taught from the viewpoints of those who are the victims of oppression. Studies of racism, sexism, classism, discrimination based on sexual orientation, and other forms of discrimination have focused mainly on oppression. More recently, however, critical whiteness studies and research on masculinities have begun to tell the other half of the story. Oppression and privilege exist in relation to each other; thus, if some group is oppressed, another group is privileged (McIntosh, 2001; Johnson, Kimmel, & Ferber 2003). Hill Collins (1990) emphasizes that the varying axes of privilege and oppression are interrelated, and form a "matrix of domination." Most of us have experienced varying degrees of privilege and oppression, and we all fit somewhere in this matrix (1990). Privilege and oppression affects each of our life chances, the impressions we make on others, and our own sense of identity. Ultimately, our approach is pro-active and inclusive. We start with the assumption that we all participate (consciously or unconsciously) in a racist, sexist, homophobic society, and have internalized some of these attitudes and beliefs. We emphasize that the first step toward change is recognizing one's position in this complex matrix; the second step is assuming responsibility for making change happen. Although we tend to focus on the manner in which discrimination in all of its various forms occurs at the institutional or cultural levels, as opposed to the individual, we de-emphasize the notion of blame, and, rather, take as our point of departure the idea that each individual is capable of realizing collective change. We encourage our Anglo and male colleagues and students to join us in this struggle by showcasing speakers (such as Becky Thompson and Michael Kimmel) and works that focus on white anti-racist, and male pro-feminist activism, in addition to the activism of those who are oppressed. From our standpoint, this approach not only diminishes resistance, defensiveness and polarization in the classroom and across campus, but it also tends to enfranchise our students and colleagues.

As a related event, we also offer at least one workshop per semester (in collaboration with our Teaching and Learning Center) in order to provide continuity and a source of on-going support. These workshops are open to all faculty, staff and graduate students, as well as to previous participants. At times we bring in guest speakers to conduct the workshops; other times we organize panel discussions about topics that range from resistance in the classroom to teaching difficult subject matter. Oftentimes we invite our own faculty members to serve as the panelists in order to minimize our costs; other times we post a reading on the web and organize an open discussion.

All faculty teaching in our programs need support networks for dealing with these issues. Although many seek us out individually, we are in the process of creating a list-serve for faculty who wish to discuss their experiences and/or provide support and mentoring for each other. We have also established a diversity teaching resource library, and we try to make available to faculty current articles and readings that address a wide range of diversity issues. On-going support is crucial, and most universities already have colleagues who possess the necessary expertise to mentor or conduct workshops. If faculty concerned with these issues can be brought together to support each other, and they are made to feel valued and supported on an on-going basis, not only will foster greater transformation of the curriculum be fostered, but recruitment and retention of diverse faculty and students will increase.

In our former capacities as Co-Assistant Vice Chancellors of Academic Diversity and Development, we constituted a campus-wide Diversity Coordinating Committee, which consists of all faculty, students, and staff who are currently involved in diversity initiatives or programming. This committee meets at the outset of each semester to share information in an effort to pool resources, exchange ideas, and disperse information. In turn, committee members are asked to supply our staff assistant with information regarding these events or programs, and the events and programs are listed in the calendar of events, which appears in our newsletter and on our web pages. In this way, we not only assist our colleagues in advertising or dispersing information regarding their events, but we avoid overlap and competition.

In addition, we worked with two Faculty Associates (both of whom were offered either a $2,000 stipend or a course off-load) in planning a faculty development program. After researching the experiences of colleagues at peer institutions, we rejected a one-on-one mentor model and adopted a more informal and inclusive approach. In addition to being present at our new faculty orientation, we have decided to offer a variety of workshops on an on-going basis that foster informal mentoring networks by featuring faculty from across campus. We also planned a Faculty Development Day that will be offered at the outset of each new academic year. This full-day, off-campus retreat will consist of a comprehensive program of faculty development workshops, keynote speakers, and information and resource booths designed to encourage networking, provide information, and support a full range of development opportunities for all faculty. Workshops and panel discussions will cover a range of topics, including research support, teaching about difficult subject matter, developing mentoring networks, a mock tenure review, etc. In addition, we are planning several panels that focus exclusively on women and/or faculty of color.

As one may gather, even small campuses with sparse resources can foster diversity and inclusivity. As Beverly Daniel Tatum points out, however, one of the greatest dilemmas we face is that "there is no vehicle to cross boundaries" on most campuses. As we foster climates of engagement, we also have to create paths "to cross the long-standing boundaries that separate us in American society" (2000, 29). To create change, we reject the long-established paths of least resistance. This can only occur if our efforts are comprehensive and campus-wide and are reinforced in the classroom, department meetings, student government meetings, committee meetings, review processes, hiring discussions, and cultural events. Our successes at the University of Colorado at Colorado Springs suggest that with persistence, patience, and a spirit of collaboration, an institution can create new paths of least resistance within the academic community.

References

Bohmer, S., & Briggs, J. (1991). Teaching privileged students about gender, race and class oppression. *Teaching Sociology, 19*(2), 154-63.

Ferber, A.L., & Storrs, D. (1995). Race and representation: Students of color in the multicultural classroom. In B. Goebel & J. Hall (Eds.), *Teaching a "new canon"? Students, teachers and texts in the college literature classroom* (pp.32-47). Urbana, IL: National Council of Teachers of English.

Hill Collins, P. (1990). *Black feminist thought: Knowledge, consciousness, and the politics of empowerment.* New York: Routledge.

Johnson, A. G. (2001). *Privilege, power and difference*. Boston: McGraw Hill.

Kimmel, M.S., & Ferber, A.L. (2003). *Privilege: A reader*. Boulder, CO: Westview.

Lesage, J., Ferber, A. L., Storrs, D., & Wong, D. (2002). *Making a difference: University students of color speak out*. Lanham, MD: Rowman and Littlefield.

McIntosh, P. (1988). *White privilege and male privilege* (Working Paper No. 189). Wellesley, MA: Wellesley College Center for Research on Women.

Tatum, B. D. (2000, Fall). The ABC approach to creating climates of engagement on diverse campuses. *Liberal Education, 86*(4), 22-29.

Valverde, L.A. & Castenell, L. (Eds.). (2000). *The multicultural campus: Strategies for transforming higher education.* Walnut Creek, CA: Alta Mira Press.

Abby L. Ferber serves as Director of Women's Studies and an Associate Professor of Sociology. **Andrea O'Reilly Herrera** is Director of Ethnic Studies and a Professor of English.

Chapter 14

Speaking a New Language: An Innovative Program Promotes Discussions in Diversity With Foreign Language Learners

Lisa Calvin

This chapter traces the path of instituting a general education language requirement. It follows the process from presentations made to governing bodies of the university to the development and implementation of a language program that fosters discussions in diversity.

As students carried their lunch trays past a smorgasbord of academic offerings, foreign language had always been merely one of several liberal arts options available at Indiana State University (ISU). In 2000, several years of dialogue and planning at the departmental and individual levels culminated in the university's institution of a general education foreign language requirement and the implementation of a beginning language program designed to move beyond the proverbial *veni, vidi, vinci* of paradigm recitation to communicative language and cultural awareness.

Creating University Support: A Case for Inclusion of a New Requirement

Just a decade ago Midwestern students who were forced to take foreign language (FL) courses could be heard grumbling, "When am I ever going to use Spanish (or any other culprit language)?" The achievements of technology and a generation drawn to the Internet for information, entertainment, and communication now bring those who use another language a computer screen away. Even more directly, shifting demographics mean that contact with a second language may happen with the person across the aisle from you at Wal-Mart. Indiana, with the growth of its Hispanic communities as documented in the 1990 census, reflects a burgeoning population of second language speakers throughout the United States. For Indiana as a whole, the Hispanic population grew by 117.2%, while seven counties alone accounted for 68% of the increase (Parra, 2001). An hour's drive from ISU's campus, Marion county and the state capital saw the Hispanic population quadruple. This is an example of growth in just one language, Spanish; however, within university language departments and language professional organizations, the trend has been to revise the nomenclature "Foreign Language" because one no longer need travel to a foreign country to speak another language, nor are the non-English speakers on our own shores necessarily "foreigners." Clearly, for the faculty at ISU the response to the question regarding when the target language is needed is, "Tomorrow, if not today."

Yet despite a world made smaller by technology and the lived experience of locally changing demographics, an administrative decision was made to remove foreign language as a liberal arts elective. The language department learned of the change when plans for the new General Education Program were unveiled: foreign language had unceremoniously disappeared. This, in turn, activated ISU's language faculty to pursue an initiative. Ultimately, this initiative led to instruction that now develops cross-cultural awareness and guides students in thinking more critically about their own cultural identity, values and assumptions, while developing the oral skills necessary to effectively communicate with native speakers this new language. After completing the two course, beginning language sequence, students have indicated a greater willingness to interact with native speakers, both on and off of campus. Many report feeling less uneasy when overhearing non-English conversations in public places. Anecdotal evidence suggests that more are watching cross-cultural programming and sharing enthusiasm for their new language and its culture with family members. These are first steps, but steps made possible because of the efforts of the language department.

According to Ronald Dunbar (personal communication, June 5, 2003), chair of the Department of Languages, Literatures and Linguistics (LLL), heretofore, no unit on campus, either by school, college, or department required foreign language study for a Bachelor of Science degree and only two percent of the student population graduated with a Bachelor of Arts degree, the degree requiring four semesters of foreign language study. Dunbar recalls that the department's first step in a push for a new requirement was to survey the admissions and graduation requirements for language at peer institutions in the state and the Midwest. They found that the lack of a language requirement was typical for state and regional peer institutions which began as normal schools, but most state and regional institutions had an entrance or exit requirement, and certainly most Colleges of Arts and Sciences had a language requirement.

The next step in the process was to identify campus advocates who would support the institution of a language requirement and to hear the voices of opponents. Allies found in expected disciplines such as Humanities and Philosophy, and most international faculty, conveyed the attitude that implementation of a language requirement was "the right thing to do," and were willing to lend support at the different governing bodies. Meeting with opponents on an individual basis, finding common ground, and allowing opponents to express concerns helped to shape the requirement's development.

Four primary concerns of faculty and administration emerged:

1) time constraints, within an unwieldy general education program that did not allow for juggling yet another set of courses, particularly in programs such as Nursing, which already carried a heavy credit hour burden;
2) fear of a reduction in enrollment among a student population of predominanty first-generation college students who may not have included language study as a part of secondary education;
3) articulation problems for transfer students and those earning degrees through technology delivered degree programs; and
4) faculty who had negative learning experiences in language or had never found a pragmatic use for hours of parsing sentences.

The compromises made to assuage these concerns modeled the cooperative spirit and bridge-building that can, and perhaps must, take place if major revisions to general education requirements are to be attempted. First, the foreign language faculty swallowed hard and conceded that the first change in a radically different beginning language sequence would be the reduction of course contact hours. The 101 and 102 courses had always been four credit hour classes meeting four days a week with an additional day for a non-credit, instructor-led laboratory section. The newly configured course would meet three times per week and be worth three credits, with an open lab or on-line virtual lab that could be conveniently accessed at all hours from computers in the dorms. These concessions meant a maximum six hour addition to general education requirements (less with some high school experience) and allowed greater flexibility in student scheduling than the 10 hour per week model. In time, courses would be offered in on-line and via televised educational formats for distance education students.

Addressing concerns about a reduced enrollment, the LLL department re-examined peer institutions that had recently instituted language requirements. Dunbar informed colleagues that at one institution, enrollment actually increased in the years subsequent to the new requirement. While this came as a surprise and allayed some concerns, a second compromise was made regarding the students who would need to enroll in the new beginning level courses. Students with a C average in two years of a single high school level foreign language would have fulfilled the requirement; all others would need to take 101 and/or 102 as placement indicators deemed appropriate. For many colleges and universities, two years of high school foreign language is an entrance requirement for admission; at ISU its equivalent would be an exit requirement for graduation. In a third compromise, students transferring from another institution with an associate's degree would be exempt from the requirement.

The first three major concerns had been pragmatic in nature. Addressing the negative feelings of professors and administrators was an affective strategy and was approached by the LLL department with logic and a promise. The extant general education core curriculum at the time of discussions required 13 hours of cultural study, five of them under the category of multicultural studies (Indiana State University Bulletin, 1998). Yet it was entirely possible to graduate from the university — indeed, from 17 years in the educational system — with a presumed knowledge of cultural diversity but an inability to greet or say good-bye to any cultural group other than one's own. Departmental spokespersons argued that cultural studies and language were inextricably linked. By its very nature language study adds a dimension to cultural study unavailable in most other disciplines because of the unique way the student must "walk in the shoes" of the speakers of the culture. Byram (1991) expresses the argument well:

> Thus under the term 'Cultural Studies' we refer to any information, knowledge or attitude about the foreign culture which is evident during foreign language teaching.... It is an important feature of the viewpoint taken here that Cultural Studies should not be considered merely as incidental to the 'real business' of language teaching. To discuss its significance as part of the general education curriculum from this basis is therefore to venture a step beyond the dominant philosophy in much foreign language teaching...to establish that Cultural Studies has a rightful place as part of language teaching, not just as an adjunct to language learning, not just as a means of creating better communication but as an integral component with appropriate aims and methods. (pp. 3-4)

In adopting the message of Cultural Studies, the department was choosing to make culture not just "adjunct to language learning," but an "integral component" to language study. The changes that the pedagogical shift would require are discussed in the section "Designing the Program."

The willingness of the foreign language faculty to compromise and the presence of allies in every governing body on campus still did not make the passage of a requirement an easy battle. To reach final acceptance, the proposal was approved by five committees or governing bodies: the LLL Academic Development Committee, Academic Affairs of the College of Arts and Sciences, the General Education Committee, the University Curricular Affairs Committee, and finally the Faculty Senate. Once the language requirement had won approval at all levels, the requirement as stated in the Undergraduate Catalog (2000) read, "Foreign Languages 101 and 102 in a single language, six hours, is required of all students, unless they have completed the equivalent of two years (four semesters) of a single language at the high school level with an average grade of C or better."

It would seem that an influx of students who had not met the requirement would necessitate an increased budget to secure more faculty. While it is true that some language sections needed to be added, these additions have led to a positive change because they enabled the department to hire several full-time, committed adjuncts who are active in curricular planning and extra-curricular events, whereas previously most adjuncts had taught only part-time. Graduate student teaching assistants who had previously taught five hours per week would now teach two sections totaling six hours. For the most part, Chair Dunbar found that attentive management of class scheduling and more compromise has required little additional funding. The department had always limited the number of students per section to 24, but agreed to bring the maximum to 30; this may be the compromise that faculty would most like to revisit, but it remains in effect. Finally, now that liberal studies credit is not offered for the 100 level language courses, fewer false beginners who have an extensive high school background in the language are looking to this route for an easy grade; not only does this leave seats for those who truly need the class, it levels the playing field and reduces the anxiety of true beginners who are otherwise intimidated by their peers. ISU has been the fortunate recipient of generous funding from the Lilly Endowment, which has provided financial resources for training workshops for faculty and teaching assistants during the introductory years of the new requirements.

Designing the Program: The Department Level

At the proposal phase of the process, senior faculty in the department had taken the lead. Now at the curriculum revision phase, a Working Committee was formed whose members represented tenured faculty, tenure-track faculty, and full-time and part-time adjuncts; to maintain a kind of "balance of power" on the committee all seven languages in the department had at least one representative, although no one who wanted to be a part of the committee was excluded.[1] The committee was chaired by a tenured faculty member, but in a democratic spirit all members were given an equal voice and encouraged to use it. At decision-making junctures, non-Romance language faculty were specifically asked for input.

The compromises of the LLL faculty had made the language requirement palatable to the rest of the university, but how would they conceptualize, implement, and assess the new program? The Working Committee's first charge was to develop program standards, or objectives, and a Statement of Teaching Philosophy. The department had promised resistant faculty that Cultural Studies would be an integral part of the language study, and that students would leave with communicative skills. Many Working Committee members themselves remembered having learned through the Grammar Translation Method and its reading and grammar orientation, the primary purpose of which "was to enable students to access and appreciate great literature, while helping them understand their native language better through extensive analysis of the grammar of the target language and translation" (Omaggio, 2001, p. 106). Modern proficiency-oriented pedagogies pursue different goals and instead promote development of the four skills – listening, speaking, reading, and writing, plus an understanding of culture. Based on the earlier commitment, the committee determined to promote oral proficiency skills in particular. Sources of information considered by the committee for insights in developing the standards included: (a) the American Council on the Teaching of Foreign Languages (ACTFL) National Standards (1996), with its emphasis on the areas of communication, cultures, comparisons, connections, and communities (b) a draft of Indiana's K-12 Standards (1999)[2] and (c) the Common Goals of the university's General Education 2000 program (2000), which were communication, critical thinking, life long learning, and issues of value and belief.

After engaging in an open dialogue, the Working Committee adopted four key standards and explained each in greater detail with subpoints. The standards were: Communication, Holistic Application, Cultural Awareness and Diversity Sensitivity. The Communication Standard stated, "Students demonstrate understanding and/or expression of meaning through listening, speaking, reading and writing using appropriate grammar and vocabulary (with more emphasis on reading and writing in Latin)."[3] The Holistic Application Standard combines the fostering of lifelong learning and the interdisciplinary connections of language and cultural study. In the other two standards, and the assessment tools for them, the ISU program sets itself apart and establishes Cultural Studies as an integral component of a beginning level sequence. The Cultural Awareness Standard states:

> Students critically examine issues of cultural differences, societal values and relationships, and critically evaluate their own culture and value systems through comparison and contrast to the target language and culture(s).

2.1 Students demonstrate awareness of uniqueness of target culture(s) in its practices, perspectives and products.

2.2 Students reflect on and compare own culture with target culture with evidence of developing critical thinking skills.

The Diversity Sensitivity Standard states:

Students develop openness, sensitivity and tolerance toward other languages and culture(s).

3.1 Students consider personal and societal prejudice beginning with the target language and culture(s) with evidence of developing critical thinking.

2.2 Students show evidence of applying sensitivity to cultural and language diversity beyond the classroom in the campus and civic community.

An understanding of the standards set by one group of people are kept relevant for subsequent groups of instructors when paired with a statement of course pedagogy and ongoing faculty development. The course pedagogy guidelines state that courses should be proficiency-oriented and student-centered, and should make optimal use of available technologies (Internet, video, CD-ROM, audio media such as CDs) both during class time and as out-of-class assignments. A notebook with sections for each language was compiled to serve as a reference for the current Working Group and those to come later. The notebook contains sample syllabi, sample daily lesson plans, cultural critical thinking activities, textbook adoption guidelines, explanations of assessment tools and rubrics for the assessment tools. As part of the notebook's development, the group decided to approach the syllabi that they were currently using from the perspective of the incoming student population of this new course; these would be students that had avoided language for some reason or had been unsuccessful in previous language study. Therefore, the instructors endeavored to use non-threatening language and offered suggestions for success, including realistic expectations for the amount of time needed to study. The daily lesson plans included in the notebook demonstrated that the instructor was not the "show" for the day, but that students would practice speaking the language and applying grammar every day by working in partnered or group activities.

One of the hallmarks of the new program was the uniformity of assessment measurements across the languages and a common percentage allocation for assessment. In 101, regardless of the language that is being taught, every student (a) writes a two page researched topic paper about an assigned cultural topic, (b) gives a 15 to 30 sentence oral presentation introducing himself/herself in the target language and telling about family, interests, classes and background, and (c) writes reflections in the Learning Journal. In 102, each student (a) gives a 10 minute researched, formal speech (in the target language) with a partner, (b) works with a partner to prepare and give a spontaneous role-play-like "oral interview" before the instructor, and (c) writes reflections in the Learning Journal.[4] Final exams at both levels include a cultural awareness section based on factual information unique to that target language culture (10 to15% of the exam), a holistic application essay question (5%), and a critical thinking essay question (5%) about increased cultural awareness and sensitivity.[5] Sample grading rubrics for the presentations, oral interviews, the learning journals, and final exam essay section are included in the reference notebook.

The mainstay of the new program may be the Learning Journal. This innovative tool finds its precursor in dialogue journals used in English as Second Language (ESL) classrooms. At ISU the Learning Journal is a document of reflectivity about the process of language and cultural learning. Students use critical thinking to answer questions that address factual, metacognitive, and affective issues of perception, planning, and personal and strategic development. Because of the complex nature of these reflections, students do not yet have the lexical or syntactic sophistication to express themselves in the target language and in English. Journal questions are assigned at pre-determined times during the semester and each set of questions includes linguistic and cultural facets ; the questions in 101 and 102 differ, but all 101 level languages answer the same set of questions. A sample of the cultural diversity aspect of the questions (see the insert) shows a deliberate chronological sequencing that moves from prejudice and perception to fact and interdisciplinary connections, to projections of changed behavior and attitudes. During the first week of class, students receive an explanation sheet and a grading rubric for the journals. (See the appendix for a sample of the rubric.) After each journal assignment the instructor gives individualized written feedback that prompts, questions, and attempts to push students to the next level of critical thinking. This interchange alone should make doing the assignment a worthwhile academic exercise for the students, but further validation of the assignment's value comes when students see that the reflectivity is thought preparation for class discussion. Instructors may discuss journal entries only as related to the assigned questions, or integrate the preparation into an in-depth study of the target language culture. In support of the goals of General Education, it is the desire of the LLL department that students increase their ability to learn to speak a language of cultural understanding as well as communicate in the target language.

Training the Instructors: Impact at the Individual Level

During the year-long discussion of curriculum revision, the Working Committee piloted different assessment tools, but when the program was officially implemented, a strong support system for faculty developed. Prior to the start of the semester and new school year, three tenured/tenure track faculty led a two day training and orientation workshop for all who would be teaching the LLL 101, 102, or both courses. Participants received information about the standards, assessment tools and the uniform percentage distribution for the tools; in short, each part of the Reference Notebook was explained. They received and read sample student learning journals, practiced using the grading rubric, and then discussed their decision-making process for assignment of point value. After a model lesson in a cultural critical thinking discussion, language groups congregated to brainstorm ideas for cultural lessons appropriate to their particular textbook. The instructors participated in a demonstration of a student-centered lesson; because more than half of the 101 and 102 instructors are from countries outside the United States, it is particularly important to model ideas such as "student-centered" and "proficiency-oriented" and not assume that everyone has the same understanding about these labels.

The Center for Teaching and Learning on campus offers another arena for faculty development for both faculty and teaching assistants (TAs). The Center holds its own orientation workshop for teaching assistants before the start of classes and offers a stipend to encourage attendance. Throughout the year faculty and TAs are invited to listen to guest speakers, and a multi-day conference is held in January; in 2003 a special weekend workshop was designed for TAs. The Center houses a library of teaching resources and has staff available for consultation.

Continued professional development is offered in a variety of ways. Monthly meetings offer a brief refresher and tips for administering upcoming assessment tools and include a presentation about a special topic such as teaching students with learning disabilities, a time to build community by sharing frustrations and asking questions, and a teaching idea of the month. The program coordinator offers assistance and support to TAs and adjuncts and observes a class each semester to provide pedagogy and management suggestions. Although the Working Committee was renamed the Steering Committee, curriculum revision is an ongoing process, and thus the committee continually reviews the efficacy of the assessment tools, addresses TA and instructor concerns, and evaluates the success of the program. One of the strengths of the program is this cooperative spirit of the instructors and their willingness to be flexible and modify the program as necessary.

Conclusion

Students who may have reluctantly entered the second language classroom at ISU may still exit with only a basic oral proficiency and a sense of conquest of another general education requirement, sharing the sentiment behind, "*veni, vidi, vinci*"—I came, I saw, I conquered. However, the innovative program at ISU has given students the tools to become life-long learners by setting the stage to help them climb the barricades of monolingualism and take steps to overcome a myopic view of culture. Via discussions about cultural diversity and language, their greatest conquest may be that of provincialism.

Endnotes

1. At the time the Working Committee was meeting, the department offered French, German, Italian, Japanese, Latin, Russian, and Spanish; Arabic and Chinese have since been added.
2. The draft copy of the document is now unavailable, but the final version is available online. See the References section for more details.
3. Latin will emphasize reading and writing, but include the other skills. Readers who are interested in the linguistic goals and assessment tools of the program are directed to the article by Calvin and Rider (Spring 2004).
4. Some modifications of assessment measurements have occurred since the program inception. The most recent revisions are explained here; earlier versions are included in Calvin and Rider (Spring 2004).
5. The diversity question is labeled as "cultural awareness" on the exam to reduce students' impulse to "tell us what we want to hear." Students receive a copy of the essay questions a week before final exams and are encouraged to review their Learning Journal entries as preparation. The question for Beginning Spanish II (Span102) is worded as follows:
   - What are some of the most interesting aspects of Hispanic culture and values and in what way has learning about this made you more aware of your own culture? If you took Span101 at ISU, how has what you learned about culture in 102 built on that course?
   - How has the course changed or expanded your perceptions about Spanish speaking peoples, their language, and their culture? How has it changed or expanded the way you might behave toward or interact with Hispanics? When describing the change, be sure to tell about the ideas and attitudes you

had before this class and whether that affected your interaction with native Spanish-speakers.

- How has what you learned influenced the way that you would react toward other foreign cultures?

The distribution of remaining sections of the final exam is: listening comprehension 10-15%, vocabulary 10 -15%, writing 8 -10%, reading 8 -10% and grammar 25 - 38%. This range of percentages allows flexibility for different languages, yet the inclusion of the four skills clearly demonstrates that the program is testing as it has taught.

Acknowledgments

Since I arrived at ISU in 1999 during the curriculum development stage, I am indebted to Dr. Ronald Dunbar for a review of the proposal phase of the change initiative.

References

American Council on the Teaching of Foreign Languages. (1996). *Standards for foreign language learning: Preparing for the 21st century.* Yonkers, NY: Author.

Byram, M., & Esarte-Sarries, V. (1991). *Investigating cultural studies in foreign language teaching: A book for teachers.* Philadelphia: Multilingual Matters Ltd.

Calvin, L., & Rider, N.A. (Spring 2004). Not your parents' foreign language class. *Foreign Language Annals*, *37*, 11-25.

Indiana Department of Education. (2000). *Indiana academic standards for foreign languages* . Retrieved September 24, 2004, from http://doe.state.in.us/standards/standards2000_lang.html

Indiana State University. (1998). *University Bulletin: Undergraduate Catalog 1998-2000*, *92*(3), 70-71.

Indiana State University. (2000). *Undergraduate catalog 2000-2002*. Terre Haute, IN: Author, p. 74.

Omaggio, A. C. (2001) *Teaching language in context.* Boston: Heinle & Heinle.

Parra, R. (2001, September) Latin population soars in Indiana. *Latino World*, *1*, 7.

State of Indiana foreign language standards implementation guide. (1999). Manuscript in preparation.

Lisa Calvin is an associate professor of Spanish in the Department of Language, Literature, and Linguistics at Indiana State University.

Appendix A

Cultural Diversity Writing Prompts in the 102 Learning Journal Questions

Week one: How might someone from your community describe a typical speaker of your foreign language, whatever "typical" means to you? Do you know any native speakers of the foreign language, or have you had any personal contacts that would lead you to agree or disagree with the general description above?

Week three: What are you learning about your own language and culture through the study of your foreign language and its culture?

Week five or six:

1) Have you talked about things related to your foreign language and/or its culture in other classes (history, environment, geography, literature, etc.)?

2) How can you use the foreign language or your knowledge of the country's culture outside of the classroom? How will you use this knowledge even when you have stopped taking classes?

Week 8, 9 or 10: Have you found yourself thinking about a new perspective or different value system since you began the study of language and culture in this class? Describe your thinking.

Week 12, 13, or 14:

1) What are three things you have learned about the culture from which your language of study originates that you think you will remember a year from now? Why do you think you will remember them? Do they tell you something important about native speakers of the foreign language? Something important about your own culture and people? What?

2) Now that you have been studying a new language for a semester, how might you react if you encountered a non-native speaker of English who needed help? Would you have responded this way before taking this class? If you would have, how might the encounter be different than before?

Appendix B

Holistic Rubric to Grade Learning Journals (portion)

Excellent *10/10 points*

- Looking for, discussing, analyzing cultural encounters or connections with other courses
- Addressing all aspects of the writing prompt
- Including specific details of personal thoughts, feelings, and applications to own life
- Showing evidence of reflection and introspection on the learning process
- Paying attention to English grammar and spelling; submitting work on time
- Writing neatly and professionally*

Good *8-9/10 points*

- Looking for and discussing cultural encounters or connections with other courses, no analysis
- Attempting most aspects of the writing prompt
- Including general details of personal thoughts, feelings, and applications
- Showing some evidence of reflection and introspection on the learning process
- Containing one minor errors of English grammar or spelling; submitting work on time
- Writing legibly*

  * The last criterion is applicable for those who choose to offer the option of submitting handwritten journals rather than on-line versions.

Chapter 15

Transforming Teacher Preparation: Changing Cultures Through Constructivism and Reflective Practices

Miguel Licona

This chapter highlights the work of a group of professors in addressing the call for improved test scores, better preparation and retention of teachers, and graduation of more students. The result of this effort is an integrated model that lessens the workload for both teacher and student, and also provides for increased understanding and meaningful experiences for students and faculty alike.

I was hired in 1999 into an isolated and fledgling secondary teacher preparation program. Secondary teacher preparation courses were independent with no overlap or interconnectedness among themselves. Along with low passing rates on the teacher certification test, student complaints of irrelevance and tremendous workloads caused me to begin dialogue with the group of professors known as the "block faculty." Students' attitudes and assumptions mirrored the disciplines from which they came. This was coupled with years of lived experience based on independent academic disciplines.

I came in with 25 years of secondary teaching experience in low performing schools from which I had emerged transformed. The last 10 years had been mired with much questioning of and reflection on the status quo schooling in which I had participated. I was beginning to break away from the transmission model, concentrating instead on impacting student satisfaction and persistence in science courses beyond the basic requirements. The early stage of this effort was based on what little I knew about current trends in school reform. It was during the last portion of this decade that I began work on my doctorate. I was overwhelmed with professional and scholarly knowledge and practices that liberated me to move in new directions. My views were broadened, and I acquired language to participate in the discourses of constructivism and critical pedagogy.

The move from the transmission model of teaching to providing learning contexts where students move to understand big concepts became the basis for transforming our secondary education program. The principles of constructivism and curriculum "backward design" guided the efforts of my colleagues and me to bridge theory and practice (Wiggins, G. & McTighe, J., 1999).

It became possible to continue the dialogue of reflection and change with the hiring of professors who had public school teaching experience and the desire to practice what they had learned during their doctoral studies. We sustained an atmosphere of collegial community learning. This atmosphere allowed us to stay in touch with the guiding principle that we must allow our student to see us "walk the talk." We became vulnerable yet believable, and we used student input to assist with programmatic changes. We talked about what was essential from each of our courses and let those things guide our assignments. We had to let go of some content. We, as the only professors from the College of Education that our students would encounter during their preparation as teachers, experienced much the same conflicts as other teachers in change initiatives. Themes that emerged were: uncertainty; intensification and limited time; subject loyalty versus team allegiance; craft pride, caring, and moral purpose (Nolan, J. & Meister, D. G., 2000).

Rewards for us, as professors, are intrinsic in nature when we actually meet the challenge to put theory into practice. Initial workload increases give way to more positive feedback from graduates, improved certification test scores, and an increased sense of community that serves to sustain our efforts.

The University of Texas at El Paso

The College of Education is comprised of three departments: Teacher Education, Educational Leadership and Foundations, and Educational Psychology and Special Services. The Teacher Education Department currently employs 29 full-time faculty. UTEP serves approximately 17,000 students on the border between Mexico and the United States with a student population that is 70% Hispanic. The Teacher Education Department currently confers around 340 elementary teaching degrees, 100 secondary teaching degrees, and 100 master's degrees each year. Educational Leadership has an Ed.D. program, and Teacher Education submitted a proposal to establish a Ph.D. program soon.

Historical Background of Secondary Teacher Education

Reform efforts are cyclical, and many of the aspects of the current teacher program at UTEP can be seen in the reform effort of the 1970s. There was an initiative to reform the teacher preparation program in 1976. The focus was directed toward a field-based initiative known as the Secondary Teacher Education Program (STEP). The traditional model that included "student teaching" was replaced with cohorts where secondary pre-service teachers moved through a field-based program that called for professor collaboration and involvement in the public schools (University of Texas at El Paso College of Education, 1976a, 1976b). This era was mired in behaviorism as a theoretical foundation for education, a teacher-centered focus in curriculum and pedagogy, and academic freedom for professors to teach autonomously.

One must ask: If it was done before and it did not work, then why try it again? What would make it work this time around? The response is that the context for the reform effort has changed, and the new effort addresses learning theory that did not exist during the last thrust for change. The constructivist foundation that has been forged recently replaces the behaviorist theories that framed teaching and learning of the past era. We now focus on learner-centered praxis rather than on teacher-centered performance. We believe that meaningful learning does not necessarily follow teaching. If we engage in experiences that result in student understanding, then we have done much toward providing a democratic educational opportunity for all students, not just those that adapted well to a hegemonic structure. This chapter will point to why moving toward a more collaborative perspective will be successful on this attempt.

The Call for Change

In 1999 many of the professors who had been at UTEP during the 1976 uprising were retiring and much research on teaching and learning now appeared over the horizon. Research on the brain and learning emerged from the neurosciences, psychology, anthropology, and sociology (National Research Council, 2000) informing new initiatives in a constructivist realm. Armed with new knowledge and a shift in paradigm from behaviorism to constructivism, the stage was set to revitalize the teacher preparation program. In 2000, a renewed effort by like-minded professors moved the secondary teacher preparation program toward the vision of integration and collaboration that is espoused by more progressive educators and scholars (Beane, 1997).

Professors began meeting regularly in 2000 to share our ideas and develop a vision of what the secondary program would look like. Some resisted the changes due to unfamiliarity with the paradigm within which this initiative was taking place. Some opted out of participating, and others refused to take part. Some participated tentatively while the group worked toward sharing ideas and strategies that would support our vision. The group of professors began attending conferences and presenting our new roles. The structure began to take a less amorphous form. We now articulate a basic philosophy of education, theories that support it, and strategies that keep it alive and thriving.

From 2000 to 2003, much maneuvering took place. The group sought to include more professors that would support this integrated approach to teacher preparation and we began an intense collaboration that moved us toward our present condition. Students participating in our teacher preparation program are now called interns. As new interns register for teacher preparation, we meet with them prior to their first block at a Teacher Education Orientation day to welcome them into the program. All involved set the stage for what we think will be an enduring, successful, and meaningful experience toward teacher certification.

Despite education professors collaborating to make this a meaningful time for the students, this schedule proved to be problematic in two ways. First, the four-course load for interns was tremendous. Each professor required one or two texts, several articles, a reflective journal, at least one student presentation, and a mid-term and final assessment. Each of the activities was based on constructivist principles and best practice, but the workload for students was overwhelming (Brooks & Brooks, 1999; Zemelman, S., Daniels, H., & Hyde, A., 1998). Second, the interns were in schools that did not align with the constructivist philosophy and practices of the university teacher preparation program. Existing school cultures were based in a tradition from which much resistance to reform emerged. The result was tremendous student resistance and confusion. As much as interns "liked" what they experienced in our classroom at the university, they did not feel they could implement these practices in places where teachers and administrators seemed to invalidate them.

In the fall of 2001, the State Board for Educator Certification placed the teacher preparation program into "accredited under review" status due to low Exam for Certification of Educators in Texas (ExCET) scores. This meant that the university teacher preparation program could be "taken over" and managed from an outside entity within three years if scores did not improve. There was a mad scramble to push test scores up so that the state would not assign an external control agent to oversee the program.

Along with the impact from high stakes testing, a recent study by El Paso Independent School District (EPISD; 2000) found that 39% of new teachers in the El Paso area districts leave teaching after the third year of teaching (50% after five years). It was obvious that something had to be done on several levels. Historically, there has been a push to graduate more teachers in order to ameliorate the "teacher shortage." It became apparent, in light of the EPISD study and low ExCET scores, that the dramatically high turnover rates called for a systemic change in the way that teachers are prepared for today's classrooms. The college was determined to help teachers pass the ExCET by calling for improvement in the quality of teachers, moving to support new teachers, and increasing the number and quality of their mentors. With a more rigorous test preparation program in place and more attention finally being directed toward the secondary education program, block faculty began a collaborative move to improve the quality of student experiences in their courses while supporting the competencies for the Texas Examination of Educator Standards (TExES). The TExES replaced the ExCET in the fall of 2002.

College administrators moved to put a rigorous test preparation program into place while asking all professors teaching in the program to modify syllabi and course content to reflect the exit test competencies. It seemed as if we were being directed to "teach to the test" much as the public school teachers have done with their high stakes tests. We were faced with the challenge of "improving" our courses, but we thought improvement could be achieved in ways that do not teach to the test. There still exists a requirement that all teacher education students attend a test preparation session weekly. Many students have voiced concern with this requirement, and it highlights a potential contradiction between what we say and do. The group feels strongly about this issue and decided to develop a program based on current research and best practice.

Prior to applying to the secondary teacher preparation program, students have attended 15 or more years in schools that were predominantly based in a behaviorist culture. We believe that their educational socialization is very much in place for these aspiring teachers and heavily influences their incoming attitude. As students enter the secondary teacher preparation program, they encounter a constructivist environment based on different principles. Many students see the block classes as mere formalities toward certification and rely heavily on teaching as they were taught. They seek and point out incongruities between professors' philosophies as a form of resistance. In 2001, a group of students submitted a letter of concern to the dean of the College of Education. In it they outlined how many texts, articles, journals, presentations, and other assignments they experienced during their one semester in teacher education. This letter caught our attention and caused us to listen and begin the collaborative process that eventually moved us to the present.

Secondary education professors met often during these developmental times. The courses were being transformed based on the feedback obtained from students. We were determined to base their experiences on learner-centered constructivist pedagogies rather than teacher-centered behaviorist context, as was historically the case. Changes in the amount of work assigned and how it fit to support the overall theme for their preparation emerged. Our discourse led to identifying the essence of our courses and deciding if we could live with assigning less reading material so that students might process the content in more profound ways. The concept of "less is more" guided our development. We were embracing content from a "depth versus breadth" perspective that would eventually liberate some of us to become even more open to other progressive ideas.

The group of professors continued meeting and sharing syllabi, negotiating content and finding ways to overlap our assignments. Two texts were identified as basic to the university program rather than to one course. *In Search of Understanding: The Case for Constructivist Classrooms* by Brooks and Brooks (1999) was assigned during the first two weeks of classes to set the philosophical foundations of constructivism. The use of this text presented a united front for professors and has had a positive impact on our students. The second text is *Joint Curriculum Design: Facilitating Learner Ownership and Active Participation in Secondary Classrooms* (1997) by Patricia Gross. Although much of this text is used in the curriculum course, it is referenced in the other three courses that interns take during their preparation at UTEP.

Time and Content

The block professors felt there was not enough time to cover all of the essentials, and because students met with us for such a short time, what we did present was not well processed. We looked at how reflective teaching and learning could inform us and began to use "deliberative inquiry" based on Henderson's *Reflective Teaching* (2001). Students still took the four teacher education classes during the Block I semester. Attempts were made to lessen the load of particular assignments by having students keep one handwritten journal for all four classes rather than for each separate class. This soon became problematic, as it was difficult for professors to access the student responses without taking the journals, thus rendering them inaccessible. As it was, we met with the students for 16 one-hour-and-fifty-minute sessions. Taking their journals did not allow students to address journaling during that time. We were moved to collaborate on what we desired for students to process during their short-lived "exposure" to education even though, at this time, it was not working well.

A Block I professor who taught Developmental Variations introduced the rest of us to an English professor who had developed a web-based journaling environment, The Journal Place. He gave us a presentation and we all agreed that this might solve the journaling issue for our program. Student pictures would be taken on the first day of class and appear clustered at the top of their electronic journal page. We collaboratively developed a meaningful question for each week of the semester and posted it on the web at an appropriate time that coincided with content from our syllabi. Quality and length parameters were set and students were clustered in groups of three. They would respond to the question in the first of three columns. In the second column, they were required to consider the content of the question in terms of their field placement. The first two columns were to be completed by the weekend so that they would have time to read their clustermates' responses and engage in a dialogue in the third column by Sunday noon. All professors could view or comment on any student response in order to share the scoring responsibilities. Each was assigned one fourth of the clusters on a four-week rotation, and he or she would interject responses and prompts to individual students before the Monday or Tuesday class. All professors worked to have a sense of inter-grader reliability and it was agreed that the journal would count 20 % of the grade in each of our courses.

Integrated Curriculum

Professors and students met during the first four class sessions as a cohort. We did not move to separate courses during this time in order to produce a sense of community and collaboration and to ensure that we would get the semester off to an integrated beginning. We created two four-hour blocks of time on Mondays and Tuesdays where all four professors were seen in the new light of facilitator rather than simply interpreters of texts and lecturers. On the first day, we took turns introducing ourselves, shared our constructivist approaches, and laid the foundation for shared content, activities, journaling, assessment, and grading. We spent "quality" time eliciting student input. We took their pictures and showed them how to log on to The Journal Place. We assigned the Brook and Brooks text to be read for the second week of classes.

Shared Common Experience

A modified version of the Atkin/Karplus learning cycle was used to structure a common experience for students early in the semester (1962). This lesson served as a reference for the remainder of the semester on two fronts. First, it was a method to engage the students in a way that they would experience a discovery lesson that modeled cooperative learning and integrated curriculum rather than telling them about the curriculum and pedagogy important to this lesson. Secondly, it allowed professors to interact and use this "hook" activity to tie their content to the Block I theme. Our role as facilitators would be to mingle within the groups to establish Socratic dialogues while never giving answers. Inspired by the level of enthusiasm, we proceeded to move through the other phases of the learning cycle. Each professor found opportunities to support the groups directly at this time while identifying potential connections for their content to be addressed at a later time.

Discussion and brainstorming of ideas occurred often. We brought up assessment, learning for understanding, choice, grading, and rubrics that set the stage for discussing curriculum and pedagogy in our individual classes during the rest of the semester. Best practice literacy strategies and suggested modifications were embedded throughout the lesson as students applied the concepts in new settings (Zemelman, S., Daniels, H., & Hyde, A., 1998).

We met for the third time as a cohort during the second week of the semester to give each group the opportunity to present its versions of the assessment phase. We used the jigsaw and expert group strategies to "process" the Brooks and Brooks text on constructivism. Students were assigned a writing activity based on the theme of Significant Past School Experiences (Adams, N. G., Shea, C. M., Liston, D. D., & Deever, B., 1998). This activity allowed us a fourth block of time as a cohort, with all professors present, to share part of their lived experiences in schooling and further build community as we moved to begin meeting in shorter blocks of time for individual courses. This activity also served to set up a common mid-term activity to support the construction of the educational context within which these students would soon begin their professional teaching practice.

Common Assessments

Aside from the 20% weight given to journaling, the mid-term and final assessments were collaboratively developed and worked to serve all four classes. A form of action research was set into place with the use of *Learning to teach: A critical approach to field experiences* (Adams, N. G. et al., 1998). Students were paired, given a choice of topics, and then asked to go into the schools and develop a collaborative mid-term presentation based on their research. They were given a rubric, and when the mid-term arrived, all professors and students met for the four-hour block of time for the presentations. Each of us, as assessors, scored the presentations and then met in conference to establish the final scores based on dialogue and negotiation. These scores would count 10% of the course grade for each of the courses. Doing this eliminated the need for students to present four separate mid-terms and allowed for us, as professors, to assess them within the context of our planned meeting times, distributing the responsibility of scoring as well as allowing for negotiation of grades. We each had a scoring rubric with specific attributes that needed to be addressed in order for a particular score to be given. This process united us and gave students a sense that they were being scored fairly. Issues of fairness still arose, but they could be attributed to the fact that most of the students had never experienced this type of assessment and they feared getting a lower grade due to the low performance of another group member. This fairness issue set up the opportunity to distinguish traditional group work with collaborative work where positive interdependence plays a distinguishing role. We gave it a 10% weight because we knew it was possibly our students' first collaboratively graded assignment. It also provided a launching point for the more heavily weighted final.

The final was similar to the mid-term in structure, but had more specific points that needed to be addressed from each of the four block courses. Groups were comprised of three students, and the work counted for 20% of the grade. Students were required to write and submit a proposal delineating precisely how they were going to address the assignment, and they were asked to be explicit about each participant's responsibility. They were to acknowledge all parameters of the assignment, including appropriate use of technology, data gathering, and assessment.

Students experienced a 50% overlap of their grades for each of the four classes. We combined our classes for six four-hour sessions, and professors seemed satisfied to have "control" of the remaining 50% to process the block experience and to develop specific readings and activities in their content areas. This combination occurred on two simultaneous tracks, a morning and an afternoon cohort with only two professors common to both. In other words, there were six different professors working together as a team, something not easily done at the university level.

The Present Initiative

As the spring of 2003 approached, more attention was directed towards the secondary teacher preparation program. This attention had implications for the Teacher Education Department, the Education Psychology and Special Services Department, other university departments, and the public schools where our interns would be placed. We had to be able to convince these communities that what we considered "best practice" was based on contemporary research and scholarly work, and that we must move on a united front based on dialogue and trust. These goals are difficult to accomplish because academic structures are rigidly fixed and associated with creators who may take personal offense when these structures are questioned and moved for altruistic purposes.

During the spring 2003 semester, the structure of the secondary program was reevaluated and divided into two blocks. Students now take two courses in each of the two semesters rather than taking all four at once as in the previous semesters. This change alleviated some of the time-constraining issues for professors insofar as being available for the four hour cohort meetings. Classes are now scheduled for three hours each on Monday and Tuesday mornings or afternoon. The morning professors teaching the Block I courses can more easily arrange to meet together, and the afternoon block can do the same. Now that students are engaged with the four professors over two semesters, we anticipate an enhancement in the socialization of the interns into education.

Contact hours per course have increased by approximately 30% when compared to the prior program structure.

Recent research has called for the institutions that prepare teachers to review their practices. Such research suggests that teachers must move beyond being content masters to revisit the pedagogical aspects of teaching and learning (Wilson, S. M., Floden, R. E., & Ferrini-Mundy, J., February, 2001). The field experience component has also come under review. There must be collaboration between the disciplines, the cooperating teachers in the field, and university professors. We are addressing all of these issues as we develop and grow to improve education for our nation's children.

We are now aligning the road to teacher preparation with input from various departments across campus that traditionally had little communication with us, even though their students ended their bachelor's program in the College of Education. These programs include art, music, and kinesiology. The years from pre-school to the senior status at the university have served to establish an uncritical mental model of what schooling is and what it is supposed to look like. Extant school cultures reify this model based on outdated behaviorist notions.

We have seen professors willing to take risks and move away from academic freedom as the reason not to collaborate. We have broken barriers across academic disciplines and are meeting face-to-face with professors whom we had only known by name prior to this initiative. The College of Education is no longer in danger of losing its accreditation since our students are now passing the exit certification tests (now known as the TExES) at a proficient level. We feel that current learning theory should inform the practices of new and existing educators and that an important threshold has been encountered, one that has the potential to address teacher retention and student drop out rates as well.

I have moved on to another university. Upon reflection of the effort described above, it is obvious that political economic forces have already begun to dismantle the gains accomplished over a half dozen years. Pressure to graduate more teachers, generate credit hours, competition with other teacher preparation programs, and lack of administrative understanding have all impacted the potential for transformation. Despite the incredible time and effort put forth by participants, less visionary administrators have regressed this initiative to a more efficient and less threatening program. I have described resistance from faculty and students, yet other issues such as faculty loyalty and tenure will undoubtedly continue to impact participation. The nature of the deep seated traditional "model" will continue the pressure to maintain the status quo. This initiative proved it could be done, just not sustained in these politically troubled times. It is disappointing to see the missed opportunity for academics to put theory into practice.

References

Adams, N. G., Shea, C. M., Liston, D. D., & Deever, B. (1998). *Learning to teach: A critical approach to field experiences.* Mahwah, NJ: Lawrence Earibaum Associates.

Atkin, J. M., & Karplus, R. (1962). Discovery or invention. *The Science Teacher, 29(2),* 121-123.

Bean, J. A. (1997). *Curriculum integration: Designing the core of democratic education.* New York: Teachers College Press.

Brooks, J. G., & Brooks, M. G. (1999). *In search of understanding: The case for constructivist classrooms.* Alexandria, VA: Association for Supervision and Curriculum Development.

University of Texas at El Paso College of Education. (1976a). *Handbook for the elementary teacher education program.* Author.

University of Texas at El Paso College of Education. (1976b). *Handbook for the secondary teacher education program.* Author.

El Paso Independent School District (2000). *Employee dropouts: Professional leavers in EPISD 1996-2000.* El Paso, TX: Office of Research and Evaluation.

Gross, P. A. (1997). *Joint curriculum design: Facilitating learner ownership and active participation in secondary classrooms.* Mahwah, NJ: Lawrence Earlbaum Associates.

Henderson, J. G. (2001). *Reflective teaching: Professional artistry through inquiry* (3rd ed.). Upper Saddle River, NJ: Prentice-Hall.

National Research Council (2000). *How people learn: Brain, mind, experience, and school.* Washington, DC: National Academy Press.

Nolan, J., Jr., & Meister, D. G. (2000). *Teachers and educational change: The lived experience of secondary school restructuring.* State University of New York Press.

Wiggins, G., & McTighe, J. (1999). *Understanding by design.* Alexandria, VA: Association for Supervision and Curriculum Development.

Wilson, S. M., Floden, R. E., & Ferrini-Mundy, J. (2001). *Teacher preparation research: Current knowledge, gaps, and recommendations.* Seattle, WA: Center for the Study of Teaching and Policy.

Zemelman, S., Daniels, H., & Hyde, A. (1998). *Best practice: New standards for teaching and learning in America's schools.* Portsmouth, NH: Heinemann.

Miguel Licona is an assistant professor in the Curriculum and Instruction Department, College of Education, at New Mexico State University.

II. Departmental or Program-Based Change Initiatives

Chapter 16
Teaching Together: Interracial Teams

Mathew L. Ouellett and Edith C. Fraser

In 1993, the masters program at the Smith College School of Social Work (SCSSW) strategically implemented interracial teaching teams in a required diversity course to address its goal of creating multiculturally inclusive classrooms, as well as linking to a broader institutional initiative to become a multicultural organization. In this study, we explore how these interracial teams managed their personal and professional differences while teaching challenging content. We also suggest best practices for team teaching gleaned from the strategies developed by these co-instructors.

Race, class, gender, sexual orientation, professional experience, economic status, and ability are some of the different social identities brought to the classroom by students and instructors that may significantly influence the teaching and learning environment (Adams, Bell, & Griffin, 1997). For many college instructors, however, even exemplary disciplinary training may not have included systematic preparation for college teaching, much less preparation for meeting the needs of an increasingly diverse student population. Addressing the needs of diverse learners has become increasingly important to professional and graduate school programs as they strive to educate scholars and practitioners that better reflect the diverse perspectives of the populations they are likely to serve post-graduation. In this context, both teaching and learning are made even more complex when the content of a course focuses on issues of race and racism, especially if a goal is to avoid classroom dynamics that replicate the type of inequities often experienced by members of over- and under-advantaged social groups.

In 1993, the Masters of Social Work program at the SCSSW implemented a program that relies on interracial teams to teach a required diversity course. This initiative served as a strategy to create multiculturally inclusive classrooms and to link to a broader institutional anti racism commitment to become a multicultural organization (Basham, Donner, Killought, & Werkmeister Rozas, 1996). The course, *334A: Race and Racism in the United States: Implications for Social Work Practice*, is taught within the *Human Behavior and the Social Environment (HBSE)* sequence in a condensed, five-week term, as are all courses. Most students take this required course in their second year of the SCSSW graduate program.

Over the years, some of these interracial teaching teams seemed to thrive and remain stable while others floundered. However, there were few efforts to systematically identify the attributes of teams at SCSSW that worked well and, conversely, of those that failed. Looking more broadly at the literature, there is currently a paucity of research on the impact of diversity and social identity (e.g., race, gender, ethnicity, sexual orientation, etc.) on the effectiveness of instructors in teaching teams, either from the instructors' or students' perspectives. Such absences in the literature are especially notable when one considers the challenges faced by interracial teams of co-instructors who teach emotionally loaded content such as race and racism, multiculturalism, or other diversity issues.

In our research, we are interested in what interracial teams at SCSCW discovered about the following subjects: themselves as teachers, indicators of success as co-teachers in interracial teams, the best pedagogical strategies for presenting race-related content, and techniques for managing inclusive classroom environments. In this study, we explore how these interracial teams manage their personal and professional differences while teaching this challenging course content. Finally, we suggest what lessons may be learned from the strategies developed by Smith College School for Social Work's interracial teaching teams.

Benefits of Team Teaching with Interracial Teams

Faculty collaboration in higher education is on the rise – both for those involved in research and classroom teaching. Today, many colleges are utilizing team teaching as a modality of educating students in light of the growing realization that team teaching promotes collegiality and collaboration, ensures successful program change and improves students' outcomes (Davis, 2002; Murata, 2002). Team teaching has been known to bring an end to "pedagogical solitude" (Benjamin, 2000), i.e., faculty members who are specialists in various disciplines can share concepts and approaches collaboratively, exposing students to new ideas and multiple perspectives. Team teaching also provides an opportunity for enhanced knowledge acquisition, and an enriched learning environment for students (Aguilar & Woo, 2000; Gately & Gately, 2001). In a classroom among peers, ideas can be critiqued as a student has the opportunity for both confrontation and cooperation in and out of the classroom. Students benefit from seeing professors who are competent and confident with such confrontation and cooperation in the service of knowledge acquisition. Furthermore, students are exposed to several ways of knowing, especially if their instructors reflect diversity in discipline as well as gender, race or ethnicity (Eisen & Tisdell, 2000).

There are a variety of models of team teaching - each of which offers different levels of collaboration (Davis, 2002). Maroney (1995) suggests that a key distinction is whether or not instructors are teaching the same students at the same time within the same classroom (model one), or working together but not necessarily at the same time, with the same students, or in the same classroom setting (model 2). Further, Maroney describes five types of team teaching that may be reflected in model one: traditional, complimentary/supportive, parallel instruction, differentiated split class, and monitoring the teacher. This article will focus on team teaching model one utilizing the model described as traditional, i.e., both teachers share in the responsibility for the preparation and implementation of classroom instruction with all students and are actively involved in all classes (Maroney, 1995).

Whether faculty teach alone or in teams, there is recognition that the topics of race and racism stimulate strong emotions to such a degree that they are frequently avoided in classroom conversation (Miller, Donner, & Fraser, 2004). This hesitancy to engage in controversial, or highly emotional, content is shared by both students and instructors alike and can affect classroom interactions and discussions, closing down important dialogue (Adams, Bell, & Griffin, 1997). Weinstein & O'Bear (1992) note several factors that increase faculty reticence to discuss issues of racism in the classroom, such as: fear of confronting one's bias, knowing how to respond to biased comments, dealing with the emotional intensity of these difficult conversations and concerns related to institutional risks. Even faculty members predisposed to take this "walk on eggshells" have consistently revealed deep fears of not knowing how to effectively respond to students when challenging moments arise in the classroom (Frederick, 1995, 2000). When faced with emotional responses to their efforts to facilitate such dialogues, faculty members often find their own feelings heightened. This may contribute to their hesitancy to broach these topics in the classroom (Roberts & Smith, 2002; Warren, 2002).

Griffin (1997) recommends interracial team teaching as a vehicle for engaging instructors and students in valuable discussions. Ideally, co-facilitation is recommended by co-teachers that represent both the target (i.e., individuals that are disenfranchised, exploited, and victimized) and the agent (i.e., individuals of the dominant or privileged group) (Hardiman and Jackson, 1997). By creating teams of co-instructors with both agent and target experiences, the instructors serve as role models for grappling with complex content, and students have an opportunity to consider the content from the perspectives of both the agent and target viewpoints (Tatum, 2000).

Under any circumstance, team teaching requires coordination, communication and cooperation to overcome inevitable "disconnects" between two individuals who are responsible for the delivery of the curricular content (Young & Kram, 1996). With interracial teams, these demands may be increased (Griffin, 1997). In addition, members of the team are likely to bring their own biases including issues related to internalized oppression or racism. Internalized oppression occurs when members of the target group internalize negative, denigrating messages that may lead to a negative self-concept, often based on stereotypic messages, derogatory comments, or concepts of inferiority propagated by the agent group (Rosenwasser, 2002). Co-facilitators who are part of the dominant, or privileged, group may struggle with internalized racism, which occurs when they manifest unconscious or previously unrecognized aspects of racism. For example, being unaware of their access to and perhaps reliance upon unearned benefits that come to them based on their dominant racial identity or by assuming "color-blindness" to the importance of race in determining access to privileges. These processes heighten the emotional stakes high for both co-instructors in interracial teaching teams.

In concert with these high emotional stakes comes the opportunity for co-instructors to provide a unique and important learning experience for students. When the interracial team of co-instructors works well, students may be provided with their first-ever role model of effective sustained interracial communication. Over the years, SCSSW students in their final evaluations have often commented that a key benefit of the class was the opportunity to observe two leaders from different backgrounds collaborate together in a spirit of mutual respect and shared leadership.

Design

The course, 334A: Race and Racism in the United States: Implications for Social Work Practice, is a five-week, required course taught in the HBSE sequence during the second year of the Smith College School for Social Work M. S. W. program. The new concept of teaching this course in interracial teams was introduced in summer of 1993, following several years of lecture format. Since then, a total of 76 sections have been taught over twelve summers, with an average of about seven sections per summer. A total of 34 instructors have been involved in teaching these sections over the years, of which sixteen instructors were invited and agreed to be interviewed for this study.

Participants

The sample of 16 interviewees included 11 women and 5 men, of whom 7 participants identify as White, 1 as biracial, and 8 as People of Color (PoC). In terms of institutional status, 14 participants are summer lecturers (adjunct professors), 1 is a resident tenured professor and 1 is pre-tenure resident faculty. While data on other aspects of social identity were not specifically collected, interviews generated information about sexual orientation. Two participants self-identified as gay men (both White), and four participants self-identified as lesbian women (2 White and 2 PoC). Nine of the instructors had no previous experience with team teaching before teaching HBSE 334A, and participants' experiences teaching HBSE 334 A ranged from 1 section to 18 sections during a period of 11 years. By far the majority of the participants in the study, 15, have taught *HBSE 334A* multiple times and teamed with a number of partners over the years.

Methodology

This study is an exploratory research study utilizing qualitative methods useful when investigating areas of education where there is little prior research (Marshall & Rossman, 1989). As noted earlier, teaching teams at the Smith College School for Social Work utilize a traditional team teaching model in which both teachers share equally the responsibility for the design and implementation of the curriculum and are actively involved throughout the class pe-

Table 1. Profile of Participants

	Social Workers	Men	Women	Sample
White	3	3	4	7
Biracial	1		1	1
People of Color *	5	2	6	8
	9	5	11	16 (44% of Possible pool of 34 instructors)

* Represents: Latino, Hispanic, African American and Asian Americans.

riod with all students (Maroney, 1995). We wanted to explore how these instructors understand of the strengths and challenges facing interracial teams, identify the strategies of effective co-instructors, and illuminate how teams in this study maneuvered internal and external tensions triggered by addressing issues of race and racism in their classroom.

Utilizing a phenomenological approach, we conducted a semi-structured face-to-face interview (see Appendix B), with each participant and each other during the academic year 2003 – 2004. Merriam defines a semistructured interview as an interview that is "guided by a set of questions and issues to be explored, but neither the exact wording nor the order of questions is predetermined" (Merriam, 1988, p. 86). All interviews were then transcribed, analyzed, and coded using the computer-aided qualitative data analysis tool Ethnograph. Ethnograph is a program designed to facilitate the analysis of text-based data collected in qualitative research methods by enabling the researcher to code the data and then to sort the coded data in multiple ways (Seidel, Friese, & Leonard, 1996).

To ensure the protection of participants in the study, Edith, Matt and the individual instructor worked together to determine which researcher (Edith or Matt) conducted the interview as well as the time and place of the interview. To the degree possible, we arranged interviews so that the interviewer mirrored the participants' racial identity to ensure the highest degree of candor possible. This was especially important in light of what we understand about the challenges of interracial dialogues in the workplace, especially when participants have important, long standing ties but are members of dominant and target groups. This also allowed Edith and Matt to acknowledge our long-standing relationships with many of the participants and our desire not to distance ourselves from either our purpose or the manner in which we undertook this research. We are as committed to exploring and understanding our perspectives as interracial co-instructors as we are to understanding the perspectives of our colleagues. At a faculty retreat in January 2005 we presented a draft of our results to a subset of the interviewees and discussed the outcomes of the study to get their feedback and perspectives. Additionally, in this chapter we have aggregated the data and selected illustrative quotes designed to protect individual identity.

Results

In semi-structured interviews, current and past co-instructors of *334A: Race and Racism in the United States: Implications for Social Work Practice* were asked to reflect on their experiences and identify factors that could help and hinder interracial teaching teams (see Appendix B). The interviewees identified a range of possible tensions that could emerge in the classroom and described several strategies they found useful in responding to such stressors. Below, we present these findings, organized in three key dimensions: Formation of Teams, Allies, and Institutional Support.

Formation of Teams

Creating teams in which the instructors balance and support each other proved to be one of the most important indicators of a team's long-term success. At Smith, co-instructor teams for *HBSE 334 A* are interracial, as well as typically interdisciplinary. At least one instructor is required to have a formal social work background while the other works and/or teaches in a related discipline, such as law, education, or social policy. Whenever possible, teams are also formed across genders. In our case, Edith has both a masters and a doctorate in social work. Matt's doctorate is in education and he was at one time a social worker and supervisor of a state-level child protective services unit.

To achieve the goal of creating diverse teaching teams (i.e., across racial identity, gender, disciplinary background, etc.), co-instructors often did not know each other before being assigned to team teach, or, if they were acquainted, it was only casually. All of the participants in this study had some form of prior teaching experience, although not always in formal higher education settings, and about half of the participants had prior experiences with team teaching, while the other half did not. Study participants also represented a range of experiences with co-instructors in that some participants taught with a single partner during one summer while other participants co-taught with different partners over many summers.

While our survey provided a wealth of data on the attributes of effective interracial teams, it also indicated that the chemistry of some teams simply never worked positively despite attributes that indicated potential success. Additionally, some individual instructors could team well with just about anyone. Of the many constellations of teams, most worked effectively and only a few did not. Some also worked well for a while, but then seemed to deteriorate for some of the reasons we describe below.

As one may suspect, no consistent definition of what makes an interracial team a "success" emerged from this study. However, we repeatedly found that the decision to teach together *again* was often a moment of truth. Some teams that appeared outwardly placid and had relatively trouble–free classroom experiences (e.g., high evaluations from their students) chose not to partner again, although each instructor went on to teach regularly with other co-instructors. In contrast, some teams had very challenging experiences in their sections, sometimes to the point of student complaints to the chairperson, but built a sustained history of teaching together and becoming allies in the classroom. Ultimately, it was the teams themselves that decided whether or not to deem their partnerships "successful." In the context of this study, therefore, consistent decisions to teach together over time and in the face of a range of challenges became the definition of success.

> All co-teachers are not the same. It takes time, investment, knowing people and their style so it doesn't trigger something in you.
>
> (Female, PoC, experienced professor)

When participants were asked for their perspectives on what leads to sustained interracial co-instructor teams, the majority identified four important attributes:

1. mutual respect,
2. congruence of expectations and flexibility,
3. ability to positively handle stressors, and
4. commitment to dialogue.

Mutual respect. Among these attributes, study participants discussed the role of mutual respect between co-instructors at length. When pressed to define this more explicitly, many talked about the importance of giving each other the "benefit of the doubt;" i.e., trusting the other person to be genuinely engaged in doing the requisite internal work to address personal issues of internalized racism and oppression. Based on this assumption, team members were able to cultivate a confidence in each other that made them willing to hear and listen to each other more deeply and across different perspectives on the core content of the course. As in most team-teaching situations, listening and hearing with respect were important pre-requisites to nurturing a positive relationship between co-instructors. However, in this context, the importance reached far beyond a general sense of collegiality to an appreciation that teaching issues of race and racism could often have more resonance at a personal level than other content areas.

Congruence. Another important attribute of co-instructor teams that endured over time was a philosophical congruence and some flexibility about how best to teach issues of race and racism. Conflicting philosophical beliefs about how to teach these issues emerged in a multitude of different ways. Conflicts commonly arose over issues like: how confrontational to be with students or with one's co-instructor; how much priority to give to lecturing versus experiential processes; how to balance social data and historical information with an emphasis on personal stories; and, the balance between creating opportunities for self-reflection and growth versus understanding the experiences and perspectives of others. While there were no clear "rules" about how to proceed with these questions, in the best of situations, co-instructors shared generally similar philosophical beliefs so that their styles and priorities "clicked." On some teams, differences over how to answer these questions became ongoing points of tension and compromise. Whatever the approach settled on by the team of co-instructors, to be successful as a team they ultimately had to find their way to complementary styles in order to achieve success.

Managing stressors. Co-instructors were able to positively respond to stressors related to interracial team teaching when their team became a source of mutual support and growth for both instructors. Participants developed such a team by knowing and trusting each others' strengths, developing the ability to "play to each others' strengths," and attending to other aspects of the –isms (e.g., gender, sexual orientation, religion, class, etc.) that intersect with power relationships so that they could support each other appropriately. The most common stressors reported included tensions over roles that emerged for teams in a variety of ways: (1) when one member felt the other expected too much personal emotional support, (2) when one member felt marginalized by his/her partner due to status inequities (i.e., gender, racial identity, sexual orientation, graduate student), or, (3) when one partner alone assumed the mantle of "expert" and began to treat the co-instructor as an assistant.

Co-instructors had a variety of strategies for addressing such tensions. First, they emphasized the need for both pre- and post-planning – especially debriefing what happened in class on a regular basis. They discussed the importance of having a ready process for how to talk about what came up and each others' responses, and how this could help ensure that both instructors had a solid handle on what would happen in the next class. Also important were strategies co-instructors used for sustaining a dialogue between them about pedagogy. Many teams talked about the benefits of having a co-instructor in the classroom to help when one of or both teachers felt socially incompetent or overwhelmed by the complexity of the teaching process.

Many participants in the study noted the importance for each instructor to demonstrate integrity in her/his own change processes, but also to avoid the trap of an expectation to know all of the answers, all of the time. Because team members strived to be sensitive to how the personal and the scholarly could become intertwined for both themselves and their co-instructors in such sustained dialogues, teams with longevity consistently proposed a similar strategy. They regularly talked about and acknowledged the importance of other dimensions of social identity differences beyond race (e.g., gender, sexual orientation, class status, etc.). The "-isms" heighten the importance of attention paid to who talked and how much, who said what and to whom, who received questions, and who answered which questions.

Dialogue. In developing the ability to work through stressors cooperatively, sharing a commitment to dialogue proved critical. Participants identified a constructive relationship with their co-instructors as essential to being able to positively handle stressors related to team teaching courses on race and racism. They described the ability to agree to disagree while continuing to genuinely listen to each other and make sense of how best to teach the material as a prerequisite to a constructive relationship. For example, many participants emphasized the importance of first acknowledging to each other, and then to the class, the power differentials within the team. And, they underscored the need to talk about what that might or might not mean to the relationship between the co-instructors and how the class responded to the team both individually and together.

In the best situations, co-instructors were eventually able to use their relationship and process of decision-making about the teaching of the course as a model of an interracial dialogue. To engage in this sort of transparency required enough confidence and trust experienced by the co-instructors to bring up discomforting issues. Sometimes, this process was particularly difficult when perceived power differentials in the team made one partner reticent to be totally honest with the other, and the class by extension. We now address the second important dimension rooted in the data analysis: becoming allies.

Allies

Interdisciplinary team members bring a wider range and better balance of theoretical perspectives, in addition to different teaching strengths, social experiences, and models for classroom application to the topics at hand. In the context of interracial teams, and especially when the content covers race, it becomes imperative that co-instructors consciously engage in relationship-building practices if they are to make the most of these riches. When the four attributes described above in the formation of teams are sufficiently present, co-instructors can then move on to collaboratively deepen and strengthen the teaching team. Participants in the study identified three key aspects of the movement from the formation stage to that of being allies:

1. shared authority,
2. shared responsibility, and
3. trust.

Shared authority. Every participant in the study emphasized a commitment to shared authority as a significant determinant in the ability of teams to develop an alliance. Because teams are deliberately paired across race, gender, and disciplines, how team members responded to socialized role expectations, stereotypes, and power as they engaged with each other defined a critical turning point in the development of the team and the learning experience for students. Clearly, it was essential for interracial teaching teams to find ways to develop a relationship in which both instructors were equally valued and validated, rather than one that replicated a traditional model of power differentials.

Participants in this study also noted that the dynamics in teaching preparation were as important as what transpired in the classroom. An important method for attending to this commitment to shared authority can be seen in the strategies used by co-instructors to build shared responsibility. This sense of allegiance to a shared authority had to be incorporated in all decisions related to course design and teaching from the selection of text books, to the design of assessment and evaluation methods.

Shared responsibility. Related to a commitment to shared authority is the commitment to shared responsibility. For participants in this study, this meant that co-instructors needed to perceive that their teammates were "pulling their weight" in the planning and implementation of course goals, management of the learning process, and in assessing and responding to students' developmental needs in an appropriate, timely fashion. Instructors cited the process of developing the course syllabus, choosing assigned readings, deciding on the appropriate preparation and delivery of lectures, facilitation of experiential components, and the collaborative evaluation of assignments as tangible expressions of shared responsibility. They noted the challenge of achieving such balance and acknowledged how easily it could go awry. Thus, instructors underscored the importance of regular, if not daily, communication about handling the load equitably.

Participants regularly noted the importance of validating each team member's role in managing the learning process and underscored the importance of establishing this balance in authority and responsibility with students from the very first contact. Common examples of this include jointly: facilitating discussions, establishing ground rules, building a common vocabulary, and defining the scope and important content of the course.

Although there seemed to be no one "best method" for presenting a unified position to students on course expectations, participants stressed the importance of working together to assess student progress and provide formal and informal feedback using developmentally appropriate methods. Some teams developed signals to alert each other that an issue needed to be addressed and they expected their co-teacher to pursue it. For example, instructors for the HBSE 334 course often decided that an important learning outcome of the course was for instructors to model being an ally to members of other racial groups. Opportunity for this arose when comments that carried stereotypical or prejudiced messages were made in class. A common strategy of interracial teaching teams was to have the instructor that most closely mirrored the speaker's racial identity to be the one who intervened.

> We had a look, the "leap from the window" look when [name] is letting me know that if I don't take on this white guy she'll leap from the window.
>
> (Female, White, experienced professor)

Despite the challenges of handling tensions in the class, teams suggested many pedagogical strategies useful in managing the affective as well as cognitive aspects of learning. They acknowledged the importance of sustaining a learning environment that encourages students to learn from each other and the instructors, and to balance increased self-reflection with increased skills in understanding the perspectives of those different from oneself. Specific learning strategies teams suggested include: case studies, journals, experiential exercises, collaborative learning groups, and assignments that ask students to reflect upon and discuss core materials in intraracial and interracial group configurations. Co-instructors provide invaluable mutual support in understanding the dynamics and implications of students' behaviors that may range from open conflict to silence. In tandem, teams are far better prepared to decode students' signals more accurately and assess and respond to their developmental needs more astutely.

For many interracial teaching teams, the ongoing commitments to collaboratively share authority and responsibility provided essential opportunities to understand each other's intellectual and scholarly perspectives, pedagogical priorities, and life experiences. Conversely, failure to incorporate these commitments resulted in embedded patterns in teaching teams that diminished their integrity and, ultimately, their survival even if they initially seemed to work. Under the right conditions, such deepening collegiality led to the third attribute essential to becoming allies: trust.

Trust. Under the best of circumstances, teaching can sometimes feel like being on a high wire without a safety net. Instructors teaching issues of race and racism in interracial teams can anticipate that their course will create compelling emotional dynamics for students and teachers alike and that co-instructor pairs can become foils for students in unique ways. To balance the cognitive and affective learning dimensions of this course, and to address the in-class process as important "content," co-instructors distinguished the importance of being able to trust and, to some degree, be vulnerable with each other.

Working collaboratively provided team members with the opportunity to debrief each other and balance emotional states of trust. In doing so, co-instructors developed the ability to be open and honest with each other and create tools to manage their own emotional "work," while recognizing the challenges their colleague may face (e.g., the possibility of being the only member of a specific ethnic group in the classroom). While it could happen intuitively, co-instructors often developed a code with which to signal the other team member when one member needed to stop and talk, debrief, or take a time-out. This involved understanding when and how to intercede as allies and when to speak versus when to support. Instructors reported that when their relationship with their co-instructor was trusting, it could promote a richer learning environment for students and a teaching experience for instructors. While they emphasized that good communication between team members in the moment ameliorated many of the stressors of interracial team teaching , some aspects of developing effective interracial teaching teams required a scope of support available only at the institutional level.

Institutional Support

Participants in this study of interracial teaching teams recognized important aspects of their teaching experiences as mediated by institutional context and priorities. They suggested important contributions to the success of interracial teaching teams could be derived from institutional support for teaching development opportunities. Modes of such support, participants suggested, should encompass both developmental (formative) and evaluative (summative) modes. Below we first describe institutional mechanisms identified by participants as helpful in supporting interracial teaching teams (i.e., regular discussions and end of semester evaluations) and, second, we describe suggestions for improvement that emerged from the study.

In this study participants noted the helpfulness of two current institutional mechanisms to help interracial teams learn about the process of team teaching: informal discussion groups and end-of-semester evaluations. All teams were invited to regular lunchtime "brown bag discussions" that afforded instructors important opportunities to share syllabi, readings and related teaching materials across sections; to generate ideas and strategies together for responding effectively to immediate teaching-related challenges; and to offer emotional support when needed. Additionally, they noted, these meetings proved not only a practical way to collaborate on complex issues, but also to introduce instructors from different teams to each other and contribute to a general sense of departmental cohesion.

Often, senior academic administrators relied on two key formats to ascertain success of teachers: student end-of-course evaluations and informal feedback from students. The SCSSW has a long-standing practice of embedding teaching assessment in all courses through the use of required end-of-course evaluations. And, because of the size and intimate nature of the graduate program, academic administrators generally had access to a steady stream of feedback from students about instructors. Participants in this study agreed on the importance of student evaluations for the growth and development of instructors and also on the usefulness of such feedback for determining general improvements to the course.

Participants stressed the value of the institutional supports described above and also suggested that such informal and formal strategies be enhanced through development opportunities for both interracial teams and academic leaders. In this study, every interviewee voiced the importance of relationship- and trust-building to the individual and collective success of instructors working in interracial teaching teams. Co-instructors also reported that due to time constraints, they often plunged into teaching before having the opportunity to build a relationship with their co-instructor likely to generate a successful experience for students or themselves. They suggested it is crucial that guided opportunities be offered for teams to talk to each other about their racial identities, important life events, and their own beliefs about how teachers can best help students to identify, articulate and reflect upon their beliefs and values especially in relationship to the historical and social implications of race in the United States. Annual "advances" (day-long faculty development opportunities) serve well the function of bringing instructors together for such guided opportunities. An example of a tool that may be of use in such opportunities can be found in Appendix A: Team Interview Guide. Such a guide might best be nested inside of a packet of related resource materials on best practices in team teaching and used in conjunction with an array of other forms of institutional support (e.g., mentors for individual instructors or for teams).

The results of this study suggest that instructors and teams also would benefit from additional opportunities for structured feedback on their teaching effectiveness. In practice, participants noted that teams may receive positive end-of-course evaluations but have unresolved issues between co-instructors. Department chairs and academic deans may never know if teams, as teams, are not working well until the situation is problematic (e.g., relationships become heated, instructors decline to work with each other again, or instructors leave the department). One strategy to address this responsibility is to offer structured debriefs for teams. For example, in the Smith College School for Social Work M. S. W. program, at the teams' request, quite often a skilled faculty consultant is asked to bring an independent perspective to mid-course support or to facilitate end-of-course team debriefs.

Additionally, participants articulated the important support institutions can provide in helping to educate department chairs, deans, and provosts that review teaching evaluations as part of personnel processes how best to support and reward such interracial team-teaching endeavors. Often the expertise required of such teams is outside the pathway of the traditional scholarly preparation within the field and, consequently, these teams are often interdisciplinary ones. Therefore, it may be more difficult to get the reward structures in traditional departments or schools to fairly reflect credit where credit may be due for such individuals and teams. This can be especially true for introduction of innovative resource materials, exercises, case studies, pedagogical strategies, and other manifestations of course improvements that ultimately benefit the department and school in important ways such as: greater representation of students of color in courses or the program, student satisfaction levels with classroom experiences, preparation of students for success in the profession, external reviews, and accreditation requirements.

Conclusion

This study investigates the perspectives of members of interracial teams who have co-taught *HBSE 334A: Race and Racism in the United States: Implications for Social Work Practice*, a required course in the M. S. W. program at the Smith College School for Social Work during the past six years. Based on the perspectives of course co-instructors, we identified what factors can help or hinder the successes of such interracial teaching teams.

Interracial team teaching is a dynamic and powerful pedagogical approach that fosters and incorporates inclusiveness. The interracial co-team encourages a more diverse class for students and professors to discuss issues, which are often taboo in the classroom, and taps professors who can discuss these issues from different perspectives. Utilizing co-teachers from both target and agent social groups provides students with models of cross-cultural interactions, several perspectives on issues of diversity, and professors who may reflect their own racial or ethnic identify. Thus, members of both minority and majority groups are represented in the class and may feel more reassured that their voices and perspectives are likely to be included in the discourse.

The act of teaching together offers interracial teams a kind of mini-learning community by sustaining a dialogue over the course of the semester that encompasses the subject area content and the classroom environment; promotes a better understanding of who we are as teachers, and who are our students; and fosters a deeply reflective perspective on the teaching process.

As this study indicates, when teams are interracial, such efforts can lead to increased self-awareness, new strategies and pedagogical practices, and better integration of interdisciplinary perspective in the core content. Such teams can also provide instructors with peer mentoring, feedback, and fresh perspectives on student interactions.

As we implement innovative pedagogical strategies, such as interracial teaching teams, this study reminds us of how important it is to acknowledge and guard against the unintentional tendency for such innovations to replicate inequities often found in the larger society. In higher education, this can inadvertently play out on both team and institutional levels in how the roles and rewards of team teaching are addressed. For instance, such interdisciplinary teams by design seek to assemble teams of co-instructors that bring a broader range of preparation and expertise with them into the classroom. However, such instructors are often part-time instructors and therefore particularly vulnerable. This may be seen in the disparities between adjunct and tenure-track faculty status, access to opportunities to write and publish on the outcomes of such collaborative work, and in invitations to represent the institution at regional, national and international conferences related to such innovations. As one example, the M. S. W. program of the Smith College School for Social Work addressed this by specifically inviting 334A instructors to participate in submission of articles for the Smith College Studies in Social Work journal special issue on pedagogy and diversity.

Finally, the authors hope that this study further contributes to the movement beyond an individual focus on teaching development. Our findings suggest that the transparent, collaborative sharing of strengths, strategies and insights that emerge across teams of co-instructors can contribute significantly to the success of program, department, and institutional-level goals related to diversity.

References

Adams, M., Bell, L., & Griffin, P. (Eds.). (1997). *Teaching for diversity and social justice: A sourcebook.* New York: Routledge.

Aguilar, V., & Woo, G. (2000). Team teaching and learning in diversity training for national services programs. In M. Eisen & E. J. Tisdell (Eds.), *Team teaching and learning in adult education* (pp. 63-71). New directions for adult and continuing education, No. 87. San Francisco: Jossey-Bass.

Basham, K., Donner, S., Killought, R., & Werkmeister Rozas, L. (1996). Becoming an anti-racist institution. *Smith College Studies in Social Work, 67*(3), 565-585.

Benjamin, J. (2000). The scholarship of teaching in teams: What does it look like in practice? *Higher Education Research and Development, 19*(2), 191-205.

Davis, J. (2002). *Interdisciplinary courses and team teaching*. Westport, CT: Oryx Press.

Eisen, M., & Tisdell, E. (Eds.) (2000). The many faces of team teaching and learning: An overview. In *Team Teaching and Learning in Adult Education* (pp. 5-14). New directions for adult and continuing education, No. 87. San Francisco: Jossey-Bass.

Frederick, P. (1995). Walking on eggs: Mastering the dreaded diversity discussion. *College Teaching*, *43*(3), 83-92.

Frederick, P. (2000, February). Approaches to teaching diversity: Successful college teaching strategies for the age of multiculturalism. *NEA Higher Education Advocate, 17*(4), 5-8.

Gately, S., & F. Gately. (2001). Understanding co-teaching components. *Teaching Exceptional Children*, *33*(4), 40-47.

Griffin, P. (1997). Facilitating social justice education courses. In M. Adams, L. Bell, & P. Griffin (Eds.), *Teaching for diversity and social justice: A sourcebook.* (pp. 281-282). New York: Routledge.

Hardiman, R., & Jackson, B. (1997). Conceptual foundations for social justice courses. In M. Adams, L. Bell, & P. Griffin. (Eds.). *Teaching for diversity and social justice: A sourcebook,* (pp. 16-29). New York: Routledge.

Johnson-Bailey, J. (2002). *Race matters: The unspoken variable in the teaching-learning transaction* (pp. 39-49). In J. M. Ross-Gordon (Ed.), New directions for adult and continuing education, No. 93. San Francisco: Jossey-Bass.

Maroney, S. (1995). Some notes on team teaching. Retrieved March 5, 2005, from Western Illinois University Web site: http://www.wiu.edu/users/mfsam1/TeamTchg.html

Marshall, C., & Rossman, G. (1989). *Designing qualitative research.* Newbury Park, CA: Sage.

Merriam, S. B. (1988). *Case study research in education: A qualitative approach.* San Francisco: Jossey-Bass.

Miller, J., Donner, S., & Fraser, E. (2004). Talking when talking is tough: Taking on conversations about race, sexual orientation, gender, class and other aspects of identity. *Smith College Studies in Social Work: Pedagogy and Diversity*, *74*(2), 377-392.

Murata, R. (2002). What does team teaching mean? A case study of Interdisciplinary teaming. *Journal of Educational Research*, *96*(2), 67-78.

Roberts, A., & Smith, K. (2002). Managing emotions in the college classroom: The cultural diversity course as an example. *Teaching Sociology, 30*(3), 291-301.

Rosenwasser, P. (2002). Exploring internalized oppression and healing strategies. In L. Yorks & E. Kasl (Eds.), *Collaborative Inquiry as a Strategy for Adult Learning* (pp. 53-61). New directions for adult and continuing education, No. 94. San Francisco: Jossey-Bass.

Seidel, J., Friese, S., & Leonard, D. (1996). *The ethnograph v4.0: A program for the analysis of text based data.* Amherst, MA: Qualis Research Associates.

Tatum, B. (2000). Defining racism: "Can we talk?" In M. Adams, W. Blumenfeld, R. Castaneda, H. Hackman, M. Peters, & X. Zuniga (Eds.), *Readings for diversity and social justice.* New York: Routledge.

Warren, L. (2002). Managing hot moments in the classroom. Retrieved March 5, 2005 from Harvard University, Derek Bok Center for Teaching and Learning Web site: http://bokcenter.fas.harvard.edu/docs/hotmoments.html

Weinstein, G., & O'Bear, K. (1992). Bias issues in the classroom: Encounters with the teaching self. In M. Adams (Ed.), *Promoting diversity in college classrooms: Innovative responses for the curriculum, faculty, and institutions*. New directions for teaching and learning, No. 52. San Francisco: Jossey-Bass.

Young, M., & Kram, K. (1996). Repairing the disconnects in faculty teaching teams. *Journal of Management Education, 20*(4), 500-515.

Mathew L. Ouellett is the associate director of the Center for Teaching (CFT), University of Massachusetts Amherst and adjunct professor, Smith College School for Social Work. **Edith C. Fraser** is professor of Social Work and director of Faculty Development and Research at Oakwood College and adjunct professor at Smith College School for Social Work and at Alabama A & M University.

Appendix A

Team Interview Guide

Purpose: This facilitation guide is designed to promote dialogue between co-instructors teaching core content related to issues of social justice. It may also be useful for co-instructors in other disciplines who are interested in intentionally managing other sorts of diversity where differentials in power are likely to emerge within teams or as a guide for self-reflection.

Instructions: The questions below address three key themes: complex identity, teaching interests, and team-building / interpersonal growth. They are designed to range from low-risk (easy to answer) to high-risk (more challenging to answer). These questions are not intended to be answered in one sitting; in fact they are likely best addressed in the context of a dialogue sustained over time. It is not necessary to answer all of them or in sequence.

It may also be beneficial for co-instructors to step back from the dialogue about these questions to reflect on their individual processes. For example, are there questions that feel too risky to answer? What questions are stressful to discuss? Did you have answers that, in retrospect, feel too "pat"?

Themes:

Complex Identity

1. What are your goals at this time in your life?
2. When was the first time you remember feeling different from others? Describe what happened and how you felt about it.
3. How would your friends describe your personality? How would you describe your personality? How do friends, colleagues and students respond to you?
4. Tell me about a time when you felt powerful socially.
5. Tell about a time when you felt disempowered.
6. What would you like me to know about how you've come to understand your racial identity? (People and events important to you and important decisions you have made.)
7. What does it mean to you today?
8. What other aspects of your social identity are important to you and how do they intersect with your understanding of race?

9. In your family, extended family, community, work institutions, and culture, what emotions do you share publicly and how do you express these emotions? What don't you share (or, only share after you trust the other person)? How does your psychological identity intersect with your social identities?
10. What brings you to teach this course at this particular time in your life?
11. What do you feel is your "ultimate purpose" in life?

Teaching Interests / Disciplinary Passion

12. What do you love about teaching? What challenges you about teaching?
13. What teacher(s) or mentor(s) of yours have influenced your thinking about how to teach issues of race and racism?
14. What strengths do you think you "bring to the table"?
15. What challenges do you anticipate?
16. What other sorts of classes (workshops, institutes, etc.) have you taught?
17. Who's theoretical and what experiences have influenced your thinking about issues of race / racism?
18. What do you think is gained by team teaching this course?
19. What do you think is lost by team teaching this course?

Team-Building and Interpersonal Growth

Team Building

20. What will you have to set aside to "be here?"
21. What do you like / dislike most about the syllabus?
22. What sorts of things do you think should be responded to immediately in class? What sorts of things should we wait on and respond to later?
23. When do you think will be the best time to prepare for class?
24. When a student takes a cheap shot at me or implies I'm not being effective, I…
25. What do you think are the most important learning outcomes for this course (content, skills, and values)?
26. How do you balance power in your team relationship?
27. What do you hope will be our relationship as co-teachers?

Pedagogy

28. How do you see yourself influencing the group process as a co-instructor?
29. What do you like / dislike most about the syllabus?
30. What do you like / dislike most about the institution in which we are teaching this class?

31. What aspects do you feel most comfortable with in the core content?
32. When the class is "silent," it may indicate that …
33. When the class is talkative, but off-topic, I often …
34. How do you balance fulfilling an "agenda" with responding to students' interests?
35. How will we decide "in the moment" what to do?
36. How will we give students regular feedback on their progress in this course?
37. How will we evaluate the written work of students?
38. How will we evaluate students at the end of the term?

Communication

39. What sort of things do you feel comfortable talking about in front of students and which do you want to do privately?
40. How do you want to divide up the work?
41. How will I know if you're unsettled or uncomfortable?
42. What aspects of conflict do you most embrace / are hardest for you? How will I see this in your facilitation style?
43. How would you feel if I interrupt you to make a point I think is important and that you may omit?
44. When do you think will be the best time to debrief the class?
45. How do you know your facilitation style is working well?
46. Describe what "being supported" means to you? And, "not being supported?"
47. This is emotionally draining work; what sustains your enthusiasm for it?
48. Who else do you anticipate you will go to for support / mentorship during this course?
49. Is it important to and / or how will we bring those discussions back into our relationship as co-instructors?
50. Are there any other questions we ought to ask each other?

Appendix B

Interview Protocol

1. What has been your experience with team teaching? How long have you used this model of teaching? (How do you manage this experience?)

2. Have you used the team teaching model in any other settings?

3. What are some of the pros and cons to the team teaching model in general?

4. What are some of the unique dimensions of team teaching in a racism course as an interracial team?

5. How have your own issues of racism or internalized oppression been triggered in the classroom experience?

6. Can you remember tense experiences in the classroom? How have these been handled?

7. How do you handle racism and internalized oppression in your students?

8. Students often discuss an interest in having a "safe environment." Is team teaching a "safe environment" for teachers?

9. What are some primary strategies for effective team teaching? How would these strategies differ for interracial teams?

10. Are there other issues of diversity which might affect team teaching, such as gender, class and sexual orientation?

11. What could the Smith College School for Social Work do to be supportive of team teaching?

12. Any questions or further reflections about the team teaching experience you'd like to add?

Chapter 17

Confronting Issues of Oppression in the University: Creating a Space for Faculty Dialogue, Reflection, and Action

Peter T. Wilson

David DeWeese, Carol Huang, Sharon Shockley Lee, Barbara O'Donnell, Laurel Puchner, Jacque Wuertenberg

The Social Justice Study Group at Southern Illinois University Edwardsville (SIUE) School of Education is a group of seven faculty members who came together to: a) deepen our understanding of multicultural education and how it should inform teacher education, and, b) increase awareness of our own issues of oppression and how to deal with them. This chapter describes and analyzes the issues and processes that constituted our first year of work as we grappled with issues of social justice and educational equity. Personal narratives illuminate the impact of the study group on ourselves, our classrooms, our institution, and our community.

In February 2002 Peter Wilson sent a memo to faculty at the SIUE School of Education, inviting them to participate in a faculty Social Justice Study Group. The purpose of the Study Group was to engage faculty who wanted to address two questions:

- Are you concerned about how racism and classism affect student achievement?
- Are you concerned with whether or not we are effectively preparing teachers and principals to work with diverse populations?

The memo went on to ask,

> Would you be interested in coming together regularly, perhaps every two weeks or so for the remainder of the semester, to examine issues of social

> justice? Group members will determine the focus, process, and schedule. One possibility is that we might function as an action research group. We might examine the culture of our classrooms, our own syllabi and instructional practices to identify strengths and possibilities for improvement. Or we may generate new possibilities for collaboration when we come together.

Five faculty (four white, one Chinese American; two male, three female, one tenured, four non-tenured) responded. The SIUE School of Education includes five departments; Study Group participants came from the Department of Curriculum and Instruction with 19 full-time faculty (all white) and Educational Leadership with 13 full-time faculty (two of Asian descent and 11 white). Peter Wilson, the facilitator, who is also white, was at SIUE as an adjunct professor to direct a federal grant. The project, "Teaching and Leading as Social Justice Advocacy" (TLSJA), engaged leadership teams from urban schools in intensive, experiential weekend retreats on racism with 20 hours of follow-up sessions. TLJSA supported the facilitator's work with the Study Group, provided copies of articles and purchased books for Study Group members. Participants received neither compensation nor institutional recognition.

The Study Group began meeting bi-weekly in April 2002. We agreed initially that the Study Group would have a dual focus of deepening our understanding of multicultural education and increasing our awareness of and ability to deal with our issues of oppression. Experiences of the Study Group members are best told by the participants themselves. Hence this portrayal of the Study Group will begin with a general description of our work, provided by the group facilitator. Following this description, each of the other members will provide his or her brief narrative, describing some part of their experience as a Study Group member.

Peter's Story: The Overview

It was clear from the start that while we were committed to this "adventure," it felt risky. We thus set out by developing a set of norms about how we would work together and what, if anything, could be shared outside the group. We also agreed that in order to pursue our dual purpose we needed to set aside time for each focus in our bi-weekly sessions.

My role as study group facilitator was multi-faceted. One facet was providing resources, readings, books, videos, and sometimes a particular conceptual tool to help group members deepen the development of their racial identity.[1] The Continuum of American Racial Thought (Singleton, 2001) turned out to be particularly powerful. I also led several exercises aimed at heightening awareness of our own issues with oppression. For example, we used the "Things I Learned and Heard" exercise to examine the source of messages about identities that have and may still be informing our responses to individuals and situations. This activity works with a matrix of identities and with sources of institutional messages (e.g., family, school, media). In addition to raising the critical problem of mis-education regarding difference, it helped us to get to know each other.

My identity as a white male who was not based in the institution impacted my facilitation is several ways. Being a white male made it easy for me to raise issues of privilege within the group and regarding the very white male culture of the institution. This, combined with my not being part of the institution, may have made it easier for the group to raise and discuss issues of concern. Some members of the group were skilled at attending to the issue of voice within the group, which made the job of facilitation considerably easier.

In my male identity I was cognizant of the dynamic between the two male members and the rest of the group. There was a constant question for me as to when and whether or not to address intra-group gender issues since our primary focus was on race and racism.

Only one member of the group identified her racial identity as other than white. Carol identifies as Asian American. In metropolitan St. Louis, racial issues are almost always defined as black/white. This is certainly the case in the context of SIUE, a predominantly white institution in which black students are the dominant minority population. I often felt that I needed to consciously, both for myself and with the group, recognize Carol's racial identity. She is critically conscious and seemed to deal with the issue quite well.

Our work with readings led to interesting and meaningful discussions. For example, a reading by Lisa Delpit (2002) led to an exchange between two members related to when and how we "interrupt" expressions of oppression by others, and the relative value of making "others" feel comfortable. Some group members suggested that a commitment to social justice necessitates making people uncomfortable, but others were not sure. We've also used *The*

---

[1]Activities included: "White Privilege: Unpacking the Invisible Knapsack" (McIntosh); Trapspotting for White Anti-Racists" (Olsson, 1997); "Things I Learned and Heard"
The readings included: excerpts from The Skin that We Speak (Delpit & Kilgour, 2002); Knowledge, Skills, and Experiences for Teaching Culturally Diverse Learners (Cochran-Smith, 1997); Community Teachers (Murrell, 2000).
The books included: *The Miner's Canary* (Guinier & Torres, 2002); A White Teacher Talks about Race (Landsman, 2001).
The videos included: Off Track (Fine, Anand, Hancock, Jordan, & Sherman, 1998); True Colors (Sawyer, 1991); The Color of Fear (Wah, 1994).

Miner's Canary (Guinier & Torres, 2002) as a text to help us address important social justice questions, reading and discussing a chapter each month.

A final facet of my facilitation involved sharing tactics and strategies for teaching difficult and controversial topics. This seemed to help faculty as they worked to engage their students of color and hear their stories. Indeed, an important theme that surfaced early in our second year was an interest in investigating the status and well-being of African American students in the teacher education program. Personal experiences of the group members led us to speculate that some of the relatively few black students in the School of Education (SOE) felt more isolated than supported among their fellow students. The question of how best to support these students occupied us for much of this year. Members talked at length with the few African American students that they have had in their classes. We also talked with the administration and with the Assistant Provost for Diversity. These discussions have led to some initial action, including providing students with information on how to establish a SOE African American Student Association, and discussion with the Metro East Advocates for Urban Learners to explore the possibility of establishing a Metro East St. Louis chapter of the National Alliance of Black School Educators. We see the latter as a possible vehicle for supporting current students and establishing a stronger tie with black educators in Metro East St. Louis school districts.

To end my story, I'll call attention to one of the most striking aspects of the Study Group's work. During discussions, a prevailing feature has been expressions of feelings of vulnerability and marginalization on the part of many of the group members themselves. The perception that the Study Group was a safe-haven for these non-tenured faculty participants to discuss work that is outside of the mainstream of the SOE appears to have been an important part of the Study Group's role.

Sharon's Story: A Critical Educator's Sense of Place

SIUE is located just 20 minutes from East St. Louis, Illinois, described as "America's Soweto" in *Savage Inequalities* (Kozol, 1991). In sharp contrast, most teacher education students are middle and working-class Caucasians from small towns and rural communities. The administration and faculty are also overwhelmingly white. As a Caucasian female still new to SIUE, the Social Justice Study Group offered me a sense of belonging and the camaraderie of critical friends as I explored the cultural intersections and collisions around me and developed a sense of place.

Small but increasing numbers of Latino and Asian children are visible in area schools, but to our teacher education students, diversity is a matter of black and white. Teacher education students routinely express culture shock as they begin clinical experiences:

> I grew up in a small town with one school, kindergarten through seniors. I saw no racial diversity. It was a shock when ninety percent of the students were African Americans.... I do not know enough about other groups of people to even call them "other." How do I know they really aren't just like me?

Most Caucasian students know little about East St. Louis. Many have seen *National Lampoon's Vacation* and echo *Savage Inequalities* (Kozol, 1991): "The ultimate terror for white people ... is to leave the highway by mistake and find themselves in East St. Louis." Kristi, a teacher education student, remembers, "I was taught that East St. Louis was... very unsafe.... I recall taking the wrong exit and ending up in East St. Louis. I remember being very scared. I locked all the car doors."

I worry that the one or two African American students I have each semester feel as "unsafe" and "scared" as Kristi felt lost in East St. Louis. Davian, the only African American student in her class, contributed quietly in the relative safety of her small literature study group, but never addressed the class of 35 white students. One Wednesday, she found her voice. Davian describes the experience:

> The conversation started as a summary of Delpit's *Other People's Children*. It ended up a personal battle against my classmates. Everyone is looking at me, the angry black woman. The silence was broken. It's me against them. I do not want special treatment. I do not need sympathy. I only want what I deserve, equal treatment.

Despite reading, writing, and talking about white privilege, oppression, marginalization, and silencing, many students could not "hear" Davian's voice. John, a white male, described the same class session from his perspective:

> The situation was blown up more than it should have been. It appeared that the white students do not let the black student have a voice. I do not believe that to be true. I don't think there is a racist climate in this room, but Davian made it out to be. I do not think that is fair. The issue of race has been going on who knows how long and will continue as long as this world continues.

Other students, however, experienced a real epiphany. Mark, also a Caucasian male, explained:

> The conversation Wednesday was unsettling.... We feel as if we are having these enlightening and meaningful discussions about diversity and differences... and then Davian shocked us all with her revelation, "I feel that in this class and every class that it is me against every one of you!"
>
> Many of us responded... defensively: "We're not racists. We're not trying to *silence* anyone." We missed a key point. Davian *DID* feel silenced. As the only black student in a room full of white students... she was acutely aware of racial differences even though many of us were not.... Our response should not be, "I'm not a racist. You misunderstand me." To respond in this way is to dispute Davian's feelings. The question is, "How can we approach race in such a way in our classrooms so no one feels silenced and each student feels empowered to voice their ideas?"

Also reflecting on the Wednesday class, Diane, a Caucasian female, wondered: "What would I feel if I were the only white person? I never thought about that. The class was inspiring. A quiet person spoke out and shared her feelings and beliefs."

I realized I had grown from analyzing Peter's skilled, sensitive facilitation of our Social Justice Study Group. As facilitator of my students' critical dialogue, I struggled to pry scales from colorblind eyes, to make the moment of insight last, to erect a symbolic monument at this key point in our shared journey.

Our faculty experience in the Study Group, I later reflected, paralleled my students' encounter one Wednesday with silence and voice, safety and risk, denial and discovery, colorblindness and diversity.

Carol's Story: The Model Minority Teaches about Social Justice

As an Asian American new faculty member on a predominantly White campus, teaching social and cultural foundations of education, I swam in rapid currents with many dangerous whirlpools. Luckily, there were some African American students in my classes. And even more fortunate for me, many of them were very outspoken about racial issues in front of their white classmates. Each semester, I prayed to have such students. They helped shoulder the critical agency that I intended to generate in my classes. Without them, I would be acting solo in representing a great spectrum of issues addressed by my classes. When we played the Horatio Alger's "Leveling the Playing Field Game," I was the one who fell far behind everyone else in class because of my immigrant background, my third world upbringing, and the racial signifier (being racially characterized) that I encountered in this country.

Students noticed their cultural and racial privileges over me, and yet I was the person of authority in the class. I was sent to convince them that they should look at the treatment of minorities in American society, and yet I was an embodiment of the positive stereotype, in that I had made it this far; I was part of the model minority, the American dream fulfilled. But was I here to remind them that I am the exception and not the norm? How could I teach about social reproduction , social oppression, and poverty to a group of rural poor whites? My predominantly rural,small-town, Catholic school-educated students looked at me with puzzlement and confusion. In addition to not knowing how to pronounce my name, they became hypersensitive and self-conscious in discussing issues related to minorities in the United States because of my race and the power that I possessed as a teacher. The Social Justice Study Group gradually became a place where I found my critical agency: I realized that I was not the only one with these issues. It was very comforting to find such a place. Like all critical educators, we want our students to be critical of the status quo and to be reflective about their practice. Through the bi-weekly gatherings, we addressed our own ideological, pedagogical, and personal struggles to make sense of the world.

Through the readings and sharing of information on teaching material and our own experience, the group became one of the major elements in my first year of teaching. In a sense it became a place where junior faculty met to discuss social issues that impacted us by examining our own ideology and reflecting on our practice, just as we were demanding of our students. It was a group of kindred spirits who were striving to think about social justice issues in education in a safe environment.

After one year of regular meetings, we tried to figure out collectively what could be done on campus to help actualize social justice issues that we saw as lacking. However, I was shocked to see the insecurity of all of our positions—as non-tenured junior faculty. We were rather limited in our ability to bring forth the issues we would like to address outside of our study group. But it was a place where political contestation and ideological struggle began. Retrospectively, the Study Group was a place for me to build a learning community and to understand my position as the only Asian American woman faculty member in the SOE and my obligation as a new member of the community.

Jacque's Story: Rendering the Invisible Visible

For 35 years I traveled as an educational consultant occasionally accepting adjunct and one-year visiting lectureships at 15 colleges and universities. SIUE made16. I knew how to work alone. *Now,* I sought to further practice Paulo Freire's "problem posing: to name, reflect critically and act" (Wink, 2000) by meeting in a newly-formed Social Justice Study Group.

Peter Wilson provided resources; the group established norms for a safe venue in which to discuss social issues such as the damaging effects of feeling marginalized and invisible. Introduced to the documentary, *True Colors*, we reflected and told our own personal stories.

I discussed *True Colors* with my class and introduced "Mr. Cellophane," the song from the musical *Chicago:* "Mr. Cellophane shoulda been my name …'cause you can look right through me, walk right by me and never know I'm there." The class sang, created a choral reading from these lyrics and the students requested, "Let's do it again!" They wrote and talked in small groups about the experiences of feeling marginalized and invisible. One African American student wrote:

I know this feeling.
I know people see me and hear me.
I know I am different and stand out.

My culture
Life and perspective
Is different.

Yet,
Many look at it
As if it is nothing at all.

I met and listened to this student's story knowing that this was the only African American student in my class of 39. At the end of the course in which many of the issues of concern to the Study Group were discussed and debated in my class, I received this note from the same student.

> I have had a long tough battle to get where I am today. I have been told that I wouldn't make it. I have had few shoulders to lean on… I have lost so many friends and seen so many go before their time in the streets. I refused to turn back… I promise not to turn my back. I shall return and give the children hope, success and a way out through education. I am blessed and so shall those I encounter. My involvement spiritually and emotionally is

> beyond words. I kept pushing and involving myself by staying, learning and absorbing. I wrote in my Day Book: *'To teach is to learn. To learn is to understand. To understand is to enhance your life, your knowledge, society and your future as well as others.'* I am learning in this class, I understand and I have enhanced my life as well as everyone who has heard me speak about my passion to educate the discouraged. Please talk to me even when I am no longer in your class!

My involvement in the Study Group better equipped me to handle the class situation of a single minority student among people who were evidently strangers to this student's situation, lifestyle and ambitions. I consider this remarkable note a tribute to the motives, aims and aspirations of our group.

Laurie's Story: Learning how to Teach about Oppression

Helping my students to understand issues of racial oppression is one of the most challenging aspects of my current job. One recent semester, I drew from Peggy McIntosh's (1988) work and began a discussion of race by asking students to come up with ways that whites are privileged. (This exercise had worked well the previous summer.) This group had a hard time creating the white privilege list, so I should have been prepared for their reaction to *American Apartheid* (Sutcliffe, 1998), a video that had also spurred a good discussion in a previous class. The first comment raised after this compelling video about racial inequity was that Jesse Jackson wasn't a good role model for blacks in America because he'd been in financial trouble in the past. I was disappointed: why would this young woman raise that issue after watching the video?Her point had absolutely nothing to do with the movie. Then came other comments: "It's ridiculous for the video to claim that when white people move to the suburbs it has anything to do with race. We move because it's too crowded in the city." When descriptions by one of the three black students in the class, about how badly he is treated whenever he walks into a bank, were repeatedly dismissed by an outspoken group of white students, my frustration peaked. "Don't assume that you know what it's like to be black," I said. "Don't assume that you have any idea what our experience is," the vocal white students said. This group of white students ended up furious with me for not allowing students to have their own opinions, for having an "agenda" about race, for being too opinionated. They complained about me to another professor. Meanwhile, one of the black students wrote to me in a journal that she hoped I'd understand it if she didn't participate when placed in a small group with any of those white students who clearly hated her for her race, and who clearly dismissed her whole life experience.

The Study Group contained people who have lots of experience talking about race. They explained to me how futile it is to cause resistant individuals to get defensive. They gave me another video (*True Colors*), one that does not elicit as much defensiveness as *American Apartheid*, and that's more likely to lead students to question assumptions about race. I read *The Miner's Canary*, and it discussed the need to help poor whites and ethnic minority groups see how they are both discriminated against in our society. Peter told us about Singleton's *Continuum of Racial Consciousness in America*, which illustrates the problems with a color-blind approach to race, and the need to move on beyond that (Singleton, 2001). This all fit in so well with the Issues in Feminism class that I was teaching in which I happened to have assigned students a reading that discusses the problems with taking a gender-blind approach in education.

The study group also fit in well with my life in general, as I shared in the group how a white woman looking at a house for sale across the street from me came over and asked, "this is a mixed neighborhood isn't it?" Her tone told me that her question was not well-intentioned, so I told her yes, but that I found the question very offensive. She angrily explained that she needs to know this kind of thing "when buying property." The Study Group suggested that a more friendly challenge would allow for meaningful discussion, and how my angry reaction just made her more likely to dismiss people like me. And so the Study Group has helped me begin to learn how to talk to people about social justice.

David's Story: Testing Old Ideas and Trying New Ones

I came to SIUE after several years of service as a public school principal and over -20 years of teaching English at a large, culturally diverse, urban high school. SIUE was attractive to me because its mission focused heavily on serving the larger metropolitan area that includes culturally diverse schools and communities. I was initially attracted to the Study Group because I was looking for colleagues who might be able to provide insight into how the university's mission was enacted in its teacher education programs.

What has been of significant value to me is our study of *The Miner's Canary*. The authors helped me gain a deeper understanding of how racism in our society is actually buttressed by limiting any dialogue on race to biological terms, a delimitation that is scientifically invalid. Guinier and Torres present abundant evidence that race is a political and socio-economic category, not a biological one, and that a belief in biological definitions impedes consideration of social, political, and economic injustices that continue to marginalize entire segments of our population.

Our Study Group tackled these matters head-on in our discussions. The members of the group helped me reflect on definitions of race, and led me to reflect on the intractable racist practices and unwritten policies followed in the educational institutions where I had previously worked. These reflections led me to incorporate more discussions and assignment options in my graduate classes that focused on issues related to teaching and learning in culturally diverse classrooms. I asked my students to consider how teachers might actually contribute to institutionally racist practices by the materials they select, by their interaction with their students and/or by failing to question policies and procedures that negatively affect some students because of their socio-economic status, their culture, or their gender. I was initially taken aback by my students' passive responses. I was hoping that they would begin to question their own perceptions of race and how they might influence their professional growth as teachers. Little meaningful discussion took place. Students seemed content to parrot back what they thought I wanted to hear, often using the exact same words I had used. I was pleased to note later, however, that close to half of my students' research papers focused on educational issues related to cultural diversity. For the most part, the papers reflected careful research and reflection. I naturally cannot ascribe this interest to the changes I made in the course content, but the increase over the previous semester was noteworthy.

In sum, the Study Group has been a welcome forum. The discussions have allowed each participant to raise questions and test old ideas in a trusting and helpful environment. It has certainly provided me with new resources that have enhanced the content of the courses I teach.

Barbara's Story: Disrupting Illusions of Harmony

Although I have taught in three institutions prior to SIUE, I have had few opportunities to work closely with culturally diverse students. When I learned of the Study Group forming, I realized this might be the way to open my mind to other cultures, question my teaching methods, and make changes in my views and practices. In the Study Group we discussed the possibility that many black students feel isolated in the SOE. I decided to investigate.

The elementary education program groups students into cohorts for their entire instructional program on campus and in the field. Cohort groups tend to be cohesive and collegial since they share the same experiences and activities, and I thought my group would not be an exception. I decided to interview the only two black students to find out if my assumptions were accurate.

Violet, an extremely quiet student, seldom talked in class. I soon realized she used this façade to protect herself. She explained that peers intentionally snubbed her, thought of her as inferior, and ignored her ideas. She actually dreaded coming to our class because she was "stuck" with this group for the entire program, remarking that only a handful of her peers are friendly. Violet felt totally alienated in our cohort and often wondered why she transferred to SIUE. She had felt very much a part of her previous college experience, but transferred because of the strengths of SIUE's elementary education program. The only saving element was that she was not alone. She had Tammy's support.

Tammy's bubbly personality hid her disappointment with the class and with treatment by her peers. She shared coping strategies her parents taught her – to put on a false happy front, to realize that she may be treated unfairly, and to take it in stride. Tammy has set long-term goals and does not let comments by peers affect her.

Talking with these students also informed me of unsettling situations in their field experiences. When in their urban school setting, Violet and Tammy were cognizant of the discord of fellow white students. They overheard comments like, "every time I leave this school, I feel like I need to take a bath." When assigned to group projects within their school, some peers found ways to avoid working with Violet and Tammy. In their rural school setting, different prejudices surfaced. Elementary students shunned Violet and Tammy, turning their chairs away from them as they taught. Although they have reported changing students' opinions, isolated events still caused them to question their decisions to become teachers.

How could I have been so naïve? The answer can be found in *A White Teacher Talks about Race* (Landsman, 2001). Although raised in a lower-middle class neighborhood on the fringes of a Hispanic neighborhood, I lived in a "white power world," attending parochial schools and living comfortably. This could be why I could not see what my students were experiencing; I have not lived what they deal with everyday.

I thought about what I can personally do to "fix" this unfairness. These thoughts brought to mind what Landsman tells her readers:

> It will come when we have lived with each other side by side, when we have heard each other's stories... We will achieve a day of freedom from racism when whites acknowledge the day-to-day privileges they and their children receive simply because of the color of their skin. (p. 161-162)

By listening to the stories of my students, I am making a start.

Conclusion: Certain Ends and Sure Beginnings

Passing Time
Maya Angelou

Your skin like dawn
Mine like musk
One paints the beginning
of a certain end.
The other, the end of a
sure beginning.

Drawn by common concerns and shared commitments to social justice, the journeys of five teacher educators and an external facilitator converged in February 2002. Evidence of our collaboration includes new instructional materials, revised syllabi, growing collegial relationships, self-reports of personal development and changes in ourselves and our students, and this chapter. The Study Group supported us as we examined and refined our efforts to address racism with our students. Influencing dynamics outside of the classroom was more difficult, however. The informal, ad hoc nature of the Study Group made it a safe place for non-tenured faculty, but the group had no structural means of influencing university policies and practices. In contrast, the facilitator is currently engaged in a similar social justice project at another university. In this instance, Peter feels that institutional funding and an explicit mandate to work with the College of Education NCATE Committee greatly increases the potential of influencing institutional policy and practice.

As we complete this manuscript in June 2003, we encounter change and continuity, endings and beginnings. The spring semester is over, and the summer term begins. The only tenured member of the group has retired. Two new colleagues have joined us. The grant project that brought Peter to SIUE has ended. One group member is an adjunct faculty member who faces constant uncertainty. Another participant was not recommended for tenure and must leave the university. The study group has agreed to meet again in the fall, but our future is unsure. We continue our journey through uncharted terrain, from understanding to advocacy to action, uncertain if this is "the beginning of a certain end" or "the end of a sure beginning."

References

Cochran-Smith, M. (1997). Knowledge, skills and experiences for teaching culturally diverse learners: A perspective for practicing teachers. In J. J. Irvine (Ed.), *Critical knowledge for diverse teachers and learners* (pp. 27-87). Washington, D.C.: American Association of Colleges for Teacher Education.

Delpit, L., & Kilgour, J. (Eds.). (2002). *The skin that we speak: Thoughts on language and culture in the classroom*. New York: The New Press.

Fine, M., Anand, B., Hancock, M., Jordan, C., & Sherman, D. (1998). *Off Track: Classroom privilege for all*. New York: Teachers College Press.

Guinier, L., & Torres, G. (2002). *The miner's canary*. Cambridge, MA: Harvard University Press.

Kozol, J. (1991). *Savage inequalities: Children in America's schools*. New York: Crown Publications.

Landsman, J. (2001). *A white teacher talks about race*. Lanham, MD: The Scarecrow Press.

McIntosh, P. (1989, July-August). White privilege: Unpacking the invisible knapsack. *Peace and Freedom*, pp. 10-12. Wellesley, MA: National Seed Project, Wellesley College Center for Research on Women.

Murrell, P.C. (2000). Community teachers: A conceptual framework for preparing exemplary urban teachers. *The Journal of Negro Education, 69*(4), 338-348.

olsson, j. (1997). *Detour-spotting for white anti-racists*. Questa, NM: cultural bridges.

Sawyer, D. (Anchor), (1991, September 26). True colors: Racial bias in American cities – focus on St. Louis [Television broadcast]. *ABC News Prime Time Live*. New York: American Broadcasting Company.

Singleton, G. (2001). *Beyond diversity: A strategy for de-institutionalizing racism and improving student achievement*. San Francisco: Pacific Educational Group.

Sutcliffe, K. (Producer). (1998). *American apartheid* [Television broadcast]. London: British Broadcasting Corporation.

Wah, L. M. (Producer/Director), & Hunter, M. (Co-Producer). (1994). *The color of fear* [Videorecording]. Oakland, CA: Stir-Fry Productions.

Wink, J. (2000). *Critical pedagogy: Notes from the real world.* New York: Addison Wesley Longman.

Peter Wilson is the President of Educational Equity Consultants, LLC. **Carol Huang** is an Assistant Professor at the City College of New York. **Sharon Shockley Lee** is a Professor of Education at Lincoln University of Missouri. **David DeWeese**, **Barbara O'Donnell**, **Laurel Puchner** and **Jacque Wuertenberg** are at the School of Education, Southern Illinois University Edwardsville.

Chapter 18

Breaking the Silence: Innovative Approaches for Promoting Dialogue About Diversity Issues Within a Communication Disorders Department

Maria Diana Gonzales and Jane A. Baran

This chapter addresses innovative approaches implemented by the authors as they embarked on a mentor/mentee relationship and a collegial effort to create a departmental environment that was multiculturally inclusive. The context in which these efforts were initiated and how these contexts changed over time are addressed, as are personal perspectives of the authors as to why they chose to pursue these endeavors. Also addressed are their perceptions of the barriers and challenges they faced and the successes and rewards they achieved as a result of their collegial relationship.

Importance of Infusing Diversity Issues within a Communication Disorders Program

The changing national demographics of the United States population underscore the need for professionals within the human services field to be prepared to work with an increasingly pluralistic American society. One only has to view the mass media to recognize that the landscape of America is changing dramatically. Current projections suggest that by 2050 the number of Americans who will fall into racial classifications other than "White" will bypass that of the "White" classification (Day, 1996). Hence, in the future there will be an even greater need for educators to be able to prepare a workforce that is capable of working with individuals who do not share a common racial and/or ethnic identity.

The American Speech-Language-Hearing Association (ASHA) has for some time recognized the importance of preparing speech-language pathologists and audiologists to work with a diverse clientele. It began its efforts to address this need in the late 1960s, first by establishing an Office of Multicultural Affairs, and later by appointing a number of committees, task forces, and boards that were charged with various multicultural initiatives. In addition, it has incorporated language into many of its cardinal documents that point to the importance of preparing professionals to work with individuals from diverse cultural and linguistic communities (ASHA, 1983; 1985; 1991; 2002; 2004). Of particular relevance to the present discussion are a number of documents that address the need for graduate students to gain competence in working with diverse populations. In the ASHA Standards for the Accreditation of Academic Programs promulgated by the Council of Academic Accreditation, one of the relevant standards is stated as follows: "academic and clinical education reflects…the diversity of the society" (3.2) (Council of Professional Standards, 2000). In the past, many academic programs have attempted to address this standard by having faculty infuse information about different cultural and/or linguistic groups into their courses, whereas other programs have attempted to meet this standard by offering a required course on multicultural and/or multilinguistic issues. However, these efforts have traditionally been limited to 1) the provision of demographic data specifying the prevalence of different disorders among various racial and ethnic groups, and/or 2) descriptions of linguistic "differences" that might be interpreted as "disorders" by professionals and students unfamiliar with the language patterns of diverse linguistic communities. Although this type of information may have provided students with some knowledge that may have assisted them in their work with culturally and linguistically diverse clients, it fell short of equipping them with the skills needed to be able to communicate and work effectively with individuals from diverse populations. This shortcoming was due to the fact that the "differences" that are commonly encountered when working and interacting with individuals from diverse backgrounds go well beyond simple variations in linguistic conventions to contrasts in learning styles, discourse conventions, and other experientially-based differences, which are often culturally-determined (Westby, 1994).

The need to move beyond the type of academic preparation that has typically been the standard in the professions of audiology and speech-language pathology is alluded to in a recent position paper that is available on-line from the ASHA website (http://www.asha.org/about/academia/changing.htm). In the paper, "In Responding to the Changing Needs of Speech-Language Pathology and Audiology Students in the 21st Century" (ASHA, 2004), the authors identify nine workplace skills that graduate students need to acquire to be successful in their professional lives. Figuring prominently is the skill of "managing diversity." The authors suggest that the person who is able to manage diversity is the one who welcomes different personal interaction styles, recognizes and acknowledges the contributions of all staff members, and is able to work with a diverse clientele by taking into account cultural differences when providing clinical services. In this document, the authors appear to be pointing to the importance of the role that faculty play, or should play, in helping students to become "culturally competent." Students clearly need to develop a competence that goes well beyond the simple recognition of the linguistic or language differences that might exist among the clients they will serve, to an understanding and appreciation of the unique personal experiences and beliefs of their clients that are likely to be culturally-shaped and central to each individual's social identity. Given the changing demographics and the need for faculty in all disciplines, especially those involved in the human service areas to assist students in becoming "culturally competent," it is essential that we begin to explore alternative methods of providing opportunities for students to achieve this type of competence.

This chapter describes the innovative approaches implemented by the authors as they embarked on a collegial effort to create a departmental environment that was multiculturally inclusive within a Communication Disorders program. Although the focus of this chapter will be on activities specifically developed for and implemented within a Communication Disorders department, many of the activities reported and the personal experiences related will have an application to a broader array of disciplinary fields.

The Development of a Collegial Relationship to Enact Programmatic Change

While it is well-documented that most junior faculty face a variety of stressors in the academy, non-majority faculty members face many additional complicated and usually invisible stressors, such as "chilly" academic climates, a "solo effect," excessive committee assignments, huge student demands, the internalization of failures, and the undervaluing of scholarship on minority issues (Moody, 2001a; 2001b). The result of these additional stressors on non-majority faculty usually causes increased loneliness and personal and intellectual isolation (Alexander-Snow & Johnson, 1999; Moody, 2001a; 2001b). In addition, non-majority faculty members may sense that majority students are more likely to question their intellectual authority (Moody, 2001b), which in turn adds to the other stressors they already face.

Reflections by Maria Diana Gonzales

Even though I was aware of the aforementioned facts, I was unprepared for my experiences as a non-majority faculty member. As a Latina faculty member with a recently acquired doctoral degree in speech-language pathology, I was so overwhelmed with my duties as an assistant professor at a Research I institution that I experienced extreme isolation and loneliness. As a result, I found that I began to withdraw emotionally and psychologically from my peers.

My initial student evaluations after teaching a graduate course on language disorders for the first time were not impressive. Some of the students commented that too much time was spent in addressing diversity issues, such as bilingual theory on assessment and intervention. I was bewildered and confounded by these observations! Since this was my area of expertise, I could not understand why the students were not as passionate about the topic as I was. In addition, it was not clear why my efforts to address cultural and linguistic diversity met with such resistance since the ASHA standards mandated that graduate students in speech-language pathology and audiology be equipped with the tools they need to manage diversity (Council of Professional Standards, 2000).

In an attempt to help me overcome the obstacles I faced, the chair of my department and the dean of our school recommended that I work with a mentor, and they assigned the second author of this chapter to take on this role. Jane A. Baran is a successful senior faculty member with a proven track record of teaching effectiveness within the Department of Communication Disorders at the University of Massachusetts Amherst.

Reflections by Jane A. Baran

When approached by the chair of the department to serve as a mentor for Dr. Gonzales, I had a number of concerns, questions, and reservations: 1) Was I qualified to be a mentor? As mentioned earlier, I did have a history of positive evaluations of teaching effectiveness, but I had no formal training in pedagogy. I worried that I might not be qualified to be such a mentor and I also wondered why the chair had asked me as opposed to another faculty member who might be teaching in an area more closely aligned with Dr. Gonzales' area. 2) What were the expectations of the administration for this mentoring activity and how would my performance as a mentor be judged? Because the department had no formal mentoring program in place, there were no internal resources to turn to for guidance, suggestions, and support. Also, not having had a "teaching" mentor as either a doctoral student or a junior faculty member, I did not even have a role model from my past to follow. 3) Did Dr. Gonzales want to enter into a mentor/mentee relationship, or was this something that was being required of her? What was her level of commitment to this relationship? Was she comfortable with my being assigned to her as her mentor? 4)

Where do we start, and what specific types of activities would make sense for the two of us to undertake?

The Evolution of Our Mentor/Mentee Relationship

Before embarking on the mentor/mentee relationship, we met to discuss our expectations of the relationship. We agreed to enter the mentor/mentee relationship only if it was likely that the relationship would be mutually beneficial and if each of us would take an active role in determining which activities would benefit our careers.

Initially, the primary focus of the mentor/mentee relationship was to focus on increasing teaching effectiveness by concentrating on teaching pedagogy. For assistance in this area, we contacted the staff of the Center for Teaching (CFT) at the University of Massachusetts Amherst and arranged monthly meetings with them. The primary purpose of these meetings was for the two of us to participate in guided discussions designed to explore teaching practices in an effort to increase teaching effectiveness since it is well documented that many faculty members enter the academy without any formal coursework in educational pedagogy (Stanley, 2000). During one of the monthly meetings, it became obvious to us that we, as well as our colleagues (i.e., other faculty within the department) were not effectively providing the foundation for student learning of the multicultural issues that were being presented in our classes. Many, if not most, of our students were not "prepared" to handle material about bilingual assessment and intervention. Infusion of diversity issues such as second language acquisition had to be much more inclusive. As a result, we embarked on a collegial relationship to improve overall teaching effectiveness as well as to enact programmatic change for the infusion of diversity issues within the department.

While both of us were motivated to engage in organizational practices that would support effective student learning about multicultural issues, we were unsure of how we should proceed. As a result of our participation in the monthly teaching effectiveness meetings with staff from the CFT, we were invited to submit a proposal to participate in a unique program that was offered through the center entitled, "Teaching and Learning in the Diverse Classroom" (Ouellett, 1999-2000). Participation in this unique program provided us with various tools to engage in departmental practices that supported effective teaching and student learning.

Challenges to be Considered When Enacting Departmental Change

Enacting programmatic change can be problematic if everyone within the department or organization is not invested in the process. Some of the challenges that we tackled as we embarked on our project included: 1) a lack of an appreciation of the dynamics of diversity in the teaching-learning process (Marchesani & Adams, 1992); 2) a lack of recognition that teaching primarily within the cognitive domain as defined in Bloom's Taxonomy (Lane, 2001) was ineffective when addressing diversity issues; 3) limited or no engagement of students and faculty in self-reflection activities to increase comprehension as to how experiences can shape an individual's view of the world; and 4) the lack of full faculty commitment to the infusion of diversity into the curriculum and the absence of consensus among the faculty as to who should be responsible for these activities. We realized that programmatic change, if it were to be successful, needed to occur without alienating any of the department's faculty or students; therefore, we had to implement strategies that were "inclusive of diversity issues."

The first challenge we faced as we undertook our efforts was how to educate ourselves about diversity dynamics in the teaching-learning process. We had to "understand and truly know" where the students and faculty were in terms of their "monocultural" versus "multicultural" socialization before embarking on programmatic change. Individuals fall along a continuum in terms of their socialization—some have a monocultural socialization, while others have a multicultural socialization. We needed to determine whether the students and faculty of the department came from a dominant cultural perspective or a multicultural perspective. Students and faculty socialized from a dominant cultural perspective might experience a sense of "cultural shock" when exposed to multicultural issues. On the other hand, non-majority students and faculty might experience a sense of alienation and/or isolation as multicultural issues are infused into the program (Marchesani & Adams, 1992). In terms of the course content that we cover, we needed to ask ourselves, "What is the content that we teach and is it inclusive?" "Have we included diverse voices and perspectives when teaching our course content, or have we strictly adhered to a monocultural perspective?" In addition, we had to understand our own socialization and how it impacted our teaching styles. In order to have a more inclusive curriculum and/or classroom, we had to implement a multicultural and inclusive approach to teaching and learning.

The second challenge we faced was recognizing the fact that continuing to teach primarily within the cognitive domain as defined in Bloom's Taxonomy was ineffective when addressing diversity issues. When infusing the curriculum with diversity issues, the affective domain as well as the cognitive domain needs to be accessed within each student if success is to be achieved and the values that are being espoused are to be integrated into the student's value and belief system. The affective domain relates to emotions, attitudes, appreciations, and values of the individual, which are manifested behaviorally as awareness, interest, attention, concern, and responsibility (Lane, 2001), all of which are essential to the professions of speech-language pathology and audiology. Without adequate attention to the affective domain, students may withdraw "emotionally" from discussions and exploration of diversity issues as they relate to the management of individuals exhibiting communication disorders, especially if the individual students within the classroom have not had the opportunity to examine their own beliefs and values about these issues.

A third challenge that we tackled was the initiation and/or engagement of the students and faculty in the practice of this life-long journey of self-reflection. Earlier we had mentioned that as educators, we had to "know" ourselves, and that meant understanding our own belief systems and biases. Before infusing our classes with multicultural issues, it became essential that we examined our own belief systems. We realized that this self-examination would be a life-long and dynamic process, one that would be needed if we were to ensure culturally inclusive teaching. Inclusiveness does not mean having a few students from culturally and linguistically diverse populations in the classroom. It is the recognition that *everyone, whether one is from a majority or non-majority culture,* has individual and deep personal differences based on culture, language background, gender, class, religious background, and learning style. Diversity awareness training, if is it to be effective, does not mean addressing only those issues that pertain to minority groups, but also diversity issues as they relate to the communication styles, the learning preferences, and the beliefs and values of *all* of the participants in the class or group. Diversity awareness occurs incrementally in each of us. All of us, teachers and students alike, have been socialized differently and will progress in our awareness of diversity at different levels. Cultural awareness cannot be forced; however, with consistent and appropriate exposure to these issues, sensitivity and competence will increase proportionately. Students are more likely to comprehend and internalize factual information about the behaviors, values, and responses to therapeutic intervention exhibited by culturally and linguistically diverse populations if they have had an opportunity to reflect on their own beliefs about these issues. Students as well as faculty members have to engage in self-reflection to understand how their socialization impacts service delivery and decision making (Marchesani & Adams, 1992).

Love (1999) recommends that faculty reflect on their own "emotional triggers" before engaging their students and other faculty in this endeavor. All of us have certain "emotional triggers" that create stress and anxiety when addressed in class. An emotional trigger may be a behavior that a particular student engages in, or it may be a particular comment or reference made by an individual. We also realized that behaviors or comments exhibited or offered by faculty within the classroom may trigger emotions within one or more of the students in the class. Before infusing the curriculum with diversity awareness, we had to recognize and understand our own "emotional triggers" and develop the ability to recognize those personal behaviors that we might exhibit in our classrooms that could trigger such responses in our students. Here we found a specific suggestion offered by Love to be useful. She suggests that individuals interested in exploring their personal emotional triggers should begin by developing a chart that lists each "emotional trigger" and one's typical response to each trigger. Next, the individuals should reflect upon each trigger and their typical responses to determine what the *desired* response would be. Once identified, these desired responses can be substituted for the typical responses so that learning takes place in the classroom and the situation does not become uncomfortable for either the faculty or the students. As faculty, identification of our emotional triggers is necessary so that when they are triggered in the classroom, we can deal with them appropriately.

The fourth challenge we faced was gaining faculty acceptance for the implementation of diversity issues within the department. Initially, some of the faculty members were very skeptical of our efforts. Some individuals hinted that we were asking for trouble and were initiating teacher-student conflicts by engaging in dialogues about these issues. We found that it was more effective to begin these diversity dialogues with faculty who already had some investment in promoting inclusiveness and hoped that other faculty would join in. In addition, majority and non-majority faculty members had to acknowledge and embrace the concept that we *all* shared the responsibility of exposing students to these issues. Addressing these issues in only *one* course or by only *one* faculty member in multiple courses is not an effective strategy for promoting cultural competence. Those faculty who did not join in initially were eventually drawn in by the very students who had participated in our attempts to promote dialogues about diversity. These students had come to appreciate the fact that if they were to develop "cultural competence," *they* had the responsibility of asking questions about culturally and linguistically diverse populations in *all* of the content courses taught within the department. They were no longer satisfied with having only a few of us address these issues.

Effective Approaches in Promoting Dialogue about Diversity Issues

The following is a discussion of some of the approaches that we found to be useful in our effort to promote dialogue about diversity issues within our department. We accessed multiple points of entry into the curriculum in a variety of different formats to promote engagement of the students and faculty. We recognized that these issues should not be addressed in one specific class and certainly should not be implemented by only one faculty member. The responsibility for exposing students to diversity issues and ensuring that they progress towards cultural competence needed to be shared by everyone, including students, administrators, and majority and non-majority faculty members. Therefore, it was important to get the entire faculty invested in the process.

We attempted to infuse multicultural issues into as many of our own classes as possible throughout the year. In addition, we provided faculty within the department with references about diversity issues within their content areas to encourage them to start the dialogue about these issues within their courses. During an introductory course in communication disorders, students were provided with the definitions for basic terminology such as racism, discrimination, culture, and culturally and linguistically diverse populations in order to give them the basic foundation to begin dialogues about diversity issues. Beverly Daniel Tatum's book, *"Why are All the Black Kids Sitting Together in the Cafeteria?"* (1997) was an excellent reference tool in this regard. In addition, we introduced these issues into upper division undergraduate and graduate courses to better prepare students to manage diversity as they provided audiology and speech-language pathology services. Targeting the students' affective domain became a priority and was accomplished by addressing societal issues and their impact on health access disparities across groups. In addition, students electing to enroll in a multicultural course that was taught by the first author were exposed in greater depth to these issues while also addressing the differentiation between language differences and language disorders and the topic of racial identity development (Tatum, 1992; 1997).

Another early entry point into the curriculum was our co-teaching of a separate two-hour workshop for graduate students. Through this venue the students had an opportunity to observe two inter-ethnic faculty members as they engaged in dialogue about diversity issues. During the workshop, the students participated in a social identities exercise that allowed them to explore the impact of group memberships in a diverse society. The students engaged in the "Multiple Identities Exercise" developed by Fair Teach at the University of

Michigan at Ann Arbor (L. Sfeir-Younis & H. Weingarten, personal communication, 1992). Small and large group discussions about diverse group memberships were held. These activities were followed by the viewing of a video entitled, "The Importance of Culture in Building Therapeutic Relationships" (University of Arizona, 1999) that addressed different ethnic groups and how the level of acculturation is a vital consideration for health care providers when working with individuals from different ethnic and cultural backgrounds. After viewing the video, the students were asked to discuss the values and characteristics of four ethnic groups in the United States (Euro Americans, Hispanic Americans, Asian Americans, and Native Americans). As an outgrowth of their discussions, the students decided that these groupings were "stereotypical" and although useful at some level in helping them to understand potential reactions to their intervention efforts that might be culturally-based, they could not be used to categorize and/or predict the reactions of all individuals within a particular group. Based on the ensuing discussion, the students recognized how culture and level of acculturation affects daily service delivery decisions.

In addition to the two-hour workshop, the authors co-taught a diversity awareness session in an undergraduate class. Again, the primary goal was to model both a majority and a non-majority faculty member dialoguing about diversity issues. We began the session with a discussion of meningitis as an etiological basis of hearing loss and then shared data with the students that documented disparities in the prevalence rates for hearing loss associated with this disorder across different ethnic groups (Nuru, 1993). The students then viewed segments of a video entitled, "Race, Class, and Health: Higher Education, Public Health and Community Partners Debate the Root Causes and Elimination of Health Disparities" (Association of American Colleges and Universities, 2000). The speakers in this video of a live satellite teleconference took a multidisciplinary approach to exploring the racial legacies and social determinants shaping the health of the nation's people. The goal of the video was to address how racial minorities and people who live in poverty are more likely to be burdened by such factors as substandard housing, poverty, pollution, and public policy decisions that contribute to health risks. After viewing the tape, the students engaged in small and large group discussions to explore possible explanations for the disparities that existed in meningitis rates across groups. Clearly much more "learning" occurred in this context than one in which the instructor would have simply presented information about the rates of meningitis and other potential causes of hearing loss across ethnic groups. Many of the students approached us after class to express their thanks, and their evaluations of the experience were very positive. In fact, more than one student indicated on course evaluations completed at the end of the semester that this particular class was the "thing that they liked most about the course."

Another entry point into the curriculum included inviting Dr. Beverly Daniel Tatum to hold separate dialogues about diversity issues with faculty and students. This experience provided the faculty and the students with the opportunity to observe and interact with an expert on social justice issues. Following her presentation, Dr. Tatum stated that she was impressed with the students' comprehension of the issues and their ability to engage in dialogue openly and freely. This commentary offered some independent testimony to the success of our efforts—at least at some rudimentary level—to help develop an inclusive, open, and safe environment where our students felt comfortable conversing about diversity issues.

Positive Outcomes of Collegial Relationships between Senior and Junior Faculty Members

The authors shared many successes and rewards and recognized the value of a collegial relationship in fostering and enhancing efforts to incorporate diversity within a curriculum as a result of embarking on this endeavor. Some of those successes included a strengthening of the relationship between a senior majority and junior non-majority faculty member that extended beyond the infusion of diversity issues into a curriculum. Co-teaching classes with a Caucasian senior faculty member allowed the junior faculty, who was from a non-majority background, to experience validation by the majority students. Furthermore, the senior faculty experienced greater acceptance by the non-majority students when addressing diversity issues in the classroom, which in turn lead to an enhanced comfort level when addressing these topics. A second outcome of the experience was that the student evaluations of the junior faculty member's teaching effectiveness increased substantially. In fact, she was nominated by her students for a campus-wide Distinguished Teaching Award at the University of Massachusetts Amherst in 1999. A third outcome, which extended the collaboration beyond teaching into the area of scholarship, was the co-authorship and presentation of a paper on this topic at a national conference, as well as the co-writing of this chapter.

A final and important outcome of the collegial relationship was the authors' ability to model the effectiveness of a mentor/mentee relationship between a majority and non-majority faculty member to students, faculty, and administrators. Others recognized that the inter-ethnic mentor/mentee relationship did not result in either of the faculty members "losing" part of her own cultural or racial identity in the process. Instead they learned from each other and flourished individually as a result of embracing their differences.

Reflections by Maria Diana Gonzales

The differences noted in my student teaching evaluations after participating in the mentor/mentee relationship and the diversity fellowship program were amazing. Student evaluations of my teaching effectiveness increased tremendously! Even though I had engaged in some minor changes in pedagogy, I felt that my overall teaching skills had not changed drastically. The changes in teaching pedagogy were subtle. However, the positive outcomes far exceeded my wildest expectations. By taking the time to provide students, faculty, and administrators with the necessary foundation to understand and embrace diversity, I sensed less resistance to multicultural issues. Furthermore, I found I did not experience the isolation and loneliness that I had experienced initially.

As a result of the excellent mentoring I received from Dr. Baran, I was awarded tenure and promoted to associate professor in 2003, exactly six years after earning my doctoral degree in speech-language pathology. I continue to treasure and value the mentor/mentee relationship that I have with Dr. Jane Baran even though I chose to leave the University of Massachusetts Amherst when I accepted a position with Texas State University-San Marcos. However, our collegial relationship continues to grow and develop beyond any of my original expectations.

Reflections by Jane A. Baran

I believe that Dr. Gonzales and I have become more effective teachers as a result of our mentoring relationship and participation in the diversity fellowship, and that our students (both those who were in our classes at the time of our fellowship award, as well as those who we have encountered in our classes since the time of our initial collaboration as faculty in our efforts to explore "best practices" in teaching) have benefited tremendously from what we have learned. More importantly, however, I believe that our students have become more effective "learners" and individuals who recognize, accept, and celebrate diversity. I have also come to realize through this experience that "ineffective" teaching evaluations of non-majority junior faculty may not be an indication of their lack of ability or experience, but rather a lack of understanding of the non-majority teacher's cultural background by the students.

I have grown tremendously both as a teacher and as a person as a direct outgrowth of my participation in this relationship with Dr. Gonzales. Although I initially entered this mentor/mentee relationship with many reservations, these concerns were quickly dispelled as Dr. Gonzales and I formed a truly "interdependent" relationship. There were many times over the course of our collaboration when I, the "mentor," became the "mentee." So much was gained from these experiences that I would not hesitate to "volunteer" to serve as a mentor for another junior colleague in the future.

Conclusion/Summary

Many valuable lessons were learned as a result of our collaboration in the mentor/mentee relationship and the diversity project. We recognized the importance of valuing each other's differences as we proceeded with our efforts to infuse the curriculum with diversity issues. We also came to recognize the importance of fostering institutional support for faculty who undertake this type of endeavor. We knew that we had university support; however, we needed to foster departmental and faculty support. Using different entry points into the curriculum and formats for sharing information allowed us to achieve the support of the faculty and students within our department.

We also learned the importance of accessing an individual's affective as well as cognitive domains when addressing multicultural issues. Cultural competence can only be achieved if students and faculty are exposed to dialogues about diversity issues in effective ways that tap into both the emotional and cognitive foundations that underlie learning.

Moreover, we learned that if the goal of one's program is to promote dialogue about diversity issues between faculty and students, then it is imperative that faculty members model skilled dialogue that includes respect, reciprocity, and responsiveness. After exposure to this type of dialogue between the two authors of this chapter, students within the Department of Communication Disorders at the University of Massachusetts Amherst were more effective in addressing these issues in the classroom, within the university community, and hopefully within their personal lives. They were also better "prepared" to address the multicultural issues that are commonly encountered within the professions of speech-language pathology and audiology.

Our efforts to develop a more inclusive curriculum additionally resulted in the understanding that the responsibility for exposing students to diversity issues should be shared by everyone within the program, including faculty and students. Faculty who were initially somewhat resistant to our efforts were eventually drawn in by the very students who had participated in our program to promote dialogues about diversity. As a result of their growing "cultural competence," students began asking the "right" questions in class, and the very same faculty who had been initially reluctant to address these issues were now being engaged in these dialogues by their students.

Finally, our experiences taught us that what might appear to be "ineffective" teaching evaluations of junior faculty, especially non-majority faculty, may not be indications of their lack of ability or experience, but rather indicators of a resistance to, or a lack of an appreciation of, cultural differences on the part of the students, faculty, and administrators, many of whom are from the majority culture. Non-majority faculty are often judged negatively by students due to a lack of understanding of cultural differences. In order to ensure more culturally inclusive departments, majority faculty and administrators need to take this fact into consideration when evaluating non-majority faculty, otherwise non-majority faculty may be denied tenure, promotion, or merit through no fault of their own (Gappa & MacDermid, 1997).

Closing Comments

To conclude, we would like to reaffirm our belief that embarking on the mentor/mentee relationship described in this chapter was mutually beneficial for us on a number of levels. It enabled each of us, both the "mentor" and the "mentee," to become more effective teachers, and it laid the foundation for collaboration between the two of us that extended beyond the initial "teaching" focus to one that also addressed scholarly activities. Although there clearly was an investment of time and energy for both of us, the rewards that we received as a result of our collaborations far outweighed the "costs" endured by either of us. As a result of our endeavors and extremely positive experiences, we are now strong advocates for the participation of *all* junior faculty members in a mentor/mentee relationship. The development of these mutually beneficial collegial relationships should be an option, if not a requirement, for all faculty. We found this experience to be so rewarding that neither of us would hesitate to become a mentor for other junior colleagues. In fact, we look forward to participating in such relationships in the future.

References

Alexander-Snow, M., & Johnson, B. J. (1999). Perspectives from faculty of color. In R. J. Menges & Associates (Eds.), *Faculty in new jobs: A guide to settling in, becoming established, and building institutional support* (pp. 89-117). San Francisco: Jossey-Bass.

American Speech-Language-Hearing Association. (1983). Social dialects: A position paper. *ASHA 25*(1), 23-24.

American Speech-Language-Hearing Association. (1985). Clinical management of communicatively handicapped minority language populations. *ASHA 27*(6), 29-32.

American Speech-Language-Hearing Association. (1991). Multicultural action agenda 2000. *ASHA 33*(5), 39-41.

American Speech-Language-Hearing Association. (2002). *Communication facts: Incidence and prevalence of communication disorders and hearing loss in children-2002 edition.* Retrieved March 1, 2004, from http://www.professional.asha.org/resources/factsheets

American Speech-Language-Hearing Association. (2004). *Responding to the changing needs of speech-language pathology and audiology students in the 21st century.* Retrieved March 24, 2004, from http://www.asha.org/about/academia/changing.htm

Association of American Colleges and Universities and the National Association of County and City Health Officials in Association with the George Washington University and Public Broadcasting Service (Producers). (2000). *Race, class and health: Higher education, public health and community partners debate the root causes and elimination of health disparities* [Live Satellite Teleconference]. Washington, DC: Public Broadcasting Service.

Council on Professional Standards in Speech-Language Pathology and Audiology of the American Speech-Language-Hearing Association. (2000). *Background information for the standards and implementation for the certificate of clinical competence in speech-language pathology.* Rockville, MD: American Speech-Language-Hearing Association.

Day, J. C. (1996). *Population projections of the United States by age, sex, race, and Hispanic origin: 1995 to 2050* (U.S. Bureau of the Census, Current Population Reports, pp. 25-1130). Washington, DC: U. S. Government Printing Office.

Gappa, J. M., & MacDermid, S. M. (Eds.). (1997). *Work, family, and the faculty career. New pathways: Faculty career and employment for the 21st century: Inquiry #8.* Washington, DC: American Association for Higher Education.

Lane, C. (2001). *Bloom's taxonomy.* In Distance learning resource network's technology resource guide. Retrieved February 21, 2003, from http://www.dlrn.org/library/dl/guide4.html

Love, B. J. (1999, September). *Issues of diversity and social justice in the classroom.* Paper presented to the 1999-2000 Teaching and Learning in the Diverse Classroom Faculty and TA Fellow Program. Center for Teaching, University of Massachusetts Amherst.

Marchesani, L. S., & Adams, M. (1992). Dynamics of diversity in the teaching-learning process: A faculty development model for analysis and action. In M. Adams (Ed.), *Promoting diversity in college classrooms: Innovative responses for the curriculum, faculty, and institutions* (pp. 9-18). New Directions for Teaching and Learning, No. 52. San Francisco: Jossey-Bass.

Moody, J. (2001a). Junior faculty: Job stresses and how to cope with them. In J. Moody (Ed.), *Demystifying the profession: Helping junior faculty succeed* (pp. 11-22). CT: University of New Haven Press.

Moody, J (2001b). Helping junior faculty, especially non-majority newcomers, thrive. In J. Moody (Ed.), *Demystifying the profession: Helping junior faculty succeed* (pp. 23-25). CT: University of New Haven Press.

Nuru, N. (1993). Multicultural aspects of deafness. In D. Battle (Ed.), *Communication disorders in multicultural populations* (pp. 287-305). Boston: Butterworth-Heinemann.

Ouellett, M. L. (1999-2000). *Teaching and learning in the diverse classroom: A faculty and teaching assistant partnership project.* Center for Teaching, University of Massachusetts Amherst.

Stanley, C. A. (2000). Factors that contribute to the teaching development of faculty development center clientele: A case study of ten university professors. *Journal of Staff, Program, and Organization Development 17*(3), 155-169.

Tatum, B. D. (1992). Talking about race, learning about racism: The application of racial identity development theory in the classroom. *Harvard Educational Review 62*(1), 1-24.

Tatum, B. D. (1997). *Why are all the Black kids sitting together in the cafeteria?* New York: Basic Books.

University of Arizona, National Center for Neurogenic Communication Disorders. (1999). *Understanding cultural diversity: The importance of culture in building therapeutic relationships* [Video]. Tucson: National Center for Neurogenic Communication Disorders, University of Arizona.

Westby, C. E. (1994). Multicultural issues. In J. B. Tomblin, L. H. Morris, & D. C. Spriestersbach (Eds.), *Diagnosis in speech-language pathology* (pp. 29-51). San Diego, CA: Singular Publishing Group.

Maria Diana Gonzales, Ph.D., is an associate professor in the Department of Communication Disorders at Texas Sate University-San Marcos.
Jane A. Baran, Ph.D., is a professor in the Department of Communication Disorders at the University of Massachusetts Amherst.

Chapter 19

Transforming Higher Education Institutions Using Multicultural Organizational Development: A Case Study of a Large Northeastern University

Linda S. Marchesani and Bailey W. Jackson

This chapter focuses on the efforts being made by the University of Massachusetts Amherst (Umass Amherst), a large northeastern research based, land grant institution, to utilize a Multicultural Organizational Development (MCOD) approach to effect systemic change based on issues of community, diversity and social justice. It illustrates how one higher education institution utilizes a MCOD framework to envision, direct, and sustain a long-term change process on its campus.

Historical Perspective on Social Diversity and Social Justice Change Efforts

A review of past efforts to effect social change in higher education revealed that the UMass Amherst campus has a long and reputable history of addressing issues of social diversity and social justice. Beginning in the late 1960s, this campus pioneered and was an early advocate of developing academic support programs for people of color and other underrepresented students (Committee for the Collegiate Education for Black and Other Minority Students, Bilingual Collegiate Program and other programs); creating a social and cultural diversity requirement within its General Education curriculum; supporting themed housing (such as a "2 in 20" Floor for Gay, Lesbian, Bisexual, Transgender, (GLBT) and ally students) within the residence life program; and promoting cutting edge campus-wide multicultural arts programming (New World Theater; Asian Dance and Theater).

Such extensive efforts often resulted in model programs that have been replicated at other institutions. However, the homogeneity of UMass Amherst faculty, staff, and student populations has been experienced by some members of underrepresented groups as unwelcoming or hostile, embedded with obstacles to full and equitable inclusion for all. For many individuals and groups who work to create a more socially diverse and socially just campus, this lack of sustained progress is disconcerting at best.

A historical analysis of change efforts on our campus reveals some of the limitations of our previous approach to change and the need to develop a new approach if we hope to successfully create long-term systemic change in higher education around issues of social diversity and social justice. Our previous approach to effecting such change can be characterized by four prevailing patterns of action:

1. *Crisis driven social diversity and social justice agenda.* Historically, the motivation to initiate change emanated from federal or state legal mandates and, more often, from student protests concerning their experiences of the campus as unresponsive to their needs, hostile towards their presence, and limited in its ability to allow them full and equitable participation in the campus community. Long standing discontent and the perception of disregard for their concerns often led to students' protest and demands for change, thereby creating a crisis-driven change agenda. Generally, such actions were directed to the chancellor and/or other senior administrators with the expectation that they would address students' demands for change.
2. *Change initiatives primarily directed towards underrepresented groups of students.* Frequently, in the aftermath of campus protests and demands, stand-alone programs were created to support students who experienced exclusion and discrimination. These programs were designed primarily to help specific groups of underrepresented students feel welcomed and included in campus life and to succeed academically. Equally critical but often ignored, were concerted efforts to assist underrepresented groups of faculty and staff who may also experience the effects of a campus culture that is neither prepared for, nor fully accepting, of their presence and participation.
3. *Change efforts focused on individual behavior change.* While many campus change initiatives were directed towards support for underrepresented groups of students, some interventions were directed towards assisting majority students, faculty, and staff with developing the competence needed to effectively learn, work, and live on a campus that espouses the values of community, diversity, and social justice. These change efforts, sponsored by various campus offices such as Residence Life, Workplace Learning and Development, Equal Opportunity and Diversity, Ombuds Offices, and the Office of Human Relations, consisted largely of education

and training programs. These programs were aimed at increasing an individual's diversity awareness and sensitivity and towards reducing incidents of "offensive" behavior. For example, forums were created where white people were encouraged to examine their values, beliefs, and behaviors towards people of color. Few interventions, however, were aimed at examining and changing the policies, practices, and procedures that create barriers to full participation and inclusion.

4. *Change agents located at the margins of the organization.* In those instances when the need for organizational change was acknowledged, the offices and centers created to advocate for change and to address the needs of underrepresented groups were often located on the margins of the "chain of command" and thus did not possess sufficient power to influence the institutional policies and practices that sustain an exclusive and unjust environment. For example, ALANA (African, Latino, Asian, and Native American) academic support programs and cultural centers,support programs for students with disabilities, and advocacy organizations for women and GLBT students were all located at the margin of Student Affairs, not within Academic Affairs.

Our experience has taught us that the university needs to evolve beyond the prevailing crisis-driven diversity agenda to a new level of proactive, systemic planning and action. Good faith efforts to comply with federal and state mandates, well-designed support programs, and opportunities for education and training are necessary but do not produce sustained systems change.

Creating a socially diverse and socially just campus means moving beyond compliance with federal and state mandates prohibiting discrimination to an understanding of multicultural competence as an educational imperative for all. In order to effect lasting systemic change, the campus has come to realize that it needs to engage in a change process that involves all parts of the campus working towards eliminating barriers to full inclusion and creating pathways of success for all. Becoming proactive in our actions, moving towards multicultural competence as an educational imperative for all, and fully engaging all aspects of the university system in our change efforts will enable us to make social diversity and social justice hallmarks of our institutional excellence.

Looking for a New Approach to Promoting Community, Diversity and Social Justice

In 1998, then Chancellor David Scott's Counsel on Community, Diversity and Social Justice released *A New Approach to Promoting Community, Diversity, and Social Justice: Aspects of Strategic Action*, www.umass.edu/

ohr/cdsj_report1.htm, which served as the conceptual foundation for the development in 1999 of the Community, Diversity, and Social Justice (CDSJ) Initiative. The purpose of the CDSJ initiative is to engage the campus community in a process that would result in proactive, systemic change related to issues of social justice and social diversity thereby moving the University of Massachusetts Amherst towards becoming more of a multicultural organization.

Specifically, the goals of the CDSJ initiative and the multicultural vision for the university include the following:

1. Create a more welcoming, inclusive, and equitable learning, working, and living environment for all members of the campus community by examining and changing policies and practices of exclusion into systems of inclusion.
2. Develop proactive management practices regarding CDSJ issues so that issues will be appropriately addressed before escalating into a crisis.
3. Increase responsibility and initiatives supporting CDSJ at the local level by locating responsibility for change within each department, school and/or college and administrative unit and by integrating change around CDSJ issues into the system's regular planning and budgeting cycle.
4. Fully integrate CDSJ into the vision, mission, and values of all teaching, research, and outreach functions, thereby increasing the centrality of CDSJ and reenvisioning CDSJ as a component of our educational excellence and a contribution to our competitive advantage.
5. Ensure that CDSJ is seen as relevant to all members of the campus community.

Utilizing a Multicultural Organizational Change Process to Guide CDSJ

In order to effect the long term systemic change envisioned in the CDSJ initiative, we needed new frameworks, models, and approaches to the change process. We looked to Jackson and Hardiman (1994) whose pioneering work integrating diversity and social justice with organizational development created the theoretical frameworks that have come to be known as Multicultural Organizational Development (MCOD). For a more comprehensive discussion of this model, see Jackson's Chapter 1 in this volume. Prior to their work with MCOD, Jackson and Hardiman each contributed significantly to the development of educational models and practices designed to raise awareness and promote sensitivity about social justice issues (2001), and their work has been used extensively in private corporations and more recently in higher education and other organizational settings. They were among the first scholars to recognize that diversity work in organizations designed to address the behaviors, attitudes, and awareness of individuals related to issues of diversity and justice was necessary – but not sufficient – to produce organizational change in support of social justice and diversity. To create real systems change, it is necessary to view the organization and/or system as the target of change, rather than focusing only on the individuals in the organization.

Multicultural Organizational Development (MCOD) developed and evolved over 20 years into a theoretical framework, a series of core assumptions, and set of change strategies that uses a systems approach to promoting diversity and social justice in organizations. The core assumptions along with three major elements – the MCOD Goal; the MCOD Developmental Stages; and the MCOD Systems Change Process – form the theory and practice of MCOD. This model, MCOD, continues to show promise as an approach for creating long-term systemic change in organizations, including higher education, and is the foundation for the CDSJ initiative.

Implementing the MCOD process in Higher Education

Our experience implementing the MCOD process in higher education will be illustrated through a case study, the Community, Diversity, and Social Justice Initiative at the University of Massachusetts Amherst. We used the MCOD process, with some modifications, to inform and guide the work of our campus wide effort, the CDSJ Initiative.

The MCOD process has four components with a number of sub components. These components are: 1) Identification of the change agents; 2) determination of the readiness of the system for an initiative of this type; 3) assessment or benchmarking of the organization; and 4) change planning and implementation. These components, while represented sequentially, are inherently part of a cyclical process meant to keep reiterating itself over time. The components of the process will be highlighted here with attention given to how the university implemented the MCOD process.

Identification of the Change Agents

There are three primary actors or change agents in this process: the internal change team, external consultants, and the leadership team. The internal change team is a group of people from within the organization who agree to take on the responsibility to manage the MCOD process for the organization. The external consultants provide technical expertise to the change team, and the leadership team champions the effort.

Internal Change Teams

The first of the three primary change agents are the internal change teams. In keeping with the goal of increasing responsibility for change at the "local level," a series of interconnecting change teams were developed to guide the CDSJ initiative in the fall of 2000. We will first describe the structure of the teams and then their functions.

1. Team Structure

- University CDSJ Team is charged with setting the overall direction for the CDSJ initiative, managing the coordination of CDSJ work, monitoring the resources and facilitating the consultant relations. Membership on the University CDSJ team consists of a liaison from each of the Executive Area Teams (EXATs) as well as additional faculty, staff, and students.
- Executive Area Teams (EXAT) are established by the senior leadership of the area to manage the change process in each of the five major organizational units in the system: Academic Affairs, Student Affairs, Administration and Finance, University Advancement, and Chancellor's Area (due to substantial budget cuts and reorganization, the University Advancement and Chancellor's Area team consolidated into one team in 2002). Teams are established in each executive area because the size of the institution requires more than one team to address the entire system. Also, members who have first-hand knowledge of the specific work environment in their area and the subculture of their part of the system populate area-specific teams. In addition, we hoped that area-specific teams would facilitate a sense of collegiality and ownership of the process among the team members and enhance the team's ability to encourage others to fully participate in the MCOD process.

  Membership on the EXAT change teams has been determined by using the MCOD change team criteria as a guideline. Of particular importance, is the cross-functional nature of each team and that each team consists of members distributed throughout the hierarchy. For example, the Academic Affairs team consists of deans, department chairs, faculty, students, and professional and administrative support staff. Regardless of position, each member's opinions are valued and generally acted upon equally; and it is recognized that each holds a unique perspective on the system. Fully engaging the faculty and academic administration in the process serves to interrupt the prior emphasis on CDSJ issues as primarily the responsibility of student development professionals.

  These 10 to 12 person teams typically meet twice monthly and are charged with developing and implementing the change process in their respective executive areas in partnership with their executive area leadership. EXATs are charged with conducting CDSJ assessments to identify areas of needed change and work with the leadership of their executive area to develop, implement, monitor, and evaluate appropriate change strategies. Each team also has a liaison that is a member of the EXAT and also a member of the University CDSJ Team.

- Cross Team Work Groups were formed with members from each of the EXATs to coordinate specific functions common to all EXAT teams. The Assessment Group provides guidance and feedback to EXATs regarding all aspects of the assessment process. The Communications and Documentation Group facilitates communication with campus constituents through the development of web pages, presentations, and news articles. Also, this group maintains the archives for the initiative. The Leadership Development Group facilitates interconnectedness between the CDSJ initiative and the leadership of the institution.

2. Team Function

The primary function of the EXATs is to work in partnership with the leadership of the Executive Area to guide and support the CDSJ initiative and to serve as role models for CDSJ goals and values. Additionally, the EXATs are charged with building and maintaining capacity to manage CDSJ issues within the executive area and with making themselves available to serve as resources and coaches regarding CDSJ issues in their area.

3. Training and Development

In order to prepare for the functions described above, each team participated in an initial two day retreat during which they engaged in team building activities, were introduced to the MCOD framework, and became familiar with the MCOD change process they would be implementing. Unlike the committee or task force structures typical in higher education, the MCOD change teams require members to be personally engaged in the team's development as well as focused on the task at hand. During the initial retreat, time was also set aside for teams to begin the change planning process.

In addition to preparing the EXATs for their role in the CDSJ initiative, "launch" activities were conducted with the management in each executive area to prepare them for CDSJ by developing their understanding of the CDSJ initiative, cultivating their commitment, and securing their support for the change process. The Administration and Finance Executive Area held a series of meetings with all the senior and middle managers to prepare them for the CDSJ initiative. This proved particularly important in this area, as many of the employees on this team required their supervisor's cooperation to participate easily in the team meetings and CDSJ activities.

Throughout the course of this initiative, All Team Meetings (ATMs) have been held to facilitate connections among the teams and to reinforce the system wide nature of this change process. During these ATMs, teams engage in ongoing team-building and skill-building activities, have an opportunity to share their progress, explore their challenges, obtain feedback on their plans, and continue to deepen the understanding and competence in facilitating the MCOD change process.

These ATMs occur regularly (once per semester or as needed), last a half a day, and have been positively evaluated by the participants. The most recent ATM was hosted by the Provost in December 2003 and was attended by the Chancellor and each Vice Chancellor. At this ATM, each team presented the results of the assessment process in their executive area, and the senior leadership of the institution was given an opportunity to identify similarities and differences of the CDSJ issues across the different executive areas.

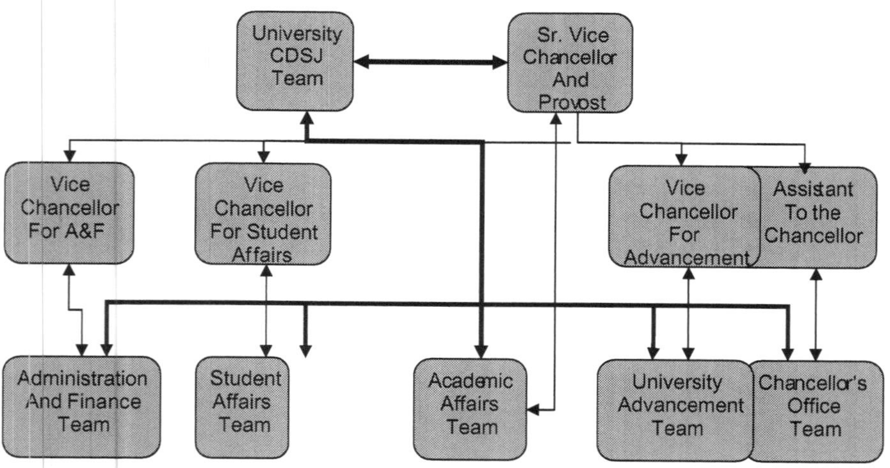

External Consultant Team

The second of the three primary change agents for a large-scale systems change initiative such as the MCOD process is the external consultant team. The external consultants can provide an outside or objective perspective of this process, assist the teams with learning the MCOD change process, and help to build the internal capacity of the team to sustain the change effort after the consultants have exited the system.

Given the complexity of engaging the whole system in an interconnected yet decentralized change process, the university's leadership agreed to support the success of this initiative by providing funds to engage an outside consultant group with expertise in facilitating MCOD change processes. After issuing a RFB (request for bid proposal), the University CDSJ team engaged the consulting company of Ramos Associates for three years (2000-2003). Ramos Associates, www.ramosassociates.com, were selected because they brought a depth and breadth of experience in social justice, diversity, and higher education. The consultant team consisted of a past Vice Chancellor for Student Affairs, a full professor of Sociology and a national expert in organizational development and systems change.

The consultants were instrumental in working with the executive leaders of the university to educate them about CDSJ and the MCOD process and to help prepare them for the implementation of the Executive Area Teams. They met regularly with the EXATs to help facilitate the team building process and conducted regular All Team Meetings (of all EXAT members) during which they helped the teams learn the MCOD process and develop their assessment plans and instruments. Furthermore, theyfacilitated connectedness and shared problem solving among the teams. At critical junctures, their neutrality in the system enabled them to intervene with the university's senior leadership in support of the CDSJ initiative on behalf of the teams.

Leadership Team

The third of the three primary agents in the MCOD change process is the leadership team. For a MCOD intervention, the leadership team must know what is going on and must have direct involvement in the manner in which the initiative is carried out, must have some understanding of the process and what its role will be, and, finally, must decide what level of involvement it will have in the process.

Engaging the CDSJs Leadership Team

After the initial New Approach document was presented to then Chancellor David Scott and the Vice Chancellors, several meetings ensued during which the CDSJ initiative was discussed, debated, and approved. University funds were made available to hire external consultants. The university leadership group engaged in a seminar during which the MCOD process was introduced. They met individually with the consultants as needed and met with the University CDSJ team on a semi-annual basis. The liaisons from each team also met regularly with their respective Vice Chancellors to keep them informed about the progress of the initiative, address any concerns from the team, and seek input and cooperation regarding implementation of the process. These strategies included writing cover letters in support of CDSJ and the importance of gathering everyone's input during the assessment process, reinforcing with supervisors the fact that working on the EXAT is considered part of one's job, and participating on occasion in the All Team Meetings.

In 2002, the university experienced a change in leadership with the arrival Chancellor John Lombardi and the appointment of an entirely new team of interim Vice Chancellors. This transition resulted in a change in the relationship between CDSJ and the leadership. The new Chancellor expressed support for the initiative; however, unlike his predecessor who had championed the initiative, he delegated responsibility for the initiative to the Provost who, in turn, has become the initiative's key champion. The UCDSJ team no longer met with the leadership as a whole group; however, liaisons did continue to meet and, for the most part, have maintained strong connections with their executive area leadership, the Vice Chancellors.

Determining the Readiness of the System for Change

The second core component of the MCOD process is determining if the organization is ready for a change initiative, especially one that focuses on the complex and potentially controversial areas of social diversity and social justice. It is especially important to know the level of support and awareness in the organization for an initiative whose goal it is to create a Multicultural Organization (MCO), and how ready the leadership is to do what must be done to support and engage in this process. Of particular importance is the readiness of the system for the rather intensive data collection phase that begins the MCOD process.

Our CDSJ initiative did not utilize the formal inventories described in Jackson's chapter to determine the university's readiness to engage in the change process. It relied instead on the UCDSJ team members who had many years of university service and were able to share information and perspective on the readiness of the system for change. Many of the campus's prior diversity and social justice initiatives that are referenced in the beginning of this chapter served as indicators that the necessary ground work had been done over many years.

In addition, then Chancellor David Scott, on regular occasions, articulated his commitments concerning community, diversity, and social justice, and these public pronouncements of support signaled to the team that we would have the support of the leadership as we moved forward with the CDSJ Initiative.

Benchmarking the System

The third key component of the MCOD process is assessing or benchmarking the system. It is worth noting that this is the first time a comprehensive assessment of CDSJ issues has been conducted at this university. Establishing the benchmark is essential to understand how far the organization has to move to become an MCO, and how it is progressing as it implements the action or change plans.

MCOD Assessment

The systems change process begins with the development and implementation of an assessment plan. In order to obtain an overview of CDSJ issues across the university, the EXATs utilized the MCOD framework to guide the development of assessment plans in their respective executive areas.

In keeping with the CDSJ goal of maintaining a locally centered change process, the assessment process for each executive area emphasized issues that were particularly relevant to their executive area while simultaneously ensuring that some elements of each assessment plan were common to all teams. For example, the Academic Affairs assessment plan sought to identify CDSJ issues that impacted the teaching and learning process, whereas other areas like the Chancellor's Area and University Advancement focused more on issues of supervision.

The EXATs utilized several data sources to gather information about the status of CDSJ issues in their executive area. As suggested in the MCOD model, most of the EXAT assessment plans used some or all of the following data gathering methodologies.

Campus Survey

Each EXAT team utilized the Comprehensive Employee Attitudes and Experiences Survey, http://www.umass.edu/wost/cdsj/survey.pdf as part of the assessment process. This survey was developed collaboratively under the direction of the Assessment Work Group and was designed to collect information from campus employees about their attitudes and experiences across a range of CDSJ issues. Within the four-page survey, three pages were identical for all executive areas and one page was customized to fit the organizational and cultural characteristics of the executive area. For example, the fourth page for Academic Affairs was designed to elicit information about the CDSJ issues related to teaching and research, whereas the Student Affairs page further probed employee's CDSJ experiences with racial profiling, stereotyping, and negative student comments.

The surveys were also administered differently in the different executive areas. For example, while the surveys were mailed to employees in Academic Affairs, they were administered in a "sit down" session within Administration and Finance.

Focus Groups

Most assessment plans incorporated data from focus groups to further clarify and illustrate the findings from the survey. In many cases, data was sought from specific identity groups such as people of color, women, classified employees, and so forth, as well as from "mixed" focus groups.

Other Data Sources

Many EXAT teams incorporated existing institutional data sets into their assessment plans. Some examples include faculty, staff, and student demographic data sets, policy reviews, and incident analysis.

Preparing the Data for Presentation

The CDSJ Initiative utilized the services of one of its on-campus assessment and evaluation offices, SAREO (Student Assessment, Research, and Evaluation Office), to compile the survey results utilizing survey research standards to arrive at verifiable and reliable results. Overall, the campus had a return rate on the survey of 57% and each executive area also had a better than 50% return rate on the surveys in their respective areas. The demographic information from the survey enabled the EXATs to obtain the survey results about the executive area as a whole, and to be able to examine specific divisions, schools, or colleges within the executive area.

The EXATs managed the data sets and worked with others to compile the data in formats suitable for most people to understand during presentations. In preparing it for distribution, the data was examined to ensure that the anonymity of individual respondents would not be compromised. This principle was applied both to the reporting of the survey results and to the qualitative or focus group data. For the survey, if there were fewer than five individuals in a particular identity grouping, we eliminated that group from the data set. For example, if there was only one African American woman in a unit, this person's identity could not be protected and therefore needed to be included with a larger body of responses from "people of color" or removed altogether. For the focus groups or open-ended survey responses, we removed any language or names that would identify an individual person or department.

The data was reviewed and the lenses of the MCOD model were used to organize and identify issues in the executive area that either contributed to or detracted from the system becoming an MCO. Each EXAT created its own assessment report and presented the results to its respective executive area, to the leadership group, and to the other EXATs in an All Team Meeting in December, 2003. An example of the report from the Academic Affairs Executive Area can be found on the University of Massachusetts-Amherst website: www.umass.edu/wost/cdsj/report or on the web page of the Provost:www.umass.edu/Provost.

Presenting the Executive Area Assessment Results to the System

Once the data was organized for presentation, it was fed back into the executive areas offering those who participated in the process an opportunity to hear and respond to the results of the assessment process. The process of systematically presenting the data for clarification and verification is to cultivate a sense of confidence in and "ownership" of the assessment results among the members of the organization.

During the spring of 2004, each of the four executive areas embarked on the process of presenting the data to their part of the university system, doing so in a manner that best fit each area's organizational culture. For example, some teams utilized senior level management to present the data to members of their respective areas. Within some divisions in Administration and Finance for example, employees were brought together in groups, given a Power Point presentation of the results by their managers and division head, invited to participate in conversations about the meaning of the data, and, finally, asked to provide managers with recommendations for critical change areas.

The Academic Affairs executive area published its report, Academic Affairs Community Diversity , and Social Justice Assessment Report in print and online at www.umass.edu/provost or at www.umass.edu/wost/cdsj and, by request, copies of the report were made available electronically. Because Academic Affairs is such a large and diverse executive area, the AA CDSJ team early on decided that once data was collected and the report written, it would be important for schools and colleges to each convene local CDSJ committees to further analyze the data, decide on change goals suitable for their school's priorities and needs, and to implement actual change plans. Once it had completed its report, the AA CDSJ committee began by first meeting with the provost and the dean's council to present the overall report and to discuss selected, campus-wide findings. This meeting provided an opportunity for the deans to confer about general themes in the data consistent across schools and colleges, for the provost to make clear her expectations for follow-up, and for the AA CDSJ team to describe the support the committee was prepared to offer schools and colleges in the next steps. AA CDSJ committee support to schools and colleges includes, for example, distribution of print and electronic copies of the executive area report, the availability of AA CDSJ team members to attend college-level meetings to explain the CDSJ initiative and to present and explain an overview of the academic affairs data, and to provide schools and colleges subsets of the data specific to their particular college. Since "local" committees are also composed of faculty, academic administrators, and classified staff members (many of which are unfamiliar with reading data sets like these), the AA CDSJ committee has also often been asked to help explain how to "read" such data and initially to walk committees through that process.

Change Planning and Implementation

The fourth key component of the MCOD process is change planning and implementation. Once the assessment is completed and the data has been presented, discussed, and understood by its contributors, the next step is to identify those things that must be changed so that the organization can become a MCO. Each executive area and its subunits are encouraged to identify those issues and problems that when addressed will affect the issues or problem in an observable and measurable way and that can be addressed within 18 months to two years.

At this juncture in the CDSJ initiative, some executive areas have begun to identify their change goals and develop change plans. By and large, however, most executive areas anticipate moving into the change planning and implementation phase in the fall of 2004. The UCDSJ is planning an All Team Meeting in the early fall to help facilitate and support the change planning process.

When the change plan has been implemented and the results evaluated, it is time to redo the assessment, renew the commitment to becoming an MCO, develop the next change plan, and implement that change plan. With each completion of this process, it is expected that the MCOD process will become internalized within the organization and its culture.

CDSJ: What has Worked Well

1. The New Approach document and the MCOD theory served to anchor the campus CDSJ initiative, providing an effective theoretical framework and practical roadmap to a new way of effecting change around issues of community, diversity, and social justice for the University of Massachusetts-Amherst.
2. The MCOD Assessment Process enabled the campus for the first time to develop a comprehensive campus-wide database concerning the attitudes, perceptions, and experiences of employees around issues of community,

diversity, and social justice. This established a benchmark against which we can measure our progress over time.

3. The CDSJ initiative also successfully distributed the assessment data back to the system. The process of engaging employees in looking critically at the results of the assessment process built support for the change process and helped silence critics who assumed they would never learn the results of the assessment.
4. Ramos Associates, the external consultants, helped develop the internal competence of the EXATS to manage their part of the CDSJ initiative.
5. The development of Executive Area Teams (EXAT) proved to be an effective way to manage the CDSJ initiative. Along with the sub-groups and regular All Team Meetings, the EXATs were responsible for conducting the assessment, developing the change plans, and implementing those change plans. The progress of the EXATs is being documented and disseminated in triennial reports. Other facets of the EXATs that worked well are:

- EXATs developed a flexible process to accommodate changing team membership.
- Membership on the EXATs cut across the hierarchy and included, for example, deans, faculty, professional, and, in the case of the Academic Affairs team, administrative support staff.
- Some EXATs successfully changed form entirely as they began the feedback and change planning and implementation stage of CDSJ. For example, Administration and Finance now utilizes its senior management team as the EXAT and encourages the development of ad hoc groups in the divisions to develop and implement the change plans. Academic Affairs, while keeping the original EXAT team formation, is supporting the development of EXATs in each of the schools and colleges of the university. In both cases, CDSJ is being "pushed" farther down in the organization, as called for by the MCOD model.

6. All aspects of the CDSJ process were tailored to the culture of the particular executive area, thereby recognizing and respecting the different norms, interests, and expectations of each area regarding this process.
7. The CDSJ initiative was able to successfully negotiate significant transitions and challenges to the University system. Since the initiative's inception, the university has appointed a new Chancellor who in turn has appointed an entirely new set of Vice Chancellors. Some of the current Vice Chancellors, most especially the Provost, have been in other key leadership positions since the inception of CDSJ, were very familiar with the initiative, and became key leadership champions. In addition, CDSJ survived the most severe budget cuts to university funding in its history.

CDSJ: Challenges to Address

1. While some areas have successfully changed the format of their EXAT, others now have ill-defined change agent teams. This makes it difficult to keep that area effectively connected to the overall initiative.
2. With the extensive change of senior campus leadership, support from the leadership varies among the different executive areas. Investment on the part of senior University officials varies, as may be anticipated. There are clear champions among the leadership group, committed leaders, loosely connected leaders, and leaders that delegate without much apparent investment in the process or the outcome.
3. We have come to realize how slow moving a systems' change process like CDSJ can be, and when that change is combined with the impact of the leadership transitions and budgetary traumas, CDSJ has taken longer than originally anticipated to generate the types of results for which everyone had hoped. For some, this delay has called into question the viability of the initiative, and we have had to work to sustain their commitment.
4. Some EXAT teams put more emphasis on learning MCOD and implementing CDSJ and less on the team-building aspects of the process. This led to a strong task but weak process orientation. In-depth team building is essential if important issues of race and class/caste that emerge are to be adequately addressed.

Concluding Comments

As noted earlier in this chapter, the University of Massachusetts-Amherst's CDSJ initiative is one of the few, if not only, attempts by a large higher education institution to take a systemic approach to pursuing the goal of becoming a MCO as an enhancement to its goal of strengthening the quality of its teaching, research, and outreach mission. While the jury is still out on the effectiveness of this approach, UMass Amherst is drawing on the successes of the implementation of the MCOD model in other large systems and is satisfied with the results it has achieved so far. It intends to continue to pursue it mission and goals to become a fully developed MCO.

References

Academic Affairs Community, Diversity, and Social Justice Team. (2004). *Academic affairs community, diversity, and social justice assessment report.* Retrieved July 26, 2004, from University of Massachusetts Amherst Web site: http://www.umass.edu/wost/cdsj/report/index.htm

Chancellor's Counsel on Community, Diversity, and Social Justice. (1998). *A new approach to promoting community, diversity, and social justice: Aspects of strategic action.* Retrieved July 26, 2004, from University of Massachusetts Amherst Web site: http://www.umass.edu/ohr/cdsj_report1.htm

Hardiman, R. (2001). Reflections on white identity development. In B. W. Jackson & C. L. Wijeyesinghe (Eds.), *New perspectives on racial identity development: A theoretical and practical anthology* (pp. 108-128). New York: New York University Press.

Jackson, B.W., & Hardiman, R. (1994). Multicultural organization development. In E.Y. Croass, J.H. Katz, F.A. Miller, & E.W. Seashore (Eds.), *The promise of diversity*. Arlington, VA: National Training Laboratories Institute.

Jackson, B.W. (2001). Black identity development theory: Further analysis and elaboration. In B. W. Jackson & C. L. Wijeyesinghe (Eds.), *New perspectives on racial identity development: A theoretical and practical anthology* (pp. 8-31). New York University Press.

University Community, Diversity, and Social Justice Team (2002). *Comprehensive employee attitudes and experiences survey.* Retrieved July 26, 2004, from University of Massachusetts Amherst Web site: http://www.umass.edu/wost/cdsj/survey.pdf

---

Linda S. Marchesani is Director of Workplace Learning and Development at the University of Massachusetts Amherst. **Bailey W. Jackson** is an associate professor in the Social Justice Education department at the University of Massachusetts Amherst.

Chapter 20
Institutional Transformation to Support Inclusive Teaching Initiatives

Murali Krishnamurthi

The success of inclusive teaching initiatives depends not only on how faculty engage their students in the learning process in the classroom, but also on the supportive climate of the institutional environment for such initiatives. As learning takes place both inside and outside of the classroom, the institution as a whole must be transformed for inclusive teaching to succeed. In this chapter, the efforts at campus wide transformation at Northern Illinois University to support inclusive teaching initiatives are presented along with a general model for institutional transformation.

This chapter describes the institutional transformation underway at Northern Illinois University (NIU) and the support systems necessary to promote such an inclusive teaching initiative, and it recommends a comprehensive model for guiding similar institution-wide transformation elsewhere. The model is based on the ongoing multicultural transformation at various levels of NIU and the lessons learned from that experience. A summary of the initiatives being implemented at various levels of the university is included along with the key results from their implementations.

Northern Illinois University is a comprehensive public institution serving nearly 25,000 students pursuing more than 70 degree programs offered through its seven major colleges. NIU's location in rural DeKalb, Illinois and its proximity to Chicago attract a diverse student body to the campus. Approximately 25% of NIU's current student body is from underrepresented groups (2002 figure), and the regional trends indicate that this population may double within the next 10 years. The campus community is cognizant of this increase in its underrepresented student body and is making every effort to transform the institution to address its needs and support inclusive teaching initiatives.

Interestingly, the initial impetus for institutional transformation to support inclusive teaching initiatives at NIU came from the student body and not from any other group. In 1994, members of the Student Association at NIU met with then Provost and expressed the need for multicultural curriculum transformation. The student leaders also emphasized the need for professional development opportunities for faculty to learn about multicultural course and curricular transformation and to address the unique needs of the underrepresented student body. This student activism resulted in the creation of the Provost's Task Force on Multicultural Transformation as the first step in institutional transformation at NIU. Since 1994, the task force has been entrusted with the responsibility for hosting a week long multicultural curriculum transformation institute every summer and has been provided the necessary funding to offer stipends to a select number of faculty participating in multicultural course transformation.

During these 11 years, several hundred faculty at NIU have benefited from the multicultural curriculum transformation institute and have transformed their courses and curricula to incorporate inclusive teaching practices. But most importantly, the institute and the curricular transformation activities have had a positive impact on various levels and constituents of NIU, which in turn has helped to sustain the support for inclusive teaching initiatives. Thus the initiative that began as a curricular transformation effort has helped to promote institutional transformation, and institutional transformation has been crucial to the continuation of inclusive teaching initiatives. This continuous loop of institutional transformation has been the key for success for supporting inclusive teaching issues at NIU.

Experiences in Institutional Transformation

The need for inclusive teaching and strategies for transforming curricula are well documented in literature (Adams & Strother-Adams, 2001; Morey & Kitano, 1997). But for inclusive teaching initiatives to succeed and receive support, the complex issues that impact such a transformation initiative must be understood and addressed at all levels of an institution (Smith, 1989). NIU's experiences during the past 20 years in supporting inclusive teaching initiatives and promoting institutional transformation span several areas and influence several constituent groups of the institution as shown in Figure 1. The areas include curricula, support programs and services, and institutional infrastructure. The constituent groups include faculty, staff, students, and administration. The involvement of all these areas and groups in the institutional transformation process has been the key to its success at NIU.

Curricula. Faculty at the departmental, college, and university levels are primarily responsible for curriculum transformation at NIU. As mentioned earlier, faculty transforming their courses and curricula are supported through the multicultural curriculum transformation institute. One of the early experiences in the curricular transformation initiative was that faculty wanted the administration to demonstrate that multicultural curricular transformation activities were valued by the institution, especially in the personnel process for merit, tenure, and promotion. This was also confirmed in an assessment of the past participants of the multicultural curriculum transformation institute conducted in spring 2000 at NIU. To demonstrate institutional commitment, the Provost annually sends an official letter to chairs of all academic departments at NIU emphasizing that multicultural curricular transformation activities are valued as part of teaching and scholarship and should be considered in the personnel process. The Provost also conveys this message annually during new faculty orientation and in meetings with academic deans and department chairs. A number of faculty who had participated in the institute during the past 11 years are also now serving in personnel committees at various levels of the university in order to help convey the importance of inclusive teaching issues and demonstrate NIU's commitment to multicultural curricular transformation activities. The curricular transformation process is also supported at the university level by the General Education Committee, which requires the incorporation of inclusive teaching issues in all general education courses at NIU, thus demonstrating once again the value the institution places on multicultural curriculum transformation.

Listed below are some of the results from the university-wide curricular transformation effort:

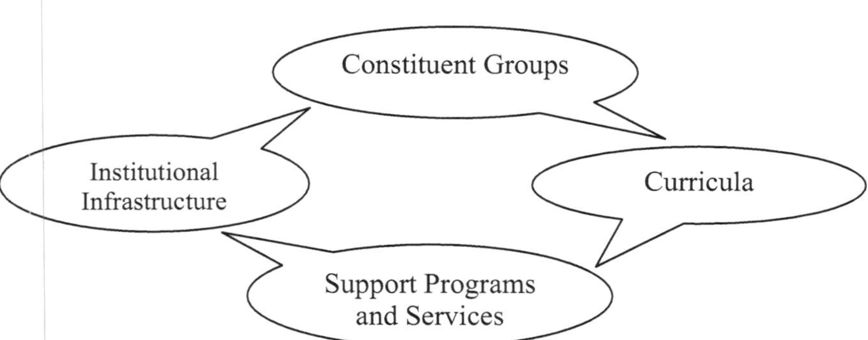

Figure 1. Four major components of institutional transformation at Northern Illinois University

1. Transformation of courses by individual faculty has resulted in the transformation of entire curriculum in some disciplines, and transformation of specific courses in others.
2. Attention paid to inclusive teaching and diverse learning styles has resulted in an increase in the number of women and minority students in courses in some disciplines – such as engineering – where their enrollment is usually low.
3. Inclusive teaching initiatives have opened up new opportunities for research and scholarly activities among faculty across disciplines. Faculty are collaborating across disciplines and pursuing sponsored research and publication opportunities on diversity topics.
4. The transformation initiatives resulted in the recognition of the need for curricular programs in Asian American studies and LGBT (Lesbian, Gay, Bisexual, and Transgender) studies along with the existing ones in Black studies, Latino and Latin American studies, and Women's studies. During the 2003 academic year, the curricular committees at NIU formally approved certificate programs in Asian American studies and LGBT studies.
5. Faculty whose curricula reflected multicultural transformation are beginning to assume administrative responsibilities and committee chair roles at various levels of the university, thus influencing institutional transformation.

These positive outcomes of the curricular effort are helping to move NIU forward in the institutional transformation process and are also aiding in transforming other areas of the institution.

Support programs and services. NIU recognized early on in the transformation process that support programs and services are essential for the success of curricular initiatives. Therefore, NIU established several support programs and services through various units on campus. The Faculty Development and Instructional Design Center plays a key role in supporting faculty and staff engaged in various teaching initiatives including multicultural curriculum transformation. Campus units such as University Resources for Latinos, University Resources for Women, and the Center for Access-Ability Resources offer programs and services, retreats , and open houses for particular groups. Affirmative Action and Diversity Resources offer diversity-related training programs and address complaints and conflicts. Student Support Services offer special tutoring and mentoring services tailored to the unique needs of underrepresented students.

Along with establishing support programs and services, NIU also recognized the need for forums to discuss diversity-related issues. For this purpose, a number of committees, commissions, and task forces were established during the past 20 years to address issues related to the status of minority groups including Asian Americans, women, persons with disabilities, and sexual orientation. These committees advise the President and the Provost on issues related to particular underrepresented groups and offer programs and services related to those groups.

Institutional Infrastructure. The institutional "infrastructure" component is addressed through NIU's commitment to diversity, policies, funding, and programs. During the past 20 years, NIU's administration has established and supported a number of facilities, programs, and services to promote Asian American studies, Black studies, Latino and Latin American studies, and Women's studies. Furthermore, NIU has provided resource centers for women, Latinos, and LGBT students, has created the earlier mentioned committees, commissions, and task forces for underrepresented groups, and has continued funding of programs such as the Multicultural Curricular Transformation Institute, minority student receptions, cultural celebrations, affirmative action and diversity resources, and faculty development. Without such ongoing support for facilities, programs, and services, it would be difficult to sustain and continue institutional transformation efforts.

Another important aspect of institutional transformation is the establishment of policies that support diversity and ensure compliance. These include the training of the university community on policies and guidelines on affirmative action, equal opportunity employment, ADA compliance, and sexual harassment. The various committees, commissions, and task forces have been instrumental in assessing diversity issues in an ongoing manner and recommending policy recommendations to appropriate bodies at NIU.

Assessment of established programs, policies, and services constitute another important institutional component. At NIU, program reviews and campus wide assessment of diversity-related issues are routinely conducted to ensure institutional goals are being met and to identify issues that require addressing. Listed below are some of the findings from assessments of past participants of the multicultural curriculum transformation institute and underrepresented groups conducted during 2000 at NIU (Krishnamurthi, 2003):

1. Faculty, staff, and students value inclusive teaching and benefit from development opportunities currently available. But diversity training for department chairs as well as leadership training for minority faculty and staff are needed.
2. Students from different underrepresented groups find the campus climate supportive of diversity. One concern that some students expressed was about the need for cultural sensitivity among campus police.
3. Curricular programs in Asian American studies and LGBT studies, and support services for these two groups are needed.

4. Lack of support from departments and colleagues for inclusive teaching initiatives should be addressed by the administration.
5. Positive outcomes of inclusive teaching and diversity initiatives should be publicized and promoted more on campus to increase everyone's awareness of these positive results.

These finding are already being addressed by appropriate bodies at NIU, and without the assessment initiatives some of these issues could not have been identified or confirmed. Assessment is an important component of institutional transformation; it helps to verify the transformation process is proceeding according to plan and allows administrators to take any necessary corrective actions.

Constituent groups. The "constituent groups" have been one of the most challenging as well as rewarding components of institutional transformation at NIU. The groups primarily include faculty, staff, students, and administrators, and the community has some influence on the diversity initiatives of the institution as well. The constituent groups have varying levels of involvement in the other three areas (curricula, support, institutional infrastructure) mentioned earlier. Faculty have the primary responsibility for curricular transformation and approval of curricular changes through various committees of the university. Not all faculty were quick to participate in the multicultural curricular transformation process. Their reluctance was often conveyed in comments such as "multicultural issues are not relevant to my course and discipline," "my syllabus is already full and if I have to include multicultural issues then I will have to sacrifice some of the content," "if students are interested in multicultural issues they can take courses on those topics from programs that offer such courses," and "there is no incentive or recognition for me to integrate inclusiveness issues in my courses." Discussions with some of these faculty helped to identify the following underlying reasons for many of these comments:

1. Misconceptions about inclusive teaching issues (that it is all about content and not about pedagogy and other aspects) and the multicultural curriculum transformation process,
2. Lack of champions in their disciplines to model the process and guide them in their efforts,
3. Lack of encouragement and recognition for the effort from their immediate supervisors and in their personnel process,
4. Lack of exposure to foundational issues in diversity such as power, privilege, and so forth, and
5. Discomfort in opening themselves up to personal transformation as the first step in transforming their courses and curricula.

Fortunately, a majority of the early adopters of the transformation process from disciplines such as education, ethnic and gender studies, health sciences, history, and sociology were able to address the mentioned concerns and motivate faculty to participate in the transformation process. Also, the initiatives taken by the Provost to demonstrate the value placed by NIU on multicultural curriculum transformation process and to recommend academic units to consider multicultural activities in the personnel process have definitely helped to address the concerns. However, as existing faculty retire or leave and new faculty join, these issues have to be addressed in an ongoing manner to sustain the transformation process.

The staff group plays multiple roles with a majority of staff functioning in support roles in various campus units, and some also teaching part time. Many of the support units provide academic support to faculty and students. NIU recognized early in the transformation process that staff should also be developed along with faculty as many of the interactions students have outside the classroom are with support staff. Due to the important role staff play in support units, they are also invited to participate in the multicultural curriculum transformation institute. Support units such as Faculty Development, Student Support Services, and Affirmative Action and Diversity Resources offer a number of programs on curricular and other diversity issues for faculty, staff, and students at NIU, and the participation of these units has been crucial for the success of institutional transformation at NIU.

The student body is represented in many of the committees at NIU, and students are the driving force in many aspects of institutional transformation including the establishment of the multicultural curriculum transformation task force and institute. Students' input is sought in the various diversity committees, commissions, and task forces at NIU, and the administration has taken their recommendations seriously. For example, the Center for Black Studies offers both academic and support services for African American students at NIU, but in response to the unique needs raised by Latino students, NIU has two separate units, Latino and Latin American Studies for academic studies, as well as a support service, University Resources for Latinos. But the experience with student groups is that they are often transitional in nature, and one set of students may be active one year, but the next set of students may not be active on the same issues the following year. Many students also find it difficult to participate in committees and forums due to their class schedules and other commitments. To address this issue, NIU has established student leadership conferences, retreats, and forums in the evenings to accommodate diverse student groups and engage them in the institutional transformation process.

The administrative body at NIU is composed of academic administrators such as deans, department chairs, and heads of support and administrative units. The administrative body plays an important role in establishing policies, allocating resources for initiatives, approving hiring of personnel, and supporting the creation of a campus climate that facilitates retention of a diverse campus community. Recognizing the impact that department chairs have on diversity issues and the need for their support of inclusive teaching issues, the Provost's Office and the Faculty Development and Instructional Design Center launched a department chair diversity initiative to help department chairs address recruitment and retention of a diverse body as part of the institutional transformation process. During the past two years, several workshops have been held on topics such as cross cultural communication, strategies for recruiting diverse faculty, and legal issues related to diverse faculty recruitment. The first workshop on cross cultural communication issues highlighted the following important issues and demonstrated the need for this special initiative for department chairs:

1. There was clearly a "disconnect" between majority (department chairs) and minority (faculty and staff) participants of the workshop. The department chairs wanted solutions to address diversity concerns, but the minority faculty and staff wanted the chairs to become aware of and understand diversity and climate issues first before developing solutions.
2. The discussions demonstrated training needs for both sides to communicate better with each other and to work together on recruitment, retention, and other climate issues.
3. Many department chairs were not aware of the strategies employed by some departments on campus to successfully recruit a diverse body.
4. The workshop revealed the general misconceptions and stereotypical opinions that various groups held about other groups even among highly educated faculty and staff.
5. Most importantly, the initiative demonstrated institutional commitment to recruitment and retention of a diverse body, and gave the department chairs the necessary impetus for addressing such issues in their units.

The experience from the first workshop was very eye opening and helped to identify issues to address in the subsequent workshops. Department chairs who participate in these workshops have also been sharing the issues with their deans and faculty and engaging them in the process. These workshops have also been instrumental in demonstrating the administration's commitment to institutional transformation and in addressing some of the concerns raised by faculty related to a lack of administrative support and recognition for their diversity efforts.

Another segment of constituent groups is the local community surrounding the university, and it has a significant impact on underrepresented groups at

NIU. In some of the open forums conducted at NIU, students from underrepresented groups expressed that their experiences in the community, especially in their interactions with police and businesses, were not positive. The local community's inexperience with underrepresented groups and its lack of services for minorities are some of the issues the university has been helping the community to address. Community and university leaders are working together to raise community's awareness of diversity issues and making the community more open and welcoming to a diverse population.

The experiences gained in institutional transformation at NIU are helping to move the institution forward, and the initiatives are beginning to pay off in the recruitment of a diverse body, development of inclusive curricula, involvement of faculty, staff, students, and administrators in diversity initiatives across campus units, and transformation of the institutional infrastructure to support inclusive teaching initiatives in the long run.

A Model for Institutional Transformation

Based on the experiences in institutional transformation at NIU, a general model for institutional transformation is proposed in this section. The model has four major components:people, curricula, support, and institutional infrastructure, as shown in Figure 2. This model is built on those proposed by Marchesani and Adams (1992) and Garcia, et al. (2001). Marchesani and Adams' model on multicultural teaching and learning focuses primarily on curricular initiatives, and Garcia, et al.'s model focuses on education and scholarship, access and success, campus climate and intergroup relations, and institutional viability and vitality. The emphasis in their model is mostly on climate, relations, and perceptions. The proposed model integrates the two, resulting in a comprehensive framework that guides institutional transformation.

People. The "people" component of the model emphasizes the importance of recruitment, retention, development, and recognition of a diverse body composed of faculty, staff, administrators, and students. As a diverse faculty and student body is critical for promoting inclusive teaching in the classroom, a diverse staff and administrative body is also equally important for the initiatives to receive support outside the classroom.

Some of the basic issues related to recruiting a diversity body are increased awareness and understanding of the importance of diversity at all levels of the institution, better communication between majority and underrepresented groups, tangible strategies for recruitment and retention of underrepresented faculty, and improved climate. Conducting a fair search and hiring faculty of color addresses only one part of the faculty diversity issue. The other and most important part is retaining the hired faculty of color. Retaining faculty of color requires a campus climate that is welcoming, supportive, understanding of and responsive to the unique needs and concerns of faculty of color (Davis, 1998).

The first line of interaction and support for faculty and staff is the department chair who is their immediate supervisor. But an overwhelming majority of department chairs and supervisors still lack an understanding of the unique needs and concerns of faculty of color and the communication skills necessary to interact with them effectively to help retain them. Faculty and staff from underrepresented groups also need training in communication, leadership, and networking skills to be able to pursue administrative and other leadership positions in academia, interact effectively and constructively in voicing their needs and concerns, and contribute to the diversity process. The relatively small number of faculty of color in administrative positions need mentoring and support to succeed in those positions. Institutions must create development opportunities to address these needs.

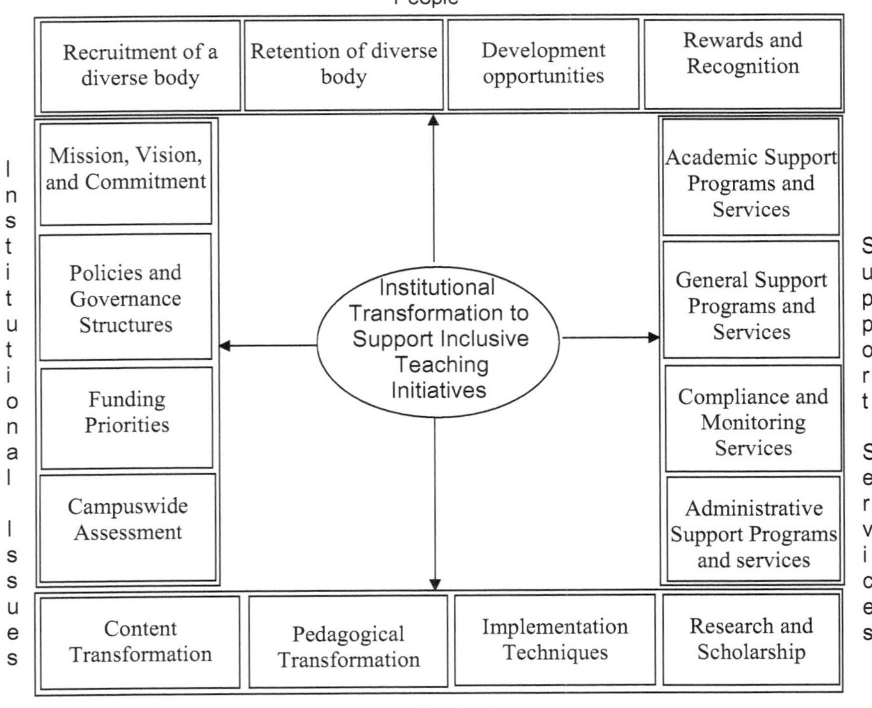

Figure 2. A Model for Institutional Transformation to Support Inclusive Teaching Initiatives

"Development" refers not only to teaching and curricular transformation-related opportunities, but also to the development of leadership skills, mentoring opportunities, and so forth. The types of development programs and support faculty, staff, and administrators need can vary based on their developmental needs during different stages of their academic careers. For this purpose, their needs throughout their "life cycle" (that is, from the time they join academia until they leave) should be analyzed, and the necessary support should be provided. Similar to faculty, staff, and administrators, students also need opportunities with regard to development and interaction with regard to diversity issues both in and outside of the classroom. The type of inclusive teaching, when pursued at an institution, may or may not provide all students with the opportunity to benefit from such initiatives, so along with classroom learning situations, students need opportunities to interact with people from diverse backgrounds outside of the classroom. These opportunities could arise in residence halls, student employment, athletics, student organizations, and other extracurricular activities. Usually student affairs offices and academic support units in academic institutions engage students in diversity-related discussions through these opportunities.

Along with developing a diverse body to support inclusive teaching issues, it is necessary to reward and recognize the efforts and accomplishments of that body. Often the same people participate in numerous diversity initiatives across levels in academic institutions and experience "burn out" after some time; therefore, rewards and recognition are necessary to encourage those involved and others to join and support the initiatives. Rewards and recognition can come in many forms including awards, funding, celebrations, and personnel actions, and these can be established at different levels of the institution for different purposes.

Curricula. The "curricular" component of the model focuses on content, pedagogy, implementation, and scholarship. Transformation of content and pedagogy is already discussed in detail in the literature (Banks & Banks, 2001) and in other chapters of this book, but implementation and scholarship also require such consideration. Implementation can depend on the type of curricular approach and should be accompanied with plans for assessment. It is also beneficial to coordinate curricular assessment along with the assessment of other programs and services related to inclusive teaching at the institution. Along with the implementation of inclusive content and pedagogy, opportunities for research and scholarly activities in related areas should be explored. Faculty are especially motivated to engage in an initiative if there are opportunities for publications and sponsored research grants.

Support. The "support" component refers to all the programs and services that support and promote inclusive teaching initiatives. These include academic support services and programs (for example, faculty and TA development, admission, records and registration, tutoring and mentoring, counseling, career planning, computing, library, and so forth); general support services and programs (for example, campus employment, housing and dining, campus recreation, fraternities and sororities, student organization, disabilities accommodation, diversity awareness and celebration programs, and so forth); compliance services (ADA, affirmative action, EEOC, and so forth); and administrative support services (for example, general counsel, administrative computing, and so forth). The staff and administrators responsible for these support services and their awareness and support of diversity issues can impact the support for inclusive teaching initiatives outside the classroom.

Institutional infrastructure. The "institutional infrastructure" component refers to mission and vision statement, funding priorities, governance structure and policies, campus-wide assessment, and so forth. Institutional issues are often transparent and more challenging than interpersonal issues. Institutional issues related to diversity are often difficult for dominant groups to understand and very frustrating for underrepresented groups to explain (Gallos & Ramsey, 1997). The institution must have a campus-wide plan and vision to promote and engage people from both dominant and underrepresented groups in pursuing inclusive teaching initiatives successfully. In many institutions, policies usually exist for fair recruitment, disabilities accommodation, curricular approval, and so forth, but policies can only ensure compliance and do not demonstrate support and commitment. Therefore, it is critical that there is administrative participation in diversity initiatives, which often demonstrates institutional commitment and priority. Funding, rewards, and recognition for diversity initiatives require balancing them with competing initiatives and planning and implementing them carefully with campus wide support. These issues require serious consideration in transforming institutions to support inclusive teaching initiatives (*Diversity Blue Print: A planning manual for Colleges and Universities*, 1998).

Campus wide assessment of inclusive teaching and the related diversity initiatives is necessary to analyze the impact of these initiatives, identify additional needs, and plan for continual improvement and support. There are several approaches for assessing diversity and inclusive teaching initiatives depending on institutional goals and needs. Chesler (1998), Levitan and Wolf (1994), and Garcia et al. (2001) provide a number of strategies for assessing diversity initiatives in academic institutions. Hayles and Russel (1997) also discuss why some initiatives fail and what institutions can do to prevent such failures.

The four components of the proposed model cover the major issues to address transforming an institution to support inclusive teaching issues. The model can be used as a general framework for guiding institutional transformation, and the issues covered by each component can be tailored to suit the unique needs of an institution.

Conclusions

Inclusive teaching initiatives require support at all levels of an institution to succeed in the long run. The success of the initiatives depends on transforming not only courses, curricula, and institutional commitment to inclusive teaching and diversity, but also the people, support programs, and services involved in the process. The comprehensive model for institutional transformation proposed in this chapter is based on the experiences in institutional transformation at Northern Illinois University. The proposed model is continuing to be implemented by campus units and groups to support inclusive teaching initiatives at all levels of the university. The implementation is an ongoing process as institutional needs change and new programs and services are created to meet the demands of a diverse body. The results obtained so far confirm the importance of institutional commitment, support programs, and services, and a diverse academic community for inclusive teaching initiatives to succeed.

Faculty development can play a key role in transforming an institution to support inclusive teaching initiatives. In addition to offering development programs and services on curricular transformation, faculty development can collaborate with other units on campus to offer programs on related issues such as recruitment and retention of a diverse body, diversity-training programs for staff and students, and participation in the development of rewards and recognition and assessment plans. NIU's Faculty Development and Instructional Design Center is engaged in transforming the institution to support inclusive teaching initiatives with the help of other units on campus, and this center has brought considerable visibility to the role faculty development can play at an institution. The ultimate benefit of the transformation process is that inclusive teaching becomes a core value and responsibility of everyone at all levels of the institution.

References

Adams, J.Q, & Strother-Adams, P. (Eds.). (2001). *Dealing with diversity*. Dubuque, IA: Kendall-Hunt.

Banks, J. A. & Banks, C.A. (Eds.). (2001). *Handbook of research on multicultural education.* San Francisco: Jossey-Bass.

Chesler, M. A. (1998). Planning multicultural audits in higher education. In M. Kaplan, *To improve the academy, 17* (pp. 171-202). Bolton, MA: Anker.

Davis, J. D. (1998). *Retaining faculty of color: The five habits of a highly effective institution.* Proceedings of the the Conference Keeping our faculties: Addressing the recruitment and retention of faculty of color in higher education. Minneapolis: Office of the Associate Vice-President for Multicultural and Academic Affairs, University of Minnesota.

Diversity Blue Print: A Planning Manual for Colleges and Universities. (1998). Washington, DC: Association of American Colleges and Universities.

Gallos, J. V., Ramsey, V. J., & Associates (1997). *Teaching diversity: Listening to the soul, speaking from the heart.* San Francisco: Jossey-Bass.

Garcia, M., Hudgins, C. A., & Musil, C M. (2001). *Assessing campus diversity initiatives.* Washington, DC: Association of American Colleges and Universities.

Krishnamurthi, M. (2003). Assessing multicultural initiatives in higher education institutions. *Assessment and Evaluation in Higher Education, 27*(3), 263-277.

Hayles, V. R., & Russel, A. M. (1997). *The diversity directive: Why some initiatives fail and what to do about it.* Chicago: Irwin Professional.

Levitan, T., & Wolf, L. (1994). Assessing diversity on campus: A resource guide. *New Directions for Institutional Research, 81,* 87-100.

Marchesani, L.S., & Adams, M. (1992). Dynamics of diversity in the teaching-learning process: A faculty development model for analysis and action. In J. R. Menges & M. D. Svinicki. (Eds.), *New directions for teaching and learning, No. 52: Promoting diversity in the college classrooms: Innovative responses for the curriculum, faculty, and institutions* (pp. 11-19). San Francisco: Jossey-Bass.

Morey, A. I., & Kitano, M. (1997). *Multicultural course transformation in higher education: A broader truth.* Boston: Allyn and Bacon.

Smith, D.G. (1989). *The challenge of diversity: Involvement or alienation in the academy?* (ASHE-ERIC Higher Education Report No. 5). Washington, DC: Association for the Study of Higher Education.

Suzuki, L. A. (2000). *The new handbook of multicultural assessment: Clinical, psychological, and educational applications* (2nd ed.). San Franciso: Jossey-Bass.

Murali Krishnamurthi, Ph.D. is an associate professor in the Department of Industrial Engineering and Director of the Faculty Development and Instructional Design Center at Northern Illinois University. Dr. Krishnamurthi can be reached at Northern Illinois University, DeKalb, IL, 60115, by telephone at (815) 753-6502, fax (815) 753-2595, or by email at mkrishna@niu.edu.

Chapter 21
Cultivating Global Understanding Through Campus-Wide Learning Communities

Bonnie B. Mullinix, Rekha Datta and Morris Saldov

Raising awareness of global issues, other cultures and alternate perspectives can serve as a first step towards cultivating an appreciation of diversity. This chapter explores the case of the Monmouth University (MU) Global Understanding Project (GUP), a campus-wide, faculty initiated and MU community-driven venture that sponsors activities throughout the academic year and culminates in a week-long convention. A brief history of the origins of the GUP initiative and a description of its key activities and events are followed by reflections on the effectiveness of this approach to creating a campus-wide learning community whose goal is establishing and sustaining an appreciation for diversity.

As travel, technology, and post 9/11 sensitivities continue to shrink our world and bring international images to our daily awareness, we should not assume that deeper connections or enduring understanding naturally follow. To appreciate how diversity can positively transform our world, we need to engage actively with the issues, concerns and the potential available in cultures and peoples from around the globe. Higher education is a natural venue for such engagement, providing opportunities for initiating scholarly dialogue and supportive programmatic initiatives with various constituencies and facilitating community networks at institutional, local, national and international levels. In the *Chronicle of Higher Education*, Green and Baer (2001) raised a series of issues for institutions of higher education to consider as they globalize the teaching and learning environments on their campuses. In 2002, diversity on college campuses in the US became a controversial issue receiving national attention as legal challenges to admissions policies at the University of Michigan moved towards the Supreme Court. As the transformation of university culture and approaches to teaching and learning is generally acknowledged to be a protracted process, opportunities to catalyze such transformation are worth nurturing. The Carnegie Foundation for the Advancement of Teaching has identified the culture of teaching and learning as a topic worthy of exploration and campus-wide learning communities as a potentially transformative mechanism in higher education (Boyer 1990; Huber and Hutchings, 2003). These realities represent our starting point and signposts that serve to guide our progress and actions.

This chapter presents Monmouth University as an interesting and relevant case study of multicultural institutional change. The substantial growth and turnover in Monmouth faculty over the past decade coupled with a growing institution provides fertile ground for building learning communities. The Global Understanding Project, described in detail in the following pages, is a grassroots initiative that has built networks and learning communities, contributed to our understanding of, teaching, learning and scholarship and, ultimately, managed to incorporate a global vision within the fabric and structure of the university.

September 11, 2001. More than any other, this pivotal day in history brought faculty, staff and students together in an unprecedented grassroots effort to educate and support each other in the face of a new world reality. Classroom instructors struggled to maintain the relevance of students' education amidst an atmosphere of uncertainty and confusion. Seeking support and collaboration, faculty came together to explore different ways to react, respond and address events using the educational tools at their disposal. Campus communities scrambled to develop new ways of thinking about the geopolitical, military, cultural, religious, social and economic circumstances as they unfolded. For colleges and universities closest to the points of impact for these events, the educational imperative of this teachable moment was strongest.

The Lay of the Land: Understanding the Context of the Case

Monmouth University is a midsized, comprehensive liberal arts university, located on the New Jersey shore about an hour's drive south of New York City. Founded in 1933, Monmouth attained university status in 1995 and has established itself as a teaching university of regional distinction characterized by quality academic programs and small class sizes. The University continues to grow and is confronted by both the opportunities and challenges that such growth engenders. It currently offers more than 50 undergraduate and graduate degree programs and concentrations situated in six schools.

Its student body of over 6,200 represents, on average 26 states and 33 countries. In 2003, MU drew only 6.7% of its undergraduate student population from beyond the state with only 0.3% representing international students.

Among the graduate students, 2.3% came from US states other than New Jersey and 6.6% were international students. As of 2002, the faculty reflected greater diversity with nearly 11% of the full-time faculty originating from 12 countries and many others bringing substantial experience in and connections to countries across the globe. Added to this mix is the fact that Monmouth's full-time faculty complement has expanded by more than 34% in the past 5 years, with 75% of the entire faculty having joined Monmouth during the past eight years. Under a 1991-1995 grant from the W. K. Kellogg Foundation, the Monmouth community collectively considered how to "educate its students for leadership and social responsibility" and continues to incorporate civic service elements into its general education curriculum. Monmouth University's core requirements in cross-cultural studies and interdisciplinary perspectives, integration of Experiential Education requirements, expanding Study Abroad programs and increasing partnering relations with NGOs and social support institutions make it possible to 'bring the world to our students' in ways that were not feasible just a few short years ago. Monmouth has the added distinction of having the first accredited Social Work graduate program in the United States to offer an International and Community Development concentration. As an independent, comprehensive, teaching-oriented institution, Monmouth University's mission clearly articulates its commitment to foster lifelong learning and promote awareness of culture and diversity with the goal of enhancing the quality of life and enabling students to contribute significantly to their profession, community, and society.[1] So while Monmouth University has little diversity to build from, with vision and hope, this offers a case context that is rich in both challenges and opportunities.

The relevant case context is obviously broader than Monmouth University. Since September 11, 2001, the world in which we live has changed drastically. On September 12, 2001, the United Nations Security Council unanimously voted in favor of joining hands to combat international terrorism. While terrorism had struck many places across the globe prior to September 11, the nature and extent of this attack shook the edifice of globalism. Policy makers were faced with determining appropriate responses to threats of terror that helped people to feel more secure. The choices reflected through early dialogue and action included: withdrawing into isolationism (a largely ineffective strategy in today's interdependent world); working multilaterally to address these challenges at a global level (a potentially protracted and seemingly passive response); or engaging with venom and preemptive military interventions against

[1]The complete text of the mission statement of the University is available at: http://www.monmouth.edu/about/ataglance/mission.asp.

peoples and countries that allegedly sponsor terrorism (which could damage international relations and reputations and possibly escalate acts of terrorism).

The more appropriate and constructive path for an educational community was to reach out and engage through inquiry and dialogue the challenges confronting us; to work to understand the motivations and appreciate the perspectives of the people and countries whose cultures and lives while different, were so intimately tied to our own.

Planting the Seeds: History, Origins and Development of the Global Understanding Project

In the Spring of 2001, a group of MU faculty and academic administrators with experience and interest in international development began to coalesce, moving from occasional informal conversations to generating ideas for formal collaborative activities to raise global understanding. Political Science Professor Rekha Datta, primary initiator of this group, captured the initial focus of the group in her June 2001 e-mail:

> ...A network of faculty, students and MU community members who are interested in issues related to international dimensions of the following: economic development, peace, history, business, gender issues, human rights, health, education and other issues. This will serve as an interdisciplinary forum/center for the study of global and UN issues. The purpose and goal of this group will be to meet and decide on strategic planning to host an annual conference on campus or a public lecture on an issue of global importance. We can decide on a theme every year and have activities around that theme...

More than twenty faculty colleagues attended the first two meetings held over the summer. These early meetings focused on brainstorming ideas regarding the mission and possible activities of the group. In the second meeting participants came closer to identifying what such an initiative might accomplish and closed with plans to meet again on September 14th.

On September 11, 2001 our world and everyone else's changed dramatically. The Monmouth community experienced even more poignant connections as many members lost family or friends or knew people who had suffered such losses. Our September 14th meeting had an overwhelming response for a committee, drawing more than fifty people from across campus (faculty, staff, and students) and filling to capacity the room where we met. Prior to that apocalyptic day, the rationale for global awareness and consciousness raising at MU could best be framed in the context of need for cultural exchanges and business needs promoting global understanding. Driven by a need to do something, the new attendees came with a broad range of ideas for how to promote international development and understanding. While the founding members of the group were reticent to let go of their nascent vision, they understood the need for a plethora of co-existing conceptions and activities. To create a truly community-driven, campus-wide learning community, we would need to allow the interest, initiatives and ideas of all volunteer members to drive our activities. From this point forward full group meetings focused on generating ideas, coordinating efforts and articulating the mission, goals and objectives of the group. Subcommittees were formed and charged to carry out specific activities. Thus was the *Global Understanding Project* born!

Taxonomy and Anatomy of a Learning Community: The Mission, Activities, Structure and Functioning of GUP

A clear mission, goals, coherent, focused activities and supporting structures ensure the health of any learning community. GUP worked from the beginning to establish these. Summarized below in their current form, GUP members revisit, reflect on and modify these as needed each year in an open annual retreat.

Mission Statement: The Global Understanding Project is a community-based effort by faculty members, staff, and students at Monmouth University to encourage and promote activities and awareness concerning global issues. Through academic programs, field experiences, institutional relationships and exchanges, scholarship, and research, the participants in the Global Understanding Project will help fulfill that part of the University's broad mission of pursuing excellence and diversity in an increasingly interdependent world.

The general structure of this initiative is one that retains and reinforces the decentralized, collaborative and individual interest-driven aspects of its roots. The overall decisions for GUP-related activities are made by the Committee of the whole through dialogue and consensus. Subcommittees are structured and restructured according to needs and activities conceptualized by the whole committee. The subcommittee structure changes as needed to better reflect the needs of the group, the interests of its members and the global issues of the day. Since its inception GUP has had between six and seven active committees (see Table 1 for listing) who spearhead a particular initiative and overlap activity categories as appropriate and needed to ensure success. This effort has received tremendous support from numerous constituencies across campus and included growing representation and direct support from many academic and administrative departments, students and student clubs, staff, and external community groups.

Fruits of Our Labor: Nurturing a Productive Learning Community

The Global Understanding Project just passed its third anniversary. Having expanded in new and interesting directions, it has grown well beyond its original conception. With flexibility, vision, member initiative, and multiple action paths as its guiding foundation, GUP currently encompasses the four major categories of goal-referenced activities identified in Table 1. The rationale for and description of the specific activities undertaken within each area is provided below.

Academic Initiatives

To maximize long-term impact and increase the potential for deep and extended learning, GUP established a Curriculum Initiatives Committee to look

Table 1. Goals, Activities and Associated Subcommittees of the Global Understanding Project

Goals	Activities	Associated Subcommittees
• To promote integration of global awareness in academic programs through curricular and co-curricular initiatives and field experiences;	*Academic Initiatives:* curricular revisions, coordinated field experiences, internships and study abroad;	• Curriculum Initiatives Committee • Convention Organizing Committee • Event and Film Series Committee • Media/Publicity Committee • Scholarship Committee • Outreach/ Funding Committee • Student Committee • Strategic Planning Committee
• To assist in supporting Monmouth University organizations to bring a greater awareness of global issues to the community;	*Campus-wide Awareness Activities:* conventions, conferences, seminars, co-curricular/community building events, student clubs and activities, newsletters, websites, film series and other community fora;	
• To support the development of Monmouth University as a regional resource for global understanding.	*Community Outreach and Service Activities:* speakers and resource persons, website dialogs; *Building and Promoting Institutional Faculty and Student Expertise:* networking faculty interests, pursuing collaborative research in grants, establishing an NGO, facilitating scholarships and competitions.	

into developing a new thread within Monmouth's undergraduate core curriculum that would accentuate global understanding through international studies. By identifying courses with comparative international orientations, the committee was able to demonstrate the existing potential for adding such a core curricular requirement as well as the possibilities for building towards developing a global studies program. Once integrated within the University's programmatic structures, such initiatives would naturally encourage the development of additional courses with global dimensions and help to ensure that global awareness and understanding touches all students who pass through the University.

Embedded within this global studies thread was the concept of globally-oriented field experiences and internships and liaison with the Study Abroad Program. To move beyond simple awareness and superficial understanding, the global studies minor/certificate would require students to experience and actively work within a cultural setting, contributing to and reflecting on the application of their particular discipline. The proposal has begun to weave its way through the University committee structure and gained clarity and preliminary approval as it contributes to core curriculum dialogue. While awaiting approval, dialogue around the proposal's development has already produced a noticeable and desirable impact. For example, discussion of operational distinctions and supportive similarities between "global", "cross-cultural" and "American diversity" orientations at a faculty retreat were facilitated by this advanced understanding. Several faculty members who were engaged in these processes or have become aware of the possibility of a global studies concentration were encouraged to continue developing their globally-oriented courses or inspired to develop new ones. International study tours and courses are being conceptualized and put into place. Criminal Justice has established one such intensive study program and, with the support of GUP, faculty in the Political Sciences, Business and Education are actively conceptualizing additional programs. All of these efforts serve to enrich the diversity of offerings that address global understanding at the University and, in turn contribute to the ever-increasing awareness of the community.

Campus-wide Awareness Activities

This is the current heart and soul of GUP. While the other categories of activities are supportive and necessary, promoting awareness encompasses the activities that visibly and collectively contribute to the construction of a campus-wide learning community. Described below, these activities include: conferences, seminars, co-curricular/community building activities, student clubs and activities, newsletters, websites, and an International Film Series.

Conferences: The Global Understanding Convention (GUC) has become the most ambitious and effective event undertaken by GUP. Early on, the subcommittee responsible for designing and organizing the first GUP sponsored conference decided to search out a term that was inherently more conducive to encouraging and encompassing a wide variety of activities. Desiring to break away from the term "conference", which in academic circles produces visions of presentations, experts and 'talking heads", GUP decided to use the term *convention* to better encompass its wide range of activities and inspire interactivity and engagement. The following categories of activities were generated and have become part of the week-long event.

- *Anchornote Speakers* – A range of guest speakers drawn from government and international institutes and organizations are invited throughout the week to share perspectives on how international development issues and efforts impact communities and individuals across the globe. Past speakers have included a US senator, UN officials, and international, national, regional and local scholars, activists, and experts on issues associated with the convention theme. With convention activities spanning a full week, thematic speakers and panels are scheduled at key points and serve to *anchor* the convention.
- *Classroom Colloquia* – Initiated by Dr. Bonnie Mullinix (a faculty development professional and adult educator at MU) this unique aspect of the global convention creatively addresses space and scheduling concerns while expanding, engaging and broadening the potential learning community. During the Convention week, faculty build a global component into their course syllabi and open their regularly scheduled classes to students, faculty, and MU community to come and explore a topic related to the convention theme and their disciplinary interests. Classroom Colloquia generally take the following forms: Faculty-facilitated sessions, student-facilitated presentations, topic-specific guest presenters or panels. Faculty may choose to open their classrooms by designating a specific number of "spaces" for visiting learners to attend and participate or open their classroom to full capacity as they require their students to attend other colloquia sessions/convention activities during class time and/or throughout the week.
- *Issue Discussions and Galleries* – Faculty and/or students, individually or as part of class projects, organize and sponsor Poster Sessions and/or Community Dialogues on convention issues and offer them in the form of panels, roundtables or other types of sessions.
- *Community Connections* – Students from area middle and high schools attend a half-day interactive workshop on issues related to the convention theme, and individuals and community groups from the surrounding area have moved from sponsoring events to active participation and facilitation of convention events.
- *UN Trip* - A guided day-long trip to the United Nations offers interested

students, faculty and staff tours and access to special sessions, speakers and discussions around critical global issues.

- *International Films* - Community members identify, arrange for and introduce films that speak to global issues and convention themes from a variety of cultural vantage points and lead reflective discussions immediately following the showing(s).

Media Coverage – Campus television, radio and newspaper have exhibited an increasing interest in covering the Convention. While the first year included publishing the Convention schedule in the student newspaper, the second year included interviews and key stories. In addition, local newspapers (Asbury Park Press, The Link) and other media have increased their coverage of GUC and GUP activities.

Occasional Co-curricular Events, Seminars and Community-building activities: In response to world events, campus needs, and faculty and student initiatives, GUP has sponsored a variety of occasional activities and events. In the Fall of 2001, shortly after its founding "Conversations about Cultures" and "Holidays of the World" were organized. Like the majority of GUP events, these half-day programs were the result of the unselfish contribution of time from volunteer members (faculty, students and staff) and resources from several offices and departments across campus. In the 2002-2003, a series of 1 ¼ hour sessions entitled "The Serious Business of War" brought the University community together to explore the issues associated with the US interventions in Afghanistan and Iraq. Discussions were framed by faculty from a variety of disciplines and touched on rationale, military strategies, media coverage, and a variety of critical current issues. On average, these events drew 100 participants from across campus. While such an audience might be considered modest on most campuses, based on past attendance at similar noncompulsory educational events these turnouts were considered excellent for Monmouth University.

Student clubs and Student-initiated activities: A number of student clubs on campus have either developed or found a collaborative home and flourished under association with GUP. The Global Service Club (previouslyG^2 or Going Global Club) is a direct off-shoot of GUP . In addition to engaging faculty to speak about international development issues at club meetings, club members have helped with GUP Convention logistics, organizing convention sessions and publicizing and actively participating in GUP sponsored events. The Amnesty International Chapter at Monmouth, the Study Abroad Club and the International Club also have direct liaisons with GUP and together they have co-sponsored a variety of events.

Newsletter: The GUP newsletter, *Global Matters,*has offered a printed mechanism for documenting the initiatives and activities of the group. Published two to three times a year, each issue highlights past and future endeavors. Contributions are solicited through GUP and the volunteer GUP member editors construct issues based on submissions from faculty, students and staff. *Global Matters* is distributed both in print and electronically across campus in an effort to both increase awareness of global issues and encourage active participation by the campus community. With publication costs funded initially through departmental contributions, *Global Matters* now constitutes a regular portion of the base operating budget of GUP.

Website: GUP has developed, maintained and regularly added to its website since Fall of 2001. This virtual community reference point began as Dr. Rekha Datta worked with the MU Instructional Technology Web Factory to develop a web-based discussion forum in the aftermath of September 11, and identified faculty willing to share their expertise and answer questions posed by MU Community members. Subsequently the website has begun to serve as a documentation point for GUP activities. (see: http://www.monmouth.edu/gup).

International Film Series: Originating as an element of the 2002 GUConvention, in 2003 a GUP committee formed to organize a year long offering of monthly films that culminated in a week's worth of film events during the Convention. GUP Faculty initiators invited MU community members to facilitate films and follow-on discussions to move the experience beyond mere entertainment and into the realm of deepening understanding of cultures and practices from across the globe. Offered free of charge and one of the first monthly film series on campus, attendance increased as word got around of the popcorn, soda and raffled video card initiated by the committee and chair Sherry Wein of the Communication Department. Well received, the committee plans to extend the series into the coming year, coordinating with courses that have international films as their central component and expanding collaboration with and sponsorship by community-based organizations. Support from the Provost and the Associate VP for Academic Initiatives, has facilitated a growing partnership with the Two River Film Festival (http://www.tworiverfilmfestival.com), that currently includes discussions of dovetailing GUP's annual convention with Two River's international film festival.

Community Outreach and Service Activities

This category represents one of the lesser-developed areas to date, but one with great potential and importance. The ability of University speakers and resource persons, website dialogs, and other outreach vehicles to help bring the issues of global awareness to surrounding communities should be nurtured. The campus-wide awareness activities and other mechanisms for building the University learning community will continue to identify individuals and opportunities for reaching out to the wider community as well as inviting the community into the University. One example of this was the team of MU faculty that met with local teachers in Long Branch to help address issues in the post 911 teaching era and work to effectively promote global understanding in the schools. The Convention's special half-day program for school children has been well received and attended (averaging 100 students per year and touching over 10 schools in six school districts) and prompted sponsorship by MU Student Government and a local education professional association (the Jersey Shore Chapter of Phi Delta Kappa). Greater awareness of the Convention itself has already filtered out to the surrounding community and spawned requests for opening Convention events to local community groups and surrounding colleges. As the reputation of GUP grows, so too does the reputation of its members and their willingness to be engaged in increasing global awareness, both on campus and off.

Building and Promoting Institutional, Faculty and Student Expertise

This category includes several of the primary interests of the founding members and remains perhaps the least formally developed of all categories. It includes: networking faculty interests; collaborative research and grants; establishing an NGO; and facilitating scholarships and competitions. There is no doubt that networking of faculty interests persists and grows as scholarly interests and expertise become more visible through presentations and session facilitation. While there are only nascent examples of faculty networking resulting in research or scholarly collaboration (this book chapter being one), there are some promising examples of international expertise and experience nurturing and facilitating grant proposal development. In 2002, the University's Social Work Department received a grant from the US State Department for an Educational Partnership with Latvia. The individuals who collaborated to conceptualize and draft this successful project were active GUP members. Other grants to extend the activities of the GUP itself have been drafted through the Office of Academic Program Initiatives, who's Associate Vice President Dr. Saliba Sarsar, has actively supported GUP since its inception. During the second year, the entire MU community was engaged in helping to define GUP by submitting their interpretive designs to a logo competition organized by the Art department. Thirty-nine MU students, faculty and staff submitted entries with many providing written descriptions of how their design reflected elements of the GUP mission. The range of design, creativity, and effort was inspiring and made

Figure 1. Global Understanding Project Logo

the task of selecting the final design particularly challenging for the six-member jury of faculty, students and staff. All designs were displayed during an interactive exhibit at the GUConvention where viewers were encouraged to record their interpretations and impressions of entries. This information was solicited to help GUP consider how to use other logo designs to represent future GUConvention themes. Posters designed in the third year helped to decorate the campus and promote the Convention, a practice slated to be expanded and increasingly showcased in future years.

Cultivation Techniques: Sustaining the Learning Community

While building a campus-wide learning community can start with little more than the seed of an idea germinating in the mind of a few individuals, to flourish it requires broad-based commitment and contributions from a wide range of individuals. Moreover, it requires institutional support for the idea, encouragement of participants, and willingness to redirect and occasionally reconceptualize and reutilize existing resources. Finally, the ability to creatively and strategically draw on relevance and current concerns can help to sustain and catalyze the growth of a learning community.

Incentives, Funding , and Administrative and Structural Support

Support for GUP has been evident since its founding. The Provost, Associate VP for Academic Program Initiatives and Deans of the School of Humanities and Social Sciences, the School of Business, and of the Graduate School were active members in early meetings and have continued their participation and support for GUP activities. Key individuals from across campus have maintained a commitment to GUP and, even when unable to attend regular meetings, have participated electronically and taken the time to assist as requested. The Provost, the President, Public Affairs and Deans and Chairs from across the University have opened their resources, financial and human, to help further the project. Indeed, in its first year all GUP Activities were accomplished through such voluntary contributions, as no operating budget or institutional home existed for the project. Even in its second year, when a budget of $5,000 was established in support of GUP, significant in-kind and cash contributions from University departments and external community sources were forthcoming to make major events like the Convention possible. The Office of Academic Program Initiatives provided a logical and nurturing home for GUP in these early years, supporting the decentralized, participatory decision making structure and facilitating committee and member involvement by coordinating primary meetings and communications and taking responsibility for communication with higher administrative levels of the University.

Perhaps more important than the donations of logistical support, meeting space, food and equipment needed to plan and implement GUP activities, was the public acknowledgement of the importance of GUP to the University. It was acknowledged early on that participation in GUP was deemed valuable service to the University and to the community. This helped faculty applying for candidacy, tenure and promotion to risk and justify participation in GUP, where they might otherwise have had to redirect their time to alternate traditional University and Community Service. The official recognition of this service value was formally announced in the 2004 GUP Retreat and practically borne out by the tenure of several active GUP members this past academic year.

The 2003-2004 Academic year saw the arrival of a new President at Monmouth University and the development of strategic plan that had positive implications for GUP. President Paul Gaffney actively participated in the GUConvention, inviting and introducing anchornote speakers, serving as a panelist, hosting luncheons and attending open events throughout the week. The strategic plan not only served to highlight the unique contributions of GUP but to identify it as a possible "Center of Distinctiveness." As a result, the coming year will include exploration of transitioning this GUProject into a Global Understanding Institute at Monmouth.

Inclusive Outreach, Strategic Communication, Active Encouragement and Experimentation

At periodic intervals through formal and informal mechanisms, at group and individual levels, community members were informed and invited to participate in GUP activities. Whether as initiators, implementers or participants, everyone was helped to feel that their contributions were important. Faculty on the GUP committee would regularly reach out to colleagues in their department and across campus to personally encourage them to participate in events. The GUConvention Organizing Committee in particular worked to invite students, faculty and staff from all disciplinary backgrounds to participate. Many of the innovative aspects of the Convention and other GUP events emerged from this inclusive and supportive outlook.

In preparing for the Convention a number of specific support strategies were undertaken. GUC Organizing Committee members provided individual consultation on convention session and colloquia design to incorporate interactive components. In the second and third years, the newly established Faculty

Resource Center hosted a planning workshop for faculty facilitating classroom colloquia during the convention.

External Events that Catalyze

The impact of unfolding events is evidenced in the themes of the week-long Global Understanding Convention (GUC); the event that has become the visible focal point of GUP activities. In order to capture interest and cultivate participation across campus, the week-long Global Understanding Convention (GUC) identifies overarching themes that encompass a wide range of disciplinary interpretations and, as illustrated below, address timely concerns.

- 2002 "Challenges in the 21st Century: Sustainable Development" – drew on the interests of the founders of the GUP community and focused on engaging people in conversations about international development from village level through to UN policy levels. Coming shortly before the World Summit on Sustainable Development, this theme was timely and flexible.
- 2003 "Challenges in the 21st Century: Liberty/Security, War/Peace" – Events resonating with Liberty/Security included: the passage of the Patriot Act and the pending Patriot Act II; the establishment of the Department of Homeland Security, to incorporate the Department of Naturalization and Immigration Services (heightening a sense of vulnerability and xenophobia in the nation). Meanwhile the "War/Peace" dialectic responded to: the military and political interventions in Afghanistan, Congressional authorization of the use of force against Iraq; the unanimous passage of UN Resolution 1331 (authorizing serious consequences if Iraq did not comply); the UN/UK's unsuccessful efforts to get UN backing for the use of military force and creation of the 'coalition of the willing'; and, finally, the US-led invasion of Iraq.
- 2004 "Freedom from Fear: Quest for a Livable World" – Influential events included: the escalating and continuing war in Iraq, the deterioration of the reputation of the United States around the world; the extension of threats to civilian targets and associated kidnappings and beheadings; ongoing terror threat alerts; human rights violations and continuing violence around the world. The goal was to engage in dialog about how to address our fundamental freedom from fear and want and instill hope in creating a livable world.
- 2005 "Making a World of Difference: Building Local-Global Connections" – Concepualized as a positively proactive convention theme, input was invited around related subthemes such as: forgotten peoples, success stories in community building, health, environment, children, security and government, freedom and democracy.

Reaping the Harvest: Assessing Participation and Outcomes

As with any learning activity, monitoring and periodically disseminating the impact of a campus-wide learning community is important. The engagement of members of the Monmouth community was highly visible throughout the year. Using the Convention as a marker event, some statistics on participation help to paint this picture. In 2002, 46 events were provided by over 47 presenter-facilitators and their supporters. In 2003 this grew to 56 events conducted by 55 presenter-facilitators while 2004 saw 66 events conducted by 80 presenter facilitators (a respective annual growth rate of 22% and 18% in events and 17% - 45% in presenter-facilitators – see Table 2 for a breakdown of session types).

Each year, MU faculty and additional staff, visiting scholars, community members and/or UN and State officials lent their leadership skills to organizing events along with approximately 11 classes of students (representing at least 250 student-presenters). While the majority of presenter-facilitators remain faculty, each year has seen a rise in the number of students organizing sessions and invited guest speakers external to Monmouth. Convention activities touched approximately 1280 Monmouth Community Members in the first year with participation in 2003 and 2004 convention sessions estimated at over 2200 and 3800 individuals respectively (approximately 73% increase each year - see Table 3 below for a breakdown of participation).

Table 2. GU Convention Events by Type

Convention events included:	GUC 2002	GUC 2003	GUC 2004
Classroom Colloquia	19	19	26
Poster Sessions and Exhibits	5	8	8
Panels and/or Speakers featuring visiting scholars, community members and/or UN and State officials	6	6	15
Special workshops or roundtable sessions	6	6	6
Large audience films or smaller in-class video sessions	3 + 5	8 + 5	8
Field Excursions	2	1	1
International luncheons, performances and/or festivals	1	3	2
Totals	46	56	66

While we have tracked total numbers and categories of participants in convention events where possible, we were unable to track individual participation and the extent to which the convention touched specific members of the University community. Thus, calculating and presenting subpopulation percentages is inappropriate. None-the-less, it is clear from overall participation data that we have touched a significantly larger percentage of the campus population in each successive year. The broader distribution of events across campus and the increase in week-long, public poster sessions, GUP logo and poster competitions, galleries and exhibits all contributed to a growing awareness of the Convention as a campus-wide event. The common theme and broad engagement helped members of the community to come together around areas of common interest and explore issues of global diversity at increasing depth during the second and third year, lending credence to GUP's stature as a learning community. There is no doubt that cumulative impact of GUP activities is starting to become part of Monmouth's landscape.

Moreover, the reports from faculty and students about the impact that GUP has had on their perceptions, understanding and appreciation for diversity and issues of global understanding has been palpable. As a campus where such

Table 3. Approximate Person Attendance at GUC Sessions

Categories of MU Community Members:	GUC 2002	GUC 2003	GUC 2004
Faculty*	160	296	284
Students*	963	1633	3233
MU staff*	44	151	158
Community members and middle school students	116	157	179
Totals	1283	2237	3854
Guest Speakers (external)	*15*	*12*	*26*

* *These figures likely include overlap of participation by same individuals in multiple events; as a mixture of estimates and actual counts, these and other categories may be under-reported.*

events have historically experienced limited attendance, it is heartening to see increasing numbers of students participating, organizing and discussing the impact that these events have on their view of issues in the world. One example of this is the response from students who participated in the trip to the United Nations. Results from a quiz reflected what students learned about the UN system and structure and from the briefing sessions on terrorism. The building of the GUP learning community was underscored by students' articulated appreciation of the rapport they developed with instructors and their peers as part of their field trip experience. Students emerging from other GUP events continued to talk about them as they walked around campus and reentered their classes. In 2004, student GUP members even reported evening conversations in the residence halls as students shared information from the convention events they attended and reviewed the program and schedule to coordinate their attendance the following day. Students also wrote reflective papers capturing their thoughts on the convention messages and session impact not only for their courses, but for publication in *Global Matters* and the MU student newspaper *The Outlook.* Faculty and GUConvention Organizing Committee members also reflected formally on the convention noting the contribution it made to their courses, their student's ability to consolidate and present important ideas to a broader audience, and their own professional development.

Planning for Next Season: Reflections on Experiences, Challenges and Lessons Learned

Inclusivity, critical for a healthy campus-wide learning community, was a dominant concern for GUP as it developed extensive agenda and activities. Leadership from initial GUP members already modeled engagement of faculty from diverse ethno-cultural and interdisciplinary backgrounds who were vigilant in their dedication to ensuring participation of all members of the University community. Personal communications and outreach helped to encourage participation. Repeat events grew as participants began to understand the range of possibilities open to them. Personal initiative that, in some sectors of the academy, may have been misinterpreted, was appreciated in the GUP environ. Interesting interdisciplinary juxtapositions and cross-community partnerships generated sessions of critical interest. In general, many of the characteristics of an effective learning organization identified by Senge (1990) were evident.

Equalizing Status and Participation – GUP has maintained a keen awareness of the need to transcend barriers and champion inclusivity. The one area where GUP's outreach strategies have resulted in only limited success has been the ability to enable the inclusion of MU staff. Proposals to encourage the ability of hourly staff to participate in GUP events and, most particularly the convention have been put forth each year. While each year we have gotten a little farther with the proposal, as we ascend the bureaucratic hierarchy the support slips back. Nonetheless, the 2004 GUP retreat continued to articulate the critical importance of staff participation to the ultimate success of GUP and voiced a renewed commitment to making it a reality.

Reflecting on Support Structures and Implementation Systems

The first year was a landmark year for tackling conceptual issues and learning how to communicate ideas associated with GUP, its activities and the Convention. Each committee determined their path using the GUP mission and principles as their guide. This self-determining, action-oriented approach appropriately values, appreciates and relies on community member expertise and interests to direct and drive GUP activities. Such decentralized control allows for certain committees and activities to flourish, others to fade and still others to work themselves out of existence. In year one the most productive committees were the GU Curriculum and Convention Committees. In year two, the Convention Organizing Committee and the International Film Series Committee increased their visible activity, while the Curriculum Committee suspended its visible activities as it awaited decisions regarding its pending proposals and the Strategic Planning Committee pushed through, concluded its contributions, and faded out of existence. This healthy dynamic structure is appropriate for large scale learning communities where the primary force behind action is the intersecting interests and commitments of its members and the challenges at hand.

Communicating Vision: The challenges associated with the logistics of organizing and implementing the week-long, campus-wide GUConvention were significant. As one of the largest, most ambitious and unique learning activities ever undertaken at Monmouth, it was definitely breaking new ground. The ability to communicate the vision for the Convention, all of its components and the variety of ways that each MU community member could participate was critically important to its success. The focus remained on engagement, at any level, and welcoming any input or participation strategy that contributed to the overall intention of increasing global understanding.

No Space.Limited Interest: Perhaps the most creative response to the challenge of lack of space was introduction and popularization of the Classroom Colloquia. To address the perpetual lack of access to classroom space, the generally low attendance at public events and the desire to engage the greatest number of community members in the week-long series of events, it was proposed that faculty identify one class session where they might integrate a global component. While this concept and its potential was only initially understood by a handful of faculty, as it was explained, nurtured and implemented, more faculty came to understand its potential.

Opportunistic Implementation Strategies - Tapping Volunteer Resources and the potential of Technology: To survive and grow, GUP relied most strongly on the dedication, vision and expertise of its founding members. Logistically, managing the submission of sessions was facilitated by the appointment of one of this Chapter's authors during GUP's first year to the Office of Academic Program Initiatives and to support the Social Work's International and Community Development Concentration. Given the support of GUP by both departments, she was able to spend a significant amount of her time over a three-month period (and smaller amounts over an 8 month period) supporting the Convention and key GUP activities. Building on the work facilitating faculty and administrative conversations around the design of a Center for Teaching and Learning she was well positioned to reach out to faculty. The first year required a significant amount of e-mail communication, database development and management and creation of templates and merge files to produce the Convention programs, schedule sheets, session signs, and personalized communications. It also provided the possibility for collecting data on participation (manually recording attendance at each event), developing photographic archives of the events and promoting the beginnings of documentation and convention proceedings. Her movement in the second year into a faculty development support position within Instructional Technology Services allowed her to develop a Faculty Resource Center (FRC) offering the ability to officially communicate with faculty and directly support learning communities on campus (http://www.monmouth.edu/frc). It also offered direct connections to the talents of personnel in MU's Web Factory who assisted in the development of a web-based session submission form and on-line session management system as well as a parallel web-based attendance reporting structure that decentralized the data collection responsibilities. These practical advances were collected and documented in the form of a Management Information System complete with guide and an accompanying CD containing all archived information from the first year and a half of GUC Management. In the interest of sustainability and continuity, the 2003 GUP Retreat helped to identify individuals interested in learning about and taking over responsibility for managing these streamlined systems.

Calculating and Considering Contributions: Beyond the example above, many other GUP members have contributed substantial amounts of time that often, when undocumented and uncalculated, become hidden costs of nurturing such large learning communities. Facilitating the printing of physical and virtual schedules and programs were handled by the University's Director of Institutional Research, who, like so many on the organizing committee, spent untold work (and often even more extensive personal) hours working to get materials ready on time.

No Place to Call Home: Even with such a loose and decentralized structure and many volunteers, the strain on the Office of Academic Program Initiatives was apparent, particularly during the second year. As one of nine initiatives overseen by this office, the size and scope of GUP activities required more administrative support than was possible to effectively sustain. While the majority of the tasks were undertaken by faculty, staff of various departments donating time and students volunteering, coordination and facilitation of communications and official requests required the attention of this one office. Proposals for appointment of a half-time secretary and the strategic use of graduate assistants to support the committee made in the second year began to come to fruition in 2005.

Projecting Next Steps

All those who have taken part in the activities of GUP agree on the critical importance of its grassroots origins, emphasis on initiative, voluntary nature, seamless blending of disciplinary boundaries, and the facilitative opportunity it provides for networking and collaborating with various constituencies on and off campus. While members are reluctant to lose this special niche, there is a realization to sustain this vibrant learning community, GUP requires identity and resources. At the 2003 GUP Retreat, a conscious decision was made not to establish an executive committee or to formalize GUP within the University's academic structure. Fears of losing the ability to be innovative, of remaining fully inclusive and of being wholly flexible were cited as factors in reaching this decision, as were the realities of a changing University administration and strategic plan implementation in the coming years. Engagement in the strategic planning process initiated by MU's new President, helped GUP to articulate a vision that is now embedded in the University's Strategic Plan: to create a Global Understanding Institute (http://www.monmouth.edu/strategicplan, Accessed 8/13/05). While still at a conceptual stage, our hope is that GUP will continue in a way that will facilitate the flexible growth and periodic rebirth of our campus-wide learning community.

Concluding Commentary

Cited by the president, provost, deans and faculty as one of the most ambitious, successful and rewarding campus-wide learning events in Monmouth University's history, this grassroots, faculty-initiated and MU community-led event is becoming part of the academic landscape at Monmouth. GUP's strategic approach to unfolding its activities is a key to its growth and success:

- Maintaining a focus that is so clearly relevant to projected learning horizons and reflective of the University's mission helps to sustain GUP's momentum.
- Opening all activities to volunteers from across campus, be they faculty, administrators, staff or students creates an atmosphere of inclusiveness.
- Allowing decentralized groups to initiate activities that operate to further the University's mission without tying them to bureaucratic approval structures encourages innovation and creativity and values GUP member interest and expertise.
- The GUConvention strategy of opening classrooms and allowing MU community members to attend sessions in on-going courses transforms the University into an open learning community focused on global awareness and international issues.

Taken as a whole, these strategies help to foster the concept of a campus-wide learning community which promotes inclusiveness, diversity and global understanding.

Now more than ever, we need a fuller understanding of global realities, ideas and ideals. We hope to keep up the spirit of voluntary cooperation among faculty, staff, and students that we have cultivated here through Monmouth University's Global Understanding Project. We hope to continue enriching campus and community understanding of global issues and inspiring young scholars and experienced community members to take action, foster global change and help make the world more livable. As a learning community, we are sustained by our belief that such understanding helps create a more tolerant world, a world of hope and peace, in which human beings across cultures will appreciate each other. A world that embraces diversity; a world where each one of us is respected for who we are, the roles we play and the contributions we make. This is the world we are working towards, from our little corner with our campus community.

References

Boyer, E. (1990). *Scholarship Reconsidered: Priorities of the Professoriate.* Princeton, NJ: Carnegie Foundation for the Advancement of Teaching.

Green, M., & Baer, M. (2001, November 9). Global learning in a new age. *Chronicle of Higher Education.*

Huber, M. T., & Hutchings, P. (n.d.). *Integrative learning: Mapping the terrain* (Carnegie Foundation). Retrieved August 13, 2005, from www.carnegiefoundation.org/LiberalEducation/integrative_learning.htm

Monmouth University Faculty Resource Center. (n.d.). Retrieved August 13, 2005, from http://www.monmouth.edu/frc

Monmouth University Global Understanding Project. (n.d.). Retrieved August 13, 2005, from http://www.monmouth.edu/gup.

Monmouth University Mission Statement. (n.d.). Retrieved August 13, 2005, from http://www.monmouth.edu/about/ataglance/mission.asp

Monmouth University Strategic Plan 2004-2014. (n.d.). Retrieved August 13, 2005, from http://www.monmouth.edu/strategicplan

Senge, P. M. (1990). *The Fifth Discipline. The art and practice of the learning organization,* London: Random House.

Two River Film Festival Website.(n.d.). Retrieved August 13, 2005, from http://www.tworiverfilmfestival.com

---

Dr. Bonnie Mullinix was a visiting professor and Instructional Design Specialist coordinating the ITS Faculty Resource Center at Monmouth University (1998-2005). **Dr. Rekha Datta** is Chair and associate professor of Political Science at Monmouth University. **Dr. Morris Saldov** is an associate professor of Social Work specializing in International and Community Development at Monmouth University.

III. Systemic Change Initiatives

Chapter 22
Moving the Mountain: Social Justice Education at the University

Julie Andrzejewski and John Alessio

This is the story of a collaborative violence prevention education project that was part of a long-term effort to influence a mid-western university to address issues of diversity and social justice.

Background

This project must be viewed in the context of important efforts that laid the foundation for its success. In the 1970s the Minnesota legislature required most teachers to have Human Relations training for licensure, establishing the seeds of an academic program that would grow into a department addressing social justice issues. In the early 1980s a precedent-setting sex discrimination lawsuit (Andrzejewski & Craik, 1995) was settled, establishing some parameters for institutional change (for example, provisions for more women department chairs, a full time Affirmative Action Officer, etc.). A few years later, the emerging Department of Human Relations and Multicultural Education established the most challenging and popular educational minor of any state university in Minnesota. Students from this minor initiated activist organizations on campus; others initiated a successful movement to require three MGM (Multicultural, Gender, Minority) courses as a component of the general education program. Faculty and staff tenaciously pressed for Women's Studies, Ethnic Studies, and various student support services based on race, gender, disability, sexual orientation, national origin, and religion.

In the 1990s, three university-wide grant projects fostered institutional change toward social and environmental justice. The first, Responsible Citizenship in a Democracy (Andrzejewski, 1993), provided small grants to students, faculty, or staff for initiating education or activities on active citizenship and participatory democracy. The second, Curriculum Transformation Through Critique (Alessio, 1996), provided reassigned time for faculty to transform a course by integrating non-western perspectives critical of dominant paradigms. The third grant project, Multicultural Perspectives and Global Understanding (Andrzejewski, 1997), brought distinguished women scholars of color to facilitate semester-long faculty seminars to deepen the critique and provide additional resources for curriculum transformation. Approximately 10 percent of the faculty participated in the seminars and changed their courses accordingly. At this same time, new student support programs were being established for women, students of color, and gay, lesbian, bisexual and transgender students.

The Problem

In spite of these significant achievements working toward social justice, St. Cloud State University (like most universities), continued to experience numerous incidents of disrespect, harassment, and hate crimes – ranging from vandalism to assault – based on prejudicial motivations. Students studying Change Agent Skills, the capstone course on activism in the Human Relations minor, first brought the seriousness of this situation to light in 1994. They collected anecdotal information indicating that incidents of harmful and degrading comments, jokes, harassment, threats, and bias crimes were occurring with some frequency in the residence halls. They noted that these events were, for the most part, not reported, and thus occurred below the radar of the university administration. Not long thereafter, the campus gained national notoriety when racist and anti-Semitic symbols and vandalism were reported. At the same university, data compiled each year by the campus women's center documented that sexual assaults most frequently involved first year students as victims and perpetrators. While a two-hour workshop on Respect and Responsibility is required of all first year students, the student study concluded that more in-depth education was needed to ameliorate these serious problems.

Developing the Project

Acting on the student recommendations, Andrzejewski developed a course for first year students called Human Relations (HURL) 101: Human Relations, Harassment, and Personal Behavior and successfully moved it through the curriculum approval process. Since no resources were available to offer the course, Andrzejewski began to explore grant support. In order to gain wide support for the project, she circulated a draft proposal of a project that would involve the residence halls, certain general education faculty, and staff of the student support services. Advice was sought from the Affirmative Action Office, the American Indian Center, the College of Education Cultural Diversity Office, the Lesbian, Gay, Bisexual, Transgender Resource Center, the Multicultural Student Program, Residential Life, Student Disability Services, Student Life and Development, the Women's Center, and the Departments of English and Communication Studies. She held several meetings with representatives of these groups during one academic year, reshaping the proposal based on their suggestions. By the time the proposal was submitted to funding agencies, detailed letters of support from many different groups strengthened the likelihood of success.

Theoretical Foundations

The educational project was based on a number of theoretical traditions. John Dewey (1916) proposed that democracy and social responsibility are predicated upon education grounded in experience, reflection, and awareness. Paulo Freire (1970) identified the liberatory role that education can play through the study of domination and subjugation, and the critical examination of underlying assumptions and life experiences. Critical theory, critical race theory, feminist theory, and critical pedagogy illuminate various aspects of challenging hegemony and violence in schools (Banks, 1996, 1997; Bell, 1997; McIntosh, 1988; Parker, Deyhle, & Villenas, 1999; Sleeter, 1994, 1996; Young, 1990), including the following contentions:

- Harassment, hate crimes, and violence are not simply a result of aberrant actions by individuals but are supported by a hierarchical social, political, and economic system.
- Ignorance, misinformation and stereotypes about various groups of people are commonly perpetuated through media, schools, and other social institutions.
- Negative attitudes and behaviors toward groups different than one's own are defended as insignificant and are commonly used as a method of in-group bonding.
- At the same time, group-based privileges are largely invisible and unexamined.

Education at all levels often fails to address the existence and consequences of common everyday prejudicial behaviors. Instead, school and university responses to violence, harassment, and bias crimes tend to focus on punishment and increased surveillance rather than educational programs to change individual behaviors and social norms.

New research and data collection about climate in schools and post-secondary educational institutions indicate that biased language, prejudicial remarks, name-calling, teasing, harassing, or bullying based on group status is a common experience in schools and on campuses (Bickmore, 2002; Dupper, 2002; Human Rights Watch, 2001). Not surprisingly, even violence and bias crimes are not rare occurrences in higher education (Stage and Downey, 1999). The seriousness and complexity of the relationship between school violence and issues of diversity and marginalization is emerging from these studies. Many students are targeted for physical, behavioral, or perceived characteristics and some of these targeted students become so affected that they respond with violence (Vossekuil, Reddy, Fein, Borum, & Modzeleski, 2000).

The Tower of Violence

A model which illustrates possible connections between everyday acts of prejudice and more serious acts of discrimination and violence is the Tower of Violence, adapted and expanded by Andrzejewski from Outfront Minnesota.[1] This model is useful as a theoretical and educational tool for exploring and reflecting upon the everyday actions of individuals and groups and the relationship to disrespectful behaviors, harassment, bias crimes, and violence, based on visible or perceived characteristics. (See Figure 1.)

The Citizenship for Diversity Project

These theoretical foundations served as the basis for an experiential educational project initiated by Andrzejewski recommended by students and revised by staff and faculty. Titled the Citizenship for Diversity (C4D) project, it would provide first-year students with an opportunity to develop leadership skills in preventing or ameliorating harassment, bias crimes, and violence. The C4D project covered issues of race, class, gender, national origin, disability, religion, sexual orientation, and physical appearance, and focused on the links between everyday attitudes, jokes, and behaviors, and an environment conducive to harassment, violence, and bias crimes. The goal of the project was to raise awareness of the prevalence of these behaviors in everyday life, to prac-

[1]A simplified version of this model was originally obtained from the Gay Lesbian Community Action Council in 1996 (now Outfront Minnesota). The model shown in this chapter has been revised by Andrzejewski. As she worked with it, she discovered the Anti-Defamation League had developed and copyrighted an almost identical model called the Pyramid of Violence. After extensive checking, neither ADL or Outfront Minnesota could identify the original source. ADL indicated Andrzejewski should continue to reference Outfront Minnesota as the source.

tice changing personal habits of oppression, and to develop leadership skills in changing the norms of daily living and learning environments.

A new course, Human Relations (HURL 101), served as the cornerstone of the Citizenship for Diversity Project. This course addressed the links be-

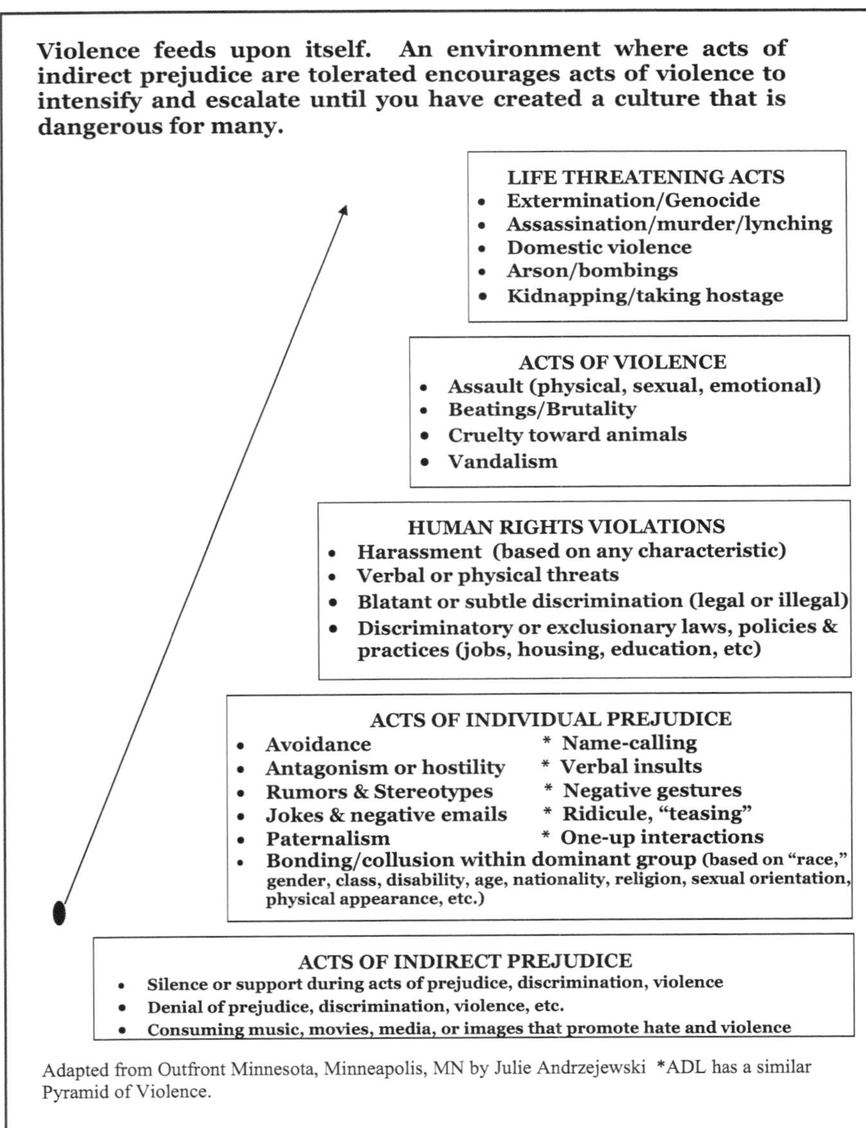

Figure 1. Tower of Violence

tween violence, ignorance, and negative behaviors toward non-dominant groups. The project provided the opportunity for first year students, living in the same residence hall, to take Human Relations 101 paired with an English or Speech Communication general education core course through a student retention program. The goal of the project was to engage first year students in developing knowledge and skills for grassroots leadership efforts to prevent disrespectful behaviors, harassment and violent bias crimes on campus. The project was supported by $75,000 from the Otto Bremer Foundation, $4,000 from the Minnesota Council Against Violence and Abuse and matched by approximately $35,000 from the university.

The project included three linked components:

1. *A core group of students living in the same residence hall.* First year students in residence halls were the first target population. Therefore, students in a student retention program who lived in the same residence hall were given the opportunity to participate. The objective was to create a knowledge and skill base among enough students to change the norms of common everyday attitudes and interactions that may unconsciously establish a biased and hostile living and learning environment for students from non-dominant groups.
2. *Enrollment in HURL 101 paired with an English or Communication Studies course.* Students in the student retention program were able to choose whether to be involved with the C4D project. From the courses available to them through the student retention program, they could select or avoid the paired courses in this project. While they were given a one-page explanation of the project, we were unable to determine how many actually read the information before making their course selections.

   HURL 101 drew upon many pedagogical traditions in content and method. In addition to readings on such topics as white privilege, male bonding, fat oppression and the like, we worked closely with the various student support service directors who recommended student speakers to share personal experiences of harassment, hate crimes, or violence with the classes. In some cases directors of the support services also came as part of the panel to share information about what services their office provided for students.

   Videos exposing the hidden influences of the media and other aspects of discrimination and violence augmented the informational component of the course (for example, Katz, 2000). Experiential out of class projects increased student awareness of each of these issues in their personal lives. Students interviewed others about knowledge of anti-Semitism, identified examples of racism and xenophobia in their personal lives, investigated myths about socioeconomic class, stepped outside gender role boundaries, examined the consequences of name calling and jokes about GLBT students, observed judgments based on physical appearance, and explored campus attitudes toward students with disabilities.

3. *General education courses in English or Speech Communication were paired with HURL 101* to broaden the research base, analytical skills, and personal development.

   Writing and communication assignments in paired sections of English and Communication Studies classes developed critical analysis skills, social awareness, and consciousness of citizenship; providing opportunities for students to process information from the Human Relations course. Essays, research projects, small group presentations, and public speeches in these classes helped students transition from egocentric perspectives to social awareness, develop critical thinking about social justice issues, and consider life goals related to making a better world.

Faculty/Staff Collaboration: Implementing the Citizenship for Diversity Project

Boyer's (1990) concepts of scholarship, especially the scholarships of teaching, integration, and application informed the faculty/staff development component of the project. About the scholarship of teaching, Boyer states, "As a *scholarly* enterprise, teaching begins with what the teacher knows.... Pedagogical procedures must be carefully planned, continuously examined, and relate directly to the subject taught.... [Great teachers] stimulate active, not passive, learning and encourage students to be critical, creative thinkers.... Further, good teaching means that faculty, as scholars, are also learners.... [T]eaching, at its best, means not only transmitting knowledge, but *transforming* and *extending* it as well..." (pp. 21-22). By design, the C4D project drew upon faculty teaching general education required courses who already had commitments to diversity and social justice, who were already involved in transforming their curricula, many of whom had participated in previous curriculum transformation projects.

We began our scholarship of teaching by considering the first semester as a pilot project, knowing that we would be revising and improving. The first faculty to teach the paired courses (one each from Human Relations, English, and Communication Studies) met a few times in advance to discuss the evolution of the project, our assumptions about the students, our goals, and initial plans. We assumed students would have had many experiences with stereotypes and discrimination, with little to no previous education to help them evaluate the consequences to themselves or others. As we focused on the long-term goal of actually reducing harassment and hate crimes, we generated questions and ideas about using experiential projects where students would use the analyses, knowledge, and skills in their everyday lives. What might motivate students to become leaders for social justice? What skills and practice would they need to make a difference in their living and learning environments? These questions guided our thinking as we left our discussions to develop curricula for our respective courses to reach our collective goals.

All the primary assignments in the Human Relations class were experiential and reflective. For instance, after readings, speakers, videos, and discussions, students were given two weeks to identify examples of racism and xenophobia in specific areas of their own lives. Many who insisted they would not be able to find *any*, returned with a raised consciousness, concern, and questions about what to do. Some students experienced dissonance. They now knew the seriousness of discriminatory language, jokes, and actions, but were afraid of changing themselves, losing friends, or offending family members. Other students were ready to learn how to change their habits and environments. Meanwhile, students in a paired Communication Studies class were asked to observe their listening habits for 48 hours. They were asked to analyze the effect of presumptions about race, class, gender, and other characteristics, to examine whether they listened as they would want others to listen to them, and what they might change if they could do it again. Those students paired with an English class began a series of writing assignments challenging them to move beyond individual and material success to critical analysis, civic-mindedness, and their interest and responsibility to a larger community. Discussions from one class often spilled over into another.

Boyer's work on the scholarships of integration and application also provided guidance to the project. Boyer suggests that "interdisciplinary *and* integrative studies, long on the edges of academic life, are moving toward the center, responding both to new intellectual questions and to pressing human problems" (p. 21). By drawing upon the expertise of faculty and staff from many academic and student life programs, the knowledge and resources from diverse perspectives enhanced the flexibility and responsiveness to student needs. Faculty teaching during a particular semester, graduate interns from the Social Responsibility program (a new program in Human Relations and Multicultural Education), and residence hall staff continued to meet on a regular basis throughout each semester to plan, re-examine, and learn from each other and our students. As we examined the strengths and weaknesses of each semester, we improved our assignments by building on our knowledge of the other classes and increasing application practice. One Communication Studies professor worked with role-playing dialogues to help students practice how one might respond to common discriminatory situations that arise. The Human

Relations assignment evolved to include the practice of educating others about social justice issues with a kind and caring approach rather than a self-righteous and judgmental one. Students chose the actions they wanted to work on from many options. It was reasoned that familiarity and practice would allow them greater flexibility upon which to base decisions about their personal behaviors when the classes ended.

Regular meetings provided a forum for faculty and staff to explore problems as they arose and to come to collective decisions about how to handle a particularly difficult teaching or student support situation. In one instance, an English professor asked for advice. In writing about her new consciousness of sexism, a student revealed in one of the essays that she had recently been sexually assaulted, but had not sought any support services. The professor wanted to discuss how she might best respond to the paper and support the student. We had an intense conversation about confidentiality, how to share resources with students, how to deal with personal experiences of bias crimes in our teaching.

At the same time, the residence hall director expressed concern about the standard protocol for supporting students who were attacked or assaulted. We began to examine whether it incorporated best practices of sexual assault victim advocacy. There was also a question about how the student might feel and react when sexual assault survivors spoke in class. A consultation with the Director of Sexual Assault Services in the Women's Center increased our own knowledge base and helped us decide which teaching methods or residence hall procedures might provide the most protection and support. While the Women's Center staff was well prepared for the responses of audience survivors, our involvement provided a stronger support network for their work as well. Because of the project, we had an opportunity which was not readily available to faculty teaching alone, or to staff working in the residence halls, to apply our collective knowledge to find the best responses for this situation.

In another instance, a residence hall director shared her observations about the project:

> The students that have participated in this project have emerged as leaders to challenge existing norms of harassment and hate and to redefine a norm that fosters social justice. In particular, participating students have become more aware, active and action-oriented in an attempt to prevent and respond to incidents of bias and hate within their residence hall and campus community. For example, when a group of students protested a bulletin board about "White Privilege," students from the project responded by challenging and educating about hidden aspects of racism in their own lives.

> On the whole, students (from the project) are more conscious of their environment and report incidents of inappropriate and bias related materials. Other students have chosen to post signs on their doors to demonstrate their intolerance for hate crimes and harassment. Several students participated in a hall diversity committee where they discuss their concerns and coordinate programs to educate their peers. (Andrzejewski et al., 1999)

By applying shared knowledge from different facets of the university to work toward the prevention of disrespect, harassment, and hate crimes on campus, the C4D project exemplified the concept of the scholarship of application as well. Boyer contends that, "such a view of scholarly service—one that both applies and contributes to human knowledge—is particularly needed in a world in which huge, almost intractable problems call for the skills and insights only the academy can provide" (p. 23). The experiential projects and opportunity to actually practice new behaviors (like not telling or laughing at racist jokes, or educating others about the impact of racist jokes, etc.) meant that the C4D project had real-life applicability. Once students decided to change their own unexamined habits, they became more in control of their own behaviors in relating to others. Further, by having a group of people they lived with going through the same experiences, they could discuss and apply their knowledge in a context where others would understand.

In some cases, however, this "cohort-like" status had its drawbacks. Sometimes, early in the semester, students might complain about having to learn about these issues or might try to reinforce denial that racism or sexism is such a big problem. However, through weekly reflection papers, negative attitudes, frustrations, and fears surfaced, were discussed openly, and were allayed in supportive ways so that student learning would not be truncated.

Assessing Student Learning

Assessment plans were built into the project from the outset to provide a basis for re-examination and revision of the project implementation as well as to report to the institution and fund agencies. The primary form of assessment was a pre-post survey of knowledge, beliefs, and behaviors (Andrzejewski & Alessio, 2001). We wanted to try to measure, using a self-report questionnaire, whether students would demonstrate changes in knowledge or could identify changes in behaviors as a result of their participation in the project. The development of the instrument and the statistical analysis provided the bases for another faculty collaboration with sociologist John Alessio.

Over the course of the three-year Citizenship for Diversity project the pre and post surveys were completed by 330 students, in their respective semester. The substantive section of the survey consisted of 72 statements to which students responded by identifying the extent of their agreement or disagreement on a scale of 0 to 10. The first 48 questions measured attitudes, beliefs, and information related to eight areas of oppression: ableism, classism, heterosexism, looksism, racism, religious oppression, sexism, xenophobia or general attitudes and beliefs toward excluded groups, hate crimes, and oppression. (See sample statements below.) Grand mean difference scores between pre and post surveys represented composite indices for each category.[2] All composite category pre-post difference scores were significant at the .000 probability level. Of the first 48 items, 11 items changed more than two full points (2.0 to 3.6 points) between pre and post surveys.

Top Knowledge and Belief Survey Items (in order of pre-post differences)

1. One of the most important factors in male bonding is the degradation of women.
2. Corporations receive more government assistance than any other group in the United States.
3. White people bond with each other through racial jokes, eye-contact, stereotypes.
4. Corporations benefit substantially from sexism by paying lower wages to women.
5. People with disabilities experience harassment, hate crimes, and physical violence.
6. Racism in the United States is a result of the control of resources by whites.
7. In the United States, many resources are distributed based on physical appearance (size, weight).

Additionally, pre- and post-test mean scores were compared on 16 items measuring the students' perceptions of how much oppression currently exists among various groups in the United States. It was hypothesized that perception of the amount of oppression would increase as students were exposed to information. A final set of eight questions measured the students' citizenship and leadership skills. (See sample statements below.) Seven pre-post difference scores were significant at the .001 probability level. Finally, students were asked

[2]Complete results and analysis of the data are available from Andrzejewski.

to evaluate different aspects of the Human Relations course and the project to help the team explore improvements. There was a very high level of satisfaction with the courses and with most of the teaching methods. A graduate student conducted interviews with 35 students five months after they completed the semester and found that the majority either maintained or increased their "awareness and involvement [in] reducing prejudices and discrimination" (Storms, 1998).

Top Citizenship Skill Survey Items (in order of top pre-post differences)

As a citizen in the community and on campus:

1. I challenge oppressive jokes and remarks on a daily basis
2. I recognize oppressive behaviors on various issues.
3. I have skills to help create a safe and just environment on campus.
4. I know how to collaborate on constructive solutions to discriminatory policies.
5. I know support systems for targets of discrimination and hate crimes.
6. I join organizations working for social justice.
7. I understand university policies and know where to report discrimination.

The results of the pre-post survey showed notable shifts in the thinking and behavior patterns of students who participated. These shifts were particularly strong among the composite variables of sexism, racism, xenophobia, and looksism. Furthermore, the results on the citizenship items suggest that students also developed a commitment and ability to do something about disrespect, harassment, and hatred.

Results of Faculty/Staff Teamwork

Through the Citizenship for Diversity project, the faculty and staff presented at a national conference and wrote a collaborative article on the project (Andrzejewski et al., 1999). Teaching methods, course objectives, resources, and content, residence hall events and support systems were all transformed toward fostering social justice. While occasional obstacles and problems surfaced, the teamwork increased knowledge and skills for students, faculty, and staff through regular meetings. While it is impossible to know or document all the ripple effects engendered by this project, there are significant reasons for our belief that it enhanced the overall institutional transformation toward addressing diversity and social justice.

References

Alessio, J. (1996). Curriculum transformation through critique. *Transformations, 7*(2), 79-92.

Andrzejewski, J. (1993). *Responsible citizenship in a democracy* (St. Cloud State University Final Q-7 Grant Report). St. Paul: Minnesota State University System.

Andrzejewski, J. (1997). *Multicultural perspectives and global understanding* (St. Cloud State University Final Q-7 Grant Report). St. Paul: Minnesota State University System.

Andrzejewski, J., & Alessio, J. (April, 2001). *Violence prevention through teaching social justice leadership skills: Pre-post survey results of a collaborative experiential education project.* Paper presented at the 2001 American Education Research Association Meeting, Seattle, WA.

Andrzejewski, J., & Craik, M. (1995). Sex discrimination litigation in higher education: Implications for women faculty. In R. Martin (Ed.), *Transforming the academy.* Canyon Lake, TX: Graymill.

Andrzejewski, J., Foster, J., Kanengieter, M., McSweeney, V., Porter, L., Tompkins, P., & Storms, R. (1999). Preventing harassment and hate crimes: The scholarship of teaching, integration, and application. *The Excellence in Teaching Journal, 5*(1) pp. 36-50.

Banks, J. A. (Ed.) (1996). *Multicultural education, transformative knowledge and action: Historical and contemporary perspectives.* New York: Teachers College Press.

Banks, J. A. (1997). *Educating citizens in a multicultural society.* New York: Teachers College Press.

Bell, L. A. (1997). Theoretical foundations for social justice education. In M. Adams, L.A. Bell, & P. Griffin (Eds.), *Teaching for diversity and social justice: A sourcebook* (pp. 3-15). New York: Routledge.

Bickmore, K. (2002). How might social education resist heterosexism? Facing the impact of gender and sexual identity ideology on citizenship. *Theory and Research in Social Education, 30*(2), 198-216.

Boyer, E. L. (1990). *Scholarship reconsidered: Priorities of the professoriate.* Princeton, NJ: The Carnegie Foundation for the Advancement of Teaching.

Dewey, J. (1916). *Democracy and education.* New York: The Free Press.

Dupper, D. R. (2002). Low-level violence, a neglected aspect of school culture. *Urban Education, 37*(3). 350-364.

Freire, P. (1970). *Pedogogy of the oppressed.* New York: Seabury.

Human Rights Watch (2001). *Hatred in the hallways: Violence and discrimination against lesbian, gay, bisexual, and transgender students in the U.S. schools.* Retrieved October 6, 2004, from http://www.hrw.org/reports/2001/uslgbt/

Katz, J. (2000). *Tough guise: Violence, media and the crisis in masculinity.* Northampton, MD: Media Education Foundation.

McIntosh, P. (1988). White privilege and male privilege: A personal account of coming to see correspondences through work in women's studies. *Working paper No. 189.* Wellesley, MA: Wellesley College Center for Research on Women.

Parker, L., Deyhle, D., & Villenas, S. (Eds.). (1999). *Race is...race isn't: Critical race theory and qualitative studies in education.* Boulder, CO: Westview Press.

Sleeter, C. (1994). White racism. *Multicultural Education, 1*(4), 5-8, 39.

Sleeter, C. (1996). *Multicultural education as social activism.* SUNY Series, The Social Context of Education.

Stage, F. K., & Downey, J. P. (1999). Hate crimes and violence on college and university campuses. *Journal of College Student Development, 40*(1), 3-9.

Storms, R. (1998). *Planting seeds for change: Assessing the impact of the citizenship for diversity project in promoting attitudinal and behavioral changes.* Unpublished thesis, St. Cloud State University.

Vossekuil, B., Reddy, M., Fein, R., Borum, R., & Modzeleski, W. (2000). *U.S. safe school initiative: An interim report on the prevention of targeted violence in schools* (p. 7). Washington, DC: U.S. Secret Service, National Threat Assessment Center.

Young, I. M. (1990). *Justice and the politics of difference.* Princeton, NJ: Princeton University Press.

Julie Andrzejewski is a professor, activist scholar, and Co-Director of the Master's degree program in Social Responsibility at St. Cloud State University in Minnesota. She represented SCSU in 2003 as the CASE Professor of the Year. She has authored numerous articles, is the editor of Oppression and Social Justice: Critical Frameworks, and coauthor of Why Can't Sharon Kowalski Come Home. Andrzejewski has a long history of social and academic activism. One of her recent projects is the collaborative development of national education standards for social justice, peace, environmental, and humane education.

John Alessio is a professor of Sociology at St. Clous State University where he teaches graduate courses in Research Methods and the Sociology of Social Responsibility. Dr. Alessio recently spent three years as an academic dean, successfully leading a major core curriculum transformation project. He has also been involved in a number of other curriculum development projects such as initiating and co-developing the MS in Social Responsibility Program at SCSU. Dr. Alessio has written many scholarly papers, and has published in numerous professional journals. His scholarship covers a wide range of topics – most recently in the areas of animal rights and gender equity.

Chapter 23
Multicultural Transformation at Macalester College

Roxane Harvey Gudeman

Macalester College is a private undergraduate liberal arts college that emphasizes academic excellence in the context of internationalism, diversity, and a commitment to service. From the Macalester Mission Statement.

Macalaster College in Saint Paul, Minnesota, has moved dramatically closer to becoming a truly multicultural learning community in the past decade. This chapter describes how several Presidential and faculty initiatives, supported by activist students, helped to make this transformation possible.

Section I: Introduction

Macalester College is a selective liberal arts college in Saint Paul, Minnesota with approximately 1850 students and 220 full-time and part-time faculty. In the past eight years the college has undergone a constellation of changes that has dramatically improved its ability to provide a learning environment that facilitates positive educational experiences enabled by racial and ethnic diversity while minimizing tensions and inequities. In this introduction, I describe diversity related characteristics of the student body and faculty and the history of multiculturalism on campus. Section II focuses on the many recent changes. Section III details faculty development programs for race and diversity funded by two consecutive three year grants from the Bush Foundation of Saint Paul, Minnesota.

In Fall 1996, a new President, Michael McPherson, came to campus committed to support the creation of a more successful multicultural learning community, a charge supported by the Board of Trustees and many students, faculty, staff and alumni. Throughout his tenure (he left in summer, 2003 to head the Spencer Foundation), the multicultural health of the campus remained a focal concern. Insufficiently successful initiatives were replaced by new ones. Over time multicultural transformation became a shared commitment for a majority of the community. Macalester's new president, Brian Rosenberg, continues to provide strong support for multicultural change.

Macalester's Students at Entry and Exit

In Fall 2003 14% of Macalester's 1884 students were from 77 countries outside the United States, 11% were domestic students of color, and 75% were White, nonHispanic. Of the domestic students of color, 22% were Black, nonHispanic; 10% were Native American or Alaskan Native, 43% were Asian American, and 25% were Hispanic American (Macalester College, 2003a).

Macalester is a "needs-blind" institution for students of color; 75% of domestic and international students receive financial aid. Socioeconomically, students are more like their public university counterparts than like those at comparable private liberal arts colleges.[1] Indeed, 29% of Macalester's entering students come from families with an income of less than $50,000, compared to 19% at comparable colleges and 25% at the University of Minnesota (UMN). Only 13% of Macalester's students come from families with incomes of $150,000 or more, compared to 31% at comparable colleges and 11% at UMN (Job, 2003).

Macalester's entering students are, on average, more liberal than students at comparable colleges or UMN. At entry 73% describe themselves as *far left* or *liberal* in comparison to 48% at comparable colleges and 39% at UMN. Only 5% describe themselves as *conservative* or *far right*, compared to 17% at comparison schools and 18% at UMN (Macalester College, 2003b).

By graduation, Macalester students report having had significantly more multicultural learning opportunities than students at similar liberal arts colleges according to the results of the National Survey of Student Engagement (NSSE).[2] Averaged across the classes of 2000, 2001, and 2002, 72% of Macalester's seniors reported *often* or *very often* having "serious conversations with students of a different race or ethnicity" compared to 53% at other colleges. Approximately 73% judged that Macalester's "institutional environment encourage(d) contact among diverse students," compared to 53% elsewhere. Finally, 85% said that courses *often* or *very often* "include[d] diverse perspectives" (Job, 2003).

---

[1]Macalester maintains a data set concerning approximately 40 selective liberal arts comparison colleges. Contact the Macalester Office of Institutional Research for additional information.

[2]In 2000, 43 BA colleges participated; in 2001, 64 did and in 2002, 70 did. Of these, about 15-20% each year came from the 40 comparison colleges listed in Footnote 1. (Job, 2003; NSSE, 2003)

Macalester's Faculty

In Spring 1998 Macalester faculty responded to a survey concerning their views about the educational value of structural diversity (Gudeman, 2000; Gudeman et al., 2000; Gudeman, 2001). Ninety-two percent of the respondents judged that "having a racially and ethnically diverse student body" was *very important* or *essential* to Macalester's mission. The faculty also overwhelmingly rejected the proposition that "too much emphasis on racial and ethnic diversity has lowered the quality of the institution" (90%) or "the quality of the students admitted" (89%). In response to the 1998 Higher Education Research Institute's faculty survey, a startling 97 % of 100 Macalester faculty judged that "a racially and ethnically diverse student body enhances the educational experience of all students" (Gudeman, 2000, pp. 48-49).

Macalester Eight Years Ago

Macalester has long had a commitment both to international and domestic diversity with multiple programs in support of both. In 1996 most international programs were located in International House, and domestic programs were supported primarily through the Office of Multicultural Affairs (OMA), which had decreased in staffing and perceived centrality for over a decade. Rapid turnover in the directorship of the OMA served as a clue to the existence of problems.

In 1991 under then President Robert Gavin, Macalester greatly expanded support for internationalism via the introduction of a new academic Dean for International Studies, new faculty positions, and increased financial aid for international students. New programs included visiting professorships, an annual conference, a publication series, and a biennial faculty international seminar, which so far has taken groups of faculty for study and academic collaboration with local scholars to Hungary, Brazil, South Africa, Malaysia, and Turkey. The flourishing of international diversity programming without a similar increased emphasis on domestic diversity was increasingly protested by some students, faculty, and alumni. As one domestic student of color argued to the Board of Trustees, "It's like they're living in Beverly Hills and we're in South Central."

Section II: The Process of Change

When President McPherson arrived in Fall 1996, students, faculty, and staff most supportive of multiculturalism were disillusioned about the ability or will of the college to undertake changes needed to create an equitable multicultural learning community. President McPherson quickly announced his commitment to diversity, supported ongoing multicultural efforts, and introduced

Table 1 Multicultural Changes at Macalester College, Fall 1996 – Fall 2003

Note: + = focal multicultural initiative; ▒ indicates term(s) initiative active; * = term initiative announced.

	F96	S97	F97	S98	F98	S99	F99	S00	F00	S01	F01	S02	F02	S03	F03	S04
College Wide Planning, Task Forces and Oversight																
+Macrocosm																
+Council for Multicultural Affairs			*													
+3 Audit Task Forces					*											
Strategic Planning Phases I - III							I		II		III					
+Multicultural Steering Committee											*					
+Multicultural Advisory Board															*	
Administrative and Structural Change																
+Asst to President for Diversity		*														
+Dean of Multicultural Life												*				
+Dean of Multicultural Studies												*	…	…	…	…
+Senior Admissions Officer														*		
Multicultural Organizational Structures and Programs																
+Culture House					*											
+Hewlett Pluralism & Unity							*									
+Lealtad-Suzuki Center											*					
+4 new multicultural staff positions																
Changes in Diversity Related Academic Programming																
+Comp No American Studies																
+American Studies																
+African American Studies Conf.						*										
Changes in Diversity Related Faculty Development																
+Bush Faculty Develop. Grant		*	…	…	…	I	-		-		-		-		…	II
Center for Scholarship & Teaching											*	…				
Other																
+Dismantling Racism Training	*	…														

new ones. Table 1 summarizes the various initiatives that took place between Fall 1996 and Spring 2004, categorized into those primarily focused on: a) college-wide planning, task forces and oversight; b) administrative and structural change; c) multicultural organizational structures and programs; d) changes in diversity related academic programming; e) changes in diversity related faculty development; and f) other initiatives. Both in the table and in the text below, initiatives whose primary focus was on multiculturalism, race, and ethnicity are marked by a "plus" sign.

College Wide Planning and Task Forces

Macrocosm, the Council for Multicultural Affairs and the Multicultural Board. In Fall 1997 President Mike McPherson asked his new Special Assistant for Diversity and Campus Community (discussed later), to head a group of faculty, staff, and students who would address issues of diversity. The group, "Macrocosm," formed subcommittees and undertook various programs. An example was the first "in-house" faculty, student, and staff conference devoted to research about pluralism. Macrocosm was internally troubled and also was treated with suspicion by some who feared that it would be an excuse for discussion, not action.

President McPherson announced the formation of a Council for Multicultural Affairs (CMA) in December, 1998. In a memo to the campus he stated his commitment to "a common vision of the College's multicultural future" (CMA, 2002, p. 12). The role of the Council was to oversee the infusion of multiculturalism into "all academic and co-curricular activities.... [and to] serve as an advocate for marginalized voices ..." (Ibid, p. 13).

As initially conceived the Council was to have 15 members with five each chosen from the faculty, the students, and the staff. Students protested that half of the Council's members should be students, and that each organization supporting students by race and/or ethnicity and sexuality should be represented. The administration was willing to revise the faculty/staff/student balance, but felt that student members should represent all students, not just those who shared specific identities. A series of sometimes heated meetings took place with some expressing distrust of the administration. Meanwhile others viewed the demands of the "radicals" as outrageous. President McPherson attended many meetings punctuated by angry, suspicious demands and personal attacks. The President's ability to "hear" the important concerns that underlay people's sometimes hostile attacks was a tremendous asset in achieving responsive multicultural transformation. When the Council finally began in Fall 1999, the membership consisted of 12 students elected by the student body, six faculty, and six staff.

The Council existed from Fall 1999– Spring 2002 when it was disbanded following the multicultural reorganization announced in Spring 2002 (see below). In its third and final year it played a strategic role by giving official voice to multicultural issues on campus. The Council drew on two multicultural audits (see below) to produce a set of recommendations to the president and to the ad-hoc Multicultural Steering Committee whose job was to recommend a new organizational structure for multiculturalism at the college (see below). The CMA document reported that a consensus viewed change as essential, then reviewed the perceived pros and cons of five models of multicultural transformation: 1) a decentralized model; 2) a continuation of the current structure; 3) a centralized model; 4) the creation of an academic dean for multicultural studies to parallel the existing deanship of international studies; and 5) the creation of a vice president for multicultural and global studies.

In Spring 2004 a new advisory and oversight group consisting of faculty and staff was formed, the Multicultural Advisory Board (MAB). Students will form a separate advisory group, with one representative serving on MAB. MAB is to be cochaired by the Dean of Multicultural Life and the Dean for the Study of Race and Ethnicity. Until the latter was chosen, the Director of the Center for Scholarship and Teaching served as cochair.

Internal and External Multicultural Audit Task Forces

In Fall 1998, President McPherson announced the formation of three President's Council multicultural audit task forces which were to provide: 1) an internal audit of the status of multiculturalism on campus; 2) an external audit of "best practices" at other selective liberal arts colleges; and 3) the integration of co-curricular and curricular multicultural initiatives. All members of the President's Council, which includes key administrators, were directed to join one of the three. In addition, the task forces were to include faculty, staff, and students. The task force charged with addressing the integration of curricular and co-curricular multicultural programming was not active.

Internal Multicultural Audit Task Force. The internal audit task force consisted of 10 administrators, four faculty, and four students who were assigned to one of four subcommittees: student audit, faculty audit, staff audit, and alumni/trustee audit. The task force developed surveys that were given to faculty, staff, and students, and the task force also made use of other research by faculty and students. The final report included research based information about: a) how all constituencies evaluated "multiculturalism" in relation to other core values; b) student multicultural experiences on campus; c) the Hughes Science Institute's programs for students of color; d) academic and social experiences of domestic and international Black students; e) White students' perceptions of Macalester's multicultural strengths and weaknesses; f) multicultural experiences and recommendations of Macalester staff; g) faculty experiences with diversity in the classroom; h) a comparison of faculty, staff, and student views on a variety of topics; and h) a summary of proposals for change made community members (Gudeman et al., 2000).

External Multicultural Audit Task Force. The external audit task force consisted of six students, eight administrators and seven faculty. Teams drawn from the committee collected data about the status of multiculturalism at comparison colleges. Faculty-staff-student teams of three made site visits to 12 campuses and collected additional information from 13 additional colleges. The external audit's final report detailed "best practices" observed on other campuses (MacKenzie et al., 2000).

Multicultural Steering Committee

The President formed a Multicultural Steering Committee in fall 2001 whose task was to propose an administrative plan for multiculturalism at Macalester. The Committee consisted of one alumnus, three students, three faculty, and three senior administrators. A consultant, Josie Johnson, the first Black member of the University of Minnesota (UMN) Board of Regents and a former UMN administrator and faculty member, chaired the committee. Through early Spring 2002, the committee sought input, then submitted their recommendations to the President. In April 2002 President McPherson announced a new administrative structure. Macalester would create two new deanships focused on multiculturalism: a Dean of Multicultural Studies and a Dean of Multicultural Life (see below).

Strategic Planning Phases I - III

President McPherson introduced a multi-year process of campus-wide, long-range planning involving all communities at the same time he was catalyzing multicultural transformation.

Planning process I: Reassess core values. In the first year of planning, 2000 – 2001, all college constituencies including alumni reviewed the core values of the college. They reaffirmed the college's historic commitment to multiculturalism, internationalism, and service in addition to academic excellence. The core values discussions led to a resolve to reduce existing barriers to enacting these values in all aspects of college life. This phase culminated in a "Strategic Directions Report."

Planning process II: Implementation task forces. In the second year of planning, 2001 – 2002, six implementation task forces were created whose charge was to plan changes that would better fulfill the college mission: a) admissions and financial aid; b) institutional identity; c) academic program quality and structure; d) student learning experience; e) resource use; and f) facilities. *All* task forces were to address the implications of their plans for "our commitments to diversity and multiculturalism" and "our commitments to promoting civic engagement" (McPherson, 2003). Members represented all college communities. Each task force produced a set of detailed recommendations.

Planning process III: Implementation. In Phase III, 2002 – the present, the appropriate campus groups worked to implement the recommendations of the task forces, modifying them as needed. The changes to be introduced were organized around seven key themes that had emerged during Phase II: 1) multicultural organization; 2) civic engagement; 3) urban opportunities; 4) academic quality; 5) strategic use of resources; 6) communications; and 7) key investments. As detailed by outgoing President McPherson in a May 2003 progress report, substantial progress had been made toward meeting the college's multicultural goals (McPherson, 2003).

Administrative and Structural Change

Special assistant to the president for diversity and campus community.

In Spring 1997, President McPherson announced the creation of a new position, Special Assistant to the President for Diversity and Campus Community. Dr. Roberto Ifill joined the administration in Fall 1997. Dr. Ifill led the Macrocosm multicultural advising group and recommended disbanding the existing Office of Multicultural Affairs (discussed later). He proposed that multicultural specialist staff positions be inserted into existing college units such as admissions, development, campus programs, and the academic support center. The Special Assistant cochaired the Council for Multicultural Affairs in its first two years. This position was effectively eliminated by Fall 2001.

Creation of deans of multicultural student life and multicultural studies.

Two new multicultural deanships were established in Spring 2002 as recommended by the Multicultural Steering Committee. The Dean of Multicultural Studies would be roughly comparable to the existing Dean of International Studies; both would report to the Provost. A new Dean of Multicultural Life would supervise all nonacademic multicultural affairs and would report to the former Dean of Students who assumed the new position of Vice President for Student Affairs.

Dean of Multicultural Life. A new Dean of Multicultural Life was chosen quickly following the establishment of the position and the Department of Multicultural Life. In its first year, the department developed a strategic plan and initiated a number of programs. The mission of this department is "to integrate the ethos and values of historically under-represented peoples, discourses, thoughts, and ideas as a catalyst for transforming the traditional ways of doing the work of the College into a more inclusive model" (Macalester College, 2003d). The Lealtad-Suzuki Center (described below) houses many of the department's programs.

Dean of Multicultural Studies/Dean for the Study of Race and Ethnicity. As initially envisioned, the job of Dean of Multicultural Studies included development and enactment of "a strategic plan by which to enhance existing curricular efforts related to multiculturalism and diversity" (Macalester College, 2002). The job was re-envisioned and retitled in Summer, 2003. The newly defined position focused the academic programs supervised by the new dean on race, ethnicity, and social justice. The Dean for the Study of Race and Ethnicity will head the new department of American Studies: Comparative Racial Formations (described below). The dean will teach two classes as well as help "develop the campus-wide curriculum in race and ethnicity" (Macalester College, 2003e). Dr. Rhodes assumed the deanship in the Summer of 2001.

New Associate Director of Admissions for Multicultural Recruitment

While Macalester struggles toward becoming a community with a critical mass of students, faculty, and staff of color, it has witnessed a series of junior multicultural admissions specialists come and go. Macalester created a more senior position in admissions for a specialist in multicultural recruitment in summer 2003. It appears that the classes of 2008 and 2009 will have a significantly higher proportion of domestic students of color than recent previous classes.

Multicultural Organizational Structures and Programs

Culture house.

When President McPherson arrived in 1996 Macalester had two buildings focused on diversity, International House and Culture House. The former was located in a large house on a beautiful boulevard. It housed offices for support services for international students and study abroad programs. Culture House was located in a much smaller, rather decrepit building. It offered a meeting place for domestic students of color and their organizations. In the summer of 1998 both had to move, International House to a large, well-located building, Culture House to small house meant to serve as an interim location pending funding for a new building. Activist domestic students of color and their supporters were outraged. The crisis about Culture House became the first major controversy addressed by the Council for Multicultural Affairs. After testimony by all relevant parties and much negotiation, support for Culture House was affirmed. For the first time the house also would serve as a residence for students interested in living in a multicultural, diversity-focused environment.

Lealtad-Suzuki Center

The Lealtad-Suzuki Center is Macalester's new home for the programs of the Department of Multicultural Life. Core foci are: a) providing "multicultural training" for all campus communities,; b) implementing "intentional multicultural programming and services," and c) offering "multicultural education through mediums such as personal consultation, literature, videos, audio, and artwork" (Macalester College, 2003d). The Center has several "signature" programs. Students, faculty and staff meet monthly for a *Soup and Substance Luncheon Series*. The Center also sponsors student collectives such as *Black Women of the Diaspora* which "are organized around racial identity groups as an entry point to ... our multiple identities ... when we look at power and privilege in today's global society" (Macalester College, 2003f). The department's programs are mentored by Center Associates, faculty and staff who help facilitate intra- and intergroup conversations. The Center also has Allies, student, faculty, and staff volunteers trained to help build a "safe environment" on campus for people of all social identities.

Hewlett Pluralism and Unity Program

The Department of Multicultural Life houses a successful Pluralism and Unity program for first year students that is designed to enhance their multicultural competence and potential for leadership. Ten international students, 10 domestic students of color, and 10 European American students participate along with three staff and three faculty facilitators. By the end of their first year, the students become multicultural collaborators as they attend two retreats, experience at least five diversity-related journeys into Twin Cities communities, and also participate in a series of events on campus designed to "probe the complexities of racial and ethnic differences and ... build the competencies necessary for effective communication, conflict resolution, and decision making in multicultural environments" (Macalester College, 2003g). The program enters its sixth year in Fall 2005.

Diversity Related Academic Programming: From African American Studies and Comparative North American Studies to American Studies

African American Studies and Comparative North American Studies. The college introduced an African American Studies minor concentration in Fall 1996. One year later a minor in Comparative North American Studies was added. The focus was diversity in America with an emphasis on understanding "race" and racism. In 1999 – 2000 an annual national African American Studies Conference was initiated.

American Studies. In the spring and summer of 2003 a core group of faculty working with consultants designed a new department of American Studies: Comparative Racial Formations. The department has three curricular emphases: 1) racial concepts and theories; 2) cultures, histories, and practices; and 3) activism and social justice. The department describes race as its main theme: "We see racial difference and racial inequality as foundational aspects of American national identity. Our curriculum allows students to explore and analyze the interrelationships between racialized notions of U.S. nationhood, citizenship, and community in a global context" (Macalester College, 2003h).

Diversity Related Faculty Development

Bush Faculty Development Grant on Race and Diversity

A group of faculty perceived a need for faculty to become better teachers and advisors across social differences, especially race and ethnicity. They received outside funding for a set of faculty development programs described in detail in Section IV.

Center for Scholarship and Teaching

During its years of self-review, Macalester developed a plan for a Center for Scholarship and Teaching (CST) which would house all faculty development programs. A grant from the Hewlett Foundation provided initial funding for the Center which opened in Fall 2002. All faculty development efforts for race and diversity now are housed in the Center. The mission of the CST is "to encourage, promote, and support the pursuit of excellence in scholarship and teaching within Macalester's distinctive urban liberal arts setting" (Macalester College, 2003i). The Center offers programs and support for the development of faculty in all core roles: scholarship, teaching, and advising while being mindful of faculty lives beyond the borders of the college and their disciplines. A goal of the Center is to infuse the values articulated in the College mission with faculty development efforts (Macalester College, 2003i).

Other

Dismantling Racism Training

In Fall 1997, following an incident of racial harassment on campus, faculty, staff, and student activists participated in a number of discussions concerning racism and formed an organization called Dismantling Racism. A staff person and eight students attended a three day preparatory antiracism workshop led by the People's Institute for Survival and Beyond in January 1998. The group then received funds from the college to attend a powerful four day national antiracism conference in March 1998 at the People's Institute in Waveland, Mississippi.

The Dismantling Racism group arranged to have an intensive on-campus antiracism training workshop in Spring 1998 under the joint guidance of staff people from Crossroads Ministry, Chicago and the People's Institute. Several subsequent antiracist workshops were held using the same facilitators. In Spring 1998, President McPherson funded travel by 38 student members of the Dismantling Racism group to a five day conference at the People's Institute. As noted by many, the President himself participated in on-campus antiracism training.

Section III: Faculty Development

Bush Faculty Development Grant I

A faculty group first conceived of a faculty development program focused on improving faculty teaching and advising across social difference during the 1997-1998 academic year. The administration endorsed their vision, and the college applied for and received a planning grant from the Bush Foundation of Saint Paul, Minnesota. In summer 1999 the college submitted a successful proposal to the Foundation for a three year grant to support faculty development on race and diversity. The grant period began in December 1999 and was extended through May 2003. Throughout, a steering committee composed of faculty supervised the programs. A faculty member served as director. During the life of the grant more than one-third of the tenure and tenure-track faculty participated in the program, as well as did several long-term adjunct faculty and teaching staff.

The faculty development program was designed to meet a number of perceived faculty and campus needs. It also offered a variety of incentives both tangible and symbolic to faculty participants. Primary goals of the programs focused on the personal development of individual faculty members with respect to their own teaching and advising across racial, ethnic, and other social differences. Program components were designed to help faculty: a) better understand *all* students; b) more effectively teach *all* students; c) more effectively advise; and, d) more effectively integrate scholarship and research about race and ethnicity into the curriculum.

Broader goals focused on providing opportunities for faculty to address many facets of multicultural life and learning at the college so that they would have the tools needed to become change agents and leaders on campus. Program components were designed to help faculty: a) learn about the effects and challenges of race and ethnicity on all facets of college life; b) participate in cross-campus discussions with others; and c) help build a more successful multicultural environment via curricular enrichment, service, community-based learning, and increased hiring and retention of students and faculty of color.

Two core programs were faculty development seminars and course development grants. Other funded activities included: a) faculty attendance at national conferences; b) resources for faculty research and travel focused on race and diversity; and c) dissemination of the results of grant related programs across campus and nationally.

The Bush Faculty Development Seminar

A total of 40 faculty participated in one of three seminars offered between Fall 1999 and May 2002. Of these, 53% were tenured, 47% untenured. That 22.5% of faculty participants were domestic faculty of color enriched the experience for all.

Each seminar met for at least ten sessions. Topics or activities included: 1) review of research findings about multicultural life at Macalester; 2) dialogue with alumni and students of color; 3) case analysis of vignettes from *Race in the Classroom*, a video produced by Harvard's Derek Bok Center for Teaching and Learning; 4) production and analysis of in-house cases pertaining to in-class or advising experiences; 5) dialogue with core administrators (for example, from admissions, student life, the student academic support office and/or residential life.); and 6) the planning of an annual spring mini-symposium.

Course Development Programs

In May, 2000, 2001, and 2002 up to 10 people were awarded grants to develop a new class or to revise extensively an existing class by incorporating diversity relevant scholarship and pedagogy. Applicants and their chairs made a commitment to offer proposed classes at least twice and to work toward inclusion in the core curriculum. Prior diversity related teaching and research experience were explicitly *not* relevant to selection. A rich and extremely varied group of 28 classes were added or modified via the grants. Bush Grant funds also supported the faculty who developed the new Department of American Studies: Comparative Racial Formations.

Campus Symposia, Workshops, and Involvement

The Bush grant sponsored several venues for program participants to participate in campus-wide development of a more successful multicultural learning community. These included: a) dialogue with key administrators within the seminar; b) participation in two faculty and staff academic issues retreats; c) sponsorship of a faculty and staff mini-symposium on race and diversity each year; and d) the offering of a science faculty workshop titled "Attracting and Retaining Students of Color in the Sciences." Finally, Bush alumni participated in many campus roles with significant responsibility for dialogue and planning about race and diversity. Indeed, the contributions of Bush alumni are astonishing. By a very conservative count, participants have filled at least seventy-five key leadership and advisory roles at Macalester subsequent to their faculty development experiences.

Evaluation

The Bush Grant programs were supervised by a steering committee composed of the program director and at least five other faculty. Progress toward achieving goals programs was monitored by an internal evaluator and an external team of two evaluators.

Internal evaluations. The internal evaluator conducted six surveys of faculty experience in the Bush programs and personal change as a result of participation. A variety of methods were used. For example, each year, faculty in the seminars were asked to indicate whether, as a result of their participation, they perceived themselves to be more knowledgeable and competent in multicultural teaching and advising context.

External evaluations. The external evaluation team came to campus twice to evaluate the Bush programs. They met with faculty participants, members of key faculty committees, administrators, and students. They provided excellent formative feedback and also conducted a summative evaluation which concluded:

Overall, our assessment of the Bush grant is that it has achieved significant success in its goal of "fostering a learning environment supportive of racial diversity" .... We are impressed with Macalester's continued commitment to the goals of the grant, its inclusive planning process, and the recent structural changes (new Deans of Multicultural Student Life and Multicultural Studies) underway at the college ... [T]he accomplishments at Macalester seem both positive and remarkable (Bonilla & Miller, 2003).

Summative self-assessment. In general, as validated by the results of our evaluations, we judge that we were able to make great progress in working toward the goals we hoped to achieve. The Bush Grant programs have had a very positive impact on participants' development as faculty sensitive to and intellectually challenged by issues of race and diversity.

An important lesson learned by faculty participants in the Bush programs is how little most faculty know about the experiences and identities of their students outside the classroom and discipline. Many faculty also learned that they knew little about the lives of others within the Macalester community, whether student, staffs or administrator, outside the parameters of their professional relationships. Most began to view this limited knowledge as detracting from their ability to teach and advise successfully and to contribute to the multicultural health of the college.

Current Faculty Development Initiatives: Bush Faculty Development Renewal Grant

In Spring 2004 Macalester received a three year renewal grant from the Bush Foundation to consolidate and expand existing faculty development programs for race and diversity. Key new components include: a) support for CST Diversity Associates and Pluralism and Unity faculty participants; b) an Urban faculty seminar; c) small grants for race and diversity development for faculty; and d) resources to develop training materials.

Urban Faculty Seminar

The goal of the Urban Faculty Seminar is to provide faculty with an opportunity to learn directly about the racial and/or ethnic, religious, socioeconomic, and other diversity of our urban area in a context of supportive community-generated initiatives. The seminar will be held in the Twin Cities in the summer. Participants will attend a one week seminar co-developed by Macalester faculty and the Twin Cities based Higher Education Consortium for Urban Affairs (HECUA). They will then spend an additional week on an independent community project. The structure in part parallels Macalester's international faculty seminars. A successful first semester was held in August, 2005.

Two Internal Grant Programs

The new Bush grant funds two programs to support faculty initiated development efforts. "Intersections" is designed for groups of faculty such as a department, interdisciplinary program, or other group with a common interest. For example, the Environmental Studies faculty might collectively apply to infuse their curriculum and in their pedagogy with issues of race and/or ethnicity and privilege . Or a department might comprehensively assess its own multicultural health. "Perspectives" is meant for individual faculty who wish to teach with another faculty member or a community partner to build educational opportunities that interweave a focus on race and ethnicity with other sources of social difference including religion, nationality, social class, sexuality, political ideology, and so forth.

Development of Training Materials

We also will develop resource materials for use in these endeavors. Our recent seminars confirmed the power of case-based learning as a faculty development tool. In them we used short, videotaped cases developed by Harvard's Derek Bok Center. However, we began to recognize that faculty at a small liberal arts college in the upper Midwest face teaching and advising situations – and student collectivities – that vary significantly from those encountered by Harvard faculty and teaching fellows.

Cases will concern faculty in their teaching, advising, research, and governance roles. We will develop two types of cases: brief encounters and elaborated cases. We also will create a facilitator's guide to help CST Diversity Associates and others elicit personal experiences and use them as the basis for discussion, analysis, and role-play.

Type 1: Brief encounters. These cases will consist of sudden moments of concern, need, conflict, or great emotion in which one must decide how to respond with little background information about the persons involved or the situation. Examples include a student in academic difficulty, "hot" moments in the classroom, or interactions with individuals at different "stages" of racial and/or ethnic identity formation.

Type 2: Elaborated cases or simulations. These cases invite faculty participants to explore multiple perspectives. Information relevant to the case is revealed to learners over time. For example, a department chair reports to a faculty member that several student in an economics class claim the faculty member has made racist, politically-biased statements in class. What is the perspective of each student, the chair, the faculty member, the other class members, the other department members, the administration, members of the board, and so forth? Who should be included in finding a resolution and by what process?

Afterword

Macalester has experienced an unprecedented constellation of changes that have improved the institutional climate for *all* students and faculty in the past eight years. Students and faculty have a much richer array of opportunities for intellectual engagement and research about the profound impact of race on every facet of life in the United States and the impact that race and ethnicity have had on the expression of other social differences. We are optimistic about continuing on the same trajectory. We know also that it is imperative to continue to devote mindful attention to our multicultural health. Multiculturalism is a process, not an outcome.

In reflecting on the future, we also noted an emerging theme, a changing relationship between domestic and international diversity. Gradually Macalester has been recruiting international students from a broader array of regions and a wider range of social classes. Simultaneously, domestic students increasingly are first or second generation "multicultural" Americans. As a result, what was once a fairly clear demarcation between two types of multiculturalism is becoming blurred in ways that allow for the emergence of creative new forms of social and intellectual dialogue.

References

CMA. (2002). *CMA report: Mission and vision for multicultural affairs at Macalester College.* St. Paul, MN: Macalester College, Department of Multicultural Life.

Gudeman, R. (2000). College missions, faculty teaching, and student outcomes in a context of low diversity. In American Council on Education and American Association of University Professors (Eds.), *Does diversity make a difference? Three studies on college classrooms.* Washington, DC: American Council on Education Press.

Gudeman, R. (2001). Faculty experience with diversity: A case study. In G. Orfield & M. Kurlaender (Eds.), *Diversity challenged: Legal crisis and new evidence.* Cambridge, MA: Harvard Education Publishing Group.

Gudeman, R., Hamre, L., Powell, I., Solon, P., Job, C., Chalco, A., et al. (2000). *Final report of the Macalester internal multicultural audit task force.* St. Paul, MN: Macalester College, Department of Multicultural Life.

Job, C. (2003). *National survey of student engagement (NSSE). Three years of results.* Retrieved May 15, 2003, from Macalester Office of Institutional Research Web site: http://www.macalester.edu/ir/private/nsse/nsse3yr.htm

Macalester College. (2003b). *Peer college data book.* Retrieved October 15, 2003, from http://www.macalester.edu/ir/private/pcdb.html

Macalester College. (2003c). *Fact book.* Retrieved October 15, 2003, from http://www.macalester.edu/ir/factbook.htm

Macalester College. (2003d) *Department of multicultural life.* Retrieved May 15, 2003, from http://www.macalester.edu/multiculturalism/

Macalester College. (2003e). *Dean for the Study of Race and Ethnicity job description.* Retrieved November 1, 2003, from http://www. Macalester.edu/provost/raceandethnicity.html

Macalester College. (2003f). *Lealtad-suzuki center.* Retrieved May 15, 2003, from http://www.macalester.edu/lealtad-suzuki/programs.html

Macalester College. (2003g). *Hewlett foundation: Pluralism and unity program.* Retrieved October 15, 2003, from http://www. Macalester.edu/grants/hewlettpluralism/

Macalester College, (2003h). American Studies Department web site. Retrieved September 15, 2003, from http://www.macalester.edu/americanstudies/

Macalester College, (2003i). *Center for scholarship and teaching.* Retrieved December 1, 2003, from http://www.macalester.edu/cst/

McPherson, Michael. (2003). *Strategic planning report.* Retrieved May 15, 2003, from http://www.macalester.edu/president/

Roxane Harvey Gudeman is an adjunct professor of psychology at Macalester College.

Chapter 24

Making the Campus Community a Safe and Affirming Space for All

Robert S. Haynor and Susan A Holton

"Never doubt that a small group of thoughtful, committed citizens can change the world. Indeed, it is the only thing that ever has."
Margaret Mead

Most faculty members know that they must be cognizant of issues of racial and ethnic diversity. Throughout the country, programs are set up to help faculty be inclusive of persons of color in the history and theory of their academic discipline. But race and ethnicity are not the only "diversities" of importance to campus communities. At Bridgewater State College, efforts at systemic interventions have successfully made changes in the campus climate and culture around gay, lesbian, bisexual, and transgender issues students, faculty and administrators have formed a coalition whose mission is to make the campus safe and affirming for all.

Despite the progress that many colleges and universities have made in the recent past, classrooms and campuses throughout the country are not yet safe for many gay, lesbian, bisexual, and transgender students, faculty, and staff.

A survey conducted by the National Gay and Lesbian Task Force (NGLTF) in May, 2003, reported in the *Chronicle of Higher Education* that

> More than one third of the respondents said that they had experienced harassment within the past year. Twenty percent said they feared for their safety because of their gender identity or sexual orientation, and 51 percent said they sometimes concealed their sexual identity to avoid intimidation. (2003, p. A31)

In this research, the NGLTF found that, "most of the colleges involved in the survey had campus centers for gay, lesbian, bisexual, and transgender students." And yet they are not safe.

The goal of the Safe College coalition at Bridgewater State College is to "make the campus safe and affirming for all." The focus is on GLBT students.

For many students, college represents their first opportunity to really explore their sexual orientation. Wall and Evans (2000) explain,

> college students typically are confronted with a variety of developmental tasks: developing competence, managing emotions, moving through autonomy toward interdependence, developing mature interpersonal relationships, establishing identity, developing purpose, and developing integrity. (p. 32)

This developmental process means that for some students, coming to terms with their sexual orientation is an additional developmental task, which can supersede or vie with normative developmental tasks and the demands and rigors of their academic career. It is important to bear in mind that GLBT students face concerns about their physical safety, being harassed, and being the targets of negative attitudes toward them. These things create a more burdensome process for GLBT students.

Although the role of supporting the developmental process for college students has been the responsibility of Student Affairs, faculty can—and should—play an equally as important of a role in this process with the GLBT students in their classrooms. Since development includes the internalization of role models, the opportunity for faculty to positively impact students' development by being affirming classroom figures can be a significant factor for students.

The efforts to make any campus "safe and affirming for all" cannot be relegated to one center, or a few staff. It must be a campus-wide effort. Although most institutional change begins as a grassroots effort, its goal must be system-wide transformation. As a means of changing the climate of homophobia and heterosexism that pervades campuses, it is vital that foundational connections between individuals, divisions, and the campus as a whole be established to work together toward systemic institutional change. That grassroots foundation for change has been established at Bridgewater State College.

At Bridgewater State College, the goal of systemic change has been achieved on some levels, but certainly not all. The change is occurring because significant purposeful and strategic efforts are being made by a coalition of students, faculty, and administrators whose mission is to provide education, advocacy, and support for gay, lesbian, bisexual and transgender students, faculty and staff. This committee is the Safe College Coalition (SCC). The presence of this Coalition has positively impacted the culture of the College by creating and facilitating conversations and opportunities that foster individual learning and professional development along with providing more visible role models for students. In a spring 2004 survey, the faculty noted a much more positive and affirming campus environment, with an increased comfort level for GLBT students.

Since the classroom is the most significant common denominator for all students, it is appropriate for faculty development centers take an active role in gathering people from all constituencies at the institution to address issues of heterosexism and homophobia. Faculty Development Centers should not, and cannot, do this work alone. They can work with other-groups to create programming addressing heterosexism and homophobia.

Bridgewater State College's Safe College Coalition actively involves the Faculty Development Program and the Center for the Advancement of Research and Teaching (CART) in an endeavor to address the campus climate through its sponsorship of relevant faculty workshops.

Because of the varied make up of the Coalition members, the lenses through which people look at GLBT issues have a wide range. Faculty members look at issues through their own disciplinary lenses and bring unique perspectives to the table. An important element of the Safe College Coalition is that it provides leadership to blend these campus voices.

Creating a safe campus community involves the participation of a diverse and representative constituency. Historically, the onus of the work to create safer campus climates has been on the members of the oppressed groups. This is also true for the GLBT community. One of the purposes of the Safe College Coalition is to engage people, regardless of sexual orientation, to address issues of homophobia and heterosexism. As a Coalition, we have accomplished this goal. Included in the Coalition are students, faculty, staff, and administrators; some are gay and some are straight. We believe that it is the responsibility of straight faculty, administrators, staff, and students to be vocal, visible advocates to work in concert with the campus GLBT community to create systemic change.

All are committed to the mission of the group, which makes the sexual orientation of Coalition members a moot point. Instead, the group is committed to the mission of the Coalition, not to individual agendas. This is one of the reasons that the group is so powerful. It is also a reason that both GLBT folks and allies feel safer working together; no one's sexual orientation is an issue in the work.

It is also critical that the work to "create a safe and affirming climate" not be relegated to student affairs, where it is most often found on college campuses. Another unique feature of Bridgewater State College's Safe College Coalition is the representation of a diversity of the institution's divisions. The committee's leadership is deliberately co-chaired by an administrator and a faculty member. The work that the group does is partly student affairs and, in part, academic affairs. Our model unifies the divisions. The concern is for the students, and that work must take place both inside and outside of the classroom.

History and Evolution of the Safe College Task Force and Coalition

Sanlo (1998) reports that almost all of the GLBT resource centers recently established on college campuses derived from one of two areas: 1) from a working committee of faculty, staff, and students that assessed the campus climate and needs of the GLBT community and reported its findings to the administration; or 2) in response to over homophobic incidents or the administration's acknowledgement of the need for such a center to address GLBT issues. The Safe College Coalition, originally called the Safe College Task Force, began in the fall of 1998 and paralleled the change taking place throughout higher education.

In part, the group's membership grew from frustration that the college's established "diversity council" was dealing with only racial and ethnic diversity. The argument given by its leadership to explain the exclusion of sexual orientation in its purview, was that under federal guidelines, sexual orientation was excluded.

The second impetus was an initiative from the Governor's office. In 1992, Governor William Weld formed the Massachusetts Governor's Commission on Gay and Lesbian Youth. Weld formed the nation's first gay and lesbian youth commission in response to the 1989 federal report identifying the epidemic of suicide by gay, lesbian, and bisexual youth. This leadership created state-supported initiatives to form and fund gay-straight alliances in high schools and colleges. Subsequently, these high school programs have made first year students both more aware of homophobia and heterosexism, and often more "tolerant" of GLBT students. As Sanlo (1998) states,

> Institutions may be at the beginning stages of reflecting upon these [GLBT] issues. Amending the values of higher education to include GLBT students is essential in the sound recruitment and retention efforts of a college or university. GLBT students are more confident and self-assured than ever before, which makes them more savvy consumers of their own education. Hardesty (1994) found that 40 percent of the students they surveyed stated that if they had had information concerning GLBT issues on their prospective campuses, their choices of where to attend college would have been different. (p. 52)

Institutions must be prepared to respond to this growing group of potential and current students.

It was clear that this was going to have to be a grassroots initiative. According to Yeskel (1991), Bailey Jackson's model for multicultural organizational development includes three things: a system approach, strong leadership, and support activities. It is important to note that while his work was on racial and ethnic diversity, it can be extrapolated to sexual orientation as well. Specifically, Jackson says, "there would need to be a spotlight on the organization's mission and values, structure, technology, management style and culture on issues of social diversity and justice" (Yeskel, 1991, p. 35). Also the organization's leadership must speak about a multicultural agenda and mission that includes (GLBT) issues. And finally, it is vital to keeping issues active that grassroots activities raise the organization's consciousness about heterosexism and homophobia, while simultaneously making the gay and lesbian agenda known. The grassroots work of the Safe College Coalition is undoubtedly the most important and, at BSC, the most visible change.

But first, why is it important to work for that change? As noted, gay, lesbian, bisexual, and transgender student campus groups have been responsible for providing education to its community that increases awareness regarding issues of heterosexism and homophobia to the campus community. This role can create a dilemma for some students in these groups when they find themselves in the public role of providing this information even though they remain uncomfortable or closeted regarding their sexual orientation. This default responsibility can interfere with the educational initiatives that remain necessary to dismantle structural heterosexism and homophobia and disrupt the supportive function of the student organization.

The recognition of the importance of shifting the responsibility of this work from the students became a primary motive for establishing a coalition with a mission to highlight awareness of heterosexism and homophobia to the campus community. Additionally, the coalition helped to shift the burden of this existing education from the few out GLBT faculty and staff to the entire community at Bridgewater State College.

It was creativity rather than choice that initiated the Safe College Coalition. In spite of the growing trend of the establishment of GLBT resource centers around the country, it was obvious that no money or staff was going to be made available to create a GLBT center or a position for a GLBT advocate at the college, so something else had to work at BSC.

History of Safe College Coalition

In 1998 and 1999, Bob Haynor, director of Outreach Education through the Counseling Center at Bridgewater State College, obtained grant funding from the Governor's Commission to develop educational and social programming to create awareness about the GLBT community on campus. This funding opportunity provided the resources to develop the seminal programming that continues to educate the campus community about the impact of homophobia and heterosexism. These programming initiatives were the collaborative effort of the gay, lesbian, bisexual, and transgender student group, AWARE, and some key individuals who supported their work and role. A call went out to the campus community to find faculty, staff, and administrators to address these issues for GLBT students. As a result, an ad hoc group of people was formed, with the primary responsibility to oversee the grant-funded programming.

The grants from the Governor's Commission on Gay and Lesbian Youth provided the foundation for the growth of the grassroots work on campus. It enabled brochures to be purchased, anti-homophobia posters to be printed, the Safe Zone program to be developed, and AWAREness Week educational programming to take place. It also provided financial support to train student activists. Unfortunately, two years later, as a result of anti-gay political activism, the money was no longer available.

It is significant to note that the work of the Safe College Coalition continues to be done without an established gay, lesbian, bisexual, and transgender center, without a dedicated staff, and without a budget. It is done with the passion and commitment of a group of volunteer faculty, administrators, staff, and students. These factors make the efforts as systemic change all the more difficult – and profound.

Efforts to Make an Impact on the Organizational Culture

Organizational culture is difficult to change; organizational climate[1] is easier and more visible. It is clear that the Safe College Coalition has made strides in changing the climate at the institution; the culture is changing more slowly.

Change can occur through a variety of contexts, from one-to-one interaction all the way through working with the entire institution. The Safe College Coalition works at every level of the institution to expedite change. Significant

---

[1]Organizational culture can be defined as "why we do what we do" organizational climate as "the way we do things around here"

changes have occurred in the classrooms, in the programming for the faculty and other constituents in the campus community, and in student programs.

In a faculty survey conducted in the spring of 2004, faculty who have been at Bridgewater State College from 25 years to less than one year commented on the changes in the campus climate and culture. Most noted a positive change, due to the work of the SCC. Specifically mentioned were the activities and opportunities, the increased discussion of the issue, awareness and programs to promote tolerance, the availability of "sanctioned programs."

Classroom

The classroom provides the most obvious climate for all students and is the site of significant cultural change, both for the academic institution and the larger world. Therefore, faculty development has been an important part of the Coalition's efforts. It is clear through a variety of research that the atmosphere in the classroom impacts – positively and negatively – more than the student's cognitive development.

Lopez and Chism (1993) found in their study of classroom issues of the gay and lesbian students on their campus that the faculty most often seemed to simply avoid the topics related to their community. Sometimes the gay and lesbian students felt that it was intentional as they perceived that their instructors wanted to avoid difficult issues and discussions. Other times, they believed that faculty reinforced heterosexism through the content of classroom discussions and assignments. Students also held faculty responsible to foster a safe and respectful classroom environment and believed they should confront subtle and overt forms of homophobia and heterosexism-much as they would any form of minority oppressive language or behavior—when they arise. To some students doing nothing is doing something; to a gay, lesbian or bisexual student, an instructor's failure to act can be perceived to be unsupportive or hostile.

This reinforces why it has been so important for the Coalition to work with the faculty development center, and with individual faculty, to create environmental change in the classroom. As Sanlo, Rankin, and Schoenberg state (2002),

> Faculty can provide a sense of empowerment to out or closeted LGBT students by including LGBT history, culture, and experiences in their curriculum. They may provide access to such information that many students are generally denied educationally. When faculty include these topics, and support individual student's interest in them, LGBT students have the opportunity to feel excitement, pride, and other positive emotions in the learning process. (p. 235)

The change needed in the classroom is transformational. It is not enough to add one gay poet, or study one bisexual chemist, or listen to the music of one lesbian songwriter. In order for the curriculum to be truly transformed, the contributions of GLBT folks need to be seamlessly and positively integrated into the curriculum.

In order to facilitate that work, faculty must learn about curriculum transformation and learn how to find and then integrate the work into their daily classroom work.[2]

Faculty also need to learn how to deal with the myriad issues that might arise in creating a GLBT friendly and safe classroom. Faculty have often said that they truly want to discuss heterosexism and homophobia in their classrooms, but do not feel that they have the knowledge or skills to do so. Through Faculty Workshops, held in conjunction with CART, members of the Coalition inform and teach their peers about issues of student development, curricular transformation, and classroom management and strategies as they relate to issues of heterosexism and homophobia. Individual consultations and classroom workshops are also offered.

Dr. Michael Kocet, a SCC member and professor of Counselor Education developed a list of tips for faculty members to make their classrooms safer environments:

1. Include Gay, Lesbian, Bisexual, and Transgender topics/issues in your course discussions/lectures/syllabi.
2. Challenge any homophobic or heterosexist comments/statements made in classes or in departmental meetings.
3. Incorporate texts, journal articles, and other relevant materials on GLBT issues into your curriculum.
4. Use GLBT sensitive language in class discussions/lectures (as in saying "partner" instead of "husband or wife").
5. Discuss GLBT people in your lectures (for example, famous GLBT individuals in your field).
6. Do not ask a GLBT student to represent an entire population.
7. Support and recognize GLBT faculty, staff, and students on campus.
8. Attend GLBT events on campus and in the community (speakers, lectures, films, concerts, and so forth).

---

[2]Curriculum Transformation work began in the 1970s with a concern about incorporating women's studies scholarship. It has expanded to race and ethnicity and now encompasses diversity in the broadest sense. The Center for Curriculum Transformation at the University of Washington is led by one of the pioneers in this work, Dr. Betty Schmitz. For more information about curriculum transformation, go to the center's website, http://depts.washington.edu/ctcenter.

9. Assure the safety of GLBT students in your classroom – provide an open forum.
10. Listen and provide support to GLBT students.

Faculty Response to Culture

Beyond the classroom, the work of the Safe College Coalition has made a difference in the retention and recruitment of faculty.

While many faculty members who responded to the spring 2004 survey said that they had been at the institution for many years, and they "were not even aware of these issues," two faculty members said specifically that the climate did impact their decision to come to the College. In addition, one faculty member, now a member of the SCC, said that the college's reputation was a deciding factor in his decision to take the job.

We can say that the positive climate at BSC has made a difference to the faculty. Again, from the spring 2004 survey, some of the comments included: "the safe and affirming environment is a fundamental necessity for learning and growth," "It is a matter of good and responsible educational practice. More than this, it is the responsibility of this college to be a safe and comfortable location for all the people who make up its community." And one perhaps flip, but telling response was, "being gay is cool in academia, man!"

There is little literature on faculty recruitment and retention based on issues of heterosexism and homophobia. The few articles that mention it merely link GLBT issues with general issues of multicultural recruitment and retention. This is certainly an area that needs scholarly investigation.[3]

One of the most important alliances in the work on campus has been between Academic Affairs and Student Affairs. It is the firm belief of the Coalition members that all aspects of campus life are important to the development, maintenance and nurturing of the campus climate for GLBT students. On many campuses, the work for and with GLBT students is strictly the purview of Student Affairs; that is not the case at Bridgewater. This alliance is obvious through everything the Coalition does, including programming.

Safeperson, Safe Place

One significant grassroots program that precipitated significant change is the BSC Safe Zone program.[4] It is one program that bridges academic and student affairs.

---

[3]More research is being done in this area. If you know of scholarly work, or want to contribute anecdotal information to this research, please contact the authors.

[4]BSC Safe Zone program, www.bridgew.edu/counselingcenter/safezone.htm

The Safe Zones program began in 1994 and was one of the first Safe Zone programs at a college or university in the country. According to Bob Haynor who lead the development the program, "as a person who was new to the institution, I observed a community that did not appear to be overtly homophobic, yet it was clearly heterosexist, which resulted in a much closeted student, faculty, and staff community at the same time."

The Safe Zone program, which presently exists at many institutions throughout the continent, was a subtle, non-confrontational way of beginning to raise the consciousness and awareness of the college community about the imbedded GLBT community. Through the work of members of the Safe College Coalition, the program evolved into a "Safe Person, Safe Place" program to reflect the recent changes in the campus climate and the GLBT community. The revised program requires that anyone wishing to display the new sticker must undergo formal training and agree be listed on the web site as a "Safe Person." This online list increases the critical visibility of positive role models and allies for students.

Anecdotally, we continue to learn from students that they feel safer seeing the stickers on campus. They perceive the people who openly display the symbol in their offices as allies and hence feel safer and more affirmed in who they were.

Co-curricular

The Coalition works with residence life to provide GLBT awareness and sensitivity programming for resident directors and assistants. Often members have been asked to do presentations for an entire group of students in the residence hall. In conjunction with the Orientation Program, SCC members provide workshops for new students and work with orientation leaders to development a skit featuring GLBT issues in student life.

The SCC provides a workshop series open to all on campus, featuring non-academic issues of GLBT rights. In the past, some of these topics have included. Being an ally, Judicial, Implications of Same Sex Marriage on Personnel Issues, Same Sex Marriage as a Civil Right, GLBT issues in the Classroom, and When Hate Equals Handcuffs: Hate Crimes.

Student Group

The student GLBT group AWARE, formerly a small and closeted group, is now highly visible and active. In part, their increased visibility is a byproduct of the involvement and work of the Coalition.

Reporting feeling more empowered by the presence of the Coalition and the Safe Person Safe Space program, the students have resumed responsibility for implementing an April AWAREness Week of educational and social programming. The programming purposefully reaches out to engage faculty and staff as well as students. From humble beginnings, the week's events now draw significant crowds to events that include a drag show, movie, panel on gay identity, and other programming for students, faculty, and staff. Faculty and staff are actively engaged in this week as well and are often found sitting at tables with students passing out literature, buttons, brochures, and stickers and answering questions.

The Rainbow Breakfast, which launches the AWAREness Week, is a Safe College Coalition and student GLBT group co-sponsored event that provides an opportunity for anyone who chooses to come to a gathering to simply celebrate community. Initially, less than a dozen people attended. At this year's event, with the President of the College as a speaker, the crowd overflowed the ballroom.

Impact on BSC and Beyond

Some key faculty and staff members heard stories of students whose parents or relatives have denied them financial and emotional support because of their sexual orientation. When this issue was brought to the Coalition, given the almost decades long efforts to provide support for the GLBT students, the Coalition felt that the institution also has a responsibility to support them when they found themselves in this situation. We felt that the mission of the institution was not only to develop students as scholars, but also as members of a diverse community. We asked how we as an educational community respond. How do we truly make Bridgewater State College a "Safe Zone"?

The answer came when an out student, active in the leadership of AWARE, went to the Financial Aid office to appeal for funding. Because of the nature of the rules for aid, and because her parents did not support her, funding was not available to her.

The Coalition determined that one of the ways the institution could support these students was by providing some funding. Therefore, an endowed scholarship for a gay, lesbian, bisexual, or transgender student at Bridgewater State College was established for a student whose disclosure of her or his sexual orientation resulted in withdrawal of family emotional and financial support. Now we work with Financial Aid to overcome the guidelines and restrictions that preclude GLBT students from accessing funds.

Through the generosity of Lucie Blue Tremblay[5] a French-Canadian singer and songwriter who gave a kick-off concert at the College and in Boston in the spring of 2000, the scholarship was launched. Lucie Blue continues to be one of the strongest supporters of the Scholarship; she mentions it at every concert and sends the money received from her appeals. It was clear that the scholarship needed to have her name.

We also felt that it should bear the name of the man whose positive work both for the College and for GLBT issues is unparalleled. Barney Frank is a local politician whose open sexual orientation has been a positive model for those facing the challenges of coming out. And so the Frank-Tremblay scholarship now had a name and some initial funds. But much more was needed to have an endowed scholarship.

The Frank-Tremblay Scholarship is specifically designed for full time matriculated undergraduate students who identify as gay, lesbian, bisexual, or transgender, who are in good standing (GPA 2.0 or higher), and who have successfully completed at least one semester at Bridgewater State College. The students must demonstrate need for this particular scholarship by providing letters of support from two individuals. A committee of members of the Coalition, including a representative from Financial Aid, was formed to review the applications and award the money. We worked with Financial Aid, the Development office, and Student Affairs to insure that the money would go directly to the student, and not to the Bursar's office to cover bills. We continually get requests from other institutions that now want to establish a similar scholarship. And so the work of Coalition extends well beyond the borders of Bridgewater.

Letters of appeal were written to campus constituents. However, the uniqueness of the scholarship fund soon caught the attention of the local media. A story was written in a small local newspaper and was picked up by national media. Our small college catapulted into the national press, which generated interest and financial support from people throughout the country. Most of these people had no affiliation with our College, but had a strong affinity for the cause of the scholarship.[6] We read letters from donors who spoke of the problems they had while going to college without financial assistance because they had "come out" to their parents. The heart-wrenching stories spurred us on to do more.

One new faculty member said that his decision to come to Bridgewater

---

[5]Lucie Blue Tremblay, www.luciebluetremblay.com.

[6]You too can send money to the Frank-Tremblay Scholarship. A check, in any amount, will be greatly appreciated. Send it to the Bridgewater Foundation, Davis Alumni Center, Bridgewater State College, Bridgewater, MA 02325. On the subject line, be sure to write Frank-Tremblay scholarship. Thanks.

State College was made, in part, because of our reputation as an open campus. He learned of the Frank-Tremblay Scholarship and the work of the Coalition through our web site. Students coming to the College sometimes mention the Scholarship. It has put us on the map of the GLBT community and has made the entire institution more aware of the ways in which GLBT students are often victims of even familiar prejudice. The organizational culture has clearly changed, through our efforts in the classroom, with faculty and administrators and staff, and with the wider community. But as the New Englander Robert Frost once said, "we have miles to go…."

Plans for the Future

Other classroom-specific efforts are underway. Currently, a survey is being conducted of all full and part-time faculty. The faculty members of the subcommittee of the Coalition who created the survey are trying to determine what currently existing courses deal with GLBT issues in more than a transitory way.

The same subcommittee is examining the creation of a GLBT studies course, and possibly a minor in GLBT studies. One course, offered by a member of the coalition, will address GLBT issues in counseling. A liberal arts course is being developed and will be available to all students. With the development of new general education guidelines, it may be possible to offer GLBT focused courses for all students.

One of the other initiatives that the Safe College Coalition is supporting is the continued drive to establish a GLBT and ally alumni group who can serve as mentors for the current students and be part of a networking system that will benefit all involved. Alumni can provide positive role models and contacts for undergraduate GLBT students. It is also important for the Coalition to bring to alumni awareness of the positive changes to the climate at Bridgewater.

In the fall of 2001, the first GLBTA (gay, lesbian, bisexual, transgender, and ally) event during the Homecoming Weekend was held. Since cultural change is slow and although that first event was not well attended, the subsequent annual event continues to grow. It is through the current work of the SCC that alumni will begin to understand the change in climate, which in turn will encourage their safe participation in the developing group.

To change the culture of the campus, the students must be empowered. Student leaders who are already involved on campus have formed a student group, representative of a cross section of campus activities. The purpose is to increase the opportunities to provide education for all students. It is often easier for students to hear messages from their peers than from faculty or staff. The Coalition members will work to identify and support this group of students.

The culture and climate of academic institutions must evolve to make classrooms and campuses safe and affirming for all students. In order for this evolution to take place, coalitions of faculty, administrators, staff, and students, regardless of sexual orientation, need to continue to work together for change.

Fleas for Change

Sojourner Truth once spoke about being "fleas for change." And perhaps that is what this coalition does. We serve, by our very presence, as a continual reminder that GLBT issues must not be ignored.

References

Chronicle of Higher Education. (2003). Retrieved October 6, 2004, from http://www.ngltf.org/library

Lopez, G., & Chism, N. (1993). Classroom concerns of gay and lesbian students: The invisible minority. *College Teaching, 41*, 97-103.

Sanlo, R. L. (1998). *Working with lesbian, gay, bisexual, and transgender college students: A handbook for faculty and administrators.* Westport, CT: Greenwood Press.

Sanlo, R., Rankin, S., & Schoenberg, R. (2002). *Our place on campus: Lesbian, gay, bisexual, transgender services and programs in higher education.* Westport, CT: Greenwood Press.

Wall, V. A., & Evans, N. J. (2000). *Toward Acceptance: Sexual orientation issues on campus.* Lanham, MD: University Press of America.

Yeskel, F. D. (1991). *Dealing with lesbian, gay, and bisexual concerns: Multicultural organizational development in higher education.* Unpublished doctoral dissertation, University of Massachusetts Amherst.

Robert S. Haynor is the Director of Outreach Education at the Counseling Center at Bridgewater State College and a member of the Governor's Council on Gay and Lesbian Youth. He can be reached at rhaynor@bridgew.edu.
Susan A Holton, Ph.D., is a Professor of Communication Studies at Bridgewater State College. She has published extensively in conflict management in higher education and works with individual institutions and international organizations on issues of conflict management. She can be reached at sholton@bridgew.edu; http://webhost.bridgew.edu/sholton. The Safe College Coalition webpage is http://www.bridgew.edu/counselingcenter/safecollege.cfm.

Chapter 25

Critical Moments: A Case-Based Diversity Project That Engages and Enlivens Campus-Wide Efforts to Teach and Work Inclusively

Diane Gillespie, Gillies Malnarich, and Tina Young

This article describes a case-based, campus-wide diversity project called Critical Moments. Using Seattle Central Community College as a case study, the authors explore how this project reinforced exemplary campus practices and stimulated institutional change.

This article describes a campus-wide, multi-faceted diversity project, supported by The Washington Center for Improving the Quality of Undergraduate Education, a public service center of The Evergreen State College in Washington State. The project's name, "Critical Moments," refers to those times when historically underrepresented students in higher education have felt challenged by their difference, set apart in ways that silenced or alienated them from the educational context in which they found themselves (Gillespie & Woods, 2000). In some cases, these critical moments lead potentially successful students to drop out of school.

The Washington Center for Improving the Quality of Undergraduate Education, a grass-roots consortium of colleges and universities, learned about Critical Moments and was keen to work with the originators of the project because of its emphasis on student voices and seldom-heard student stories. First developed in The Goodrich Scholarship Program at The University of Nebraska at Omaha, Critical Moments dovetailed with Washington Center's campus diversity initiatives (*Washington Center News*, 1998), including its work with state agencies and two- and four-year institutions to improve the academic success of students of color and to foster equitable campus cultures.

For the past three years, a William and Flora Hewlett grant has allowed the Washington Center to develop Critical Moments on four partner institutions' campuses—three community colleges and one four-year college — and to seed work at a number of other sites (Malnarich, 2002). Although the project exists on more than one campus, in this article we will focus on Seattle Central Community College — the most diverse campus in Washington State — as an example of Critical Moment's potential to influence an institution's practices. We briefly describe the project and the implementation process and then turn to our primary focus: the effects of Critical Moments on the practices of involved faculty, staff, and administrators at Seattle Central, already known for its leadership in diversity work. Critical Moments spurred faculty development through exposure to student voices and innovative curricular materials; increased communication between faculty, staff, and administrators about the institutional implications of underrepresented students' experiences; reinvigorated diversity work across institutional boundaries; and connected the college to a Critical Moments network of educators implementing the project on their respective campuses.

Critical Moments: The Process

In brief, the Critical Moments project has a generic template, developed from pilot projects and practice that schools use as a guide in the implementation process. The template contains the following steps:

1. forming a campus-wide multicultural team;
2. identifying and interviewing resilient, historically underrepresented students;
3. interpreting the interview and choosing a generative theme(s);
4. writing cases from the dilemmas those students found almost insurmountable;
5. teaching these cases to enhance critical thinking, cultural awareness, and social advocacy;
6. creating a book of such cases to serve as a reference text in a multicultural learning community; and
7. assessing all aspects of the project.

In the Washington Center inter-institutional Critical Moments' project, an additional step has been added: using cases to promote reflection and change within and across educational institutions.

The template can be modified given the particular institutional context, but the first step — forming a campus-wide multicultural team, composed of faculty, staff, and administrators interested in and involved with diversity — cannot be skipped or left until later in the process. This team oversees all steps of the project. The diverse composition is essential for hearing all student voices, whose narratives are at the heart of the project. In interviews devoted to recapturing students' lived experiences on campus, students tell stories about when they considered leaving college because of the pressures resulting from their race and/or ethnicity, gender, social class, disability, and/or sexual orientation. As interviews are conducted, the team meets Human Subjects guidelines to protect the anonymity of the students interviewed. The team interviews a variety of underrepresented students whose stories are about different dimensions of campus life. Over time, the team makes sure that representative groups of students have opportunities to tell their stories.

The team (or a subset of the team) then takes up each interview transcript for analysis. Paulo Freire's (2002/1980) term "generative theme," has been especially useful as an interpretive tool. Such themes are places of contradiction in lived experience where power and inequities collide. He believed that those who have been underrepresented have also been marginalized in ways they themselves cannot quite fully grasp. For Freire, oppression occurs through situational limits that are both empirical and psychological. These limits come to be perceived by the oppressed as "insurmountable barriers" (p. 99). Liberation occurs through re-perceiving the situation so that barriers are reconfigured and/or removed making new action possible. The action of individuals then transforms the situation itself. In the interviews, the team looks for those places of contradiction – for example, being highly visible and yet invisible as a person of color.

Once the team has found the generative theme(s) in the student's interview transcript, writers from the team use the student's language to write a case story (about five to six pages in length) that embeds the generative theme in a problematic situation. Writers take special care not to create villains and to make room for multiple interpretations. The case needs to sustain a lively introductory discussion for about 35 to 40 minutes. All discussants need to have opportunities to think holistically and critically about the dilemmas the case presents. Often readings accompany the case to provide historical and cultural background. Case stories become entries into deeper, more challenging conversations about the meanings of diversity and inclusivity.

The complexity of the case discussions requires trained facilitators who guide small groups in ways that promote critical thinking, such as being open to multiple perspectives while appreciating ambiguity; being able to employ social skills, such as empathy; and being cognizant of cross-cultural sensitivity, such as recognizing significant differences. Case discussions better promote theoretical understanding if they are part of an ongoing curriculum devoted to broader issues of social justice.

From the start, the project needs to include assessment. The assessment process is the means for refining and improving the team's work together, the students' development over time, and the significance of students' stories for making the campus's working and learning environment more equitable and hospitable. A critical component of assessment is to track the quality of student discussions. For example, do students' capacities for critical thinking increase over the course of their case discussions? (For analyses of such case discussions, see Gillespie, Seaberry, & Valades, 1997; Valades, Gillespie, Seaberry, & Okahamfe, 1997. For samples of Critical Moments cases, see Gillespie & Woods, 2000. For faculty discussions of cases, see Hanson & Gillespie, 1998; Seaberry & Gillespie, 1997; Valades, 1996.)

The goals, then, of the Critical Moments project are fourfold: to send the message to underrepresented students that their stories matter and can become a means for instructional and institutional change; to enable faculty to hear the voices of underrepresented students as a means for developing their abilities to teach more inclusively; to train all participants to problematize diversity as a means for action in particular educational circumstances; and to develop a diverse and inclusive team of campus leaders — students and educators — who are able to facilitate difficult dialogues as a means of transforming oppressive practices on campus.

The above description is an idealized version of Critical Moments that becomes messier and more challenging as campuses wrestle with implementation in their local settings. The process becomes at once more complex and simple. Each campus's culture leads to a constellation of variables that are historically situated and unique; Critical Moments has to be adapted to each campus's circumstances. Still, when campus teams exchange accounts of their work with each other at Washington Center inter-institutional project meetings, it is evident that good Critical Moments practice has essential features: campus teams must be diverse in their composition; students' testimonials, especially those based on students interviewing one another, are a complementary pedagogical practice but not substitutes for cases; cases with a carefully embedded generative theme provoke the most powerful and transformative discussions; and cases supplemented by a surrounding curriculum, in the broadest sense, lead to deep learning.

The Critical Moments' model at Seattle Central Community College continues to promote lively dialogues between students, faculty, staff, and administrators interested in and concerned about diversity and cultural pluralism. The outcomes of these dialogues are multiple: a network of educators aware of ways in which institutional practices and policies can constrain or foster the academic success of underrepresented students, white students better equipped at difficult dialogues, and stakeholders moving the institution toward better alignment with their espoused mission statement and goals. Such awareness and reflection help shape new policy and change institutional practices. (See Seattle Central Community College Critical Moments' Team, Annual Narrative Reports, 2001-2003.)

Critical Moments at Seattle Central Community College

At Seattle Central, Critical Moments fits naturally with another institutional action research project entitled "Untold Success Stories of Students of Color." The project outcome, a photodocumentary exhibit of diverse students' stories, was displayed in various settings, both on and off campus. The newly formed Critical Moments' team analyzed the narratives for potential critical incidents and decided to re-interview several students. The additional information became the basis for their initial discussions about creating a case. In addition to "Untold Success" stories, the team adapted some of the Goodrich case stories and invited people to discuss them as a means of broadening team membership. Early on, team members also interviewed Seattle Central students based on referrals from staff in student support services, other faculty, and administrators.

Seattle Central's Critical Moments' team first introduced Critical Moments' case stories in a student leadership seminar after team members recruited the students who they thought would be interested in participating in such a seminar. After learning how students responded to case discussions, team members decided to create a pilot seminar that would be facilitated by a faculty member familiar with teaching methodologies and a staff member versed in multicultural student issues, both from different race/ethnicities and both trained in Critical Moments. After receiving permission from students, non-teaching team members were welcome to observe class sessions and share feedback at team meetings. In the evaluations of the first pilots, facilitators appreciated the wisdom of this early decision to team teach: "Some stories . . . are so emotional that they need a team. If there was a silence from one [facilitator], the other, with a certain distance from the issue, was able to step in." Although the composition of the teaching team changes over time, this practice continues to be a central motivator for bringing faculty and staff together and for stimulating professional development.

After the two pilot seminars, the four facilitators identified "honesty and straightforwardness of the students and themselves" as a critical outcome of the Critical Moments' process:

> There is value in using the case stories in individual classes, but the complete case story curriculum, with a team teaching it, has an even greater potential for learning. With regard to retention, it shows students that they have options and can do things for themselves, and it enables them to ask if they are making the right choices. This class can have significant impact on success in other classes—deepening reading skills, enabling students to listen to divergent points of view, encouraging greater textual analysis, providing collaboration opportunities, and strengthening critical thinking, especially students' ability to empathize and articulate ideas. (facilitator comment)

From the perspective of the facilitators, the cases introduced students to topics that they might otherwise avoid in classrooms or other dialogues about diversity. In particular, discussions of cases such as "The Photo Album," a case on a lesbian student deciding whether or not to come out to her sociology class, and "The White Teacher," a case where two students of color are trying to decide whether or not their white teacher is racist, were opportunities for students to discuss, more thoughtfully, issues that often spark uncritical, stereotypical responses in the public domain.

As the project evolved on the campus and the team began to write Seattle Central student cases, the intense discussions of interview transcripts and the nature of the generative theme deepened all team members' understanding of power imbalances and inequities in the institution. Building on already existing inclusive curriculum and teaching practices, the team chose to extend the conversations from the classroom to the institution by developing "companion cases." These stories were based on interviews with faculty and staff who held different perspectives than students on Critical Moments' issues. The paired case stories highlighted multiple realities and institutional practices that constrain everyone's actions. The Critical Moments team used these companion cases for professional development workshops for the entire Seattle Central community. A Seattle Central case, "A Math Moment," became the occasion for meeting with math faculty to explore what could be done so women and underrepresented students could perform better in math classes. The development of a "toolbox" of resources for use in the Critical Moments seminar involved librarians more directly in Critical Moments. All along the way, students' comments and feedback from the pilot seminars helped to refine the project.

For students, some cases had more meaning than others. One student singled out "Annette's Dilemma," a case about a woman who cannot say no: "I put myself in Annette's shoes as a single mom and all the responsibilities I have on top of school. I decided not to overwhelm myself and not put extra responsibilities on my children that would interfere with their studies and add stress" (student comment). Another student liked the discussion about "The White Teacher": "I think everyone opened up more than usual. We got down to it!" Several students were moved by "The Photo Album": "The issue of gay rights has to be addressed in a non-threatening manner"; "[the case] forced me to look closely at my values and beliefs." Students also mentioned "Between A Rock and A Hard Place," a case that depicts the conflicting demands on a Latino student whose family does not understand what it takes to be a successful student. As one student put it: "The case made me feel I'm not alone."

In the first pilots, the students found the one-hour class time too limiting: "Allow the class to be a full three hours so that there is ample time for group discussions." Students wanted to hear the full expression of their classmates' views in a context where they felt safe. As one student noted, "Everyone was able to voice their opinion without feeling bad about how they thought." For many, the most valuable part of the seminar was listening to other classmates' opinions. One student felt "inspiration to do more critical thinking." Even in the limited time frame, students recognized the importance of the process: "I'm more open-minded to others' opinions." "All the things I've learned . . . I can apply to my life when I feel like I'm going through a critical moment." One student valued "seeing how the various minority groups within [the seminar] related to each other. I felt we all shared the same struggles in so many ways, yet our perceptions are so different. I think anger—cultural angers—have a lot to do with different perspectives." By chance, only students of color were in one pilot, and a student made this recommendation: "Open the class up to white students so that we can get another American cultural perspective." Although the pilot seminar *was* open to all students, this student recognized the absence of a perspective. In response, the team made a concerted effort to recruit a wider range of underrepresented students, including working-class whites.

Not only the composition but also the size of the Critical Moments' course affects relationships among the participants in the seminar. As one team of facilitators noted,

> Larger classes might make it easier to get to a point of intense and deeper discussion. If classes are too small, it is difficult to build alliances between students. And if the class met more often, students would have interacted with less restraint. We didn't achieve that level of trust that would have opened up class dialogues a lot more; but we were moving toward those levels, and the students were getting more comfortable with each other.

What might appear to be only a matter of organizational detail has far reaching pedagogical implications for trust and alliance building among students.

Well into the third year of the project, the team expanded the three-credit hour course to five-credits. Still team-taught, it now meets three times a week. Throughout the quarter, non-teaching team members, serving as college resources, assist with role-playing, fishbowl dialogues, and interviewing techniques. Case writers observe class discussions to gain valuable feedback on their cases. Colleagues who are not members of the Critical Moments team have been invited to join case story discussions. For example, a deaf faculty member helped facilitate "Struggles in the Classroom," a Goodrich case about a deaf student whose instructor is unfamiliar with disability policies. In the seminars, case stories and videos produced by partner institutions enrich the classroom as well.

Students involved in Critical Moments recognize in their evaluations that class discussions can be messy and hard, especially as they struggle to feel safe enough to trust their peers. In one student's view, "Some issues [were] sugar-coated and [discussants] just scratched the surface." These challenges are common ones in multicultural classrooms. Because the Critical Moments team includes more than faculty, an administrator on a teaching team experienced the challenges faculty face first hand. During the discussion of "The Photo Album," two gay students came out, a Christian fundamentalist self-identified, and other students talked about being survivors. The class became a catalyst for disclosure for some students who felt it was a safe space and a place of support, yet one student did not want to talk about anything having to do with sex, either about homosexual or heterosexual issues. This administrator realized that:

> the more complex and emotion-laden case stories required adept facilitation of the dialogue to avoid being at cross purposes with the skills goals. The students became so engaged that some lost sight of the goals of strengthening their abilities to listen, respond empathically, and exchange perspectives.

As facilitators gain experience moving with students to deeper levels in their thinking about the meanings of diversity, the expertise of the Critical Moments' team supports the work of the teaching team.

Collaboration in the classroom underscores the need for collaboration throughout the institution. Educators cannot afford to work in units that are isolated — for example, in academics, student affairs, or administration — if the aim is to radically reduce the critical moments vulnerable students experience in educational institutions. Although Seattle Central has had faculty members from different disciplines team teach, barriers exist for faculty, staff, and/or administrators who want to teach together. For example, staff cannot be paid overload stipends and sometimes cannot be freed from regular work duties. A further difficulty has been finding a source of origin for the course so that students from different academic areas can take and receive credit toward their degree program and/or transfer credit. The Seattle Central team is working hard to legitimize institutionally diverse teaching teams (for example, faculty and staff) and give Critical Moments cross-curricular status. Without transfer credit, first-generation students hesitate to pay for the class. The work to expand the class from two to three and now five credit hours and to find a place for this kind of seminar in the curriculum illustrates how difficult it is to modify established organizational practices.

Even though the implementation proved to be challenging, Critical Moments is taking root. English, ESL, and Humanities faculty members continue to incorporate Critical Moments case stories into their own classes in their respective disciplines. The Critical Moments Project is connected to a number of other college-wide activities. The Retention Task Force includes the project as one of numerous retention efforts being conducted on campus. A leadership institute for students of color incorporates Critical Moments into its program. The College's Structural Planning Committee lists Critical Moments work as an objective under one of its goals. The Office of Multicultural Initiatives, in which Critical Moments is organizationally housed, functions as a central station through which many administrative, academic, and student support services pass. This centralizing function leads to more coherent diversity efforts across campus and has strengthened Seattle Central's ability to develop diversity work along multiple tracks.

The Inter-Institutional Critical Moments' Project and Campus Work

Seattle Central Community College's campus work on Critical Moments has been enriched through its participation with partner institutions Tacoma Community College, The Evergreen State College, and South Puget Sound Community College at Washington Center retreats. Through campus oral and written reports, teams have shared useful practices. This cross-fertilization produces more robust local work since entry points for implementing Critical Moments differ. While one campus might be involved in writing case stories, another might be piloting and developing a Critical Moments curriculum in a particular course. Campuses adopt each other's project innovations. Throughout all meetings and retreats, ongoing conversations bring people together, making campus teams feel less alone. These larger conversations have been grounded in shared readings and continued discussions of student interviews and campus cases and work. As new institutions join the project, team members distill what they have learned, even as they are stimulated by the questions posed by newcomers to Critical Moments.

Campus teams grapple with what is distinctive about their campus culture and what is general to all institutions striving to become more pluralistic. The institutions in the project include one that is among the most diverse in the nation and one that is among the least visibly diverse in the State. After the project's first year, the campus teams decided to study together to develop a shared sociological understanding of systems of entitlement and privilege. In book seminars sponsored by the Washington Center, the teams discussed the following works: Alan Johnson's (2001) *Privilege, Power and Difference*; Gary Howard's (1999), *We Can't Teach What We Don't Know*; and Robert A. Ibarra's (2001) *Beyond Affirmative Action: Reframing the Context of Higher Education*. Each of these books contributed to the Critical Moments' cross-campus efforts by identifying, through various theoretical lenses, the contradictory cultural contexts in which *underrepresented* students often struggle. Concomitantly, the works also show how historically *represented* students can be deceived by accepting surface understandings of power relationships, often presented uncritically in the culture at large. In particular, Johnson's notion of small, doable acts informs our teaching of the cases and our ability to help students strategize for the future. And his notion also empowers us to value our own small, doable acts as we work on our campuses to implement Critical Moments.

The drawing power of the Critical Moments approach for educators is the central place it gives to students' voices. As educators listening carefully to students' stories, whether in the original interview or by reading the transcript of it, we are granted entry into students' experiential worlds. As witnesses, we are invited to re-live with them what happened, to understand their generative themes, and to imagine with them what might have made a difference so that our own practices can become more inclusive and our institutions more hospitable. And the generative themes that make cases dynamic for teaching and learning also turn out to be dynamic for institution-wide conversations that are equally hard and messy. The teams are beginning to appreciate that their own campus cultures can be "read" much like a student interview. Differing perspectives on how to get institutions to be responsive to all students can lead to an organizational generative theme(s). For example, the absence a multicultural center can hamper campus-wide diversity efforts. Discussions of such issues can uncover places in the system where practices are less equitable than one might wish. Meeting with the cross-campus team members emboldens us as educators. We go back to our own settings to advocate for more equitable practices.

References

Freire, P. (2002). *The pedagogy of the oppressed.* (30th Anniversary ed.). M. B. Ramos, (Trans.). New York: Continuum. (Original work published 1970).

Gillespie, D., Seaberry, J., & Valades, J. (1997). From student narratives to case studies: Diversity from the bottom up. *Journal of Excellence in College Teaching* 7(2), 25-42.

Gillespie, D., & Woods, G. (2000). *Critical moments: Responding creatively to cultural diversity through case stories* (3rd ed.). Olympia, WA: The Washington Center for Improving the Quality of Undergraduate Education.

Hansen, D. E., & Gillespie, D. (1998). Struggles in the classroom: A deaf student's case. *Journal of College Reading and Learning, 28*(2), 132-136.

Henning, D., & Gillespie, D. (1996). The First Amendment: A case study. *The National Teaching & Learning Forum, 5*(5), 4-5.

Howard, G. R. (1999). *We can't teach what we don't know: White teachers, multiracial schools.* New York: Teachers College Press.

Iberra, R. A. (2001). *Beyond affirmative action: Reframing the context of higher education.* Madison: The University of Wisconsin Press.

Johnson, A. (2001). *Privilege, power, and difference.* Mountain View, CA: Mayfield.

Malnarich, G. (2002). Empowering students and their communities. *Critical Moments Newsletter, 1.* Olympia, WA: Washington Center for Improving the Quality of Undergraduate Education.

Seaberry, J. S., & Gillespie, D. (1997). The white teacher. *National Teaching and Learning Forum, 6*(3), 11-12.

Seattle Central Community College. (2003). *Annual Narrative Reports, 2001-2003.* Seattle: The Washington Center for Improving the Quality of Undergraduate Education. Olympia, WA.

Valades, J. A. (1996). Misunderstood. *National Teaching & Learning Forum, 6*(1), 8-9.

Valades, J. A., Gillespie, D., Seaberry, J., & Okahamfe, I. (1997). A critical case study approach to questions of identity and racialized mixed heritage [Electronic version]. *The Journal of Critical Pedagogy, 1*(1), 1-19. Retrieved December 11, 1997, from http://www.lib.wmc.edu/pub/jep/jep.html

The Washington Center. (1998). Multicultural efforts project: Academic success of students of color, a collaborative project between the State Board for Community and Technical Colleges and The Washington Center, 1996-1998. *The Washington Center News, 12*(1). Retrieved on October 5, 2004, from http://www.evergreen.edu/washcenter/resources/fall1998/fall1998.htm

---

Diane Gillespie is professor and Associate Director of Interdisciplinary Arts and Sciences at the University of Washington Bothell. **Gillies Malnarich** is Co-Director of the Washington Center for Improving the Quality of Undergraduate Education, Evergreen University. **Tina Young** is Director of Multicultural Initiatives at Seattle Central Community College.

Chapter 26

From Reading Group to Faculty Change Team: The Hamline University Lido Group

James Francisco Bonilla

Multicultural institutional change can be a daunting task when attempted in isolation, especially when one attempts to engage faculty. However, when done as part of a diverse collegium committed to improving the teaching and learning experience for all students, small changes can and have led to systemic change. This chapter tells the story of a racially diverse, interdisciplinary faculty cohort called the Lido Multicultural Teaching Group, which was part of the Race, Gender, and Beyond Project at Hamline University.

Institutional Context

Hamline University is a small, private, comprehensive university in St. Paul Minnesota consisting of a College of Liberal Arts, Graduate Schools of Education, Public Administration and Management, and Liberal Studies, as well as a School of Law. In 1997, Hamline was also an institution ripe for addressing racial diversity. Contrary to popular belief that Minnesota is as White as Vermont, the actual demographics can startle the casual observer. For instance, the number of racial minorities currently graduating from the Minneapolis and St. Paul public schools hovers at 70%. Fortunately, these numbers have not been lost on Minnesota's higher education leaders, including those at Hamline. While initially slow to respond to the growth of the potential student of color market, complacency has been replaced by sober scrutiny of the bottom line. To compete and survive, institutions like Hamline are realizing they must fashion themselves into more welcoming places for people of color.

In 1997, this author and a colleague, Professor Patricia Palmerton in the Communications Department, conducted a study of the classroom racial climate entitled *Hamline Faculty & Student Voices: Race, Gender and Ethnicity in the Classroom*. Among the key issues uncovered were: a) a lack of classes addressing diversity; b) a lack of time for faculty to develop such classes; and c) student and faculty desires to be more competent in the area of learning and teaching about diversity. The release of the *Voices* study also coincided with an evaluation report by the Mid-States Association critical of Hamline's curriculum for its paucity of course offerings addressing Cultural Breadth. Administration began to get the message loud and clear. With the undergraduate College's enrollment figures for students of color nearing 15% and the Graduate School's Public Administration and Management program nearing 25% people of color, the changing demographics helped set the stage for action. The confluence of these events led to the Race, Gender & Beyond Project, initiated in 1999.

Project Description

This Project consisted of two distinct but related initiatives, *The Training of Trainers* Program and the *Faculty Development* Program. The Race, Gender, and Beyond Project consisted of five complementary sets of activities:

1. The first was the on-going development and support of a pre-existing core group of faculty committed to multicultural teaching known as the Lido Group. The Lido Group met each month, initially to familiarize itself with the newest scholarship on teaching and learning about diversity.
2. With Lido serving as the ad hoc advisory committee for the project's coordinator, a series of faculty development seminars were organized each spring featuring a nationally known consultant addressing a different aspect of curriculum transformation and diversity. These seminars were scheduled deliberately to serve as part of the annual publicity campaign for the next component of the program.
3. The third component of the faculty development program was the *Race, Gender, and Beyond* Faculty Development Grants program. The goal of this activity was to provide interested faculty with curriculum development grants of up to $4000 so they could have the time and resources to integrate the newest scholarship on diversity into existing courses or develop new courses.
4. The fourth component of the Project required all grantees to share their curricular innovations with their colleagues at the Annual Awardees Luncheon in April of the year following funding of a proposal.
5. The fifth and final component was a consulting service to faculty (and, on occasion, staff, and administration) interested in addressing diversity in the classroom or in their workplaces. This later expanded into consulting and

training on and off-campus as the reputation of the Race, Gender, and Beyond Project grew locally and later, nationally.

The Training of Trainers Program resulted in the development of a campuswide team of skilled leaders from the faculty, students, and staff focused on improving the larger campus climate for diversity. Support for this component has been financially sustained by Hamline since 2000 and coordinated through the Office of Minority and International Student Affairs.

The faculty development component, and specifically the Lido Multicultural Teaching Group, is the subject of the remainder of this chapter.

The Lido Group: From Reading Group ...

The intent from the outset was to gather a multicultural cohort of colleagues committed to deepening their ability to successfully address diversity in the classroom. This author served as Lido's principal coordinator and recruited both the junior and senior faculty, primarily through word of mouth and reputation. The first meeting was a dinner convened at an off-campus restaurant in the fall of 1997, a restaurant called "Lido," which eventually became the group's namesake. Over its eight year history, Lido has grown to include over 22 faculty from over a dozen disciplines (including African American Studies, Biology, Chemistry, Conflict Studies, Economics and Management, Education, English, Philosophy, Religion, Social Justice, Theater and Communications, and Women's Studies).

The success of the Project has been due to the collaborative work of the Lido Faculty participants. Lido has intentionally kept its members' responsibilities fluid and defined principally by their passion for creating inclusive curriculum and/or climate change across campus. When the Race, Gender, and Beyond Project was reviewed in 2003, the external reviewer observed:

> The faculty's desire to teach their disciplines well to diverse students and to teach with interdisciplinary and multicultural content and perspectives has led them to become resources for each other, for both intellectual study and moral support, and to generate coordinated efforts, structured and informal. Lido has been careful to keep its membership small enough to foster open and risk-taking discussions and personal mentoring. (LaBare, 2003)

No one in Lido foresaw the many ways in which it was to later become the force for change that it grew to be. Initially, the recruitment pitch to prospective Lido members was simple: "Come, join our book group. Let us feed you, and while we eat, let's discuss teaching and learning in a diverse classroom." Reflecting back, with the benefit of 20/20 hindsight, several of the organizing principles employed in assembling Lido became unexpected predictors for its future success.

One was that Lido had the good fortune of having several tenured and well-respected faculty among the first to accept the invitation to join the book group. A second ingredient was the decision to make Lido as racially diverse as possible. The pitch for faculty of color to join was to appeal to faculty of color's need not to work in isolation (Sotello, Viernes, Turner, & Myers Jr., 2000). Several young, White, untenured faculty also responded favorably to an opportunity to address social justice as they met and broke bread with their new colleagues. For some, Lido became the supportive departmental culture they lacked (Geok-Lin Lim & Herrera-Sobek, 2000; Sotello, Viernes, Turner & Myers Jr., 2000). It also became a teaching shop of sorts, a place to raise uncomfortable teaching dilemmas without fear of being made to feel incompetent or labeled "misguided," or worse still, "a racist." As one junior member of color recalled:

> I like the discussion of readings and diversity teaching in the classroom. There are many aspects of teaching and critical thinking I didn't get to explore, so it is quite interesting to hear senior Lido members' thoughts about those issues. The monthly meetings were also a great channel to vent my frustrations (seemed like I had a lot) among many kind people who are always willing to listen and exchange ideas.

While much of higher education is a place where faculty of all colors labor in relative obscurity (Birnbaum, 1988), Lido became a place that offered senior and junior faculty, White faculty and faculty of color, male and female faculty a place to experience a community run by consensus. As the group's initial reading choices broadened from classroom racial dynamics to include institutional racism in the academy, Lido transformed into a community that embraced both reflection and action (Friere, 1970).

... To Change Agent Team

In only its second year, Lido moved beyond merely being a multicultural reading group. As a "community of peers" (Birnbaum, 1988), Lido evolved into an informal campus change team addressing systemic issues of race. It unexpectedly became the prime vehicle for recruiting faculty to apply for the Project's curriculum development grants program. Lido also became a critical sounding board on policy and strategic directions, a political pressure group, and a support system that helped maintain both programmatic and institutional momentum for change. Central to this journey were the stories that were brought to the table about both student and faculty experiences with diversity. One of Lido's most significant accomplishments is its annual dialogue with students concerning the classroom climate for diversity.

The range of classroom issues students brought to the table varied and often depended on the social identities and developmental stage of the students involved (Adams, Bell, Griffin, 1997). What follows are three sample perspectives that represent a broad range of student concerns heard at a recent Lido luncheon:

1. A student of color shared with Lido faculty the challenge, as she put it, " of being a nurse for White students encountering [racism] for the first time."

2. A White student expressed a related, but very different classroom frustration: "For students who aren't at a basic level and want to go deeper, there is no place for them to go because it seems [many] faculty don't go deeper."

3. A third student from the Gay, Lesbian, Bisexual, Transgender (GLBT) community explained that her concern was that many faculty teaching diversity utilized a strict theoretical approach to the material that remained abstract, impersonal, and rational. However, precisely because she is personally connected to the material, she learned the content best experientially, engaging in a teaching approach that connected for her emotionally through self-disclosure.

As one Lido member recently commented:

> The session with the student groups was interesting. It was very helpful to hear what students think about living and learning around Hamline because I usually don't get to hear the students from diverse groups discuss that with me. I only have three advisees and all of them are White.

As issues like those above were raised in Lido, junior as well as senior faculty became more knowledgeable and confident and increasingly agitated for action beyond simple discourse. Supported and sometimes mentored by their senior colleagues, Lido faculty experienced increased classroom success and its reputation grew university wide. Some (non-Lido) faculty were overheard at times grumbling about Lido being a "clique," but administration and faculty took note of both Lido's concerns and growing expertise.

Lido's critical role as a sounding board was established early on in the drafting of the aforementioned *Voices Report* in 1997. The authors of the report utilized Lido to gauge how well the draft might be received by the faculty-at-large. Lido criticized the first draft for lacking an upfront recognition of the many strengths of Hamline's faculty. This initial feedback proved essential as it resulted in edits to the report that both included the strengths as well as problems associated with the Hamline classroom. Rather than focus excessively on what was wrong, the report struck a balance that included the many instances where students had also "caught the Hamline faculty doing things right." This made the reception the report received upon its final release vastly more meaningful to its faculty audience.

Throughout the life of the Project, Lido has raised issues, challenged assumptions, and helped the coordinator recognize and understand new directions for change. One example of a direction that emanated from the Lido membership was the idea of inviting the Dean and the Provost to what would later become an annual luncheon to discuss the campus climate. This proved not only helpful to Lido in establishing itself as a collective voice (and power) to be reckoned with, but both the Dean and Provost later reported the meetings to be helpful for them as well, using Lido as a "Diversity think-tank."

As a result, careful, collectively worded emails on racial issues crafted by group consensus often found their mark among key leaders. Lido also brought its influence to bear on Hamline's Strategic Planning process. As several Lido colleagues served on the Strategic Planning Committee, Lido was able to assert some influence to assure that issues of diversity remained central to the University's unfolding vision of itself.

Each year Lido has grown in size and reputation as invitations have been extended to one or two new faculty and the group has grown from its original nucleus of 11 to 22. One quarter of the group remained faculty of color by design. In her 2003 report, LeBare noted, "Lido seems to function very well for itself and for the university by being simultaneously on the fringe and at the center of ongoing work." The range of issues Lido tackled grew to include recruiting and retaining faculty and students of color, faculty reward systems for diversity work, and campus response systems to hate incidents. The common thread among all these campaigns was an empowered group of colleagues doggedly determined to see things improve for students of all colors. In this author's 20 years of teaching and consulting experience in higher education, it is rare to be part of a group that has reached the type of synergy Lido has achieved.

Lido and Its Relationship to the Larger Race, Gender, and Beyond Project

Lido served as the Ad-Hoc Advisory group to the larger Project by recommending speakers, flagging emerging campus issues, and being the "eyes and ears and collective brains" of the Project. Because of their developing knowledge base, members of Lido also reviewed grant applications and recommended awards for the curriculum grants project, significantly all of which were distributed to faculty outside of the Lido Group. This grants project later proved essential as it served to extend the support for and impact of diversity work more broadly across the campus. In so doing, Lido also answered the skeptics who felt the group would accomplish little beyond "preaching to the choir." "It's alive, not just goals on paper," was a sentiment Lido's outside reviewer heard expressed by both participants in and outside of Lido. Faculty were impressed that resources supported diversity work not only in the "usual" disciplines of the humanities, but also in science and in fine arts and communication. They were impressed the Project and Lido focused on gender, extending diversity concerns beyond statistics about race. Interviewees also saw that infusion of diversity happened not only in classroom settings, but also in university committees in which Lido members provided leadership and vision. They saw Lido adding to the embrace of new faculty who arrived at Hamline with more background in diversity. As one junior faculty member recounted, "Just knowing there are other people on campus who will be supportive of my work has been great." In the 2003 evaluation, faculty described it as having momentum: it moved ahead and beyond faculty whose absence might be a form of resistance. There was agreement that even those who had not participated directly in the Project and Lido had been affected by it.

University support has extended the Lido and grants initiatives, such as the dean's funding of a seven-week workshop on Teaching Diversity for Social Justice in summer 2002, with representation from each school of the university; readings on diversity issues; workshops on how to change courses; and brainstorming on syllabi. The individual pieces are themselves effective, but in the words of the Project's external reviewer, "in their combination and extensions, the whole of the Project is greater than just the sum of its parts" (LaBare, 2003). [1]

---

[1]Summary statistics show a growing impact over the three years of the project. Statistics include: 181 consultations on diversity to faculty, staff, and students locally and nationally; over 3000 participant educational contacts on issues of diversity (averaging 1-1/2 hours each); and nearly 100 development activities on and off campus for faculty, students, and staff.

Successes as a Change Team

Counted among the successes of Lido as a change agent team were the following:

- It became a place where faculty could safely discuss classroom dilemmas involving difference (including race, gender, ethnicity, religion, sexual orientation, disability, and socioeconomic class).
- It evolved to become a support group for faculty of color. One faculty member of color volunteered that when he first came to Hamline, everyone looked "very White." Colleagues in the Lido Group gave him a context of shared philosophy and were open to his perspectives. When he experienced racism on campus, he found Lido colleagues provided invaluable professional and personal support.
- It evolved to become a support group for weary and sometimes disheartened senior faculty of all colors.
- It also became s support group for bewildered new faculty that included informal mentoring.
- It served as a the programmatic sounding board for the work of the larger Race Gender, and Beyond Project.
- It served as an unofficial set of "eyes and ears" on campus regarding diversity issues. For example, Lido became an informal entity on campus where concerns about hate incidents were communicated and therefore became a catalyst for developing clearer response protocols between the faculty and Student Affairs.
- "Lido-ites" became co-conspirators for campus climate change by serving on several influential faculty and university-wide committees and communicating crucial information.
- Lido was able to influence campus administration and policy, particularly with the support of its senior, tenured colleagues.
- Lido members became recruiters that encouraged the next tier of faculty to apply for Race, Gender, and Beyond curriculum development grants.
- Lido members served as reviewers for the grant proposals on curriculum development.
- Lido was symbolically important as a multicultural community of scholars committed to teaching excellence.
- It was a locale where faculty leaders for diversity were nourished and where "the choir" become nurtured and simultaneously had its limits stretched and its skills refreshed. As one Lido colleague put it:

  > I think this group is tremendously important. It provides a support system, even when people aren't actively involved. We know this group of people exists. We know there are people we can turn to that are in this group.

We've managed to function without having to agree on everything and that is so important.

- It was where leaders engaged the newest scholarship on diversity in the classroom and then worked to apply that knowledge.

Change Team Dilemmas

Lido was not without its share of dilemmas. Some of the more persistent problems with which Lido has struggled are:

- Expanding Lido while maintaining group intimacy and trust. Deciding who and how many to invite at year's end to next year's gatherings became an annual rite of spring. Sometimes sabbatical leaves helped by making spaces at the table available. As one member commented in the annual year-end evaluation:

  > I appreciate the smaller size of Lido as it currently stands, and also recognize the concern to include more people. I hope that more discussion will happen among current members to evaluate the impact of increasing Lido numbers. I worry that a group too large will complicate the open discussions I have found so valuable in Lido this year.

- The on-going tension between creating a group environment where members could feel both safe, and also challenged. This is where early attention to building group trust has often paid off. The spirit of "I mean you no harm" became a Lido norm. Members evolved into Lido leaders through their demonstrated willingness to take risks in front of the group in order to discuss their own classroom foibles. As one senior member commented, "[Lido is a] group of friendly, supportive, honest people I can trust and work out my own issues related to these difficult matters. We don't all have to agree, for example; we respect each other even when we don't agree. That makes it possible to explore more depth."
- The competing demands and many diversity needs on campus. These tugs often pulled Lido in myriad directions at once and ranged from addressing recruitment and retention of students to faculty recruitment and retention, to addressing classism, to responding to hate incidents. What helped ground the group at these times was its focused commitment to improving the classroom climate for diversity and teaching excellence. Minus this touchstone, Lido could easily over-extend itself and become doomed to fail. The decision to keep the focus on teaching has led to resentment on the part of some staff who claim that Lido limited its membership to faculty. This charge led to rumblings about "elitism" and "classism." The group's response remains that it is not within Lido's powers to be all things to all people, but that Lido would and has advocated for a staff version of its own Lido.

- A formal or informal role? Some students and staff focused on social justice know the group and its members and want Lido to be more visible, more like an official committee. Lido members recognize this but most see Lido as a "behind the scenes" activist group, one working within and across systems, acting as constant support for each other in this work. Responding to these concerns for visibility, it has become tradition for Lido to host a student luncheon each year to facilitate closer working connections.

Key Lessons Learned

Lido and the larger Project present a number of overall insights into what went well and what could be done better in the process of developing a multicultural faculty cohort. The following six lessons are among the most instructive:

Lesson 1: Know the Culture of Your Institution. Hamline's culture consists of a student centered faculty that values its independence from administrative dictates (perceived or otherwise). The choice to keep this initiative informal and peer-driven has been key in helping Lido avoid some of the potholes (as in arguments over infringement on academic freedom or on faculty autonomy) that have hobbled others attempting to create a more diverse curriculum and classroom climate.

Lesson 2: Keep the Effort Faculty Driven. From its inception in 1997, faculty have been the ones who have guided and designed Lido and the subsequent Race, Gender, and Beyond Project, including awarding curriculum grants and deciding upon speakers and workshop leaders. This faculty-driven focus has resulted in significantly higher levels of faculty buy-in and participation, and it has reduced the level of resistance by non-participants.

Lesson 3: Nurture Your Diverse Leadership. Keeping Lido diverse as well as making sure all members are challenged as well as nurtured has kept faculty enthusiastic about participating, teaching, and leading. The tendency on many campuses has been to ignore the need to "nurture the choir" which is often synonymous for not supporting its faculty diversity leaders. By actively embracing and lifting up the level of competency of Lido leadership, the group has been able to go beyond "simply preaching to the choir" to become more effective teachers and leaders.

Lesson 4: Always Connect to Excellence. Faculty in institutions that value excellence in teaching are drawn like moths to projects that light the way toward improved teaching. By linking diversity in the classroom with overall teaching excellence, Lido has moved beyond tired arguments of "political correctness" or "just doing diversity for diversity's sake." At Hamline, an excellent education is increasingly understood as one that fully embraces diversity in and out of the classroom.

Lesson 5: Involve Students of All Colors. Nothing has galvanized the faculty more than hearing from the students annually about their perceptions of the classroom climate (strengths as well as concerns). Many faculty may dismiss administrative calls from on high to diversify the curriculum. Lido demonstrates that one of the most effective means for engaging faculty is designing a process that gives consistent and meaningful voice to students.

Lesson 6: Money is Symbolically Important. In difficult financial times many may ask, "Can we afford such an undertaking?" This cohort's lesson is that a little money can go a long way toward improving both the quality and reputation of an institution (for example, Lido's 2003-04 luncheon budget was under $1200). Most significantly, monetary compensation sends a crucial institutional message. It is a message that says, "we value our faculty," "we value diversity," and most importantly, "we value our faculty who fully embrace diversity."

As the competition in higher education for a diverse and culturally competent faculty and student body increases, these are dollars wisely spent. This is especially true when the alternative is higher faculty and student turnover, lowered revenues, critical external reviews, diminished reputations, and less than enthusiastic teachers and learners. One final recommendation is that perhaps the work of building multicultural institutions requires that we no longer work alone and in isolation, but rather begin the work by fashioning our own multicultural cohorts for change.

References

Adams, M, Bell, L., & Griffin, P. (1997). *Teaching for diversity and social justice: A sourcebook.* New York: Routledge.

Birnbaum, R. (1988). *How colleges work: The cybernetics of academic organization and leadership.* San Francisco: Jossey-Bass.

Bonilla, J., & Palmerton, P. (2000). Hamline faculty & student voices: Race, ethnicity and gender in the classroom. *The Hamline Review: A Faculty Annual. 24,* 72-94.

Bonilla, J., & Palmerton, P. (2001). A prophet in your own land?: Using faculty and student focus groups to address issues of race, ethnicity and gender in the classroom. In D. Lieberman & C. Wehlburg, (Eds.), *To improve the academy,19,* 49-68. Bolton, MA: Anker.

Geok-Lin Lim, S. & Herrera-Sobek, M. (2000). *Power, race and gender in the academe: Strangers in the tower.* New York: Modern Language Association.

Freire, P. (1970). *Pedagogy of the oppressed.* New York: Continuum.

LaBare, M. (2003). *Engaging America 2010 at Hamline University: Race, gender & beyond. An external evaluation report*. St. Paul, MN: Hamline University.

Turner, C.S., & Myers, S. (2000). *Faculty of color in academe: Bittersweet success*. Boston: Allyn & Bacon.

James Francisco Bonilla is an associate professor of Conflict Studies in the Graduate School of Public Administration and Management at Hamline University.

Chapter 27
But How Can I Talk With Faculty About That? Approaches to Consulting Around Multicultural Issues

Matthew Kaplan and Beth Glover Reed

This chapter provides a model for approaching multicultural issues in any consultation around teaching, whether they are raised by the instructor or not. It includes illustrative cases, questions to guide practice, and consideration of various approaches to consulting related to multicultural pedagogy.

Consultation about teaching occurs in multiple ways among people in quite different roles. In some instances the consultant is a professional educational developer located in a center focused on enhancing teaching and learning. In some institutions and situations, faculty members are consulting with each other, or an instructor has a part-time responsibility for strengthening teaching and learning in his or her unit or institution. Or an instructor may be mentoring or supervising a graduate student teaching assistant. In addition to the roles and locations of consultants, the types and circumstances of the consultation also differ. Sometimes the educational developer becomes involved because of a crisis, dilemma, or problem in the classroom. In other instances, an educational developer works with an instructor over time, providing assistance in planning a course, conducting midterm observations, assessments and feedback, and/or assisting an instructor in reviewing and evaluating student feedback and learning. Contact may be in person, in the classroom or in an office, or may occur over telephone or email.

Whatever the roles and relationships, we assume that educational developers encounter diversity issues in *all* consultations with instructors. Although many definitions of multiculturalism exist, they can be clustered into a few categories:

- the *celebration of diversity* that entails accommodating and appreciating different learning and cultural styles

- a focus on *societal power dynamics*, especially those associated with race, gender, and so on, how they are replayed in the classroom and become barriers to teaching and learning
- a concentration on *social justice learning* with the explicit aim of preparing students to work towards a more socially just world

All of the above definitions are relevant in consulting situations but may be more or less visible and acknowledged in any given interaction. Moreover, these are issues we need to learn to address if we assume that teaching should optimize learning for everyone and prepare students for participation in a diverse society and global environment. Marchesani and Adams (1992) make clear that diversity is part of all aspects of teaching. It affects instructors, students, course goals and content, and instructional methods, and it often involves interrelationships among them.

To help us navigate the complexities of consulting on diversity, we will explore specific examples of how these issues arise in consulting. To organize, we use a Concentric Circle Model with three categories defined by how central the diversity issue is within the goals of the consultation and how aware the instructor is of the diversity related issues (see Figure One). Before turning to

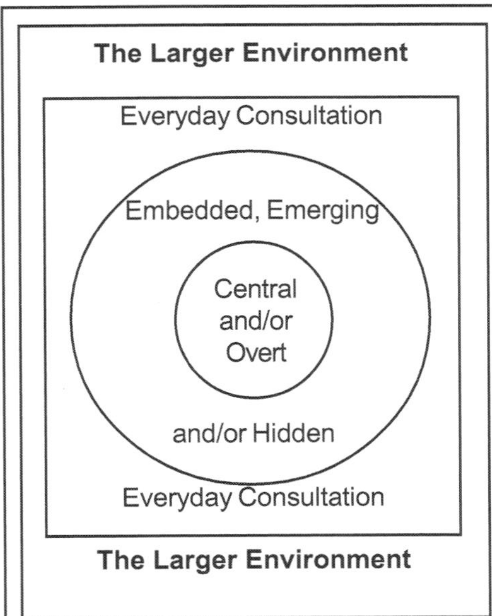

1. *Central and/or overt.* Sometimes some aspect related to diversity or justice is the major concern in a consultation—the instructor is aware of and concerned about a diversity question.
2. *Embedded, Emerging, and/or Hidden.* In this type, a diversity element is a major component in a teaching situation, or is emerging as an issue, but is not recognized by the instructor or a major goal of the instructor in the consulting situation.
3. *Everyday consultation.* This term characterizes all other instances in which diversity issues are not recognized as important by the instructor nor overt in the situation but are relevant within the larger context.

Figure 1: Concentric Circle Model of Multicultural Consulting

a fuller discussion of our model, we offer two caveats. First, there is no formula for this process, no one right way to address diversity in consulting. Each of us will approach these issues based on our own comfort level, knowledge, and skills as well as our relationship to the instructor and the nature of the situation. Our purpose here is to provide a framework that can help us to think about, recognize, and become more aware of the multiple ways that multicultural and social justice issues can arise in consultations, with some ideas of how they can be handled once they come up. Second, although we have included the organizational unit and larger environment in the diagram and believe that it is always important to place consultation within the larger context, in this article, because of space limitations, we focus primarily on situations in which the consultant is working with an individual faculty member.

Using the Concentric Circle Model

I. Consultation Situations in which the Multicultural Issue is Overt

In the following case examples, both the instructor and the consultant recognize that diversity issues are central elements in the situation. Thus, the tasks within consultation are twofold: to understand the issues and how they manifest themselves in the instructional situation; and to consider how the consulting process can assist the instructor to address them successfully.

Classroom Dynamics

Chris, an instructor for an introductory chemistry lab course, has come to see you about a situation in the lab. One of the students has a severe physical disability. "But this is a lab course," Chris says, "and that means that the students need to be physically engaged in various ways over the four hours of class time. They need to manipulate instruments, go back and forth to the hood, write down results, and so forth. I spoke to this student at the beginning of the term to find out if he thought he could manage, and he insisted that he needed the course as a prerequisite for a career in the health professions. He's never come to talk to me since then, but I can tell that he's having trouble keeping up. He's confined to a wheelchair, which makes it difficult for him to get up to the lab benches, and he sometimes has trouble with fine motor skills. His lab group started out sympathetic, but lately they've been ignoring him and getting the work done without including him. Whenever I go over to the group, the three other students are all working together and he is generally working on his own, usually on a much earlier part of the lab. So it's hard for me to ask the group questions that include him because it's like they're almost doing two different experiments. I also call on students to present their group's work, and I don't ever feel I can call on him, not because he's disabled, but because he's not up to speed. What can I do? I don't want to single the student out or be discouraging, but I'm also not sure that he can really succeed in the course."

Questions to Consider

1. How comfortable are you with the topic of disability? What knowledge do you have and what do you know about the resources on your campus for students with disabilities?
2. How do your own attitudes toward disability affect how you would approach this consultation?
3. What would you want to find out about the instructor and the instructor's attitudes toward disability?
4. What are the issues for the student? Why might the student not be asking for help? What responsibility does the student have?
5. What are the group dynamics issues in this case? How can the instructor work to improve group dynamics?
6. What else would you like to know about the course or the students in question?
7. How would you approach this consultation? Would you begin with practical suggestions, questions and discussion of the issues involved, other approaches? Why?

Discussion

The case raises obvious pedagogical issues. One approach involves helping the instructor consider carefully which issues are specifically related to disability and which raise more general pedagogical concerns (Border, 2001). For example, the inaccessibility of the lab, the need to physically manipulate instruments, and student reactions and attitudes all relate to the issue of disability. On the other hand, the case involves a set of questions around teaching methods more generally, such as the set-up and function of groups, the intervention by the instructor in negative group process, and dealing with students at different levels of competence. By helping delineate between the two, the consultant can refocus the instructor, who, at this point, has concluded that all of the difficulties stem from the student's disability (implying some blame, as if the situation would disappear if the student did). Instead, this case demonstrates that concentrating on students at the margins can lead to wider insights that benefit the whole class. (For more information on Universal Instructional Design, please see chapter 29 by Burgstahler, Faculty Development and Students with Disabilities.)

Such an approach enables the consultant to talk candidly with the instructor about his or her attitude toward and knowledge of disability, since the instructor's attitudes and lack of knowledge could well explain the tendency to view a complex teaching issue through the single lens of student disability. Studies on the learning environment for students with disabilities indicate that the instructors who are aware of local campus policies (such as the possibility of making rooms accessible or changing locations, or the use of lab aides to help with fine motor tasks) and the rationale behind them, are more likely to be helpful and accommodating (Rickman, 1995). Moreover, it is important for faculty to understand that their attitudes set the tone in class and that students with disabilities find negative faculty attitudes to be a major barrier to their full participation in higher education. Finally, in order to be effective, the consultant needs to know about institutional policies on and support for students with disabilities (or at least know how to get hold of them) and have the skill to begin an honest discussion about the source of Chris's discomfort and ways to overcome it.

Challenges

Angela is a young, Latina assistant professor who has come to you about a large introductory anthropology course she teaches. Over the past few years, she has revamped the course, making the content both more rigorous and more relevant to students' lives (by including guest speakers, demonstrations, and relevant films on the topic). Enrollment is up substantially, to the point where the department is turning away students. The number of majors has also risen.

These positive outcomes have been marred for Angela by the presence of a small but vocal group of students who are disaffected and disrespectful, and almost all of whom are male. Sometimes these students can be downright aggressive. For example, at the beginning of the term Angela had to turn away some students who wanted to add the course. One student this past term refused to give up, eventually yelling at her and getting really angry. Angela was intimidated by this behavior and finally felt she had to yell back at him to get him to back off.

In addition, there are problems with classroom dynamics. Angela teaches in a large lecture hall that seats 400. Last term, a group of students sat in the center of the hall and talked throughout the lecture. They also asked questions that seemed to challenge Angela's knowledge of the subject. After stopping several times to ask politely for quiet, she finally lost her temper and yelled at this group of students. On the end of term ratings, a small subset of students mentioned this incident, and some used disparaging language about her. Angela also tells you that when she team taught the course with a male colleague, these disruptions never came up during his lectures. Her department appreciates the good work she is doing but worries about the student ratings and her interactions with students. She would like to know how she could avoid these situations, and she has come to you for suggestions as she plans the course.

Questions to Consider

1. What issues does this case raise for Angela? Where would you start?
2. What is your own experience with challenges to authority? How might that affect your consultation?
3. What else would you want to know about Angela, her teaching, and this course?
4. How might gender and race be interacting in this case? How would you raise the issues of race and gender, if Angela did not name them first?
5. What do you know about the challenges to their authority that women and people of color often face in the classroom? How might you use this knowledge in a consultation?
6. What might Angela do to avoid this behavior in the future?
7. How might Angela handle problems that arise during the term?
8. Would you advise Angela to let her department know about the challenges she faces? If so, who and at what level? Why? Why not?

Discussion

Angela, like Chris, faces difficult, general pedagogical issues, such as classroom incivility, the consumer-oriented attitude of today's students, and the many challenges of teaching large classes effectively. Unlike the lab instructor, Angela seems keenly aware of her own identity and how it might contribute to the obstacles she faces: her authority in the class is being challenged by the male students in particular. What is not clear is the degree to which there is an intersection between gender and other identity characteristics, such as age, physical stature, and race. A growing body of literature has documented similar challenges faced both by women and faculty of color teaching in predominantly white institutions (Basow, 1998; Benokritis, 1998; McGowan, 2000; McKay, 1995; Smith, 1999; Thomas & Hollenshead, 2002; Vargas, 1999).

Obviously, Angela cannot change who she is. However, if the consultant is willing to discuss the challenges faced by underrepresented faculty (either based on research findings or personal experience), the issue can be normalized. It would no longer be a problem based solely on the instructor's individual skill or competence, but one that reflects a wider pattern based on students' expectations of who does or does not have authority in the classroom. The shift from the personal to the structural could help Angela put the experience in a larger context and be better able to develop strategies to address student attitudes and behavior. The literature on such strategies is less well developed than the descriptions of the problems. Recommendations tend to focus on being clear about all the administrative aspects of the course, maintaining a professional distance from students, and emphasizing one's background in the subject area.

Another possibility would be to make the cultural expectations at play in the class a subject of inquiry or discussion. Such an approach would depend upon a match between these issues and the course content. One of us (Reed) has taken a similar approach in social work, making the teaching and learning process both transparent and an object of inquiry for class discussion. In a discipline such as anthropology (or sociology or social psychology) Angela might find ways to turn classroom dynamics into a case study to promote student self-reflection and learning. Many humanities courses could do this through reading selections. In areas where teamwork or leadership skills are important (for example, engineering and business), direct attention to group dynamics would also be relevant.

Finally, while we concentrate in this article on individual consultations, Angela's situation raises systemic questions of organizational development. While Angela holds the institutional authority in the classroom, students' voices exercise a significant influence since they affect the department's perspective on Angela's viability as a faculty member. Faculty executive committees, department chairs, and other administrators need to be aware of the challenges affecting underrepresented faculty so that information (such as comments on student ratings) is not interpreted naively. Strategies need to be developed to support junior women faculty and faculty of color. The strategies used to raise administrative awareness will depend on the consultant's role in the institution.

II. Consultation Strategies with Embedded, Emerging, and/or Hidden Issues

In situations we have defined as embedded, emerging, or hidden, the consultant perceives that a diversity issue is a major element of the teaching situation, but the instructor is less aware of this issue and has not defined it as a goal for the consultation. In these types of situations, the consultant must decide whether and how to raise the issue and how to assist the instructor to recognize, accept, and understand its importance. Then, depending on how this discussion goes, a major task is to assist the instructor to decide how to approach the issue. The following case and the subsequent discussion offer an example of the steps involved.

Laying the Groundwork for Multicultural Learning

Paul, a TA in English, is teaching the introductory writing class in the fall. Paul is an experienced TA who is about to finish his degree and start looking for a faculty position. He has taught this course several times before and says that he has always enjoyed it and done well with it. He has come to you in the summer to review his syllabus with you and get your advice particularly about issues of workload and using groups effectively. At the beginning of your meeting, Paul explains his concerns about the course. He has used peer review of compositions on several occasions, and he would like to now move this process online using the university's courseware system. In addition, Paul wants to integrate online discussions into the course to extend student thinking about discussion topics and to give them practice with informal, "low stakes" writing. After Paul finishes his explanation, he gives you a few minutes to look over the syllabus. You notice that the course is divided into major sections devoted to writing for different types of audiences: writing for popular culture, exploration of public issues, and disciplinary writing in academia. As you read over the assignments and activities Paul has sketched out in the syllabus, you notice that he has focused the "public issues" section of the course around the issue of gay marriage. The readings include very recent editorials both pro and con, with a range of titles including pieces that use inflammatory language. These readings introduce the section, and students are then free to write an essay on a public issue of their choosing. As you look back over the syllabus, you notice that this is the only sensitive issue dealt with overtly in the course. You are still considering the implications of Paul's choice as you finish looking through the syllabus, and he says, "So now that you've got a sense of the course, I'd like to talk about the Web. Have you worked with other TAs or faculty who have their students give feedback online?"

Questions to Consider

1. How can you determine how aware Paul is of the potential issues that his choice of topics may raise?
2. How can you assess whether Paul is prepared to handle the ways that class members may react to these topics, or to recognize the teaching issues likely to arise?
3. In what ways might Paul help to lay the groundwork in earlier sessions that can support productive learning?
4. How can you frame your perceptions so that Paul can hear them and learn from them?
5. How does your own identity affect your approach to this situation?
6. How ready is Paul to recognize and consider how to handle issues he previously has not recognized?

The consultant notes elements of the course content that are likely to need preparation and contextualization for students for optimal learning. It is not clear from the syllabus and interactions with the instructor thus far how much the instructor has explored his own identities relevant for the proposed topic, how much experience this instructor has in using controversial topics to promote learning and in managing the classroom dynamics likely to occur, or whether the instructor has anticipated students' reactions to proposed topics and assignments. The instructor's explicit goals focus much more narrowly on the use of technology. In addition to all of the topics considered earlier, the consultant must consider at least three additional sets of concerns: instructor readiness, consultant styles and approaches, and the values and ethics of raising or not raising the issue.

Readiness for Change

Originally developed by studying successful self-changers trying to modify undesired behaviors (such as smoking), psychologists have outlined common stages of change (Prochaska, Norcross, & DiClemente, 1994) that can provide a useful framework for thinking about working with instructors on diversity issues. Although the model delineates stages of change, it also stresses that change can be cyclical and that people may move back and forth a number of times. The stages are:

1. *Precontemplation.* No recognition or acceptance that change is necessary.
2. *Contemplation.* Awareness that issues require change, but no action yet taken.
3. *Transition.* Instructor actively deciding to change, gathering resources and information to support change.
4. *Changing practice.* Change process is underway along with attendant difficulties, struggles, and so forth. Often new practices are inconsistent with some that have not changed.
5. *Maintaining progress and deepening change.* Sustaining, consolidating, and extending new practices over time.

A consultant's awareness of these stages can help her identify the type of support a client needs, and can lead to careful questioning, listening, and observation to determine whether a client recognizes the issues, and what, if any, action has already been taken. Obviously, different strategies will be needed at different stages: education to raise awareness in precontemplation; information about options in contemplation; during transition, help with assessment, planning, and feedback on plans; and while changing and consolidating changes, assistance handling the struggles of success and failure. Although we might assume that an instructor facing an overt or emerging multicultural issue would need at least to be aware of the need for change, responses from the instructor might make it clear that he or she wants the issue to "go away" without any change. While level of readiness is important in other levels of our concentric circle diagram as well, it is especially important in this middle level of embedded issues.

For example, the consultant should expect some defensiveness when raising news that is unexpected, or experienced as "bad" by the recipient, especially if these were not the reasons why the instructor sought consultation. Defensiveness may arise for many reasons—because of embarrassment, not wanting to face the extra work and learning, not feeling support from the larger environment, or worry about not having the skills or courage to address the issues. Jumping straight to strategies without discussing the underlying resistance could ensure that any change is poorly implemented and could possibly make a situation worse.

Working with a client who is resistant might challenge a consultant's view of his or her role in the consultation process. Brinko (1997) describes five "models" of consulting, most of which involve providing resources, expertise, or support. However, she also includes a "confrontational model," in which a consultant must challenge existing practices and reframe and focus attention on issues not yet recognized by the instructor. While this approach may take us outside our comfort level, it might be necessary when an instructor does not see (or ignores) an issue of diversity, or assumes that no change is necessary. Confrontation does not need to be aggressive. In fact, confrontations are heard and accepted better if they occur within a context of empathy, with a careful assessment of the constraints and barriers the instructor faces. Nonetheless, there are times that a consultant has to consider ways to raise and actively pursue topics and issues that were not put on the agenda by the instructor and that some instructors will not want to hear or address.

Values and Ethical Issues

Mintz (1994) and Mintz, Smith, and Warren (1999) discuss some ethical and value guidelines for instructional developers. The consultant must consider what the consequences are for students and student learning if the emerging issue is or is *not* recognized and addressed. What are the implications for the instructor if the issue is not identified, or if it is? What should the consultant's role be in relation to diversity and social justice issues if these are not identified by the instructor, and especially if the instructor is reluctant to recognize them? We know that barriers to learning and teaching related to race, gender, culture, sexual orientation, and other factors occur partly because they are invisible. In fact, some believe that we are "taught" not to see them and that the many barriers that exist to recognizing them are part of the forces that sustain inequitable social structures and processes. Even when we "see" them, we often do not have the knowledge and skills to address them, and recognizing them can increase feelings of helplessness and guilt if we do not know how to address them. The instructional consultant will need to weigh all these things while deciding whether or not to raise embedded or hidden issues and to consider when and how to do this. If an instructor is dealing with other crises, for instance, the consultant may want to wait until things have subsided, when the instructor may have more time and energy to consider additional difficult issues. If the consultant feels that an issue must be raised and confronted (perhaps because of the likeliness of negative consequences if the issue is not addressed), there is also an obligation to be available to assist the instructor and students to navigate what happens subsequently.

III. Everyday consultation

This category includes the wide range of consultations that do not seem to raise multicultural issues overtly either for the consultant or the instructor. Consultants have an obligation to carefully consider raising issues of good multicultural practice in any consultation for two reasons. First, as seen in the cases in sections one and two, the impact of identity, inclusive classrooms, and multicultural content will affect the teaching and learning process whether or not they are raised. When we are proactive, we can help instructors plan and think through ways to use diversity and power differences as positive forces that can enhance the learning of all students. Second, as stated at the outset, preparing students to participate in a multicultural society – both in the political arena and the workplace – is now seen as a major responsibility for higher education. While the presence of a diverse student body is a necessary condition for promoting such goals, they cannot be fully realized unless students and faculty deliberately and skillfully engage with multicultural issues in as broad a spectrum of classes as possible. Many of the issues raised in the previous section about readiness and resistance also apply to these cases. In particular, the following questions can help consultants make the decision about whether to explore multicultural issues with a client:

1. What are the pros and cons of raising or not raising multicultural issues?
2. How ready do we feel the instructor is to engage with these issues?
3. How urgent are other issues? Can the instructor handle having these issues raised simultaneously? Can you schedule a later time to follow up with a discussion of multiculturalism?
4. How much support can you provide if you do raise these issues?

For example, for TAs about to enter the academic job market and for faculty considering promotion, tenure, or the search for a new position, self reflection is inherent to the writing of a teaching philosophy. Consultations about teaching statements involve conversations to help instructors begin formulating (or refining) their ideas about teaching and learning. In addition, consultants often provide faculty and TAs with exercises to help them start making implicit values and assumptions about teaching explicit (Chism, 1997-1998; Goodyear & Allchin, 1998; Coppola, 2000). Questions about multicultural topics can be easily incorporated into both one-one-one discussions and worksheets along with some discussion of the current focus at institutions across the country on creating a successful learning environment for an increasingly diverse student body (Kaplan, 2001-2002). Senior graduate students represent the next generation of academia. Helping them to consider their thoughts on such issues has the potential to create a new ethos in the professorate; not raising the issue ensures the status quo.

The consultant can also raise multicultural topics as part of the range of issues discussed about a course or curriculum change. Such an approach normalizes a topic that might seem unfamiliar and threatening to some faculty and validates the concerns of other faculty who consider the issues central to teaching and learning but are unsure of how the consultant (or the institution) will react to their interest. Perhaps most importantly, curriculum – whether that means an individual course or a set of courses in a degree program – is a primary area of intellectual engagement for faculty and students. If we are concerned with institutional change, we need to find ways to generate productive conversations about the impact of multiculturalism and diversity on the curriculum.

Discussion and Conclusions: Getting Started

Effective consultations involve a complex set of skills, knowledge, and attitudes that, as we have argued, include the ability to raise and react effectively to multicultural topics in teaching and learning. In many cases, consultations around multicultural topics can ask us to stretch beyond our comfort zones. Unfortunately, faculty and faculty developers involved in consulting often have little training in multiculturalism. Kardia (1998) outlines a number of reasons for this disconnect and then suggests strategies to build competence and confidence around multicultural work by expanding our knowledge base, pedagogical strategies, professional skills, and self reflection. In particular, she suggests three steps for getting started: developing a working definition of multiculturalism, talking to colleagues who share a similar background about these issues, and talking with colleagues who are different from us. The cases in this article could provide an entry point for such exchanges, either within the context of a teaching center staff, among a group of faculty or graduate students who regularly consult on teaching, or as part of a mentoring program in which junior and senior faculty meet to discuss pedagogical issues. Such discussions can help novices gain confidence in their ability to talk about multiculturalism within and across differences and can highlight resources for developing a broader knowledge base. More experienced practitioners would gain the insights that always come with teaching and mentoring and the energy that comes from cultivating an expanded group of allies on campus.

Productive discussion among consultants will depend in part on the degree of self knowledge and reflection of participants. Just as we ask faculty and TAs to consider their identities and perspectives and how they affect the teaching and learning process, we need to ask ourselves how these same issues play into our approaches to consulting. Figure Two contains a set of questions to help faculty and developers begin the process of self reflection.

Finally, we must note that our narrow focus on one-on-one consulting is in many ways artificial and contrary to best practice, especially concerning multiculturalism. Oftentimes consultants will need to ask themselves when the topics raised in a consultation have broader implications for a department, a group of instructors, or an institution as a whole. While such considerations are beyond the scope of this chapter, we do need to think carefully about how and when we—and the instructors with whom we work—can take issues beyond the privacy and safety of individual conversations to forums that have a potential impact on organizational development.

Describe what instructors will see when you step before them as their consultant.

What will they first notice about you?

What additional information or impressions do you intend to give them?

How might instructor reactions to you support or enhance your role as consultant?

How might instructor reactions be a challenge for you as you advise and consult?

How much have you explored various aspects of your own identity? What information about yourself do you share and/or plan to share with instructors? (for example , socio-economic background, religious affiliation, educational background, political views, family, sexual orientation, teaching experience, popular culture experience.)

To what extent have privilege and oppression played a role in your life outside the academy? Within the academy?

What do you need to learn? How can collaborators assist you to expand your comfort zone and body of knowledge and skills?

Figure 2. Negotiating Consultant Identity

(Adapted from workshop materials developed by A.T. Miller, Center for Research on Learning and Teaching, University of Michigan.)

References

Banks, J. A. (1995). Multicultural education: Historical development, dimensions, and practice. In J. A. Banks & C. A. M. Banks (Eds.), *Handbook of research on multicultural education* (pp. 3-24). New York: Macmillan.

Basow, S. A. (1998). Student evaluations: The role of gender bias and teaching styles. In L. H. Collins, J. C. Chrisler, & K. Quina (Eds.), *Career strategies for women in academe: Arming Athena* (pp. 135-156). Thousand Oaks, CA: Sage.

Benokraitis, N. V. (1998). Student evaluations: Working in the ivory basement: Subtle sex discrimination in higher education. In L. H. Collins, J. C. Chrisler, & K. Quina (Eds.), *Career strategies for women in academe: Arming Athena* (pp. 3-36). Thousand Oaks, CA: Sage.

Border, L. L. B. (2001, October). *Case study: Instructors with disabilities*. Workshop presented at the meeting of the Professional and Organizational Development Network in Higher Education, St. Louis, MO.

Brinko, K. T. (1997). The interactions of teaching improvement. In K. T. Brinko & R. J. Menges (Eds.), *Practically speaking: A sourcebook for instructional consultants in higher education* (pp. 3-8). Stillwater, OK: New Forums Press.

Chism, N.V.N. (1997-1998). Developing a philosophy of teaching statement. *Essays on teaching excellence: Towards the best in the academy*, *9*(3). Athens, GA: The Professional and Organizational Development Network in Higher Education.

Coppola, B. (2000). How to write a teaching philosophy for academic employment. *American Chemical Society, Department of Career Services Bulletin.* Washington, DC: American Chemical Society.

Goodyear, G. E., & Allchin, D. (1998). Statements of teaching philosophy. In M. Kaplan (Ed.), *To Improve the Academy, 17* (pp. 103-22). Stillwater, OK: New Forums Press.

Kaplan, M. (2001-2002). The multicultural teaching portfolio. *Essays on teaching excellence: Towards the best in the academy, 13*(3). Athens, GA: The Professional and Organizational Development Network in Higher Education.

Kardia, D. (1998). Becoming a multicultural faculty developer: Reflections from the field, In M. Kaplan (Ed.), *To improve the academy, 17* (pp. 15-33). Stillwater, OK: New Forums Press.

Marchesani, L. S., & Adams, M. (1992). Dynamics of diversity in the teaching-learning process: A faculty development model for analysis and action. In M. Adams (Ed.), *Promoting diversity in college classrooms: Innovative responses for the curriculum, faculty and institutions* (pp. 9-20). New Directions in Teaching and Learning, No. 52. San Francisco: Jossey-Bass.

McGowan, J. M. (2000). African-American faculty classroom teaching experiences in predominantly white colleges and universities. *Multicultural Education, 8*(2), 19-22.

McKay, N. Y. (1995). Minority faculty in [mainstream white] academia. In A. L. DeNeef & C. D. Goodwin (Eds.), *The academic's handbook* (2nd ed., pp. 48-61). Durham, NC: Duke University Press.

Mintz, J. (1994). Challenging values: Conflict, contradiction, and pedagogy. In E. C. Wadsworth (Ed.), *To improve the academy, 13* (pp. 177-190). Stillwater, OK: New Forums Press.

Mintz, J., Smith, R., & Warren, L. (2001). Ethical guidelines for educational developers. In D. Lieberman (Ed.), *To improve the academy, 19* (pp. xvii-xxiii). Bolton: MA: Anker.

Prochaska, J. O., Norcross, D., & DiClemente, C. (1994). *Changing for good.* New York: W. Morrow.

Rickman, J. C. (1995). The microculture of disability. In J. Q. Adams & J. B. Welsch (Eds.), *Multicultural education: Strategies for implementation in colleges and universities, 4* (pp. 177-186). Macomb: Illinois Staff and Curriculum Developers Association.

Smith, R. (1999, Spring). Walking on eggshells: The experience of a black woman professor. *ADE Bulletin, 122,* 68-72.

Thomas, G. D., & Hollenshead, C. (2001). Resisting from the margins: The coping strategies of Black women and other women of color faculty members at a research university. *Journal of Negro Education, 70*(3), 166-175.

Vargas, L. (1999) When the "other" is the teacher: Implications of teacher diversity in higher education. *The Urban Review, 31*(4), 359-383.

Matthew Kaplan is Associate Director of the Center for Research on Learning and Teaching at the University of Michigan. **Beth Glover Reed** is a faculty member affiliated with both the Women's Studies department and the School of Social Work at the University of Michigan.

Chapter 28

Mainstreaming Feminist Perspectives

Carol Lauer and Lynda M. Glennon

Many educators would agree that one of the more effective ways to introduce the feminist perspective to students is to diffuse it across the curriculum; however, faculty with little or no background in Women's Studies are often unsure of how to incorporate a focus on gender fairness into their courses. We have developed and conducted a series of workshops to facilitate this inclusion of feminist thinking across the curriculum, in which faculty from various disciplines meet to discuss basic issues of feminist methodology and perspective and to review discipline-relevant resources, incorporating the results of the workshop into their curriculum. Introducing these "feminist modules" into courses opens up a world of gender-based issues in the classroom; students are empowered to ask questions about gender bias in the course curriculum and in the classroom.

Deep-seated attitudes about gender do not usually change because of a single course experience—they are more likely to be changed by an entire curriculum infused with gender-fair ideals. The following describes a workshop that we designed to prepare diverse faculty to participate in such a curricular experiment.

History

The impetus for this workshop and its particular style came from two historical trends at our liberal arts college. The first trend is a long history of workshops run by faculty and by invited consultants. Our traditional in-house workshops, which typically last for a week or more, train faculty to incorporate in their courses the skills mandated by our general education curriculum (for example, public speaking and writing across the curriculum).

We both have taken several of these workshops and have come to appreciate some of their methods. Because the workshops last for more than a day or two, faculty are frequently given a series of assignments. The most effective of these assignments asks participants to share their plans and experiences in trying to implement the relevant skill introduced by that workshop. Often faculty members are invited to do a presentation based on a course syllabus and planned projects. In critiquing these proposals, workshop participants point out pitfalls in proposed methods, give examples of their own attempts to implement such changes, and suggest revisions. Because these discussions are based on work with a single population of students, Rollins College undergraduates, the success and/or failure of methods may be idiosyncratic, but that is exactly what makes the information valuable. The suggestions made during the workshop are frequently relevant to teaching in courses beyond those involving the particular skill under discussion. We both felt that this report-and-critique format would work well in training faculty to include gender-related issues in their courses.

The second historic thread that shaped the nature of our gender workshop comes from our experiences within the Women's Studies program at our college. Since the inception of the program in the 1980s, we have never had a full-time coordinator or a single faculty member whose locus of tenure was in Women's Studies. In the early years, faculty with no formal training in Women's Studies (then a rare specialization) would be recruited from across the disciplines to teach these courses. While we now have faculty with advanced degrees in Women's Studies, we never have enough to cover all the courses needed for the program. Thus by necessity, we have been required to keep encouraging people to retrain and to teach courses in Women's Studies and to incorporate issues of gender and diversity in courses not focused on these topics. As a result of these ongoing retraining needs, we have each led and/or participated in about ten colloquia over the past 20 years on issues of gender and diversity.

During the 2001-2002 academic year, the college embarked on a "Year of Gender Matters," an initiative underwritten by the President of the college. Its focus was on creating a more equitable environment across campus and encouraging discussions of gender-based issues. Our workshop, entitled "Gender Issues in the Classroom," was conducted at the request of the organizers, representatives of the Rollins College Women's Studies program as part of the initiative to foster gender equality in the classroom. The Gender Matters program included 70 initiatives ranging from women's football to sexual assault awareness.

Selection of Participants

Our first challenge was attracting participants. To train the dedicated core of Women's Studies faculty to include gender issues in their courses, when they had been doing so for years, would not be useful or change anything. Therefore, when we sent out invitations for our workshop, we explicitly told this group not to apply. Some did anyway, and they were politely turned away. Incentives seemed a good way to encourage other faculty to apply, so we offered a $300 stipend and three lunches to anyone who would take the three afternoon-long workshops and compose a one- or two-page summary of their efforts to be posted on the Gender Matters Web site.

Enlisting people was the most difficult part of the process. Even with only three meetings, scheduling problems meant that several interested faculty could not attend. While we sent out written invitations to all faculty, we also tried the personal invitation approach with several. Sometimes this worked, sometimes it did not. We approached one science professor we thought would be amenable to attending, but she declined our invitation saying that gender and diversity issues were not relevant to her discipline. Even after providing her with several specific examples and a pamphlet detailing case histories that reveal problems with gender bias in introductory science courses, she rebuffed our efforts to persuade her to reconsider. We describe this case because it illustrates that convincing faculty to think about gender bias is not easy.

We hoped to enroll between eight and 12 participants to ensure small group dynamics where all would be able to contribute to the discussion. In the end, eight people agreed to participate, all white males from humanities and social science disciplines, representing various career stages from newly-hired to those nearing retirement, in ranks from assistant to full professor. What they did have in common was that they heretofore had never included gender issues specifically in their courses and were willing and eager to find a way to do so.

Description of Project: Gender Issues in the Classroom

The workshop consisted of one meeting per month for three months. At the first meeting, we distributed resource material and discussed some basic issues of feminist thinking and methodology. At the second, participants were asked to present plans for a gender-focused unit for their ongoing courses. At the third, participants presented and critiqued the results of their completed course units. Having three meetings over several months was essential for the design of the workshop. We wanted participants to have time to think about how they could integrate gender issues into their classes, experiment with their ideas, and critique the results. Too often, workshops are compressed into a day or two, and participants have no opportunity to discuss the results of their attempts to implement change. Also, reporting back to a group is a strong incentive to go beyond planning change to actually instituting change.

To foster an atmosphere of camaraderie, we met in a roundtable format in a seminar classroom, and we purposely avoided the now often caricatured trappings of sessions with outside consultants: flip charts, overheads, and PowerPoint presentations. Our working lunches served as tangible rewards, and this "breaking bread" over deliberations further bonded the group.

Resource Meeting

In the introductory meeting of our first workshop, we explained expectations for individual projects, asked about reasons for participating, handed out resource material, and discussed some basic principles of feminist pedagogy. We tried in several ways to avoid the characterization of the workshop as an exercise in political correctness training. In an effort to practice what we preach, we made our meetings as non-hierarchical as possible. We explained that we were modeling the feminist philosophy of classroom discussion as a sharing of information between equals with attention given to the value of personal experience. To that end, we relayed anecdotes about our own successes and failures in attempting to enlighten our student body about gender issues. We gave dramatic details about how the "chilly classroom" functions for female students, its impact on female faculty, including ourselves, and, without violating confidences, we recounted some of the horror stories of how sexual harassment and other ills are alive and well on our campus. These accounts helped to define the workshop as a problem-solving endeavor, rather than an abstract exercise in social justice awareness.

We also explained that the non-hierarchical and non-competitive style was one that many female students found more comfortable and more conducive to learning than that of the traditional lecture. One participant was amazed that changing the style of his classroom was in and of itself a gender focused change. We spent some time discussing the issue of gender-neutral language in the classroom and in texts. We discussed the use of the term "human" versus "man," of "he/she" or "they" versus "he," of using gender neutral language to refer to jobs: mail carrier and fire fighter, for example. We thought this would be a five minute discussion and not new to anyone, but we learned that this was not the case. Many of the participants had not thought about these issues nor had their disciplines. While Anthropology and Sociology texts have used gender-neutral language for over two decades, we were surprised to learn that this was not the case in other disciplines. (One participant, for example, wrote on his evaluation form for the workshop that the discussion of gender-neutral language was one of the most helpful aspects of the workshop.) We then turned to the importance of using inclusive examples, explaining that the use of white men in all examples discounts the experience and importance of women and minorities. Again, as group facilitators, we did not expect this to be news to anyone, but it was.

We also discussed the basics of gender-biased interactions in the classroom: how females' ideas are ignored more than males'; how males are called on more than females; how females are interrupted more frequently than males (Gmelch, 1998). We were able to provide examples from our own Arts and Sciences faculty meetings where these dynamics commonly play out.

In Anthropology and Sociology, we commonly look for the hidden curriculum, for the underlying and unquestioned assumptions upon which analyses are based. We felt that modeling this deconstructing perspective would give workshop participants skills to apply to their own disciplines and to help students do this with the texts and articles they read as course work. We selected several brief articles for this exercise. One was an article on human paleontology from *Time* (M.D. Lemonick & A. Dorfman, 2001) that includes a summary of a theory developed in the 1980s in order to explain the evolution of bipedalism in humans. The argument is that bipedalism evolved so that men could bring food to women and children. Our point was that the theory remains in circulation not because it is accurate, but because it fits conventional, taken-for-granted notions of what gender roles should be. We also used Sue Rosser's "Feminist critiques of biology" (1997) as a model for examining the hidden assumptions of texts. She notes: "the use of biology to justify political and social inequalities" (p. 25); the assumption that "genes explain everything about an organism" (p. 33); and the implication that sperm (and thus males) are as important as eggs in the formation of children. The latter is a view that reflects American androcentrism rather than biological fact. We wanted participants to consider whether their own disciplines were making similar androcentric assumptions. Two of the participants were economists and they pointed out that the underlying assumptions for their whole discipline are androcentric. One of the economists argued that the basic economic theories are biased by a Western view of human nature as competitive and acquisitive that is based on the behavior of idealized Western businessmen. He thought that female students were so rare in basic Economics classes and their Economics major because the models presented did not necessarily fit their worldview. This was one of many cases where participants provided the most telling examples.

We ended the session by handing out resources, which are listed in the Appendix. We also were able to give people discipline-specific pamphlets published by the National Center for Curriculum Transformation Resources for

Women. There were two sets of pamphlets that were handed out. One set, available for 16 disciplines, provides brief discipline-specific overviews of the impact of new scholarship on women, references for further reading and lists of resources (Hedges, 1997). The other set, available for seven disciplines, provides more narrowly focused essays, "examining ways in which the study of gender, race, ethnicity and class has been slowly transforming the curriculum of the university" (Helly, 1997, p. v). Finally, we provided participants with a long bibliography of discipline-specific resources and made it clear that we were available to help find further resources. In several cases, as faculty developed their projects, we were able to provide them with course readings. These handouts and offers of help were key facets of the workshop. Through years of discussions about the inclusion of a gender focus in courses, a chief faculty complaint has been that they do not know where to begin their search for resources, or that the search is too time consuming. We would like to think that our assistance, the bibliography provided and the discipline specific pamphlets, went far in remedying this problem. Certainly no one in the workshop complained about difficulty finding resource material.

Project Proposals

A month later, participants reconvened with plans for their projects. Some were more developed than others. A professor from the English Department, who wanted to model his project with the group, led us through a discussion of feminist literary criticism using a chapter from Charles Bressler's *Literary Criticism* (2001), a text that he provided before the meeting. We then turned our attention to Sir Arthur Conan Doyle's *A Scandal in Bohemia* (1993), the only Sherlock Holmes story where a woman outwits Holmes. The idea was to look for the underlying assumptions about gender roles. It was a worthwhile exercise, partly because Victorian England is different enough from 21st century America that the underlying biases are easy to pick out, and partly because it came from and was led by one of the participants. The exercise built on the work of our first meeting in teaching the skill of "deconstruction."

We then proceeded to a discussion of each project proposal. Participants provided almost all the critiques and made suggestions about pedagogy and specific assignments. As is typical of these kinds of discussions, each person's presentation and the critique of each presentation provided ideas that the rest of the group could use to modify their own plans.

Plans varied from a lesson plan for a single class to a plan for several weeks of discussions. As coordinators, we took the stance that whatever participants did was fine. We hoped that the plans for one day would lead to bigger things in later courses.

Project Results

Another month passed before we met again, and by this point most participants had completed their projects. We had their perceptions of what had happened to consider, as well as their students' perceptions, since the organizers of the Gender Matters initiative had asked us to distribute evaluation forms to these students. Their intent was to empower students to be more than passive receivers of knowledge by demonstrating respect for their voices. The forms were distributed to students at the end of the projects, filled out anonymously, collected and reviewed by the classroom instructor, and returned to us for further review and safekeeping. Faculty were also given forms to evaluate the workshop and were asked to write up one- or two-page summaries for posting on the Gender Matters Web site. Following our protocol for the earlier meetings, we had faculty participants report on projects. The rest of the group made comments and suggestions for future improvements.

All the units were based on classroom discussion. Given our earlier emphasis on the non-hierarchical nature of feminist pedagogy, we saw this as a positive sign. Generally, faculty were pleased with their results.

From our English professor who had his students read and analyze the gender assumptions in *A Scandal in Bohemia* (Doyle, 1993):

> Afterwards, the students became more sophisticated as readers but more cynical about Doyle's constructions of women in his stories and Sherlock Holmes's attitudes toward women in his cases. Several students began to resent the absence of admirable women from the series, but experienced difficulty in determining where to direct their anger and disappointment. They see the sexism in the stories as a reflection of a social and cultural phenomenon, but they tend to locate that sexism in Victorian Britain and to deny its existence all around them. (Cohen, 2002, p. 1)

Another exercise, this one in an Environmental Studies course, was on how models shape our worldview. The professor had the students look at a series of maps. Some, for example, had the Atlantic in the center and some had the Pacific in the center. After a discussion of how these and other models influence worldview, they turned to a discussion of how gender models shape views:

> On the positive side, the vast majority of students responded that the activity changed the way they thought about gender, maps, models, and bias. An overwhelming number of students also stated that the activity helped them gain a better understanding of gender, maps, models, and bias as well as sparked a desire to learn more about them. (Gunter, 2002, pp. 2-3)

In an Anthropology course about the culture of China, the professor asked students to compare Chinese gender roles to those in the U.S.:

> The lines of debate were not strongly marked by gender. In other words, female students occasionally took the ameliorating line that suggested not too much more needs to be done since, though gender inequality is a continuing problem in both the U.S. and the P.R.C., the trend is in the right direction. Things are getting better. Other females argued vigorously about the effects of discrimination in levels of pay and promotion that they had heard or read about, and they were supported by one or two male students. The point was also raised that even if things are getting better, what justifications are there for improvements to be delayed? It doesn't seem right that fairness should be something that people would have to get used to. (Moore, 2002, p. 4)

The student evaluations for all of the projects were generally positive, but the faculty participants were disappointed that most students did not see their future behavior changing as a result of these gender-focused exercises. As coordinators, we were not surprised. Behavior usually changes as a result of many experiences; rarely because of a few days in a classroom. We saw these results as good illustrations of the need to include gender and diversity discussions in the classes of many disciplines. We discussed with the group how they were experiencing the frustrations shared by all Women's Studies faculty and how the results reinforced the need for collective and sustained efforts.

Unexpected Consequences

From the first session, the workshop involved lively discussion and active participation by the whole group. Faculty for our undergraduate liberal arts programs are interested in pedagogy as well as their students, and these concerns drove our discussions. As academic women of a certain age we were used to being the only women in a faculty group, but as coordinators, we were hesitant to appear as "preaching" for a feminist perspective. This fear quickly became moot because the participants' stories and analyses made the relevant points with maximum impact. As in any good interdisciplinary conversation, we learned a lot from each other. In our first meeting, an economist pointed out the underlying gender biases in his discipline and therefore its lack of appeal for female students. This led to a broad discussion of the gender-segregated nature of many of our disciplines, undergraduate majors, and courses. We discussed the causes for this segregation and the impact of mostly male or mostly female enrollments on the nature of particular courses. With each new proposal and critique, we discovered more about our own work with gender issues by seeing them anew through the various interdisciplinary perspectives represented in the group.

In later meetings, when we discussed the class responses to projects, the results sometimes went beyond the immediate impact of the class discussion. In discussing the impact of the Sherlock Holmes story on his students, our English faculty member wrote: "They see the sexism in the stories as a reflection of a social and cultural phenomenon, but they tend to locate the sexism in Victorian Britain and deny its existence all around them" (Cohen, 2002). This professor was delighted to later report that a student had questioned the use of the term "Women Romantic Poets." She had wanted to know why the syllabus assumed that "Romantic Poets" referred to men and that women had to have a separately labeled category. In another course, there was a similar discussion about the NBA (National Basketball Association) versus the WNBA (Women's National Basketball Association).

Discussions about gender bias made at least some students feel comfortable bringing up concerns that had not been voiced to these faculty members before:

> Sad stories regarding [specific departments] suggested that not all faculty were enlightened. In [one department] one woman reported being told that the medical schools would prefer a man, and therefore she should take up another major. This was a former high school valedictorian, to make matters worse. She had never in her life been exposed to such sexism, and it happened on our campus. In [another] department stories of borderline harassment and assault were told in class. (Morris, 2002, p. 6)

When the faculty member discussed these stories at our meeting, the participants were surprised. As coordinators and teachers of Women's Studies courses, we were not. We were able to bring up some of the many cases with which we were familiar. The discussion certainly shocked and appalled the group and showed them a new side of campus life. We discussed how a focus on gender in their courses would empower students to share stories of harassment episodes with all of them. We emphasized that as white males they could have tremendous impact on legitimizing students' complaints. While they would become aware of a part of students' lives on campus that we would prefer did not exist, their power as white men could help change that reality.

Shortly after our last meeting, we were invited to do a presentation at our "Faculty Scholarship Day." This is an annual, in-house conference where faculty members report on discipline-based and pedagogical research. All of the workshop participants said they wanted to personally report on their work, and the session was one of the best-attended at the conference. It was generally agreed that the easygoing camaraderie set the stage for fruitful collaborative work on the evolving projects and their assessment. This first run of the project bodes well for future workshops because of its reputation as a fulfilling, engaging educational experience in which colleagues meet to try new ideas and share pedagogical concerns.

References

Bressler, C. (2002). *Literary criticism: An introduction to theory and practice* (3rd ed.). Upper Saddle River: NJ: Prentice Hall.

Cohen, E. (2002). Reading Sherlock Holmes. Retrieved May 10, 2003 from Rollins College Gender Matters Web site: http://www.rollins.edu/gendermattersyear/facworkshop_report.htm

Doyle, A.C. (1993). A scandal in Bohemia. In J. A. Hodgson (Ed.), *Sherlock Holmes: The major stories with contemporary critical essays* (pp. 32-52). Boston: Bedford/St, Martin's.

Gmelch, S.B. (1998). *Gender on campus*. Piscataway, NJ: Rutgers University Press.

Gunter, M. (2002.) The politics of the environment. Retrieved May 10, 2003 from Rollins College Gender Matters Website: http://www.rollins.edu/gendermattersyear/facworkshop_report.htm

Hedges, E. (1997). Preface. In B.B. Spanier, *Biology discipline analysis* (p. iii). Baltimore, MD: Towson University, National Center for Curriculum Transformation on Women.

Helly, D. O. (1997). Preface. In B. B. Spanier, S. V. Rosser, J N. Muzio, & E. B. Tucker (Eds.), *Biology CUNY panel: Rethinking the disciplines* (pp.v-vii). Baltimore, MD: Towson University, National Center for Curriculum Transformation on Women.

Lemonick, M.D., & Dorfman, A. (2001, July 23). One giant step. *Time,* 54-61.

Moore, R. (2002). Modern China in film. Retrieved May 10, 2003 from Rollins College Gender Matters Web site: http://www.rollins.edu/gendermattersyear/ facworkshop_report.htm

Morris, R. (2002). Health and wellness classes. Retrieved May 10, 2003 from Rollins College Gender Matters Web site: http://www.rollins.edu/gendermattersyear/ facworkshop_report.htm

Rosser, S. (1997). Feminist critiques of biology. In B. B. Spanier, S. V. Rosser, J N. Muzio, & E. B. Tucker (Eds.), *Biology CUNY panel: Rethinking the disciplines* (pp.18-42). Baltimore, MD: Towson University, National Center for Curriculum Transformation on Women.

Carol Lauer, is a Ph.D. professor of Anthropology at Rollins College. **Lynda M. Glennon**, is a Ph.D. professor of Sociology at Rollins College.

Appendix

Resources Distributed

Bressler, C. (2002). *Literary criticism: An introduction to theory and practice* (3rd ed.). Upper Saddle River: NJ: Prentice Hall.

Doyle, A.C. (1993). A scandal in Bohemia. In J. A. Hodgson (Ed.), *Sherlock Holmes: The major stories with contemporary critical essays* (pp. 32-52). Boston: Bedford/St, Martin's.

Glennon, L.M. (1983). Synthesism. In G. Morgan (Ed.), *Beyond method* (pp. 260-271). Beverly Hills, CA: Sage.

Hall, R.M., & Sandler, B.R. (1984). *Out of the classroom: A chilly campus climate for women?* Washington, DC: Association of American Colleges.

Martin, J.R. (Ed.). (1999). Higher education as filter. In *Coming of age in academe: Rekindling women's hopes and reforming the Academy* (pp. 85-115). New York: Routledge.

Rich, A. (Ed.) (1979). Taking women students seriously. In *On lies, secrets, and silence: Selected prose 1966-1978* (pp. 237-245). New York: W. W. Norton.

Sandler, B.R., & Hall, R.M. (1986). *The campus climate revisited: Chilly for women fac*ulty, *administrators, and graduate students*. Washington, DC: Association of American Colleges.

Chapter 29

Faculty Development and Students With Disabilities: Accommodations and Universal Design

Sheryl Burgstahler

Overall, students with disabilities experience less success in postsecondary education and careers than their non-disabled peers. Because faculty members have little expertise and experience in teaching these students, there is a need for professional development in this area. This chapter reviews the literature and introduces two approaches — accommodations and universal design — that can be combined into a single framework for creating inclusive learning environments.

Today, postsecondary campuses are populated by students who have a wide range of characteristics with respect to age, race, ethnicity, gender, and ability. Teaching this diverse audience presents challenges in both on-site and on-line learning environments. Legislation, improvements in precollege teaching, medical breakthroughs, technological advances, and changing attitudes have resulted in increasing numbers of students with disabilities attending postsecondary institutions (Gajar, 1998; Henderson, 2001; Horn & Berktold, 1999; National Council on Disability, 2000). Six percent of undergraduates report having a disability (Horn & Berktold, 1999). Of these, the largest group (29%) report having a learning disability; 23% report a mobility or orthopedic impairment; 16% report a hearing impairment; 16% report a visual impairment; and three percent report speech or language impairments (Horn & Berktold, 1999). Overall, students with disabilities experience less success in postsecondary education and careers than their non-disabled peers (Blackorby & Wagner, 1996; National Council on Disability, 2000; Phelps & Hanley-Maxwell, 1997; Stodden & Dowrick, 2001).

Faculty members are generally willing to accommodate students with disabilities, but lack knowledge about legal obligations, disabilities, assistive technology, accommodation strategies, and resources and have few experiences teaching students with disabilities (Anderson-Inman, Knox-Quinn, & Szymanski, 1999; Burgstahler, 2002b; Burgstahler & Doe, 2004; Dodd, Fischer, Hermanson, & Nelson, 1990; Dona & Edmister, 2001; Hill, 1996; Leyser, Vogel, Wyland, & Brulle, 1998; National Center for the Study of Postsecondary Educational Supports, 2000a, 2000b; Thompson, Bethea, & Turner, 1997). The most difficult accommodations for faculty to understand are those for students with learning disabilities (Burgstahler; Burgstahler & Doe; Vogel, Leyser, Wyland, & Brulle, 1999). Some faculty members are confused about issues related to the confidentiality of disability-related information and about how to maintain academic standards while providing reasonable academic accommodations (Burgstahler & Doe; National Center for the Study of Postsecondary Educational Supports, 2000b). Faculty members have little knowledge about how the poor design of Web pages, online distance learning courses, and other electronic resources can erect barriers to students with disabilities (Burgstahler, 2002a; Schmetzke, 2001).

Faculty members have a wide range of interest levels, of scheduling challenges, and of perceived needs for information regarding inclusion of students with disabilities in their courses. They are interested in a variety of professional development delivery methods, including short printed publications, on-site presentations, Internet-based resources, as well as individual support in specific situations (Burgstahler & Doe, 2004; Leyser et al., 1998; Salzberg, Peterson, Debrand, Blair, Carsey, & Johnson, 2002; Scott & Gregg, 2000).

Section 504 of the Rehabilitation Act of 1973 and the Americans with Disabilities Act of 1990 prohibit discrimination against people with disabilities in covered entities, which include postsecondary institutions. According to these laws, no otherwise qualified individuals with disabilities shall, solely by reason of their disabilities, be excluded from the participation in, be denied the benefits of, or be subjected to discrimination under any program or activity of the institution. Students who are "qualified" with respect to postsecondary education, include people who meet the academic and technical standards required for admission in the education program, with or without reasonable modifications to rules, policies or practices; the removal of architectural, communication or transportation barriers; or the provision of auxiliary aids and services (Section 504, 1973). Assuring that faculty members are aware of disability-related legislation and policies can help institutions avoid the costs of being included in the large numbers of court cases and complaints made by students with disabilities to the U.S. Department of Education Office of Civil Rights (Dona & Edmister, 2001).

Conceptual Framework: Universal Design and Accommodations

In order to create the most inclusive instruction for all students, both proactive (universal design) and reactive (accommodation) strategies should be employed. The following paragraphs describe each approach and then a conceptual framework that incorporates both in the creation of inclusive learning environments.

Accommodations

In postsecondary settings it is the student's responsibility to request disability-related accommodations. Typically, students with disabilities present documentation regarding their disabilities to a central office that approves accommodations and communicates with each faculty member, often through a letter that the student presents to the instructor. A faculty member can create a welcoming environment for students with disabilities by including a statement in the course syllabus that invites students with disabilities to request a meeting if they require disability-related accommodations. Examples of academic accommodations commonly used by students with different disability types include the following (Disabilities, Opportunities, Internetworking, and Technology, 2004):

Visual Impairments. Students with low vision may need to have large print handouts and equipment labels, use TV monitors connected to a microscope to enlarge images, have class assignments made available in electronic format, and/or use computers equipped to enlarge screen images. Students who are blind often need audio-taped, Brailled or electronic-formatted lecture notes, handouts, and texts; verbal descriptions of visual aids; raised-line drawings of graphic images; Braille lab signs and equipment labels; auditory lab warning signals; adapted lab equipment (for example, talking thermometers and tactile timers); and/or computers with speech or Braille output.

Hearing Impairments. Students who are deaf or hard of hearing may need sign language interpreters, real-time captioning, or FM systems; note takers; captioned films; visual aids, written assignments, lab instructions, and/or demonstration summaries; visual warning systems for lab emergencies; and/or electronic mail for discussions.

Learning Disabilities. Students with learning disabilities may need note takers; audiotaped class sessions; extra time on tests; alternative testing arrangements; visual and tactile instructional demonstrations; and/or computers with speech output, spell checkers, and grammar checkers.

Mobility Impairments. Students with mobility impairments may need note takers; lab assistants and/or group lab assignments; classes, labs, and field trips in accessible locations; adjustable tables; lab equipment located within reach; class assignments made available in electronic format; and/or computers equipped with special input devices (for example., speech input, Morse code input, alternative keyboard and/or mouse).

Health Impairments. Students with health impairments may need note takers; flexible attendance requirements; extra exam time; assignments made available in electronic format; and/or use of email to facilitate communication.

Most faculty members consider accessibility issues only after students with disabilities enroll in their courses and request accommodations (Burgstahler, 2002b; Silver, Bourke, & Strehorn, 1998). They provide accommodations in response to the needs of a specific student with a disability. The next section describes a more proactive approach to making courses accessible to everyone, including students with disabilities.

Universal Design of Instruction

"Universal design" is the process of making design decisions to assure that a course, facility, product, or service can be used comfortably by people with a wide variety of characteristics, including those related to gender, race/ethnicity, age, native language, and level of ability to see, hear, move and speak (Bowe, 2000; Burgstahler, 2002b; Center for Applied Special Technology, 2002). Universal design is defined by the Center for Universal Design at North Carolina State University (Connell, Jones, Mace, Mueller, Mullick, Ostroff, et al., 1997) as "the design of products and environments to be usable by all people, to the greatest extent possible, without the need for adaptation or specialized design." For example, a standard door is difficult or impossible to open by some individuals who use walkers or wheelchairs for mobility, have little strength, or are carrying boxes. Installing sensors that signal the door to open when anyone approaches makes the entrance accessible to everyone. This method of opening a door is an application of universal design (Connell, Jones, Mace, Mueller, Mullick, Ostroff, et al., 1997).

Universal design principles can be used in the design of instruction at all academic levels (Bowe, 2000; Burgstahler, 2002b; Center for Applied Special Technology, 2002; Silver, Bourke, & Strehorn, 1998). They can be applied to lectures, classroom discussions, group work, handouts, Internet-based instruction, computer and science labs, fieldwork, and other academic activities and materials. When instructors consider the wide range of characteristics of potential students when designing courses, they make course content and activities more accessible to students with a wide range of abilities, disabilities, ethnic/racial backgrounds, ages, language skills, and learning styles.

Universal design allows for multiple means of representation, expression, and engagement (Center for Applied Special Technology, 2002). Discussed below are examples of instructional methods that employ principles of universal design (Burgstahler, 2001, pp. 2-3).

- *Class Climate.* Create a classroom environment that respects and values both diversity and inclusiveness. Encourage students to meet with you to discuss disability-related accommodations and other special learning needs. Avoid segregating or stigmatizing any student. Respect the privacy of all students.
- *Physical Access, Usability, and Safety.* Assure that classrooms, labs, and fieldwork locations are accessible to individuals with a wide range of physical abilities and disabilities. Make sure equipment and activities minimize sustained physical effort, provide options for operation, and accommodate right- and left-handed students as well as those with limited physical abilities. Assure the safety of all students.
- *Delivery Methods.* Alternate delivery methods, including lecture, discussion, hands-on activities, Internet-based interaction, and fieldwork. Make sure each is accessible to students with a wide range of abilities, disabilities, interests, and previous experiences. Face the class and speak clearly in an environment that is comfortable and free from distractions. Provide printed materials that summarize content that is delivered orally.
- *Information Resources.* Use captioned videos. Make printed materials available in electronic format. Provide text descriptions of graphics presented on Web pages. Provide printed materials early to allow students to prepare for the topic to be presented. Create printed and Web-based materials in simple, intuitive, and consistent formats. Arrange content in order of importance.
- *Interaction.* Encourage different ways for students to interact with each other and with you. These methods may include in-class questions and discussion, group work, and Internet-based communications. Strive to make course interaction accessible to everyone.
- *Feedback.* Provide effective prompting during an activity and feedback after during steps of an assignment as well as the assignment is complete.
- *Assessment.* Provide multiple ways for students to demonstrate knowledge. For example, besides traditional tests and papers, consider group work, demonstrations, portfolios, and presentations as options for demonstrating knowledge.

Universal design of instruction benefits students other than those who have disabilities. Making syllabi, short assignment sheets, and reading lists available on an accessible Web site benefits all students, not just those who use text-to-speech computer systems because they are blind. Enunciating clearly and facing the class when speaking benefits others besides those who read lips. Writing lecture outlines on a whiteboard benefits all learners, not just those with hearing and learning disabilities. Using clear and simple language in handouts and on Web pages benefits students for whom English is a second language, not just people with learning disabilities. Captions on video clips benefit a distance learning student working late at night and wishing to avoid disturbing other members of the household and people for whom English is a second language, not just students who are deaf. Text descriptions of content presented using multimedia are accessible to students who cannot access graphics because of computer system limitations as well as to blind students using text-to-speech technology.

Model Framework: Universal Design and Accommodations

Universal design provides a proactive approach to meeting the needs of students with a wide range of abilities and disabilities, as compared to the individual, reactive approach used in providing accommodations. It is an intentional process where access to students with disabilities is considered routinely as instruction is designed. Universal design minimizes, but does not eliminate, the need for accommodations. For example, even if a faculty member does a good job of enunciation to facilitate lip reading and provides key content in printed form, a student who is deaf may still require the use of a sign language interpreter to fully participate in class pesentations and discussions. Both proactive and reactive approaches are needed in order to maximize the inclusion of students with disabilities in college courses. A campus committed to both applying universal design to instruction and offering effective accommodations as a framework for assuring access to the curriculum promotes the success of all students. Such an approach requires effective communication between faculty, students, and the disabled student services office and should be reflected in policy and practice throughout the organization. Issues of accommodations and universal design should be addressed in professional development offerings to faculty.

Successful Practices for Professional Development Delivery

In response to the diverse content and scheduling needs of faculty, in a project funded by the U.S. Department of Education (grant #P333A990042), the University of Washington's Disabilities, Opportunities, Internetworking, and Technology (DO-IT) Center worked with a team of 23 other postsecondary institutions to create and deliver six research-based models of professional development nationwide (Disabilities, Opportunities, Internetworking, and Technology, 2004). Content includes legal issues, campus resources, and accommodations for students with disabilities, and promotes the application of universal design of instruction. Rigorous formative and summative evaluations with stakeholders resulted in products of practical use on campuses with a wide variety of racial/ethnic, socio-economic, and other characteristics, including the status of two-year/technical and four-year, private, public and private, and small and large (Burgstahler, 2004). Handouts, scripts, videos, online lessons, and other support materials for all models are available on the project website at http://www.washington.edu/doit/Faculty. Permission is granted to modify and duplicate project materials, in total or in part, as long as the source is acknowledged.

On-site Instruction

The first three professional development models are designed for on-site training. Model one is a 20 to30 minute presentation on basic legal issues, accommodation strategies, and campus resources. It is designed to be delivered as part of general faculty development sessions. Model two is a one- or two-hour comprehensive presentation with special focus on universal design, accommodations, legal issues, and campus resources. A cooperative relationship between the student, the instructor and the campus office that supports students with disabilities is promoted. Model three consists of ten tailored workshops for in-depth training on specific areas identified through a needs assessment – accommodating students with learning disabilities and with psychiatric disabilities; universal design of instruction; creating accessible information resources in the form of Web pages, computers, distance learning courses, and computer labs; communicating with students who have disabilities; and including students with disabilities in science, mathematics and engineering courses.

Twenty-four presentations of Model one, 146 presentations of Model two, 31 presentations of Model three, and 62 other presentations were delivered to more than 11,000 individuals during the three years of the project. Of the attendees, 34% were faculty members, 25% were administrators, and six percent were teaching assistants. As a result of the training, participants reported that they:

- were better able to find resources on their campuses to accommodate students with disabilities;
- gained knowledge about legal obligations; and
- gained knowledge about accommodations for students with different types of disabilities.

Televised Instruction

Model four is televised instruction. Project video presentations are freely available to a national audience through the Research TV network of television stations hosted by postsecondary institutions. Videos can also be freely viewed from the DO-IT website and purchased from DO-IT.

Email-Based Distance Learning

Model five is a distance learning course delivered via a series of electronic mail messages that can be copied from the DO-IT website. In this model, the instructor, usually a disabled student services staff member, sends an electronic mail lesson approximately every five days to a cohort of faculty members for up to 10 weeks. Each lesson includes a question to discuss online before the next lesson is delivered. The series of lessons is well suited for and has been tested with groups of new faculty members and teaching assistants.

Web-based Instruction

Model six is comprehensive Web-based, self-paced instruction. Located at http://www.washington.edu/doit/Faculty/, *The Faculty Room* includes case studies, frequently asked questions, universal design, and accommodations typical in lectures, labs, field trips, distance learning, and other postsecondary academic settings. Disabled student services offices, departments, and units that deliver professional development to faculty are encouraged to link to this resource from Web sites that include the specific contact and procedural information from their own campuses.

Systemic Change

Input provided by team members at the end of the project suggests that their training efforts resulted in long-lasting change on their campuses. Documented changes include (Burgstahler, 2004):

- Greater faculty awareness of campus resources and promotion of collaborative relationships between faculty and the office of disabled student services.
- Faculty acceptance of responsibility and of increased understanding and practice of accommodation strategies.
- Increased application of universal design.
- Inclusion of disability-related topics in postsecondary courses.

Students with disabilities also reported positive change in professor attitudes, knowledge, and actions as a result of faculty training. Team members provided the following quotations from students (Burgstahler, 2004):

Attitudes: "Since the sharing of your DO-IT presentation, a willingness to provide assistance has become greater."

Knowledge: "My instructors seem to understand accommodations better this year."

Actions: "I think it is really neat that my instructor now asks about disabilities in their syllabus."; "My faculty this semester are better at articulating what they display on the overhead."

Implications for Practice

Lessons learned from the project described in this article can be applied on other campuses that wish to assure that faculty are prepared to fully include students with disabilities in their courses. These lessons include (Burgstahler, 2004):

- Tailor length, format, and content to the needs and interests of specific audiences.
- In the delivery of training to faculty, model the principles of universal design and employ strategies that encourage active participation.
- Have students with various types of disabilities share their academic challenges and successful accommodations in person or via video.
- Using a tested collection of flexible Web-based, video and printed materials, such as those described in this article, can significantly reduce preparation time.
- Explore ways to systematically provide training and institutional change. For example, a distance learning course could be offered each fall to new faculty members; accessible design concepts and practices could be integrated into regular Web development courses; accessibility topics could be incorporated into ongoing teaching assistant orientations (Burgstahler & Jirikowic, 2002).

Conclusion

Current faculty members have little experience or expertise in how to fully include students with disabilities in their classes. Ultimately, increased knowledge and skills of instructors regarding legal issues, universal design, accommodations, and resources can lead to more positive postsecondary and career outcomes for students with disabilities. Adopting universal design strategies can make courses more accessible to other students as well. The positive correlation between college participation and career success make efforts to assure that postsecondary programs are accessible to students with disabilities of critical importance.

References

Americans with Disabilities Act of 1990, 104 STAT. 327. Retrieved February 15, 2004, from http://www.usdoj.gov/crt/ada/statute.html

Anderson-Inman, L., Knox-Quinn, C., & Szymanski, M. (1999). Computer-supported studying: Stories of successful transition to postsecondary education. *Career Development for Exceptional Individuals, 22*(2), 185-212.

Blackorby, J., & Wagner, M. (1996). Longitudinal postschool outcomes of youth with disabilities: Findings from the National Longitudinal Transition Study. *Exceptional Children, 62*, 399-413.

Bowe, F.G. (2000). *Universal design in education: Teaching nontraditional students.* Westport, CT: Bergin & Garvey.

Burgstahler, S. (2001). *Universal design of instruction.* Seattle: DO-IT, University of Washington. Retrieved February 15, 2004, from http://www.washington.edu/doit/Brochures/Academics/instruction.html

Burgstahler, S. (2002a), Distance learning: Universal design, universal access. *Electronic Technology Review, 10*(1). Retrieved February 15, 2004, from http://www.aace.org/pubs/etr/issue2/burgstahler.cfm

Burgstahler, S. (2002b). Accommodating students with disabilities: Professional development needs of faculty. *To Improve the Academy: Resources for Faculty, Instructional, and Organizational Development, 21*, 179-195

Burgstahler, S. (2004). *Lessons learned in The Faculty Room.* Submitted for publication.

Burgstahler, S., & Doe, T. (2004). Improving postsecondary outcomes for students with disabilities: Designing professional development for faculty. Manuscript submitted for publication.

Burgstahler, S., & Jirikowic, T. (2002). Supporting students with disabilities: What every teaching assistant should know. *Journal of Graduate Teaching Assistant Development, 9*(1), 23-30.

Center for Applied Special Technology. (2002). *Universal design for learning.* Wakefield, MA: Author. Retrieved February 15, 2004, from http://www.cast.org/udl/

Connell, B.R., Jones, M., Mace, R., Mueller, J., Mullick, A., Ostroff, E., et al. (1997). *The principles of universal design.* Raleigh: North Carolina State University, Center for Universal Design. Retrieved February 15, 2004, from http://www.design.ncsu.edu/cud/univ_design/princ_overview.htm

Disabilities, Opportunities, Internetworking, and Technology. (2004). *The faculty room.* Seattle: Author. Retrieved February 15, 2004, from http://www.washington.edu/doit/Faculty

Dodd, J.M., Fischer, J., Hermanson, M., & Nelson, J.R. (1990). Tribal college faculty willingness to provide accommodations to students with learning disabilities. *Journal of American Indian Education, 30*(1), 8-16.

Dona, J., & Edmister, J.H. (2001). An examination of community college faculty members' knowledge of the Americans with Disabilities Act of 1990 at the fifteen community colleges in Mississippi. *Journal of Postsecondary Education and Disability, 14*(2), 91-103.

Gajar, A. (1998). Postsecondary education. In F. Rusch, & J. Chadsey (Eds.), *Beyond high school: Transition from school to work* (pp. 383-405). Belmont, CA: Wadsworth.

Henderson, C. (2001). *College freshmen with disabilities: A biennial statistical profile.* Washington, D.C.: American Council on Education.

Hill, J.L. (1996). Speaking out: Perceptions of students with disabilities regarding adequacy of services and willingness of faculty to make accommodations. *Journal of Postsecondary Education and Disability, 12*(1), 22-43.

Horn, L., & Berktold, J. (1999). Students with disabilities in postsecondary education: A profile of preparation, participation, and outcomes. *Education Statistics Quarterly, 1*(3) 59-64.

Leyser, Y., Vogel, S., Wyland, S., & Brulle, A. (1998). Faculty attitudes and practices regarding students with disabilities: Two decades after implementation of Section 504. *Journal of Postsecondary Education and Disability, 13*(3), 5-19.

National Council on Disability. (2000). Transition and post-school outcomes for youth with disabilities: Closing the gaps to post-secondary education and employment. Washington, D.C.: Author.

National Center for the Study of Postsecondary Educational Supports. (2000a). *National survey of educational support provision to students with disabilities in postsecondary education settings.* Honolulu: University of Hawaii at Manoa.

National Center for the Study of Postsecondary Educational Supports. (2000b). *Postsecondary education and employment for students with disabilities: Focus group discussions on supports and barriers in lifelong learning.* Honolulu: University of Hawaii at Manoa.

Phelps, L.A., & Hanley-Maxwell, C. (1997). School-to-work transitions for youth with disabilities: A review of outcomes and practices. *Review of Educational Research, 67*(2), 197-226.

Rehabilitation Act, Section 504, 29 U.S.C. § 794 (1973).

Salzberg, C.L., Peterson, L., Debrand, C.C., Blair, R.J., Carsey, A.C., & Johnson, A.S. (2002). Opinions of disability service directors on faculty training: The need, content, issues, formats, media, and activities. *Journal of Postsecondary Education and Disability, 15*(2), 101-114.

Schmetzke, A. (2001) Online distance education – 'Anytime, anywhere' but not for everyone. *Information Technology and Disability Journal, 7*(2). Retrieved February 15, 2004, from http://www.rit.edu/~easi/itd/itdv07n2/axel.htm

Scott, S.S., & Gregg, N. (2000). Meeting the evolving education needs of faculty in providing access for college students with learning disabilities. *Journal of Learning Disabilities, 33*(2), 158-167.

Silver, P., Bourke, A., & Strehorn, K. (1998). Universal instructional design in higher education: An approach for inclusion. *Equity and Excellence in Education, 31*(2), 47-51.

Stodden, R.A., & Dowrick, P.W. (2001). Postsecondary education and employment of adults with disabilities. *American Rehabilitation, 25*(3), 19-23.

Thompson, A., Bethea, L., & Turner, J. (1997). Faculty knowledge of disability laws in high education: A survey. *Rehabilitation Counseling Bulletin, 40,* 166-180.

Vogel, S., Leyser, Y., Wyland, S., & Brulle, A. (1999). Students with learning disabilities in higher education: Faculty attitude and practices. *Learning Disabilities Research & Practice, 14*(3), 173-186.

Acknowledgements

This chapter is based upon work supported by the U.S. Department of Education, Office of Postsecondary Education (grant #P33A990042 and grant #P333A020044) and Funds for the Improvement of Postsecondary Education (grant #P116D990138-01). Any opinions, findings, and conclusions or recommendations expressed in this material are those of the author and do not necessarily reflect the views of the federal government.

Sheryl Burgstahler is the director of Accessible Technology Services and Outreach of Computing and Communications at the University of Washington and the founder and director of DO-IT (Disabilities, Opportunities, Internetworking, and Technology) and an affiliate associate professor in the College of Education.

Chapter 30

A Catwalk for Kitano: Highlighting Kitano's Paradigm for Multicultural Course Transformation in Consultations With Individual Faculty

Natasha Flowers

This chapter describes the benefits and lessons learned from an emphasis on Kitano's Paradigm for Multicultural Course Transformation as a resource for faculty consultations on diversity. The author explains Kitano's Paradigm, provides a rationale for its use and details how the author experimented with the paradigm to identify its potential as a trend or "supermodel" for multicultural course design. The author also reflects upon how the model can be used to orient instructional consultants to specific strategies for multicultural course design and the development of related modules and workshops.

Without drawing a strange analogy between fashion and multicultural course transformation (MCT), I will at least suggest that faculty developers can take something from the traditional catwalk used by fashion designers worldwide. The parading of someone's take on slacks and dresses has nothing to do with effective teaching or student success, but it does remind us how influential a little show and tell can be. The catwalk is actually more than this parading and sashaying; it is an artistic statement. However, the point is to compel people to envision and desire. Frankly, no one is pining over the latest model for multicultural change, but there is a need to demonstrate what is so attractive and provocative about diversity in higher education. Sure, there are faculty who want the technical advice in the form of quick tips and basic how-to's. These are undoubtedly acceptable resources. However, for faculty developers, there is a bit of artistry that comes with experience and education. That artistry, in the form of a consultation, may start with and go beyond the catwalk. Here is where the analogy breaks down: the catwalk is just the show while the artistry of consultation for multicultural change may begin with a grand presentation but must end with a substantial plan for course transformation.

The designers of inclusive instructional models seem to write articles and books without much reaction from faculty developers on effectiveness or appropriateness. However, these models for inclusive classrooms take backseat to general talk about diversity, inclusion, and cultural awareness. Many faculty developers may argue that this is the plight of any theory of learning and teaching. However, this issue is complicated by two obstacles: little to no knowledge of the distinct qualities of inclusive teaching models and little to no knowledge of how to make inclusive teaching an integrated force in course design. Hence, there is a need for a bigger stage to show off and a larger audience to take notice of inclusive teaching models as a viable way to transform college classrooms. Here is where local faculty development should continue to take notice of national voices on multicultural faculty development. Kardia (1998) reminded colleagues that they are "uniquely skilled and situated to integrate diversity and academic excellence" because:

> In order to engage in successful faculty development efforts of any kind, we as faculty development practitioners must be able to carefully attend to the opportunities and challenges present within our institution in order to take strategic, appropriate, and effective steps in promoting faculty, instructional, and organization development. We must be able to introduce new concepts, perspectives, and pedagogical priorities in a non-threatening manner that is responsive to the realities, values, and needs of the specific faculty members with whom we work. (p.18)

Past president of the Professional and Organizational Development Network, Christine Stanley (2002), strongly recommended researching and applying a working definition of inclusive teaching and a conceptual framework in outlining the domains of multicultural teaching. She offered Four Dimensions of Multicultural Teaching (adapted from Jackson and Holvino (1988) and Marchesani and Adams (1992). To support her notion that individual consultations are ample opportunities to initiate and resolve gaps in the course content where cultural issues could be integrated, Stanley also mentioned Banks' (1995) levels of integration of ethnic content as one approach for curriculum change. Her endorsement supports the notion that more faculty developers should be accepting "the call to action" in designing and implementing multicultural faculty development activities. As a wake-up call for some and a reminder for others, Stanley's essay is not an analysis of how she integrated these models into her own consultation and workshop design. However, her deliberate mentioning of these models and practical strategies for the challenging work ahead is part of the catwalk. She offered a very descriptive outline for a multicultural faculty development workshop. In this outline, her topics are central to the diversity in the classroom but commonly accepted as general topics that may be discussed in any consultation: ground rules for participation, self-assessment exercises, and classroom assessment techniques. What is unique about this work plan is that she inserts Marchesani and Adams' (1992) Four Dimensions of Multicultural Teaching as an example of a conceptual framework for defining the problem. Lastly, Stanley includes the critical component of evaluation as part of the workshop design. She simply identifies the purpose of the workshop evaluation as "formative feedback in order to better structure and facilitate further workshops in this area" (p. 203). This statement is exactly what happens after the show is over. There has to be some reflection on the impact of the workshop and content, such as the integration of a particular model to help faculty understand MCT.

The Four Dimensions of Multicultural Teaching model is undoubtedly appropriate for assisting faculty in examining and designing inclusive classrooms. Marchesani and Adams, et al. (1992) give faculty and faculty developers permission to go beyond what is in the syllabus and what is in the classroom. In reflecting on assumptions and stereotyped beliefs, faculty (and students in their classroom) have the opportunity to see connections in their reaction to and application of course content and their own identity and beliefs. This is not a simple feat. In consulting on beliefs and values, faculty developers may use this model to help faculty understand how those components factor into the curriculum, their interaction with students, and their pedagogy. From that perspective, benefits are outstanding. The challenge is how those conversations are broached. If the faculty member enters a consultation or workshop about course design, for example, and the faculty developer presents strategies for inclusive teaching, the faculty member "may treat direct discussion of multicultural issues with suspicion" according to Kardia (1998).

Besides any suspicion that may arise, faculty may also feel that they need more time to reflect on issues of race, gender, ethnicity, and sexual orientation before they begin to redesign a course. These factors are all valid.

Knowing that suspicion may arise, it is still important to obtain one weapon for poor integration of diversity issues in instructional design: information. Fortunately, Bonilla and Palmerton (2001) shared the results of three faculty focus groups (as well as three student focus groups). This particular study examined issues of race, ethnicity, and gender in the college classroom. In this study, faculty identified five professional development needs. Three of those needs included "help in untangling issues of fairness, favoritism, and equity in the classroom," "creation of a more supportive environment rather than a change in academic standards," and "refinement of the cultural breadth requirement and expansion of opportunities for additional course creation" (p. 59). This data alone could be used as the first step in understanding how models assist faculty developers in helping faculty with their own courses.

What is also important to consider is how we as faculty developers perceive and deal with the issue of diversity when consulting and presenting workshops. As an African American woman, I often find myself in unplanned, yet highly charged discussions regarding diversity on campus. In some instances, I feel caught off guard and anxious about how emotional the discussion may become in a matter of minutes. Therefore, I suspect that those consultants who are beginning to introduce diversity issues in their own consultations and workshop curriculum would appreciate the opportunity to prepare for the emotional aspects of these discussions. Here is where faculty developers and faculty face the same possible fears. Therefore, in accurately preparing ourselves to broach concepts such as social justice, prejudice, marginalization and privilege, we look for solid facts and strategies on which to stand . These things may help to eliminate whatever barriers that cause hesitation in that first step toward multicultural faculty development.

Consequently, there may be fear that there is no supermodel for multicultural education in higher education. To follow this line of thinking, perhaps there should be a greater fear that there is not enough investigation on the topic. As faculty development continues as an appropriate tool for exploring multicultural education, it is important that teaching centers strongly consider models that reach a variety of disciplines in need of more inclusive teaching practices. As a novice to faculty development and a long-time student of curriculum and instruction, I decided to take a chance on a model that may influence my work as an instructional designer and the work of the faculty members that I helped. I should also be candid in revealing that my own cultural background made it easy for me to be self-reflective about how faculty see me in the role of instructional consultant. As an African American female, I have worked hard to find the substance and action behind the words diversity, inclusion, multiculturalism, and community. However, I have had the misfortune of finding out that some people perceive a person of color as an agenda-packing civilian outside her territory. Furthermore, I have had to become more conscientious about my role in campus-wide initiatives related to diversity. I am not afraid to be labeled an activist, but I do not want to become a general activist with no contribution to make toward policy and curriculum change. Frankly, I want any contribution I make to the multicultural professional development on my campus to be aligned with my skill set and not just the color of my skin and my perceived cultural values. As Turner and Myers (2000) discovered in their in-depth study of faculty of color, many felt trapped by the university's expectation for them to take on diversity issues, and others revealed that their colleagues questioned their biases as they involved their research and classroom practice. In my experience as a faculty member and a staff member, these assertions are not absurd.

In my current work as an instructional consultant, I welcome the charge of contributing to a better climate and classroom environment for diverse students, faculty, and staff. However, I work hard to find the scholarship and the best models to support my cause.

My First Steps

I am fortunate to work at a university where there is ongoing discussion and action centered on the retention of diverse students. There have been many town hall meetings that allow faculty to discuss their concerns and their best practices for engendering a sense of success in their students. The "Why not both?" asked in our local marketing and publicity efforts applies to more than just having the choice of two prominent schools as one's alma mater. That question initiated the Diversity Inquiry Group, in which faculty and staff researched multicultural education in higher education and designed workshops to help spread the good news of MCT. That question also initiated the Diversity Indicators, a newly developed assessment that will "present to the community inside and outside of IUPUI a set of measures and benchmarks by which to stimulate and evaluate IUPUI's progress in attaining the goals of its diversity initiatives" (http://www.imir.iupui.edu/projects/project_diversity.asp). Furthermore, another collaboration among faculty, staff, and administration is currently recognized as the Diversity Institute. Even in its infancy, it has combined new and experienced leaders to continue the work of the Diversity Inquiry Group and to have a more active role in multicultural issues among departments across campus. I am definitely not reinventing the wheel here. However, I feel very much a part of the maintenance of that wheel.

The more consultations I received that dealt with including more student voices, integrating more diverse cultural content, and dealing with biases and discrimination within disciplines, resulted in an increased need to have some answers for some frequently asked questions about diversity. I was also very curious about how well multicultural models fit and distinguished themselves within basic instructional design models. That curiosity led me to a place where I had to select a model and try it on for size.

Understanding Kitano's Paradigm for Multicultural Course Transformation

When I found Kitano's paradigm for MCT, I was consumed with the desire to fit diversity into any general consultation. I was also looking for a balance between emotional and intellectual reactions to diversity. I saw Kitano's paradigm as a way to focus faculty's attention on what their students might see in their syllabi, reading lists, and assignment sheets. In doing so, those tangible items could be revisited so that many faculty members could textually identify their biases, their hopes for their students, and their own cultural values.

In the chapter's introduction, Kitano provides the mission behind such a model: "This chapter argues for consistency between syllabus and course implementation with the idea that the syllabus represents a tentative course guide. Moreover, all course goals, including multicultural goals, should be made explicit to students, actualized in content and instruction, and their attainment monitored" (p. 19). This statement resembles the goal of any solid instructional design model: matching the goals with the actions of the course.

I clearly saw this paradigm as a major acquisition for my own growing repertoire of instructional design models. I began endorsing Kitano's paradigm as a great starting point for MCT. Before delving into what is present in the course and the syllabus, Kitano's paradigm is designed to suggest a type of foundation-building and reflection involving multicultural education. Kitano (1997) strongly asserted that the principles of learning and principles of multicultural education serve as the "workable underpinning for course change" (p. 20). With this foundation, the goals are derived as the way in which these principles are filtered into the course. Furthermore, the goals become the determining factor for which course components will be transformed and at what level the transformation will occur.

Indiana University Purdue University Indianapolis's (IUPUI) own Principles of Undergraduate Learning (PUL) have moved in status from words on a website and bookmark to explicit expectations presented on course syllabi and a topic of campus-wide dialogues regarding assessment of student learning.[1] A respect for diversity is the value embedded in the fifth principle of undergraduate learning, Understanding Society and Culture, which is trans-

[1] The Communities of Practice (CoP) are defined as "a cross-disciplinary community engaged in an active, collaborative, curriculum focused on enhancing and assessing undergraduate learning with frequent activities that promote learning, development, scholarship of teaching, and community." These CoPs are specifically designed to involve faculty in the closer examination and the infusion of the PULs. More information can be found at http://www.opd.iupui.edu/coil/goals.htm.

lated as "the ability of students to recognize their own cultural traditions and to understand and appreciate the diversity of the human experience, both within the United States and internationally" (IUPUI, 2001). Many universities include this sentiment in their mission statements and general education requirements. Nevertheless, faculty developers interested in diversity in college classrooms must commit to some investigation of their university's thoughts on diversity. In workshops, I have used this principle to remind faculty that a respect for diversity stands boldly beside academic goals such as critical thinking, problem solving, and civic responsibility.

Finding the most appropriate information on multicultural education is challenging when dealing with faculty from various disciplines. However, like Stanley (2000) and other scholars have suggested, the mission is not to overwhelm them with definitions and frameworks. The mission is to help them create a working definition of what it means to provide multicultural education.

In terms of assisting faculty in creating multicultural goals, these consultations must rely on resources that are already available to faculty developers. One well-respected and commonly used tool is Cross and Angelo's Teaching Goals Inventory (TGI). The TGI helps initiate conversations about an instructor's goals for students in a particular course (Angelo & Cross, 1993). Here is where our general expertise in creation of goals and learning objectives helps to transform a vision of multiculturalism in a feasible action.

After the goals are brainstormed and drafted, faculty can advance to the next component in this paradigm, which is reflection upon the "nature of the course" as presented in the schematic of the model. Kitano addresses this briefly as she states, "applicability depends to a great extent on the specific discipline and course" (p, 25). The content for the rest of the book illustrates this notion broadly and specifically as it reveals the various ways instructors transform one or all of the course components.

In asking instructors to reflect upon and act based on the kind of course they have, instructors are allowed to think about the elements of the course (and the discipline) that welcome and dismiss diversity. This component should appeal to any faculty developer who plans to meet the faculty member at a certain comfort level. In asking faculty members to deal with how they teach the course and the disciplinary values related to the content and instruction, instructional designers can ask certain questions regarding the four course components as identified by Kitano: content, instruction, assessment, and classroom dynamics. In these questions, an instructional designer and the faculty member can continue to uncover what multiculturalism is to the instructor and to the students in the classroom.

The three levels of MCT as presented by Kitano are the substance of the paradigm. Each level focuses on the four elements of any course: 1) content,

2) instruction, 3) assessment, and 4) classroom dynamics. Kitano provides a summary of how each course element looks at a certain level of transformation. In this process-oriented portion of the model, the faculty member (and the instructional consultant) get a glimpse of how Kitano defines a transformed multicultural course. A summary of each course component at the transformed level is illustrated in Figure 1. Kitano revitalizes constructivist thought by reminding faculty that there are voices in the classroom that should be heard as well as various ways to assess whether or not those voices are engaged and comprehending the content of the course. Kitano's explanation of each element is balanced with feasible methods to make a course more student-centered.

As I was mulling over Kitano's paradigm and comparing it with other models, I was also presenting it before faculty in workshops. After such a global, interdisciplinary exploration of Kitano's paradigm, I accepted the re-

Component	**Transformed**
Content	Reconceptualizes the content through a shift in paradigm standard; presents content through nondominant perspective
Instructional Strategies and Activities	Change in power structure so that students and instructor learn from each other; methods center on student experience/knowledge such as • analyzing concepts against personal experience • issues-oriented approaches • critical pedagogy
Assessment of Student Knowledge	Alternatives that focus on student growth: action-oriented projects; self-assessment, reflection on the course
Classroom Dynamics	Challenging of biased views and sharing of diverse perspectives while respecting rules established for group process; equity in participation.

Adapted from Kitano & Morey

Figure 1. Course Components at the Transformed Level

sponsibility of consulting with a more vigorous approach to inclusive teaching regardless of the instructional issue brought by individual faculty. For the record, I never said to myself, "you will spread Kitano's word and convert the masses." The only thing I can admit is that I told myself that I would remember Kitano's paradigm when I consulted on any teaching and learning issue. Consequently, in over a year's time, I was able to extract four examples of consultations that dealt with content, instruction, assessment, and classroom dynamics.

Consultant as the nondominant perspective.

Content is often regarded as the easiest target for MCT. Find any underrepresented minority or nontraditional ideal and insert it in the course readings. If it was that easy, faculty would do it and there would be little argument about whether any scholarship is inclusive of all voices. Content is the most delicate because it is about voice: who is speaking and who is listening. When a professor came to the Center to discuss ways to make his course on a particular ethnic identity more interactive and interesting, he was not looking for more articles to assign. He was looking for more videos and more ways to engage the students. We discussed his syllabus and I saw that he was covering Black English. I told him about the African American studies seminar course I took on Black English and how I grappled with it as an African American woman from Mississippi who was an instructor and supervisor for student teachers. He asked if I would be willing to visit his course and give a lecture.

Of course, the lecture turned into a provocative discussion about blackness from a professional and personal view. My voice was biased and informed, so they heard the complexity of Black English from an African American voice within the first five minutes of my introduction. Later I realized that I also modeled a more engaged style of teaching for this professor. I asked the students to role play scenarios where they had to deal with Black English as a speaker or a listener. Students pretended to be parents, teachers, coworkers, students, and employers and they realized the impact that Black English had on everyone's ideas of cultural awareness, cultural sensitivity, and cultural pluralism. Also, the voices from the students became part of the content as they openly discussed the privilege and prejudice behind Black English. However, it became an opportunity for this instructor to see how students' ideas bring another dimension to the classroom.

Student growth in instruction and assessment.

"Doing Diversity" was the title of one professor's goal to give students more eyes-on and minds-on cultural awareness. Lecture and small group discussions were not enough for the more than 30 students in her course. She was pursuing a modest professional development grant that would help her students demonstrate cultural awareness. I immediately focused on how the project would be an instructional tool to facilitate more student-controlled research on diversity. I encouraged her to refine her project so that students would have more voice and time to reflect upon how the overall project influenced their own cultural biases. I soon asked her to further explain what "doing diversity" meant for her course. The consultations became focused around what students would be responsible for and how their voices and their opinions would be an integral part of the project. This professor was never opposed to more student-centered projects, but she did admit that she had become comfortable with the style of teaching she experienced as a graduate student: lecturing and some small group discussion. As we continued to talk about alternatives, it became clear that she wanted an end product as illustration of their hard work and comprehension of culture's impact on general areas like marriage, coming-of-age rituals, body adornment, and food. Ultimately, the professor designed a website group project for students to display their annotated bibliography that included links to other websites. In groups, students had to work collaboratively to research and provide details regarding the source's cultural relevance. This website captured the research, but it also prepared them for a presentation in which they had to explain why they chose a particular cultural group and its impact on their general topic area.

The assessment of this website project led the professor to consider ways in which she could assess students' reflection of their own cultural awareness. With this turn to assessment, I remembered that Kitano's configuration of a transformed course included a focus on student growth and action-oriented assignments. I presented her with various examples of rubrics that assessed cognitive ability and then I introduced her to Grant Wiggins' example of a rubric that assessed empathy and reflection as components of understanding (1998). The professor was intrigued by these aspects, but was not prepared to use the entire rubric for her own course. She decided to create a rubric using language from her own discipline while considering the levels between egocentricity and maturity as presented by Wiggins. She then came to me interested in a way to present the grid so that students would grasp her approach to evaluation easily. I then showed her a handout based on Zeichner and Riston's (1987) Reflective Teaching Index.[2] She liked the types of questions that were asked at each level of reflection. The final version of her own rubric outlined

[2] Sue Kiger, Ph.D., a professor in the School of Education at Indiana State University, uses a handout based on this index to help clarify the levels of reflection required in her pre-service students' reflective exercises during a teaching practicum.

students' progress toward cultural awareness using terms from her own discipline. This tool would reinforce her students' conceptualization and application of concepts rather than the haphazard placement of those concepts in an essay. In a few consultations, the project was enhanced to a highly reflective activity that required more than cool pictures of a cultural group and correct citation of the sources. The development of this project was due to the professor's enthusiasm and patience during the consultations. However, I do take credit for supporting her creation of an assignment that was student-centered and for having a few resources up my sleeve that helped her draft an assessment of students' reflection of their cultural awareness.

Conflict management for group work.

Classroom dynamics was the focal point of another social science professor who wanted to experiment with intensive small group work and more student accountability. He was very concerned about the horror stories he heard from students. I should note that this professor conducted end-of-the semester focus groups with his students wherein they discussed those aspects of the course that were helpful and others that were not. Working with this professor was not difficult because he had established a classroom where students helped him evaluate his own effectiveness as an instructor. However, he wanted help in designing a structure for meaningful small group activities for his large classroom.

Kitano's description of a transformed classroom included the phrase, "challenging of biased views and sharing of diverse perspectives while respecting rules established for group process" (p. 24). This phrase resonated strongly as the truth behind positive and productive collaborative exercises. The rules of respect within a group are the foundation for any interaction. Without any hesitation, I asked the professor about how he would set up the learning teams as he described them and how he was going to monitor the group work. His plan was solid. He spoke in length about how students would be able to get out of their respective groups if things did not work out. Looking at the number of teams he had and the number of individual students he may have to accommodate, I returned to the notion of "respecting rules." I recommended a student and faculty-generated list of rules of engagement that is very popular as collaborative learning becomes more pervasive across disciplines. However, there is a silent problem that can override the respect each student should have for those rules. That problem is the inability to work out those tense moments of miscommunication, disrespect, or total disregard for the team. I suggested that he consider proposing a conflict resolution process in the course syllabus so that students would come to him only if the process had failed. He began writing down a few steps that students must take before they asked for a new group assignment. Ultimately, the list proved to be an illustration of what it means to respect the rules established for group process. Students were required to show some commitment to group process that went beyond just completing their portion of the group's work. Also, Kitano's ideas regarding classroom dynamics support any faculty member's attempt to teach multiculturalism through group process.

Some Good Practice for Multicultural Faculty Development

In doing such an experiment, I have learned a few things about possible ways to introduce and orient other faculty developers to MCT by meeting them where they are as instructional designers, instructional technologists, and the like.

Strength-based model for designing multicultural faculty development.

As faculty developers, we often reject the deficit-model used to design courses and assess students' comprehension. In our own work, we have to be careful not to use this same line of thinking when we consider our own shops as support systems for multicultural faculty development. The number of consultants, support staff, and resources will always be an issue, but we have to continue focusing on the strengths of our centers.

In the center where I work, our outreach strategy evolves around a school-based system, wherein each instructional consultant becomes the liaison for particular schools across campus. Consequently, long-lasting relationships between the CTL and individual schools and departments are formed. This school-based structure does not require that every consultant be an expert in all areas of teaching and learning. However, there are certain areas, such as classroom assessment techniques, active learning, and syllabus design that are considered a general knowledge base for all consultants. We began to discuss our own concerns about being the front-line person for so many different disciplines. We decided as a group to begin in-service professional development where each consultant led a discussion, during our regular staff meeting, in specific areas of solid interest, research, or practice. This decision made it possible for me to offer an in-service on MCT . This in-service allowed me to briefly explain the models I used and the responses I received from faculty members. It also allowed some time for my colleagues to share their own concerns and experiences with diversity as faculty developers. This unit in-service along with ongoing whole-office professional development in general diversity issues assists consultants in the awareness they need for future high-quality programming as suggested by Cook and Sorcinelli (1999).

After my colleagues brainstormed how they would present a workshop on diversity, we discussed our individual consultation style, what kind of consultation on multicultural classrooms they would consider, and how we can help each other to enhance our own skills in the area. That one hour was very fruitful because it resulted in a pilot assignment of critical friendships[3] (Costa & Kallick, 1993) that would help us revise our own consultations and workshop delivery.

The last lesson I learned came from my role in the design of two online resources, *Teaching in Support of Student Success*, a series of faculty development modules and the *Multicultural Classroom Resource Guide*, an online database of research, websites, and essays regarding multicultural issues. Before I offered the in-service, I was managing the early design phase of an online module on inclusive teaching for university faculty. It was critical that instructors enter the inclusive teaching module and find a space where they could reflect on their worldview, but more importantly that they continue to think about how to transform their course in appropriate, practical ways. Therefore, it was important that the module end with an example of an action plan for MCT. Again, Kitano's paradigm served as the best model for explicitly demonstrating how all four components of the course help to transform the faculty and students involved.

The most interesting aspect of this experience was my interaction with a colleague who was responsible for helping me design an interface and the interactivity for this module.

She became a critical friend because she probed me about my vision, my biases, and my hopes for the module. Surprisingly, we had many debates about the affective and the cognitive transformation embedded in MCT. Her question, "Why are you focusing on course design. Isn't this topic more about values and biases?" led me to really think hard about why Kitano's paradigm was so attractive, and I finally realized that I really wanted to figure out a way to introduce MCT as an approach that any discipline could use. I also hoped that faculty would begin to talk about perceived obstacles in transforming one or all of the four course components. In essence, I made the decision that I was more comfortable with consulting from this angle because it was always easier

[3]"A trusted person who asks provocative questions, provides data to be examined through another lens, and offers critique of a person's work as a friend. A critical friend takes the time to fully understand the context of the work presented and the outcomes that the person or group is working toward. The friend is an advocate for the success of that work"

for me to start her with faculty and with colleagues. As a new consultant, I always needed any buy-in to be about good teaching first before the discussion moved to more personal matters. My colleague continued to engage me with questions and insight and helped me shape my own voice in this work. I do not know if this conversation would have happened if I had not had to create this module.

As a member of the design team for the *Multicultural Classroom Resource Guide*, I continued to have conversations about which framework made sense for multicultural faculty development. I did not insist on the use of Kitano's paradigm as the guiding framework, but I chose to focus on the sections related to pedagogy and the classroom. These sections were more comfortable because my job requires that I consider the "nature of a person's course" even if I am not familiar with the content. Therefore, Kitano's assertion that one should consider the course's "amenability to MCT" (p. 20) is critical during consultations that begin with, "How can I do this with *my* course?". As the only instructional consultant on this design team, I had the responsibility of researching articles that would help faculty see the variety of course types and disciplines that had undergone a transformation to help diverse students learn.

What really works?

In less than three years as an instructional consultant, I know that I am as much of a work in progress as is MCT. What is comforting is that I do not feel deprived of a mission or information. Also, my advice to any consultant or staff member ready to take the step in promoting and assisting with MCT across their campus, the following list summarizes my journey that has been shared by many others in this field:

- Continue to research and examine those principles and conceptual frameworks for your consultations in MCT. You do not have to be an expert but you should at least have your own list of resources for the need. (Trust me, it will find you even if you are not looking for it.)
- Make MCT an ongoing opportunity to learn. Consider MCT as one approach to good teaching and actively seek out ways in which to integrate at least one aspect or principle of a model for MCT.
- Share some reflective time as an individual and with other colleagues. Take advantage of an easy-going week, a critical friend, or a staff meeting where there are conversations about current issues related to teaching and learning. If you do not evaluate your own biases, needs, and goals, you will never feel empowered to learn and help faculty with MCT.
- Experiment and then experiment more. Let new ideas continue to excite your work and do not be afraid to label a workshop or consultation as your

opportunity to try on a model for MCT. Our work as faculty developers continues to evolve so this is great practice in remaining flexible and amenable to change.

In conclusion, it is about time that we allow models of diversity to be put on display for public consumption. We often think of fads when we think of the latest models, strategies, and jargon, but the basic notion of student-centered teaching is still a strong sell. Any current concept, such as MCT, has the potential staying power if there is more practice and evaluation of the appropriate ways to assist faculty in accomplishing it. Even if the glitz and glamour of the fashion industry is no match for the serious talk of diversity, there has to be some awe and excitement about the theory and practice in the area of helping diverse learners succeed in higher education. To follow Ouellett and Sorcinelli's (1995) advice regarding building multicultural faculty development opportunities into programs like their successful Faculty and Teaching Assistant Partnership Program, begin with commitment, not expertise. Even before you or the faculty member find every available model on MCT, agree to be committed to the effort! With enthusiasm and wide-eyed anticipation, faculty developers can help set the stage for the ideas and strategies that include and retain more diverse learners in our multicultural classrooms.

References

Angelo, T. A., & Cross, P.A. (1993). *Classroom assessment techniques: A handbook for college teachers* (2nd ed.). San Francisco: Jossey-Bass.

Bonilla, J.F., & Palmerton, P.R. (2001). A prophet in your own land? Using faculty and student focus groups to address issues of race, ethnicity, and gender in the classroom. In D. Lieberman (Ed.), *To improve the academy, 19*, (pp. 49-68). Bolton, MA: Anker.

Cook, C.E., & Sorcinelli, M.D. (1999, March). Building multiculturalism into teaching-development programs. *AAHE Bulletin, 51*(7), 3-6.

Costa, A.L., & Kallick, B. (1993). Through the lens of a critical friend. *Educational Leadership, 51*(2), 49-51.

Gillespie, K.H., Hilsen, L.R., & Wadsworth, E.C. (2002). *A guide to faculty development: Practical advice, examples, and resources.* Bolton, MA: Anker.

Indiana University Purdue University Indianapolis. (2001). *IUPUI portfolio: IUPUI principles of undergraduate learning.* Retrieved on October 15, 2004 from http://www.iport.iupui.edu/teach/teach_pul.htm

Jackson, B.W. (1988, October). *A model for teaching to diversity.* Unpublished paper from faculty and teaching assistant workshop, University of Massachusetts, Amherst.

Kardia, D. (1998). Becoming a multicultural faculty developer: Reflections from the field. In M. Kaplan (Ed.), *To improve the academy*, *17*, (pp.15-34). Stillwater, OK: New Forums Press.

Marchesani, L.S., & Adams, M. (1992). Dynamics of diversity in the teaching and learning process: A faculty development model for analysis and action. In M. Adams (Ed.), *New Directions in Teaching and Learning*: Vol. 52, *Promoting diversity in college classrooms: Innovative responses for the curriculum, faculty, and institutions.* San Francisco: Jossey-Bass.

Morey, A.I., & Kitano, M.K. (1997). *Multicultural course transformation in higher Education: A broader truth*. Boston: Allyn & Bacon.

Ouellett, M., & Soricinelli, M. D. (1995). Teaching and learning in the diverse classroom: A faculty and TA partnership program. In E. Neal (Ed.), *To improve the academy, 14,* (pp. 205-219). Stillwater, OK: New Forums Press.

Turner, C.S.V., & Myers, S.L. (2000). *Faculty of color in academe: Bittersweet success.* Boston: Allyn and Bacon.

Zeichner, K., & Liston, D. (1987). Teaching student teachers to reflect. *Harvard Educational Review, 57*(1), 23-48.

Natasha Flowers is the acting director of the Office for Multicultural Professional Development and an Instructional Design Specialist, Office of Professional Development, Center for Teaching and Learning, Indiana University Purdue University Indianapolis.

Chapter 31

Proving Diversity Classes Make a Difference: Effective Assessment of Students' Learning

Sherwood Smith

This chapter presents information on a particular aspect of the assessment of student learning from a diversity requirement course focusing on social justice and issues of diversity. The assessment of the course focuses on measuring how well it achieved the stated objectives, and the evaluation focuses on collecting information to improve effectiveness so that "the result of this process are data, which when systematically analyzed become the basis for determining policy and practice" (Schuh & Upcraft ,1998, p. 3).

There were multiple sections of the course each semester with the enrollment limit at 20 students per sections. The courses ran for seven weeks and met in three hour sessions once per week, plus one session each semester during which all students enrolled attended. The course is one of several university diversity required courses the author taught at the graduate and undergraduate level. The focus of the course was to examine social justice issues through the lens of race using *Experiencing race, class and gender in the United States* edited by Virginia Cyrus (2000) as the course text. The intention was to foster critical self-reflection on individual identities (Helms, 1984; Sue & Sue, 1990) and to understand issues of power and privilege (McIntosh, 1995; Spring 1994) that would reduce prejudice and encourage behavior that supports equity. According to Banks "A key goal of multicultural education is to help individuals gain greater self-understanding by viewing themselves from the perspective of other cultures" (p.1).

The material presented in this essay focuses on the assessment of students' learning, attainment of stated course objectives and self-reported changes in students' awareness or understanding relating to racial and cultural issues.

This chapter aims to:

1. Define the course and the rationale for the evaluation process
2. Present the ethical, political, and logistical concerns of assessment

3. Describe the evaluation outcomes
4. Summarize the key concepts in the process

The readers will gain:

1. Understanding of the purposes of creating an assessment tool to measure the success of a diversity and social justice curriculum.
2. Understanding of the political issues that impact the design of an assessment tool.
3. Understanding of a framework to utilize in considering the effectiveness of different responses in "leveraging" support for social justice curriculum

Purpose of the Program

The curriculum fits within the general field of multicultural education because it seeks to increase students' understanding of multiple cultural perspectives within personal systems of values and beliefs as part of the fundamental process of higher education's institutional structures (Adams & Welsch, 1999). Multicultural education is a central component because it "is not intended to simply teach about people but to enhance such cognitive capacities as analysis, synthesis, perspective taking, and ultimately, to enable critical interpretation and contextual understanding" (Adams & Welsch, 1993, p. i). For the purpose of this chapter, I will not provide in depth theories of moral development (Perry, 1981), transformative learning (Mezirow, 1978 & 1991), college student development (Austin, 1993), or racial and ethic identity development (Helm, 1984; Ortiz, & Rhodes, 2000; Ponterotto & Petersen, 1993). Each of these areas can impact the classroom in a variety of ways (Wahl, 2000). In general, it should be understood that there are a range of developmental issues related to all aspects of individual and group identities that affect classroom climate (Tatum, 1992) and learning outcomes (Hansman, Jackson, Grant, & Spencer, 1999). One major theme in the literature that is not covered in this chapter is the impact of the over-representation of faculty of color in diversity focused courses. There is significant evidence that students respond differently to faculty of color, both in the classroom and on evaluations (Turner & Meyers, 2000).

Assessment, like any evaluation process, has multiple levels of focus ranging from describing student reactions to measuring predefined outcomes (Brown & Kysilka, 2002; Tuckman, 1988). According to Carr and Kemmis, "one of the obvious reasons why decisions about education 'means' are always value laden is that they always incorporate attitudes towards other people and, therefore, they cannot be assessed in terms instrumental values alone" (1986, p.76). This is especially true of the assessment of a required diversity course at the university level. Entire books such as *Discrimination: Opposing View Points Series* (William, 1997) or *Debating Points: Race and Ethnic Relations* (Tischler, 2000) are dedicated to the debates concerning multicultural issues that are in danger of being over simplified into two opposing viewpoints. This is especially true of the assessment of a required diversity course at the university level. Entire books such as *Taking Sides* (Monk, 1996) or *Discrimination: Opposing View Points Series* (William, 2003) are dedicated to the debates of diversity and multicultural education being a benefit to US society, or a liability to our national identity. It is a debate often framed as a conflict between the freedom of the individual and the need of particular groups. This framing ignored the embedded issues of power and privilege regarding who gets to frame the issue.

Ethical, Political and Logistical Concerns to Assessing the Course

The goal of effective education is the alignment of assessment frameworks with clearly defined course objective and educational mission. In this manner, curriculum, teaching, and assessment are woven together (Brown & Kysilka, 2002). The questions about effective education reflect the desired outcomes of specific efforts toward a defined set of concerns. By applying a variety of categories and criteria of evaluation, educators attempt to understand the qualitative and quantitative impacts of actions, attitudes, and social dynamics of particular contexts. To do this, one must raise specific questions about the issues of power, culture, and context that impact on our methods of evaluation (Brown & Kysilka, 2002; Cerervo, 1988). The present study works from the belief that assessment in a social justice diversity curriculum begins with defining points of power around who decides that certain experiences are meaningful and that certain measurements are valid. For this reason, a separate instrument was designed with input from faculty and students.

One goal for the Race and Culture course was to obtain a permanent course number and a formal academic department home. The course had been listed as a "Special Topics" course within two different departments. In order to pass review for a permanent course number, there had to be approval from both college and university curriculum committees. The university approval process involved a review of curriculum content, course quality, student demand, and course placement within the mission of the department and institution.

The course was clearly linked to the institutional goals, mission, and vision. These connections were critical to building the justification for permanent course status as part of meeting the mission in the form of "Our Common Ground " statement (http://www.uvm.edu/about_uvm/?Page=values.html). The University's goal "to promote the examination and understanding of diverse perspectives and experiences to prepare our students to live in harmony with others in an increasingly pluralistic society" (http://www.uvm.edu/about_uvm/?Page=mission.html) for example.

Rationale for Assessment Methodologies

This assessment process addresses four areas (Cervero, 1988, p. 145):

1. Program characteristics associated with outcomes
2. Learner satisfaction
3. Learner knowledge, skills, and attitudes
4. Application of learning after course completion

A decision was made to use an evaluation specific to this course rather than the standard institution form. This was done for two reasons. First, the standard form did not address the special politics of the content of the course. Second, part of the purpose of the evaluation was to support the process of gaining committee approval for a permanent course number. Course evaluations had been done since the program's inception in 1988. However, there was no process for summarizing the data over time, and questions needed to be reworked over the years to be consistent with the current course curriculum goals and objectives. The revision to the course standardized the curriculum and clarified the course's four learning objectives:

1. To be able to reflect on the development of [students'?] understanding and awareness of race, gender, class, sexual identity, and culture in their lives.
2. To be able to critically examine how people of ethnically diverse cultures have shaped the U.S. culture, and to make explicit the impact of those cultural factors in our present day U.S. society, specifically by using race and racism as examples.
3. To be able to speak to the interrelationships of racism and other forms of social injustice.
4. To be able to identify further areas of study on issues of social justice.

A limitation to doing the course evaluation was the concern about the evaluation taking too much time from the course. A combination of qualitative and quantitative methods was used to more effectively record the students' experience. Summary evaluation by students was all the more critical given the social and political issues. For many of the quantitative questions, a five point Likert-type scale was used to clarify the strength of agreement and disagreement with the questions. The scale intentional allowed for the "undecided" option so as to assess the level of ambiguity.

Quantitative data provides information that permits graphic representations of larger pools of information in traditional graphic displays and allows for statistical analysis of the questions and responses. The limitations to the quantitative data were recognized due to the lack of contextual information the students can provide with their answers. According to Sue and Sue, "statistical criteria may seem adequate in specific instances, but they are fraught with hazards and problems. For one thing, they fail to take into account differences in time, community standards, and cultural values" critical to the process (1990, p.9). The qualitative section focused heavily on the stated learning objectives and less on students' own development perspectives. Given the use of the evaluation as a measure of the course's success at meeting its described objectives, public image requirements and limits of time, money and size, this was a conscious decision (Lambert, 2003).

Qualitative evidence/data was collected from open-ended questions. It gives voice (Belenky, 1997) to student experiences that are both cognitive and emotional. It also avoids the problem of creating an instrument of assessment solely based on predefined questions. In addition, by asking questions that address the same issues in both the quantitative section and qualitative sections, open-ended responses act as consistency checks for the results from the information obtained from the Likert-type scales. For example, qualitative and quantitative questions intentional covered the same concepts:

Quantitative:	I felt the instructor treated me with dignity and respect.
Qualitative:	In this class did you feel a sense of mutuality, participation, passivity or alienation among participants? Please explain.

Figure 1

This question acknowledges power relationships as an important issue in the evaluation and explores students' responses.

In addition to student assessment of course aspects, their overall political outlook about multicultural education provides rich data about the politics involved with this type of work. The debate continues as to whether a multicultural curriculum is beneficial or is "an irritant" (Adam & Welsch, 1993, p.53), or whether multicultural courses like "diversity-training programs are counter productive" (Damask, N. & Damask, J. 1993, p.185). The negative critiques of multicultural education range from the more popularist critique (Limbaugh III, 1992; D'Souza, 2002; Sowell, 1981) to the more academic challengers calling it "compulsory chapel" (Ravitch, 1990), a "menace," and "Trojan horse" (Schmidt, 1997). Its purposes are described as damaging for White Americans (Auster, 1993) or as a crutch for minorities (Steele, 1990). Others have claimed that it represents the "disuniting of America" (Schelesinger Jr., 1991) through the disruption of common beliefs and values central to our country. Because it is thought to possess any one of these negative attributes by some university faculty, part of the role the assessment plays is to disprove these accusations where possible.

Multicultural education's social justice focus requires that it seeks to present information that conflicts with the historically dominant canon in U.S. education, and as such it has a social action component (Banks, 1994).

Students cannot learn to think critically if they are not provided with multiple perspectives for analysis and contrast. When educators adopt "a framework that's process of self-understanding excludes critically questioning the content of such understanding, the interpretive approach cannot assess the extent to which any existing forms of communication may be systematically distorted by prevailing social, cultural, or political conditions" (Carr & Kemmis 1986, p. 135).

Much of the collected data could be analyzed using traditional forms of analysis beginning with the basic median, mean, and mode. This approach can be flawed in that it discounts the importance of cultural, social or political variables (Carr & Kemmis, 1986).

Unlike more traditional courses, the students partaking in multicultural education are engaged at an emotional level (Hansman, 1999; Tatum, 1992). The data can present the positive outcomes of this self-reflection (Schon, 1983) and the transformative processes that occur (Meizrow, 1991). This does not mean that the course imposes a narrow set of political values on the students (Ravitch, 1990) but rather challenges them to understand a larger set of perspectives than they had previously known or understood. It is impossible for students to an understanding of multiple perspectives and critical analysis of information if they are provided with a homogeneous and culturally limited perspective. Such a notion is a contradiction to excellence in education.

Evaluation Outcomes

The evaluation questions fall into three large categories:

Demographic Questions

1. To benefit a more detailed analysis based on different population variables
2. To support instructors to better understand changes in the population of students
3. To help students understand the differences within and outside their own group
4. To address institutionally specific concerns.

In this case it was important to understand which colleges had students enrolled in the course and in what proportions. The population demographics serve to address the political issue of who was being served by the course (and who lacked representation). The course design represents an introductory level of complexity. The intention was to serve students as early as possible in their academic career. Data showed that students, especially those in the arts and sciences and graduate students, were taking the course even though it was not a requirement. Overall the demographics mirrored the university in terms of the numbers of gender and race giving validity to the results accurately reflecting the overall population. A unique issue was the in-state to out-of-state ratio. Since this institution has a 55:45 ratio, there was a question as to whether the attitudes of in-state versus out-of-state students represented a significant difference from the overall population. As Table 1 illustrates, they did not. There was also an interest in understanding the amount of preparation through related courses the student had prior to this course. This understanding aimed to demonstrate the need for this introductory course at the college level.

Course assessment examines whether the course met the stated goals.

Course Student Objectives

1. To increase one's awareness and understanding of the current issues in American (U.S.) society with regard to racism, sexism, homophobia, and classism.
2. To increase one's understanding of the historical roots of racism, sexism, homophobia, and classism in American society.

Table 1. Attitudes of In-state Versus Out-of-state Students

Example Question 6

The course increased my understanding of the historical roots of race relations and the impact of that history on the present structure of U.S. society.

The course increased my understanding of the historical roots of race relations and the impact of that history on the present structure of U.S. society.	4.13	4.0	4		36.3	48.1	8.4	6.4	0.8
	Average	Median	Mode		SA=5	A=4	U=3	D=2	SD=1

3) To enhance one's understanding of how people of different cultures have been affected by, adapted to, and shaped by U.S. culture.

Example Question 7

The course increased my understanding of institutional racism.

This course increased my understanding of institutional racism.	4.19	4.0	4		37.9	47.7	10.3	3.3	0.8
	Average	Median	Mode		SA=5	A=4	U=3	D=2	SD=1

4) To increase one's understanding of how language, values, beliefs, and behaviors contribute to racial, cultural, and gender conflict.

Example Question 8

The course explored ways in which language, attitudes, values, beliefs, and practices contribute to racial and ethnic conflict.

The course explored ways in which language, attitudes, values, beliefs and practices contribute to racial and ethnic conflict.	4.37	4.0	4		46.8	45.8	5	1.3	0.3
	Average	Median	Mode		SA=5	A=4	U=3	D=2	SD=1

Table 1 (continued)

5) To strengthen one's knowledge and skills base for living in a multicultural society, combating racism, and dealing effectively with cultural conflict in a variety of settings.

Example Question 23

I have thought about my role in stopping oppression and discrimination in new ways.

I have thought about my role in stopping oppression and discrimination in new ways.	4.20	4.0	4		41.3	43.1	10.3	4.8	0.5
	Average	Median	Mode		SA=5	A=4	U=3	D=2	SD=1

Example Question 9

The course increased my understanding of the contributions of people from racially diverse cultures.

The course increased my understanding of the contributions of people from racially diverse cultures.	4.11	4.0	4		36.2	45	11.5	5	0.6
	Average	Median	Mode		SA=5	A=4	U=3	D=2	SD=1

6) Student Outcomes examine students attitudes about the course experience overall

Example Question 16

To understand the course content, I found the text [*Experiencing Race, Class and Gender in the United States*] was very helpful

To understand course contents, I found the text was very helpful to me.	3.73	4.0	4		26.4	41	21.3	7.4	3.8
	Average	Median	Mode		SA=5	A=4	U=3	D=2	SD=1

Example Question 21

This is an important course and I believe it should continue to be a requirement for UVM students.

This is an important course and I believe it should continue to be a requirement for UVM students.	4.23	5.0	5		54	25.8	11.8	5	2.6
	Average	Median	Mode		SA=5	A=4	U=3	D=2	SD=1

Summary of Key Concepts

The assessment tool served multiple purposes:

1. Program characteristics associated with outcomes

   * The assessment addressed the specific critiques of the program as being disconnected from the academic mission of the institution, as anti-White, not respecting students' perspectives, or lacking in academic quality of instruction. The data showed that the majority of students agreed that a variety of teaching materials and methods were used (92.6%). They were able to complete 76.6%of the readings for the course.

2. Learner satisfaction

   * Measuring students' attitudes about the course instruction and content showed that almost all students (95.1%) felt included and able to express their opinion; 95.4% felt the instructor treated them with dignity and respect.

3. Learner knowledge, skills, and attitudes

   * Measuring self-assessment of changes in their awareness or knowledge in regards to several types of bias illustrated that students reported an increase linked to the course in their understanding of sexism (86.7%), institutional racism (84.7%), homophobia (73.3%), Affirmative Action (52.9), race relations, and other issues of cultural diversity (87.8%).

4. Application of learning after the course

   *Students' self-reported awareness of the possibility for social justice actions was measured by the percentage who had thought of their role in stopping oppression (84.4%).

Outcomes of the assessment demonstrated that:

Assessment and evaluation have social, cultural, and political components, as was stated at the beginning of this chapter (Brown & Kysilka 2002; Tuckman, 1988). The Race and Culture course has challenged our national attitudes and beliefs about how people are different and has encouraged students to think critically about and reflect on their personal and professional actions (Ayvazian, 1997; Berger, 1967; Banks, 1995). The quantitative and qualitative evidence clearly proved that the course increased student self and social awareness, comfort with the complexity of social issues, and the understanding that as citizens they have a responsibility to act when they know of an injustice.

The quantitative data showed that student views of the professor (78%) were positive. They experienced significant new learning on issues of discrimination they had never considered (73 % agreed), and the overall impact on the on the campus environment was positive (75% agreed the course should be required).

The qualitative information collected indicated that students were satisfied, felt significant learning had occurred, and were able to articulate the role they play in maintaining a just community:

1. There is significant opportunity to develop critical thinking skills by the presentation of information on the historical, political, psychological, and social nature of prejudice and discrimination.

   "How to think more about what I say or do before I do it."

   "To take a step back and look at the big picture."

   "Discrimination is a problem that can be solved by talking about and discussing the issues."

2. That ALL students benefit from a diversity requirement in that they obtain new knowledge, critical thinking, and motivation to act in ways that promote social justice.

   "Racism exists and we all need to be aware and need to stand up to people who say things that are hurtful to others."

   "Discrimination is something that can effect everyone. It is a simple matter of opening your eyes to view it."

   "Respect people as I want to be respected."

   "That people need to continue to discuss cultural problems that exist and how we can

   deal with them."

3. Students are aware of both the limitations and benefits of a one-course requirement.

   "That is only a five week course."

   "Long class, needed a little bit more variety of activities."

   "Hard topic because there are no right answers."

   "It is too short."

4. The climate was not one that silenced students, especially White students, and learners felt free to express the viewpoints and were open to reflecting those espoused by others.

   "I felt that the group bonded well and fed off each other

   I felt like I could express myself

   Mutuality, I think that there was a lot of trust

> I felt we were for the most part participative and interested in what we were discussing."

The quotes of students above contained in the qualitative evidence that gives a personal voice to these social and developmental issues. Student viewpoints in the form of direct quotes provide challenges to any questions of misinterpretation and misrepresentation of our students' experiences or learning. Bank's model of multicultural education would label these students as getting involved in social action (Banks, 2000) and increasing in their social justice awareness (Sleeter,1996). Both concepts explain how new knowledge has impacted students' understanding of their own identities (Helms, 1984) as linked to responsibility for their action or inaction. The assessment proved that students' understanding of cultural, historical, and social issues changed in the positive ways that students were more aware of their own biases and more critical of the information they received from all sources.

References

Adams, J.Q., & Welsch, J.R. (Eds.). (1999). *Cultural diversity: Curriculum, classroom and climate*. Maccomb: Illinois Staff and Curriculum.

Astin, A. W. (1993). *What matters in college?* San Francisco: Jossey-Bass.

Auster, L. (1993). Multiculturalism discriminates against whites. In M.E. Williams (Ed.), *Discrimination: Opposing viewpoints series*. San Diego, CA: Greenhaven Press.

Ayvazian, A., & Tatum, B.D. (1997). Diversity-training programs are productive. In M.E. Williams (Ed.), *Discrimination: Opposing viewpoints series*. San Diego, CA: Greenhaven Press.

Banks, J. (1995). The historical reconstruction of knowledge about race. *Educational Researcher, 24,* 15-22.

Banks, J. (2000). *An introduction to multi-cultural education* (3rd ed.). Boston: Allyn & Bacon.

Benkley, M., Clinchy, B., Goldberger, N., & Tarule, J. (1986). *Women's ways of knowing: The development of self, voice, and mind.* New York: Basic Books.

Berger, P., & Luckman, T. (1967). *The social construction of reality: A treatise in the sociology of knowledge*. New York: Anchor Books.

Brown, S.C., & Kysilka, M.L. (2002).*Applying multicultural and global concepts in the classroom and beyond.* Boston: Allyn & Bacon

Caplan, P. (1993). *Lifting a ton of feathers*. ON: University of Toronto Press.

Carr, W., & Kemmis, S. (1986). *Becoming critical: Education, knowledge and action research*. London: Falmer Press.

Cervero, R. (1988). *Effective continuing education for professionals*. San Francisco: Jossey-Bass

Cyrus, V. (Ed). (2000). *Race, class and gender in the United States*. Mountain View, CA: Mayfield.

D'Souza, D. (2002). *Letters to a young conservative*. New York: BasicBooks.

Damask, N., & Damask, J. (1993). Diversity-training programs are counterproductive. In M.E. Williams (Ed.), *Discrimination: Opposing viewpoints series*. San Diego, CA: Greenhaven Press.

Hansman, C.A., Jackson, M.H., Grant, D.F., & Spencer, L.E. (1999). Assessing graduate students' sensitivity to gender, race, equality and diversity: Implications for curriculum development. *College Student Journal, 33,* 261-268.

Helms, J.E. (1984). Towards a theoretical explanation of the effects of race counseling: A black and white model. *The Counseling Psychologist, 12,* 153-164.

hooks, b. (1993). Multiculturalism can help end discrimination. In M.E. Williams (Ed.), *Discrimination: Opposing viewpoints series*. San Diego, CA: Greenhaven Press.

Lambert, R.G. (2003). Considering purpose and intended use when making evaluations of assessments: A response to Dickinson. *Educational Researcher, 32,* 23-26.

Limbaugh, R. III. (1992). *The way things ought to be*. New York: Pocket Books.

McIntosh, P. (1995) White privilege, male privilege. In M.L. Anderson & P.H. Collins (Eds.), *Race, class, gender* (2nd ed.). Belmont, CA: Wadsworth Publishing.

McIntyre, A. (1997). *Making meaning of whiteness: Exploring racial identity with white teachers*. Albany: State University of New York Press.

Mezirow, J. (1978). Perspective transformation. *Adult Education, 28,* 100-109.

Mezirow, J. (1991). *Transformative dimensions of adult learning*. San Francisco: Jossey-Bass.

Ortiz, A.M., & Rhodes, R.A. (2000). Deconstructing whiteness as part of multicultural education framework: From theory to practice. *Journal of College Student Development, 41,* 81-91.

Perry, W. (1981). Cognitive and ethical growth: the making of meaning. In A. Chickering (Ed.), *The modern American college: Responding to the new realities of diverse students and a changing society*. San Francisco: Jossey-Bass.

Ponterotto, J., & Pedersen, P. (1993). *Preventing prejudice: A guide for counselors and educators*. Newbury Park, CA: Sage.

Ravitch, D. (1990). Multiculturalism: E pluribus plures. *American Scholar, 59,* 337-354.

Schlesinger, A., Jr. (1991). A dissent on multicultural education. *Partisan Review, 58,* 630-634.

Schmidt, A. (1997). *The menace of multiculturalism: Trojan horse in America*. Westport, CT: Praeger.

Schuh, J.H., & Upcraft, M.L. (1998). Facts and myths about assessment in student affairs. *About Campus, 3,* 2-8.

Schon, D. (1983). *The reflective practitioner: How professionals think in action.* New York: Basic Books.

Sleeter, C.E. (1996). *Multicultural education as social activism.* Albany: State Univeristy of New York Press.

Steele, S. (1990). *The content of our character: A new vision of race in America.* New York: HarperCollins.

Sowell, T. (1981). *Ethnic America: A history.* New York: Basic Books.

Spring, J. (1994). *Deculturalization and the struggle for equality: A brief history of the education of dominated cultures in the United States.* New York: McGraw-Hill.

Sue, D. W., & Sue, D. (1990). *Counseling the culturally different: Theory and practice* (2nd ed.). New York: John Wiley & Sons.

Tatum, B.D. (1992). Talking about race, learning about racism: The application of racial identity development theory in the classroom. *Harvard Educational Review, 62,* 1-24.

Tischler, H. (2000). *Debating points: Race and ethnic relations.* Saddle River, NJ: Prentice Hall.

Tuckman, B. (1988). *Testing for teachers.* SanDiego, CA: Hardcourt Brace Jovanovich.

Turner, C.S.V., & Meyers, S.M., Jr. (2000). *Faculty of color in academe: Bittersweet success.* Boston: Allyn & Bacon.

University of Vermont Race and Culture (2002). *Course information and syllabus.* Retrieved September, 15, 2000, from http://www.uvm.edu/~culture/site/frameset/frameset_course_info.html

Wahl, A-M., Perez, E.T., Deegan, M.J., Sanchez, T.W., & Applegate, C. (2000). The controversial classroom: Institutional resources and pedagogical strategies for a race relations course. *Teaching Sociology, 28,* 316-332.

Williams, M. (1997). *Discrimination: Opposing viewpoints series.* San Diego, CA. Greenhaven Press.

Sherwood Smith is an assistant professor in the College of Education and Social Services at the University of Vermont.

Chapter 32

A Framework for Inclusive Teaching in STEM Disciplines

Lois A. Reddick, Wayne Jacobson, Angela Linse, and Darryl Yong

A wide body of literature exists recounting the ways in which inclusive teaching practices and principles benefit students and positively impact learning, student retention, and professional development across disciplines; however, Science, Technology, Engineering and Mathematics (STEM) faculty do not readily accept the traditional approach of examining course content from multiple perspectives. In this chapter, we propose a Framework for Inclusive Teaching in STEM Disciplines that reflects the contexts of teaching in these disciplines and extends James Banks' Five Dimensions of Multicultural Education to the distinct needs of STEM faculty in their classes.

Different Ways of Approaching This Chapter

In this chapter, we provide faculty developers with a framework for promoting more inclusive teaching in their work with faculty in Science, Technology, Engineering, and Math (STEM). Depending on your background, you may find it useful to start at different points in the chapter (Figure 1). After reviewing Section 1, people more at home with the literature of diversity and multiculturalism might want to go directly to Section 2, where we briefly describe James Banks' Five Dimensions of Multicultural Education (1996). People familiar with the STEM literature may want go from Section 1 directly to Section 3, where we propose a conceptual framework for inclusive teaching in STEM disciplines. Instructional development specialists may fit into both these categories (or neither very comfortably); people primarily interested in helping STEM faculty develop more inclusive teaching practices will find these concerns addressed in Section 4, where we provide examples of entry points for talking about inclusive teaching with STEM faculty.

Section 1: Why Focus on Inclusive Teaching in STEM Disciplines?

The lack of racial and ethnic diversity among students and faculty in STEM disciplines is a well-documented, persistent challenge for leaders in STEM education, business, government, and industry (American Association for the Advancement of Science [AAAS], 1989; Commission on the Advancement of Women and Minorities in Science, Engineering and Technology Development [CAWMSET], 2000; George, 1996; National Science Foundation & Department of Education [NSF/DOE], 1980; Rutherford & Ahlgren, 1990). Many variables impact the population of STEM degree recipients, but three in particular inform our discussion of the need for a specific focus on inclusive teaching in STEM: demographic patterns, retention related issues, and economic trends.

Demographics

Current and predicted statistics for student populations in the U.S. highlight the need to attract a more representative sample of students to the STEM disciplines. U.S. citizens are currently the primary student population in postsecondary institutions in the U.S.[1] (National Center for Education Statistics [NCES], 2003), and the white male segment of that population serves as the primary source of students in STEM disciplines. However, trends in the U.S. population indicate widespread changes for future student populations. The U.S. Census Bureau predicts a decrease in the white (non-Hispanic) segment of the U.S. population from 74% in 1995 to 64% in 2020, and to 53% in 2050. By 2050, the Latino population will have grown the most, and the Afri-

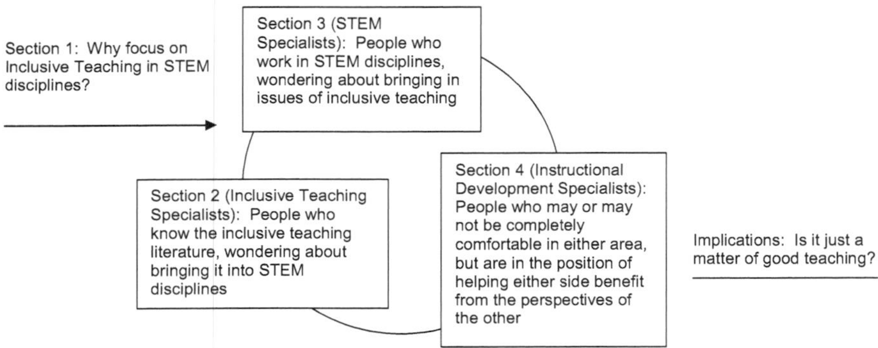

Figure 1. A Reader's Guide to Whose Questions are Addressed in Each Section of the Chapter

can-American population will nearly double in size. The traditional college-age population will grow by 16% between 2000 and 2015 and, of these potential new students, 80% will be non-white and nearly 50% will be Hispanic (Business-Higher Education Forum [BHEF], 2002).

Even without the predicted changes to future populations, the student demographics are already shifting. Over the past 20 years, the proportion of white students enrolled in U.S. undergraduate institutions decreased, falling from 80 % in 1978 to 70 % in 1997, while the numbers for underrepresented minorities increased from 16% to 22% (National Science Board [NSB], 2002). Additionally, women outnumber men in undergraduate enrollment for every racial and ethnic group (NSB, 2002) and over 57% of undergraduate students have characteristics that identify them as non-traditional students (NCES, 2002).

Retention

The number of degrees awarded in the natural sciences and engineering has steadily decreased since the mid-1980s (NSB, 2002), and projected increases in the population of 18 to24 year-olds will not reverse this trend without attention to the ability of STEM fields to attract and retain a broader, more representative portion of the population. Of particular concern are the lower completion rates for women and students from groups traditionally underrepresented in STEM fields (Cohoon, 2001; Montgomery & Barrett, 2002). Students from underrepresented groups switch to other disciplines at higher rates and have lower completion rates than white and Asian American students (Clewell & Campbell, 2002; Seymour & Hewitt, 1997). The National Science Board reports lower retention and degree completion rates in science and engineering for both women and students from underrepresented groups (NSB, 2002).

Some might assume that retention and completion rates are low because the students who change majors or drop out of college are underprepared or incapable of meeting rigorous STEM requirements. In fact, many of those who switch are academically equal to or more advanced than students who stay (Seymour & Hewitt, 1997) and these "switchers" may be opting out of STEM based on negative experiences in college and discouraging observations of STEM professionals (Clewell & Campbell, 2002; Nauta, Epperson, & Kahn, 1998). Still others suggest that non-majority students are simply not interested in STEM careers. However, studies of entering freshmen indicate a relatively even dis-

[1]In 1999-2000, foreign-born students in postsecondary institutions constituted only 11% of the undergraduate student population.

tribution of interest in science and engineering (NSB, 2002), and that white, African American, Asian American, and Latino high school seniors take similar numbers of science and mathematics courses (Clewell & Campbell, 2002).

Economics

The systematically low completion rates for women and minorities, even during economically prosperous times, belies the oft-repeated anecdote that first-generation students attend college and select majors in order to achieve economic prosperity. If future earnings were a promising means to attract students from under-represented groups, we would not have students from groups under-represented in STEM entering the less lucrative social sciences at higher rates (NSB, 2002). It is evident that we cannot rely on the prospect of lucrative careers to rectify the imbalance between general population, student population, and STEM demographics.

Overall, the decrease in degree production by U.S. institutions of higher education has resulted in a failure to keep up with the demands of business, industry, and government for qualified employees (NCES, 2002). In 1998, Dr. Vernon Ehlers, Representative and Vice Chairman, Committee on Science, U.S. House of Representatives, pointed out at a National Science Policy Hearing that a crisis is looming in the U.S. science and engineering enterprise. He predicted that the demand would soon exceed the supply of new scientists and engineers and that the economic health of our nation would suffer as a result. Projections indicate that by 2028, there will be 19 million more jobs than workers adequately prepared to fill them (BHEF, 2002).

Section 2: Banks' Five Dimensions of Multicultural Education

In light of these demographic, retention, and economics related trends, it is important for instructors in STEM disciplines to teach in ways that include all students and encourage them to continue in these disciplines. The reasons that students feel excluded are likely numerous and complex. Our goal is to provide a framework to help instructors identify, assess, and improve teaching practices that are likely to have the greatest impact on retaining underrepresented students in STEM. In developing our Framework for Inclusive Teaching in STEM Disciplines, we have drawn heavily from James Banks' (1996) Dimensions of Multicultural Education.

According to Banks, multicultural education involves attention to five major areas: Content Integration, Knowledge Construction, Prejudice Reduction, Equity Pedagogy, and Empowering School Culture (Table 1). Content Integration promotes the examination of course content from a range of cultural perspectives and is frequently viewed as the salient feature in multicultural education. Knowledge Construction, which extends thinking beyond content, requires both faculty and students to uncover and explore the value-laden assumptions and biases within a discipline. The knowledge construction process challenges the thinker to examine critically not only what is taught, but also the contexts of who, how, why, when, and where.

Prejudice Reduction involves attention to the characteristics of students' racial attitudes and values, and focuses on relationships with and among students. For faculty, prejudice reduction involves identifying potential barriers to student success, emphasizing students' individual strengths, and creating clear expectations for learning in the classroom. Equity Pedagogy addresses the

Table 1. Dimensions of Multicultural Education (Banks, 1996)

Content Integration	*Utilize resources from a diverse range of cultures and groups to illustrate course concepts and ideas.*
Knowledge Construction	*Facilitate students' understanding of the value-laden assumptions and biases operating within a given field or discipline.*
Prejudice Reduction	*Create learning environments that foster students' rejection of negative racial attitudes and values.*
Equity Pedagogy	*Adopt, integrate, and develop a set of teaching skills and techniques that reflect consideration of the full range of cultural perspectives and practices that influence student learning.*
Empowering School Culture	*Re-envision and restructure educational institutions to promote equity in learning and cultivate respect for students' backgrounds and cultural experiences.*

utilization of teaching strategies and techniques that reflect a multiplicity of learning styles and a comprehensive knowledge of the pedagogical skills and practices that have proven effective for the recruitment and retention of underrepresented students.

Finally, Empowering School Culture involves re-envisioning and restructuring educational institutions to promote equity in learning and to cultivate respect for students' backgrounds and cultural experiences. Attention to students' learning on an organizational level implies questioning assumptions about student achievement, and also providing opportunities for meaningful interactions with and among students both academically and socially.

Banks' model has become widely recognized for its relevance to K through 12 settings, and we believe it also has profound implications for STEM disciplines at the college level. However, we have also observed that many STEM faculty do not readily recognize its relevance to teaching in their disciplines. For example, it may not be clear to individual faculty members what their role is in Empowering School Culture or what shape that might take at a research university. It may not be apparent on the surface that issues of Knowledge Construction are also relevant in fields driven largely by scientific and mathematical laws, or how Content Integration, the first of Banks' five principles, is an important consideration when teaching content centered on equations and experimental design.

Section 3: Framework for Inclusive Teaching in STEM Disciplines

We can appreciate the perspective upon which these perceptions are based, and we think it is unfortunate that these misperceptions might cause people to miss the underlying principles upon which Banks' framework is based. As a result, we propose a Framework for Inclusive Teaching in STEM disciplines that draws heavily on Banks' five principles, but extends and applies them to the context of STEM disciplines in higher education. This framework consists of five interrelated dimensions, outlined in Table 2, begins with Accurate Problem Definition.

Accurate Problem Definition

With Problem Definition, we ask STEM faculty to examine course design through a process of inquiry. We begin with two familiar first steps, identifying what is important for students to know, and explicitly articulating why that information is important, but we extend this process by asking faculty to consider the ways in which students achieve mastery in their particular discipline.

This consideration includes the examination of students' learning patterns, the conditions under which students adopt new models of thinking, and the relationships among students' mastery of conceptual knowledge, problem-solving ability, and levels of engagement. We also ask faculty to establish consistency between these learning issues and their course goals, content, activities, and evaluation methods through attention to what is taught, modeled, and graded, since students typically identify what is important by observing these three areas. For example, research shows that expert problem solvers develop conceptual maps prior to tackling problems while novices begin by immediately

Table 2. Dimensions of Inclusive Teaching in STEM Disciplines

Accurate Problem Definition	*Clearly identify goals, rationales, starting conditions, appropriate design, and principles of implementation to achieve optimal learning outcomes.*
Iterative Design	*Recognize that an effective process is designed to adapt to changing conditions, monitor and respond to feedback, and provide alternate strategies when processes do not function as intended or other obstacles are encountered.*
Expert Practice	*Establish that your design and approach to teaching support effective learning of course content for all students.*
Management of External Constraints	*Anticipate, minimize, or compensate for ways in which teaching and learning processes and outcomes are influenced by environmental factors and other external constraints.*
Comprehensiveness	*Maintain thoroughness and rigor of what is taught, grounded in actual (rather than idealized) conditions.*

attempting to find solutions (Breslow, 2001). Another study indicates that successful problem solvers view mistakes and failure as necessary steps to improve problem solving skills (Born, Revelle, & Pinto, 2002). Armed with this knowledge, an instructor may identify conceptual thinking as a stated goal and discourage students from viewing mistakes as failure. However, if class time, projects, and tests emphasize memorization, repetition, and summative forms of evaluation, then students will likely conclude that memorization, repetition, and perfection are most important.

Iterative Design

The second dimension of our Framework for Inclusive Teaching is the provision of Iterative Design. This dimension asks STEM faculty to recognize that an effective process is designed to adapt to changing conditions, monitor and respond to feedback, and provide alternate strategies when processes do not function as intended or other obstacles are encountered – often making it necessary to provide more than one means to a desired end. This realization can stimulate the need for closely monitoring student learning, and require consideration of multiple means of facilitating student success: for example, some students learn relatively more from interactive lectures, others through peer collaboration, and still others from hands-on experience. Ultimately, this dimension of the framework asks instructors to design learning experiences based not just on how they have taught before or how they originally learned the material themselves, but on the complexity of the learning goals and full range of students' capacities to learn.

A second implication of Iterative Design is that instructors should be prepared to provide appropriate support for those learning outcomes that require particular learning experiences. To return to the example of collaborative design, students who prefer to learn through interactive groups may need little or no additional support to learn effectively on a design team. However, students who prefer to work individually are unlikely to benefit from collaborative work simply by being told to "form a group." Students in this situation are much more likely to learn how to work collaboratively if they are given well-designed support to help them define tasks, assign individual roles and responsibilities to the team, and assess outcomes of the team's work. For example, Born, Revelle, and Pinto (2002) found that successful interventions for improving student performance in biology included weekly workshop groups that were academically rigorous (non-remedial), cooperative (non-competitive), and facilitated by trained student peers who had successfully completed the course and who provided encouragement and guidance without giving answers.

Expert Practice

The third dimension of our Framework for Inclusive Teaching is Expert Practice, defined here as the demonstration that teaching practices are not biased to favor particular outcomes for particular learners, but rather are designed to support effective learning for all students who do what is required for the course. Many instructors may believe that their classrooms provide neutral conditions for learning, but research (Marx, Brown & Steele, 1999) demonstrates that some learners come into STEM classrooms expecting to find it biased against them. Students often expect classrooms to favor students who are most like the instructor (traditionally white and male). With Expert Practice, instructors proactively demonstrate that all students have equal opportunity to learn (not just those who are similar to the instructor).

This demonstration can be as straightforward as making explicit statements that the course design and approach to teaching support all students who do what is required for the course. Another useful practice is for the instructor to make explicit statements about his or her own content related challenges and to identify specific behaviors that led to successful learning. In this way, instructors remind students that the subject matter did not "come naturally" to them, but required learning particular sets of skills, over a certain period of time, and perhaps with a considerable amount of effort. Within this context, effective strategies also include providing students with feedback that is task-specific and not a general confirmation of natural ability. For example, an instructor may tell a student that her thinking demonstrates a clear understanding of a given concept rather than responding with general statements like "good," which can associate performance with student identity and not specific learning.

Management of External Constraints

The fourth dimension of our Framework for Inclusive Teaching is the Management of External Constraints, which involves minimizing or compensating for direct and indirect environmental affects on processes and outcomes. This dimension aids STEM faculty in dealing with the numerous factors, which may only be indirectly related to the instructor's teaching practices, but are affecting the students before they take a course and while they are taking it.

One critical external constraint is student preparation. Students' prior learning experiences are clearly beyond an individual instructor's control, but that limitation does not preclude gathering data on those experiences and taking them into account while teaching. In a study of the predictors of women's higher level career aspirations in mathematics, science, and engineering majors, Nauta, Epperson, and Kahn (1998) found that the relationship between ability and higher level career aspirations could be positively influenced through attention to students' feelings of self-efficacy. They noted that female students had the tendency to view their STEM performances less positively and less accurately than male students, and that aiding these women in developing more accurate and positive pictures of their performances strengthened their commitment to future endeavors in STEM disciplines. While STEM faculty may be unable to control the quality of students' prior STEM experiences, with knowledge of such studies, they can positively influence the ways in which students view their learning potential and their past and present performances.

Another important external constraint on student learning is the presence of other students. Montgomery and Barrett (2002) found that negative peer interactions (for example, feelings of isolation and perceptions of resentment from male students) have detrimental effects on female students in undergraduate science and engineering courses. If particular students are left on their own, or are routinely assigned less desirable roles on project teams, these students will quickly get the message that their contributions are not valued. Similarly, students who volunteer answers or raise questions during lecture, but observe that other students routinely disregard or disrespect their contributions, may easily conclude that they are not welcome in the class.

Outside the classroom, External Constraints include departmental factors such as advising practices and mentoring opportunities. Women, for example, generally report fewer opportunities for positive student/faculty interactions and supportive advising (Montgomery & Barrett, 2002). Department facilities can also be a factor, such as whether there are adequate facilities for students to work together between classes, or even a sufficient number of women's restrooms. In another case, a department review revealed female students' frustration over the number of male students using the computer lab to access Internet pornography.

For an individual instructor, control over these External Constraints is limited, but minimizing their effects or otherwise compensating for them is still possible. Those that are related to classroom learning can be addressed by the instructor's decisions about how to establish groups, for example, or how to respond to individual students' contributions to class. Out-of-class constraints may be harder to deal with, but instructors can bring departmental issues to the attention of appropriate decision makers (in the case of issues such as study areas or restrooms), or take the lead in establishing an ethic of professionalism, respect for fellow students, and compliance with the university's stated policies (in a case such as Internet pornography).

Comprehensiveness

The fifth dimension of our Framework for Inclusive Teaching is Comprehensiveness: ensuring that what is taught is rigorously grounded in actual (rather than idealized) conditions, which include contexts in which learning outcomes, applications, or practices will be used, and also the ethical or social implications of such practices. Instructors who avoid discussing the ethical and social relevance of their work do a disservice to their students by communicating that students who are concerned with these issues are somehow less important members of the professional or scientific community.

Similarly, it may not occur to some instructors that the history and development of their discipline has been shaped by a diverse community of professionals and scholars, and attention to thoroughness and rigor requires that these contributions to the profession be duly acknowledged. In a course, the emphasis remains on what one does as an expert in the field rather than on who one is; however, it is still important to proactively demonstrate that people of all types have been successful. To give one example, a white male professor can show through attention to principles of Expert Practice that successful learning is not contingent upon being either white or male. He may also utilize scholars of color as guest lecturers, or former students of color as peer mentors. One study found that the mere presence of women proctoring a difficult mathematics exam diminished the impact of stereotype threat and underperformance for female test takers (Marx, Brown, & Steele, 1999). This attention to Comprehensiveness adds the positive message that it is possible to succeed as a female or a person of color, provided that the learner is willing and enabled to do the work of learning in the discipline.

Section 4: Talking about Inclusive Teaching with STEM Faculty

We suggest that faculty developers can provide leadership to help bring more inclusive practices into STEM classrooms. To support that goal, we propose our Framework for Inclusive Teaching as a tool for faculty developers with two distinct uses. First, this framework provides a set of guiding questions that directly relate to contexts of teaching in STEM disciplines, allowing faculty developers to address issues such as course goals, rationale, starting conditions, and appropriate design – areas in which many faculty developers are already successfully working. Beyond that, we suggest using this framework to define not just what we talk about with STEM faculty, but how we talk about it when we work with them.

Our framework begins with Accurate Problem Definition (Table 3) because knowledge construction for many in the STEM disciplines involves questions of inquiry: problem definition, design, data collection, and analysis. Since problem definition provides a familiar language for STEM faculty to reflect on knowledge construction, faculty developers can begin by making our case to them on these terms.

In addition to using familiar terminology, we also propose establishing a case for inclusive teaching by drawing on a central feature of knowledge construction within these disciplines: referral to evidence and recognized sources of data. For example, faculty developers may use criteria from the National Science Foundation (NSF), the Accreditation Board of Engineering and Technology (ABET), career surveys that show the importance of working collaboratively, or discipline-specific arguments for greater diversity within the

Table 3. Dimensions of Inclusive Teaching in STEM Disciplines and the Dimensions of Multicultural Education (Banks, 1996) to which they are most closely related.

Dimensions of Multicultural Education		Inclusive Teaching Framework
Knowledge Construction Process	⇔	**Accurate Problem Definition**
Equity Pedagogy	⇔	**Iterative Design**
Prejudice Reduction	⇔	**Expert Practice**
Empowering School Culture	⇔	**Management of External Constraints**
Content Integration	⇔	**Comprehensiveness**

field. Other sources of data could include research on the effectiveness of current programs and practices. For example, Seymour and Hewitt (1997) identified reasons females leave STEM disciplines as including changed interest, being "turned off," poor teaching, and inadequate advising. By starting with the data, and making faculty aware of the large body of research available to them, it is possible to present exclusive teaching as a problem for which they need to design a solution. Faculty developers can also challenge STEM faculty to plan their courses in ways that allow them to collect data on the inclusive nature of their own teaching. Because of the ways that knowledge is constructed within these disciplines, this approach opens an avenue for change that is both familiar and valued.

Our framework also proposes approaching faculty with consideration for Iterative Design, acknowledging that faculty learn and change in different ways and at different rates. Some will change on the basis of empirical evidence while others may be more motivated by assessing student outcomes. In any case, faculty change, like student learning, is rarely immediate or completely based on a single experience.

Our own Expert Practice as faculty developers must include a healthy respect for faculty defenses against perceived prejudice and help STEM faculty manage the threat of talking about diversity. Just as students may feel a learning situation is prejudiced against their success, so faculty may feel they have been pre-judged as resistant to change, uninterested in diversity, or unconcerned about social justice. (Just as students may have good reasons for their perceptions of prejudice, so too faculty may have experienced being labeled in these ways.) One approach is to explicitly acknowledge unspoken accusations and share experiences managing this perceived threat. Another approach is to point out ways in which faculty are already teaching inclusively, even though they might not have thought of their teaching within this framework.

Additionally, we need to acknowledge the External Constraints influencing faculty change, and be prepared to extend our consulting beyond an individual instructor. Key elements for consideration include the departmental climate for faculty — not only for women and faculty of color, but also for those who place a higher value on learner-centered teaching, Scholarship of Teaching and Learning, and non-traditional STEM approaches to achieving learning outcomes (for example, group processes, interdisciplinary problem-solving, communication, and decision making). We can also help faculty who are committed to inclusive teaching become their own advocates by helping them gather and present data in ways that will help them make effective cases for change within their departments.

Finally, we have found that faculty members who equate inclusive teaching with content integration often conclude that the literature on inclusive teaching is not relevant to their teaching. We challenge this conclusion, but also recognize that for many faculty members it is not the most compelling place to begin. Our model recognizes this by addressing the issue in terms of Comprehensiveness, and by allowing the other four dimensions to establish a context for inclusive practices, rather than by placing it first where it may more easily be seen as the primary focus of the model.

Section 5: "Is Inclusive Teaching Really Just Effective Teaching?"

We recognize that it might be possible to review our Framework for Inclusive Teaching in STEM Disciplines and conclude that inclusive teaching is synonymous with effective teaching. We can agree with that conclusion, but only in part. We are not suggesting that someone who is teaching effectively is, incidentally, also teaching inclusively. Inclusive teaching represents a set of principles, goals, and practices grounded in research, experience, and commitments to social justice. Within this broader set of principles, goals, and practices is a subset that might be identified as effective teaching practices. Because effective teaching fits within this broader framework of inclusive teaching, there will not be a conflict between the two, and in fact it may be difficult to distinguish one from the other simply by looking at a random sample of teaching practices.

However, inclusive teaching adds to effective teaching a particular definition of effectiveness, and also a framework for understanding why teaching is effective. This framework in turn helps solve problems, extends effective practices to other contexts, and facilitates adapting to change. For example, a faculty member may teach a course effectively without consciously considering inclusiveness, but by defining the problem well, this faculty member has created a learning environment that effectively welcomes and includes all students. However, being effective in one course does not guarantee being effective in a different course, at a different level, or with a different group of students. Inclusive teaching provides categories for description and analysis when something is discovered to be ineffective (even though that instructor has been effective at another time, in another course, or with another group of students), and helps faculty to be explicit in their decision making about teaching and going beyond "doing what worked last time."

The Inclusive Teaching framework also provides entry points for faculty who wish to be proactive in promoting inclusive practices, in both their classes and their departments. It is probably always a good idea to encourage people to teach more effectively; the Inclusive Teaching framework suggests which effective practices are likely to be most strategic in creating a more inclusive teaching and learning environment.

As faculty developers, we want the faculty we work with to teach effectively, but we would also like to see them do better than that. By using this Framework for Inclusive Teaching to guide our work and even the nature of our interactions with STEM faculty, we hope to provide them with a way to understand what is effective, and why, for including all students in opportunities to learn.

References

American Association for the Advancement of Science (1989). *Science for all americans*. New York: Oxford University Press.

Banks, J.A. (1996). Multicultural education: Historical development, dimensions, and practice. In J.A. Banks & C.A.M. Banks (Eds.), *Handbook of research on multicultural education* (pp. 3-23). San Francisco: Jossey Bass.

Born, W.K., Revelle, W., & Pinto, L.H. (2002). Improving biology performance with workshop groups. *Journal of Science Education and Technology, 11*(4), 347-365.

Breslow, L. (2001). Transforming novice problem solvers into experts. *Teach Talk, 13*(3). Cambridge, MA: MIT, Teaching and Learning Laboratory.

Business-Higher Education Forum (2002). *Investing in people: Developing all of America's talent on campus and in the workplace*. Washington, DC: Atlantic Computational Excellence Network.

Cohoon, J.M. (2001). What causes women to discontinue pursuing the undergraduate computer science major at higher rates than men: Toward improving female retention in the computer science major. *Communications of the ACM, 44*(5), 108-114.

Clewell, B., & Campbell, P.B. (2002). Taking stock: Where we've been, where we are, where we're going. *Journal of Women and Minorities in Science and Engineering, 8,* 55-284.

Coley, R. J. (2001). *Differences in the gender gap: Comparisons across racial/ethnic groups in education and work*. Princeton, NJ: Educational Testing Service.

Congressional Commission on the Advancement of Women and Minorities in Science, Engineering and Technology Development. (2002). *Land of plenty: Diversity as America's competitive edge in science, engineering and technology*. Washington, DC: United States Congress. (ERIC Document Reproduction Service No. ED449963.)

Ehlers, V.J. (1998). *Math/science education II: Attracting and graduating scientists and engineers prepared to succeed in academia and industry.* National Science Policy Hearing, April 1, 1998. Retrieved March 31, 2004, from http://www.house.gov/science/ehlers_04-01.htm

George, M. (1996). *Shaping the future: New expectations for undergraduate education in science, mathematics, engineering, and technology.* Washington, DC: National Science Foundation.

Marx, D.M., Brown, J.L., & Steele, C.M. (1999). Allport's legacy and the situational press of stereotypes. *Journal of Social Issues, 55*(3), 491-502.

Montgomery, S., & Barrett, M.C. (1997). Undergraduate women in science and engineering: Providing academic support. *Occasional Papers, 8.* Retrieved November 12, 2002, from University of Michigan Web site: http://www.crlt.umich.edu/publinks/CRLT_no8.pdf

National Center for Education Statistics (2002). *Special analyses 2002: Nontraditional undergraduates.* The condition of education 2002. Washington, DC: Department of Education.

National Center for Education Statistics (2003). *The condition of education 2003.* Washington, DC: Department of Education.

National Science Board *(2002). Science and engineering indicators – 2002.* Washington, DC: National Science Foundation.

National Science Foundation, & U.S. Department of Education. (1980). *Science and engineering education for the 1980s and beyond.* Washington, DC: National Science Foundation.

Nauta, M.M., Epperson, D.L., & Kahn, J.H. (1998). A multiple-groups analysis of predictors of higher level career aspirations among women in mathematics, science, and engineering majors. *Journal of Counseling Psychology, 45*(4), 483-496.

Rutherford, F. J., & Ahlgren, A. (1990). *Science for all Americans, American association for the advancement of science.* New York: Oxford University Press.

Seymour, E., & Hewitt, N.M. (1997). *Talking about leaving: Why undergraduates leave the sciences.* Boulder, CO: Westview Press.

Lois Reddick is a Ph.D. candidate at New York University's Steinhardt School of Education. **Wayne Jacobson** is the associate director at the Center for Instructional Development and Research at the University of Washington Seattle. **Angela Linse** is director of the Teaching and Learning Center at Temple University. **Darryl Yong** is an assistant professor of mathematics at the Harvey Mudd College.

Chapter 33
The Multicultural Lab: Diversity Issues in STEM* Classes

A.T. Miller

The traditional view that the STEM disciplines are empirically based, and thus culturally neutral, has meant that many instructors in these fields often do not see, or cannot imagine, a connection between their classrooms and laboratories and multicultural initiatives. At the same time, most instructors see that there continues to be a gender imbalance in these areas and a notable under-representation of people of color and other identities that face social discrimination. Unfortunately, patterns of retention in these disciplines show that the imbalances grow wider as coursework proceeds. This chapter outlines some of the ways instructors can approach these issues in their practices in and outside of the classroom, to enhance the retention and achievement of under-represented students (and future professionals) in the STEM disciplines.

The Dynamics of Group Work

Problem sets, labs, projects, and sequential courses that produce "cohorts" all lend themselves to situations involving working in groups or teams, large and small. How an instructor sets up and manages such groups can play a major role in encouraging the success of all students. Several basic principles for success are that groups should be assigned or chosen by the instructor, they should change (including lab partners) at least once during a semester, there should be procedures to encourage balanced and respectful participation by all group members, and each group should be heterogeneous in perceived ability or performance.

Allowing students to choose their own groups immediately places pressure on the social dynamics of difference in the classroom and foregrounds students' own attitudes and preferences. It creates unnecessary anxiety in

*Science, Technology, Engineering, Math

those students who are unfamiliar to the majority, or who are on the margins, and raises that marginality even higher. Furthermore, instructors all know the irritations of having some students in the lab operating inappropriately, mainly as sets of friends or buddies, rather than as scientists or technicians. Rather than have the instructor try any form of "social engineering," before one knows much about the students and their academic performance, a clearly fair and random assignment will probably produce the best results. Mixed-achievement grouping, discussed further below, can also be achieved by consulting student records, though some may not wish to perpetuate impressions of students that may have come from prior instructors.

These kinds of random assignments, of course, may not always work well for some individual students, and that is why it is important for the groups to change at least once during the semester. Change also allows for any distracting social dynamics within groups, whether positive or negative, to be dispelled in order to keep the focus of the course on the subject matter. Later in the term, when the instructor has some direct knowledge of student performance, making some assignments that pair those doing well with those who are struggling will make the entire class perform better and allow the course to proceed at the quickest pace that remains inclusive.

Instructors might hesitate to make these mixed-achievement pairings, and some students might balk. However, most instructors have also had the experience of feeling a real mastery of their fields and particular topics at the point of having to teach them. Furthermore, cognitive research shows that the ability to explain and the practice of actually explaining a concept, lead to greater comprehension and clarity of thinking. It is for this reason that heterogeneous groupings are of special benefit to the strongest students, who when paired with each other can become bored or disengaged in the lab or classroom because they have no opportunity to teach their peers. For the other students, having strong partners stimulates sharing, opens up ways for them to get many questions answered without monopolizing the instructor's time, and avoids dividing classrooms into obvious groups of those expected to succeed and go on, and those who are just trying to survive the course. It also helps to make students responsible to each other, a kind of behavior that will prove invaluable in future professional group work.

Another way of grouping students is by learning style, a method that quickly proves its value to the students involved, often to their own amazement. This practice is also a valuable classroom technique because it clearly reinforces the benefits of having a diverse team in any scientific or problem solving situation. Mixed learning-style groupings can come from having students take quick diagnostic tests, some easily available on the internet, and then assigning students accordingly. The notes they share and different observations and insights they bring to their teams will be enlightening both for them and for the instructor (see Finelli, et al., 2001).

In courses where students are assigned to groups or labs where they have partners, it is important that for at least some, if not all, of the collaborative assignments a single grade be assigned to the group or partnership. Some instructors ask for student input regarding weighting their own and their partners' contributions to group products. Incorporating some strategies for group-based assessment can be especially helpful to build positive interdependence as an important motivator for high-achieving students who otherwise may resist collaborative learning. Just as scientific research or technological products are given a single evaluation for group efforts, it is important for students to learn early that science is collaborative in nature and cumulative in comprehension (see Ohland, et al., 2001).

Gatekeeping

In many STEM disciplines, there are particular courses or stages within courses that instructors see and sometimes intentionally design as key benchmarks where students prove their ability to continue in the field. While such essential building blocks of skills and abilities do exist in these areas, and while not all students who desire to achieve a degree in a particular area will be capable of doing so, the approach of the instructor to these key concepts or procedures can play a major role for all students.

Instructors who take a "Darwinian" approach of leading students to the hurdle, and then stepping back to see who makes it, often fail to understand the role of social expectation in determining outcomes. Some instructors with deep concerns for diversity issues express their repeated disappointment that "the women" or "the minority students" just "can't make it" even with their genuine good will. Other instructors take a more active role in seeing it as their duty to weed out the students that they feel will not do well at higher levels, and the instructors often see themselves as doing such students a favor. The anxiety and stress created by both of these approaches that assume that "not all of you are going to make it" are particularly acute for those students who already know that demographically they are unlikely to emerge in the lead on the other side of the hurdle. The sense of competition also reinforces a dynamic of "winners and losers" that plays into feelings of demoralizing fatalism, ideas of luck or chance, and a focus on meeting the instructor's expectations rather than mastering the material.

The renowned high school calculus instructor in urban Los Angeles, Jaime Escalante, has made no secret of his method for success in getting African American and Latino youth from impoverished communities to pass the Advanced Placement Calculus examinations in large numbers and with high marks. He makes it clear in his classroom and in his own expectations that everyone is expected to make it through the exam. He is not the judge of the students, but the coach who makes sure they all get over the hurdle.

Part of this type of coaching is recognizing that academic achievement is based on teamwork and a group approach. If all of the students in a class see themselves as united in an effort to master the material, the class will be lively, and the instructor will feel the rewards of focusing on accomplishment. Lab partners who see themselves truly as partners who need to assist each other to get through the material with confidence and understanding will be well-suited to higher level work in these fields. Success in STEM research and professions depends on groups, intellectual communities, replicable findings, and shared knowledge. This team approach is true from the very beginning stages in introductory courses, and instructors can play an important role in socializing students early to the collaborative nature of intellectual inquiry and achievement. Grading that is based on clear standards and expectations, and not based on relative competitive performance, (for example, grading on a curve) is an important factor in building this shared sense.

Problem-Based vs. Concept-Based Instruction

Many STEM disciplines are dominated by textbooks and teaching traditions that place great emphasis on working problem sets, making calculations, and memorizing long lists of formulae or specific terms, structures, or data. It is a rather specific personality disposition that will easily take on this kind of fact-based skill-building without a clear understanding of why such efforts are being made. Conceptual approaches to knowledge in the STEM fields provide solid undergirding to a much broader range of students, who will then be able to undertake the cultivation of the necessary skills to move to higher levels in these disciplines. When one does not understand why a given experiment or project is relevant, it is difficult to apply the knowledge and connect it to the course, syllabus, readings, and calculations. Instructors need to insure that there is a balance between inductive and deductive reasoning, both in the student assignments and activities, as well as in the class lectures and demonstrations (Tobias, 1990).

Because any real world scientist, engineer, technician, or mathematician would have ready access to charts and tables, it is important to avoid pointless memorization and instead to favor higher-level cognitive skills. The old "plug-and-chug" classroom of solving problem after problem without a larger context, varied approaches, and clear opportunity for application and comprehension is quite alienating for many students, in addition to being dull for instructors. Further, the pitfalls of missed steps or miscalculations common when an instructor is repeatedly working examples on a board or overhead are particularly dangerous. The all-too-frequent similar errors in textbooks of this sort and their "typos" can lead to even greater student confusion and be significantly counterproductive. Overall, the constant repetition of "how" without a clear concept of "why" also discourages the creativity necessary for succeeding in scientific and technical fields.

It is very typical of under-represented students, both women and students of varied backgrounds, to work out their own ways of doing problems that also arrive at the correct answers. Instructors who insist on only one order to the steps that reach an answer, or only one method of problem solving, may close themselves off from important creativity and insight, as well as discourage the promising young scholars for whom their fields purport to be searching. Such rigid behavior on the part of instructors will also blind other students to the possibilities for creativity and intellectual engagement with examples that, when taught with an insistence on uniform procedure, will look to many students like only rote learning. The number of times one encounters under-represented students in STEM disciplines who work out their own methods and shortcuts only to hide these skills because they are embarrassed or ashamed of doing their work differently from the way prescribed by instructors is surprising and discouraging.

Conceptual knowledge is also not individuated into discrete problems and answers, but can be elaborated, explained, and applied, which then presents the instructor with much greater opportunity to employ cooperative, collaborative, and other forms of participatory and peer instruction. An experiential and interactive classroom provides much better retention and comprehension for students and allows an instructor to devote attention to those most in need of it, thereby keeping the entire classroom operating at a closer-to-common pace. Placing the problems and demonstrations out in the classroom and dependent upon students' collective observations, interpretations, examples, and suggestions rather than keeping them on the board from a single hand, makes them real, dynamic, and creative. Passive learning becomes active, and the monotony of teaching or lecturing on "the basics" becomes more rewarding for the instructor.

Study Groups

One of the main factors in student success in STEM disciplines is the participation in out-of-class study groups (Fullilove, et al. 1990). Instructors should not only encourage students to form such groups, but give such groups tasks, provide study aids for group work, and check up on when and if they are functioning well and actually meeting together. As noted earlier, groups assigned by the instructor in a random manner are most effective, but they can also be assigned according to the convenience of campus residential geography or other considerations. It is helpful if such groups have within them students with differing academic or departmental majors or goals and that they not be based on preexisting social cliques or past study groups from previous courses. Again, having the study groups change once in a semester is a healthy practice that promotes broader learning and mediates any tension or distracting dynamic that might develop within one particular study group. To the degree that it is possible, it is also a healthy practice not to isolate under-represented students as single members of different study groups.

Instructors should also reinforce the message that working together is expected and that excluding anyone, as well as operating as a "loner," is not acceptable. Meeting with every group as a whole at least once in a semester will allow the instructor to monitor the group dynamics and get feedback on the balance of participation and roles within the group. Leaving groups alone to negotiate their own ways of operating is likely only to replicate some of the negative social dynamics found on campus and in society for some groups of students. While it may be appropriate to have certain problems designated to be solved on an individual basis for assessment purposes, instructors should also make sure to provide a good number and range of problems for study group work.

Under-Teaching

Many instructors are quite conscious of those students with identities that are under-represented in their disciplines, and sympathize with both their possible isolation as well as conspicuousness. One well-meaning response is to try not to put such students "on the spot" during class or in front of others. It is important to recognize that this sympathetic action runs the danger of depriving these students of important practice, modeling, and teaching attention and opportunities. National studies have shown, for example, that both male and female instructors typically walk a male student through a problem eliciting next steps and allowing him to figure things out and possibly make mistakes along the way. Female students are more typically told the answer or instructed what to do next, thus depriving them of clear coaching through the learning process. Women are also less often asked to explain answers or their reasoning, thus additionally depriving them of opportunities to demonstrate mastery of the material. It is important that a classroom not only be open to the participation of all students, but that the kind of ways that students participate also be comparable, fair, and balanced, so that the attention and resources of the instructor are evenly distributed among all students and that students of all types and backgrounds can clearly be seen to be valued in the classroom (Musil, 2001).

Modeling, Relevant Problems and Projects, and Examples

While the particular concepts and building blocks of comprehension and skills within more empirical disciplines like the STEM fields are often accepted as standardized and universal, their presentation and teaching always take place in a cultural context. Furthermore, their applications are also always culturally bound when carried into the "real world," whether that world is portrayed in the classroom through hypothetical problems, a research agenda, or a social or institutional context. It is therefore important that instructors pay attention to the variety and types of examples, applications, problems, and research settings included in any given course. This attention is also important when listening to student responses and examples, especially when students draw from experiences or settings that might be unfamiliar to the instructor. This is an area where diverse faculty colleagues in these disciplines can readily share experiences and ideas with each other for more varied approaches, in addition to paying attention to student interests and ideas.

Making room for student-identified examples or even problem definition can assist an instructor to cover more varied, multiple, and diverse considerations and contexts. It also introduces or enhances the team building and cultural exchange skills that are so necessary to successful work in scientific or technical research in academia or industry in an increasingly globalized economy, student body, and workforce. It is also valuable to have technical projects, sponsored research, and scientific problems come into the classroom from community groups and organizations. Many campuses rely on industry sponsorship for such projects, internships, and design experience, but community nonprofits can supply additional ideas and projects, and such partnerships provide productive and different settings for learning. The incorporation of academic service learning into scientific and technical fields has been very successful at Purdue and the University of Michigan, and has produced a very high level of student satisfaction with real-world projects and work with clients on very human terms.

Conclusion

In this short chapter, I have sought to outline a number of areas in which the STEM disciplines can and have achieved real progress and made strong contributions in multicultural teaching and learning. It is also important to notice that all of the suggestions given here are focused on the classroom. While many schools and colleges have very valuable support programs, student organizations, special recruitment activities, scholarships, and summer bridge programs to recruit and retain students from under-represented backgrounds to their degree-earning majors, the more support that can come from within the classroom, the better. Of course, it is also important that all instructors be familiar with these programs and organizations in their departments and fields as a part of being an effective advisor and mentor to all students. These are not remedial programs for the students, but rather programs to solve the institutional deficiencies that lead to the phenomenon of under-representation in the first place. Instructors, as significant members of the institution, have an important role to play in these efforts at institutional change.

Building the multicultural lab is a challenge for all scientists and technicians, but one that meets a strong demand for scientists and technicians able to operate easily in a diverse society and the world. Direct modeling and clear descriptions of these and other practices are essential for faculty, nearly all of whom were not educated in the multicultural lab. My experience teaching physics using many of these methods has convinced me that the demographics of the STEM disciplines can and will change profoundly as the pedagogical concerns in these areas also incorporate the issue of inclusion.

Faculty developers need to invite more of their STEM discipline faculty to replicate these results and to move the multicultural agenda across campus into the lab, senior design project, and introductory calculus. Teaching inclusively is not only a matter of curriculum, distribution requirements, good will, common sense, and pedagogy, though all of these are important. It is also a matter of praxis, where faculty members experience their disciplines as sites of diversity and all students find and notice the experience of inclusion in all settings, including the multicultural lab.

The author thanks Connie Cook, Vilma Mesa, John Norton, Matt Ouellett, Honor Passow, and Derrick Scott for their comments and suggestions.

References

Elliott, R, Strenta, C, Adair, R, Matier, M, & Scott, J. (1996). The role of ethnicity in choosing and leaving science in highly selective institutions. *Research in Higher Education*, *37*(6), 681-709.

Finelli, C., Klinger, A, & Budny, D. (2001, October). Strategies for improving the classroom environment. *Journal of Engineering Education, 90*(4), 491-497.

Fox, M. A., & Hackerman, N. (Eds.), (2003). *Evaluating and improving undergraduate education in science, technology, engineering, and mathematics*. Washington, DC: National Academy Press.

Fullilove, R., & Treisman, P. (1990). Mathematics achievement among African American undergraduates at the University of California, Berkeley: An evaluation of the mathematics workshop program. *The Journal of Negro Education, 59*(3), 463-478.

Hines, M. (2003). *Multicultural science education: Theory, practice, and promise*. New York: Peter Lang.

Musil, C. M. (Ed.), (2001). *Gender, science, and the undergraduate curriculum*. Washington, DC: Association of American Colleges and Universities.

Ohland, M., & Finelli, C. (2001). Peer evaluation in a mandatory cooperative education environment. *Proceedings of the 2001 American Society for Engineering Education Annual Conference*. Session 3230.

Roberts, H., Gonzales, J, Harris, O, Huff, D., Johns, A., Lou, R. et al. (1994). *Teaching from a multicultural perspective*. Thousand Oaks, CA: Sage Publications.

Tobias, S. (1990). *They're not dumb, they're different: Stalking the second tier*. Tucson, Arizona: Research Corportation.

A.T. Miller is Coordinator of Multicultural Teaching and Learning at the University of Michigan.

Chapter 34

Science in the Interest of Social Justice: Untangling the Biological Realities of Race and Gender

Leslie S. Jones

Social constructions of race and gender receive unwarranted validation from widespread misunderstanding of scientific information. Myths and exaggerations reify notions of biological human differences, but these fallacies can be effectively dismantled with established scientific information. This chapter suggests approaches to teaching life science content in ways that more accurately represent the biological facts about race/ethnicity and sex/gender.

While I would never deny that social activism motivated me to address race and gender in biology content classes, it is only honest to admit that I initially raised the issues as direct responses to student interest. Part of my first college teaching assignment involved large lecture halls full of somewhat disinterested students who took life science only to fulfill a university requirement. The description for "Life: Continuity and Change" prescribed coverage of human biology for nonmajors with emphasis on heredity and reproduction. One day during an explanation of sexual differentiation, I realized that there was a great deal of confusion about sex and gender. After quick modification of my lecture plans, I concluded the unit by exploring these terms and some of my students' questions about sexual behavior and orientation.

I wish I had been sharp enough to have looked for a topic of similar interest in the genetics unit that followed. I am embarrassed to admit that I dutifully regressed to coverage of standard information, boring my audience with long explanations of what chromosomes do during mitosis and meiosis. Fortunately, I was again prompted to reconsider scheduled lecture topics after noticing the students' curiosity about the inheritance of skin color. Sensing another teachable moment, I spent an entire weekend researching the way race is covered in biology and genetics textbooks. In subsequent semesters, gender and race became the "interest anchors" for the respective units. Race and gender visibly changed student attitudes toward the course material. I found I could delve into other challenging subject matter by relating information to these subjects they found so interesting. Student comments and formal course evaluations indicated that these presentations gave a dreaded science course some semblance of personal relevance. I literally stumbled into an excellent way to take a feminist and antiracist approach to science teaching.

In the Context of Science Coursework?

While there are certainly no monolithic definitions of race or gender, these categories take on very different meanings when viewed in light of current scientific knowledge. Attention to diversity and social justice assumes a great deal of academic credibility when scientific information about race and gender is incorporated into the mainstream science curriculum. Both of these social classifications are confounded by fundamental misunderstandings of biological information and confusion over the interaction of genetic and environmental influences. Mistaken assumptions about human variation operate in insidious ways to reinforce stereotypes and distort the causes of human difference. The heart of the problem is the tendency to confuse the fairly consistent molecular transmission of inherited morphological features with the much more complex determination of social characteristics. My goal is to help students recognize that biological information has been distorted to legitimate social inequities attributed to race and gender. Basic education in reproduction can expose the complex intersection of physiological aspects of sex and the social inscriptions of gender. A straightforward explanation of inheritance shows how race is nothing more than a superficial geographical phenomenon.

Race and gender are volatile concepts that are rich with sociocultural power and laden with scientific ambiguity. Since these topics have always been obscured in scientific education, most people are not aware of how the nature of human biology has been distorted in the context of these issues. Confusion over the fundamental basis of human similarities and differences makes it difficult to recognize how misinformation about race and gender has been used to justify discrepancies in social power. Outside of the natural sciences, attention to these social constructs almost never includes key scientific information that would expose the unjustified use of biology in the magnification of difference. By keeping race and gender out of life science classrooms, we not only fail to clarify that racial hierarchies and sex discrimination lack a scientific basis, but we also avoid taking responsibility for social injustices that biological science has been complicit in supporting.

Since one of the basic components of "The Scientific Method" is the epistemological premise of objectivity, it is hardly surprising that race and gender fall outside of the comfort zones of most biologists. Scientists are enculturated to believe that science generates value-free knowledge, and this assumption is relayed to the general public as a predominant theme within science education. Whether the effort is explicit or not, science is presented as a process in which the nature of the world is presumed to be accurately revealed through scientists' rigorous adherence to a mathematical script. Experimental design and statistical analyses limit the chances that real differences will be confused with something that is random. Scientific ideas are respected because they are presumed to have been proven. Much of the confidence in scientific knowledge arises from underlying belief in the goals of the enterprise and the impartiality of the methodology used in its production. The presumption of neutrality is perpetuated when we present science to the public through written and/or visual media or when we enter classrooms to share information with students.

Course descriptions reveal implicit disciplinary cannons regarding appropriate subject matter and show the expectation that instruction stays close to scripted presentations of facts about natural phenomena. For the most part, we actively avoid touching on the messy complexity of issues that are inherently subjective and raise sociocultural questions that are outside of the traditional realm of investigations of the natural sciences. Even though issues-based approaches have been touted among the suggestions for improving the delivery of science education, instructors who actually use such approaches are the exception rather than the rule. Modern science textbooks, especially those for non-majors courses, have begun to contain obvious references to the connections between science and society, but these are not critical explorations of political topics such as race and gender. Biological scientists think of our discipline as being outside of the realm of social phenomena. I have always been careful of the stance I take as a biologist explaining race and gender. Instinctively, I use the credibility of my position in the scientific community to overshadow the political nature of the issues.

The inclusion of race and gender is a radical departure from conventional biological subject matter; in my case, there was nothing subtle about pressure to remain close to the cannon and cover traditional subjects in traditional ways. Faculty autonomy is relative to seniority, and I knew better than to create reasons that could be used to forbid me to teach the way I wanted. I started out cautiously, monitoring student reception with full recognition that any complaints would give my department head an easy excuse to sanction me for doing something unorthodox. I was questioned about what I was covering and told that it was very important that we all cover the same material (even though this was obviously the terminal life science course for most of these people). Apparently, coverage of race and gender constituted a move outside of disciplinary boundaries, and I was expected to justify how I could connect biological science with these unpopular social conundrums.

Parallel Pedagogies

Without realizing it, and even though both initiatives were spontaneous, my approaches to these subjects developed around almost identical teaching strategies. While gender always seems like the easier subject because the science is more familiar to me, the advantage of talking about race is that nobody can accuse a white woman of having an agenda based on self-interest. Knowing how the rhetorical stance can make a tremendous difference in the reception, I attempt to give the impression that I am merely dispensing information and allow the authority of science to back up the reasonable claims that I make. Whether I am teaching in my own classroom or giving an invited talk, it seems important to adopt a discursive style that is congruent with audience expectations of how a natural scientist should act.

The opening I use for lessons on race and gender involves spontaneous, in-class writing assignments. Students are asked to take five to seven minutes to respond to the following questions:

> How many Races are there?
> What are they and how are they distinguished?

or

> Is there any difference between Sex and Gender?
> Define each of these terms.

It takes assurance that this is not a quiz and there is no right or wrong answer before students seem to believe that they are actually being asked to express their own opinions. Once they have written out their own impressions, they are invited to share their opinions with others students sitting in close proximity. This always involves awkward neck and body contortions in lecture halls, but since students are so glad to break out of the uniform direction of communication, the room is usually filled with a roar of animated dialog. Asking for a collection of different views provides anonymity because people can say, "we discussed the idea that..." and individuals do not have to make public proclamations of their own potentially controversial viewpoints.

The responses to these introductory questions vary little. On the subject of race, the majority of these college students mention four or five categories with predictable labels and descriptions. There are usually a few radical thinkers who proudly declare that there is one human race. There is also usually an anthropology major who might declare that more than thirty have been designated in some schemes. When it comes to sex and gender, most of students are baffled to be asked about the difference. They seem to realize that the words must have individual meanings, but they have been asked so often to state their own gender as male or female, they are unable to make a distinction in the terms. Students who have had exposure to Women's Studies will eagerly point out that one is biological and one is cultural. With both race and gender, existing views become the springboard for me to use scientific information to demonstrate the fallacy of racial categorization and the inaccurate conflation of sex and gender. I carefully select well-established scientific information for the presentations that follow. The subjects are controversial, but there is enough solid science to support deliberate teaching for social justice in the context of a biology classroom.

A Critical Look at the History of Science

An important justification of my inclusion of subjects like race and gender in a biology content course lies in showing that there is a reason so many people hold mistaken assumptions of gender and racial difference. The scientific community that has provided so much productive information about our species has also been complicit in the social construction of race and gender. The history of science reveals an unfortunate pattern of participation in the assembly of racial hierarchies and the justification of sexism. Members of the scientific community took an active interest in human difference starting in the Enlightenment of the 18th Century. As part of the emerging belief that human reason could be used to provide explanations for social and natural phenomena, the idea of inherent variation served as a convenient excuse for social inequities.

Scientific attention to race and gender blossomed at precisely the same time the natural sciences happened to be moving into a position of greater academic credibility. Scientists implicitly demonstrated their usefulness by providing explanations that justified discrepant treatment of women and people from different ancestral groups. The construction of unfounded biological explanations for difference rationalized practices of segregation and discrimination in a society that considered itself to be egalitarian. One of the earliest and most clearly documented examples of scientific racism can be found in the system of classification, devised by Carolus Linnaeus (1758), which divides *Homo sapiens* into distinct racial categories that are delineated more on the basis of social behavior than physical characteristics. Scientific sexism is even easier to document, and one of the classic examples was medical literature that cautioned that the education of women would jeopardize their reproductive capacities (Bullough & Voght, 1973). These and enough other gendered and racial cants accumulated under the pretext of scientific studies make it obvious why it is so hard for the public to discern the truth about the biological reality of human difference.

While I know why Audre Lord (1984) cautioned that "The master's tools will never dismantle the master's house," I also see real possibility for using my insider status to use them for that very purpose. The exaggeration of biological difference may be a case where socially-active science instruction is the only device that can begin to undo the damage that has been done. The science classroom is an effective site to undermine the social power that racism and sexism gain through the perpetuation of a mythology of fundamental biological difference. Since scientific information has been distorted to justify these forms of discrimination, the scientific community can be part of attempts to rectify this ignorance. Scientific contradictions are likely to be the only source of information powerful enough to counteract the erroneous construction of race. Scientific misinformation is so firmly woven into the fabric of racism and sexism that only concerted disciplinary based, instructional efforts are going to untangle fiction from reality.

The Complex Intersection of Nature or Nurture

Attempts to categorize people are based on mistaken assumptions that aspects of character are governed strictly by genetic inheritance and that these qualities are inherently linked to the physical appearance. A collection observable physical characteristics that are common to one particular group of people and distinct from others provides the markers for sexual or racial categorization. The obvious transmission of these visible traits from parents to offspring left little doubt that such features were inherited. Since the physical traits were immutable, behavioral patterns were also assumed to be fixed at birth, linked in inheritance and, therefore, unquestionably typical of different sexes or geographical groups. The importance of using biology to help people understand the cultural implications of both race and gender is the need to decipher some of the confusion over the natural and experiential constituents of each. As is the case with so many human characteristics, we wonder, Is it innate or is it learned? Is it genetics or is it environment? Is it heredity or is it training? The answer is yes, no, and both at the same time. There is no clear separation of these spheres of influence, but there is a critical need for clarity regarding what can be attributed to inborn characteristics and what is acquired. A great deal of the social power that both race and gender carry is due to the fact that confusion exists over what is inherent and what is attained.

Attention to mechanisms of genetic regulation has overshadowed the fact that environmental conditions play such a critical role in the expression of inherited tendencies. Some characteristics are not indelibly determined at conception and are modified by non-genetic factors during prenatal development as well as after birth. The observable constitution of an organism is known as the phenotype. By definition, this expression of variable features in individuals is a consequence of the interactions between the genotype (genetic template) and the environment. Genetically, only a limited number of characteristics are qualitatively determined strictly by the presence of certain forms of a single gene. Most variation is initiated by polygenic inheritance or the effects of several genes. When the range of expression of an inherited trait is further enhanced by a multitude of potential environmental influences, it is known as a multi-factorial trait.

Many mistaken beliefs about gender and race are based on confusion over multi-factorial influences. Human attributes have provoked considerable debate over the relative significance of innate and external influences. The matter is part of the nature or nurture controversy that questions whether genetics or the environment is ultimately more important. Actually, phenotypic variance is usually the product of the interactions of both the genetic template and environmental changes. Genetic factors create the potential for particular phenotypes. Environmental impacts can range from subtle to strong and are likely to modify various genotypes in different ways. Thus, the complex interactions of both nature and nurture are responsible for phenotypic variance. The fundamental goal of my instructional approach is to use well-documented scientific information to help students begin to discern what is actually known about human inheritance. In the science classroom, I am interested in putting these people in a stronger position to make their own rational social critique.

There is No Biology of Race

My approach to race is based on showing students how race has never been a valid biological category. I make it clear that I want them to recognize that there are absolutely no genetic or physical criteria that distinguish different racial groups. I suggest the examination of different sources for definitions of the word, rather than taking for granted there is agreement as to what race means. I explain that few current life science textbooks even mention race because the ambiguity of the word renders it biologically useless. Even though race is presumed to have anthropological significance, there has never been agreement, even within that field, as to the number of races or how to distinguish them. Racial divisions have ranged anywhere from two to several hundred depending on whether the Nazis or anthropologists were counting.

The concept of race was based on the mistaken assumption that populations could be "pure," because they inherited a collection of distinct traits as a whole. Not only is this idea of the mode of inheritance flawed, but genetic evidence indicates that human populations have always shared genes through cross-mating. Models derived from studies in population genetics explain how noticeable differences in human groups were shaped by environmental pressure and by the fact that geographically and socially separate gene pools ended up with divergent gene frequencies. Furthermore, as former geographical and social mechanisms for isolating human populations break down, genetic pools are blended and physical traits become even less useful as markers of difference. In this global society, populations are mixing so rapidly that intermediate gradations may eventually replace the morphological distinctions that were used in attempts to define races.

Skin color is both the primary marker of racial categories and an excellent example of racial misconceptions. Color has been used as the single criterion for dividing people into "Black, White, Yellow, Brown, and Red" races. The fallacy of such a system is the absence of any lines of demarcation. Skin colors actually range across a broad spectrum from dark to light and also spread out to include a wide variety of differing tones or hues. Patterns of skin color correspond to the latitudinal distribution of indigenous people due to variation in the quantity and type of the pigment melanin, which regulates the penetration of sunlight. People with common ancestry, even full siblings, often have somewhat different skin colors. Other people, such as Africans and Australian Aborigines, can have similar skin color in spite of having little recent ancestral connection.

Another way I negate any legitimacy of racial separations involves showing the distribution of the familiar blood markers in the A, B, and O blood groups. These blood types provide valuable genetic information because the patterns of inheritance are simple, straightforward, and well documented. A global database exists because blood typing has been carried out on large numbers of people all over the world. Gene frequencies vary among different indigenous populations, but the patterns of distribution do not correspond to geographical regions occupied by racial groupings based on morphological features. In fact, the A, B, and O blood markers distribute in basically longitudinal patterns that are perpendicular to the latitudinal distribution that is characteristic of skin colors. This demonstrates the fallacy of assuming people are genetically segregated according to skin color, because if traditional racial categories had a genetic basis, the frequencies of these blood types would be congruent with the patterns of distribution of skin color categories.

The Conflation of Sex and Gender

In the unit on reproduction, introductory questions about sex and gender lead right into a discussion of biological sex. Part of my deliberate interrogation of existing ambiguity in these terms is to prompt students to recognize that gender actually ranges along a continuum between masculine and feminine.

There are usually a few good laughs when we talk about the stereotypes that epitomize each extreme. To emphasize how gender is inscribed, I touch on the social punishments for those whose behaviors are incongruent with social expectations. Once we have outlined gender, I ask them to compare the labels that describe sex. Placing the words male and female below masculine and feminine is a way to prompt them to compare the way these descriptors are used. There has never been anything other than consensus that male and female are mutually exclusive, dichotomous categories. Everyone clearly thinks I have lost my mind when I ask if they are sure there are only two sexes. The next question is, "What do we call something that is both male and female at the same time?" All it takes is mention of the earthworm to bring up the word hermaphrodite, and an explanation of intersexuality takes off in a direction these students never anticipate.

Most students have no idea that variations in sexual differentiation occur in humans. True hermaphroditism is a very rare, but due to developmental anomalies, individual anatomy can range from ovotestes (with both male and female tissue) to the presence of one male and one female gonad. While less is known about this infrequent situation, the partial manifestations known as pseudohermaphroditism are caused by genetic mutations that occur frequently enough to be better understood. Explaining both the incidence and the etiology of Type I – Female Pseudohermaphroditism (Congenital Adrenal Hyperplasia) and Type II – Male Pseudohermaphroditism (Androgen Insensitivity Syndrome) alerts students to the fact that sex difference is not anywhere near as clean as they have been led to believe.

In all the years I spent training as a reproductive physiologist, I never dreamed I would be teaching that there were more than two sexes. In fact when my graduate Cultural Studies professor assigned a paper called "The Five Sexes" by Anne Fausto-Sterling (1992), I remember thinking the premise was absolutely absurd. It is very powerful to generate the following diagram:

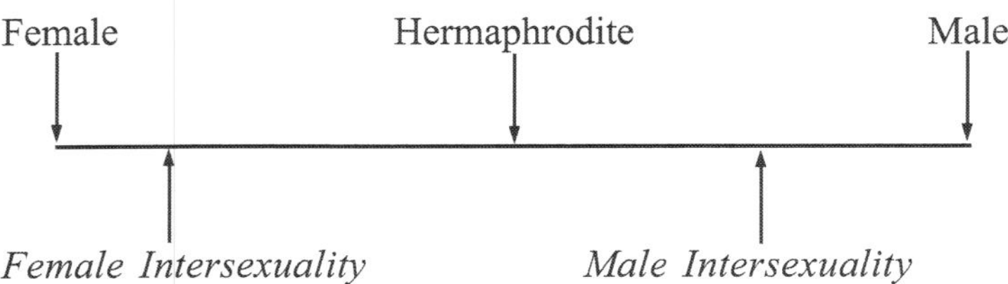

While creating disequilibrium is not one of my favorite classroom activities, I make exception in this case. By purposely disrupting their naïve but comfortable certainty, I encourage these young people to think differently about sex and gender. Whether the final interpretation comes down to simple math

(2+3=5) or the idea of a range of sexes along a continuum, the idea of absolute sexual categories is disrupted.

A widespread myth that contributes to confusion over sex and gender is the idea that there are completely different male and female hormones. Part of a premise of sexual duality is based on ignorance of the fact that the same chemical messengers regulate different sexual functions. From the protein hormones (GnRH, LH and FSH) released by the brain to the steroids (Progestins, Androgens, and Estrogens) produced in the gonads, the same molecules are present in both sexes. A basic lesson in reproductive endocrinology corrects the erroneous impression that masculinization and feminization are strictly due to separate actions of male and female sex hormones. Explanation of the well-documented stages of sexual differentiation provides a powerful picture of the fundamental physical similarities of male and female bodies. This is especially brought home by the fact that human sex reversal can take place at puberty in individuals with a genetic condition that disrupts production of an enzyme (5 Alpha-Reductase) that is part of the steroidogenic pathway. Explanations of hormonal regulation of sexual behavior seem to help them appreciate the complexity of sexual orientation and transgender situations.

Emphasis on Human Unity

In these lessons on race or gender, I point out that I hope students recognize how inordinate attention to difference distracts us from recognizing the significance of the common characteristics of all human beings. The best case I can make for this is reference to biodiversity. Comparison of *Homo sapiens* to other species of living organisms demonstrates how clearly the resemblance among humans far outweighs any collective differences between us. I realize that it is mind-boggling for students to hear that the DNA of a chimpanzee is more than 97% identical to that of humans. This cross-species comparison helps to make the case that, on the biological level, there is far more similarity among every member of our species than there is difference between groups with dissimilar physical features and lifestyles or those with different reproductive organs.

Recent determination of the full sequence of the human genome provides indisputable evidence of fundamental human similarities. By spelling out the chemical details of the "Book of Life," scientists have confirmed that the DNA of every human is more than 99.99 percent identical. Of the 3 billion nucleotides or molecules that make up chromosomal DNA, only one in every 12 thousand is estimated to be different. Since only about 10% of the total DNA is functional, many of the single variations occur in sections that are of no consequence with respect to inheritance. Approximately 30 thousand human genes have been identified, but 75 % of these templates are known to be monomorphic or completely identical in every individual.

One of the most common activities in biological science is the practice of comparing and contrasting the characteristics of living organisms. I see these feminist and antiracist approaches to science as another way to explore "unity and diversity of life." Applying critical theory to life science may be seen as a departure from disciplinary norms, but it is important to help students learn to separate social from biological reality. Emphasis on these cultural implications of science employs an alternative to the usual style of presentation of scientific information. Most explanations of the living world are made with a reductionist approach, breaking down systems into smaller and smaller components for the sake of clarity. The human genome is a classic example, since knowledge of the complete sequence allows for description of structural genetic regulation down to the level of every atom in DNA molecules. Evaluations of the biological fallacies of race and gender require an explanatory shift in the opposite direction to a holistic perspective. Appreciation of the intersection of inherited and environmental influence comes by considering genetic and physiological information in the context of social values to generate a larger or more expansive concept of humanity.

Science for Social Responsibility

To ensure the credibility of these lessons, both race and gender are treated as substantive content topics in my biology courses. Over time, each issue has expanded to more than one class session and numerous cross-references made during the discussion of other aspects of the units. In the eyes of an undergraduate student, anything "that is going to be on the test" is important, so I leave no question that they will be held responsible for this material on examinations. Even in the multiple choice format, I have been able to discourage rote learning with demanding conceptual questions, so queries that raise social issues do not seem out of place. Regardless of the size of my classes, I use writing assignments to facilitate learning. When students are required to produce a single-spaced, one-page essay on a subject, they have to think about what was covered in class. The importance that students spend time "writing to learn," so I have developed a system for giving 10 point scores for compositions that are well organized around a clear thesis that is built on some approach to the scientific and social information that has been discussed. Usually, it is most effective to repeat the questions that were used to open the coverage of race and gender. I get a clear sense of the efficacy of this instruction because many are open about how their thinking about the legitimacy of race and the distinctions between sex and gender have changed.

While the idea of scientific literacy has been overworked to the point that it has almost become a cliché, there are aspects of the idea that should not be ignored. The American Association for the Advancement of Science (AAAS) report, *Science for All Americans* (1989), states that

> ... the scientifically literate person is one who is aware that science, mathematics, and technology are interdependent human enterprises with strengths and limitations; understands key concepts and principles of science; is familiar with the natural world and recognizes both its diversity and unity; and uses scientific knowledge and scientific ways of thinking for individual and social purposes (p.4).

Ideally, college science coursework would come closer to achieving this goal by opening up critical conversations about the biological fallacies that are used to justify racism and sexism. In spite of the fact that non-major's science courses have progressed far beyond the days when they were merely "watered or dumbed down" versions of introductory majors courses, many students are still not exposed to much more than a content-intensive exposure to scripted biological information. The traditional emphasis of most postsecondary science courses tends to obscure other important aspects of disciplinary knowledge that students find more personally relevant. I am convinced that memorizing the Krebs cycle or photosynthetic pathway is far less important than understanding why there are mistaken assumptions about the magnitude of human racial difference.

Progressive movement toward a more equitable educational system depends upon the development of a more sophisticated understanding of the nature of race and gender. Current approaches to education provide little explanation of the interdependence of the biological and sociocultural components of these subjects. The neglect of these important topics in biological education can be overcome when instructors assemble and disseminate concrete information about the extent of human similarities and difference. Most people have an intuitive understanding of the social consequences of race, sex and gender, but few people have an accurate perception of the biological realities of these issues. Subjects such as gender and race generate student interest in required science courses because they have to do with the "Three S's". Anything that is Sexy, Scary, or Scatological works to grab the attention of young people. Gender is obviously sexy, racism can be very scary, and since the consequences of both forms of oppression are definitely scatological, they seem to work with this audience.

References

American Association for the Advancement of Science. (1989). *Science for all Americans*. Washington, DC: Project 2061 – National Council on Science and Technology Education.

Bullough, V., & M. Voght, (1973). Women, menstruation and 19th century medicine. *Bulletin of the History of Medicine, 47*, 66-82.

Fausto-Sterling, A. (1993, March/April). The five sexes. *The Sciences*, vol?, 20-25.

Linnaeus, C. (1758). Systema Naturae, Editio decima. Laur Salvius, Holmiae.

Lorde, A. (1984). *Sister outsider.* Freedom, CA: The Crossing Press.

Leslie S. Jones is an assistant professor in the Biology Department at Valdosta State University.

Chapter 35

Faculty Development and Organizational Change: Moving From "Minority Relevant" to Intersectionality and Social Justice

Beth Glover Reed and Melissa R. Peet

This chapter describes the structures and educational processes that facilitated and/or inhibited faculty development during a curriculum change in a graduate school of social work that has worked on these issues for more than 20 years. A recent initiative targeted clusters of required courses and reframed goals from incorporating knowledge/skills for particular groups (e.g., race, class, gender, sexual orientation) to an intersectional approach (multiple interacting dimensions) that also envisions social justice and analyses/challenges unearned privilege and oppression. A formative and implementation evaluation is illuminating the range of changes required, barriers arising, and critical issues important in faculty and student development.

Much writing on faculty development tends to focus on individual faculty members, the development of teaching skills, and/or conceptualizing and implementing particular courses. These approaches pay less attention to important organizational, collegial, and curricular issues that directly impact teaching. This shortcoming is particularly problematic in professional schools where faculty teach within a highly sequenced curriculum designed to foster specific knowledge and skills through a series of courses. These types of curricula require collaboration among faculty and well-structured institutional processes.

Diamond (2002) proposes three alternative ways to improve instructional quality: faculty development, instructional development (focused on students via courses and the curriculum), and organizational development (focused on the structures and processes of the institution). We agree with Diamond's assertion and argue that 1) all three approaches are necessary to increase inclusive teaching; 2) they must occur simultaneously and iteratively; and 3) student mobilization and on-going evaluation make improvements in instructional quality much more likely. In this paper, we use data and lessons learned from four years of curricular revision to:

1. Illustrate interconnections among faculty, student, instructional and organizational development;
2. Describe the underlying assumptions and principles that guide the curriculum change, including the role of participatory evaluation, as well as some specific activities;
3. Illuminate some challenges, tensions, and opportunities faced in integrating the new curriculum using the lenses of practice (structuration) theory, praxis, and organizational innovation; and
4. Discuss implications and recommendations for faculty development.

Underlying Assumptions, Rationales, and Conceptual Frameworks

Criticisms within the field of Social Work assert that social workers are often educated to aid, treat, empathize, and give comfort, but *not* to respond to the larger social and economic inequalities creating illness and despair in the lives of the people they serve (Reisch & Andrews, 2001). Furthermore, some critics argue that *not* educating social workers to address these inequalities translates into practitioners who unknowingly and unconsciously perpetuate the dynamics of cultural, social, and economic oppression (McGoldrick, 1999; Freire, 1990).

In the curriculum change that provides the context for this paper, the University of Michigan graduate School of Social Work (SSW) added another element to this critique—the need to envision possibilities and develop skills that lead to social and economic justice. Previous approaches to diversity in the SSW emphasized the development of "culturally competent" practitioners [professionals with knowledge, skills, and awareness to work effectively with people from different cultural, ethnic, and racial groups (Sue & Sue, 2002; Arredondo, 1999)] with some attention to understanding and combating oppression and its effects. The revised curriculum emphasizes multiple intersecting identities, social justice, and the development of practitioners as "critically conscious" social change agents.

This shift is complex and paradigmatic—requiring fundamental changes in the ways that faculty, students, and professionals think about their professional roles, the nature of knowledge, the types of awareness and skills needed for effective practice, and even our responsibilities as citizens and workers. It also reflects many recent political, epistemological, and ethical debates within higher education as a whole (Rhoads & Black, 1995).

Although several professional schools seem to be struggling with the need to educate practitioners to be more socially conscious, very few practical and/or theoretical models and approaches exist for curriculum, student, and/or faculty development that are informed by social justice goals. With few explicit models to guide us, knowledge about practice (structuration) theory (Giddens, 1979), praxis (Freire, 1972), and organizational innovation (Rogers, 1995) influenced our decisions to use participatory action research methods.

A structuration framework illuminates how people embody, create, and recreate social structures in their everyday consciousness and actions through focusing on the interplay of organizational norms and structures with group processes, and individual's interpretations of those organizational and group influences (Giddens, 1984; Ortner 1996). Since human actions create social structures and because we are always acting, we are always producing and/or reinforcing social structures and being influenced by them. Therefore, "action" and "structure" are not separate phenomenon, but *are interconnected parts of the same thing* (Giddens, 1979). Creating or reinforcing social structures through our everyday actions is referred to as the *process of structuration.* This process links the cognitive roots of human action to larger organizational and group processes, therein providing a multidimensional framework for studying complex changes (adapted from Giddens, 1984, and Orlikowski, 2000). We emphasize three elements.

- *The activation of interpretive schemas.* How individuals make meaning out of their experiences and perceptions, including feelings, cognitive patterns, actions, and meanings given to ideas, norms, resources, actions, and events (Ortner, 1996).
- *The practice of group processes and organizational norms.* Assumptions that guide, control, or regulate acceptable behavior and patterns of communication among members of a particular group, including collaboration, conflict, and so forth (Emirbayer & Mische, 1998).
- *The integration of organizational structures.* Formal and informal processes relating to the functioning of an organization: faculty recruitment policies, promotion and tenure criteria, leadership and curricular structure, and so forth (Hays, 1994).

In this project, structuration theory is being used to examine how faculty members' (and students') interpretation and engagement with the new curriculum (an organizational structure) interacts with the organizational norms, structures, and group processes within the SSW to affect how they construct meanings (their interpretive schemas) that lead to specific actions.

Using praxis emerged from our emphasis on critical consciousness. Through the work of Marx, the concept of critical consciousness emerged in the U.S. from Paolo Friere's philosophy of education, which argued that learning should serve to liberate people from what he referred to as the "amnesia of political fatalism," the belief that social inequalities are a natural, unfortunate, and inevitable fact of life (Freire, 1990, p.16). Theoretically, critical consciousness addresses social inequality through praxis: an iterative process of engaging in knowledge, action and reflection in an effort to understand and transform the world (Freire, 1990, p.36). As used here, critical consciousness includes:

- Reflecting on oneself historically, in relation to others, including an awareness of "intersectionality," how one's race, gender, class, and other group identities simultaneously work together to create one's perception and experiences (Freire, 1972, p.16; Collins, 2000);
- Developing "structural perception," the ability to see or "unveil" the social, political, and cultural forces that shape our everyday experiences (Freire, 1985);
- Developing "critical epistemology," a radical curiosity with regard to the nature of knowledge and how different truth claims support social inequalities (Freire, 1972, p.18; Agger, 1998).
- A commitment to "learning dialogically" in specific contexts with others (Freire, 1972);
- A commitment to "ethical actions to end injustice" (Freire, 1972).

The assumptions and principles of praxis, intersectionality, and critical epistemology underlie all elements, particularly the choice of evaluation methods and the interweaving of information gathering and theorizing with educational and organizational change activities.

These approaches are also consistent with knowledge about how organizational innovations are created, adopted, and institutionalized (Daft, 2001; Mayer & Davidson, 2000; Osbourne, 1998; Rogers, 1995). Any change tends to surface unspoken and often unrecognized unexamined beliefs as well as cultural and power-related issues within an organization and among participants that can either facilitate or impede desired changes and learning. When changes emphasize issues of social justice and diversity, the stakes are raised further (Cox, 2001; Fine, 1995). Thus, while faculty development is essential for initiating, defining, and implementing a multicultural curriculum change process, attention to overall organizational issues is also important. Useful strategies include chances to try out new procedures, learning from initial efforts, making that learning visible within the organization, and developing leadership and "champions" for the changes at all levels. These champions can help to sustain motivation and work to realign other aspects of the organization that are needed to support the desired changes.

Curriculum changes can also be greatly facilitated by student involvement. Students' feedback and interactions with each other and faculty can assist or resist course revisions and implementation.

For all these reasons, the SSW approached its curriculum change effort through a formative "learn as we go" approach, including collaborative development of courses, and on-going evaluation and feedback using action-research methods (Whyte, 1991; Greenwood, Whyte, & Harkavy, 1993; McNiff & Whitehead, 2002). The on-going evaluation generated insights regarding the strengths, opportunities, and challenges involved in implementing the curriculum change, and provided faculty with valued research-based information to keep them intellectually engaged in the process.

Methods for Change and Evaluation

The context. The curriculum change is occurring within a two-year Masters of Social Work (MSW) program intended to prepare students (about 300 in a cohort, four semester program) to perform effectively in multiple types of roles: working directly with individuals, families, and groups; developing social policies; conducting program evaluations; acting as administrators in human service organizations; and/or assisting communities to accomplish desired goals. Students earn one quarter of their credits in community-based and governmental field settings (more than 400 sites supervised by up to 600 field instructors). Forty-plus tenure-track faculty and another 40 adjunct faculty teach in any given term.

The curriculum change. The curriculum change is called Intensive Focus on Privilege, Oppression, Diversity and Social Justice (PODS) and involves 25 courses in specific concentration areas (overseen by faculty work groups) including a component of students' field experiences (25% of credits for graduation). These PODS courses replaced the previous "minority relevant" requirement where students took one of several designated courses (designed by individual instructors) that devoted 50% of their content to a minority group (for example, a group determined by race, gender, or sexual orientation), and/or mechanisms of oppression.

Activities Over Time. Five types of activities are involved in this change process: 1) organizational development, 2) student development, 3) faculty development (classroom), 4) faculty development (field-based), and 5) assessment/evaluation. We divided faculty development into classroom and field-based since the processes and tasks differ substantially. Assessment and evaluation activities preceded and informed every other activity to guide and monitor progress.

Organizational development. A faculty/student committee has provided extensive leadership for the PODS change effort – facilitating different areas of development, functioning as liaisons to administrators, and supporting several forums and events designed to build school-wide support and awareness for PODS. For example, in 2003, responding to recommendations from the evaluation, approximately 400 students and faculty attended a school-wide "all-day" event designed to address conflict: how to stay engaged, communicate, and work with differences.

Student development. In 2001, student activism helped to shape the PODS curriculum change. Since then, students have participated on school committees, created workgroups for implementing school-wide events, and been heavily involved in a multicultural orientation designed to introduce PODS to incoming students and recruit volunteers for further PODS-related efforts. In the past year, students have been working on learning portfolios (Brown, 2002; Gibbs, 2004; Miholic & Moss, 2001; Willis & Davies, 2002) designed to help them integrate their course and field learning and help the SSW to evaluate how PODS is being incorporated in different courses and its impact on learning.

Instructional development. In year one, curricular workgroups used a course planning grid to assess PODS courses and guide planning (See Appendix 1). One axis delineated the components of PODS; the other delineated different course elements (readings, class activities, resources, assignments, evaluation and/or grading criteria, and ways of linking with students' field experiences). In year two, we created an evolving list of overall PODS competencies. Since then, workgroups have been creating measurable PODS competencies for each course and concentration area.

Faculty development. Faculty development occurred through presentations, short workshops, discussion at faculty meetings, and longer seminars and retreats. Each event included written materials, mini-presentations, activities designed to increase learning about PODS-related knowledge and skills, and a follow-up evaluation. In seminars, faculty reviewed work-to-date and evaluation results and engaged in experiential activities to illuminate various issues related to PODS such as different interpretations of the terms and teaching challenges. For instance, in a 2003 seminar, faculty engaged in interactive theater activities designed to "try-out" different approaches to PODS issues in the classroom.

Field instruction development. In 2003, we engaged in a year-long effort to understand how to expand PODS to field settings. Through focus groups, students and field educators produced recommendations for a multi-step learning and implementation process.

Implementation evaluation. The motion for the curriculum change included an evaluation of progress during the planning and phase-in period, and an assessment of student outcomes at the end of the implementation period. Primary goals were to triangulate different types of data and methods and to illuminate multiple perspectives on progress and problems (Denzin, 1989). Methods include: focus groups (42-to-date), interviews (40+), a survey for students to self-assess their knowledge, skills and confidence on PODS competencies (repeated several times), analyses of workgroup minutes, reports, and syllabi, and evaluation of all events and activities. Data analyses included inductive thematic coding of central themes and issues (Glaser & Strauss, 1967; Glaser, 1992), as well as deductive summary and analysis of responses to specific questions using a grounded theory approach (Strauss & Corbin, 1998).

Results

Interpretive schemas. In a structuration framework, interpretive schemas are seen as the individual "space" wherein organizational, cultural, and group dynamics come together to influence a person's underlying assumptions and beliefs, and order how a person perceives, interprets, and assigns meanings to information, experiences, and actions (thereby influencing the types of actions that will follow). Through various forms of feedback, faculty and students reported on what influenced their interpretation of and responses to the curriculum change.

Although most faculty strongly supported the curriculum change, differences among their interpretive schemas created challenges to implementation. Faculty differed in how they conceptualized and applied PODS terms. The variations seemed to reflect larger differences in underlying assumptions about the nature of knowledge, how students learn, and the methods of teaching that best facilitate learning.

For example, some faculty believe that knowledge is socially "constructed" through dialogue, discourse, and debate among people from different perspectives, viewpoints, and positions within social structures. For them, creating dialogue with others in an effort to reveal these differences is a legitimate form of knowledge-making. These faculty assume that definitions of PODS terms are also "constructed" and likely to change in different contexts. "Expertise," then, includes the ability to engage in and/or facilitate a knowledge-making process with others. This assumption places students at the "center" of their learning—generating questions and insights by applying different theories, approaches to knowledge, and critical perspectives to different situations and contexts.

Conversely, most faculty members' training prepared them to approach knowledge, teaching, and learning as "content experts" who impart knowledge and skills to students in areas of their expertise. These faculty were more likely to want definitions of the PODS terms that apply *across* contexts. Some of these faculty felt that conflicts and differences emerging in PODS courses detracted from achieving course objectives, rather than seeing conflict as a means to teach the content and reach the objectives.

Of course, not all faculty clearly fit into these two distinct "camps" in terms of their assumptions about teaching and learning; many embodied beliefs from both perspectives or had different perspectives for different courses. Since these differences had not been recognized or articulated explicitly among faculty before the curriculum change, as the change unfolded, the tensions between these paradigms permeated many interactions among faculty.

Faculty also struggled with another tension. On one side is a strong valuing of academic freedom and a belief that good teaching happens when faculty members can express initiative and build on their strengths. On the other is the need to create a sequenced, integrated curriculum, with agreed-upon goals and components for particular courses, expressed by some as "organizational accountability."

Students also had diverse perceptions and definitions of the PODS terms and varied a great deal in their expectations for faculty teaching and how they wanted to learn. Despite these differences, students agreed that optimal learning about PODS occurred when faculty: 1) addressed conflicts and promoted dialogue across differences, 2) facilitated self-reflection in multiple ways, 3) integrated course content with practice experiences, and 4) used multiple instructional approaches.

Faculty and students' perceptions differed a great deal in terms of the best methods for teaching PODS material. Many faculty stressed conceptualizing PODS as ethical questions and/or engaging students in the theoretical complexities of PODS. Students overwhelmingly reported that they learned PODS best by having to *apply* PODS knowledge and principles to specific action-based assignments—*not* by primarily talking, reading, or theorizing.

Group Processes Among Faculty and in the Classroom

In a structuration perspective, group processes influence 1) how people create meaning from their experiences and 2) how people make sense and take action in a particular context.

Faculty interactions. Faculty working to transform their courses felt both negatively and positively influenced by their peers and the group processes within the SSW. Some said they felt a great deal of intellectual and practical support from their colleagues, counting on others for references, feedback on decisions regarding syllabi, ideas for various teaching strategies, and lively discussion about the meaning and implications of the PODS themes. Conversely, some faculty did not have peer support. These faculty either prepared their PODS course on their own because no other faculty were in their area or because they did not agree with their peers. Even though preparing PODS courses required a great deal of work for all participating faculty, those who had supportive peer processes felt more positively about the curriculum change than those who lacked support.

Handling conflict and silence. In general, nearly all students and faculty felt the climate of the school did not support group dynamics that constructively address conflict and differences. For example, even outside the context of course planning, nearly all faculty remarked that the biggest barrier to curriculum change was how they communicated with each other—their difficulties in engaging and building on differences and the lack of collective will to deal with conflict directly. This barrier allowed differences and misunderstandings about the meaning of PODS terms and the best ways to implement PODS and other epistemological differences between faculty to intensify unnecessarily. Nearly everyone suggested faculty development sessions, seminars, or other structured opportunities to learn, dialogue, and practice conflict-related skills together, for use in faculty groups and in the classroom.

Students also reported that group dynamics in the SSW created barriers to open exchange and dialogue. With the exception of particular classes, students across the spectrum of social identities and political orientations reported many complex and difficult group dynamics in which they were reluctant to talk and interact openly in classes. Students self-censored and withdrew for a variety of reasons (for example, fear of offending or being misunderstood and wanting to protect cherished values from challenge). Students of all racial groups identified faculty members' lack of comfort and skill with handling conflict as a major barrier to implementing PODS goals. Conversely, students reported that faculty who had skills in facilitating conflict were able to promote dialogue and constructive debate.

Organizational Culture and Norms

In a structuration perspective, the norms of an organization—the "assumptions and values guiding and facilitating acceptable behavior and patterns of communication among members of a particular group" (Emirbayer & Misch, 1998, p.9)—shape group and individual actions. These expectations, often invisible, are affected by gender, cultural and racial group statuses, professional roles, expectations of the workplace, the dynamics of work teams, and so forth.

Faculty and students reported ways that the schools' culture and climate—mostly in terms of its norms and values—had an impact on the curriculum change process and its effects. Norms of "niceness" (being kind and respectful of each other) were valued but were also associated with difficulties in addressing the differences described above.

Many faculty reported that the University's culture (as well as the SSW) over-emphasized particular values—expertise, individualism, and competition—that in some ways undermined the schools' efforts to integrate PODS into the curriculum. The competition and prestige of a research environment was perceived to reward individual research efforts, not collaboration and dialogue. Some felt that these values contributed to a competitive and hierarchical environment that overemphasizes the opinions of senior faculty at the expense of important input from junior and adjunct faculty on PODS issues (as well as students). This hierarchy also interferes with a sense of community and the ability to engage in the dialogue and collaboration necessary for integrating PODS into the curriculum. Some faculty described the SSW as a building where some colleagues focus on individual research agendas and ignore issues pertaining to the school as a whole. They also noted disconnections between the amount of time needed to transform a course and the value given to such efforts in annual performance criteria.

Despite these challenges, faculty reported that the curriculum change process was valued and supported by the collective will of their colleagues overall, many of whom held a deep commitment to the values of social justice. Even though there were vast differences among faculty in terms of how they thought the curriculum change should be implemented, most believed in the value of the change and worked towards its goals despite beliefs that these efforts were not adequately rewarded.

Organizational and Course Structures

In a structuration perspective, organizational structures refer to the formal and informal frameworks (for example, the curriculum of a school and/or the roles and expectations placed on faculty, admissions processes) for the functioning, norms, values, and group processes of an organization. In an academic environment, these informal and formal "structures" also include the tools of teaching and learning: course syllabi, course objectives, assignments, class activities, methods of evaluation, and so forth.

Faculty roles. Due to competing demands, nearly all faculty felt they lacked the time necessary to engage fully in the curriculum change process. Some were surprised by the time required to transform and teach revised courses to emphasize PODS. Additionally, the status and roles of different types of faculty impacted their participation. For example, adjunct faculty had less time and resources than governing faculty for the change process; because they did not attend SSW faculty meetings, they had little information about the changes being made or how they were supposed to change their teaching. They also had significantly fewer resources available to them (for example, libraries, conversations with other faculty).

Curricular alignment issues (the structure of the curriculum). Both faculty and students reported that the curriculum change effort "surfaced" problematic structural issues in the curriculum—how a particular PODS course "fit" into the curriculum or concentration area as a whole, especially related to the linear progression of courses over time. Faculty teaching advanced courses felt they could not count on students having any shared PODS knowledge from previous courses. Similarly, with the exception of an evaluation course taken in their last term, most students reported the curriculum failed to develop their PODS knowledge and skills over time. They reported that the PODS knowledge they were receiving was often not tailored for particular courses. To address this problem, faculty workgroups are developing competencies that build upon each other, and distribute across courses.

Within course alignment issues. Students also reported that PODS content, issues, and skills were not being integrated well into applied situations. This criticism was consistent with other indicators of difficulties in operationalizing PODS elements. Using the course planning grid (described earlier) to identify how PODS was being implemented, faculty discovered many problems with alignment of course elements (Cohen, 1987): PODS was most often incorporated into course content (readings), but much less into class activities, assignments, grading criteria, and linkages with the field.

Social Work students tend to be focused on developing concrete skills and are primarily interested in theory and knowledge when they can see its practical application. Thus, gaps between knowledge and application affect their interest and motivation and decrease the likelihood that PODS will inform their work. These gaps led many students to report feeling quite powerless; their consciousness about PODS was raised but they did not know how to act on or apply their growing knowledge and awareness. Conversely, students who were assisted to apply PODS concepts and skills in assignments and field placements expressed more confidence and agency.

To learn more about these disconnects and how to address them, including how to operationalize PODS and link all course elements, faculty developed course portfolios (Cerbin, 1994) for some of the PODS-targeted courses. Participants felt that what most helped them to make stronger linkages among course elements was to start with desired student learning outcomes—specific expectations about what they wanted students to be able to do after the course.

Then they could work "backwards" to evaluate how they were 1) eliciting and assessing these (including giving feedback to students to improve their performance); and 2) using readings, class activities, and assignments, and 3) making linkages with professional practices.

The process of developing course portfolios also uncovered many implicit goals within courses that are not defined in course statements or objectives [often related to overall professional development (like teamwork and ethics issues)]. Many PODS issues are embedded in these implicit areas and were not being directly recognized or assessed.

Implications for Faculty Development (in an Organizational Context)

Although some of our learning is particular to this profession and school, much, including the conceptual frameworks and methods, also has broader applicability.

Interpretive schemas. We have stressed here interpretive schemas that reflect underlying epistemologies about PODS dimensions and the nature of learning and teaching, but many others are also relevant. Activities are needed in which schemas can emerge and be identified, with discussion of their sources and underlying epistemologies and implications. These should not be just intellectual debates, however, and must include not only opportunities to conceptualize and name experiences but also to examine, revise, and make operational interpretive schemas, concepts, and ideas. In our situation, it is not yet clear whether everyone needs to agree on particular terms and approaches.

Group processes. Most planning, implementation, and learning activities occur in groups of different types and sizes. Dynamics within groups can either promote or inhibit learning and change. For example, forces that promote silence and suppression of conflict and differences among faculty and students and the larger environment impede change. Effective faculty development for multicultural teaching requires an understanding of group dynamics and ways to manage power and other differences within groups, and the impact of the larger organizational context on these differences. Activities are needed in which faculty and students work together to engage in group activities, identify group dynamics, and work to change those that inhibit desired learning and change. In our case, participants needed to learn new frameworks and skills for continuing to engage with each other despite serious differences of opinion and approaches.

Organizational culture and norms. Group processes and individual interpretive schemas are both influenced by *and* influence organizational culture and norms. These must be assessed and examined in many contexts (some of them school or department-wide and not just within individual classrooms) for the ways that they promote or interfere with desired changes. Administrators, students, faculty (all kinds), and staff must work together if organization, culture, and norms are to change.

Organizational structures. These include curricular and course structures, as well as overall policies, elements, and arrangements within the larger organization. Here we have stressed within-course and curricular alignment difficulties, as well as standards for performance evaluation, promotion, and tenure. Examining alignment can help to identify how unchanged elements are undermining the effectiveness of changes already made. In every effort we have made to transform a particular course or assist a faculty member to implement PODS more effectively, we have encountered difficulties arising from other courses and the larger environment.

Interrelationships among all the above. All our experiences reinforce our initial assumptions that we must attend to multiple levels of the organization simultaneously with faculty development and curriculum revision. If we don't, issues at one level interfere with progress on others. Mechanisms must also be in place to anticipate and understand previously unexamined and sometimes unexpected organization-level elements that surface. We did not anticipate concerns about academic freedom, or fully understand how much our "learn-as-you-go" approach to change violated organizational norms. We are still working on ways to handle meetings and relationships as strong differences among faculty are becoming more explicit.

The importance of praxis and action-research methods. Although very labor intensive, evaluation activities have been invaluable in helping to uncover and make visible our progress, best practices, challenges, and underlying factors that need attention. Elements include gathering multiple types of data; distributing data reports, knowledge, and theory to everyone involved; reflecting on the meaning of the data (across all constituencies); developing action steps informed by data; and creating many ways to get feedback and to circulate information. Every faculty development effort should include a review of past activities and learning, new knowledge, an interactive and experiential component, and ways to evaluate and learn from the experience.

Structuration, praxis, organizational innovation, and action-research methods all require persistent, iterative, incremental steps over time. Identifying challenges and sources of resistance are important, as is recognizing and building on promising practices. Building on successes recognizes those who are successfully innovative and can generate much momentum.

Involving students. And finally, we cannot stress enough the importance of involving students extensively. Their feedback, collaboration, and impatience (as shorter-term members of the organization) were very useful to inform, support, and motivate faculty.

We are just beginning work on extending these efforts to our field sites and do not yet know what our eventual outcomes will be. We have learned a great amount, however, about what works and what does not, and hope that we have captured some of this in this paper.

References

Agger, B. (1998). *Critical social theories: An introduction.* Boulder, CO: Westview Press.

Arredondo, P. (1999). Multicultural counseling competencies as tools to address oppression and racism. *Journal of Counseling and Development, 77*(1), 102-108.

Brown, J. O. (2002). Know thyself: The impact of portfolio development on adult learning. *Adult Education Quarterly, 52*(3), 228-245.

Cerbin, W. (1994). The course portfolio as a tool for continuous improvement of teaching and learning. *Journal on Excellence in College Teaching*, *5*(1), 95-105.

Cohen, S.A. (1987). Instructional alignment: Searching for a magic bullet. *Educational Researcher, 16*(8) 16-20.

Collins, P. H. (2000). *Black feminist thought: Knowledge, consciousness, and the politics of empowerment* (2nd ed.). New York: Routledge.

Cox, T., Jr. (2001). *Creating the multicultural organization: A strategy for capturing the power of diversity*. New York: John Wiley.

Daft, R. L. (2001). *Organization theory and design* (7th ed.). Cincinnati, OH: South-Western College Publishing.

Denzin, N. (1989). *Strategies of multiple triangulation in the qualitative research act.* New York: Sage.

Diamond, R. M. (2002). Faculty, instructional, and organizational development: Options and choices. In K. H. Gillespie, L. R. Hilson, & E. C. Wadsworth (Eds.), *A guide to faculty development: Practical advice, examples and resources* (pp. 2-8). Bolton, MA: Anker.

Emirbayer, M., & Mische, A. (1998). What is agency? *American Journal of Sociology, 103*(4), 962-1023.

Fine, M. E. (1995). *Building successful multicultural organizations*. Westport, CT: Quorum Books.

Freire, P. (1972). *Education for critical consciousness*. New York: Continuum.

Freire, P. (1985). *The politics of education: Culture, power, and liberation.* Hadley, MA: Bergin & Garvey.

Freire, P. (1990). A critical understanding of social work. *Journal of Progressive Human Services, 1*(1), 3-9.

Gibbs, H. J. (2004). Student portfolios: Documenting success. *Teaching Techniques, 79*(5), 26-32.

Giddens, A. (1979). *Central problems in social theory: Action, structure, and contradiction social analysis*. Berkeley: University of California Press.

Giddens, A. (1984). *The constitution of society: Outline of the theory of structuration.* Berkeley, CA: University of California Press.

Glaser, B. G. (1992). *Emergence vs. forcing: Basics of grounded theory analysis*. Mill Valley, CA: Sociology Press.

Glaser, B, G. & Strauss, A. (1967). *The discovery of grounded theory.* Thousand Oaks, CA: Sage.

Greenwood, D. J., Whyte, W. F., & Harkavy, I. (1993). Participatory action research as a process and as a goal. *Human Relations, 46*(2), 175-191.

Hays, S. (1994). Structure and agency and the sticky problem of culture. *Sociological Theory, 12*(1), 57-72.

Mayer, J. P., & Davidson, W. S. (2000). Dissemination of innovation as social change. In J. Rappaport & E. Seidman (Eds.), *Handbook of community psychology* (pp. 421-438). New York: Kluwer Academic/Plenum Publishers.

McGoldrick, M. (Ed.). (1999). Introduction. In *Re-visioning family therapy: Race, culture, and gender in clinical practice* (2nd ed.). New York: Guilford Press.

McNiff, J., & Whitehead, J., (2002). *Action research: Principles and practice* (2nd ed.). London: Falmer Press.

Miholic, V., & Moss, M. (2001). Rethinking portfolio applications and assessment. *Journal of College Reading and Learning, 32*(1), 5-13.

Orlikowski, W. (2000). Using technology and constituting structures: A practice lens for studying technology in organizations. *Organization Science, 11*(4), 404-428.

Ortner, S. B. (1996). *Making gender: The politics and erotics of culture.* Boston: Beacon Press.

Osborne, Stephen P. (1998). Innovations, innovators and innovating. *Voluntary organizations and innovation in public services* (pp. 20-68). London & New York: Routledge.

Reisch, M. & Andrews, J. (2001). *The road not taken: A history of radical social work in the United States.* Philadelphia: Brunner–Routledge.

Rhoads, R. A., & Black, M. A. (1995). Student affairs practitioners as transformative educators: Advancing a critical cultural perspective. *Journal of College Student Development, 36*(5), 413-421.

Rogers, E. M. (1995). *Diffusion of innovations* (4th ed.). New York: The Free Press.

Strauss, A. L., & Corbin, J. M. (1998). *Basics of qualitative research: Techniques and procedures for grounded theory*. Thousand Oaks, CA: Sage.

Sue, D. W., & Sue, D. (2002). *Counseling the culturally different.* New York: Wiley.

Willis, E. M., & Davies, M. A. (2002). The promise and practice of professional portfolios. *Action in Teacher Education, 23*(4), 18-27.

Whyte, W. F. (1991). *Participatory action research.* Thousand Oaks, CA: Sage.

Beth Glover Reed is a faculty member in social work and women's studies at the University of Michigan. **Melissa R. Peet** received her MSW from the School of Social Work and is a doctoral candidate in the program in higher and post-secondary education at the University of Michigan.

Appendix 1

The University of Michigan School of Social Work
Intensive Focus on Privilege, Oppression, Diversity and Social Justice
Course Preparation and Assessment Worksheet

Course #/Name: ______________________

For both the Knowledge and Skills sections below, please check which course elements will deal with which of the following criteria. Attach a brief narrative explanation of how the criteria will be implemented.

Knowledge	*Readings*	*Class* *Assignments*	*In-Class* **Exercises & Activities**	**Links Between Readings, Class Activities & Assignments**	**Student Grading Criteria and Other Methods of Evaluation**	**Link Between Classroom Experience & Field**
Social justice & visions of what social justice could look like						
Systems (and mechanisms) that create & support oppression & privilege						
Limitations & strengths of social justice paradigms & framework that are used & how they are learned						
Practice approaches to create steps that move in the direction of social justice						
Diversity & human differences & how they intersect with each other including cultural & ethnic differences (inclusive of African, Hispanic, Asian, Native/First Nation, & Arabic ancestry & culture), social construction of race, economic class, disability status, sexual orientation, gender, religion, age & others relevant for a particular practice area.						
Diversity & human differences & how they are linked to issues of societal power, access to resources & mobility						
The importance of historical, global & other contexts of human difference						
Ways to effectively work within cultural & other social group contexts						
Diversity between different groups, within different groups and the strength and resilience of different groups						

Additional Comments:

Skills	*Readings*	*Class Assignments*	*In-Class* **Exercises & Activities**	**Links Between Readings, Class Activities & Assignments**	**Student Grading and Other Methods of Evaluation**	**Link Between Classroom Experience & Field**
Identify mechanisms that support oppression & privilege & how they intersect with each other in the context of the multiple & intersecting categories that people occupy.						
Critique knowledge, research methods & practice methods in terms of what cultural frameworks are represented, illuminated or obscured.						
Disrupt systems & mechanisms that create & support oppression & privilege.						
Implement collaborative interventions that assist client systems within their cultural & other social group contexts						
Promote social justice goals & diversity issues & incorporate them into practice						

Additional Comments:

Pedagogy From Maurianne Adams, Lee Anne Bell and Pat Griffin (1997) *Teaching for Diversity and Social Justice*. New York: Routledge.	*Please discuss how the overall concentration and each course statement and implementation incorporates these, and any other comments*
Balancing the emotional and cognitive components of the learning process - In what ways does the learning experience pay attention to personal safety, classroom norms and guidelines for group behavior? Does it protect ignorant or diverse views and avoid singling out persons of difference to represent all persons of the same difference?	
Acknowledging and supporting the personal (the individual student's experience) while illuminating the systemic (the interactions among social groups) - How does the learning experience call attention to the here and now of the classroom setting, grounding the systemic or abstract in an accumulation of concrete real-life examples?	
Attending to social relations within the classroom - How does the learning experience help the students name behaviors that emerge in group dynamics, understand group process and improve interpersonal communications without blaming or judging each other?	
Utilizing reflection and experience as tools for student-centered learning - How does the learning experience recognize the student's world view and experience as the starting point for dialogue or problem-posing?	
Valuing awareness and personal growth - In what ways does the learning experience accommodate and balance different levels of awareness and learning styles?	
Integrating social justice, diversity and change - How does the learning experience integrate goals of social awareness, knowledge development and social action?	
Critical thinking / critical consciousness - In what ways are students encouraged to critique models, frameworks and materials in the context of IF dimensions? In what way does the instructional experience support critical consciousness? (Is there support for students to not only question the questions but also question the answers (Freire's notion of the 'liberatory')?)	

Additional Comments:

Appendix I is a working document that has been revised several times. It was first developed in Fall, 2001 at the University of Michigan School of Social Work. R. M. Ortega was the original drafter with input from many others.

Chapter 36

Interactive Theater as a Multicultural Change Agent in Faculty Development

Diana Kardia, A.T. Miller, and Jeffrey Steiger

Interactive theater is used at the University of Michigan to engage instructors in effective discussions about classroom climate and the experience of teaching students on the margins. This approach utilizes principles of multicultural teaching to open conversations which have become routine or reactive in other arenas, and is especially effective with non-voluntary audiences. Theater provides a powerful, yet non-threatening, mechanism for summarizing research findings, and makes the implications of such findings immediate and tangible. The interactive format empowers instructors to articulate problems, generate solutions, and examine how inclusive teaching benefits all students.

Overview

In the past decade, multicultural programs in faculty development have grown in number and in sophistication as faculty development professionals have explored the complexities of engaging diverse disciplinary audiences in this work. A high degree of success has been actualized in work with those faculty who identify multicultural teaching as a recognizable and worthy goal. The collaboration between such faculty and faculty development professionals has resulted in a variety of effective curricular and pedagogical strategies that promote the learning and success of all students in diverse (and mixed) classrooms across the university.

Within this context, however, both faculty and students lament that many instructors who need greater awareness, knowledge, and skill development to teach inclusively are not at the table. Furthermore, the methods that work successfully to engage committed multicultural teachers often do not translate to interactions with instructors who do not see the relevance of these issues to their own teaching. These methods are also often not employed by those who may be willing to consider multicultural issues, but who are disillusioned with multicultural programs that they feel do not speak to the reality of their classroom experiences. In our own experience, we faced continued frustration with the multicultural segments we embedded in our more general programs, such as faculty orientation, which routinely received mixed reviews and did not achieve our intention of reaching instructors and classrooms across the university.

This track record began to change through the use of interactive theater as a medium for our multicultural work in these settings. In 1997, the Women in Science and Engineering Program (WISE) at the University of Michigan received a grant from the Sloan Foundation to develop an interactive theater program designed to promote awareness among Graduate Student Instructors (GSIs) of the factors leading to a high attrition rate among women in the sciences. Our faculty development center, the Center for Research on Learning and Teaching (CRLT), began collaborating with this program as it developed. While still under the auspices of WISE, this program generated such enthusiasm among GSIs, faculty, and administrators that CRLT was granted central and unit based funding to adopt this program when the grant funding ran out in 2000. The CRLT Theatre Program continues to developed scripts (15 at the time this volume want to press) and numerous other specialty performances that are regularly offered as a faculty development resource on campus. During its first four years as a CRLT program, we have conducted a total of more than 150 performances reaching over 7500 instructors.

In the early stages of our use of interactive theater, we performed the sketches in breakout sessions at events like faculty orientation, hoping to attract a more diverse audience through the attraction of this unusual medium, but still unsure it would be received well across the board. Encouraged by the strong evaluations these breakout sessions received, we moved the theater into the plenary sessions, performing for all participants. The evaluations remained strong, and these performances often receive a higher rating than any other component of the program. Thus we have enhanced our overall success while effectively achieving our intent to present multicultural programming to the broad cross-section of the university that attends such events. Follow-up evaluations, done three to six months after such events, confirm the success of this program. Instructors repeatedly tell us that the program raised their awareness and changed their practices in the classroom.

How Interactive Theater Works

A basic interactive theater performance consists of a typical dramatic performance followed by a facilitated discussion between the audience and the characters from the sketch. The set piece drama is short (approximately 10 minutes) and portrays a classroom scenario in which students and an instructor act out situations documented by research. For example, in the Gender and the Classroom sketch originally created by WISE, questions posed by a female student are answered in a peremptory fashion while male students are given an opportunity to work through their answers with assistance from the instructor. The facilitated discussion is an opportunity for the audience to explore the dynamics occurring in the sketch by asking the characters questions about their motives and reactions. Audience members also offer feedback to the instructor and the students about how to improve this classroom environment. In many cases, this discussion is followed by a second performance depicting a transformed classroom that reflects the points raised in the discussion.

Because the actors must improvise answers to a wide variety of questions, some anticipated and some unexpected, it is important that they are well versed in the research being presented, and on-board with the multicultural mission of the theatre program. We have learned the importance of doing extensive cast development on the specific issues covered, as well as on the purposes of multicultural faculty development and institutional responsibility. While participants are actors playing characters, they also are part of the larger university program, and must therefore understand and embrace the larger objectives if they are to be convincing and reliable during improvisation.

The facilitator plays a key role by reinforcing and elaborating on the underlying research base reflected in the sketch. Before the sketch is performed, the facilitator sets the stage by defining the concept of classroom climate (which is typically the focus of these sketches) and by preparing the audience for their participation. During the interactive discussion, the facilitator role is limited to directing the flow of the conversation between the audience and the characters. At the end of this discussion, the facilitator may add information about research findings or pedagogical strategies that bring further integration to the discussion.

While most of our performances limit participation to the interactive discussion, some performances allow the audience to take a more involved role in the performance itself. Drawing on the concept of Forum Theater developed by Augusto Boal (see below), a problematic scene is portrayed by actors, and then audience members are invited to play the role of the instructor and act out their solutions. Numerous audience members are invited into this role (in succession) in order to get ideas on the table and avoid any sense of acting competition or defining a "right" answer. The nuances of each intervention are discussed among participants and new strategies are formed based on the previous conclusions. Hence, a dialogue of showing *and* telling is created through a quick succession of scenarios. Preparation for these performances may include the development of short scenarios that focus audience attention on specific issues, or the actual scenario itself may be generated by the audience. In both of these cases, theater games and warm-up exercises are utilized to ready audience members for going on stage.

Why Interactive Theater Works

The development of the CRLT Theatre Program has been guided by three underlying sets of principles: the work of Augusto Boal, who originated the concepts of interactive and forum theater in his work (called "Theatre of the Oppressed" in Brazil); faculty development principles; and the principles of multicultural teaching. The use of humor has also been a key component of the success of this program and is described below. Each of these arenas highlights important aspects of why this program works.

Augusto Boal was inspired to use interactive theater by his friend and Brazilian compatriot, Paolo Freire. He was concerned that performances simply for entertainment or amusement did not serve audiences or society well, and that "social cause" theater was often perceived as didactic or preachy. Like Freire, Boal assumes that the fundamental form of knowledge and wisdom is dialogical and inherent. Thus, the instructor's, or actor's, job is to present information and then problematize the information in order to search for knowledge as a source for inspiration and action. At its most basic form, the actors and director do not even choose the theme or issue for the performance, but that too comes out of the experience, concerns, issues, and ideas held by the audience. Boal's terminology helps further indicate the dynamics of his approach. Attendees of a Boalian performance, actors and spectators alike, are all dubbed "Spect-Actors"—both spectator and actor. The likelihood that real ownership and inspired action are elicited by such performances is raised significantly, and the respect demonstrated for the audience creates an alliance between artist and audience, rather than an alienating elitism.

There is much in common between Boal's approach to theater and many of the basic premises of faculty development work. Given the independent nature of the teaching endeavor, faculty development programs are most successful when they engage instructors on the problems that matter most to them and in the generation of their own solutions. Multicultural programs in faculty development have struggled with how to honor this principle while also naming issues and dynamics that may not yet be visible or meaningful to instructors. The difficulty of maintaining this balance is evident in participant criticisms of such programs: too often instructors say that these programs feel like lectures, condescension, or provoke feelings of guilt.

Interactive theater avoids these criticisms by creating a forum in which problems are simply demonstrated (or may even be generated by the audience themselves) and the participants themselves take full responsibility for naming and resolving these problems. In this way, the intelligence and analytical skills of the audience are employed, and the audience is more invested in the solutions that are generated. Interactive theater also avoids misunderstandings about motivation or intentions, or the impression that any particular person is being criticized or put on the spot, since the scenario being discussed is familiar but removed from the individual experience of audience members. This focused distance creates the space for discussion.

A second key faculty development principle utilized by this program is the use of research as a central foundation and resource. A significant portion of our audiences report that the informed discussion of research was crucial to their willingness to participate in the program. Having a common intellectual problem to analyze and discuss also creates an alliance among faculty members in the audience. Thus this approach engages faculty in a familiar activity: reviewing and analyzing data. Typically, audience members combine their own experiential knowledge with the scenario depicted in the sketch as they consider the problems and implications of the classroom dynamics.

Fundamental principles of multicultural teaching that underlie this program are having a setting that is open to participation by everyone, laying out common ground rules and parameters for exchange, and avoiding assumptions about or placing expectations on any particular participant. Providing a common scenario and a clear method for participation in interactive theater fulfills all of these principles and allows each performance to adapt itself to the interests and needs of any given audience. This approach allows for the specific needs, experiences, and identities of an audience to be expressed voluntarily, and in reference to a text and the dramatic presentation. This format provides considerably more comfort and safety when working with colleagues, all of whom have recognized expertise in particular subject areas, as well as a voice in the institutional setting.

Being willing to use humor as a medium to discuss complicated and problematic issues has been key to our success. Humor bonds an audience in common emotion and releases tension around subject matter that is often seen as touchy, controversial, or inflammatory. Humor is unexpected and therefore keeps an audience interested and focused. It makes people comfortable both with the presenters and with each other and frees thinking to go deeper, rewarding those who pay attention with amusement as well as new view points. Finally, humor breaks down a key form of guardedness typical of multicultural discussions: the fear of saying something wrong. It models that learning is possible and does not always have to be painful.

Without making light of the pedagogical issues being addressed, humor is typically utilized in these presentations. In "Gender in the Classroom," one student is continually coming up with offbeat ideas and smart comebacks, both within the script and within the interactive portion. He wants to be called a note taker for his group, not a secretary, he accuses the instructor of stringing random words together in a homework problem, demands a decoder ring, and plays up the drama of having to learn new material 24 hours before an exam. Another character in this script plays the role of a student who sets high priorities on getting all the answers right and following the rules. Characters such as these are easily recognized by the audience; they bring a playfulness to the presentations that realistically broadens the classroom dynamics beyond the specific issue examined, and their humor can invite participation. Other kinds of humor spring from portrayals of collectively shared but unspoken situations. In a sketch on gender dynamics in a faculty meeting, audience laughter emerges as a form of recognition of the plight of the female character as she struggles to be heard amidst departmental politics and gendered dynamics. In this case, laughter serves as a pressure release valve, allowing audience members shared recognition that a problem exists even while solutions still seem amorphous and complex.

Two Examples

The following section highlights two sketches currently in use in the CRLT Theatre Program. Each of these descriptions includes an overview of the purpose of the sketch and typical audience questions and reactions. The first sketch presented, "Gender in the Classroom," is a standard interactive format consisting of an initial sketch, audience interaction, and follow up sketch. The second sketch, "Conflict in the Classroom," incorporates principles of forum theater to engage the audience in resolution of these classroom issues.

Gender in the Classroom

This sketch consists of two ten-minute scenarios, separated by an interlude in which the audience interacts with the actors (who stay in character). In the first scenario, Chris, the only female student in a small physics class, experiences a variety of classroom situations that lead to a chilly or problematic classroom environment. (These conditions have been associated with decreased self-esteem and a decrease in retention among women in science, math, and engineering, and these conditions can negatively affect the learning experience of women students in other disciplines as well.) The second version of this scenario demonstrates how general good teaching practices correct many inequities in the classroom and improve the learning environment for Chris and for the other students as well.

Theater allows the layering of many issues simultaneously, and different audiences respond to different classroom dynamics played out in this sketch. There is, however, a set of key issues in this sketch typically identified and discussed by all audiences. Some examples include:

- *Instructor professionalism and boundaries.* In the first scenario, Chad, the instructor, runs a very informal classroom including such behaviors as joking with the students about holding office hours in a bar, chiding students with phrases such as "C'mon guys, you've got to show some effort here!", and responding to those students who shout out rather than calling on hands. This buddy-buddy approach is demonstrated to primarily reward and engage the animated males in the classroom while creating tensions and barriers between Chad and other students. In the second scenario, Chad tries less hard to be liked by the students and becomes a more effective teacher to the whole classroom.
- *Instructor tone.* Chad speaks to Chris in the first scenario in ways that are likely to undermine self-esteem. Examples include: "Did some of this not make sense to you?" "I think we've just covered that stuff, Chris." "Oh, that's simple." (This is said in response to a question Chris raises about the homework. By the reactions of the other students, it is clear that no one agrees with Chad's assessment, but no one is likely to ask additional questions based on this dismissal.) Furthermore, Chad's responses to Chris are often pre-emptive, cutting her off as she formulates a question or answer. This tone has a direct effect on Chris, and dampens other student contributions as well. A more uniform and encouraging tone in the second sketch promotes stronger class discussion all around.
- *The instructor's role in peer interactions.* A variety of problematic peer interactions affect Chris in the first sketch including: a male student who is continually asking her on dates, hesitation by other students to be in a group with her, and willingness on the part of other students to interrupt and override her participation in the class. Chad's classroom leadership in the second sketch resolves these issues through behaviors such as proactively assigning groups and group roles, and redirecting students who interrupt, thus protecting and ensuring Chris's participation in the class.

Chad initiates and motivates all changes between the two scenarios in this sketch. Changes in student behavior are an organic response to the difference in Chad. Before seeing the second sketch, audiences typically explore the ways in which students might be responsible for these changes. In particular, many audience members want Chris to change, to become more assertive and exhibit behavior that is more likely to be rewarded in this environment. These sketches deliberately challenge that assumption. When confronted with this suggestion in the interactive portion, Chris asserts her right to engage in what she considers to be more polite and appropriate behavior and points out ways in which she does attempt to interrupt and be heard, but to no avail. The second scenario effectively demonstrates the responsibility and ability of the instructor to shift the circumstances of engagement so that teaching and learning can happen for all students in the classroom.

Conflict in Classroom

In this sketch, a problem given for homework in a statistics class unexpectedly raises self-disclosure and controversy among the students, leaving the instructor at a loss as to how to repair the human relations and move on, and whether to engage with a hot social topic the instructor feels ill-equipped to discuss. The initial sketch closes with stony and tense silence in the stand-off between four students, one of whom naively blundered into controversy, another of whom is highly offended, a third who wants to move on with stats, and a fourth who has seen "all of this" before and knows it never comes out well. Complicating the dynamics are the perceived social and racial identities of the characters, some of which are intentionally ambiguous and open to audience interpretation or interrogation. It is obvious in the initial presentation that the instructor's attempt to move on quickly to another problem has failed. The sketch is performed additional times allowing any audience member to stop the action at any time and intervene as the instructor as the characters improvise realistic responses to the strategies employed. At least five or six audience members are invited to handle the overall situation, or any aspect of it, and in many cases 10 or more audience members take to the stage.

Inevitably, several audience members demonstrate various ways that such a classroom "blow-up" can be directed as a teachable moment, and the actors keep the scenario complex by making it clear that the needs of every character must be addressed. Facilitation in this model involves inviting the audience to identify, discuss, and debrief each strategy that is attempted, and to weigh what sorts of methods fit their styles, situations, and comfort levels. The characters can also be asked how various strategies work for them as students, thus every audience member gets that "second chance" so many of them only mull over on sleepless nights in response to real classroom experiences. This method also highlights the benefits of working through teaching problems with colleagues and consulting one another about teaching—two areas faculty development professionals often try to promote among faculty, but areas that the usual campus culture around classroom autonomy tends to discourage.

Beyond the specific strategies instructors try out and evaluate in this interactive theater experience, the audience is also invited to engage in some self-examination in its responses to the different student characters. A typical division in any audience is between those who find David – the student who naively raises the issue and thus reveals his prejudice – - "the cause" of the incident, and those who feel that the student who "calls" David on his prejudice is the source of conflict. When the facilitator points out this split in audience interpretation and experience, he or she makes real the ways that different students can see and feel an incident or situation quite differently. It is also more often the case that this audience division breaks along identity lines, and so the facilitator is also able to demonstrate how to serve as a bridge when there is a disagreement that might have some implications for those on the different social sides of privilege and oppression. Thus larger principles of multicultural practice are communicated and experienced in the course of exploring a specific classroom situation.

Conclusion: Changing Classrooms, Changing the Institution

Those responsible for multicultural climate change on college campuses often despair about being able to get into the classrooms of any faculty beyond the already convinced. The staff and administration can change orientations, student services, and many other institutional practices and programs, but they usually cannot change courses and curriculum without the cooperation of many faculty members across the institution. Complicating this need for cooperation are the conflicting tensions and motivations of faculty members as autonomous intellectuals and as busy professionals for whom teaching is only one facet of their work. We work hard to balance the demands for direct and prescriptive advice and solutions with the need to respect and cultivate allies who will make informed decisions on what is appropriate for their own diverse classrooms and teaching situations.

What we have found with interactive theater is a way to reach many faculty in a memorable and convincing format that is actually producing change in classrooms across our university. Interactive theater has also served for many instructors as a valuable gateway to our center's many other multicultural teaching and learning services. The engaging presentation of research and strategies opens the door for instructors to see that inclusive teaching is not just a matter of good will and common sense, but that there are real issues and techniques that should be considered, skills to develop, and approaches to be learned. Not only has the interactive theater program expanded our reach and been effective on its own, but it has also strengthened the whole array of our multicultural offerings.

Diana Kardia worked with the CRLT Theatre Program for its first five years. She is now a freelance writer and founder of Diversity By Design, a consulting, coaching, and training resource for higher education. **A.T. Miller** is coordinator of multicultural teaching and learning at the Center for Research on Learning and Teaching (CLRT) at the University of Michigan Ann Arbor, and **Jeffrey Steiger** is director of the CRLT Theatre Program.

Appendix

Resources for Creating an Interactive Theater Program

Research summaries and further information about teaching strategies demonstrated through the CRLT Theater Program can be found on the CRLT website: www.crlt.umich.edu

The following will be of particular relevance:

CRLT Occasional Paper #8: *Undergraduate Women in Science and Engineering: Providing Academic Support,* by Susan Montgomery and Martha Cohen Barrett
http://www.crlt.umich.edu/occ8.html

Creating Inclusive College Classrooms, by Shari Saunders and Diana Kardia
http://www.crlt.umich.edu/F6.html

Multicultural Teaching Resources
http://www.crlt.umich.edu/multimain.html

Teaching Strategies and Disciplinary Resources
http://www.crlt.umich.edu/tsmain.html

The CRLT Theatre Program
http://www.crlt.umich.edu/theatremain.html

Chapter 37

Dissemination of Peer-Led Team Learning (PLTL) and Formation of a National Network: Embracing a Common Pedagogy

Pratibha Varma-Nelson and David Gosser

For several years we have been part of a coalition that has been involved in design, implementation, evaluation and dissemination of a new pedagogy called Peer-Led Team Learning (PLTL). Evaluations indicate this pedagogy is accessible and effective for students from diverse backgrounds and cultures with a variety of learning styles. We describe a four-tier model for dissemination and the role that the Workshop Project Associate (WPA) mini-grant program has played in building a national network of faculty who have implemented PLTL.

Unmet demand for mathematics and science graduates poses a potentially serious problem for American industry and society. While the National Research Council (NRC) predicts that the U.S. demand for scientists and engineers will increase at more than double the rate for all other occupations during the next decade, both increasing difficulties in attracting students into math and science fields and high attrition rates of enrolled students have contributed to the increasing deficit in quality math and science professionals.

In 1993, a study by Astin reported that 40% of college freshmen in science, mathematics, and engineering switched out before their senior year. The first math class a student takes in college can, therefore, be a pivotal experience, affecting career ambitions and self-esteem (Seymour & Hewitt, 1997). Seymour and Hewitt also showed that "the most effective way to improve retention among women and students of color, and to build their numbers over the longer term, is to improve the quality of the learning experience for all students—including non-science majors who wish to study science and mathematics as part of their overall education."

They also found that while almost all students value collaborative learning, students from underrepresented groups "appreciate it more and miss it when [it is] unavailable." Their research identified interactive collaborative learning as key to improving student performance. Treisman (1992) showed that students often fail to excel in science and mathematics because they do not know how to work effectively with peers to "create a community for themselves based on shared interest and common professional goals." Treisman found that remedial programs and those specifically targeted at minority groups often do not increase success rates, suggesting that programs to improve learning that include all students are more successful.

To enhance the success of students in the sciences, in addition to emphasizing mastery of content, instruction should engage students in debate and discussion of scientific ideas, arriving at a consensus, which underlines current understanding of scientific process. Traditional and institutional barriers do not always make this possible. The traditional lecture-oriented model of science instruction makes it difficult to actually achieve desired engagement. How can students be involved in serious debate and discussion in the context of a large lecture hall? How can they be engaged in critical thinking and problem-posing if their curriculum is driven by content coverage and the time constraints of three 50-minute meetings per week? How can students develop leadership and communication skills as part of learning science? We posit that the answer lies with peer-led team learning.

A Tremendous Untapped Resource

Peer-Led Team Learning is a model of instruction that was first introduced in general chemistry classes at The City College of New York (CCNY), part of the City University of New York (CUNY) system (Woodward, et al., 1993). In the early 1990s, CCNY introduced formally scheduled, student-led workshops that were an integral part of the course. The first group of leaders was recruited from advanced chemistry students. Thereafter, it was found that many new leaders could be recruited from those who had done well in the class, had good communication skills and a desire to assist other students. The weekly structure was fairly simple: student leaders prepared for workshops by discussing the material with the faculty teaching the course. Following this preparation, the leaders would meet with their student group to lead a discussion and debate chemistry concepts and problems. This model was then expanded to other colleges in the CUNY system.

There was an unforeseen explosion of enthusiasm for these peer-led workshops. In focus groups, students and student leaders voiced support for the model. In contrast to lecture, where students "might not say anything the whole semester," students felt that workshops reduced anxiety, leaders were accessible, and peers became supportive. The leader was viewed as a peer and sometimes a friend. It was frequently remarked that the leader explained things "in a different way...using different vocabulary and examples." Students also said leaders were successful because they were close in age and "know where you are coming from" and "the way you understand things." There was agreement that in all groups, students started out feeling and acting alone, bringing with them their traditional classroom attitudes, but after a few weeks, their behaviors changed. Workshop leaders asked their students to explain problems, and as these students became increasingly confident, they in turn began questioning and helping one another. They found it beneficial that "the same idea would often be expressed in different ways by different students." The importance of mistakes came up. The workshops provided students with "the chance to make a lot of little mistakes," helping to "make connections in the brain." Students regarded their peer leaders as less threatening than their professors, so they felt free to express themselves and explore different ideas, to see where they led, and "to see what worked."

Becoming a Pedagogical Method

While it may be said that the concept of using more advanced peers to lead small group learning is not entirely original, it has not until recently really been formally recognized as a pedagogical model. Student interactions may have taken place in "the little red schoolhouse" where necessity required more advanced students to assist others, and small group learning promoted by Uri Treisman and the Keller plan (Cracolice & Roth, 1996) pioneered such innovative teaching more formally. Workshops led by a peer certainly share many features of active student engagement with various models of student assisted learning (Miller, et al., 2001). The unique feature of the PLTL model is the specific role of a student (peer) as a leader of the group discussion. The PLTL model retains the advantages of small group learning, but introduces several important qualities that make team learning more accessible by utilizing the tremendous untapped resource of college undergraduate students. By carefully defining PLTL, it becomes amenable to study, accessible to employ, and easier to maintain and institutionalize.

Steps in Implementing Peer-Led Team Learning

A. Recruitment, selection and training of peer leaders. In preparing to implement a PLTL course, one of the first tasks is to find undergraduate leaders, one for each six to eight students who will take the course. The first time around, faculty are likely to look for advanced students (majors) and for students who have done well in a recent class. It is helpful to have a formalized application and acceptance process. This will serve to clarify the roles and responsibilities of the faculty and the leaders and will be a first step in leader training. One method of interviewing students that has been successful is a group interview, where a number of applicants are interviewed in a workshop style setting. Their responses to questions relating to typical workshop settings will provide a strong indication of their potential for group leadership (communication skills, listening skills, and attitudes towards assisting other students). At most campuses, the leaders are compensated at a level that is commensurate with local standards. Peer leaders typically earn $400 to $500 for a semester leading a group in a course. The time commitment is the actual workshop (two hours per week) and participation in leader training (one to three hours per week).

Leader training will often begin with a one or two day pre-semester meeting, led by a team consisting of faculty, experienced leaders, and a learning specialist. New peer leaders become acquainted through participatory workshops, with introductory content of the first workshop; diversity of learning styles; principles of collaborative learning; and active listening. In this setting they have a chance to voice their concerns and apprehensions and also to work with experienced leaders in preparing possible solutions and answers to their questions such as, "What should I do if a student demands answers?", "What should I do with a dominant student or a shy student?", or "What are the boundaries that I can set in interacting with my group?"

Following this introductory meeting, students need to have follow-up preparation and training in both content and leadership. This can be obtained in a number of ways, but in any case the direct involvement of the faculty is critical. The most common manner in which students are prepared is for the faculty to lead a workshop each week with the peer leaders as the members of the group. In this way the faculty can model the desired listening and collaborative learning skills. Peer leaders can be prepared in the content and can see what is expected of them in a workshop setting. The peer leaders are expected to facilitate discussion and debate among the group members, and are discouraged from lecturing. To this end, it is very helpful for leaders to have explicit instruction in various collaborative learning methods such as pair problem-solving, structured round robin, brainstorming, and so forth. Leaders are asked to write reflective journals, which often illustrate their own personal growth through the experience of peer leadership.

On several campuses there is a formal PLTL leader training course, which may have one or two credits. The course can be offered in collaboration with a learning assistance center or school of education. This collaboration introduces a partnership outside the discipline that can be very productive. The learning specialist, a generic term that denotes an individual whose specialty is in the areas of student assistance, cognitive science, science education, or adult learning, can bring an important perspective and provide great assistance to the faculty in balancing the content with an attention to group leadership and pedagogy. The partnership also can introduce assistance in forming alliances and obtaining institutional funding to do PLTL workshops.

B. Materials for workshops. The selection and/or construction of appropriate workshop materials is critical to the success of the workshop. They will be the tools of the peer leaders' work and should be constructed with the specific structure of the workshop in mind. In fact, the existence of the two-hour workshop offers an opportunity to think more deeply about the objectives of the course and how they can be fostered through problem-solving activity in the workshop. Central concepts are introduced by the instructor in lecture. The workshop units are carefully designed to promote deeper understanding of the material. Students are expected to attend lecture, complete readings and do a self-test and/or assigned problems prior to the workshop. Typical peer-led workshops will begin with a brief review of the self-test, and then proceed by tackling the problems of the workshop unit.

It is possible to transform traditional textbook problems into questions that will be suitable for group discussion which will explicitly raise more fundamental questions than are typically found in textbooks. A straightforward question in a text that simply requests a numerical answer can be improved by structuring the problem into parts, asking the group to explain each part, reflect on the answers, explain to their neighbors, compare methods, and create flowcharts and visual representations of their thought processes. The workshop is a very good environment to explore various models and representations of concepts and problem solving. The small group setting is perfect for the introduction of model building and intellectual processes characteristic of the discipline, including more traditional items such as molecular model building (important for the understanding of tetrahedral carbon and DNA) as well as "games" of simulation based on assumptions and rules. The role of such intellectual model building coupled with concrete representations can be very helpful for developing students' understanding of concepts that appear more abstract (for example, equations of kinetics).

C. Examining outcomes. Based on the evaluation and reflections of the original implementers, the factors noted as important ingredients for peer-led workshops – including involvement of the instructor, training and supervision of leaders, the quality of materials, and others – became codified as six critical components:

1. The peer-led workshop is integral to the course;
2. The faculty teaching the course meet regularly with the leaders to ensure content preparation and integration of the workshop into the course;
3. The peer leaders are trained in content, pedagogy, and group facilitation;
4. Materials used are appropriately challenging and useful tools in small-group problemsolving;
5. Space, time, and the environment are conducive to learning;
6. Institutional support is provided (Sarquis, et al., 2001).

Several years of new adoptions and evaluations have demonstrated that these components are indispensable to the implementation of PLTL in ways that will lead to increased student academic performance, positive experiences for the peer leaders, and overall satisfaction for the faculty members involved. Extensive analysis has revealed the model's positive impact on student attitude and success in the study of science and mathematics (Gafney & Varma-Nelson, 2002; Tenney & Houck, 2004). Surveys have indicated that when the method is introduced with fidelity to the model, students place a high value on the workshops. Surveys of peer leaders several years after graduation have revealed that they view the experience as highly beneficial, not only as an aid to learning but also as excellent career preparation, providing experience and confidence in making presentations and working in teams. Further studies in this area are in progress.

Tien, Roth and Kampmeier (2002) conducted a study on groups of students who were in Jack Kampmeier's traditional organic chemistry course at the University of Rochester from 1992 to 1994 with those who were involved in PLTL Workshops from 1996 to 1999. Although the control and treatment sections were not taught in the same year, they were similar in many ways. The same instructor taught the course, with the same textbook, lecture style, class size, and level of difficulty. It was found that the workshop participants outperformed the control group on exams in all cases. For overall means, the scores were significantly different with $P < 0.01$. When broken down by gender and ethnicity. the results show that all PLTL groups outperformed their counterparts in the more traditional course. While such rigorous statistical analyses have not been performed in all cases, at least 20 similar studies have been conducted involving PLTL workshops at other institutions involving several disciplines (Table 1). As stated by Lyle and Robinson (2003), "although there may be flaws in a study, if the study is repeated, taking into account the flaws that have arisen and the same general results occur, the results can be considered useful" (p. 132).

While the PLTL Project's primary assessment of student performance was based on grade comparisons and surveys of 1500 students at thirteen

Table 1. Comparisons of Percent of Students Achieving ABC Grades

Institution	*Non-PLTL % ABC*	*PLTL % ABC*
Historic Comparisons		
University of Rochester (Org)	66 (n=1450±)	79 (n=1554)
St. Xavier, Chi (Org/Bioch)	72 (n=95)	84 (n=116)
City College 103.1 (G Ch 1)	38 (historic)	58 (n=484)
City College 104.1 (G Ch 2)	52 (historic)	66 (n=137)
University of Portland (Chem)	44 (%AB, historic)	73 (%AB,n=99)
Prince George's CC (A&P)	39 (historic)	53 (n=34)
Prince George's CC (Gen C)	51 (n=173)	66 (n=156)
University of Miami (Int Bio)	82 (n=1471)	85 (n=1584)
Evergreen CC (Chem)	65.3 (n=269)	74.4 (n=74)
Randomly Assigned		
Univ. of Pittsburgh (G Ch 2)	83 (n=113)	90 (n=130)
Self Selected Groups		
University of Rochester (Org)	2.68 (Ave grade, n=171)	3.09 (n=119)
University of Kentucky (Gen Chem)	63 (n=1072)	84 (n=92)
U of OH, Athens (Gen Chem)	76.5 (n=292)	83.6 (n=65)
Sierra College (Inorganic)	72.5 (n=62)	94 (n=82)
Sierra College (Organic)	70.8 (n=24)	94.8 (n=19)
Portland State University (Gen Chem)	74 (n=119)	89 (n=44)
Miami of Ohio (Gen Chem)	70 (n=236)	75 (n=116)
State University of West Georgia	35 (n=78)	49 (n=145)

institutions, many new adopters of PLTL are in the process of collecting and reporting additional data from a variety of perspectives. The most commonly-used instruments other than grades have been the Student Assessment of Learning Gains (SALG) (Seymour) and the American Chemical Society's (ACS) General Chemistry exams. Goodwin and Gilbert (2001) reported higher scores on the ACS exam for PLTL students. Blake (2001) compared the performance of former workshop leaders (n=42) with those of non-leaders (n=144), and found that former leaders scored 20% higher than non-leaders, even though the non-leaders who had been tested had taken more advanced chemistry courses.

Gafney and Varma-Nelson (2002) conducted a study of past leaders (n=26) to determine how they viewed their PLTL experience after having graduated from college. Sixteen respondents reported that acting as a peer leader was their most valuable undergraduate experience and that it increased their confidence and early success in gaining entry to and making progress in science-related careers and made them more effective in interacting with people in a variety of situations – giving presentations, participating in discussions, and working as members of a team.

A strong theoretical base for understanding why PLTL models are successful can be found in the works of L.S. Vygotsky (1978), who viewed learning as a profoundly social process that emphasizes dialogue, language, and mediated growth. The PLTL model, with its emphasis on peer-assisted instruction, maps well onto Vygotsky's theoretical framework (Cracolice, 2000). In addition it draws from other well-established areas of educational design and research such as group learning, reciprocal teaching, power of explanatory knowledge, and studio instruction (Varma-Nelson & Coppola, 2004).

D. Disseminating the model. From the initial implementation in general chemistry at several CUNY campuses in the mid 1990s, the PLTL workshop model was adopted, further developed and refined by a group of chemistry faculty from the University of Rochester, New York City College of Technology (CUNY), and St. Xavier University, Chicago (Gosser, et al., 1996). Areas of substantial effort by this leadership group included the development of leader training and materials, institutional issues, and evaluation of the model. This group expanded further, and by 1999 the PLTL Workshop Project's core dissemination group now included the University of Montana, Prince George's Community College (MD), the University of Miami, San Jose City College (CA), Glendale Community College (CA), and Portland State University (OR).

Even by conservative estimates, the PLTL Workshop method is now in use by more than 150 faculty, teaching all of the physical sciences and mathematics disciplines at more than 60 institutions in 25 states. More than 15,000 students are taking PLTL courses led by more than 1400 peer leaders. Published Project materials include a five volume Peer-Led Team Learning Series (Prentice Hall, 2001) comprised of workbooks in General Chemistry, Organic Chemistry, General Biological and Organic Chemistry, A Guidebook, and A Handbook for Team Leaders. Fifteen issues of the Project newsletter, *Progressions*, have been published, and an ISSN designation has been obtained. The Project website, www.pltl.org, contains a listing of events, contacts, and information about peer-led team learning, including a dissemination manual that provides overheads and speaker's notes for disseminators. The Project leadership and faculty associates have given over 115 formal presentations and have 15 publications in books and professional journals.

Early on in the start-up of the "Workshop Chemistry" Project, a precursor to PLTL, the Project's leadership team decided that a good way to present PLTL was to engage peer leaders both in presenting to faculty and conducting sample workshops with faculty playing the role of "students." The results revealed that students' passion for and eloquence about being a peer leader could be key factors in disseminating the model.

The poise and confidence that the leaders exhibited while presenting their views to sometimes skeptical faculty quickly and easily convinced us that students could indeed be partners beyond what we had initially imagined. Inclusion of students in most major presentations has been a hallmark of the PLTL Project. Since the start of the Project over 100 peer leaders have been co-presenters with Project faculty at local, regional, and national meetings and Chautauqua Short Courses. Peer leaders have also taken an active role in sharing their knowledge. Fifteen leaders from seven colleges met in April 2001 at the State University of West Georgia to compile their tips and suggestions for new leaders. This information appeared as an entire issue written by peer leaders in *Progressions* (Spring 2001).

Based on the experiences of the PLTL leadership team and the grant's resources, a four-phase approach to dissemination was developed and implemented. From the perspective of the potential adopter these phases or stages include:

1. Initial familiarity and motivation based on presentations, articles, collegial contacts and the like;
2. Grounding in the method, usually based on a two- to three-day conference and personal contact with experienced PLTL faculty;
3. Implementation of PLTL using the critical component model and with the guidance and support of the PLTL network;
4. Successful experiences such that some adopters emerge as leaders promoting the method through local, regional, and national presentations.

This approach to dissemination has had considerable success. In particular, consultation with those experienced in the method has been invaluable in dealing with a number of problems that are common in initial implementation such as developing materials, training leaders, working with administrators, and seeking funding.

Preliminary Results of Dissemination

The evaluation of dissemination itself is different from the evaluation of a program or grant, but some of the same principles can be employed. Success

Table 2. Number of Peer Leaders and Students Using PLTL Workshops

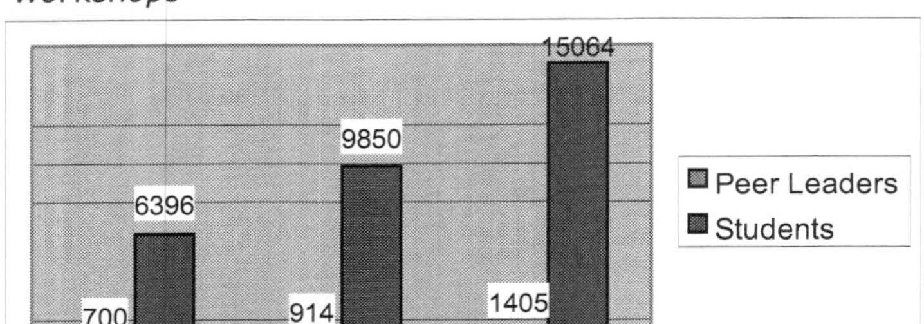

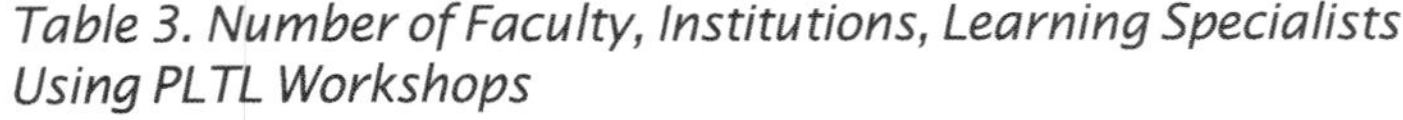

Table 3. Number of Faculty, Institutions, Learning Specialists Using PLTL Workshops

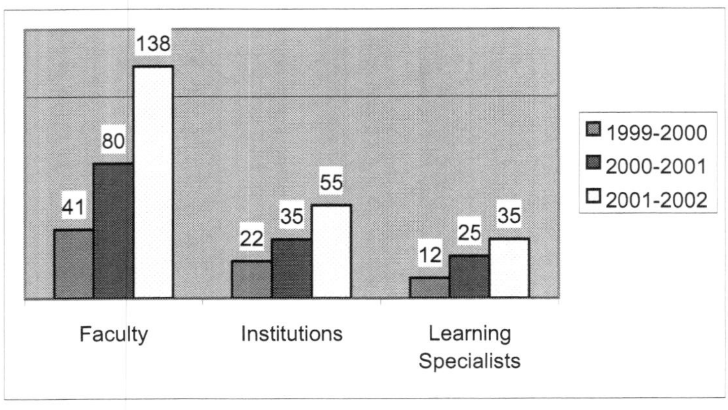

of the dissemination efforts should not be difficult to measure. If large numbers of faculty adopt PLTL across the quantitative disciplines and through courses continue to outperform those not in PLTL courses, and if institutions support the program, making PLTL part of the regular course of studies, then we will judge dissemination a success. But just as attention must be paid to the implementation of a new program in order to identify how the pieces fit together and how to account for successes or failures, in a similar way attention has been paid to the dynamics of dissemination in order to discover how implementation takes place.

Table 4. PLTL Courses by Discipline

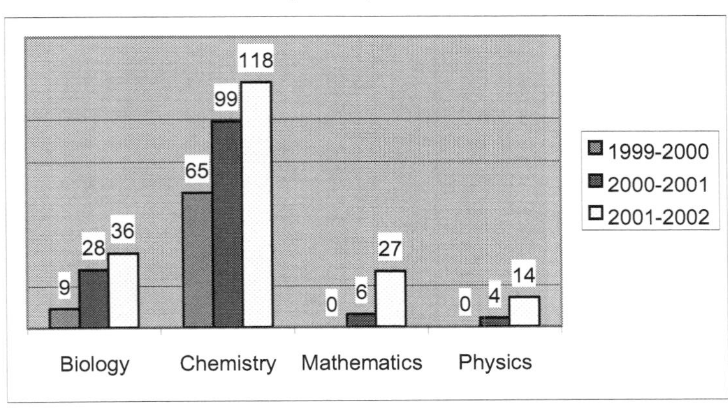

Table 5. Concerns

Concerns About Adopting PLTL	
Institutional, departmental, and collegial support	24.3%
Cost/funding	20.7%
Logistics and organizational arrangements	13.5%
Time for all aspects of implementation	12.6%
Recruiting and training peer leaders	9.9%
Developing materials	9.1%
Pedagogical fit/Student interest	7.2%
Institutionalization	2.7%

The four-tiered plan for dissemination has functioned very well. Response survey forms were used to gather data about participant reaction to a number of the two- and three-day PLTL conferences. In general, participants found the conferences to be highly informative. Using a 1 to 5 scale, respondents at four conferences gave the "presentation of the PLTL model," an average rating of 4.5 (n=66). When asked to indicate how close they were to implementing PLTL using a 1 to 10 scale, responses averaged 7.2 (n=66). Table 5 displays the concerns about implementing PLTL as tabulated by Leo Gafney, the PLTL project evaluator, from written responses (111 comments from 83 respondents at five conferences).

The response to PLTL from faculty members in biology, physics, and mathematics has been favorable. Adopters are beginning to make presentations at local and national conferences in these disciplines. Adoption of PLTL has been modest in these areas due in part to the start-up time in accessing the network of potential adopters and, as indicated in the table above, because they have a number of concerns related to PLTL start-up. Nevertheless, biologists, physicists, and mathematicians connected to the project have been developing materials suitable for workshops and the number of adopters is growing steadily.

Workshop Project Associates (WPA) Program

A central strategy in the dissemination of PLTL has been the awarding of mini-grants to faculty members interested in adopting the method. Pratibha Varma-Nelson, in consultation with others in the project, developed a set of guidelines for processing applications and administering WPA mini-grants to initiate PLTL. The proposals are reviewed by at least three members of the PLTL leadership team before the awards are granted.

Although these grants provided an average of only $5000, there has been a large number of applicants, and over three years (1999-2002) 72 grants were awarded. At the conclusion of their project, the WPA recipients are required to submit a brief report. A form was devised to collect information about the WPA project from those receiving the mini-grants and implementing PLTL. Data gathered from these reports are currently being analyzed.

Institutionalization

The widespread adoption of PLTL has brought to light issues related to institutionalization. Professors starting workshops have appreciated the availability of materials in chemistry but have generally adapted them to their own needs, adjusting the level, topics, and approaches. Those teaching disciplines other than chemistry have found it necessary to develop their own materials. Through this activity, the PLTL Project has gained important experience and new insights into the role of materials in PLTL. In physics, an attempt was made to write a curriculum that would bind those adopting PLTL. This turned out to be an unnecessary constraint linking PLTL to a particular perspective and reducing the program's flexibility. For biology, coordinated efforts have been made to write modules that are clear, practical, and flexible. The work is progressing and because there are so many approaches to introductory biology, it took time to find common ground. For mathematics there is a wealth of problem materials at all levels, and these continue to be adapted to PLTL's needs. Those already involved in mathematics have made modules available in calculus and college algebra.

Successful implementation of PLTL requires the active support of the administration. Implementers of PLTL can better gain administrative support if they can show that the outcomes of PLTL are coincident with the mission of the college, division, and departments. Certainly, increased student retention and performance in coursework are uniform concerns among colleges, and implementers can point out their own experience and results with PLTL and also correlate those with the national evaluation.

It has become clear, however, that successful implementation consistent with the critical components does not guarantee institutionalization. The institutional culture, the administrative approach to curriculum and to change, the collegial atmosphere regarding pedagogy, and the availability of funding are also critically important. An individual or several individuals can successfully implement PLTL, but programs may be discontinued when those few individuals leave or when the project encounters barriers. Experience in the implementation of PLTL has given rise to a new question: What is required for the institutionalization of the project? This question is the basis for a new study currently underway.

The PLTL Network

To maintain the momentum and to support the large number of adopters, a mechanism has been put in place for the consolidation and expansion of the network of faculty, peer leaders, and learning specialists that has formed around this common pedagogy. The PLTL website and the quarterly newsletter enable project affiliates to write articles about their own implementations. Five resource centers strategically located in different regions of the country have been established (see www.pltl.org). Each resource center director has been involved in the development, implementation, evaluation, and dissemination of the PLTL model. Having a core of experienced leaders at five centers helps accelerate the rate of dissemination in new disciplines as well as at a larger number of institutions. The regional centers have been involved in establishing local networks by conducting workshops, establishing a mentor system within the region, and providing assistance through face-to-face meetings and electronic communication.

Conclusion

We are now entering into a phase in the project in which PLTL has an institutional presence and support on individual campuses. PLTL is a model of teaching that increases student participation dramatically; engages students in debate and discussion of scientific ideas; creates a sense of community among students and faculty; and leads to greater retention and success of students in science coursework. It introduces into coursework authentic teamwork, collaboration, and communication with diverse groups. It also provides an extraordinary opportunity for students to engage in a meaningful leadership role in partnership with faculty, in an effort that has major impact on instruction and the institutional culture; and it fulfills a need of higher education to educate leaders of society, not merely technically trained individuals. It is adaptable to many different visions of content and learning goals and pedagogical methods. For these reasons, Peer-Led Team Learning has the potential to play a major role in the transformation of undergraduate science education in the United States.

Acknowledgments

We would like to acknowledge the students, faculty and learning specialists across our coalition for their participation in the development and support of the peer-led team learning model. We are particularly grateful to Jack Kampmeier, Victor Strozak, Ellen Goldstein, Mark Cracolice, Leo Gafney and A.E. Dreyfuss for their contributions to the shared vision of the peer-led model. In addition we would also like to thank Michael Gaines, Joseph Griswold, Dennis Bartow and Madeline Adamczeski for their contributions to the PLTL model and its dissemination. In addition we would like to thank A.E. Dreyfuss for her help in the preparation of this manuscript.

We are pleased to acknowledge support from the National Science Foundation, Division of Undergraduate Education, Course and Curriculum Development Program through the following grants: NSF-DUE 99722457, $2,394,555, 9/1/99 to 8/31/02, Peer-Led Team Learning: National Dissemination by the Workshop Project; and NSF-DUE 0004159, $474,791, 9/1/00 to 8/31/02, Peer-Led Team Learning: Community College Supplement. A continuation of the National Dissemination grant was funded in 2003 (NSF-DUE 0231349).

References

Astin, A. (1993). *What matters in college? Four critical years revisited.* San Francisco: Jossey-Bass.

Blake, R. (2001). What are the benefits of PLTL for student leaders? *Progressions: Peer-Led Team Learning, 3*(3), 6. Retrieved on September 24, 2004, from www.pltl.org

Cracolice, M.S. (2000). Vygotsky's zone of proximal development: A theory base for peer-led team learning. *Progressions: Peer-Led Team Learning, 2*(1), 3. Retrieved on September 24, 2004, from www.pltl.org

Cracolice, M.S., & Roth, S.M. (1996). Keller's "old" personalized system of instruction: A "new" solution for today's college chemistry students. *The Chemical Educator, 1*(1). Retrieved on September 24, 2004, from www.chemeducator.org./bibs/0001001/00010004.htm

Gafney, L. & Varma-Nelson, P. (2002). What happens next? A follow-up study of workshop leaders at St. Xavier University. *The Workshop Project Newsletter: Progressions: Peer-Led Team Learning, 3*(2), 1, 8-9.

Gosser, D.K., Cracolice, M.S., Kampmeier, J.A., Roth, V., Strozak, V.S., & Varma-Nelson, P. (Eds.). (2001). *Peer-led team learning: A guidebook.* Upper Saddle River, NJ: Prentice Hall.

Gosser, D., Roth, V., Gafney, L., Kampmeier, J., Strozak, V., Varma-Nelson, P., et al. (1996). Workshop chemistry: Overcoming barriers to student success. *The Chemical Educator, 1*(1). Retrieved on September 24, 2004, from www.chemeducator.org./bibs/0001001/00010002.htm

Gosser, D.K., Strozak, V.S., & Cracolice, M.S. (2001). *Peer-led team learning: General chemistry.* Upper Saddle River, NJ: Prentice Hall.

Goodwin, J., & Gilbert, B. (2001). Cafeteria-style grading in general chemistry. *Journal of Chemical Education, 78*, 490.

Kampmeier, J.A., Varma-Nelson, P., & Wedegaertner, D.K. (2001). *Peer-led team learning: Organic chemistry.* Upper Saddle River, NJ: Prentice Hall Inc.

Lyle, K.S., & Robinson, W.R. (2003). *The Journal of Chemical Education, 80*, 132.

Miller, J.E., Groccia, J.E., & Miller, M.S. (Eds.). (2001). *Student-assisted teaching: A guide to faculty student teamwork.* Bolton, MA: Anker.

National Research Council. (1998). *From analysis to action: Undergraduate education in science, mathematics, engineering, and technology.* Washington, DC: National Academy Press.

Roth, V., Goldsteing, E., & Marcus, G. (2001). *Peer-led team learning: A handbook for team leaders.* Upper Saddle River, NJ: Prentice Hall.

Sarquis, J.L., Dixon, L.J., Gosser, D.K., Kampmeier, J.A., Roth, V., Strozak, V.S., & Varma-Nelson, P. (2001). The workshop project: Peer-led team learning in chemistry. In J.E. Miller, J.E. Groccia, & M.S. Miller (Eds.), *Student-assisted teaching: A guide to faculty student teamwork.* Bolton, MA: Anker.

Seymour, E. (2004). *Student assessment of learning gains (SALG).* Retrieved on September 24, 2004, from http://www.wcer.wisc.edu/salgains/instructor/

Seymour, E. & Hewitt, N.M. (1997). *Talking about leaving: Why undergraduates leave the sciences*. Boulder, CO: Westview Press.

Tenney, A., & Houck, B. (2004). Learning about leadership: Team learning's effect on peer leaders. *Journal of College Science Teaching*, 25-29.

Tien, L., Roth, V., & Kampmeier, J.A. (2002). Implementation of a peer-led team learning instructional approach in an undergraduate chemistry course. *Journal of Research in Science Teaching, 39*(7), 606-632.

Treisman, U. (1992). Studying students studying calculus: A look at the lives of minority mathematics students in college. *The College Mathematics Journal, 23*, 362-372.

Varma-Nelson, P., & Coppola, B. (2004). Team Learning. In N. Pienta, M. Cooper, & T. Greenbowe (Eds.), *The chemists' guide to effective teaching*. Upper Saddle River, NJ: Prentice Hall.

Varma-Nelson, P., & Cracolice, M. (2001). *Peer-led team learning: General, organic, and biological chemistry*. Upper Saddle River, NJ: Prentice Hall.

Vygotsky, L.S. (1978). *Mind in society*. Cambridge, MA: Harvard University Press.

Woodward, A., Gosser, D., & Weiner, M. (1993). Problem solving workshops in general chemistry. *Journal of Chemical Education, 70*, 651.

Pratibha Varma-Nelson is professor of Chemistry and chair of the Departments of Chemistry, Earth Science and Physics at Northeastern Illinois University, and Co-Principal Investigator of the PLTL National Dissemination Project grants. **David Gosser** is professor of Chemistry at City College of New York, CUNY and Principal Investigator of the Workshop Chemistry Project and the PLTL National Dissemination Project grants.

Chapter 38

Service Learning, Study Circles, and Problem-Based Learning: Student-Initiated Efforts to Confront the Concept of Race

Larry E. Greeson

Education is your most powerful weapon.
With it, you are the White man's equal.
Without it, you are his victim.
Chief Plentycoups[1]
Last Crow Chief

We must be the change we wish to see.
Mahatma Ghandi[2]

This chapter addresses questions regarding problem-based learning (PBL) and the concept of race. For instance, what is PBL and how can it be applied to problems concerning race? Must PBL problems be teacher defined and formally stated? Or, can problems emanate from informal student study circle discussions and involve ongoing, real world concerns? What role, if any, can students play in problem identification as well as analysis and resolution?

These questions emerged as a result of my participation in a Miami University Faculty Learning Community on PBL. Our faculty learning community attended PBL 2000, An International Conference on Problem-Based Learning in Undergraduate and Professional Education; took part in presentations on

[1] *Spirit of the dawn.* A documentary by Heidi Schmidt.
[2] *A fight for survival: Voices on poverty.* A documentary by Dhruvi Kakkad and Johanna K. Peters-Burton.

PBL at the 2000 National Lilly Conference on College Teaching; and had numerous lively, and sometimes heated, discussions on PBL. Through these experiences, I came to understand that PBL is not a "cookbook" style pedagogy but rather a "way of perceiving" the teaching and learning process—a way that differs dramatically from the traditional, teacher-centered, test-oriented methods prevalent in many colleges and universities today.

As Lee Shulman (October, 2000) indicated in his PBL 2000 keynote address, PBL should be a "pedagogy of engagement" that encourages students to explore areas of uncertainty, unpredictability, adventure and surprise. For Wilkerson and Gijselaers (1996), good PBL is complex and engaging, ill-structured yet meaningful, and, above all, compels students to seek problem resolution and understanding.

What follows is an attempt to apply student-initiated cooperative learning principles common to service learning, study circles, and PBL to a real world issue of educational and societal concern. The issue will be the concept of race andits social construction and consequent effects upon human relations in the form of racism, stereotyping, prejudice, discrimination, equality of educational opportunity, and civil and human rights. The concept of race is particularly significant for teaching, as it affects the everyday lives of teachers and students alike through proficiency testing practices, labeling, expectations, tracking, and the social construction of perceived racial, ethnic, and cultural differences that affect the teaching and learning process itself.

First, possibilities for applying student-initiated study circle principles to service learning and PBL will be discussed in relation to the social construction of race. Next, some noteworthy examples of pedagogical practices and outcomes involving students and teachers cooperating to confront the concept of race will be described. Finally, suggestions will be made regarding problems and prospects for future consideration.

Context

The Corporation on National and Community Service defines service learning as an active learning method "through which citizenship, academic subjects, skills, and values are taught...drawing lessons from the experience of performing work" (Saunders, 1998, p.56). Often the purpose of service learning has been to address the needs of poor people, people of color, and other disenfranchised populations (Rhoads, 1997).

I have been drawn to service learning as well as to study circles and PBL because of my background in cognitive-developmental, social, and humanistic psychology—fields that emphasize active, mindful, engaged, and cooperative learning, as well as critical thinking (for example, Greeson, 1988; Johnson, Johnson, & Smith, 1998; Langer, 1997; Mierson & Parikh, 2000; Piaget, 1974; Rogers & Freiberg, 1994). Several study visits to Scandinavia have enabled me to perceive important connections between service learning, the Scandinavian concept of "study circle," and PBL (Greeson, 1994).

Jacques Delors' (1996) UNESCO Education Commission Report concludes that the university should be "a place of culture and learning open to all" in which "each person should be both teacher and learner." Ellen Langer (1997) advocates for "mindful" learning, involving the "continuous creation of new categories, openness to new information, and implicit awareness of more than one perspective" (p. 4). As Byström (1994) suggests, study circles can provide ideal opportunities for such active, mindful, and service-oriented PBL to occur.

Byström describes the study circle as "a circle of friends or associates assembled for the study of a predetermined subject or problem" (p.5827). Study circles, developed in Scandinavia in the early 1900's to address perceived societal inadequacies, are "learner organized and implemented" and "immediately relevant and applicable" to learners' everyday lives; people learn to "discuss, argue, show consideration for others, and share responsibilities" in attempting to address real world problems that "cannot be foreseen in advance" (Byström, 1994, p.5828).

Recently, study circles have been adopted in the U.S. and Canada to help students talk constructively about race (Ruenzel, 1997). In response to a cross-burning and rally by the KKK in Springfield, Ohio, high school students were taught how to moderate study circles in order to address "controversial issues rationally and respectfully." The ultimate purpose was a change in student and teacher consciousness—"to break down barriers and rework the internal process that happens when stereotypes are formed" (Ruenzel, 1997, p.23). Meaningful cross-racial dialogues occurred with teachers and students alike sharing "powerful stories" about themselves and the issues under discussion.

Mierson and Parikh (2000), in a collaborative teacher/student work, have shown how PBL methods can engage students in a manner similar to study circles—students "functioning independently," (p.21) "taking charge of their [own] learning," (p.23) and deciding for themselves how to seek solutions to complex problems of real-world significance. Everyone becomes a teacher *and* a learner, and both students and teachers seem to really care about addressing and understanding the problems presented (Wilkerson & Gijselaers, 1996).

Ongoing societal problems addressed in my educational psychology classes often concern human diversity issues, particularly questions of race (for example, Clark, 1964; Nieto, 2000; Ruenzel, 1997; West, 1994). Students have opportunities to analyze 1) How the concept of race has been constructed and defined; 2) For what reasons, and with what effects, particular definitions of race have been employed; 3) How various definitions of race have influenced other aspects of human relations, such as racism, stereotyping, prejudice, discrimination, race relations, equality of educational opportunity, and civil and human rights; and 4) How educators can encourage greater student understanding of these concepts and promote action to affect positive change. By integrating student-initiated study circle, service learning, and PBL activities, effective pedagogical strategies may be developed that enable students to critically analyze and actively engage with each other in addressing these issues.

Brown's (2002) Teaching for Social Justice Series volume raises particularly important questions regarding how the "lie of race" as a biological construct has come to be so deeply embedded in our culture that it has become a social, economic, political, and educational reality. Brown questions why so little is known and acknowledged about the lives of influential White allies in the struggle for civil rights. Cornel West (1994) raises similar questions regarding how much *race* has mattered in our American past and how much race *matters* mean to America's present and future. For West, the problem is urgent, involving fundamental issues of power and morality; "for others, it is an everyday matter of life and death" (West, 1994, p. xvi; see also Jones, Newman & Isay, 1997). For LeAlan Jones, a young Black teenager from a ghetto area on the South Side of Chicago, it is "living in a second America where the laws of the land don't apply and the laws of the street do" (Jones, et al, 1997, p. 7). It is being someone supposed to "be a loser...[and] make it only because of affirmative action" (p. 177). As LeAlan, now a college student, disturbingly concludes, "I'm not supposed to be positive. I'm not supposed to be educated. I'm not supposed to know what I know. *But I do*." (p. 177) [italics added].

In arguing for the importance of such a self-narrative, Rhoads (October, 2000) discusses his own life growing up poor in terms of the "hidden injuries of social class," such as having to use free lunch tickets in the school cafeteria or waiting in line at the grocery while his mother used food stamps. With some anger and sadness, Sonia Nieto (2000) recalls her tenth grade teacher asking the patronizing and stereotyping question, "Are you in a *special* English class?" "Yes," Sonia replied. "I'm in *Honors* English" [italics added]. Nieto describes the feeling of being "silenced" or rendered "invisible" as a result of such biased, prejudiced, and discriminatory practices. This phenomenon may be related to what Peggy McIntosh (1988) refers to as "White (and male) Privilege," whereby opportunities and experiences taken for granted by some segments of society must be consciously fought and struggled for by others.

Kenneth Clark (1964) states in *Dark Ghetto* that both Whites and Blacks "have been required to learn the language and behavior of prejudice at the same time that they learned the words and ideals of democracy" (p. 233). Perhaps, through student-initiated service-based cooperative learning experiences, we can engage in a different dialogue—one that takes the message of Jones', Newman's, and Isay's, *Our America*, to heart—that we begin to "tear some holes" in the invisible fences surrounding ghetto communities and come to know "the people who live behind them…magnificent people blessed with the remarkable human capacity to adapt to the bleakest of circumstances" (p. 22).

In this regard, Garcia (1991) advocates for a type of "democratic teaching" in which the teacher is "legally and morally bound to managing a classroom that protects the fundamental right of all students to equal educational opportunity" (p.8). Perhaps the concept of democratic teaching may be best understood through the lens of critical pedagogy (see McLaren, 1998; Giroux & McLaren, 1986). For teachers, this perspective means beginning to "candidly and critically" face our society's complicity in the roots, structures, and reproduction of inequalities and injustice, and to empower students to overcome their "cultures of silence" and to become agents for social change (McLaren, 1998, p.xxi). In such a process, "student experience and student voice" are valued and students and teachers become "transformative intellectuals" working together to democratize and reform schools (Giroux & McLaren, 1986, p.213). It is unclear whether critical pedagogical approaches may be compatible with or co-opted by PBL and other related cooperative teaching and learning strategies, including study circles and service learning. In either case, student-initiated learning opportunities would seem to be ideally suited for critically engaging issues related to the socially constructed concept of race.

Some Noteworthy Approaches and Outcomes

Garcia (1991) and Nieto (2000) have written teacher preparation texts based upon principles of critical pedagogy and multicultural literacy. Nieto describes how critical curricula and teaching methods can result in the collective empowerment of students, simultaneously reducing racism, discrimination, and low academic expectations. Garcia presents pluralistic teaching models and methods that can result in the development of cultural pride and intergroup understanding. Each text cites the seminal contributions of James Banks and bell hooks to the development of transformative multicultural educational practices based upon engaged and reconstructive pedagogy and authentic learning.

Along with Garcia's and Nieto's books, my students and I have employed *Foxfire* Appalachian culture material and resources from the Southern Poverty Law Center Teaching Tolerance Project, including the video, *The shadow of hate*, and its corresponding publication, *Us and them: A history of intolerance in America*, which present "the story of some Americans who were hated by others simply for who they were, what they looked like or what they believed" (p. xxiv). These materials serve as powerful tools in empowering students to act as change agents combating racism, prejudice, and discrimination. In fact, *I* learned about some of these materials from *my students*!

Other materials that I have used to introduce issues and encourage active student-initiated inquiry relevant to issues of poverty, culture, and race include documentaries such as *Spirit of the Dawn*, *We Want Them to be Safe*, *Voices on Poverty*, and *Diary of a Harlem Family*. Gordon Parks's (1966) classic, *Diary of a Harlem Family*, interspersing love and family with hopelessness, violence, and despair, is particularly disturbing for White students who tend to initially perceive the film's content in a rigid oversimplified manner. Books and articles that are used for similar purposes include Clark's *Dark ghetto*; Jones et al.'s *Our America*; Kozol's *Amazing grace*; Page's *Showing my color*; Tatum's *Why do all the black kids sit together in the cafeteria?*; Takaki's *A different mirror: A history of multicultural America*; Staples's *Parallel time*; Fish's (1995) *Psychology Today* article, "Mixed Blood"; Jacobson's (1976) "IQ: Myth and Reality" in *Demythologizing the inner city child*; and an American Indian mother's letter, "Respect my child: He has a right to be himself," appearing in *Media & Methods* (1978).

I learned of Ronald Takaki's work through a series of workshops that he conducted here at Miami University a few years ago. Dr. Takaki is a renowned diversity scholar and founding director of the American Cultures Center at the University of California, Berkeley. His own personal story, as a child of Japanese American immigrants, provided important experiential as well as intellectual perspectives for teachers and students alike. These perspectives are mirrored in his book, which provides a thought provoking historical analysis of the interconnectedness of economic, political, and social developments influencing the lives of American Indians, African Americans, and Chinese, Japanese, Irish, and other immigrant labor populations. Staples's equally compelling book depicts the "concurrent" lives of a Black student attending the University of Chicago, bordered by the South Chicago Ghetto. For Staples, this meant learning the consequent conflicted lived experience of "Scatter the Pigeons" (p.203)—frightening affluent Whites because of his blackness—as he approached them on downtown streets.

Sometimes students view feature films that portray issues relevant to human development, education, and cultural difference such as *Smoke Signals*, *Ghandi*, *Malcom X*, *Dangerous Minds*, and *Do the Right Thing*. Spike

Lee's, *Do the Right Thing*, for example, opens with Public Enemy's rap lyrics, "you got to Fight the Powers that be," and closes with quotes by Martin Luther King endorsing principles of "nonviolence" and Malcom X defending the concept of "freedom by any means necessary" including violence, leaving viewers left with the question, "What *is* the right thing?".

One of the most remarkable aspects of "student-initiated" PBL has been the tendency for groups of students to independently plan and undertake study visits to local, regional, and national sites of educational, cultural, and historical significance. These study visits are always student-initiated and involve aspects of cooperative learning (for example, planning, discussing, and reporting on the visits) that can be connected to issues and processes relevant to study circles and PBL (for example, problem identification, solution seeking, critical discussion, and debate). Students visited the National Afro-American Museum and Cultural Center located in Wilberforce, Ohio, around the same time that a wooden cross emblazoned with hate messages was burned on the museum grounds. Students have also traveled to Berea College, in Kentucky and to the Museum of Appalachia in Tennessee to learn more about Appalachian heritage and culture; and to the Cherokee Indian Museum in North Carolina and the Eiteljorg Museum of American Indian Art and Culture in Indianapolis, Indiana for similar purposes. These study visits both "inform" students and promote critical thinking and PBL as well.

I am especially proud of student-initiated study visits that have involved trips to civil rights sites in Montgomery and Birmingham, Alabama and Memphis, Tennessee.

In Montgomery, students visited the Southern Poverty Law Center Civil Rights Memorial, a moving depiction of people who fought and died for civil rights during the 1950s and 60s, accompanied by the engraved words of Martin Luther King, Jr., "Until justice rolls down like waters and righteousness like a mighty stream." They also visited the Dexter Avenue King Memorial Baptist Church, located near the memorial, where Dr. King first preached. In addition to learning about important events in the history of the civil rights movement, the students met the Reverend Mary Jo Smiley, associate pastor of the church and friend of the King family. Subsequent to their trip, the students arranged for Reverend Smiley (in her 70s) to visit our campus where she gave informal talks to students as well as a community-wide keynote presentation documented by the local press.

I requested that students write about and discuss their experiences. Their responses were voluntary; neither their papers nor their class presentations were graded. Some of the more poignant and insightful reflections are included below.

"Jaime C." writes,

> Our experience on the trip to Memphis, Birmingham, and Montgomery created memories that we will carry with us for a lifetime. We saw the place where Dr. Martin Luther King was assassinated, sat in the very same church that he had once delivered sermons, and walked the ["Freedom Walk"] path once marched by Dr. King, now known as Kelly Ingram Park. We sat on a bus with Rosa Parks and listened to conversations that took place, saw the remains of a bus bombed during the Freedom Rides, and touched the cell where Dr. King wrote "Letter from a Birmingham Jail." No words can express the intense feelings, thoughts, and emotions we felt during this trip."

"Aaron B." writes,

> It has been about two weeks since my friends and I made the trip to Memphis. It has taken me that long to process all that I took in. I feel that this trip helped bring to light how naïve I am and how much I still have to learn about humanity. I journeyed to Memphis thinking that I was going to a place of racial harmony and peace. I learned that we as a society are not doing enough to educate people about the fallacies of racial bias and prejudice. Looking over the journal entries that I made and reflecting on the whole experience, I am left to feel disheartened and disgraced by our society. I was made to feel this way by all. African Americans called us "cracker" and "honky." Whites referred to us as "N——r lovers." I had no peace. I know that we are not as close to racial harmony as social science textbooks would have us believe.

One year later, Jaime reflected,

> If I learned anything at all on the trip, I learned that one person can make a difference. I felt much sadness for the lives lost during these events. However, in all of this sadness and struggle, I found inspiration. A year later I still find myself eagerly sharing and teaching many of the events, quotes, and experiences that I learned with somebody new almost every day. This is the message that I hope to share with others and to carry on to the students I may encounter as a teacher.

Less dramatic but, nonetheless equally worthwhile are student-initiated visits to a local Underground Railroad Museum and corresponding historical sites. "Megan W." writes, "One of the best things we did in class was the Underground Railroad.... I couldn't believe all that history is right down the road." "Lisa K." saw the Underground Railroad Museum as "the most memorable experience of the semester." "Tracy S." remarked that both she and her son (who accompanied the class) "learned more about [their] own [African American] cultural heritage in one afternoon than in years of school." Interestingly, a national Underground Railroad/Freedom Center opened in the summer of 2004 in Cincinnati, just a short drive from our campus. I am sure that our students were among the first to experience this new museum and learning center.

At the end of the semester "Marty W.", a White female, asks, "What have I gained from this course?" In response, she replies,

> Racial issues have become more than regrettable issues written about in the papers, but an ugly reality still prevailing in our society... I have come away with a deeper understanding of the prejudices and misconceptions that I have harbored, and where those prejudices come from...you were so right when you observed how much we were able to learn from each other in such a short amount of time.

"Douglas P.", now a teacher, writes,

> I hope that you find the fact that I am applying the knowledge gained in your class a success story...this [cultural diversity] information has become key to my classroom.

"Jennifer S's" story dramatically illustrates the power such experiences have to transform individual lives as well as classroom learning. In a class discussion subsequent to her trip down South, Jennifer tearfully conveyed how she had learned that a lynch mob picture in one of the museums included one of her distant relatives. She had noticed the name in the picture caption and later discovered from her parents that, indeed, the man had been a member of their family. The whole class was moved as she discussed her feelings of personal confusion and dismay. I am certain that this story is being conveyed to others as my students move into student teaching experiences and full time positions of their own.

Future Problems and Prospects

Whether traveling out-of-state to sites of national prominence or just around the corner to neighboring communities, student-initiated experiences such as the ones described above illustrate a power and depth of learning, empathy, and insight not often apparent in traditional teacher-centered, content-oriented college classes. Models of PBL that afford possibilities for *student identification* of problems and *student-initiation* of problem solving activities, within real-world study circle contexts may be expected to promote self-determination skills as well as cooperation, critical thinking, and academic achievement. This approach may be referred to as student-initiated PBL or SIPBL.

Nieto (2000) believes that the lack of relationship between many school curricula and principles of democracy shows the "chasm that often exists" (p.99) between expounding on democratic teaching and the lack of democratic actions in classrooms. West (1994) notes that there is no escaping our interracial interdependence. Both of these issues pose challenges appropriate for SIPBL, including analyzing how different cultural, ethnic, and racial categories are constructed and exploring ways that different groups might work together to achieve greater democratic decision-making in America's schools.

According to West (1994), "without the presence of Black people in America, European-Americans would not be White—they would be only Irish, Italians, Poles, Welsh, and others engaged in class, ethnic, and gender struggles over resources and identity...[conversely]...Blackness [would have] no meaning outside of a system of race-conscious people and practices" (pp. 37 and 80). LeAlan Jones pleads that "you must learn our America and we must learn your America, so that maybe, someday, we can become one" (p. 7). His plea reflects Clark's (1964) conclusion that "[Black Americans] will not break out of the barriers of the ghetto wall unless Whites transcend the barriers of their own minds" (p.240). As Clark indicates, it has become increasingly clear that the supposed "*facts* about the ghetto are not necessarily synonymous with the *truth* of the ghetto" [italics original]—figures on malnutrition tend to lose significance when one is directly confronted with a starving child. Langer (1997) believes that the "lack of ability to see different perspectives" (p.139) may really be a learning "disability" within contexts requiring multiple interpretations and understandings. Incorporating student voice and self determination into the teaching and learning process through student-initiated service learning, study circles, and PBL experiences would appear to provide a rich means by which greater multicultural interaction, insight, and understanding might be attained.

Students *can* identify and define race-related educational and social problems relevant for SIPBL. Students *can* initiate and direct SIPBL activities designed to address ongoing issues of educational and societal concern, including questions involving the concept of race. Ironically, faculty attempts to define, structure, and initiate PBL may sometimes serve to impede the very self-directed learning, critical thinking, and problem solving skills that they are designed to enhance.

References

Brown, C. S. (2002). *Refusing racism.* New York: Teachers College Press.

Byström, J. (1994). Study circles. In T. Husén & T. N. Postlethwaite (Eds.), *The international encyclopedia of education* (2nd ed., Vol. 10). London: Pergamon.

Clark, K. B. (1964). *Dark ghetto: Dilemmas of social power.* New York: Harper & Row.

Delors, J. (1996). *Learning: The treasure within.* Paris: United Nations Educational, Scientific and Cultural Organization.

Garcia, R. L. (1991). *Teaching in a pluralistic society* (2nd ed.). New York: HarperCollins.

Giroux, H., & McLaren, P. (1986). Teacher education and the politics of engagement: The case for democratic schooling. *Harvard Educational Review, 56*, 213-238.

Greeson, L. E. (1988). College classroom interaction as a function of teacher- and student-centered instruction. *Teaching & Teacher Education, 4*, 305-315.

Greeson, L. E. (1994). Torsten Husén: A case of ethnocentrism in U. S. educational research? *Interchange, 25*, 241-259.

Johnson, D. W., Johnson, R. T., & Smith, K. (1998). *Active learning: Cooperation in the college classroom* (2nd ed.). Edina, MN: Interaction Book Company.

Jones, L., & Newman, L., with Isay, D. (1997). *Our America: Life and death on the south side of Chicago.* New York: Washington Square Press.

Langer, E. L. (1997). *The power of mindful learning.* Reading, MA: Addison-Wesley.

McIntosh, P. (1988). *White privilege and male privilege: A personal account of coming to see correspondences through work in women's studies.* (Working Paper No. 189). Wellesley, MA: Center for Research on Women, Wellesley College.

McLaren, P. (1998). *Life in schools: An introduction to critical pedagogy in the foundations of education* (3rd ed.). New York: Longman.

Mierson, S., & Parikh, A. A. (2000, January/February). Stories from the field: Problem-based learning from a teacher's and a student's perspective. *Change, 32*, 21-27.

Nieto, S. (2000). *Affirming diversity: The sociopolitical context of multicultural education* (3rd ed.). New York: Addison Wesley Longman.

Piaget, J. (1974). *To understand is to invent: The future of education.* (G. Roberts, Trans.). New York: Grossman.

Rhoads, R. A. (1997). *Community service and higher learning: Explorations of the caring self.* New York: SUNY Press.

Rhoads, R. A. (2000, October). *Writing the self into educational research and narrative: The role of self-narrative.* Paper presented at the Laurie McDade Lecture, Miami University, Oxford, OH.

Rogers, C. R., & Freiberg, H. J. (1994). *Freedom to learn* (3rd ed.). New York: Merrill.

Ruenzel, D. (1997, Spring). Crucial conversations: Study circles help students talk constructively about race. *Teaching Tolerance, 6* (1), 18-23.

Saunders, M. D. (1998). The service learner as researcher: A case study. *Journal on Excellence in College Teaching, 9*(2), 55-67.

Shulman, L. (2000, October). *From problem to learning: The promise & perils of problem-intensive pedagogies.* Keynote Presentation at PBL 2000—A Conference on Problem-Based Learning in Undergraduate and Professional Education, Birmingham, AL.

West, C. (1994). *Race matters.* New York: Vintage.

Wilkerson, L., & Gijselaers, W. H. (Eds.). (1996). *Bringing problem-based learning to higher education: Theory and practice.* San Francisco: Jossey-Bass.

Larry Greeson is a professor in the educational psychology department at Miami University Middletown.

IV. Best Practices and Methods

Chapter 39

Developing Diversity Management Skills in a University Context: A Direct or Indirect Approach?

Philip Frame and Jennifer O'Connor

This chapter presents two approaches to learning about diversity, which have been developed within the context of the United Kingdom (UK) and experience with MBA learners at Middlesex University Business School (MUBS). Our students learn about diversity either by a direct/content or an indirect/process approach. We define the direct/content approach as one that has explicit objectives and provides the learner with knowledge concerning diversity learning. Conversely, the indirect/process approach provides the learner with real life experience of this area and the tools to reflect and learn from this experience.

We believe it is important to contextualize our work from multiple perspectives: legislation, learner diversity Middlesex University, the MBA Program, and finally ourselves. Why? Because it provides a backdrop for the developments reported here and a framework for the process of staff development.

We became interested in a proactive approach to diversity development in part because of our backgrounds, partly because of change in the demographic of our student population, partly in response to policy changes at government and at university level, and finally because of our commitment to offer our students the best possible learning opportunities that take account of them and their needs as well of those of their instructors. In fact, we developed our approach almost by accident some years ago. We were running a module where students learned in small groups and were assessed on their reflection of this process. While analysing these reflections, it became apparent that by working together our students were learning about the diversity of group members or what made them different and devising strategies to manage this diversity, that is, to work effectively with these differences. As a result, we determined to make diversity a more explicit element of one learning experience and leave it implicit in the other. Thus in terms of the developments reported here, our action preceded our reflection (Kolb, 1984).

The methodology utilized here is based on a content analysis of learners' reflections that have been submitted as part of the assessment process. It is consistent with the approach we have adopted in our previous work in the field of Human Resource Management, for both a professional audience (Frame & O'Connor, 2002a, 2003a) and an academic one (Frame & O'Connor, 2002b, 2003b).

The Diversity Context in which we Operate

This section describes the external and internal environment within which we, as a typical modern UK university, currently operate from three perspectives:

1. The legislative framework in the UK has long outlawed less favourable treatment on the grounds of ethnicity (Race Relations Act, 1976 and subsequent amendment, 2000), gender (the Equal Opportunities Act, the Equal Pay Act, and subsequent amendments) and disability (The Disability Discrimination Act, 1995). Economic Union directives prohibiting discrimination on the grounds of religion and sexual orientation, for example, supplement these laws.
2. Learner diversity has further increased as a result of successive government attempts to increase student numbers and widen participation. Thus government departments, such as the Department for Education and Skills, support initiatives such as "Aimhigher," which aim to encourage traditionally under-represented groups to undertake a university education. In addition to creating a fairer society, such attempts from successive governments are underpinned by the belief that the provision of equal opportunities for all is an engine for economic growth. European Union initiatives such as Erasmus encourage intercountry study. There is a resultant reduction in the proportion of traditional students, who McNay (1994) characterises as white, male, and middle class in undergraduate degree courses living away from home.

   Modern universities, of which Middlesex University is an example, now have a greater gender and racial mix, with students from a range of social classes and with a range of qualifications. European and international students are much more in evidence, while patterns of study and domestic arrangements are increasingly varied. In respect of the former. students now receive tuition on a part-time basis, on an evenings-only basis, on weekends, at summer school, and at a distance. More of our students now live at home (57% of Middlesex students live in the London area). As result, their domestic arrangements include family responsibility for children, either their own or those of their extended family, and/or for elderly and infirm relatives.

3. Middlesex University is a large, multi-campus, modern, higher education institution with more than 25,000 students. It offers a wide range of programs at undergraduate, postgraduate, doctoral, and post-experience levels. Middlesex University Business School (MUBS) is one of five Schools at the University. MUBS has approximately 3600 undergraduate students, 1150 postgraduate students, and 60 doctoral students. It has 157 permanent academic staff and also employs 45 part time staff.

   MUBS's mission is to be a leader in delivering challenging business, management, and related programs in order to prepare a culturally and internationally diverse body of students who will contribute professionally in business and the community. A socially inclusive approach to university education is one of its aims.

   The demographics of MUBS as reported in the Middlesex University's 2002/2003 Statistical Digest shows that in terms of gender, the Business School has a balance between men and woman at 46% and 54% respectively. Interestingly these proportions are reflected at the postgraduate level as well. In respect of ethnic origins, the source referred to above confirms that 56% of the British-born student body was made up of non-white students who originated from Asia, Africa, the Caribbean, and China. Most surprisingly, only 19% of our students reported themselves as being White. We believe this reflects the particular nature of Universities located in our major cities. Disappointingly, 29% chose not to disclose their ethnicity. In respect of social class mix, 97% of our students attended state-funded schools and only 3% were privately educated.

The Context: The MBA Program

According to a recent self-audit document (which was produced for the re-accreditation of the program by the relevant professional body, the Association of MBAs):

> The overall mission of our MBA program is to develop managers who can lead change and manage strategically, ethically, and sensitively in a range of organizations in an increasingly global and rapidly changing environment. "Ethical management" requires an appreciation of the factors that potentially influence the behavior of an organization while "managing sensitively" refers to the emphasis of the program on managing by persuasion, rather than by edicts or direction.

The aim of the MBA program is to develop an integrated and strategic view of business and enhance awareness of social, cultural, and ethical issues. The program both implicitly and explicitly addresses leadership, change, ethics, diversity, and personal skills. These issues are addressed specifically within the module Personal and Managerial Effectiveness and the Group Consultancy Project, which are the foci modules of this chapter.

The structure and content of the MBA was reviewed in 1999, and the revised program consists of four basic themes that are mandatory for all students. These are:

1. *Personal and professional development.* Here a range of skills related to study and personal development are enhanced. The Personal and Managerial Effectiveness module is aligned to this theme.
2. *Business enablers.* Here students are furnished with the knowledge and skills to lead business operations, manage resources, and meet customer needs.
3. *Strategy and the business environment.* Here students' ability to create a vision, gain competitive advantage, manage integratively, and operate in an international setting are developed.
4. *Applied and vocational subjects.* Here students are supported in developing the capability to apply and practice theoretical perspectives and techniques. A major feature of this theme is the Group Consultancy Project.

The teaching and learning strategy focuses on active as opposed to passive learning. Whenever possible, we attempt to teach concepts and theories in the context of real life concerns and issues. A problem-based approach to learning is preferred to a dialectic approach

The Context: The Authors

According to Adams et al. (1997) "whilst much has been written about how to engage students in social justice course little attention has been paid to the teachers in the classroom" (p. 299). While our primary interest is not in social justice per se, we agree with the authors' observations with respect of teachers. Below we offer a framework for instructors to develop their diversity capabilities using our practice as an example. This framework consists of four elements, two process-based activities and two products or outcomes: pedagogic values, disclosure, diversity dimensions, and biographical motivators.

Pedagogic Values

Our educational values foreground real-life action and experience as a source of learning, and we draw on a strong and developed pedagogy in this area to inform our practice. Authors such as Revans (1980), Kolb (1984), Honey and Mumford (1992), and Heron (1999) emphasize the value of experience as the basis for learning. For example, Keaton and Tate (1978) state "experiential-based learning means learning in which the learner is directly in touch with the realities being studied" (p. 1). Heron (1999) refers to experience as "the ground of experiential knowledge" with which the student has a "felt acquaintance" (p.16). This process approach is often contrasted with the product approach (Joplin, 1995) that is first hand experience transformed into meaningful knowledge as opposed to passive learning that focuses primarily on reproducing received information in a descriptive manner. We agree with Bligh et al. (1998) that education benefits both students and the community as a whole and that higher education should involve itself in three domains of learning: affect, cognition, and adaptable occupational skills. We are persuaded by the case they make for the development of attitude and emotional integrity as well as intellect. Indeed, a process approach is one that facilitates the former, while a product or content approach encourages the latter.

Disclosure

We feel that perhaps with diversity, more than any other subject matter, an appreciation of the history of the instructors is of paramount importance. Why? We believe that self-reflection leading to self-disclosure is a prerequisite for effective development of diversity management skills both in the facilitator and the learner. Mortiboys (2003) makes this point with respect to faculty members, and Johnson and Redwood (2000) make this point for training and development professionals. We suggest that the process of self-disclosure should ideally occur both between the instructor team and the students. However, the individual must retain the right to determine the boundaries of their openness. In support of this we make explicit our own diversity and in doing so we exemplify the process of creating and maintaining an open climate that is essential for those involved in this subject area. The identification of self-disclosure as a prerequisite is, we believe, a relatively new feature of learning and development in business-related scholarship.

Diversity Dimensions

We believe that the effective management of diversity should take a holistic approach rather than focusing on one or two diversity domains such as gender, socioeconomic class, or race. It should also recognize that there are similarities as well as differences between all of us. Putting this assertion into practice involves two stages: Stage One involves applying to ourselves the Twelve Step Typology that we developed from Middlesex University's Equal Opportunities Policy, and set out below in Table 1.

Our approach differs markedly from that recommended in *Teaching for Diversity and Social Justice* (Adams et al., 1997), not least because the focus of our attention is the post-graduate student. Additionally, the perspective therein is one that works towards increasing social justice, that is, helping to ameliorate historic disadvantage, whereas ours is one that underlines the business and employability case for utilising "differences," that is, the benefits to the organization, and the individual employee, of productive diversity. This difference in approach is perhaps not surprising, given that we have developed our practice in a University Business School context. Social justice may well be a by-product of our activities – indeed we hope it is – but it is not our primary aim.

Many of the areas identified by Adams et al. (1997) are ones that we would consider to be relevant to all instructors whatever their subject area, such as "am I competent?", "the need for learner approval" and "negotiating

Table 1. Twelve Step Typology

	Criteria	**Similar**	**Different**
1	Age		X
2	Ethnic Origin		X
3	Family responsibility	X	
4	Marital status		X
5	Race		X
6	Color		X
7	Nationality	X	
8	Disability	X	
9	Socioeconomic status	X	
10	Religion	X	
11	Sexual orientation	X	
12	Gender		X

authority." In contrast, the table set out above addresses one area that they too identify as significant, which is "social identity awareness". We believe, though, that our approaches go further, by encouraging instructors to consider their own motivation in offering the topics that constitute "diversity" in the first place.

Biographical Motivators

Stage Two explores our motivation for becoming involved with diversity development by identifying a number of significant factors from our biographies.

Philip Frame

There are three reasons why I, as a white male with a working class background, am actively committed to encouraging the recognition and utilization of diversity to enhance the student experience in Higher Education.

Firstly, I benefited from the recognition of diversity when applying for my undergraduate courses at the University of Sussex in the mid 1960s. At that time, all those who wished to become undergraduates were required to possess a foreign language. As a result of failing a major exam at the age of 11, I attended a Secondary Modern School and was unable to attain this qualification. However, Sussex had a dispensation for students such as myself: no foreign language was required. I thus obtained a university place on the basis of Sussex recognizing the potential of students who had a non-traditional background, and their attempts to achieve a more diverse student intake. Secondly, my undergraduate degree in Social Anthropology taught me, via the study of non-Western societies, to recognize, understand, and value different practices and beliefs, and to become less Eurocentric in my views. Finally, I worked for the Race Relations Board in the 1970s. This was a government department, which was charged with seeking compliance with the 1968 Race Relations Act. The Act outlawed discrimination on the grounds of race, color, ethnic, or national origins. My job was to encourage organizations such as the Post Office, British Gas, and the TUC to develop and monitor equal opportunity policies. In effect this was an attempt to help employers to recognize and manage the requirements of an increasingly diverse workforce.

Jennifer O' Connor

There are a number of reasons why I have developed an interest in diversity. Firstly, I am a Black, British middle class woman who lived in an affluent country area for 20 years. During my secondary education (aged 11 through 18), I attended a comprehensive school where I was the only Black pupil in the year. Secondly, I believed there were weaknesses inherent within the Equal

Opportunities philosophy. Anecdotally, I knew people who refused to apply for jobs that included an Equal Opportunities statement as they did not want to be hired as a "token" or by virtue of a belief that being black was their only valued characteristic. Thirdly, equal opportunities suggested targeting groups that were classified as "disadvantaged." Being classified as such felt offensive. In addition, such a classification appeared to absolve organizations and educational institutions from taking responsibility for recognizing, valuing, and managing the diverse characteristics of an individual at all stages of the employment relationship. Fourthly, as a mature undergraduate with a hidden disability, my individual needs were not always adequately addressed within a system geared towards traditional undergraduates (McNay, 1994). Finally, since becoming a lecturer on the Executive MBA program, it is become increasingly apparent that the diverse student population presents opportunities to enhance teaching, learning, and assessment practice by exploring the impact of diversity on learning while learning about diversity.

What we have done here is to reflect on and identify significant factors in our own histories that have led us to develop the practice of learning about and with diversity.

***

We would recommend that all instructors and indeed learners follow a similar process as an introduction to developing their diversity skills, by thinking about and articulating what motivated them and what in their history has influenced their interest in diversity. One potential danger is that diversity teaching provides the primary means for the instructor to seek closure on negative personal experiences of discrimination, or it becomes the primary vehicle for pursuing a limited personal agenda in this area. Such narrow and self-focused motivation could well limit the effectiveness of the resultant learning experience.

We will now present case studies of the diversity interventions that were developed as a response to the complex and dynamic context within which we work. As noted above they comprise two compulsory elements of an MBA program, both of which last for 11 weeks.

The Modules

These MBA modules are entitled Personal and Managerial Effectiveness (PME) and Group Consultancy Project (GCP) and have been run successfully for four years. We will now compare the two modules in terms of their similarities and differences. Both modules are similar in that they utilize workshops as their main learning vehicle, the parameters of which are determined by the tutor. They both provide the opportunity for extensive inter-student interaction, via team and group work, with the academic instructor as facilitator for this form of social learning. Both modules use a range of assessment methods, but a reflective learning review is common to both. This involves recording and analyzing learning in the following domains: attitudes, skills, knowledge, and emotions (see appendix 1 for the ASKE model (Frame, 1991)). In terms of delivery, one tutor, Jennifer O'Connor, teaches these two modules; however, Philip Frame supports their ongoing development.

The modules differ, however, in a number of ways, and in particular with respect to the two inter-linked dimensions identified previously: direct-indirect and content-process.

Direct-Indirect

All Middlesex University modules have learning objectives or outcomes in terms of knowledge and skills. The learning objectives, as stated in the module handbook for Personal and Managerial Effectiveness (PME), are explicitly related to diversity: "explain the meaning of diversity," "distinguish between diversity and equal opportunities," and "explore personal attitudes and perceptions toward diversity."

Similarly, there is an explicit requirement that students' individual learning reviews, which are assessed by the instructor, include a section that refers to learning about diversity. Students are directed to use theory as a means of reflecting on their experience and of identifying their diversity management skills, including their strengths and the challenges they face, as the quotations which follow clearly demonstrate.

In comparison, Group Consultancy Project (GCP) has no such specific diversity-based learning objective. Instead, a more general objective around working in a team is identified. Similarly, students are required to produce a learning review, which identifies the areas of attitudes, skills, knowledge, and emotions as useful to report. (See appendix 1 for the ASKE typology (Frame, 2001)). Diversity, as such, is not mentioned.

Thus in relation to content inputs, identified learning outcomes and the focus of assessment, these modules differ significantly.

Content-Process

The content, or the "what" of learning in PME includes attitudes, perceptions and, importantly, equal opportunities and diversity.

In contrast, GCP focuses on team building, organizational culture, and the consultant role. Diversity is touched on only in the introductory session when students are advised not to "work with their friends, flatmates, or lovers". Instead we strongly recommend that no single gender or overseas nationality teams are formed, for, as we explain, these tend to limit the experience of those involved. We rely on the experience or the process of working in a diverse team as the means for developing our students' diversity capabilities. Diversity is not specifically and formally referred to again, either as a topic or as the basis for an exercise, during the rest of the module.

We do, however, provide content input on teamwork, team roles, and team contracting. It is in this context that students begin to make sense of their experiences as we monitor team development. Additionally we organize team-building exercises and require all teams to produce an agreed contract of behavioral ground rules. We give teams the power to exclude free loaders, and we, the instructors, provide a process consultation facility if relations within a group become counterproductive. Thankfully, nearly all teams work well most

Figure 1. Dimensions of Diversity Delivery

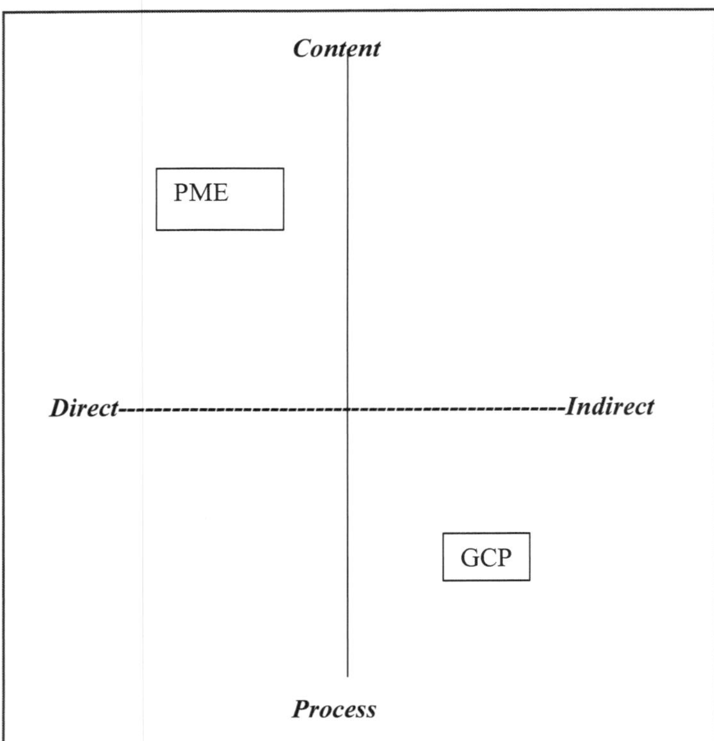

of the time: expulsions infrequently happen and effective team processes develop.

We can combine these two dimensions to create a model for mapping a range of diversity-related learning experiences, and using our case study modules as an example of this process (Figure 1).

We would suggest that instructors utilize the above figure of a means of locating and understanding their own actual or potential diversity classroom practice.

The Student Voice

What then were the outcomes from these two different learning experiences as reported by students? We believe the most meaningful and illuminatory comparisons can be made by first examining the way in which students wrote about diversity. We then consider strategies identified by the students for managing diversity.

Writing about Diversity

Those who experienced the explicit approach invariably used the term "diversity" in their learning reviews. Typical examples are as follows:

> *In relation to managing diversity by striving to understand the root cause of them and then to change or adapt my behavior, I believe I will be better equipped to manage all forms of diversity, even diversity of opinion or approach in order to get the best out of persons, situations, or projects* (PME Student, 2002).

> *Even though my previous attitudes appeared rational, justifiable, and based on fact, I now see they restricted the true diversity potential* (PME Student, 2002).

> *After diversity was brought to my attention, I can really see that my attitude in this situation did not bring out the best in each individual team member. If I had really understood diversity I could have achieved more* (PME Student, 2002).

In contrast, those who experienced the implicit approach spoke of diversity much more in terms of their behavior when working in their school-based co-operative learning teams, as the following quotations confirm:

> *These differences were at times a source of conflict, frustration but at the same time strength, creative and diverse knowledge.... At the end of the*

> *day the group was able to overcome the negative consequences arising from our differences and make better use of its positive aspects* (GCP, 2003).

> *Recognising diversity within the group was an essential element in aiding the management of the group effectively. This was demonstrated by the group as a whole as roles were shared out according to individual perception of others and themselves* (GCP, 2003).

> *Even though a diverse team can have a positive impact on the performance of the team if managed properly, it can at the same time create interpersonal problems that can negatively impact task effectiveness* (GCP, 2003).

Here there was a recognition of the pluses and minuses on working with diversity, which is an important step forward, from either ignoring the negatives or blaming them on others and absolving oneself.

But we wondered whether there was in reality such a stark contrast between "learning the language" of diversity and "changing behaviour." By examining what students in both groups had identified as strategies for diversity management, we were able to reveal that members of both groups identified behavioral changes.

Strategies for Managing Diversity

Start with Self-knowledge

Learners on both modules evidenced a willingness to self disclose, the importance of which we noted above with respect to ourselves as instructors. For PME students:

> *It is also important for me to be aware that I am different too and that my makeup has been shaped and once I have an understanding of this complex arena, I will be in a better position to help my team* (PME Student, 2002).

> *Sometimes I tend to stereotype, for example,. ... people are lazy, ...people are difficult to do business with* (PME Student, 2002).

The quotations below from GCP students demonstrate a degree of self-knowledge.

I had to learn the emotional makeup and deal with their responses. This was difficult (GCP 2003).

I developed the skill of valuing others' views and suggestions (GCP, 2003).

Value Individuality

This was a strategy identified by students in both cohorts:

My focus now needs to be on each individual's real talents, strength,s and what he or she brings to the table by tapping into those areas (PME Student, 2002).

My current approach will be the recognition of the unique contribution each employee can make to an organization as opposed to concentrating on distinct, mutually exclusive groups such as White/non-White, financial/clerical, junior/senior (PME Student, 2002).

It is therefore necessary that a leader accepts and recognizes different perceptions, attitudes, and emotions and deals with them in a productive way in order to enhance total performance (GCP 2003).

As a group it was realized that we need to recognize and harness the full potential talents of each individual (GCP 2003).

Be Flexible

Taking on the role of the leader also changed my perspective of the group members; my perspective changed from recognizing weaknesses of group members to recognizing capabilities of the individual (GCP 2003).

To understand the root cause of them and then to change or adapt my behavior (PME Student, 2002).

Finally, what might be termed "multi-strategies" were identified by PME students.

Multi-strategies

I believe diversity should be managed through Attention, Respect, and Communication. Attention helps me to perceive differences, Respect brings me acceptance, and Communication permits me to solve conflicts that can be generated due to differences (PME Student, 2002).

> *After I received the basic principles of the perceptual process. I realized that a fundamental rethink in the way I judge people's behavior would be necessary for diversity management to succeed. For diversity to thrive, the human touch is needed:*
>
> T stands for Trust,
>
> O stands for Openness,
>
> U for Understanding,
>
> C for Consideration
>
> H for Honesty
>
> (PME Student, 2002).

These two quotations are from the learning reviews of students who studied PME that we have presented as an example of a direct/content approach. No such similar quotations were apparent in the work of students who studied GCP. We therefore speculate that these multi-strategies represent a more sophisticated and informed approach to the issue of diversity.

Outcomes

Given the nature of their respective learning experiences, it is perhaps not surprising that both groups of students wrote about diversity in different ways, which we term informed (PME) or experienced (GCP). However, both groups identified similar strategies, which may suggest that either an explicit or an implicit approach achieved the same outcomes. Perhaps the most striking feature to emerge is the contrast between the "intentionality" of the PME students, who talk about what they *will do*, and the "actuality" of the GCP, who talk about what they *have done*. We asked ourselves why this difference should be apparent.

We suggest that this was, in part, a result of the different learning experiences that students were provided with on these two modules. It would appear that an explicit approach that focuses on content such as literature on diversity, attitudes, and perceptions, results in a much more theoretically informed perspective, but not necessarily in any action towards changed behavior. Given that PME students were all in full time employment, it could be argued that they had ample opportunity to put their intentions into practice, and indeed they refer to future action at their place of work. Conversely, their employed status could well have been a barrier to behaving differently, at least in the short term, because the context in which they operated may have been uninterested or hostile to diversity management developments. In contrast, GCP students developed their strategies of practice by experiencing the process of working with diversity in a theoretically uninformed way. They worked together as a consultant team with the goal of solving their client's problem, but not of learning explicitly about diversity. But in fact they did so as a means of getting the task done. Also, they did this exercise as students rather than in their role of being employed and the attendant constraints that this role may entail. They perhaps had more freedom to experiment and to do so in a safe environment.

Conclusion

In this chapter we have looked at the diversity-development implications of two approaches to teaching diversity-related content in an MBA program at Middlesex University. We began by identifying the contexts within which we operate – the external and internal environments – and the changes therein. We went on to emphasize the significance of self-knowledge, motivators,and disclosure as pre-requisites to effective learning in this area. We then explored the importance of these two seemingly different approaches when we outlined two case study modules, and we identified the direct-indirect and content-process dimensions, utilizing the "student voice" as a means of identifying what diversity learning had taken place.

We do not argue for an either/or approach but rather suggest that the essential elements of diversity development should involve disclosure, action, and reflection on the part of both instructor and student, facilitator and facilitated, and that this should take place in a safe environment. Our data suggest though that the direct/content approach is likely to lead to intentionality whereas an indirect/process approach is more likely to produce action. We will now explore the implications of these diversity experiences to inform and enhance faculty development.

We suggest the case studies reported here can be used for staff development in four ways:

1. staff themselves can engage directly in facilitating their students working with diversity through the type of modules outlined above.
2. They can use elements of our approach, such as organizing groups based on diverse participants or introducing an element of self-disclosure into their classes. The Twelve-Step Typology that we have provided here may well be a useful starting point.
3. Staff themselves can engage in processes similar to those experienced by our learners by, for example, working in diverse project teams and reflecting on those experiences both within the institution and the community.

4. The collection, analysis, and sharing of information based on the "student voice" may well encourage colleagues who are managing diverse groups to experiment, based on the positive outcomes noted above.

For those who have been working with diversity for some time we suggest that Figure 1: Dimensions of Diversity Delivery can provide an effective means of locating and reviewing current practice and of developing this practice further.

However, for any staff development to be robust and meaningful, there must be recognition in the institution's formal systems that such development is worthwhile and valued. Thus, it would be appropriate to include a diversity element in both staff appraisal and the observation of teaching.

References

Adams, M., Bell. L.A., & Griffin, P. (1997). *Teaching for diversity and social justice.* New York: Routledge.

Bligh, D., Thomas. H., & McNay, I. (1999). *Understanding higher education: An introduction for parents, staff, employers and students.* Exeter, England: Intellect Books.

Frame, P. (2001). Learning from part time work: The process. In L. Probus (Ed.), *Proceedings of the 9th annual teaching and learning conference* (pp. 80-90). UK: Business School, Nottingham Trent University.

Frame, P., & O'Connor, J. (2002a). Beyond the rhetoric: Embedding diversity through teaching and learning. Paper presented at the Chartered Institute of Personnel and Development Professional Standards Conference, Keele, United Kingdom.

Frame, P., & O'Connor, J. (2002b). From the 'high ground' of policy to 'the swamp' of professional practice: The challenge of diversity in teaching labour studies. *Society in Transition: Labour Studies in Transition, 33*(2), 278-292.

Frame, P., & O'Connor, J. (2003a). Workplace diversity training. In J. Rolph (Ed.), *Reflections: New developments in training* (pp. 14-19). London: Chartered Institute of Personnel and Development.

Frame, P., & O'Connor, J. (2003b). Developing diversity management in the HE context. *Proceedings of the Second annual US/UK scholarship of teaching and learning conference* (pp. 127-137). London: UEL, City University and the Carnegie Academy for Scholarship of Teaching and Learning.

Heron, J. (1999). *The complete facilitators handbook.* London: Kogan Page.

Honey, P., & Mumford, A. (1992). Cited in M. Reid, & H. Barrington. (2004), *Resource development: Beyond training interventions* (7th ed.). London: CIPD, 57.

Joplin, L. (1995). On defining experiential education. In K. Warren, M. Sakofs, & J. S. Hunt Jr. (Eds.), *The theory of experiential education.* Dubuque, IA: Kendall/Hunt.

Johnson, R., & Redmond, D. (2000). *Diversity incorporated: Managing people for success in a diverse world.* London: Pearson Education.

Keeton, M. T., & Tate, P. J. (1978). Cited in Davies, L. (1990), *Experience-based learning within the curriculum.* (pp. 13-29) Association for Sandwich Education and Training, London.

Kolb, D. A. (1984). *Experiential learning: Experience as the source of learning and development.* Upper Saddle River, NJ: Prentice-Hall.

McNay, I. (1994). The future student experience. In S. Haselgrove (Ed.), *The student experience* (pp. 167-179). Buckingham, UK: Society for Research into Higher Education and Open University Press.

Middlesex University (2003). *2002/2003 Statistical Digest.* London: Author.

Mortiboys, A. (2003). *The emotionally intelligent lecturer.* London: Staff and Educational Development Association.

Revans, R. W. (1980). *Action learning: New techniques for managers*. London: Blond and Biggs.

Rogers, C. (1983). *Freedom to learn for the 80's.* Columbia, OH: Charles Merrill.

Philip Frame is a Principle Lecturer in the Human Resource Management group at Middlesex University Business School London. **Jennifer O'Connor** is a senior lecturer in the Management Strategy group at Middleses University Business School.

Appendix 1

The ASKE Typology

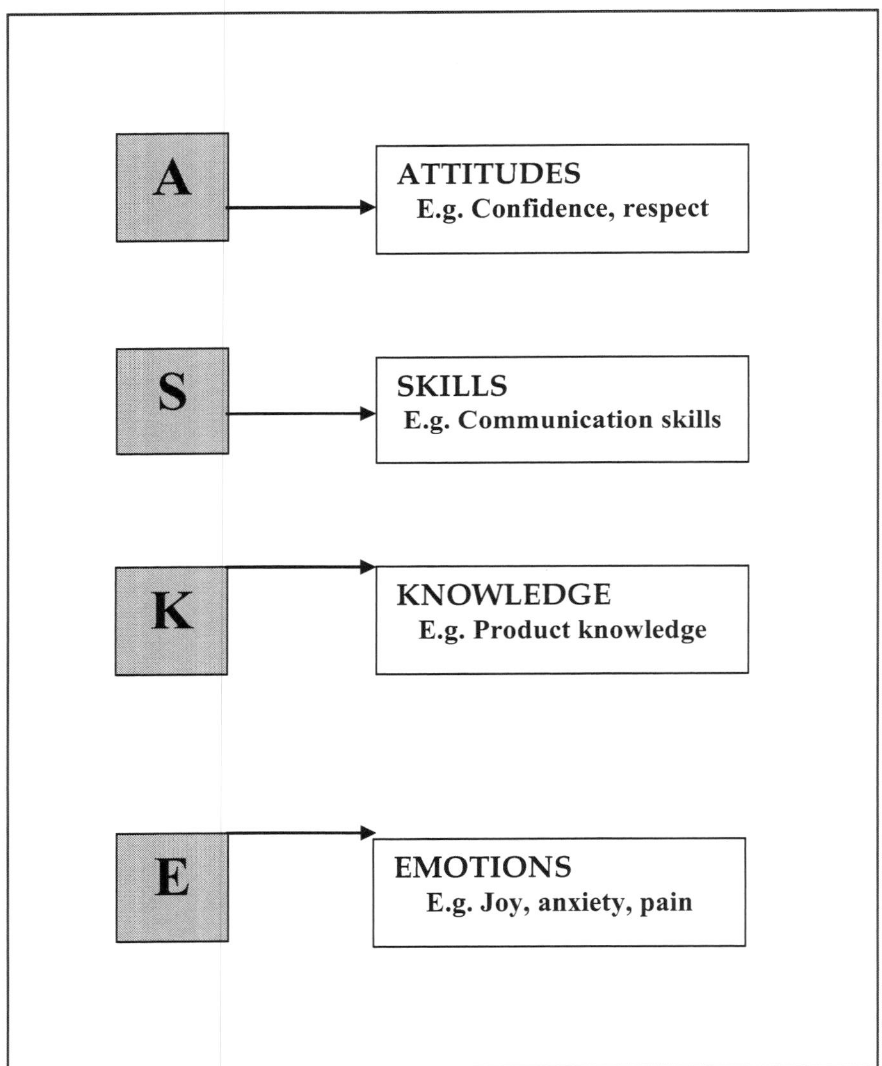

Chapter 40

Creating Inclusive Classrooms: A View Through the Student Lens

James Greenberg and Andre Perry

As teachers, our view of good teaching and important dimensions of classroom climate tends to be self-centered. We rely on "the literature" in the field, on colleagues, on our experiences and on experts; but, if you talk to students about the number of times teachers have consulted them on their knowledge and insights related to good teaching, few report any number greater than ZERO. This chapter explores, through the student lens, attempts to balance some of the expert opinion on the topic of "inclusive classrooms" with the insights, reflections, and recommendations straight from the students themselves.

What Others Have Written about Student Views

Perhaps the best known work that speaks directly to listening to student voices and using those voices to improve college teaching is Cross and Angelo's *Classroom Assessment Techniques* (CATS) (1994). Most faculty developers in the U.S. have utilized CATS in teaching colleagues how to structure the solicitation of student feedback to gain specific useful data related to their own teaching goals, including classroom climate and inclusiveness goals. More recently, Marcia Baxter Magolda completed a study focusing on learning from student voices, *Making Their Own Way: Narratives for Transforming Higher Education to Promote Self-Development.* (2004). This unique contribution to the literature on student development and the impact of the college experience grounds recommendations in an extensive longitudinal research process and uses the results to provide concrete insights and direction for reform. Another recent work more specifically aimed at issues of inclusiveness as seen through the student lens is *How Minority Students Experience College* (Watson & Terrell, Eds., 2003). In this book, minority students on seven predominantly white campuses were interviewed and their voices are the basis for the study's findings.

Finally, there are a number of programs at college campuses that help utilize student voices to provide insight and direction for classroom climate and curriculum and instruction improvement. One of the most outstanding programs was developed by Christine Stanley and colleagues at The Ohio State University. The Commitment to Success Program uses a variety of methods to listen to student voices and to use the results for faculty development and support. As the program's mission statement says, "Using such methods as focus groups, unit and classroom-based and online climate assessment surveys, classroom observations with feedback, and a review of curricular materials, consultants can assist with the development of long-term strategies and action plans for fostering an inclusive teaching and learning environment for all students." (http://ftad.osu.edu/CSP/overview.html) Mark Chesler, at the University of Michigan, has been a leader in FAIRteach (Faculty Against Institutional Racism-Teaching), and he conducted a study of student voices as part of that program's development effort. From fifteen focus groups with undergraduate students of color, certain themes emerged. Among the themes were concerns about low expectations from faculty, exclusion from the curriculum, and lack of understanding about diversity among students. Chesler and the FAIRteach program used the student voices to create recommendations and direction for faculty development on their campus (Chesler, 1997).

The general literature on diversity in higher education provides a broader context for this chapter and helps to put the students' voices we heard in perspective. All the work on the educational benefits of diversity (Milem & Hakuta, 2000; Milem, 2003; Chang, 1999, 2002; Hurtado, 1996; Bowen & Bok, 1998) has given us evidence and rationale for understanding diversity as a positive element in contributing to positive learning outcomes in higher education. But as Patricia Marin says, "most college environment studies focus on the overall institutional environment or campus climate, not the classroom environment" (2003, p.61). In her case study research on college classrooms, Marin analyzed student and faculty voices in order to provide a richer understanding of how and why particular outcomes result from diverse classrooms.

Faculty voices provided Marin a clear rationale for seeing a diverse classroom as a teaching and learning asset. Faculty in her study made it clear that a diverse student population actively engaged in an interactive classroom environment could produce a clear increase in the quality of student learning in the classroom environment in which such learning occurs. As one professor said, "The last thing I want is to be the person that tells people what the diversity in the world is. I want it to speak for itself, and, therefore, it has to be represented. I can share what I've heard about other people, and seen about other situations, but I can't really be that" (p. 63).

Student voices in Marin's study strongly supported the benefits of diverse classrooms. Marin says,

> Students compared their experiences in interactive, multi-racial/multi-ethic classrooms with their experiences in non-integrated environments. They said that in interactive, multi-racial/multi-ethnic classrooms, they not only learned more about others and acquired a broader perspective on issues, but they also learned more about themselves.... In general, multi-racial/multi-ethnic classrooms expand on course content by engendering more perspectives, more complicated discussion, and more sophisticated analysis. (pp. 69-70)

Jeff Milem offers us a conceptual framework for understanding the role and benefits of diversity in higher education as well as multiple dimensions through which diversity is expressed or experienced on campuses. In his framework, Milem identifies four benefits:

1. Individual benefits, such as benefits to students and teachers
2. Institutional benefits, such as benefits to curriculum, research, and other components of the mission
3. Economic benefits, such as benefits to the workforce and employers
4. Societal benefits, such as benefits reflected in enhanced equity, social welfare, and democratic values (2003, pp. 130-131)

The current chapter, which looks at the question of creating inclusive classrooms from the vantage point of the student lens, emphasizes Milem's first framework component, individual benefits, and the "diverse interactions" dimension of his complex concept of diversity.

Conversations with Students

Our most recent discussions with students revolved around a few simple questions. We started with a basic clarifying question to check our own assumptions and to make sure it was the student lens, not our own, through which the responses would be expressed and understood. We then asked students to characterize their experience in terms of inclusive classrooms, both generally and with regard to specific positive and negative examples. We followed with questions arising from their responses, including questions about how relationships with faculty were formed and if such relationships were considered important to an inclusive classroom climate; and we also asked students if it mattered – all things being equal – whether the teacher was like them in terms of gender, ethnicity, or other characteristics. Undergraduate students and graduate students were both included in the discussion groups, usually separately, and the insights that emerged will be discussed accordingly.

Undergraduate Students

Some distinct themes emerged from students' responses to our questions and these themes both reinforced what we had found in the literature and expanded our notions of what students thought. Certain clear themes emerged in all groups when we asked about their definition of an "inclusive classroom" and the ingredients of such an classroom from their point of view:

Valuing different perspectives and demonstrating respect for my voice. In the first discussion we held with a mostly African-American group of students, the importance of including different perspectives emerged as a crucial parameter of an inclusive classroom. In response to the question of how these students would define an inclusive classroom, an African-American government and politics major said: "Several points of view and a lot of participation; you don't want a small minority to dominate the class discussion; you need the basic pros and cons included in a discussion; different reference points to argue on."

Another African-American student summed up the issue in a somewhat more philosophical way: "An inclusive classroom has access; getting inside the classroom door doesn't mean you have access. If you don't feel empowered to say what you want to say, you don't have access and you are shut out."

Respect is an issue that kept surfacing in different ways, and the sense of being respected, as essential to having an inclusive classroom, seemed inextricably tied to the "professor" and the type of atmosphere he or she helped to create for the class.

An Asian-American student made respect of student voice a reason for going to class:

> Professors need to leave their egos at the door.... The most effective professors are those that walk into that classroom as a peer.... They feel they need to earn the respect of the students, and they get students' respect... . One of my most effective professors on the first day of class walked in to the classroom and [sat] down and [said], "alright, I'm going to give you guys an hour, tell me how you want the class set up for the rest of the year... ." A lot of it comes down to setting the tone on the first day so students know what to expect.... I never missed Dr. G's class because I knew if I missed that class I felt like my voice would be missed . . . whereas a lot of other classes I don't go to [because] I felt that if I didn't go, it wouldn't matter .

A number of student comments made specific reference to building relationships as a critical element in appraising what a teacher does or doesn't do in order to create inclusive classrooms. This issue, which some students felt was dependent on the professor's initiative, was raised by several students as follows: "I think the professor has a lot to do with it.... That's like whether the professor is out there to build personal relationships and make the education more personal or whether he just wants to relate information and be neutral."

Teaching styles and classroom format. While it seems fairly obvious that themes emerging from student voices don't fall into strictly exclusive categories, comments about teaching styles and strategies related strongly to the personality and relationship characteristics noted above, but also had a distinct place in pinpointing specific "how to's" as seen through the student lens. The first day and first impressions emerged as a sub-theme in the area of teaching strategies, but most comments picked up on the larger messages and enduring value that a positive first day can have. For example an AsianAmerican student showed how much students understand about why teachers do what they do and how important those decisions about teaching strategies can be to learning outcome goals:

> Being able to understand the different sort of people you have in your classroom really helps, out and if you do that early on it really helps ease the tension in the classroom. One of my classes deals with government issues in inner cities. [The professor] started out by going around the room and asking everyone in the class to start talking about different stereotypes you hear about different cultures, and she tied this in to the whole class so everything relates to race in some way...and how we can break down these stereotypes to help us learn more about how things function within the world.... It made a lot of people feel at ease because she knows that it is a difficult topic to talk about, but just to let it out on the first day really helped the atmosphere of the class. Setting the tone on the first day of class is really important.

Other students showed us that they understand such teaching methods can be effective regardless of the discipline:

> It depends on who the professor is.... In my General Chemistry class it is a very large lecture, but the professor works to get people involved.... He picks people out of the audience... . It depends how the class is set up and how the professor sets it up.... It doesn't feel like I'm lost in the crowd in that class at all; I'd have to say it's all because of the professor.

There were many comments related to physical set-up of the classroom space and arrangements that promote inclusiveness (for example, circles) or that inhibit inclusiveness (for example, rows). One student summed up the comments in this sub-category nicely:

> It's the small things...like whether the teacher is behind one of those lecture things or is sitting in front of the table, like whether they are part of you, or teaching at you. When they teach the class, are they reading off their paper or are they having a discussion and engaging with you? It's the little things that affect us. Physical setup is really important, like the circle.

Composition of the class and background of the teacher. In listening to the voices of these students, it was apparent in every group of undergraduates – Asian-American, Latino, African-American, and Caucasian, males and females – that sensitive teachers who cared about all their students used methods that facilitated engagement, respected student voices and ideas, and therefore made the most difference in creating inclusive classrooms. However, we probed in our discussions to see what students felt about other issues that persist as priority concerns in the discourse around diversity and college teaching. We asked them how important it was to have students like themselves in class, and how important the gender, ethnicity, or other characteristics of the teacher were to their sense of inclusiveness. Some examples of student responses about the importance of teacher identity follow:

> I'm getting my certificate in Asian-American studies.... I know ahead of time...that the teacher will have something in common with me. For certain types of classes, you know that the teacher will be a little more receptive to your concerns. I really think it depends on the kind of the class, but I think that in the back of the class the ethnicity and gender of the professor do matter.

> It's hard for me to say what it takes to include the quiet students because I am not a quiet person and I will make myself included regardless... but in all the classes I have felt most included, the teacher was either Black or Latino...

> ...definitely makes a difference because I can relate more to a professor who is a Latino.

> I'd be more inclined to go to a Black teacher for help...

> I notice that when we are saying professor we are all saying "he".... It's important to be exposed to different kinds of professors.... We say that it is important to have diversity among the students and curriculum, but in terms of the faculty it is important too, so that you have other people to look up to and learn about because we all probably have the same picture of the professor in our minds when we are all saying "he."

A number of students who expressed such sentiments clearly had a concern about diversity of the faculty when asked if it made a difference to them. However, many students were also quick to respond somewhat differently:

> I think it's more that the professor is open-minded and know that not everything applies to everyone. It doesn't matter if they are old... male, female.... It doesn't matter if they can show that they can reach all people in all kind of ways.
>
> I'd rather have a teacher that can teach me something than one I can relate to; I came to college to get a degree and get a job. Adding diversity into it is nice...but if we keep concentrating on that we may end up turning away teachers that can really teach simply for the sake of diversity.

and from an Asian-American female undergraduate:

> You can't force inclusiveness; people have to be interested. It's more important to have quality teachers who can relate to the students. I had one Asian American female professor that I did not relate to at all. In general, I think it is better to have quality teachers that are interested in the students. [We] shouldn't be forced to have minority teachers.

A group of predominantly Caucasian students had some interesting responses on this topic, particularly in regard to having teachers of a different background from their own.

> My English teacher is Asian and gay, and the very first day he established a relationship with the class and made it really comfortable for everyone. I think that having race or sexual orientation differences in the teacher really helps to get ideas out in the class; no one will be like, "we're not gonna go there because the teacher can't relate."
>
> My African American literature class is taught by a Jewish male.... I thought that was interesting to see a different race dealing with other race specialties. I think that it is still an effective class; he has a very open view; he is very knowledgeable about the subject matter. I think I like it that it is a white male because it broke my stereotype and it makes it more comfortable that there are people that care about other races.

While students generally felt that good teaching and a positive attitude toward inclusion were of paramount importance, having a teacher with whom students felt comfortable – often because of similarity in ethnicity or related background experience – also was important to many and a plus for almost everyone. Some similar views were expressed around the question of diversity of students in classes and how important that was to a sense of participating in an inclusive classroom:

> I think it's extremely important because college is the time where you are supposed to discover yourself and get this identity.... I think that if you talk to people who were in diverse classrooms they will say that they learned a lot more.... A lot of times we end up learning more from our peers than from the course itself.... It's extremely important to be with other APAs and also people of other color and gender and everything else, not just people who look like you, people who are different from you.

Some comments highlighted the problem of stereotyping and of feeling uncomfortable because of the nature of the discourse in certain classes. In each case, the peer group or mix in a particular class was a significant factor rather than the overall diversity at the institution:

> I don't want to be the one Black guy who doesn't know what's going on.

> I think a lot of time students may censor themselves because they don't want to offend someone from another background. Being White Protestant, a lot of times I feel bad about expressing opinions because someone who may have a different background from me, either racial, religious, [or geographical].... I don't feel comfortable because I'm afraid that someone is going to take this the wrong way or be offended.

Listening to these undergraduate student voices reminds us that we just can't generalize about "students" regardless of their age, gender, ethnicity, or other aspects of identity. They have complex views, they have drawn from different experiences, and at times they have come to different conclusions. However, their voices are so instructive in emphasizing the importance of the quality of the learning experience and the kinds of things that we can all do to affect that quality – most of which require more of a change in attitude and approach than in the budget.

Graduate Students

In all, undergraduate and graduate students shared many of the same sentiments with regards to their conceptualizations of inclusive classrooms as well as how they believe those spaces are created and maintained. This section reiterates and supports many ideas that were expressed by the undergraduates. Nonetheless, responses we received from graduate students differed most notably in their abilities to locate, articulate, and conceptualize inclusive classrooms. In general, graduate students provided more analytical and specific responses to our questions. We attribute these distinctions to developmental, positional, and academic differences between the two groups.

Composition of the classroom. Graduate students express that demography plays significant roles in how inclusive a classroom can be as well as how instructors can influence classroom climate. They reiterate the importance of who is in the classroom in terms of race, gender, social status, and sexual orientation.

A lesbian, named Kim, stated:

> When my professor told the class in not so many words that she is a lesbian, I felt so much more comfortable in the class. In my other classes, you can see professors freak out when I tell them I'm lesbian.... You feel more engaged in the material when you know you don't have to defend who you are as a person whenever you make a point.... [The professor] also brings in authors that my straight faculty don't even mention.

This theme supports scholarship that highlights the significance of the numerical representation of various social groups on classroom inclusiveness, climate, and participation (Allen, 1995; Hallinan & Smith, 1985).

Kim's statement brings to the fore important variables on inclusiveness: teacher identity and self-disclosure. These factors combined are generally explored in the scholarship on teaching and sexual orientation (Allen, 1995; Barnard, 1993; Fonow & Marcy, 1991).

The racial composition of students in the classroom also plays a significant role in the level of inclusiveness in the classroom. A Black, female, Math doctoral student stated, "I am in a discipline that is dominated by White men. I didn't know how important it was to see people who looked like me until I went to grad school".

When asked how that situation affected diversity in the classroom, she responded:

> Well, no one is really "included" in Math classrooms. Everyone has to listen and learn what the professor is teaching. It sounds funny hearing other students talk about bringing in different perspectives. You can question material in all these other fields. We have to master what we are taught. No one questions the content of our courses so I guess everyone is in the same boat.... I guess I just need to see that there are others like me who are doing Math. I am actually inspired by being one of the few, but it's something you shouldn't be inspired by.

Content, pedagogy, and structure. Having "representatives" of various social groups does not in itself ensure inclusive classrooms (Hurtado, 1992). As we know from the writings on identity, individuality is not neatly encapsulated in one's racial designation, sexual orientation, or socioeconomic status (Cerulo, 1997).

Many students stated that graduate schools' smaller class sizes, emphases on class discussion, and the closeness with the faculty generally allow for positive personal interactions with the variety of bodies in the classroom. More often than not, students feel personally connected to the people in their programs. Graduate students did not report incidents of sexist or racist language, harassment, or other hostile acts of discrimination that are commonly found on college campuses (Fassinger, 1995; Feagin, 1992; Myers & Dugan, 1996). For many of the graduate students involved in this study, inclusiveness primarily involves the institutional aspects of their programs that limit the freedom to pursue certain research topics. By institutional, we mean the assumed traditions that are entwined in the fabric of the postsecondary enterprise. Graduate students interviewed in this study suggest that the curriculum and graduation requirements affiliated with the dissertation measure the overall level of inclusiveness.

A White doctoral student stated:

> I have Black instructors, but I can't tell any difference between them and my White professors. I fully expected that I would have had a different learning experience. Out of the classroom, my Black instructors are so different from my White or Indian teachers. In the classroom, they're all the same.

When asked if she was saying that her professors teach the same things in the same way, she responded:

> Yes and No. I've taken African American literature courses from people of different races and it seems that they all emphasize the same points. I've learned Morrison from multiple instructors and they basically taught it the same way.... How is that inclusive?

When the group was asked if it was correct to say that they feel limited by Western standards, a Black student in English stated, "In classes we learn how to critique Western norms. I even consider some of my faculty quite progressive. But when it comes down to the dissertation, we have to toe the line to [Western standards]."

These comments reflect a consistent sentiment among many graduate students, particularly among doctoral students in the social sciences, humanities, and education. Students feel less limited by professors' race, gender, sexual orientation or teaching style than their course offerings and methodological approaches to research. As one student put it, "the curriculum and dissertation are where you'll find how inclusive we are." Another student said, "It's not just Maryland. Higher education is an institution that believes in its product. They have no intention on giving up on its main product." A cynical student responded, "Some of these comments are incredible. People act as if colleges and universities haven't been selling the same thing for years. Did people do their research of what getting an advance degree entailed? They're not going to change because a few Blacks and Latinos came to town." Most graduate students do not wave white flags as an unconditional surrender to the curriculum and dissertation. However, these structural features of their programs pose tremendous barriers for the attainment of inclusive classrooms.

Students did not limit their comments to inclusiveness in the classroom. For doctoral students especially, the dissertation as well as comprehensive examinations or qualifiers represented the most exclusive exercises of the graduate school experience. These customs expose traditional values that faculty regularly practice. A Black doctoral student in Education stated:

> Your faculty can control every aspect of your research. I wanted to take an Afrocentric approach to my dissertation, but it turned out being another critical analysis on my subject. My advisor and committee pretty much forced me to learn all the traditional critical theorists. I finally gave in because they weren't trying to accept my literature base as valid.

Throughout the interview on inclusive classrooms, doctoral students consistently moved the discussion away from classroom dynamics towards their research interests. Tinto asserts that lines between academic and social requirements of persistence are blurred (1993). The tendency incorporate research in a discussion on classroom inclusiveness supports Tinto's general notion that the various components of the graduate school experience are inextricably linked. In addition, the dissertation may be considered graduate education's primary means of socializing students in the profession, making it one of its most hallowed traditions (Golde, 2000; Isaac, Quinlan, & Walker, 1992). We also attribute this shift to graduate students' central frustration with their inability to explore alternative methodological strategies they can employ towards dissertation data collection and analysis.

Talking about methods seems to generate the most visceral reactions to the subject of inclusiveness among various focus groups. Methodological approaches establish and ensure standards of quality by which the research is measured. Embedded within most recognized methodological approaches in American higher education is a tradition that has Western philosophical roots: "The principal characteristic of scholarly and scientific inquiry, as opposed to informal, intuitive kinds of inquiry, is the use of rationally grounded procedures to extend knowledge that a community of scholars regards as reliable and valid" (Organization Development Program of the Fielding Institute, 1998). What is rational and formal is most often defined by Eurocentric models of inquiry. In the previous quote, we can reasonably assume that this student's frustration stems from a scholarly community's rejection of Afrocentric methods, which he equates to a rejection of cultural, academic, and personal difference.

This is certainly not news for anyone who received or is receiving a doctorate. The dissertation reflects a specific academic and intellectual culture (Isaac et al., 1992). Limiting curricular offerings to traditional standards begs the questions posed by Henry Louis Gates, "Must academic inquiry be subordinated to the requirements of national identity? Should scholarship and education reflect our actual diversity, or should they rather, forge a communal identity that may not yet have been achieved" (1992, introduction, xiv). Changes in numerical diversity transformed the complexion of American higher education, but these changes seem not to have a major effect on what is assumed to be a valid, rigorous education.

Nevertheless, the cultural differences that numerical diversity brings will also usher cultural challenges to the dominant mode of scientific inquiry. Occasionally, the ability to self -express intellectually is challenged by educational institutions. Graduate students in this study illustrated that self -expression in the classroom is mitigated by traditional Western standards. Those who question the dominant curriculum question the dominant culture's prominence throughout American education and its political and economic priorities. Students who question feel the resistance of traditional curricular standards.

Several other graduate students suggest that the inflexibility of the curriculum and the academy's conceptualization of scholarly work contribute to the shortage of underrepresented groups in the faculty (Anderson et al., 1993). A Black student in Education stated:

> I can't wait till my advisor gets tenured, if she gets tenured. I came here because she was doing some cutting edge stuff, but she has been publishing in the Black journals. I don't know if she's going to make it.... She is the only one who will support my research.

These comments reflect another key variable in creating inclusive classrooms, the presence of tenured faculty members who conduct non-traditional research and employ alternative research methods. A group of Chinese doctoral students commented on their appreciation of a Chinese, associate professor who incorporates Eastern philosophies in her coursework:

> Professor Y teaches peace education, and he uses many different perspectives. Sometimes he uses writings from some of the great Chinese philosophers. I am not in international education so I don't get the opportunity to learn about other Eastern philosophers.

This quote makes two important points. First, although it is no guarantee, different racial, ethnic, religious, sexual, and socioeconomic identities can translate into diversity in curricular offering and teaching styles. Second, the comments suggest that the culture embedded within the content of the course is an attraction in itself. Course content is not neutral. Students often relate culturally to what is taught. The group of Chinese graduate students noted that their professor's teaching methods are very different from the rest of their professors. In this regard, inclusive classrooms are spaces in which faculty have the freedom to teach beyond the boundaries of the curriculum.

Summary and Recommendations

The students' voices and the literature on the factors and dynamics related to inclusive classrooms offer powerful guides and suggestions for individual and institutional change. There is nothing radical or totally surprising in what we have reviewed in this chapter. Rather, the variety of undergraduate and graduate student perspectives have provided helpful and significant texture to the basic concepts underlying inclusive classroom settings and the behaviors that can have enormous influence on student attitudes and student learning. Our recommendations are simple:

1. Listen to student voices. Just listening can help teachers learn so much, and valuing student voices helps to create inclusiveness.
2. Engagement is critical to learning. Students feel engaged or become engaged largely because they feel included in the teaching and learning process. They will do what is required anyway, but they will be more engaged, and they will learn more if their views are respected and if they feel included.
3. Specific concern for, and sensitivity to, diversity issues and diverse learners helps create inclusive classrooms and learning experiences. However, basic principles of good teaching and student-centered learning, such as emphasis on learning rather than on the teacher, are probably most important and most valued by students.

4. Documented advantages of diversity to the quality of education will not be realized to their full potential unless we do our part. The advantages can be tremendous, as our students have told us, but if we don't help to make our classrooms inclusive and supportive of the diverse individuals, talents, and views that inhabit them, we are missing a great opportunity.

References

Allen, K. (1995). Opening the classroom closet: Sexual orientation and self-disclosure. *Family Relations, 44*(2), 136-141.

Anderson, M. et al. (Autum 1993). Why the shortage of Black professors? *The Journal of Blacks in Higher Education,* 25-34.

Barnard, I. (1993). Bibliography for an anti-homophobic pedagogy: A resource for students, teachers, administrators and activists. *Feminist Teacher, 7*(3), 50-52.

Baxter-Magolda, M. (2004). *Making their own way: Narratives for transforming higher education to promote self-development.* Sterling, VA: Stylus.

Bloom, A. D. (1987). *The closing of the American mind.* New York: Simon & Schuster.

Cerulo, K. A. (1997). Identity Construction: New issues, new directions. *Annual Review of Sociology, 23,* 385-409.

Cheney, L. (1992). *Telling the truth: A report on the state of the humanities in higher education.* Washington, DC: National Endowment for the Humanities.

Chesler, M. (1997). Perceptions of faculty behavior by students of color. *CRLT Occasional Papers, 7.* University of Michigan.

Cross,P., & Angelo, T. (1993). *Classroom assessment techniques.* New York: Jossey-Bass

Fassinger, P. (1995). Understanding classroom interaction: Students' and professors' contributions to students' silence. *The Journal of Higher Education, 66*(1), 82-96.

Feagin, J. (1992). The continuing significance of racism: Discrimination against black students in white colleges. *Journal of Black Studies, 22*(4), 546-578.

Fonow, M. M., & Marcy, D. (1991). The shift from identity politics to the politics of identity: Lesbian panels in the women's studies classroom. *National Women's Studies Association Journal, 3,* 402-413.

Gates, H. L. (1992). *Loose canons: Notes on the culture wars.* New York: Oxford University Press.

Gates, H. L., Jones, R., Austen, R., Wolfenstein, E., & Baker, J. (Winter 1993/94). Does academic correctness repress separatist or Afrocentrist scholarship? *The Journal of Blacks in Higher Education,* 40-48.

Golde, C. (2000). Should I stay or should I go? Student descriptions of the doctoral attrition process. *The Review of Higher Education, 23*(2), 199-227.

Hallinan, M., & Smith, S. (1985). The effects of classroom racial compostion on students' interracial friendliness. *Social Psychology Quarterly, 48*(1), 3-16.

Hurtado, S. (1992). The campus racial climate: Context of conflict. *The Journal of Higher Education, 63*(5), 539-569.

Isaac, P., Quinlan, S., & Walker, M. (1992). Faculty perceptions of the doctoral dissertation. *The Journal of Higher Education, 63*(3), 241-268.

Levine, L. (1996). *The opening of the American mind: Canons, culture, and history*. Boston: Beacon Press.

Myers, D., & Dugan, K. (1996). Sexism in graduate school classrooms: Consequences for students and faculty. *Gender and Society, 10*(3), 330-350.

Nemec, M. R. (1997). The role of curricular debate in the university. *The Review of Higher Education, 20*(2), 215-227.

Nieto, S. (1999). *The light in their eyes: Creating multicultural learning communities*. New York: Teachers College Press.

Ohio State University. (n.d.). *Commitment to Success Program.* Retrieved May 3, 2004, from http://ftad.osu.edu/CSP/overview.html

Organization Development Program of the Fielding Institute. (1998). *Inquiry and research knowledge study guide.* Santa Barbara, CA: Author.

Rust, P. C. (1993). "Coming out" in the age of social constructionism: Sexual identity formation among lesbian and bisexual women. *Gender and Society, 7*(1), 50-77.

Sizemore, B. (1990). The Politics of curriculum, race, and class. *Journal of Negro Education, 59*(1), 77-85.

Tinto, V. (1993). *Leaving college: Rethinking the causes and cures of student attrition* (2nd ed.). Chicago: University of Chicago Press.

Watson, L. & Terrell, M. (Eds.). (2002). *How minority students experience college: Implications for planning and policy.* Sterling, VA: Stylus.

Willie, S. S. (2003). *Acting black: College, identity, and the performance of race*. New York: Routledge.

James Greenberg is the director of the K-16 Partnership Development Center in the College of Education at the University of Maryland, College Park and was the founding director of the University Center for Teaching Excellence. **Andre Perry** is an assistant professor in the Department of Educational Leadership, Counseling, and Foundations at the University of New Orleans.

Chapter 41
Multicultural Course Transformation

Christine A. Stanley, Shari Saunders, and Jamie M. Hart

Multicultural course transformation necessitates a look at what we teach, how we teach, and who we are as instructors in the teaching and learning process. It entails assessing core principles of the content area, discussing representation in course materials, using a variety of methods to present course content, and engaging students in activities to promote reflection and learning. This chapter addresses the dimensions of multicultural course transformation and the implications these have for enhancing teaching and learning.

What Do We Mean By Multicultural Course Transformation and What Does It Take to Do This Work?

Multicultural course transformation is the conscious, meaningful effort given to modify a particular course to appropriately include multicultural content, perspectives, and strategies (Morey & Kitano, 1997). It takes much mental, emotional, physical, and spiritual energy to engage in multicultural course transformation as well as multicultural teaching. There is so much to know in order to do this work well, yet we must move forward, even with incomplete knowledge and skills. A critical starting point for knowledge and skill building is for those who do this work to begin by knowing themselves and engaging in ongoing self-development.

We have continually relied upon several frameworks for our own understanding and work on multicultural course transformation. A useful faculty development framework for conceptualizing how we teach and assess the learning of multicultural content by diverse learners is a model derived from Marchesani and Adams (1992) that we have adapted and used in conversations with faculty, students, staff, and administrators on how diversity impacts teaching and learning. This model addresses the complex interaction among four distinct dimensions in teaching and learning, including:

1. Knowing who we are as educators and/or faculty
2. Knowing our students
3. Examining our teaching methods and assessment measures
4. Reviewing our course content

Knowing who we are as educators and/or faculty. This dimension requires educators to reflect on our socialization and its relevance to this work, examine assumptions and stereotyped beliefs, and to mentor students in the process. Educators must regularly examine their attitudes, values, behaviors, thinking, points of view, and reactions in and outside of educational contexts. Goodman (2001), who focuses on working with people from privileged groups, identifies factors that can affect our educational effectiveness when working with students (for example, where we are in terms of our own social identity development, our triggers, our stance as advocate or missionary, and our stereotypes and biases (pp. 169-179)). She also discusses what can be done to increase our educational effectiveness (for example, ongoing personal work in both content and consciousness, and developing and maintaining respect and compassion). Our learning and self-work is never ending, and we need to regularly examine the fit between our philosophies and our practices as they pertain to multicultural teaching and learning. We, as educators, are only part of the complex teaching puzzle.

Knowing our students. This dimension requires educators to work at learning more about our students, to get students to reflect on their socialization around multicultural issues, and to examine assumptions and stereotyped beliefs. We are working with groups of students who are on their own developmental paths. To facilitate students' learning about where they are developmentally, educators might consider looking at the following: social identity development theory (Hardiman & Jackson, 1997, pp. 23-29), intellectual development (Goodman, 2001, pp. 47-53) and racial identity development (Wijeyesinghe & Jackson, 2001, pp. 8-152; Tatum, 1997). Educators might also consider learning about the characteristics of intergroup dialogue (Schoem, Hurtado, Sevig, Chesler, & Sumida, 2001). Because students can facilitate or hinder the learning of their peers, educators may find it useful to get a sense of students' experiences with intergroup dialogue around multicultural issues and the skills they have for engaging in intergroup dialogues about multicultural content within a classroom context. To do this, educators could adapt the *Facilitator Per-*

sonal Assessment Chart (Beale, Thompson, & Chesler, 2001, pp. 233-235) that looks at knowledge, skills, awareness, and passion competencies for peer facilitators.

Examining our teaching methods and assessment measures. This dimension requires educators to examine the implicit messages and the culture of the classroom and develop classroom norms that emphasize respect and equity. We must consistently explore the ways in which the social and cultural identities of the students and instructors can be used to facilitate or pose challenges to the teaching and learning process and assessment of learning when the content is multicultural. It is important to consider the complex interaction among content, social identities, teaching methods, and learning styles, and to provide multiple ways for students to learn and demonstrate their mastery of course content (Adams, Bell, & Griffin, 1997; Marchesani & Adams, 1992).

Reviewing our course content. This dimension requires educators to examine the explicit messages we send in the curriculum through content emphases, perspectives, examples, and illustrations. It is useful for educators to be knowledgeable about multicultural content and processes that can facilitate the learning of multicultural material. This can be more difficult than it sounds, as many of us may not have learned through our formal educational preparation the knowledge we need to do this work well. One conference that we have found particularly helpful for acquiring new knowledge, skills, and resources is the annual National Conference on Race and Ethnicity in American Higher Education (NCORE) that is sponsored by the Southwest Center for Human Relations Studies in the College of Continuing Education at the University of Oklahoma. In addition to issues of race and ethnicity, attendees can usually find sessions addressing other social identity characteristics such as sexual orientation, physical and/or learning ability, age, socioeconomic status, and religion.

It is important to note that for the purposes of this chapter, we are focusing on transforming a course, but it might also be possible for someone to use this framework to develop an entirely new course. And although we are discussing courses at the individual level in this context, we do not want to exclude the possibility of multicultural course transformation at a much broader level. Such an effort might involve a group of people who collectively work on multicultural course transformation to affect the content, teaching methods, and climate throughout their educational setting.

How Can We Transform Our Courses Using Multicultural Content?

Our perspectives on multiculturalism influence the decisions we make about content, materials, and instructional strategies, and are also interconnected with the kind of classroom climate we are trying to develop. Therefore, it is essential that we as educators make our perspectives on multiculturalism explicit to see how they inform the core principles and multicultural goals of the courses we teach, and if there is truly a fit between our philosophy and our practice.

There are many working definitions of multiculturalism, multicultural education, and multicultural teaching. In a broad sense, multiculturalism may be defined as a "celebration of racial and cultural diversity, seeing other cultures, (especially those traditionally excluded) on their own terms," and as embodying the belief that "with words and ideas, marginalized groups can be empowered and justice be brought to the world" (Herbert, 1997, pp. 154-155). Taking this definition yet a step further, Schoem, Frankel, Zuniga, Ximena, & Lewis (1995) define how multicultural teaching must explicitly address the backgrounds of the students and the power relationships in the classroom. They suggest, "an individual's gender, race, ethnicity, and cultural background significantly influence her or his worldview and the way he or she experiences and understands course content and classroom experiences." They go on to argue that "power relationships in the classroom define, in large part, students' participation, sense of trust and safety, and classroom interactions." Therefore, it becomes the teacher's responsibility "to create a classroom environment that fosters the full participation and development of all students." Finally, they suggest that a "non-deficit approach to education that recognizes, validates, and incorporates the insights, perspectives, and cultural knowledge of diverse student populations benefits all students in the classroom" (p. 281).

The underlying commitment to empowering and respecting students is woven throughout definitions of multiculturalism. Yet to an educator, the often perceived high-level of responsibility for the well-being and future actions of our students can appear to be a daunting task. So how do we begin to articulate our individual perspectives on multiculturalism and use this articulation to inform and guide the development of our courses? Throughout our various experiences working with educators on multicultural course transformation, we have found that it may be helpful to think about a number of issues when considering our individual perspectives on multiculturalism. First, what categories of human diversity do you include when thinking about multiculturalism? Do you emphasize any of these more than others? Second, what role does self-awareness and personal reflection play in your perspective? Third, how are power relationships, oppression, and privilege addressed in your perspective? And finally, what kinds of actions do you want your perspective to elicit in others (no action; self-education; educating others; initiating events programs; changing policies; and so forth)? (See *Action Continuum* (Wijeyesinghe, Griffin, & Love, 1997, p. 109).)

Once this internal working definition of multiculturalism is made explicit, we can begin to articulate what we consider to be the core principles of our course. (For our purposes in this section, we will focus on content rather than pedagogy.) Defining core principles such as our beliefs, philosophy, and ideology related to content, we must ask ourselves, what is at the center and/or core of our course–without which none of the rest would have integrity? Thinking about both disciplinary (such as themes and models) and multicultural issues (such as subject areas, topics, units of analysis), it is helpful to consider the following when beginning to redesign a course:

- *What are your assumptions about what is important for your students to know?* We have expectations about what must be taught and learned, both from our own beliefs and those of our disciplines. We also have an idea of what knowledge, skills, and beliefs we would like to see our students have as a result of our course. And we are generally aware of the beliefs, philosophy, and ideology of our discipline and how these things may either complement or conflict with our own.
- *How does your social identity impact your course?* Our experience and background greatly influences how we choose content materials, how we organize the overall course, and how we incorporate multicultural content. Our first instinct may be to choose content and materials with which we are both familiar and comfortable.
- *How do your assumptions about your students' social and cultural identities impact your course?* Our assumptions about their motivation for being in our classroom or about the social identity mix of the students may affect our choices in terms of content, materials, organization, and/or teaching strategies. We may make decisions about the order in which we present the course content based on the perceived background or knowledge-base of the students, choosing to "warm them up" to certain more multicultural (or controversial) perspectives over time or deciding to cover more controversial content right away to model behavior for (hopefully) more honest and open discussion as the course goes on.
- *In what ways are your perspectives on multiculturalism reflected in the core principles of the course?* This is where we see if there is truly a fit between philosophy and practice. Many of us can recognize that a student's background greatly influences the way that he or she experiences and un-

derstands the course content and classroom interactions, yet we may not acknowledge the impact of our own background and training on the materials we choose or the way we traditionally teach a course.

This initial phase of determining what is at the heart of a course can be very helpful in providing context for our efforts and helping to define our multicultural content goals. Kitano (1997) suggests the logical place to begin incorporating multicultural content in a course is with intended outcomes or multicultural goals. Such goals may include:

- Supporting "diverse students' acquisition of traditional subject matter, knowledge, and skills"
- Helping "students acquire a more accurate or comprehensive knowledge of subject matter"
- Encouraging "students to accept themselves and others"
- Helping "students value diversity and equality"
- Equipping "all students to work actively toward a more democratic society" (p. 19).

Once we are clear about our definition of multiculturalism, the core principles that form the foundation of the course, and the goals that we hope to achieve in the classroom, we must then determine which method of multicultural course transformation is most appropriate within this context. Our faculty development work has proven time and time again that students' views can be broadened in any context, but that in terms of content, it is easier to modify courses in some disciplines (particularly those within which knowledge is socially constructed, such as sociology or education) than in others (particularly those considered to be "objective," such as math and the sciences). Specific examples of multicultural course transformation in the sciences and professional schools can be found in Schoem, Frankel, Zuniga, and Lewis (1993) and Morey and Kitano (1997).

There are several models on multicultural curriculum transformation. We recommend the following sources: Banks (1993), Green (1989), Schoem, Frankel, Zuniga, and Lewis (1993), Ognibene (1989), and Jackson and Holvino (1988). Although it was developed for the K through12 course context, we have found Banks (1993) model particularly useful in our work. The four levels of curriculum transformation include:

- **Level 1**: *The contributions approach.* The course presents traditional views with the mention of the activities of various groups and/or perspectives.
- **Level 2**: *The additive approach.* The course presents traditional views with alternative perspectives added in, and encourages students to analyze why such viewpoints have been excluded in the past.

- **Level 3**: *The transformation approach.* The course challenges traditional views and assumptions and encourages students to think in new ways. The field is reconceptualized as a result of the new content and process.
- **Level 4**: *The social/action approach.* The course has been entirely transformed and provides students with the social action and decision-making skills to be agents for social change.

It is up to us as educators to determine which level of modification we are ready to undertake , and to then look into the available resources to support our journey (for example, teaching and learning centers, colleagues, materials).

Ultimately, we must recognize the power we have as educators to determine what is important to us, to understand what is important in the eyes of our discipline(s), and to ensure that various experiences and perspectives are represented. Saunders and Kardia (2000) suggest that in multicultural teaching, "content is presented in a manner that reduces all students' experiences of marginalization and, wherever possible, helps students understand that individuals' experiences, values, and perspectives influence how they construct knowledge in any field or discipline" (p. 21). Therefore, it is essential to include diverse voices, perspectives, and scholarship by utilizing multiple perspectives on each topic within the course and including materials written or created by people of different backgrounds and/or perspectives. It is also essential to truly respect the way these perspectives and experiences are being represented by including materials that do not trivialize or marginalize the experiences of underrepresented groups, being aware of (and responsive to) the portrayal of certain groups in the course content, and avoiding the tendency to dichotomize issues of race into black and white (Saunders & Kardia, 2000). In the end, we must choose the materials creatively, yet carefully, and it is also our responsibility to make sure students are aware of the limitations of the materials and to help facilitate their ability to read and think critically.

There are challenges and opportunities within every teaching endeavor, but we must now consider these in light of a course that has been transformed to have multicultural goals at its core. At the student level, we may face resistance to learning about content that is new and unfamiliar and that may challenge students' values or beliefs (or those of their parents). At the individual level, we may have to overcome our lack of motivation for revamping yet another course, or address the very real limitations in some disciplines for addressing the experiences of various groups, or move past our fears of branching out into new territory and putting ourselves at risk of failing in front of our students and our colleagues. At the administrative level, our colleagues and administrators may not find value in multicultural teaching, may not provide the necessary support (both tangible and intangible) that is required to undertake the transformation process, and may in fact perceive that our efforts are challenging the very structure they hope to maintain.

So why even bother with multicultural course transformation? First and foremost, it can serve to open the minds and broaden the perspectives of all students. It can also give voice to those who have been marginalized and disempowered by both the educational system and greater society. It can also serve as a model of good teaching for other educators, and provide proof that there is great benefit to breaking out of the norm and no longer doing things the way they have always been done. And although we must come to grips with the fact that teaching involves "unknowability," we can look at multicultural course transformation as a dynamic process that is forever changing and enhancing our ability, as well as our students' ability, to continue to learn and grow. Most importantly, multicultural teaching is effective for *all* students. It is not teaching that is less rigorous or watered down. It is not teaching that is conducive to some disciplines and not others. As Morey and Kitano (1997) articulate, "it is simply an attitude that is inclusive, a repertoire that is broad, and commitment to infusing pluralism into all aspects of teaching and learning. It is intellectually challenging, personally rewarding, and academically sound" (pp. 70).

What Methods Can We Use to Teach and Assess Multicultural Content to Diverse Learners?

Once we have developed our goals and transformed the content of our course, how do we effectively translate this new message to students, and at the same time, help our students become an integral part of the transformation process? Typically, many of us tend to teach the way we were taught or the way we learn. Marchesani and Adams (1992) and Kuh and Whitt (1988), argue that many faculty model unexamined teaching methods that require learners to gain an understanding of disciplinary content and knowledge by the transmission of information via the lecture as the teaching method of choice and the assessment of learning demonstrated by individual performance criteria. These are not culturally neutral teaching, learning, and assessment practices. Rather, they reflect a curriculum that is often unfamiliar and unwelcoming to students who are coming to college campuses with different values, norms, behavioral expectations, and ways of knowing and thinking in the world.

Teaching does not occur in a vacuum. Parker Palmer author of *The Courage to Teach* refers to teaching as making connections. Palmer says,

> Good teachers are able to weave a complex web of connections among themselves, their subjects, and their students so that students can learn to

> weave a world for themselves. The methods used by these teachers vary widely: lectures, Socratic dialogues, laboratory experiments, collaborative problem-solving, creative chaos. ... As good teachers weave the fabric that joins them with students and subjects, the heart is the loom on which the threads are tied, the tension is held, the shuttle flies, and the fabric is stretched tight. Small wonder, then, that teaching tugs at the heart opens the heart, even breaks the heart–and the more one loves teaching, the more heartbreaking it can be. The courage to teach is the courage to keep one's heart open in those very moments when the heart is asked to hold more than it is able so that teacher and students and subject can be woven into the fabric of community that learning, and living, require. (1998, p. 11)

In order to teach and make learning connections with a diverse student population we have to consider the role and positionality of the teacher and learner in this process. The positionality of the teacher means being aware of our own social and cultural identities. In most traditional classrooms, the social and cultural identities of the teachers and learners usually remain in the background. Sometimes, they are hidden. However, in a diverse classroom, we argue that the significance of who we are as teachers and learners is important and can pose challenges to as well as opportunities for teaching and learning. For example, as Black women educators, when we enter the college classroom, we do not leave our social and cultural identities at the door. We are a blend of multiple identities race and ethnicity, gender, sexual orientation, class, religious affiliations, ability status, and the like. When we are teaching courses from a multicultural perspective, particularly with regard to African American issues, we are constantly reminded of the tensions that exist between being a member of that group and a person of authority as college professors who teach primarily to a predominantly White student population (Stanley, Porter, Simpson, & Ouellett, 2003). We have turned these tensions into opportunities by offering data based on our experiences, research, and expertise. We have found that these strategies stretch the boundaries of knowledge and provide an opportunity for us to model what we are asking them to do in fulfilling learning outcome goals.

Teaching multicultural content to diverse learners must be linked to explicit learning outcome and pedagogical goals and appropriate assessment measures. Morey and Kitano (1997) argue in their proposed model for multicultural course and syllabus change, that an instructor's multicultural course goals should be derived from sound principles of multicultural education and learning. Chickering and Gamson (1987) outlined seven principles for good practice in undergraduate education that are valuable when considering strategies for teaching multicultural content. Good practice encourages:

1. Student/faculty contact
2. Cooperation among students
3. Active learning
4. Prompt feedback
5. Time on task
6. Communicates high expectations
7. Respect for diverse talents and ways of learning

Learning and assessment objectives for multicultural content address cognitive (how students think and process information), affective (how students understand and relate the role of self and others in the learning process), and behavioral (how students develop and apply appropriate skills in learning) domains (NCSS, 1992; Sawchuk, 1993). We must provide multiple ways for students to demonstrate their mastery of course content. Examples of these ways might include self-evaluation of progress reports and learning projects that require students to apply their learning in ways that produce change. Ann Christy, Associate Professor of Agricultural Engineering at Ohio State University, for example, has used student portfolios as a way for them to make meaning and connection with course topics and to assess their own progress in learning course content.

Effective teaching of multicultural content depends on an educator's willingness and ability to draw from a repertoire of instructional strategies to reach a variety of learning styles in the classroom. The literature on learning styles suggests patterns of learning for African American, Asian, Native Americans, Latinos, and women that point to the necessity of using alternative teaching strategies (Anderson & Adams, 1992; Tharp, 1989; Irvine & York, 1995). These alternative teaching strategies include collaborative and cooperative learning to balance traditional expectations of competition; visual, auditory, or kinesthetic modes as alternatives to the use of verbal and written expressions; study groups and group projects to enhance in and out of class student relationships instead of individual study; and active learning activities, simulations, and role plays to balance other passive modes of learning and teaching such as the lecture (Marchesani & Adams, 1992).

As educators, we are constantly reminded of the need to stretch our own preferred ways of learning and teaching when we teach students and/or prepare to facilitate workshops and seminars for faculty, staff, and administrators. We know from Sadker and Sadker's (1992) review of research in higher education classrooms (as cited in Morey and Kitano, 1997) that

> (1) compared to White males, female students of all backgrounds and males from underrepresented populations are more likely to remain quiet in the

> classroom and are less likely to be assertive in discussion; (2) most teachers, regardless of gender, race, or ethnicity, are unaware of their biased interaction patterns; (3) wait time after questioning is related to achievement, type of discourse, and participation; and teachers give White males more wait time than they give to women students and to students of color; and (4) informal segregation by race, ethnicity, and/or gender increases patterns of unequal participation because teachers are drawn to the part of the room where White males cluster. (pp. 28-29)

The methods we use to teach to and assess multicultural content for diverse learners involve planning, experimentation, revision, and a willingness to be patient when an instructional strategy is tried in the classroom with limited success. Broadening our repertoire of instructional strategies requires change. The courage to embrace change is a dynamic process. It takes time. It might be useful to outline small learning goals when working toward multicultural teaching. Faculty development specialists can be especially helpful in this endeavor, as this process will require challenge and support to do this well.

How Can We Create and Sustain Climates that Support the Teaching of Multicultural Content and the Learning of Diverse Students?

Now that we have transformed the content of our course and worked to develop creative methods to teach the material to our students, we must strategically think about how to create a supportive learning climate to carry forth our goals. We have found that creating a space in which students (a) feel their voices have a place and can enter, (b) are willing to take risks to share their thoughts and feelings honestly, (c) are willing to listen to views that differ from their own, and (d) make comments intended to forward understanding rather than to prove rightness or wrongness is one of the most challenging facets of multicultural teaching. Creating such a space, in which all want to participate, is an issue of climate.

When we talk about climate in this chapter, we mean the learning environment that is co-constructed through the interactions among faculty and students as they use a variety of instructional methods to engage with multicultural course content through intergroup dialogue. We think climate is intimately connected with content and instructional process.

Classroom climate is not static—it is a dynamic, ever-changing process. The type of climate created by educators can open up or limit (and often times both) the opportunities for learning about multiculturalism. It is important for faculty to provide opportunities for students to give attention to issues of climate in deliberate and routine ways. Faculty cannot simply address climate and try to build community solely during the first class or the first week of classes. To sustain the positive aspects of the climate developed during this time and to address emerging needs for support and relatively "safe" (though not necessarily comfortable) spaces, faculty need to continually assess the climate and reaffirm their commitment to do the work needed to allow the kind of intergroup dialogues that will promote growth and understanding about multicultural issues.

So often, we expect college students to enter our courses with the skill set needed to engage in discussions of multicultural content. There is so much content to cover, we may be tempted to choose to ignore or give minimal attention to teaching students process techniques. For a more in-depth discussion about the content/process balance in intergroup dialogue, see Beale and Schoem, 2001. Students will benefit from learning strategies that allow them to engage in an inclusive-divergent dialogue—such a dialogue has two characteristics: "a generally cooperative, tolerant spirit, and a direction toward mutual understanding" (Burbules, 1993, p. 112). Specifically, students need to learn how to listen and speak with those with whom they have strong differences of opinion on an issue due to knowledge, values, beliefs, and so forth (for example, see information about the LARA method in Schoem and Saunders, 2001). They also need strategies for communicating with and giving critical feedback to classmates (Bidol, 1986; Porter, 1982); and techniques for responding to their triggers (for example, Griffin, 1997, pp. 78-79). Simply giving students handouts that describe strategies without giving them opportunities to practice those strategies and to receive feedback means the techniques in the handouts do not get read at worst, and get read but not practiced at best.

Faculty as well as students must make a commitment to define the kind of space needed to support and sustain difficult conversations about multicultural issues and content, and everyone needs to be held accountable for doing the work needed to make these dialogues possible. It requires everyone to take risks and to be willing to stretch with their discomfort. Sometimes this means speaking when one is fearful or refraining from talking to allow for other voices to be heard when one tends to dominate conversations. Faculty can set up an initial set of guidelines in class that facilitate intergroup dialogues about multicultural issues. Faculty should expect that these guidelines might change throughout the course as new issues arise. Individuals can identify ways in which they need to stretch and provide evidence that they are doing this stretching or why they are not. Again, as with the initial guidelines, individuals may revise the areas in which they need to stretch as they acquire information about their struggles stretching, as new areas emerge and as they achieve success with areas they initially identified.

Kumashiro (2000) summarizes and critiques four approaches to anti-oppressive education that can inform educators' thinking about the multicultural course transformation process:

1. Education for the other
2. Education about the other
3. Education that is critical of privileging and othering
4. Education that changes students and society

In particular, this publication offers characteristics of anti-oppressive education and teaching that can inform our development of classroom climates that support the teaching of multicultural issues and content from the first day of class and beyond.

- Teaching involves unknowability
- Anti-oppressive education involves crisis
- Anti-oppressive education involves self-reflexivity
- Anti-oppressive education involves overcoming resistance to change and learning, instead, to desire change, to desire difference.

As we plan the work of developing a supportive and "safe" classroom climate in which a diversity of voices is shared and heard, keep in mind the unknowability of teaching. We can never fully know what is going to happen from day to day in terms of how participants will respond in any given situation and which participants will struggle with a topic being discussed. This unknowability is one of the things that can make teaching interesting and challenging! Although we will not always know what is going to happen, we can be prepared with strategies to manage difficult dynamics (Griffin, 1997, provides examples of some useful strategies in the *Discussion Leadership Tasks* (see pp. 286-291 section of her chapter)).

Creating a safe and supportive classroom climate requires building in the expectation of crisis. As Kumashiro says, "learning about oppression and unlearning worldviews can be upsetting and paralyzing to students" (p. 24). Faculty must plan for these reactions. Griffin (1997) addresses common student reactions to social justice education (pp. 292-298): resistance, anger, immobilization, distancing, and conversion and what can be done to address them. If you would like a more in-depth discussion about resistance, you might want to read the following chapters in Goodman (2001): "Understanding Resistance" (pp. 61-78) and "Preventing and Reducing Resistance" (pp. 79-101). Kardia and Sevig (2001) address the conflict between individual and group identities as they can play out in intergroup dialogues.

Instructors also need to build in opportunities for self-reflexivity as it pertains to how individuals and the group engage in intergroup dialogues. Students need not only to reflect on their role in the dynamics of the oppression of voices in classroom dialogues, but need to also use what they learn to change who they are and how they participate. (See Appendix A for questions Shari used during three weeks of a summer course to begin a process of self-reflection and self-reflexivity). Educators can create questions that specifically move students to greater self-reflexivity as they move through any given course.

Faculty and students need to engage in discussions that acknowledge and explicitly address resistance to change and learning as well as how to create a climate that desires, acknowledges, and supports change and difference. Of course, how students respond to resistance on the first day may be different from how they respond to resistance at various times throughout the course.

If we want to create climates that are welcoming though not always comfortable, we need to be flexible. It is important to remember that creating classroom climates is not a one-time event. It is necessary to think about issues of climate as we create courses as well as during every class session. Course instructors do not bear sole responsibility for the classroom climate. Developing supportive classroom climates is the result of cooperative efforts between faculty and students. For a successful climate to be developed instructors must build students into the process of creating and assessing the climate, and instructors and students need to be held accountable for their role in making the climate what they want it to be.

Conclusion

An end result of multicultural course transformation is to prepare all students to function in an increasingly diverse and global society. Whether we are preparing to engage in this endeavor at an individual or broader conversation level, course transformation focuses on posing critical questions about and realizing how the interconnected dimensions of ourselves as educators in the process, our assumptions about teaching and learning, what and how we teach, and classroom climate affect teaching and learning outcomes. We believe that multicultural course transformation is a long-term, complex, and probably never-ending process. What we have shared in this chapter comes directly from theory, research, and much work and practice. We hope that educators such as faculty, staff, students, and administrators find this chapter useful in conceptualizing the work involved in multicultural course transformation. It is important to begin at the point of entry where we are most comfortable, but also with an understanding that we can only grow and stretch in our ways of knowing and thinking about teaching and learning in our disciplines. Simply put, and as the title of Morey and Kitano's (1997) book suggests, it is work that seeks to arrive at an understanding of a much "broader truth."

References

Adams, M., Bell, L. A., & Griffin, P. (1997). *Teaching for diversity and social justice: A sourcebook.* New York: Routledge.

Anderson, J. A., & Adams, M. (1992, Spring). Acknowledging the learning styles of diverse student populations: Implications for instructional design. In L.L.B. Border & N.V.N. Chism (Eds.), *Teaching for Diversity* (pp. 19-34). New Directions for Teaching and Learning, No. 49. San Francisco: Jossey-Bass.

Banks, J. A. (1993). Approaches to multicultural curriculum reform. In J.A. Banks & C.A.M. Banks (Eds.), *Multicultural education: Issues and perspectives* (pp. 195-214). Boston: Allyn & Bacon.

Beale, R., L. & Schoem, D. (2001). The content/process balance in intergroup dialogue. In D. Schoem & S. Hurtado (Eds.), *Intergroup dialogue: Deliberative democracy in school, college, community, and workplace* (pp. 266-279). Ann Arbor: The University of Michigan Press.

Beale, R. L., Thompson, M. C., & Chesler, M. (2001). Training peer facilitators for intergroup dialogue leadership. In D. Schoem & S. Hurtado (Eds.), *Intergroup dialogue: Deliberative democracy in school, college, community, and workplace* (pp. 227-246). Ann Arbor: The University of Michigan Press.

Bidol, P. (1986). Interactive communication. In P. Bidol, L. Bardwell, & N. Manring (Eds.), *Alternative environmental conflict management approaches: A citizen's model* (pp. 205-209). Ann Arbor: University of Michigan School of Natural Resources.

Burbules, N. C. (1993). *Dialogue in teaching: Theory and practice.* New York: Teachers College Press.

Burbules, N. C. (1993). Four types of dialogue. In N.C. Burbules (Ed.), *Dialogue in teaching: Theory and practice* (pp. 110-130). New York: Teachers College Press.

Chickering, A., & Gamson, Z. (1987). Seven principles for good practice in undergraduate education. *AAHE Bulletin, 39.* Washington, DC: American Association for Higher Education.

Ferdman, B. M., & Gallegos, P. I. (2001). Racial identity development and Latinos in the United States. In B. W. Jackson, III, & C.L. Wijeyesinghe (Eds), *New perspectives on racial identity development: A theoretical and practical anthology* (pp. 32-66). New York University Press.

Goodman, D. J. (2001) *Promoting diversity and social justice: Educating people from privileged groups.* Thousand Oaks, CA: Sage.

Green, M. F. (Ed). (1989). *Minorities on campus: A handbook for enhancing diversity.* Washington, DC: American Council on Education.

Griffin, P. (1997). Introductory module for the single-issue courses. In M.A. Adams, L.A. Bell, & P. Griffin (Eds.), *Teaching for diversity and social justice: A sourcebook* (pp.61-81). New York: Routledge.

Griffin, P. (1997). Facilitating social justice education courses. In M.A. Adams, L.A. Bell, & P. Griffin (Eds.), *Teaching for diversity and social justice: A sourcebook* (pp.279-298). New York: Routledge.

Grant, K, & Sachs, J. (1995). In B. Kanpol, & P. McLaren (Eds.), *Critical multiculturalism: Uncommon voices in a common struggle* (p. 176). Westport, CT: Bergin & Garvey.

Hardiman, R. (2001). Reflections on white identity development theory. In B. W. Jackson, III, & C.L. Wijeyesinghe (Eds), *New perspectives on racial identity development: A theoretical and practical anthology* (pp. 108-128). New York University Press.

Hardiman, R., & Jackson, B. W. (1997). Conceptual foundations for social justice courses. In M. Adams, L.A. Bell, & P. Griffin (Eds.), *Teaching for diversity and social justice: A sourcebook* (pp.16-29). New York: Routledge.

Herbert, P. (1997). *The color of words: An encyclopedic dictionary of ethnic bias in the United States*. Yarmouth, ME: Intercultural Press.

Horse, P. G. (2001). Reflections on American Indian identity. In B. W. Jackson, III, & C.L. Wijeyesinghe (Eds.), *New perspectives on racial identity development: A theoretical and practical anthology* (pp. 91-107). New York University Press.

Irvine, J. J., & York, D. E. (1995). Learning styles and culturally diverse students: A literature review. In J.A. Banks, & C.A.M. Banks (Eds.), *Handbook of research in multicultural education* (pp. 484-497). New York: McMillan.

Jackson, B.W., III (2001). Black identity development: Further analysis and elaboration. In B. W. Jackson III, & C.L. Wijeyesinghe (Eds.), *New perspectives on racial identity development: A theoretical and practical anthology* (pp. 8-31). New York University Press.

Jackson, B. W., III, & Holvino, E. (1988). Developing multicultural organizations. *Journal of Religion and the Applied Behavioral Sciences, 9*(2), 14-19.

Kardia, D., & Sevig, T. (2001). Embracing the paradox: Dialogue that incorporates both individual and group activities. In D. Schoem & S. Hurtado (Eds.), *Intergroup dialogue: Deliberative democracy in school, college, community, and workplace* (pp. 247-265). Ann Arbor: The University of Michigan Press.

Kim, J. (2001). Asian American identity development theory. In B. W. Jackson, III, & C.L. Wijeyesinghe (Eds.), *New perspectives on racial identity development: A theoretical and practical anthology* (pp. 67-90). New York University Press.

Kitano, M. (1997). A rationale and framework for course change. In A. I. Morey, & M. Kitano (Eds.), *Multicultural course transformation in higher education: A broader truth* (pp. 1-17). Needham Heights, MA: Allyn & Bacon.

Kuh, G. D., & Whitt, E. J. (1988). *The invisible tapestry: Culture in American colleges and universities*. (ASHE-ERIC Higher Education Reports, No. 1). Washington, DC: Association for the Study of Higher Education.

Kumashiro, K. (2000). Toward a theory of anti-oppressive education. *Review of Educational Research, 70*(1), 25-53.

Marchesani, L. S., & Adams, M. (1992). Dynamics of diversity in the teaching-learning process: A faculty development model for analysis and action. In M. Adams (Ed.), *Promoting diversity in college classrooms: Innovative responses for the curriculum, faculty, and institutions* (pp. 9-20). New Directions for Teaching and Learning, No. 52. San Francisco: Jossey-Bass.

Morey, A. I., & Kitano, M. K. (1997). *Multicultural course transformation in higher education: A broader truth*. Needham Heights, MA: Allyn & Bacon.

Lynch, E. (1997). Instructional strategies. In A. I. Morey, & M. Kitano (Eds.), *Multicultural course transformation in higher education: A broader truth* (pp. 56-70). Needham Heights, MA: Allyn & Bacon.

NCSS Task Force on Ethnic Studies Curriculum Guidelines. (1992, September). Curriculum guidelines for multicultural education. *Social Education, 56*, 274-294.

Ognibene, E. R. (1989). Integrating the curriculum: From impossible to possible.*College Teaching, 37*(3), 105-110.

Porter, L. (1982). Giving and receiving feedback: It will never be easy, but it can be better. In L.C. Porter, & B. Mohr (Eds.), *Reading book for human relations training* (pp. 42-45). Alexandria, VA: NTL Institute.

Sadker, M., & Sadker, D. (1992). Ensuring equitable participation in college classes. In L.L.B. Border, & N.V. Chism (Eds.), *Teaching for diversity* (pp. 49-56). New Directions for Teaching and Learning, No. 49. San Francisco: Jossey-Bass.

Saunders, S., & Kardia, D. (2000). Inclusive classrooms: Part one of a two part series. *The Hispanic Outlook in Higher Education, 10*(15), 21-24.

Saunders, S., & Kardia, D. (2000). Inclusive classrooms: Part two of a two part series. *The Hispanic Outlook in Higher Education, 10*(16), 45-48.

Sawchuk, M. T. (Ed.). (1993). *Infusing multicultural perspectives across the curriculum*. Los Angeles: Prism.

Schoem, D., Frankel, L., Zuniga, X., & Lewis, E. A. (1993). The meaning of multicultural teaching: An introduction. In D. Schoem, L. Frankel, X. Zuniga, & E.A. Lewis (Eds.), *Multicultural teaching in the university* (pp. 1-12). Westport, CT: Praeger.

Schoem, D., Frankel, L., Zuniga, X., & Lewis, E. A. (1993). Roundtable discussion: The insiders' critique of multicultural teaching. In D. Schoem, L. Frankel, X. Zuniga, & E.A. Lewis (Eds.), *Multicultural teaching in the university* (pp. 279-292). Westport, CT: Praeger.

Schoem, D., Hurtado, S., Sevig, T., Chesler,M., & Sumida, S.H. (2001). Intergroup dialogue: Democracy at work in theory and practice. In D. Schoem, & S. Hurtado (Eds), *Intergroup dialogue: Deliberative democracy in school, college, community, and workplace* (pp. 1-21). Ann Arbor, MI: The University of Michigan Press.

Schoem, D., & Saunders, S. (2001). Adapting intergroup dialogue processes for use in a variety of settings. In D. Schoem, & S. Hurtado (Eds.), *Intergroup dialogue: Deliberative democracy in school, college, community, and workplace* (pp. 328-344). Ann Arbor: The University of Michigan Press.

Stanley, C. A., Porter, M. E., Simpson, N. J., & Ouellett, M. L. (2003). A case study of the teaching experiences of African American faculty at two predominantly White research universities. *Journal on Excellence in College Teaching, 14*(1), 151-178

Palmer, P. (1998). *The courage to teach.* San Francisco: Jossey-Bass.

Tatum, B. D. (1997). *"Why are all the black kids sitting together in the cafeteria?" And other conversations about race.* New York: Basic Books.

Tharp, R. F. (1989). Psychocultural variables and constants: Effects on teaching and learning in schools. *American Psychologist, 44*(2), 349-359.

Wijeyesinghe, C., Griffin, P., & Love, B., (1997). Racism curriculum design. In M. Adams, L.A. Bell, & P. Griffin (Eds.), *Teaching for diversity and social justice: A sourcebook* (pp.82-109). New York: Routledge.

Wijeyesinghe, C. L., & Jackson, B. W., III. (2001). *New perspectives on racial identity development: A theoretical and practical anthology.* New York University Press.

Wijeyesinghe, C. L. (2001). Racial identity in multiracial people: An alternative paradigm. In B. W. Jackson III, & C.L. Wijeyesinghe (Eds.), *New perspectives on racial identity development: A theoretical and practical anthology* (pp. 129-152). New York University Press.

Christine A. Stanley is Assistant Dean of Faculties and Associate Professor of Higher Education Administration in the College of Education and Human Development at Texas A&M University. She teaches courses on College Teaching, Professional Development in Higher Education, and Diversity and Social Justice in Higher Education. Her research interests include faculty development, college teaching, and multicultural organizational development in higher education. She is a Past President of the Professional and Organizational Development (POD) Network in Higher Education and Past Chair of the POD Diversity Commission. She serves as Senior Editor for the New Forums Press series on faculty development.

Shari Saunders is Assistant Professor of Educational Practice and Coordinator of the Master of Arts with Certification (MAC) Program, Cohort B at the University of Michigan, Ann Arbor. She also served as Coordinator of Multicultural Teaching and Learning Services at the Center for Research on Learning and Teaching (CRLT) at the University for several years. In that role, she consulted individually with faculty and graduate student instructors on multicultural issues in teaching and learning contexts and co-facilitated multicultural workshops and sessions for units throughout the University. Her areas of interest include: social justice education, multicultural education, and teacher education.

Jamie M. Hart is Director of the Intercultural Health Practice Area at Health Systems Research, Inc., in Washington, D.C., and telecommutes from her home in Austin, Texas. She provides program and technical support to clients at the federal, state, and local levels in relation to health disparities, homelessness, family planning, HIV/AIDS, STDs, substance abuse, mental health, and criminal justice. Prior to joining HSR, she worked as an instructional consultant at the University of Michigan's Center for Research on Learning and Teaching (CRLT) in Ann Arbor, and was involved in multicultural curriculum transformation, workshop design and facilitation, and assessment and evaluation activities.

Appendix A

Self-Reflections on Participation

Session A

1. Describe your participation in this week's sessions.
2. What did you do in this week's sessions that contributed to creating opportunities for others to speak?
3. In what ways did you stretch with your discomfort in this week's sessions?
4. What future concerns do you have about your in-class participation based on the nature of your participation in this week's sessions?
5. What concerns do you have about how we as a group will participate in class in the future based on the ways we participated in this week's sessions?

Session B

6. Describe the variety of ways you participated this week (e-mail, small group, large group, and so forth).
7. Describe the ways you participated in terms of content-related contributions or learning experiences (reading, note taking, sharing ideas, and so forth).

8. If it tends to be easy for you to talk in large groups, what did you do in this week's sessions that contributed to creating opportunities for others to speak in the large group?
9. If it tends to be difficult for you to talk in large groups, what did you try or what did others do that facilitated your entry into the large group discussion?
10. If you feel your participation in the large group is balanced, in what other aspect of participation do you feel you can improve?
11. What else do you want instructors to know about your participation this week?

Session C

12. Pair up with someone for the week. Give each other feedback on your perceptions of each other's participation in the large group. What did you learn from this experience in terms of a) your own participation, b) giving feedback to your peer about her or his participation, and c) responding to feedback given to you about your participation?
13. Each day, choose one person who is in a small group with you to be your feedback partner for the small group discussion. Give feedback to one person on your perceptions of her or his participation in the small group. Another person will give you feedback on his or her perception of your participation in the small group. What did you learn from this experience in terms of a) your own participation, b) giving feedback to your peer about her or his participation, and c) responding to feedback given to you about your participation?
14. In this week's discussion, did anyone present a perspective with which you do not agree? What did you observe about how you responded to the person and/or perspective (for example, feelings, thoughts, behaviors)? What did you like about your response, and what would you like to change about your response?
15. In this week's discussion, did you present an opinion that you feel was not well received by others? What did you observe that led you to think this? What did you do to check to see if your perception was accurate?
16. In this week's discussion, did you hesitate to share a perspective that you perceived was different from that of the majority of the group? What made you hold back? What needs to happen to facilitate your willingness to publicly share a different perspective?

Chapter 42

Teaching With a Social Justice Perspective: A Model for Faculty Seminars Across Academic Disciplines

Maurianne Adams and Barbara J. Love

"We know that ... changing what we teach, means changing how we teach" (Margo Culley and Cathy Portuges (1985), *Gendered Subjects: The Dynamics of Feminist Teaching*, Routledge & Kegan Paul, p.2).

In this chapter, we suggest various ways our faculty colleagues can create more inclusive classrooms and interact more effectively across social and cultural differences. We do this by suggesting models and frameworks we find particularly useful for examining equity and excellence in college teaching and the social justice perspective that binds them together. We identify the knowledge and skills helpful in succeeding in such endeavors, and we offer strategies useful to faculty, faculty developers, and academic administrators who are interested in supporting greater social justice in college and university classrooms.

Faculty Teaching for Diversity and Social Justice

The two of us are often asked by colleagues at our own university and elsewhere to assist them in their efforts to create more inclusive classrooms and to interact across social and cultural differences more effectively. We begin with the premise that building socially and culturally inclusive classrooms has both discipline-specific and interdisciplinary characteristics. The questions posed most often by our faculty colleagues also point to issues of curriculum and process. Although we acknowledge that our colleagues teach across many disciplines with a range of curricular content, we have found that their success in building inclusive classrooms depends in large part on their willingness to develop a social justice perspective within both their curricular content and pedagogical process. In this chapter, first, we explain, what we mean by a *social justice perspective*, second, how we approach the analysis of teaching and learning utilizing such a perspective, and third, we offer some of the self- and curricular-assessment models helpful in looking at teaching practice across a range of disciplines. Additionally, throughout the chapter we offer examples and practical exercises designed to help instructors apply these frameworks and models.

1. A Social Justice Education Framework

The social justice education perspective that we bring to our teaching is based on an analysis of the process of schooling that includes an understanding that the overarching social structures are characterized by domination and subordination, and that social and cultural differences are used to justify that inequality. The social justice framework includes analysis of domination and subordination at different societal, institutional, and interpersonal levels. It includes an analysis of the ways in which structures of domination and subordination are reproduced in the classroom, following patterns of social and cultural difference found in the larger society.

A social justice education framework recognizes that the patterns of domination and subordination are manifest throughout and across social institutions. Among these institutions, education plays the dual role of *reflecting* these stratified relationships as well as *reproducing* them through curriculum and pedagogy. Education also offers the unique opportunity of *interrupting* these unequal relationships both by helping people understand social inequality, and by *modeling* more reciprocal and equitable relationships in the classroom.

As social justice educators, we work from an understanding that schooling presents educators with choices, either to reproduce unequal social relationships or to interrupt and transform those relationships. These choices are reflected in both curriculum content and in pedagogy. As students in different disciplines learn new course content, they also learn to prize certain knowledge and devalue other knowledge or ignore it entirely. Thus a social justice perspective on course content enables us to scrutinize curriculum in order to see the implicit judgments about social relationships embodied in the curriculum.

Similarly, a social justice perspective enables us to recognize patterns of domination and subordination in teacher-student, or student-student relationships, as well as opportunities to develop reciprocal and equitable relationships. This perspective explores the reproductions of race, gender, class, and other identity-based power inequities and to analyze these in the context of other power relations in the classroom. Such an analysis enables instructors to clarify the specific kinds of relationships we choose to model and endorse in the classroom.

As we work with our colleagues, we share our perspective on social justice education not because we necessarily expect that they will include specific social justice content in their curriculum, but because every component of teaching and learning can potentially be informed by this social justice perspective. We are not asking our colleagues to teach social justice content. Rather, we are asking that our colleagues develop a social justice perspective upon their own teaching.

2. A Four-Quadrant Analysis of Teaching and Learning

Teaching and learning are fluid, interactive processes that can be characterized in many different ways. To facilitate our social justice analysis, we conceptualize teaching and learning processes as falling into four interactive quadrants, each one of which can be analyzed from a social justice perspective. These four quadrants are based upon what (1) our students, as active participants, bring to the classroom, (2) we, as instructors, bring to the classroom, (3) the curriculum, materials, and resources convey to students as essential course content, and (4) the pedagogical processes are through which the course content is delivered (Marchesani & Adams, 1992).

As an overall organizer, this model provides opportunities for us to take snapshots (our students, ourselves, our subject matter, and our pedagogical process) of an extraordinarily complex moving picture in which in real life each quadrant interacts simultaneously with the others. When we take each quadrant by itself, as we do in order to focus attention in an organized and coherent manner, we cannot represent the complex interplay among and within these dimensions as they occur in real time classroom interaction. The use of this teaching and learning model allows us to reflect both our need for order, and our recognition of the complexity of the dynamics of teaching and learning.

Quadrant 1: What our students as active participants bring to the classroom

It is often easier for faculty to begin the conversation with stories about their students, rather than about themselves. Focusing upon one's students can allow faculty to examine the assumptions we make about our students, especially when their visible social identities are different from our own. We encourage faculty to focus upon their dynamic interactions with all students, to recognize the ways that those interactions may be different with students holding different social identities.

Participants may describe classroom situations in which students interact or fail to interact with each other on the basis of their social identities and the attitudes and expectations that have become attached to those social identities. They may describe many familiar student-to-student scenarios. For example, when students form small groups for projects or study, they may follow the patterns of separation along social identity group lines that are manifest in the larger society. Patterns of residential segregation may show up in the interaction patterns in the classroom. In small groups, women may take notes, while men speak. In class discussions, men may appear more visible, vocal and take up greater space. Women, on the other had, may appear to follow traditional patterns of female socialization by speaking less often, with less certainty, confidence or authority than men, and may take up less time or space. Women may appear less comfortable challenging the authority of the teacher; the same may appear with students of color. White men may appear more likely to challenge the authority of the teacher and to feel that it is within their right to do so. White male faculty may appear to feel more comfortable with a challenge from a white male student than from a Black male student or from women. However, for faculty to anticipate, intervene in, and transform these recognizable student scenarios, we find it useful to refer to Quadrant 2, in order to explore their own socialization and their unexamined assumptions about the "other," who, in this case, might be their students.

Before doing so, however – and especially if we are working in seminars with faculty who appear initially uncertain how to interpret and deal with these or similar classroom scenarios, and who may belong to social groups that have traditionally had a place in higher education — there are a few questions we may use to probe faculty analysis of who their students are, and what their students bring to the classroom. Depending on the scenarios that faculty describe, we may select one or two from among the following questions:

- What have been manifestations of multiple and interacting social identities of students in the classrooms you describe?
- What are examples of possible student-to-student interactions based on those social identities?
- What have faculty noticed – and if noticed, how have they accounted for developmental differences in how students of different social identities understand their own and each other's ways of being, knowing, and communicating?
- What differences in student worldview and values have faculty noticed in their classrooms, that may be rooted in part in differing social group memberships?
- What differences have they noticed in cultural and individual learning styles, communication, and interaction styles?

- What happens when they ask students to reflect on their differing perspectives or their interactions on "hot button" social issues?
- What strategies do they utilize in their planning for different levels of skill, readiness, and comfort on the subject matter in their classes?

In faculty seminars in which "knowing one's students" is the focus for discussion and analysis, we introduce various organizers to engage faculty with considerations such as learning style and/or cognitive and social identity development (Adams, Jones, & Tatum, 1997; Hardiman & Jackson, 1997; Marchesani & Adams, 1997). *Learning style models* help faculty to design a range of learning environments that match some preferred cultural or individual student learning styles while stretching others. We suggest that faculty change the learning environments from one week to the next so that no students are "matched" or "stretched" all of the time (Anderson & Adams, 1992). *Cognitive development models* help faculty to understand the different ways that students take in and process knowledge. For instance, these models help faculty to anticipate the tendency of some students to dichotomize complex questions, and reduce multiple perspectives to simple either/or right/wrong choices, while other students (often in the same classroom) work with the inherent messiness of real-world social issues and appreciate the multiple, differing perspectives held by their peers (Adams, Jones & Tatum, 1997; King & Shuford, 1996; Marchesani & Adams, 1997). *Social identity models* enable faculty to understand what the social identities are and some of the implications of these identities for the communication and interaction in the classroom. For instance, these models also enable faculty to anticipate that the ways they and their students understand and experience their multiple, often intersecting social identities, are likely to change over time. These models also help account for the possibility that students connected by seemingly same social identities may express very different response (denial, anger, pain) to social issues in the classroom (Adams, Jones & Tatum, 1997, p. 321; Hardiman & Jackson, 1997; Tatum, 1992; Wijeyesinghe & Jackson, 2001).

There are many ways to gather information about one's students. Faculty can gather information formally and informally, at the beginning as well as throughout the semester. Sometimes it is useful to ask that students fill out identity sheets on which we have allowed ample room for students to describe themselves however they wish to do so, whether racially, ethnically, by gender, by class, by first language or national origins. We take special care with sexual identity, however, explaining that because of the hostility and physical danger many environments hold for students who are "out" as bisexual, lesbian, gay, transgender or queer, we will not ask for that information, although we welcome it if a student feels comfortable conveying it to us.

There are less formal modes of gathering information, however. We might design interactive small group activities based on how students complete the sentence stem "I am …." by referring to whatever social identities are uppermost for them in that specific classroom context and at that moment. Similarly, group activities such as "Common Ground" (Adams, Jones, & Tatum, 1997, p. 316) provide rich opportunities to acknowledge whose social and cultural identity groups are present in the room and to note those that are absent. Self-selected work-groups based on specific social identity topics provide faculty with on-going information about identities that might not appear visible or especially salient to the instructor, but are important to the student (Adams, Jones, & Tatum, 1997, for further examples).

Information about social identities is not only important to the instructor. It is important information for students to have about each other, as a context for understanding their different perspectives on social justice issues. Further, it is important information for students to have about themselves.

Sometimes questions of social identity are new to students. Students may experience the process of personal self-reflection about these social identities as a new cognitive skill. In these cases, the gathering of information about students on the part of an instructor is in itself an important pedagogical intervention to stimulate the student's self-awareness – and it constitutes a contribution to the inclusive subject-matter within the curriculum.

Quadrant 2: What we as instructors bring to the classroom

We place the teacher (professor, instructor, facilitator, mentor, coach) as an integral part of the classroom dynamics, and not, as in more traditional accounts of teaching and learning, separate from considerations of subject matter and pedagogy, or teacher/student interactions. Faculty come from a range of disciplines, with knowledge and skills developed in graduate training relevant to those disciplines. This academic discipline-based knowledge and skill, while necessary for successful classroom teaching, is not sufficient for what we have described earlier as a social justice education perspective (Adams, 1992). This perspective can be achieved in many different ways. Faculty have often reflected on their social interactions with people who are different from them. They have noticed domination and subordination within the larger society and within the academy, as well as within their own personal relationships and interactions. They may have already examined some of their stereotypes about others, and the roots of those stereotypes in their earlier experiences within their extended families, neighborhoods, schools, religious education, and workplaces.

These faculty appreciate the opportunity to reflect more systematically upon this prior socialization in a structured setting with colleagues not from their home institution, with whom they can examine their prior socialization – that is, their early experiences of themselves and others within their extended families, neighborhoods, schools, religious education, and workplaces. The opportunity to analyze this prior socialization in a structured seminar setting enables them to develop and extend their social justice perspective to their own classrooms and home institutions.

We believe that it is important for us to emphasize, in this chapter, that as co-facilitators of faculty development seminars, we establish the same ground rules to ensure mutual respect and safety that we employ with our students at our home institutions (see Adams & Marchesani, 1997, pp. 268-269). We use the same activities to identify participant hopes and concerns. We ask them to write their hopes and concerns on 3x5 cards, scramble the cards, and conduct a "read around". The norms and behavioral ground rules fairly jump out as areas of group consensus emerge from these discussions and as we create guidelines that help us to achieve our hopes and avoid or diminish our concerns. As noted above, faculty participants become actively engaged in this activity, insofar as it clarifies their own norms and guidelines, while the process we experience together also models how they might use this activity to generate norms and guidelines in their own classes.

We have found that faculty understand the importance of engaging in self-knowledge exploration in order to create learning communities characterized by social justice. Faculty seminar participants also appreciate seeing self-knowledge exploration as an on-going process modeled by the two of us as co-facilitators, so that they, too, can think about how to model self-awareness for their students. As facilitators, we model this behavior by our own willingness to disclose important aspects of the development of our social identities. For example, we may choose to share one of us has her doctorate in Curriculum Studies, the other in English Literature. One of us was born in Philadelphia, PA, and the other in Dumas, Arkansas. Between us we have a taught a total of 80 years in public schools and universities and small private colleges. In addition to our work as Social Justice Education faculty, we have been faculty in English Literature, Human Development, Organization Development, Staff Development, and Student Development departments. We have also worked as department chair, program chair, chair of local school boards, school and college committees, and a range of task forces and committees dedicated to multicultural and social justice institutional change. We were born and raised rural working-class and urban professional middle-class, European- and African-American, Baptist and Jewish, with English our sole language although with local dialects and accents that signal racial, class and geographical differences. We are married and the single mother of a college-bound daughter; our educational and professional status currently locates us in the upper middle class; and as we grow older we are no longer as able-bodied as we once were. These social identities and experiences help to position us in relation to our students, colleagues at our home institutions, and the faculty whom we join in seminars that explore a social justice perspective upon our teaching practice.

Various organizers, such as models of social identity awareness, models of socialization processes, self-awareness, and knowledge of social justice (content) issues are all components of this second quadrant on participant self-awareness as social justice educators. We select and sequence from among the organizers listed below, on the basis of participant interest and awareness, and the time available (see Bell, Washington, Weinstein, & Love, 1997 for further discussion).

1. *Social identity awareness* includes analysis of one's multiple and interacting social identities (race and ethnicity, gender, sexuality) as well as one's identity statuses (dominant or subordinate), and the impact of those identities and identity statuses on various dimensions of their classroom practice (subject matter, pedagogical process, interactions with students).
2. *Socialization awareness* includes analysis of how we come to know ourselves as persons holding the particular identities that we wear, and the socialization impact on us of institutional and cultural systems, structures, and practices (see Harro, 2000a & b, Love 2000, for texts that help generate discussion).
3. *Social justice issue awareness* includes analysis of the consequences of societal structures of domination and subordination on the life chances and opportunities for people from different identity groups based on race, gender, class, sexuality, (dis)ability, religions, primary language. This includes an examination of the ways that power and privilege is connected to those identities and how power and privilege are reflected in the classroom and in the academy. In our faculty seminars, we focus on racism, sexism, classism, heterosexism, ableism, religious oppression, and linguicism (see Goodman, 2001; Pharr, 1988; Wildman, 1996; Young, 1990 for useful texts to prompt discussion).
4. *Social justice facilitation* issues include assessment of readiness (support, passion, awareness, knowledge, skills), establishing effective learning environments, choosing appropriate leadership roles, and attending to a variety of leadership tasks (Griffin, 1997a; Appendix E).

Our analysis of one or more of these organizers in our faculty seminars enables participants to generate data they can use in their action planning for their own classrooms. For example, we may use self-assessment instruments such as *The Multicultural Life Experience Profile* (Appendix B) to generate information about their early identity socialization and to better understand how their current patterns of domination and subordination affect their classrooms. On these and related issues, faculty have demonstrated willingness to challenge their own comfort zones and learning edges (Griffin, 1997b, p. 68).

Here are some areas where we encourage faculty to engage in deeper analysis, using questions they have raised or classroom scenarios they have described or the data generated from one of the self-assessment instruments:

- Awareness of the ways in which power and privilege based on social group memberships affect student learning and teacher/student interactions.
- Awareness of the ways in which power and privilege based on social group memberships are compounded by the power and privilege connected to faculty's educational status and institutional role.
- Knowledge of the many different consequences of social domination and subordination between and among students, and between teacher and students, such as access to schooling, residential segregation, access to employment, health care, legal protection, and the like.
- Practice with models that enable faculty to transform curriculum and teaching
- Knowledge and skills to create intervention and action strategies for students, peers and self, such as interrupting racist jokes, heterosexist innuendoes, and collegial evaluations of each other based on stereotyped assumptions (Delgado Bernal & Villalpando, 2002)

Faculty participants may understandably express frustration and anxiety when faced with the daunting task of developing their own self-awareness, correcting misinformation and misguided stereotypes, and developing new cross- or inter-group communications skills to better "read" the social dynamics of diversity and social justice within their own classrooms. As facilitators, we agree that this is indeed a formidable task. It is also a life-long task, whereby our goal is not to be "experts" but seen by ourselves and our students as "works in progress" (Bell, Washington, Weinstein, Love, 1997; Love, 2000).

To strengthen the participant group's sense of shared challenge and common cause, we utilize a check-list and self-assessment we have devised, based on a compilation of bias issues that faculty members in the past have reported to be most fearsome or formidable (Weinstein & Obear, 1992). Although the check-list was compiled more than a decade ago, we find confirmation of these fears and fantasies whenever we raise the subject with faculty participants. Participants are often reassured by knowing that others before them faced the same fears and anxieties and express humor in responding to this checklist (Appendix L). They are inspired to share stories that document their own experience or that illustrate their own fears. We treat this checklist as "fears," whether or not they have happened (Weinstein & Obear, 1992).

Quadrant 3: The curriculum, materials, and resources that convey course content to students

As noted earlier, our social justice and diversity faculty seminars are typically cross-departmental and cross-disciplinary. This cross-fertilization is in itself a powerful experience for participants. It enables faculty to talk without fear of repercussion at their home institutions about the challenges they face in developing inclusive curricula. Our role as social justice co-facilitators is to ask questions designed to prompt insight and information. We ask questions such as:

- What specific course content, exploratory issues, examples and perspectives can be brought into your formal curriculum to create an inclusive experience in which students can see their social group perspectives valued and represented?
- What are the ways that the curriculum can provide ways of de-centering the dominant worldview and incorporating multiple perspectives that reflect underrepresented peoples' viewpoints? Are multiple perspectives presented through histories of the field, contributors to the field, the application of theories in the field, the information sources for the field?
- What strategies or models do you as instructor use to examine your curriculum for inclusivity (e.g. readings, films, videos; written, oral, visual assignments and outside projects; modes of assessment and examinations for final grades; collaborative and group communication skills; perspectives, information, and examples presented in lectures)?

We have not found it useful for us, in our co-facilitative role, to attempt to "keep up" with the literature in specific disciplines dealing with inclusion. This literature is more effectively conveyed by participants sharing with each other the resources they have discovered that challenge the insularity of their disciplines – and where they might find other resources. We have noticed that it has been easier for faculty in the social sciences and humanities to find resources on inclusivity, diversity and social justice, than for faculty in mathematics and the natural sciences. However, increasingly there are resources to support the efforts of faculty in science and math to create more inclusive curriculum, such as *Math and science across cultures* (Bazin, Tamez, and Exploratorium Teacher Institute, 2002), *Ethnomathematics* (Powell & Frankenstein, 1997), and *Multicultural science education* (Hines, 2003) which we found at recent conferences and bookseller's catalogues. Robert Moses' book on *Math literacy and civil rights* (2001) came from word of mouth.

Other valuable resources for inclusivity have been known more generally. Takaki's *A different mirror* (1993) continues to open new perspectives on

U.S. history for graduate students or undergraduates, as does Spring's *Deculturalization and the struggle for equality* (2001) for the study of education in the U.S. Rogoff's *The cultural nature of human development* (2003) provides an inclusive understanding of human development. Walker and Snarey's *Race-ing moral formation* (2004) places Kohlberg's classic texts into active dialogue.

A range of journals now address faculty concerns about social justice and diversity, along with other concerns about teaching, in specific academic disciplines. Faculty participants provide useful resources for each other as they talk about the challenges and opportunities for creating inclusive curricula across their various disciplines.

We ask faculty participants to commit themselves to carry out one specific curricular "change" project in at least one course the following semester. We provide guidelines for them to specify the elements in their curricular change project, one step at a time, and use focused instruments to further document the sequence of proposed changes that constitute their course-change project (examples in Appendix C). We ask that participants think of their curricula as works in progress. This perspective on curricular change means that each change they make in their courses will lead the instructor to consider a new, previously unimagined set of changes in an on-going process of transformation toward inclusivity.

We still find useful a curriculum transformation phase model that was originally developed some years ago for women's and ethnic studies (Butler & Walter, 1991; Green, 1989; Schuster & Van Dyne, 1985). This model encourages participants to slow down and not to attempt to transform their entire curriculum all at once. Instead, we suggest an incremental step-by-step process of curricular reform rather than a big-vision all-at-once overhaul.

Quadrant 4: The pedagogical processes through which the course content is delivered.

There are many ways to bring a social justice framework to classroom pedagogy. We contend that *all* social justice education pedagogies lead to the central insight that *how* we teach shapes *what subject matter* the students learn. More generally, we argue that the other three quadrants also lead back to quadrant four, *how we teach and interact* with our students and subject matter.

This overarching principle of social justice education practice may sound counter-intuitive, given the content-focus of most academic disciplinary and professional training. The *how* of learning that many faculty still assume without question is the lecture-and-listen mode through which they experienced much of their own undergraduate and graduate coursework. Because of this challenge to our principles of practice from within much of academic socialization (Adams, 1992), we devote a significant part of faculty development seminars to quadrant four and to questions of *how* we teach what we teach.

It does not work for faculty to convey new information or perspectives about prejudice, discrimination and oppression to students in lectures or through readings, or even to discuss with students their beliefs, attitudes or opinions, as if these were abstractions. *Active learning*, then, is a second, overarching principle of social justice education practice. This means that students will need to question their previously held beliefs about themselves and socially different "others" in light of new perspectives and information. Students will also need to acknowledge and engage with contradictions in their current ways of knowing and seek ways to translate new learning into action. This transforms students from consumers to active subjects in their own meaning-making.

Third, we know that our teaching about topics such as oppression and liberation, racism, sexism and other issues of inequality and empowerment, cannot be thought of as neutral activities. These topics are emotionally loaded for students and for us as faculty, and linked to our strongly held — and sometimes vehemently differing — beliefs, values and feelings. *Acknowledgement of the feelings that attach to beliefs and perspectives* is a third, overarching principle of social justice educational practice.

Beyond these three overarching principles, we draw upon other pedagogical organizers. One organizer is grounded in bodies of literature derived from pedagogies such as feminist pedagogies, Freirean, multicultural, cross-cultural, intergroup, intercultural, anti-racist, experiential, and T [Training]-group pedagogies, and pedagogies rooted in cognitive and social identity development (explored in Adams, 1997). Examination of these pedagogical practices has resulted in the development of a social justice pedagogical framework consisting of five convergent principles of social justice practice (Adams, 1997).

(1) *Balance the emotional and cognitive components of the learning process:* Social justice education pays attention to personal safety, classroom process, and group norms and guidelines. It emphasizes student-centered, interactive, and collaborative learning modes. This principle is grounded in the theory and research of the laboratory, intergroup, feminist, experiential, humanistic, and developmental literatures.

(2) *Acknowledge and support the personal (a person's individual experience) while also illuminating the systemic (the interactions among social groups)*: Social justice education pays close attention to the here-and-now of the classroom setting. The systemic or abstract is grounded in an accumulation of concrete, real life examples. This principle is grounded in the theory and research of the laboratory, cross-cultural, Freirean and critical, Black studies, feminist, experiential, and developmental literatures.

(3) *Attend to social relations within the classroom*: Social justice education involves a "process" orientation (group interactions, who speaks, who remains silent) and attention to multicultural group dynamics. Students' behaviors in the group setting of the classroom may serve as a microcosm of the social relations among agent and target group members more generally. Teaching helps students name behaviors that emerge in group dynamics, understand their group processes, and improve interpersonal communications without blaming or judging each other. This principle is grounded in the theory and research of the laboratory, multicultural, feminist, Freirean and critical pedagogical literatures.

(4) *Utilize reflection and experience as tools for student-centered learning*: Teaching starts from students' worldviews. Experience constitutes the starting point for dialogue or problem-posing, and provides examples for broader abstractions. Students are helped to reflect upon and clarify their learning — this principle is grounded in the theory and research of the Freirean and critical, experiential, and developmental literatures.

(5) *Value awareness, personal growth and change as outcomes of the learning process:* Teaching balances different learning styles and provides opportunities for "processing" or "debriefing," as well as questions and discussion. Teaching is explicitly organized around goals such as social awareness, social knowledge, and social action and transformation, although the exact proportions among the three goals may well change in relation to student interest and readiness. This principle is grounded in the theory and research of the laboratory, humanistic, experiential, Black and multicultural studies, feminist, and critical pedagogical literatures.

In addition to these five principles of social justice practice, we also rely on other organizers noted above, such as learning styles and cognitive or social identity models.

We draw upon *Learning style models* (discussed above with reference to *Quadrant 1: Knowing One's Students*) , such as the Kolb learning style model, to focus attention on the "how "of learning and the variety of strategies that can achieve active student engagement (Kolb, 1984; Smith & Kolb, 1986; Svinicki & Dixon, 1987). Although the Kolb learning style model is not in itself a model of social justice practice, attention to the specific learning strengths designated by each quadrant in the Kolb model helps faculty to vary their teaching designs to alternatively match or stretch students with different cultural communication and learning styles, particularly when those styles are rooted in social identities (Anderson & Adams, 1992; Griffin, 1997, pp. 56-57). The same can be said of the Witkin model of *field sensitive* (sometimes called relational) and field independent (or *analytical*) learning styles (Anderson, 1988; Anderson & Adams, 1992), which more explicitly than Kolb helps focus on socially-rooted and gendered learning styles.

Cognitive development and *social identity development* models provide organizers for teaching practices that support and challenge students who bring dualistic, right/wrong , individualistic perspectives to the classrooms, as distinct from those who may be more engaged with the contradictions and dissonance that multiple or systemic perspectives bring to the classroom (Adams, 1997, pp. 39-42; Adams, Jones, Tatum, 1997, pp. 320-322; Bidell, Lee, Bouchie, Ward, & Brass, 1994; King & Shuford, 1996). Social identity development models enable faculty to better understand and respond appropriately to differing patterns of interaction resulting from differing patterns of prior socialization (Hardiman and Jackson, 1997; Tatum, 1992).

Faculty Self-Assessment and Action Planning

In our seminars, we find that faculty share a commitment to developing a more comprehensive and far-reaching social justice education perspective on their teaching practice. They acknowledge and appreciate the various resources each participant brings to the seminar. They demonstrate a readiness and a commitment to identify specific dimensions of their teaching practice for change.

Our focus is on assessment, not on evaluation. When we introduce assessment, it has been important for us to clarify the distinction between assessment of one's practice and evaluation of one's students for purposes of grading. We use assessment instruments to generate information that helps faculty determine where to focus attention on self-awareness, curriculum, their students, and their teaching practice. The assessment instruments correspond to specific dimensions within the four quadrant model.

Self-Assessment Instruments:

In the Appendices we include sample assessment instruments that we use to generate concrete information in our seminars.

"Knowing Ourselves as Social Justice Educators" (Appendix A) is designed to provide a bridge between faculty self-knowledge on the one hand, and their knowledge of their students on the other. Feedback from this instrument includes social identity and socialization as well as learning style.

"The Multicultural Life Experience Profile" (Appendix B) is designed to give participants a snapshot of their multicultural life experiences. This is also an assessment they can use with their students, for the same purposes.

"Creating an Inclusive Curriculum" (Appendix C, derived from Schuster & Van Dyne, 1985) provides participants with an overview of the characteristics of each phase in the movement from an exclusive to an inclusive or transformed curriculum. This is an assessment they can use with their departmental or home institution faculty colleagues. It is in two-parts: Steps I have taken, and Steps I will take.

The "Five Principles of Social Justice Pedagogical Practice" (Appendix D, derived from Adams, 1997) enable participants to clarify the specific skills they might want to develop to become more effective social justice educators. It also asks that they assess the challenges that stand in the way of such practice and their opportunities to develop and practice new pedagogical skills. This is an assessment faculty can use with their departmental or home institution faculty colleagues.

"Social Justice Education Facilitator's Readiness Worksheet" (Appendix E, derived from Griffin, 1997a) provides information on five dimensions of facilitator readiness. By gaining insight onto these dimensions of facilitator readiness, faculty can better determine the content of their change plan. This instrument is useful with colleagues at the home institution as well.

"Dynamics of Diversity – Risk Self-Assessment" (Appendix F, derived from Marchesani & Adams, 1992) enables faculty to determine which of the four quadrants presents the highest level of challenge or risk at this stage of their growth and development. Some faculty will want to start with the area of highest risk, while others will find it more productive to start with the quadrant of lowest risk. This assessment provides an initial indicator of the focus of the change plan they take out of the seminar.

"Developing a Liberatory Consciousness" (Appendix G, derived from Love, 2000) encourages participants to reflect on four components of a liberatory consciousness and to consider how these might be applicable to a social justice classroom.

"Dynamics of Diversity Change Plan" (Appendix H, derived from Marchesani & Adams, 1992) reviews participant experience with the four quadrants in order to prioritize the content of the change plan they take back to their home institution. It asks a series of questions that address the four quadrants and provoke self-reflection about how they can begin the change process.

"Individual Change Plan" (Appendix I) asks participant to select the quadrants that represent their challenges and to describe steps they might take to increase their skills and effectiveness in that quadrant.

"Learning Development Plan" (Appendix J) encourages faculty to identify new knowledge or skills they would like to develop to increase their effectiveness. It asks them to not only describe *what* skills will be developed or knowledge gained and *how* this can happen, but to also describe the support and the resources they need to sustain their growth and development.

"Instructional Activities for Aspects of the Kolb Learning Styles Model"

(Appendix K, derived from Anderson & Adams, 1992) assesses instructor's prior use of various structured learning activities that can match or stretch each of the four learning style modes.

"Instructor Fears & Challenges" (Appendix L, based on Weinstein & Obear, 1992) asks faculty to identify areas in which they feel personally and professionally vulnerable in the social justice classroom.

Individual and Institutional Support Systems

In this chapter, we have tried to provide instructors, faculty developers, and academic administrators with a range of social justice frameworks for examining equity and excellence, an overview of the knowledge and skills useful to faculty interested in teaching more inclusively, and models for strategies for change. Embedded in each of these sections we have tried to offer applied examples and exercises many of the instructors we have worked with found useful in promoting self-reflection and new skill acquisition. While this chapter reflects only our approach to diversity and social justice, we hope that the methods and exercises we have developed through our years as faculty in schools and in institutions of higher learning may prove useful to you, as well. We leave the reader with a few overarching suggestions for gaining the support that will be required to implement and sustain changes:

- First, we encourage faculty to seek out and build support for this process as an on-going endeavor. When faculty try to maintain their change process alone, they too often become discouraged and burn out. We find that the group experience shared within the faculty development seminar is illustrative of the kinds of bonds and support nets they would like to nurture on their home campuses. Many faculty are willing to go back and seek out possible allies, both on the faculty and elsewhere on their campuses.
- Second, we encourage faculty to link their individual goals with the goals of the department or of the campus in order to garner more sustained institutional support for their change effort. For example, campus resources such as Centers for Teaching, Community Service Learning, and Residence Life or Campus Outreach programs are valuable campus-wide resources for faculty networking and support.
- Third, where colleges and universities exist in geographical proximity to other institutions, these connections can be developed across different campus networks. Although traditionally classroom teaching has tended to be experienced as an isolated endeavor, we urge that faculty seek out every opportunity for conversation about their teaching and support from colleagues and through Centers for Teaching.

- Finally, we encourage faculty to use web-based communication, including bulletin boards, listserves, other online resources, and email as powerful tools for the exchange of ideas and resources that can make a difference in their change efforts.

References

Adams, M. (1992). Cultural inclusion in the American college classroom. In L.L.B. Border and N. V.T. Chism (Eds.), *Teaching for Diversity* (pp. 5-17). New Directions for Teaching and Learning, No. 49. San Francisco: Jossey-Bass.

Adams, M. (1997). Pedagogical frameworks for social justice education. In M. Adams, L.A. Bell, & P. Griffin (Eds.), *Teaching for diversity and social justice: A sourcebook* (pp. 30-43). New York: Routledge.

Adams, M., Bell, L. A., & Griffin, P. (Eds.). (1997). *Teaching for diversity and social justice: A sourcebook.* New York: Routledge.

Adams, M., Jones, J., & Tatum, B. (1997). Knowing our students. In M. Adams, L. A. Bell, & P. Griffin (Eds.), *Teaching for diversity and social justice: A sourcebook* (pp. 311-325). New York: Routledge.

Adams, M., & Marchesani, L. (1997). Multiple issues course overview. In M. Adams, L.A. Bell, & P. Griffin (Eds.), *Teaching for diversity and social justice: A sourcebook* (pp. 261-275). New York: Routledge.

Anderson, J. A., & Adams, M. (1992). Acknowledging the learning styles of diverse student populations: Implications for instructional design. In L.L.B. Border, & N.V.T. Chism (Eds.), *Teaching for Diversity* (pp. 19-33). New Directions for Teaching and Learning, No. 49. San Francisco: Jossey-Bass.

Bell, L. A., Washington, S., Weinstein, G., & Love, B. (1997). Knowing ourselves as instructors. In Adams, M., Bell, L. A., & Griffin, P. (Eds.), *Teaching for diversity and social justice: A sourcebook* (pp. 299-310). New York: Routledge.

Bidell, T.R., Lee, E.M., Bouchie, N., Ward, C., & Brass, D. (1994). Developing conceptions of racism among young white adults in the context of cultural diversity coursework. *Journal of Adult Development, 1*(3), 185-200.

Butler, J. E., & Walter, J. C. (1991). *Transforming the curriculum: Ethnic studies and women's studies.* Albany, NY: SUNY Press.

Delgado-Bernal, D., & Villalpando, O. (2002). An apartheid of knowledge in academia: The struggle over the 'legitimate' knowledge of faculty of color. *Equity & Excellence in Education 35*(2), 169-181.

Goodman, D. J. (2001). *Promoting diversity and social justice: Educating people from privileged groups.* Thousand Oaks, CA: Sage.

Green, M. F. (Ed.) (1989). *Minorities on campus: A handbook for enhancing diversity.* Washington, DC: American Council on Education.

Griffin, P. (1997a). Facilitating social justice education courses. In M. Adams, L.A. Bell, & P. Griffin (Eds.), *Teaching for diversity and social justice: A sourcebook* (pp. 279-298). New York: Routledge

Griffin, P. (1997b). Introductory modules for the single issue courses. In M. Adams, L.A. Bell, & P. Griffin (Eds.), *Teaching for diversity and social justice: A sourcebook* (pp. 61-81). New York: Routledge

Griffin, P. & Bell, L. A. (1997). Designing social justice education courses. In M. Adams, L.A. Bell, & P. Griffin (Eds.), *Teaching for diversity and social justice: A sourcebook* (pp. 44-58). New York: Routledge.

Harro, B. (2000a). The cycle of liberation. In M. Adams, W. J. Blumenfeld, R. Castañeda, H. Hackman, M. Peters, & X. Zúñiga (Eds.), *Readings for diversity and social justice (*pp. 457-463). New York: Routledge.

Harro, B. (2000b). The cycle of socialization. In M. Adams, W.J. Blumenfeld, R. Castañeda, H. Hackman, M. Peters, & X. Zúñiga (Eds.), *Readings for diversity and social justice (*pp. 15-21). New York: Routledge.

Hines, S. M. (Ed.). (2003). *Multicultural science education: Theory, practice, and promise.* New York: Peter Lang.

King, P.M., & Shuford, B.C. (1996). A multicultural view is a more cognitively complex view: Cognitive development and multicultural education. *American Behavioral Scientist, 40*(2), 153-164.

Love, B. (2000). Developing a liberatory consciousness. In M. Adams, W. J. Blumenfeld, R. Castañeda, H. Hackman, M. Peters, & X. Zúñiga (Eds.), *Readings for diversity and social justice* (pp. 463-470). New York: Routledge.

Marchesani, L. & Adams, M. (1992). Dynamics of diversity in the teaching-learning process: A model for analysis. In M. Adams (Ed.), *Promoting diversity in the college classroom* (pp. 9-21). New Directions for Teaching and Learning, No. 52. San Francisco: Jossey -Bass.

Moses, R. P., & Cobb, C. E. (2001). *Radical equations: Math literacy and civil rights.* Boston: Beacon Press.

Pharr, S.(Ed.) (1988). Common elements of oppression. In *Homophobia: A weapon of sexism* (pp. 53-64). Inverness, CA: Chardon Press.

Powell, A. B., & Frankenstein, M. (Eds.). (1997). *Ethnomathematics: Challenging eurocentrism in mathematics education.* Albany, NY: SUNY Press.

Rogoff, B. (2003). *The cultural nature of human development.* UK: Oxford University Press.

Schuster, M. R., & Van Dyne, S. R. (1985). *Women's place in the academy: Transforming the liberal arts curriculum.* Totowa, NJ: Roman & Allanheld.

Spring, J. (2001). *Deculturalization and the struggle for equality. A brief history of the education of dominated cultures in the United States* (3rd ed.). Boston: McGraw Hill.

Tatum, B. (1992). Talking about race, learning about racism: The application of racial identity development theory in the classroom. *Harvard Educational Review, 62*(1), 1-24.

Walker, V. S., & Snarey, J. R. (Eds.). (2004). *Race-ing moral formation: African American perspectives on care and justice.* New York: Teacher's College Press.

Weinstein, J., & Obear, K. (1992). Bias issues in the classroom: Encounters with the teaching self. In M. Adams (Ed.), *Promoting diversity in the college classroom* (pp. 39-50). New Directions for Teaching and Learning, No. 52. San Francisco: Jossey-Bass.

Young, I. M. (1990). The five faces of oppression. In *Justice and the politics of difference* (pp. 39-66). NJ: Princeton University Press.

Wijeyesinghe, C. L, & Jackson, B. W. (2001). *New perspectives on racial identity development: A theoretical and practical anthology.* New York University Press.

Wildman, S. M. (1996). *Privilege revealed: How invisible preference undermines America.* New York: University Press.

Maurianne Adams is a professor in the Social Justice Education concentration, School of Education, at the University of Massachusetts Amherst. **Barbara J. Love** is an associate professor in the Social Justice Education concentration, School of Education, at the University of Massachusetts Amherst.

Appendix A

Activity: Knowing Ourselves as Social Justice Educators

Step 1: Jot a few first thoughts on each of these questions:

What aspects of my own experience – my cultural experience – and/or my learning style – have helped me engage (all) (some of) (a few of) my students on issues of social and cultural diversity, difference, and inequality?

What aspects of my own experience – my cultural experience – and/or my learning style – have seemed especially useful to me with students who seem most similar to me culturally or socially?

What aspects of my own experience – my cultural experience and/or my learning style – have helped me build bridges to students who seem different from me culturally or socially?

What aspects of my own experience – my cultural experience – and/or my learning style have made teaching about diversity or teaching students different from me seen especially challenging and difficulty?

Step 2: Join up in dyads or triads to talk for a few minutes about any initial insights that came out of this brief activity.

Appendix B

Multicultural Life Experience Profile

Please rate the level of multiculturalism for the organizations of your life, using the scale:

1 = Completely monocultural
10 = Completely multicultural

		1	2	3	4	5	6	7	8	9	10
1	Home of origin										
2	Community/neighborhood where you grew up.										
3	Elementary school										
4	Religious organization Church, Temple, Synagogue, Mosque Tabernacle, etc										
5	Civic Associations: Scouts, Brownies, etc.										
6	High school										
7	College										
8	Fraternity, Sorority										
9	First Work Organization										
10	Professional Association										
11	Current work organization										
12	Neighborhood/community where you reside										
13	Current home/family										
14	Current Religious Organization										
15	Other:										

Appendix C-1

Creating Inclusive Curriculum: Steps I have Taken

For this exercise, select a course that you have taught in the past two semesters. Describe steps that you have taken to create a more inclusive curriculum in that class. This may include a range of strategies in addition to those listed below.

Strategy	Steps taken
Course content	
Teaching/facilitation style: e.g., more interactive, flexible	
Varied methods of student learning assessment	
Reading assignments	
Using students as resources for class	
Guest speakers	
Video and other resources	
Examining language patterns used in the classroom	
Analysis of group work	
Analysis of student /student interactions	
Analysis of interaction patterns with students	

Use back of page to describe additional strategies.

Appendix C - 2

Creating Inclusive Curriculum: Steps I Will Take

For this exercise, select a course that you plan to teach on the next two semesters. Describe steps that you might/plan to take to create a more inclusive curriculum in that class. This may include a range of strategies in addition to those listed below.

Strategy	Steps I plan to take/steps I might take
Course content	
Teaching/facilitation style: e.g., more interactive, flexible	
Varied methods of student learning assessment	
Reading assignments	
Using students as resources for class	
Guest speakers	
Video and other resources	
Examining language patterns used in the classroom	
Analysis of group work	
Analysis of student /student interactions	
Analysis of interaction patterns with students	

Use back of page to describe additional strategies.

Appendix D

Five Principles of Social Justice Pedagogical Practice
Personal and Intergroup Skill Identification Worksheet

(1) *Balance the emotional and cognitive components of the learning process*. What personal skills would I need? What stands in the way of my making this balance? How might I practice these skills?

(2) *Acknowledge (support) the personal (the individual students' experiences) while illuminating the systemic (the broad conceptual organizers, such as inequality among different social groups)*. What personal or intergroup skills would I need? What makes it difficult to coordinate the individual & personal, with the systemic?

(3) *Pay attention to social relations and communication patterns that emerge in the classroom or in small groups. Note interpersonal and intergroup dynamics*. What personal or group development knowledge or skills would I need? How might I develop and practice these skills?

(4) *Utilize personal reflection and individual or group experience as tools for experiential student-centered learning. Use as starting points for dialogues or problem-posing*. What personal, interpersonal, or group development skills would I need? How might I develop and practice these skills?

(5) *Explicitly value the development of awareness, personal growth and change (new skills, new behaviors, and efforts to make effective interventions) as demonstrable outcomes of the learning process*. How might I build these goals into my curriculum? How might I help students to learn and to practice skills related to these goals? How might I assess these skills?

Appendix E

Social Justice Education Facilitator's Readiness Worksheet

Support:

Climate:	Very Supportive	Could be better	Not supportive
Administrative Support:	High	Could be better	Not supportive
Colleagues & Friends:	High	Could be better	Not supportive
Someone to talk to:	Always	Sometimes	Not at all

Passion: Use scale of 1 (very high), 2 (somewhat), 3 (not at all)

Importance of SJE issues:	1	2	3
Clarity of your SJE rationale:	1	2	3
Willingness to risk controversy:	1	2	3
Consideration of students' perception of you in relation to SJE issues:	1	2	3
Comfort level re SJE issues:	1	2	3

Awareness: Use scale of 1 (very high), 2 (somewhat), 3 (not at all)

Work on own awareness:	1	2	3
Awareness of school climate:	1	2	3
Awareness of interrelationships of social justice issues:	1	2	3

Knowledge: Use scale of 1 (very high), 2 (somewhat), 3 (not at all)

Information on SJE issues:	1	2	3
Preparation on SJE issues:	1	2	3
Resources re SJE issues:	1	2	3

Skills: Use scale of 1 (very high), 2 (somewhat), 3 (not at all)

General SJE skills level:	1	2	3

Briefly list the skills you regularly use in leading SJE discussions:

1.

2.

3.

List the skills you'd like to better develop to facilitate SJE discussions:

1.

2.

3.

Comfort with different viewpoints:	1	2	3
Listening to prejudice without giving way to your own "triggers":	1	2	3
Helping students challenge their own stereotypes and fears:	1	2	3
Comfort with disclosure of your own uncertainties	1	2	3

Adapted from P. Griffin. (1997a). "Facilitating Social Justice Education Courses."

Appendix F

Dynamics of Diversity
Risk Self- -Assessment

(1) While listening to the presentation about the four quadrants of teaching and learning, reflect on what are for you the risks and challenges involved in imagining change in your own classroom on each of these four dimensions.
Use the scale for assessment: 1 = Low Risk, 5 = High Risk.

(low) 1 2 3 4 5 (high)

Knowing your students
(their social identities)

Knowing yourself
(your socialization)

More inclusive curriculum
Building in multiple perspectives

Flexible teaching repertoire

(2) Note which quadrant has the lowest risk for you, and which has the highest risk. Jot down what you believe are some reasons for these different risk levels.

(3) Use the risk levels – and the reasons for them – to consider what challenges or difficulties you may experience in making changes in any one of these four quadrants. Note your challenges or difficulties.

(4) Turn to the person next to you and talk about whatever insights you wish to share out of steps #2 or #3 in this activity.

(5) Brief open discussion about some of the challenges noted in your paired-sharing.

NOTE: As you think about your own "change plan" for tomorrow, consider which quadrant you wish to focus on.

Adapted from L. Marchesani and M. Adams. (1992). "Dynamics of diversity in the teaching-learning process: A model for analysis."

Appendix G

Developing a Liberatory Consciousness

	Personal Examples
Awareness	
Analysis	
Action	
Accountability/ Ally-ship	

Adapted from B. Love. (2000). "Developing a Liberatory Consciousness."

Appendix H

Dynamics of Diversity Change Plan

Refer back to your risk assessment to focus on what poses the greatest challenge for you. Use that as a barometer to indicate where change would need to be most intentional.

Knowing your students (their social identities):

- What strategies or activities can I use to learn about my students' social identities?
- How can I help my students develop their own self-awareness of social identities?
- How can I enable my students to interact more effectively & consciously across their social identities?
- How can my students' social identities become a positive and intentional part of my classroom dynamics?
- Other areas I wish to explore?

Knowing yourself (your socialization):

- How can I develop greater comfort in exploring my own social identities?
- How can I learn more about how my social identities affect my classroom comfort levels and presentation?
- What are the obstacles that prevent my developing a more flexible, interactive classroom pedagogy?
- What skills do I feel I should develop more fully to be a more effective classroom instructor & facilitator?

Inclusive curriculum (Building in multiple perspectives):

- What specific aspects of my course curriculum can I make more inclusive?
- How can I make my readings & resource materials more inclusive?
- How can I make my instructional examples more inclusive?
- How can I draw upon the diversity in my classrooms to bring multiple perspectives into my course content?
- Other possibilities?

Flexible teaching repertoire:

How can I begin to practice new, different instructional strategies?
How can I begin to develop new facilitative skills?
How can I remind myself to use a range of activities that may match or stretch different student learning styles, as well as my own?
How can I encourage myself to try strategies that do not meet my own comfort zones?

Support and encouragement for change:

How can I establish the support I need from professional friends and colleagues?
How can I build the support I will need from my department and home institution?

Adapted from L. Marchesani and M. Adams. (1992). "Dynamics of diversity in the teaching-learning process: A model for analysis."

Appendix I

Individual Change Plan

Making the transition to an inclusive social justice education curriculum and practice is an ongoing process based on an ongoing commitment. To help you think of steps that you might take along the way, use the four quadrants of the model to determine next steps.

Reflecting on your prior work with these quadrants, select one area to work on in the near future.

Select the quadrant that represents the highest risk or might be the most challenging for you; or

Select the quadrant that could yield the highest results for the investment of time and resources.

Determine what steps you would like to take. Describe the steps in as much detail as possible. What support/resources will you need to be able to effectively take these steps?

Quadrant	
Steps	

Appendix J

Learning Development Plan

In the space below, describe steps that you can take to increase your capacity to create more inclusive curricula (a curriculum characterized by social justice) and practice

Skill Development		
What	How (Activities)	Support and resources required and a strategy for acquiring that support.
Knowledge Development		
What	How	Support and resources required and a strategy for acquiring that support
Experiences I want to create as part of my learning development plan.		

Appendix K

Instructional Activities for Aspects of the Kolb Learning Styles Model

CONCRETE EXPERIENCE	Yes	Never tried

(Note 3 that stand out for you.)

Readings
Examples
Fieldwork
Laboratories
Problem sets
Trigger films
Observations
Simulations and games
Primary text reading
Fishbowl discussion & turn-taking
Concentric circle discussions
Other

REFLECTIVE OBSERVATION:	Yes	Never tried

(Note 3 that stand out for you)

Logs
Journals
Dyads, small group discussions
Whole class brainstorming
Thought and reflection questions
Rhetorical and challenging questions
Peer panels and invited speakers
Trigger films
Observations
Simulations and games
Primary text reading
Fishbowl discussion & turn-taking
Concentric circle discussions
Other:

ABSTRACT CONCEPTUALIZATION: Yes Never tried
(Note 3 that stand out for you)

Lectures
Readings
Papers
Projects
Analogies
Model building
Recognition, discussion and analysis of real life experiences
Application of organizing frameworks across multiple examples
Analysis of films
Other:

ACTIVE EXPERIMENTATION: Yes Never tried
(Note 3 that stand out for you)

Real-world projects (group or individual)
Fieldwork
Homework
Laboratory
Case study
Simulations
Discussion, analysis, reconstruction of real situations
Identification of key individual & group skills needed
Practice of key individual & group skills needed
Practice of feedback and cross-cultural communication skills (most important: learning to listen)
Other:

PLEASE TURN TO THE PERSON NEXT TO YOU TALK ABOUT WHAT SEEMS MOST CHALLENGING OR DIFFICULT ON THIS LIST.

Adapted from L. Marchesani and M. Adams. (1992). "Dynamics of diversity in the teaching-learning process: A model for analysis."

Appendix L

Instructor Fears and Challenges

Write "yes" (I have felt this) or "no" (I have never felt this) next to each bullet.

1. Confronting my own social and cultural identity conflicts

- Unexpectedly confronted stereotyped attitudes toward my social identity
- Felt guilty, ashamed, or embarrassed for behaviors or attitudes of others in my social identity group

2. Confronted my own biases [Respond "yes" or "no" regarding whether you *feared* these things would happen, whether or not they actually did]

- Being labeled racist, sexist, etc. by others
- Finding prejudice within myself while conducting a class
- Having to question my own assumptions in the midst of teaching
- Being corrected by members of targeted group
- Having to face my fears of targeted group while teaching or preparing to teach

3. Responding to biased comments [Respond "yes" or "no" regarding whether you *feared* these things would happen, whether or not they actually did]

- Having to respond to biased comments from targeted group
- Hearing biased comments from dominant group members in presence of target group members
- Having to respond to bias from members of my own social group

4. Doubts about my own competency

- Having to expose my struggles with these issues
- Not knowing the appropriate terms or language
- Feeling uncertain about what I am saying
- Feeling like I can't unravel the complexities of the issue
- Being told that I don't know what I'm talking about
- Making a mistake

5. Need for learner approval

- Fear making students feel frustrated, frightened, or angry
- Leaving students feeling shaken, confused, and unable to fix things

6. Handling intense emotions in classroom, fear of losing control

- Not knowing how to respond to angry comments
- Having a discussion blow-up
- Having anger directed at me
- Being overwhelmed by my own strong emotions
- Losing control of the classroom

Adapted from G. Weinstein & K. Obear. (1992). "Bias issues in the classroom: Encounters with the teaching self."

Chapter 43
Strategic Action in Hot Moments

Lee Warren

Most of us, when hot moments occur, simply react. Our minds stop working. We revert to our oldest fallback behaviors, usually some version or other of fight or flight. Some of us lash out and say things that we later regret. Others retreat, check out, and take themselves and their ideas out of play. The objective, instead, is to be strategic — to get one's mind working again and to devise a response or an intervention that is effective.

Hot Moment Scenarios

- In a political science class, the teacher was discussing with students why a nation might go to war. All of the usual reasons surfaced early: to protect itself, to maintain borders, to provide safety to citizens. He asked a number of questions to take the discussion further, finally asking, "Well, what about genocide? What about the Holocaust? If we had known it was happening, would that have been a reason to go to war?" When no one answered, he called on his most vocal student, an African American woman. She said, "No." "Why?" he asked. She answered, "I'm not sure it happened like they said it did, and if it did maybe they had their reasons."

  The teacher's mind stopped; he could think of no response to this, and three years later, when I interviewed him, he was still uncertain how he might have responded. At the time, he retreated from the moment and addressed neither the issues nor the student.

- A choral director recently led a dress rehearsal of a very complicated piece of music that involved four pianos, six percussionists, four soloists, and an amateur chorus of 100. Things did not fall into place easily; the man was intent on a good or nearly perfect performance, and he became increasingly frustrated with the chorus. Not all mem-

> bers were as well prepared as they should have been, and many were still stuck in the music, rather than being free enough to look up at the director.
>
> The director got more and more frustrated. His mind stopped. He remained enmeshed in his feelings. Instead of getting some perspective on the moment and thinking strategically about how to pull the thing together, he ended up yelling at the chorus, frequently and at length.

The central task is to maintain some distance from the loaded situation, and by so doing to think more clearly in order to see how to use the moment to enhance the learning of the students or of the group.

These things are of course, much more easily said than done. This essay will suggest some techniques for achieving this goal, while also recognizing how difficult this process is and how long and through what painful experiences it takes to learn such techniques. As a bumper sticker I saw on a car parked outside a therapists' office read: "Oh no, not another learning opportunity!!" Opportunities to do this work lie all around us all the time, ready for the taking.[1]

Tips for Being Strategic

1. Stop!!

When a hot moment arrives, and we realize that our mind has ceased functioning, the first thing to do is simply to stop. Pause for as long as you need to, in order to get up and running again. Breathe deeply, from the center, and get your breath moving again. When we are under stress, our breath becomes shallow, which leads in a circular fashion to increasing feelings of stress. So our objective here is to calm ourselves through deep breathing, and thus to get our minds functioning again.

---

[1]Many of the ideas discussed here have come from my work with Professor Ronald Heifetz and Marty Linsky at the Kennedy School of Government at Harvard University, from Heifetz' first book, *Leadership Without Easy Answers* (1994). Cambridge: Harvard University Press, and from the book he wrote with Marty Linsky, [(2002). *Leadership on the Line*. Boston: Harvard Business School Press]. Ideas and concepts derived from this work include: Holding Steady, Getting on the Balcony, Self vs. Role, The Song Beneath the Words, Allies and Confidants. I am also deeply indebted to the work on "Strategic Performance" that I do with Nancy Houfek, Head of Voice and Speech at the American Repertory Theater at Harvard University.

Once we are breathing deeply, we need to Hold Steady. To be still and at one with ourselves. To be centered. If we can hold ourselves steady, we have a shot at holding the group steady and thus enabling it to do some work. If, on the other hand, we seem to be flustered or off our center, the group will be unlikely to learn together from the experience.

2. Get up on the Balcony

In order to gain the distance necessary to be strategic, get up on the balcony and off the dance floor, and observe carefully. Most of the time we are on the dance floor, in the thick of things, dancing with our partners, moving with the music, bumping into people from time to time. And we can see very little while on the dance floor — just the few people who are near us. So we need to get up on the balcony, to see what the patterns are: who is dancing with whom, what are the groupings or factions, whether the music is working for everyone or only for a few, and who is not dancing.

If the teacher in the political science class had been able to get up on the balcony and out of the confusion of his own personal reaction to the student's remarks about the holocaust, he would have been more likely to have found a way to turn her remarks into an important learning experience for all the students. Likewise, if the choral director had been able to get up on the balcony and off the dance floor of his own emotions, he might have been able to devise a strategy for leading the group through the difficult music.

Once on the balcony, we need to listen for the song beneath the words: who is saying what, who gets to speak, and what is the subtext. Often students are unable to say things clearly, as they are just beginning to be able to articulate their thoughts and feelings. So listening carefully for what they are really saying can help us deal with the real issues, not with the clumsily stated issues. And of course, sometimes people in groups deliberately hide their true agenda. Listening for it can, again, help to develop an effective strategy. Who knows what the student in the political science class was really thinking, or how figuring that out might have led to a more productive follow-up conversation in the class?

Only when we are sure we know what is going on should we make a move, and even then we need to check carefully on our timing, our tone, and our word choice. Acting too fast, moving in without careful planning when things are hot, can often make things worse, whereas a carefully timed and worded intervention can often turn the situation around.

- ☐ A faculty member, who is known for barging in at faculty meetings and stating her views up front and then wondering why no one ever follows her lead, tried a new strategy recently.

Her department was meeting to decide who to hire for a joint appointment between their department and the women's studies program. Going into the meeting, her agenda was to see if there might be a way to get both of the top two candidates. But instead of speaking right up with her agenda, she stopped and she listened. What she heard was lots of bashing of the number two candidate, even though that person was a very strong candidate.

After some time, she stood up, walked to the door, and said, "I have to leave; students are waiting for me. But before I go, I have something to say. I notice that we have been bashing the number two person for some time now." And she stopped, after her simple, descriptive sentence. The group stopped and was astonished to recognize that this was true. And then she said, "And if we continue to do this, we might close doors that we would like to leave open in the future. For example, we might at some time wish to have both of these women on our faculty." At this plainly stated, non-aggressive, suggestion, the group made this idea its agenda item and discussed it for the next three hours, and for the next three months.

Her timing, her word choice, and her tone were perfectly chosen for this situation, and meant that her agenda indeed became the agenda of the group.

3. Don't Personalize!

Personalizing hinders us from seeing the situation clearly and thinking strategically about what to do. Yet most of us tend to personalize situations and we do this in several ways.

A. Self vs. Role

One of the ways we personalize is that we do not clearly enough distinguish self from role. So when someone attacks us in personal terms, we take it personally. But almost always, the attack is REALLY about us in a specific role and/or about the issues we represent. As the teacher, for example, we are the authority in the room and represent authority to students. Or we represent something else in our role to any particular student or group of students. So an attack is likely not about us as individuals, no matter how personal it sounds, but about us in role. Usually the attack is more about the attacker and his or her preoccupations than about us.

- ☐ I was once teaching a class with a famous professor, a man who was senior in rank to me. We taught the class together, both sitting in the front of the room. About half way through the semester, it became evident to me that half the women in the room thought I walked on water, and that every word I said was a pearl. The other half thought I was the worst possible example of how women work with men, a devastating criticism.

After considerable thought, I realized that the women who liked what I said were women in the their 30s and 40s, with considerable work experience, who were able to hear what I was saying. The women who thought I was terrible were young women in their early 20s, who had little or no work experience, and who were terrified of how they were going to interact with men in the work place.

So the reactions of these women to me had more to do with them, and who they were and at what life stage, than with me personally. There was certainly room for reflection in the criticism, but although it sounded personal, interpreting it in personal terms would have inhibited me in the classroom and would have prevented a discussion of the topic. Interpreting it as a role issue made it possible to discuss it openly and for all of us to learn from it.

Sometimes we are attacked because we represent a particular issue, faction, or perspective that the attacker does not like. He or she attacks personally and very effectively takes the attention of both the individual and of the group off the issue. Because the attack distracts the group, the issue is not dealt with, or the perspective is lost. Taking the attack personally keeps the focus on the individual rather than on the issues.

☐ A woman who was the Head of Environmental Affairs at the state level received a phone call one day from the leader of the state senate. He inexplicably started yelling at her, so loudly that people down the hall from him thought he was having a heart attack, so loudly she could not hold the phone to her ear. She had no idea why he was doing this, and afterwards consulted with others and tried to find allies, in vain. The Senate leader repeated this many times, and blocked her at every point. The only reason she could find for his actions was that she was a "new girl" and he was an "old boy" who did not want women in state government. Her hands were tied; she was unable to accomplish much in the following three years of her tenure.

Several years later, during a debriefing, she was asked what issues were on the table that might have made him so angry and so determined to block her way. She had never asked the question and had no answer. After about 20 minutes of questioning, she was astonished to remember that there had been an issue: it had to do with park fees for handicapped people. The senate leader had a nephew with a handicap.

It would have been much easier to deal with that issue than to have taken it personally, attributed the problem to gender (about which she could do nothing), and be immobilized for the next three years. It is almost always easier to be strategic about issues than about the personal.

B. Psychologizing

A second way we personalize is when someone else behaves badly. When they are immoral, destructive, self-aggrandizing, and preventing the group from getting work done, we get caught up in judging their character. Often, we psychologize. We meet our friends at lunch or over coffee and analyze the personality of the person at length and with great pleasure; we conclude that the person is obsessive, or manic, or borderline, or had a lousy childhood. Or they are simply unethical human beings, bad people. We go on and on with the analysis, sometimes believing that we are being especially insightful or even kind in our understanding.

But psychologizing in this way, while lots of fun, is not useful. It does not advance the work we are doing, or move us towards our purpose. It is far more important to pay attention to the issues. Almost always, such people represent an issue, a faction, or a perspective we do not want to think about or acknowledge. By focusing on his or her character, we avoid the issue. We forget that it is *much* easier to deal with issues than with character. We cannot change another's psychology; we can think strategically about issues.

Sometimes in the classroom, when a student acts out or seems to have an agenda of his or her own, or makes an outrageous or off-topic comment, it is easy to get caught up thinking about the student's personality, rather than thinking about what issues he or she is raising that need to be aired in order to have a full range of perspectives on a topic, or in order to know how students are reacting to the course or the classroom dynamics.

□ I once worked in an organization in which a woman came to work who just did not fit in. She never seemed to grasp the environment in which we were working and would consistently blunder, to the detriment of our department, which was already a little fragile in its hold on the institution. She would stay home on Tuesdays to write poetry. She did not pull her weight. She did not work well with her peers. We were a group where people brought an idea to the table, everyone worked it over, and then the person who proposed the idea left with a better fleshed-out plan of action. This woman would bring her idea, we would all discuss it, and she would say, "You don't trust me." She was trouble.

We reacted by psychologizing about her. We diagnosed her psychological and her moral character. The situation escalated, to the point where one colleague changed the locks on her door. We scapegoated her. And finally, we drove her out.

In retrospect, I think she probably was not a good fit for the organization. And she was, I am sure, a borderline personality. But I am ashamed of our collective scapegoating behavior, and I believe that by focusing on her character, we avoided the issues that she represented. This was an organization where the rules for working and the rules for success were very unclear: What exactly was the job? How did you get the boss' approval? How was success defined? Was this a nine to five job, or a job that was defined by the task? How many tasks were expected, and how hard did you have to work?

These are serious questions, and this woman, by her behavior, represented these issues. We scapegoated her; consequently, we never dealt with the issues. The personal was much too juicy and much too seductive, and the issues were much too difficult. The result was that we practiced a common form of work avoidance.

C. Internalizing

A third way we personalize is by taking others' behavior personally. When someone else behaves badly, we react emotionally by internalizing their behavior. We get mad or depressed, or we let their behavior beat us down, and we give up. Here again we lose sight of our purpose and get locked into emotions that lead nowhere. The other's behavior has been successful at keeping us from our agenda.

- A professor who is the only woman in her department has a long history of reacting energetically to the bad behavior of some of her colleagues. When one of them does or says something she considers unfair or immoral, she explodes. She goes directly into fight mode, moves immediately to the extreme position, and threatens a trip to the dean at the drop of a hat. As a result, she has no allies in the department meetings, as it is not safe to ally with her publicly, although people do in private.

  One day recently, she told me that now she "gets it." When someone behaves badly, she doesn't react at all. She notices their behavior and begins immediately to think about how to achieve her purpose despite this behavior. She begins to think strategically: Can she go around him, over him, through him? How can she get the job done, knowing that this person is likely to continue to behave badly? Her dispassion allows her to move forward effectively.

- In an Afro Am class, close to the end of the semester, the group was discussing Louis Farrakhan. Near the end of the discussion, a Jewish woman said that she could see how Farrakhan appealed to many black men, but that she was certain he would not appeal to educated black men. In the class were six African American men. They turned on her, attacking her verbally. At the end of the class, she fled down the hall, in tears.

  The teacher was an African American man. He could have taken the woman's comments personally — it would have been easy to do. Instead, he ran down the hall after the woman, and said to her, "Rachel, if you are going to get it about African American life in the 21st century, you are going to have to really listen to what those guys have to say and think about why they are saying it." And then he went back into the room, where the six men were still talking, and said, "Guys, if you are going to get it about life in the 21st century, you are going to have to really listen to what Rachel is saying, and think about why she is saying it."

  By not taking Rachel's comments personally, this teacher managed to turn a very hot moment into a tremendous learning opportunity.

4. Prepare!!

One of the best ways to keep one's mind in action when a hot moment arrives is to prepare oneself beforehand — in several ways. It is when we are blindsided by the unexpected that our minds most often stop.

A. Predict

The most obvious form of preparation is to think ahead, to see what could possibly arise, given the topic at hand. Some topics easily lead to hot confrontations, and part of the preparation for the class can be thinking through what might come up and what one would do or say in the event. Some classrooms, regardless of the topic, are known to be more difficult for some students: the sciences are often unfriendly to women and minorities, for example, in part because of insensitivities of some of the young men in the room. A teacher intent upon keeping all students in the room, will foresee this and prepare strategies for dealing with it.

B. Know Yourself

One of the best, and least addressed, ways to prepare for teaching is to know yourself. For hot moments, it is important to know what pushes your buttons, what biases you have, and what kinds of things said or done can make your mind stop. Knowing these things allows you to devise strategies for handling hot moments in advance. Simply recognizing such a moment and your familiar reaction to it is a first step. The next step is to have strategies such as the following in mind in advance:

- Stop and take a breath
- Acknowledge the moment, name the elephant on the table
- Check that you have heard and/or understood correctly — restate, or ask the other to restate
- Model respectful listening and engagement
- Take the issue off the individual; make it a general one
- Ask students to get up on the balcony and think about what they have learned from the moment
- Use the moment as an opportunity to discuss the learning environment in the group
- Have partners to debrief with afterwards
- Defer — tell students you will deal with the issue, but deal with it later — in order to gather your wits and make a plan that will be effective

C. Know Your Purpose

In addition to knowing oneself, it is very important to have a clear idea of what your purpose is as you enter a classroom or a meeting — your purpose for the course overall and your purpose for that specific session. This is easier said than done but is critical to success in hot moments.

Most of us enter the classroom with a general sense of what we hope to accomplish, for example, a discussion about Napoleon's march on Moscow or about some aspect of micro-economics. But what specifically do we want students to learn, to walk away with at the end of the hour? What is the big takeaway?

Knowing your purpose, and keeping your eye on it, will enable you to turn the hot moment into a learning opportunity that is on target with the topic of the day. It will enable you to look for the part in the hot moment that reflects your overall game plan.

- ☐ The teacher of the student who said she did not think it was a good idea to go to war to prevent the Holocaust might, if he could have thought in the moment, have used her comment to launch a discussion exactly in line with his topic of why nations go to war: Should

> we go to war for others when we have not taken care of our own business? Should we go to war to protect groups other than our own? Both these questions are at the heart of current foreign policy: think of the recent debates over action or non-action in Bosnia, Rwanda, and Iraq.

D. Know your Students

It is also critical to know your students, if you are to effectively manage them in hot moments and help them to deep learning. This means knowing both how the group works as a group and knowing the students individually. Knowing the group will help you know how to handle the group, what tone to take, what boundaries to draw, and what strategies might be more or less effective in the moment. Knowing students as individuals will help you know how best to help them learn from the moment. Failure to know your students can lead to a missed opportunity, or worse, to damage and misconceptions.

Some prepare their students for the hard places by addressing easier issues first, coaching them in skills for intergroup dialogue, and modeling such behaviors as respectful listening, holding steady, learning from the moment, asking questions, and not personalizing the issue. We rarely think that it is our job in the college classroom to teach social skills, but in fact that is one of the most important things that students do learn, mostly by watching the professor and learning how to debate and contribute and disagree and challenge productively. Coaching explicitly and consciously could only enhance this process. Our purpose here is to help students to have constructive, cross-racial dialogue.

E. Have Allies and Confidants

It is always important to have allies when we are heading into unknown or hot territory, people who can support us, give us advice, sympathize, tell us what we have done wrong or right without animus or judgment. This is especially true when working across race, class, or gender lines, when it can be lifesaving to have people of the other group to help us understand and manage the situation in the most effective ways. We all need help getting out of our own heads and our own, by definition, limited perceptions, to see the larger picture and to understand what is really going on in any loaded situation. We all need help in thinking about how to handle the tough places. Doing this kind of work alone can be an invitation for disaster and martyrdom.

We also need confidants, people who are usually outside the workplace and who are on our team no matter what, who care more about us than about the issues at hand. They are the people we can vent with, cry with, to whom we can say the most awful things about the situation, and who will tell us how wrong we have been or how wonderful we are, because they care about us.

Do not confuse allies with confidants. Allies are people who are with us on particular issues, and not with us on others. Allies are critically important, but it is also critically important to remember the limits of the alliance. Do not tell allies everything; use confidants for that purpose.

Conclusion

These suggestions are not easy to accomplish. They are very hard and, for many of us, take a lifetime of practice – many trials, many errors. It is important to remember that we do not have to be perfect when we approach the hard places; we never will be. Having some ideas of different ways of approaching mind-stopping moments, however, can help us begin to turn the corner toward effective and even, finally, pleasurable strategic responses to hot moments. This surely is the goal: to take away the terror many experience in the face of a hot moment, and to increase the chances of turning it into a learning opportunity.

Lee Warren is an associate director of the Derek Bok Center for Teaching and Learning at Harvard University.

Chapter 44
Inclusive Teaching for Our Queer Students: A Workshop

Michele DiPietro

"The first question is: Can learning take place if in fact it silences the voices of people it is supposed to teach? And the answer is: Yes. People learn that they don't count."

–H. Giroux, 1992, p. 16

This is not a generic workshop on heterosexism and homophobia. Rather, it challenges participants to understand the issues queer students face and how they impact their classroom performance and to develop attitudes and behaviors to make their classes inclusive. The workshop balances cognitive and affective components, starting with identity development models as means of understanding their students and continuing with a guided journey to bring relevant emotions out on the table. In keeping with the Marchesani-Adams model, participants then reconsider their teaching methods and content through video-clips, brainstorming and student quotes, and generate strategies.

Picture the following scenario. A class is discussing Tennessee Williams's "Cat on a Hot Tin Roof" in small groups. One group has a very productive discussion, using the gay undertones in the play to delve into the complexities of the main character Brick. In the second group, one imposing and vociferous student hijacks the discussion, dominating on the other students with his homophobic jokes about the characters in the play. Most students look uncomfortable, but laugh lukewarmly – all but one, that is. A diminutive student at the table tentatively tries to focus the discussion back on the play, to no avail. Under the barrage of derogatory comments this student becomes progressively withdrawn, in speech and body language. The instructor comes by to check on the group, and the student looks up hopefully for vindication, but the professor laughs wholeheartedly at the jokes. Defeated, the student has shrunk into his chair and is looking down dejectedly, hurt painted on his face. This is a fictional scenario from a videotape (Critical Incidents V, Learning and Teaching Center, University of Victoria, 2001), but similar situations are unfortunately more common than one would expect in college and university classrooms. Some instructors have deeply held beliefs against any kind of sexual diversity, whereas others simply don't know how to react to offensive student comments and choose the easy way out. Furthermore, data from Croteau and Talbot (2000) shows that most instructors are largely ignorant of issues pertaining to gay and lesbian students.

Homophobia and heterosexism can create a very inhospitable climate in the classroom, which in turn has a profoundly negative impact on learning; therefore, it behooves us as faculty developers to address them in our practice, while acknowledging that some developers might be as uncomfortable and as much in need of education as the faculty they serve.

Introduction and Terminology

This chapter describes a module I developed and offer at Carnegie Mellon as a diversity seminar in the graduate student teaching seminar series, but it is suitable for faculty as well. Because there is no agreement on the terminology to use, I need to define the terms I will use throughout.

I use "gay" and "lesbian" to indicate male and female same-sex orientation, respectively. I use "transgendered" as an umbrella term for all the gender-crossing and gender-bending identities, including transsexual and transvestite. In order to be inclusive of all sexual minorities I use the acronym LGBT (lesbian, gay, bisexual and transgendered). The only exception to this is in the title, where I use "queer" simply to avoid using an acronym without defining it first. I rarely use "homosexual" because its negative clinical connotations can be offensive to some; however, this term was more popular in the past and therefore it is present in some of the classic literature on the subject which I reference. This is more than a lexicon exercise, because some of these words are loaded and can impact people in unpredictable ways. For instance, the first time I ran the workshop, two graduate coordinators took issue with the word "queer" and did not want to advertise the seminar in their departments, because they felt it could be offensive to some of the students. In fact, "queer" seems to be the preferred word in academia (there are many queer studies departments and queer theory professors and textbooks), and this was a chance to start important conversations with those departments, but faculty developers should be aware of potential implications of their choices.

This seminar is not a generic workshop on heterosexism and homophobia; rather, it specifically addresses LGBT issues in the classroom, as they pertain to learning theory and motivation.

The objectives for the workshop follow three vectors:

- To introduce a rationale for inclusive teaching strategies that acknowledge and welcome lesbian, gay, bisexual and transgendered (LGBT) students.
- To understand the development of social identities (for example, LGBT identities as compared to heterosexual ones) and how they can impact the learning experiences of students.
- To discuss proactive teaching behaviors that create an inclusive learning environment and bring marginalized perspectives to the center of the classroom.

As with all other diversity seminars, I find it very useful to frame this one according to the four dimensions of the Marchesani-Adams (1992) model: know oneself, the students, what we teach, and how we teach.

Know yourself/know your students

The first half of the quote which opens this chapter is also used to open the workshop. Students are usually tempted to reply in the negative, and the second half of the quote already gets them thinking about implications of non-inclusive teaching. I acknowledge up front that the theme of the workshop can evoke feelings of hurt, anger, or fear, and that I want this to be a safe environment. Therefore, I always start with ground rules about participation, which include voluntary sharing of information, confidentiality of what is shared in the session, and respect of all opinions. As an ice-breaker I ask them to volunteer their name and department, to tell one thing LGBT students can't do that straight students can, and to share anything else they feel appropriate. They start to get to know each other and usually come up with a very thoughtful list, which I use to introduce the concept of privilege. This is a non-threatening way of introducing a difficult but central topic in diversity, but by examining the legal inequities that face the LGBT population the concept of privilege becomes evident. After this discussion, students are more responsive to racial and other forms of privilege in other seminars.

I also show some statistics to highlight the importance of inclusive teaching for LGBT students. From the study of LGBT students by Brown University Faculty Committee on the Status of Sexual Minorities (1989) we know that 66% feared harassment or discrimination by classmates; 40% feared harassment or discrimination by professors; 60% did not feel safe being open about their sexual orientation in class; and 53% censored their academic speech, writing, or actions in order to avoid anti-gay harassment or discrimination. Even the more recent study by Rhoads (1995) found that 100% of the LGBT students surveyed reported living "in constant fear." (p.A56)

I then introduce theoretical models to frame the discussion. Of the several available, I prefer the Cass (1979) model of Homosexual Identity Formation, because it combines psychological and social aspects, and because there is some statistical evidence in favor of it (Cass, 1984). The model hypothesizes six stages in the development of one's identity:

1. Confusion. In this stage, thoughts and feelings that are incongruous with one's taken-for-granted heterosexuality create conflict that can either be repressed or lead to the next stage.
2. Comparison. In this stage, individuals gather information on homosexuality through media or contact with LGBT people. Such information may resolve the internal conflict ("Who am I?") but it creates external conflict ("Should I tell people or try to hide?"). This new conflict forces further development.
3. Tolerance. People in this stage have increased contact with the LGBT community, leading to strong identification of themselves as gay, but keep putting forth a heterosexual persona, at least in the heterosexual world, leading to more conflict.
4. Acceptance. At this stage the conflict is at its peak and either leads to resignation to spend one's life trying to conform, or propels the individual into the coming out process. LGBT identity is disclosed to selected individuals only. Some people manage the conflict effectively at this level.
5. Pride. The LGBT identity and community are embraced as a good lifestyle. At the same time, people at this stage distance themselves from the heterosexual world, which is seen as the source of discrimination, hatred and bigotry.
6. Synthesis. People who get to this stage resolve the dichotomy by realizing that sexuality is only one part of their identity and that they don't need to direct their anger at heterosexual society as a whole. This stage is facilitated by positive interactions with heterosexual individuals.

Competing models as well as models specific to the formation of lesbian and bisexual identities are reviewed in Levine and Evans (1991). For theories of transgendered identity, see Bornstein (1994).

I present the Cass model and then prompt participants to start thinking about what stages their students are likely to be in and the degree of conflict they carry around, and how these variables can impact their learning experience. I also briefly go through the Hardiman-Jackson (1992) model of Social Identity Development to show that heterosexual people also go through stages of developing an identity as members of the dominant heterosexual group and the assumptions that go with it. The model starts with a *naïveté* stage, with no awareness of sexual orientation, much less judgment of it. For example, young boys often think nothing of holding hands until they are socialized not to do so. The socialization brings about the second stage, *acceptance,* where heterosexist norms are internalized. This process can happen passively (people pitying LGBT individuals as sick) or actively if people feel the need to act on their beliefs (for example, hate crimes). Eye-opening encounters with LGBT people can bring about the next stage, *resistance.* This process too can be passive, leading to feelings of injustice but powerlessness to stop heterosexism, or active, if people are willing to work on their own as well as societal homophobia. The third stage, *redefinition,* happens as people struggle to define their identity as heterosexual individuals as a positive one now that they understand how heterosexism, of which they have been part, oppresses other people. The final stage, *internalization,* marks the integration of the new values acquired in this trajectory in all aspects of life. The person now has a positive self-perception as a heterosexual individual who recognizes that everybody gains from ending heterosexism and who works to that end. College students are likely to be in stages two or three, so the conversation at this point moves on to what kind of attitudes such students bring to our classes, and one can start anticipating what problems can arise and what strategies might be effective.

Part of our Center's philosophy is always to attend to both the cognitive and affective aspects of a topic, especially with such emotional topics. Emotions are already in the room, so it's best to explore them fully, whether these emotions include our own fear of the other, our hurt at being marginalized, or our frustration at not understanding what differences we have with each other. A useful instrument for this is the "Guided Journey" exercise described in Wall et al. (2000). During this activity, the facilitator prompts the participants to write down on index cards things or people of great significance in their life (for example, a best friend growing up, a favorite memory from college, a dream for the future). The facilitator then reads episodes from the story of a gay man who lost all such things because of his homosexuality. One by one, at the right time, the facilitator collects the appropriate index cards and rips them in half (this short description doesn't do justice to this very powerful exercise). In the subsequent debriefing, participants have a chance to process their emotions. For many of them, this is the first time they put themselves in the shoes of an LGBT person and tried to empathize with the hurt, anger, or hopelessness LGBT people often experience. The main point I try to drive home with this activity is that an issue specific to LGBT people is that of "grieving loss of membership in the dominant heterosexist culture and entry into a permanently stigmatized status" (Dillon, 1986). Several graduate students singled this activity out in the seminar evaluations as the most effective segment of the workshop.

What we teach/how we teach

This is the challenging part of the workshop because it aims to change behavior. Even the best-intentioned participants acknowledge that they want to be receptive to these ideas but that it is hard to do so in the classroom ("What does chemistry have to do with all of this?"). I approach it from Connolly's (2000) continuum of classroom experiences, from marginalization to centralization, both explicit and implicit.

- *Explicit Marginalization.* In this classroom, homophobic or heterosexist comments are overt, from the instructor, other students, readings, or other instructional material, and they are never challenged.
- *Implicit Marginalization.* Messages in this classroom are not overt, but they are still being sent in a subtle way, for instance through systematic exclusion of the LGBT perspective and use of non-inclusive language.
- *Implicit Centralization.* In this classroom, the messages sent are positive, but still subtle. The instructor might challenge a homophobic student comment, or tackle an LGBT issue when prompted by a student. But the nature of these contributions is haphazard and unplanned, signaling that a systemic change has not occurred yet.
- *Explicit Centralization.* This environment sends an unequivocal message that LBGT students and their perspectives are valued and central to the course, and that homophobic behaviors are not accepted. This happens in a systematic way through explicit discussion of ground rules for participation, explicit statement in the syllabus, choice of topics or perspectives represented, inclusive language, and so forth.

Several points come up during the discussion of this framework. Students realize most of their behaviors are not in the first and most oppressive stage, but that they might still send some implicit non-inclusive signals. They also realize that even when they think they are supportive, their support arises from the serendipity of the moment, because usually none of them are in the final stage. While many TAs do not have final control over the syllabus, this discussion prompts them to think of other ways they can make their support more explicit. I make sure the discussion includes learning issues as well by introducing Renn's (1998) considerations of how the experiences of LGBT individuals can affect the four pillars of learning theory: involvement, motivation, emotions, and construction of meaning.

- *Involvement.* The atmosphere of intolerance or support affects involvement. LGBT students facing the daily possibility of harassment have less energy to devote to class. For instance, if a student is always monitoring her comments for fear of betraying her orientation, she won't be as likely to contribute meaningfully in classroom discussions. On the other hand, the process of coming out might unleash new energies, especially in a supportive classroom environment.

- *Motivation.* According to one motivational framework, motivation is influenced by students' needs and their expectations of success. Students' needs usually include self-actualization, achievement, competence, self-worth and personal goals. Unfortunately, societal messages negatively influence the sense of competence and self-worth of LGBT students, which in turn can influence their expectations about future achievement. Coupled with negative reinforcement in the classroom environment, these societal messages can lead to a cycle of learned helplessness. On the other hand, some LGBT students can take refuge in academic achievement as the only source of self-worth. Such students are quite successful, but the knowledge they generate can be very detached from the self.
- *Emotions.* Some emotions – surprise, excitement, pride, anger, embarrassment, fear, anxiety and grief – are central to the learning process. Fear of harassment can interfere with learning, and anxiety and alienation are very common among closeted students, who experience a public-private dichotomy. On the other hand, supportive instructors who include LGBT experiences in the curriculum can provide a sense of empowerment, along with excitement, pride, and other positive emotions.
- *Construction of Meaning.* An essential part of learning is the unlearning of misconceptions and inadequate paradigms and connecting new information to prior knowledge. Depending on their developmental stage, some LGBT students may already have needed to do significant unlearning and relearning in their personal life, so they can capitalize on the experience. At the same time, students who are trying to make meaning of new material in terms of their own LGBT identity might be discouraged to do so by their instructors, impeding the construction of "meaningful" personal knowledge.

This discussion of learning leads directly to strategies instructors can employ to foster a safe environment. To make the concepts more concrete, I anchor the discussion to the three minute video-clip with the Tennessee Williams vignette I described in the beginning of this essay. Careful facilitation of what has happened in the two groups is needed to help seminar participants begin to recognize and respond to issues in the classroom with which they perhaps have had no personal experience. For instance it is easy to make the assumption that the withdrawn student is gay, but this is not necessarily the case. Maybe the reason he's withdrawing is because he has a gay sibling. Maybe the homophobic student is himself gay and self-loathing. As usual in diversity work, we need to check our own assumptions at the door. Many participants feel sorry for the student, and argue that the instructor should have nipped the disruption in the bud. True enough, but many also don't realize that the whole group is suffering. In this case, the jokes create an environment that does not allow anyone in that group to genuinely engage with the full scope of the material. The analysis can move to inclusive teaching strategies such as using appropriate language, avoiding tokenism, setting ground rules, and being an ally (Washington & Evans, 1991; Broido, 2000). After talking about teaching methods, I briefly discuss what a curriculum that explicitly includes the LGBT perspective might look like in various domains (see Appendix I).

As a final point of the workshop, I introduce Harro's (2000) cycle of socialization. The circular diagram illustrates the various steps through which we are socialized into the existing biased culture. The diagram is especially powerful because it shows that we are part of the culture and, without taking further steps, we can't help but reinforce it and transmit it, inertia being the operative principle. Only by actively interrupting the cycle, educating ourselves, and taking a stand can we induce any change. As an immediate way of interrupting the cycle, I suggest participants get involved in the SafeZone program on campus. SafeZone (present on many campuses nationally) is a network of allies committed to providing a safe and affirming environment for anyone dealing with issues of sexual orientation and gender identity. I invite the associate dean of student affairs and the coordinator for LGBT concerns to the seminar to illustrate the role of allies and to describe the related resources available on campus. I recommend faculty developers to partner with these student service providers to maximize their impact. In this specific case, representatives from student affairs helped to broaden conversation to include support to students outside the classroom (for example , advising) and seminar participants made contact with the right point persons so that if issues arise in their classrooms in the future they can contact them for help. Concluding the workshop in this way also leaves participants with a sense of efficacy and some very concrete strategies they can implement immediately.

Conclusion

As faculty developers, we have the potential to bring to the forefront a topic that is central to education but too often stays invisible. The impact we can have is significant in terms of outcomes and behaviors. Several participants shared in their evaluation comments that they think of the Center's workshop as an oasis, one of the very few places on campus where important issues in the classroom can be discussed. Moreover, other participants have acknowledged the sense of empowerment that comes from learning the language to talk about these issues and acquiring tools to promote inclusiveness or deal effectively with potentially hurtful situations in class. Several of the workshop participants took the SafeZone training, and one participant commented that the things they learn in the Center's workshops not only make them better instructors, but more importantly better people.

References

Bornstein, K. (1997). *My gender workbook: How to become a real man, a real woman, the real you, or something else entirely*. New York: Routledge.

Broido, E. M. (2000). Ways of being an ally to lesbian, gay, and bisexual students. In V. Wall, & N. Evans (Eds.), *Toward acceptance: Sexual orientation issues on campus* (pp. 345-369). Lanham, MD: University Press of America.

Brown University Faculty Committee on the Status of Sexual Minorities (1989). *Lesbian, gay, and bisexual students on the Brown University campus: A Study in progress*. Providence, RI.

Cass, V. C. (1979). Homosexual identity formation: A theoretical model. *Journal of Homosexuality, 4*, 219-35.

Cass, V. C. (1984). Homosexual identity formation: Testing a theoretical model. *Journal of Sex Research, 20*, 143-167.

Connolly, M. (2000). Issues for lesbian, gay and bisexual students in traditional college classrooms. In V.A. Wall, & N.J. Evans (Eds.), *Toward acceptance: Sexual orientation issues on campus* (pp. 109-130). Lanham, MD: University Press of America.

Croteau, J.M., & Talbot, D.M. (2000). Understanding the landscape: An empirical view of lesbian, gay, and bisexual issues in the student affairs profession. In V.A. Wall, & N.J. Evans (Eds.), *Toward acceptance: Sexual orientation issues on campus* (pp. 3-28). Lanham, MD: University press of America.

Dillon, C. (1986). Preparing college health professionals to deliver gay-affirmative services. *Journal of American College Health, 35*(1), 36-40.

Giroux, H. (1992). *Border crossing: Cultural workers and the politics of education*. New York: Routledge.

Hardiman, R., & Jackson, B. W. (1992). Racial identity development: Understanding racial dynamics in college classrooms and on campus. In Adams, M. (Ed.), *Promoting diversity in college classrooms: Innovative responses for the curriculum, faculty, and institutions* (pp.21-37). New Directions for Teaching and Learning, No. 52. San Francisco: Jossey-Bass.

Harro, B. (2000). The cycle of socialization. In Adams, et al. (Eds.), *Readings for diversity and social justice* (pp. 15-21). New York: Routledge.

Learning and Teaching Center (2001). *Critical incidents V: Diversity and inclusion*. University of Victoria, Canada.

Levine, H., & Evans, N. J. (1991). The development of gay, lesbian, and bisexual identities. In V.A. Wall, & N.J. Evans (Eds.), *Beyond tolerance: Gays, lesbians and bisexuals on campus* (pp.1-24). Lanham, MD: University Press of America.

Marchesani, L., & Adams, M. (1992). Dynamics of diversity in the teaching-learning process: A faculty development model for analysis and action. In Adams, M. (Ed.), *Promoting diversity in college classrooms: Innovative responses for the curriculum, faculty, and institutions* (pp.9-20). New Directions in Teaching and Learning, No. 52. San Francisco: Jossey-Bass.

Renn, K. A. (1998). Lesbian, gay, bisexual, and transgendered student in the college classroom. In Sanlo, R.L. (Ed.), *Working with lesbian, gay, bisexual and transgendered college students.* (pp.231-237). Westport, CT: Greenwood Press.

Rhoads, R. A. (1995). The campus climate for students who leave the closet. *The Chronicle of Higher Education, 41*(20), A56.

Wall, V, Washington, J., Evans, N., & Papish, R. (2000). From the trenches: Strategies for facilitating lesbian, gay, and bisexual awareness programs for college students. In V.A. Wall, & N.J. Evans (Eds.), *Toward acceptance: Sexual orientation issues on campus* (pp.157-189). Lanham, MD: University Press of America.

Michele DiPietro is the Associate Director for Graduate Support, Eberly Center for Teaching Excellence and an Instructor, Department of Statistics, Carnegie Mellon University. He has presented nationally on topics of diversity in the classroom and teaches a variety of statistics courses, including a freshman seminar titled "The Statistics of the Gay and Lesbian Population."

Appendix I

"Queering" the Curriculum: A Starting Point

While some disciplines (for example , English, history, religion) seem more easily open to the incorporation of LGBT concerns and to surfacing homophobic and heterosexist assumptions, the "obvious" disciplines are not the only ones that merit such attention. The ultimate judgment is left to those who are experts in their own field.

Accounting

Accountants can be trained to effectively respond to the needs of gay clients, particularly couples. Such couples do not have the right to file taxes jointly, and will probably need advice on how to navigate the system. Also, they might need to be counseled about joint accounts and joint ownership of property. They might also be looking for politically correct funds in which to invest their money.

Art

Both classic and modern art incorporates LGBT themes or undertones, lending itself to various levels of analysis, from artistic to social to moral.

Architecture

Classes like Urbanism or American Neighborhoods can incorporate a unit about gay neighborhoods, why they are present in most major American cities, why they developed in specific locations, how this phenomenon influences the life in those cities, and so forth.

Biology

There is some research demonstrating that the shape of the brain differs slightly from straight to gay males. These findings give credit to the theory that homosexuality is at least in part induced by our chromosomes rather than by the environment, and reopens the "nature vs. nurture" debate. Ethical issues in "gene therapy" or "genetic counseling" can be addressed as well.

Criminology

Assaults against LGBT people are one of the most common forms of hate crimes. A unit on this topic could include nationwide statistics over time, the problem with unreported/misclassified crimes, the current ways of prosecuting such crimes, the status of hate crime legislation across different States, which minorities are included in different laws, political and historical reasons for discrepancies, and other related issues.

Demography

The general public is rather ignorant about the demography of the LGBT population. Queers are assumed to cluster in the big cities, yet the 2000 Census shows that there are gay couples sharing households in every county of the U.S., even the most rural (with the exception of a handful). Related topics are: level of education, income, and all other demographic indicators.

Geography

For such classes as Human or Social Geography, see Architecture.

Law

Queer unmarried couples are not afforded several basic rights that heterosexual couples have. Such couples need legal advice on how to bypass the law (in terms of wills, power of attorney, and so forth). Basic training for lawyers should enable them to advise such couples in the steps they need to take for their financial security. Family law classes should include discussions of Vermont same-sex unions, the rights they grant and the ones they don't.

Marketing

Many firms today are trying to enter the gay market in their effort to diversify, because most gay couples are DINK (Double Income No Kids). Gay money does not come cheap, however, as it appears that gay customers are quite discriminating about where they rest their loyalties. Gay market consultants have developed guidelines for firms wishing to position themselves in this market; among other things, they advise the firms to at least offer domestic partner benefits to their own employees. Such techniques easily constitute a unit on market strategies.

Modern Languages

For more advanced classes, where the course covers both language and culture, some instructors have introduced units about the gay culture in foreign countries in terms of gay life abroad or famous queer personages from specific countries.

Nursing/Medicine

Sensitivity training for people working with LGBT patients is in order, especially those with HIV/AIDS (and even heterosexual patients at that). It is very common to hear complaints from patients claiming to have been mistreated and even blamed for the disease they carry.

ROTC

The leadership classes are especially suitable to an honest analysis of the "Don't ask, don't tell, don't pursue" policy regarding gays in the military, its meaning, its significance, the way it is currently applied, and the genuine way the Clinton administration envisioned its enforcement.

SDS

An instructor in the Social and Decision Sciences taught for a number of years a class called "Applied Social and Policy Theory: The case of AIDS." The class was built around understanding how risk perception and decision theory can explain the spread of the epidemic and what policies would be in treating it. While AIDS is not an LGBT disease, including this course in the curriculum might address the concerns of queer students who find themselves in a statistically high-risk group. Also, courses on human rights (habitually offered in the department) could incorporate a unit on the gay rights movement.

Statistics

There are many surveys dealing with LGBT issues that could be used in class to illustrate various statistical points. I use the study on gay teen suicides as reported by some magazines to illustrate how the media misinterpret statistics and propagate false notions. The Kinsey study itself can be used to illustrate sampling bias, as he did not use a random sample but recruited many participants from gay bars. The problem of estimating the percentage of queers in the population is an open research problem, because many people will lie and say they are heterosexual, thereby providing a biased estimate. Ways to correct the bias are methodologically very interesting and can definitely be illustrated in class as a hands-on activity.

Zoology

Several animal species practice homosexuality, habitually or in view of special circumstances, for sexual or social purposes. This gives a new meaning to "natural" sexual behavior, and could easily be incorporated in the curriculum.

Chapter 45
Key Resources on Diversity for Faculty Developers: An Idiosyncratic Annotated Bibliography

Stephanie Nickerson

This is an idiosyncratic list of resources—books, articles, videos and websites. This chapter encompasses many issues, and my primary concern is creating environments in classrooms, in departments, and on campuses that encourage learning for everyone. Some of the resources listed here focus on several aspects of diversity, others only on one. I have not required each resource to be comprehensive. I chose these materials with faculty developers new to diversity issues in mind; however, those resources with an * should be most useful to faculty developers who are experienced in diversity issues.

1. *American Association of Colleges and Universities* (AAC&U). Retrieved June 11, 2004, from http://www.diversityweb.org/

Originally developed with University of Maryland, this site has been run by AAC&U since 2002. It is a comprehensive website that seeks to be a central clearinghouse for information relating to diversity on campuses in higher education. The website addresses macro-issues, for example, broad political issues and policies and institutional visions. At the same time, it examines more micro-issues, such as strategies for teachers who want to learn to address diversity effectively in homogeneous classroom settings. This is a good place to start a search on any topic related to diversity in higher education.

2. *American Indian Higher Education Consortium* (AIHEC). Retrieved August 21, 2005, from http://www.aihec.org/

Here is a starting place for learning more about the Tribal Colleges. AIHEC's mission is to "maintain commonly held standards of quality in American Indian education; support the development of new tribally controlled colleges; promote and assist in the development of legislation to support American Indian higher education; and encourage greater participation by American Indians in the development of higher education policy" (from website). There are over 30 colleges in AIHEC. On the main page is an article,

Under a link called "The Colleges" is a document called "Tribal Colleges: An Introduction," which lays out what the Tribal Colleges are, the 30 year old Tribal College Movement, who and how many students they serve, what makes them unique, and what the pressing issues are facing Tribal Colleges.

3. Anderson, R.W. (n.d.) *Queer in the Classroom.* Retrieved June 11, 2004, from http://home.earthlink.net/~andersonrob/Bibliography.html

This is a large semi-annotated bibliography of sexuality in the classroom, focused primarily on "queer issues in the college classroom." It is not dated, but the last reference is 1998, and it is still regularly cited.

4. Belenky, M.F.; Clinchy, B. M.; Goldberger, N.; & Tarule, J. M. *Women's ways of knowing: The development of self, voice, and mind.* New York: Basic Books.

This is a classic study. It is a response to William Perry's (1970) *Forms of intellectual and ethical development in the college years* (NY: Holt, Rinehart & Winston), a study of college men–also a classic. The book is an attempt to understand women's intellectual development and how women learn. Essentially, what the authors posit is that women, in general, develop differently than men. The authors' argument is that many women know with their whole beings. They do not separate the head and the heart, or if they do, they do not feel complete. *Women's Ways* is a mushy book, in the sense that concepts are not fully clarified, and there is an exciting, exploratory quality to the work.

I saw my own epistemological grappling and many of my students' as well reflected in the excerpts of interviews with women at different stages of development. Several women I know claim the book changed their lives because they felt understood for once, and they could make sense of some of their difficulties in traditional classroom settings.

5. Border, L. & Chism, N. V. N., (Eds.). (1992). *Teaching for diversity.* New Directions for Teaching and Learning, No. 49. San Francisco: Jossey-Bass.

This issue of *New Directions* is often cited in the literature on faculty and teaching development and diversity, and appropriately so. It contains key articles for faculty developers. Some are worth special mention:

James A. Anderson and Maurianne Adams's "Acknowledging the

Learning Styles of Diverse Student Populations: Implications for Instructional Design" describes research on learning styles and suggests the kind of instructional strategies that students with different learning styles would tend to prefer. I have used this article in several productive workshops on other topics to incorporate diversity into the discussion.

In "Ensuring Equitable Participation in College Classes," Myra and David Sadker outline some of the faulty assumptions faculty often make about student learning and classroom climate and suggest strategies for making the classroom more inclusive, for promoting equality of participation.

Border and Chism include an annotated bibliography (including videos) on demographic patterns, cultural and cognitive characteristics, particular demographic groups, classroom communication, and curriculum issues. It is more than 10 years old, and some of the articles have become classics. (For annotation of the complete volume, see the Center for Research on Learning and Teaching, University of Michigan, Multicultural Teaching Services website, later.)

6. Center for Instructional Development and Research and Instructional Media Services. (1991). *Teaching in the diverse classroom* [Motion picture]. Seattle, WA: University of Washington.

This video suggests four things that college instructors need to do to teach effectively in diverse classrooms: include all students in the learning process; recognize and address different ways of learning; promote a climate of respect among students; and recognize diversity through curriculum choices. The 37 minute video shows ways instructors can do all these things.

*7. *Center for Research on Learning and Teaching, University of Michigan, Multicultural Teaching*. Retrieved June 11, 2004, from http://www.crlt.umich.edu/multiteaching/multiteaching.html

In addition to linking to occasional papers, annotated bibliographies, and support services within the University of Michigan, all connected to multicultural issues in teaching, this site also has links to many external sources on discipline-based and topic-based teaching and learning concerns. One of the innovative offerings from Michigan is the CRLT Players – an interactive theater troupe. The group develops vignettes related to multicultural issues and brings them into the classroom to engage students and generate discussion.

*8. Derek Bok Center for Teaching and Learning. (1992). *Race in the classroom: Multiplicity of experience* [Motion picture]. Cambridge, MA: Harvard University.

This video consists of short vignettes of difficult racial incidents in classrooms. These episodes last from 20 seconds to several minutes. They are useful for generating discussion about how to manage such classroom events. Total playing time is 19 minutes, and a comprehensive instructor's manual is included.

9. Derek Bok Center for Teaching and Learning. (1992). *Teaching in America* [Motion picture]. Cambridge, MA: Harvard University.

This 34 minute videotape describes strategies different international teaching assistants use to make their class sections useful and successful for their students and for themselves. It is useful for new international faculty as well as for international teaching assistants. The suggestions are concrete and practical. See Sarkisian for a companion book.

10. *Disability studies in the humanities, American studies crossroads project, Georgetown University.* (2000). Retrieved June 11, 2004, from http://www.georgetown.edu/crossroads/interests/ds-hum/index.html

This rich website contains disability-related listservs, syllabi, announcements, directories, bibliographies, descriptions of films, and other resources. For example, one can link to the American Sign Language (ASL) Browser to see many words signed in ASL.

11. *DO-IT program: Disabilities, opportunities, internetworking, and technology.* (2005). University of Washington. Retrieved August 21, 2005, from http://www.washington.edu/doit/

This is a comprehensive site for people with disabilities and for people who work with people with disabilities. One important section of the site is called The Faculty Room, (Click Postsecondary Education at the top of the site) which is directed to faculty members and administrators and advises them on "how to create classroom environments and academic activities that maximize the learning of all students, including those with disabilities" (from site). There is lots of information for instructors about accommodations for students with specific disabilities, and web links, slide-show presentations, case studies, short videos, and FAQs. The Faculty Room has much of the key information on the DO-IT site for faculty and faculty developers. However, it is not the only section related to teaching and learning in college. There is a large section on making distance learning optimally accessible. There is a science, technology, engineering and math section that addresses such issues as teaching lab courses with students with disabilities, "AccessSTEM."

There are dedicated parts of the site addressed to high level administrators, to K-12 teachers, to high school and college students. There are also parts of the site focused on helping people with disabilities get into and succeed in college and choose careers.

12. Fiol-Matta, L. & Chamberlain, M. K. (Eds.). (1994). *Women of color and the multicultural curriculum: Transforming the college classroom.* NY: The Feminist Press at the City University of NY.

This book came out of a 1985 series of colloquia hosted by the Ford Foundation, which concluded that too little consideration had been given to roles, perspectives, and contributions of women of color in the college curriculum. Ethnic and racial studies programs focused on men, and women's studies programs focused on whites. Ford decided to fund more work and developed a series of grants and programs. The National Council on Research on Women coordinated the overall project, and the book is part of the dissemination activities of the multifaceted program.

There are three main sections: "Faculty Development," which has two general chapters and then describes the curriculum transformation "faculty seminar models" for various disciplines, primarily at the University of California-L.A.; "Model Undergraduate Curriculum" includes a number of course syllabi, annotated bibliographies, and course assignments from many different colleges and universities; the "Focus on Puerto Rican Studies" section is a compendium of materials from various disciplines focused on Puerto Rican women.

The book treats "gender, race, and class as sources of social stratification rather than as mere difference. Adequately doing so requires that we understand the social meaning attached to those constructions and treat them as categories for analyzing social experience.... Race, gender and class, then, become analytical categories rather than merely empirical variables" (Leslie I. Hill, p.17).

*13. Fisher, B. M. (2001). *No angel in the classroom: Teaching through feminist discourse.* New York: Rowman & Littlefield.

Reading this book is like having a conversation with a highly empathetic, experienced, and well-read teaching mentor. I do not teach courses concerned explicitly with social justice, and teachers of courses related to social justice are Fisher's audience. However, I love this book because it is dense with questions and ideas with which many teachers grapple as we think about how to teach our own material: What is the nature of authority in the classroom? What does the ethic of care have to do with teaching? How does one demonstrate care without abusing one's power?

Community in the classroom, autonomy, self-disclosure, safety, creating a safe place, and "safety for whom?" are all issues Fisher raises. She examines the facets of each issue. It is not in any way a "how to" book. Rather, Fisher raises questions and analyzes the issues relating to those questions. She sometimes describes why she chooses a particular way to respond. It is a well-reasoned, well-grounded book.

Fisher takes several chapters to trace the development of her intertwined theory and practice of furthering social justice through "feminist discourse." In the process, she also maps out a history of the women's movement. One can read this book on many levels and benefit.

14. Frederick, P. (1995). Walking on eggs: Mastering the dreaded diversity discussion. *College Teaching, 43*(3): 83-92. Reprinted in B. A. Pescosolido & R. Aminzade (Eds.). (1999). *The Social worlds of higher education: Fieldguide.* Thousand Oaks, CA: Pine Forge Press.

Aimed at helping teachers help themselves and their students to work with multicultural content in the classroom, Frederick's focus is on nine strategies to engage students with each other and with multicultural issues. He describes these strategies, such as using powerful evocative quotations, and gives examples of how they might be used. He also describes strategies – such as establishing guidelines for discussion early on in the course, grounding discussion in a close reading of a text – to create a climate conducive to such discussion. Frederick also offers strategies for dealing with classroom crises arising from discussion of such issues.

15. Friedman, E. G.; Kolmar, W. K.; Flint, C.B.; & Rothenberg, P. (Eds.). (1996). *Creating an inclusive college curriculum: A teaching sourcebook from the New Jersey Project.* NY: Teachers College Press.

This book consists of articles written by participants in the New Jersey Project, a curriculum change project, funded by the Higher Education Department of New Jersey. It started in 1986 and originally focused "on the integration of women and issues of gender into the higher education curriculum...[but it] rapidly adopted a more inclusive orientation, recognizing that it is neither possible nor desirable to separate gender from race and ethnicity, class, sexuality, or culture" (Rothenberg, p. 14).

There are 47 chapters divided into three parts: "Creating a statewide curriculum project;" "Rethinking course content, perspective, and pedagogy;" and "Syllabi and narratives." This third section of 32 chapters comprises the bulk of the book.

16. Gillespie, K.H. (Ed.). (2002). *A guide to faculty development: Practical advice, examples, and resources.* Bolton, MA: Anker.

In this primer on faculty development, Gillespie has included three chapters on diversity issues: "Conceptualizing, Designing, and Implementing Multicultural Faculty Development Activities," by Christine A. Stanley, is a useful chapter for a newcomer. Stanley describes factors one needs to consider, offers her four-dimensional model of multicultural teaching, and outlines specific ideas about how to design multicultural faculty development activities—on workshop and individual levels.

"What we Value, We Talk about: Including Lesbian, Gay, Bisexual, and Transgender People," by Christine Imbra and Helen Rallis, gives resources and definitions related to this specific topic. Again, the material is sufficiently clear and basic that it will put a newcomer to these aspects of diversity on the right track.

"Methods for Addressing Diversity in the Classroom," by Lee Warren, describes how she uses written and videotaped cases and what she calls "case-in-point experiential learning" in which the "case" becomes what has been happening in the class as students actually take it. She also describes what she has termed "The Class Workshop," in which participants discuss their own perceived socioeconomic class and share with others what the benefits and drawbacks are of being from a certain class. She makes the point that the U.S. likes to think of itself as a classless society, but in fact there are rigid class differences that affect us all.

In order to do "case-in-point" activities well, one needs to know something about facilitating groups and group dynamics. Warren makes group facilitation sound easier than it is, in fact.

In addition to these three articles, the rest of the book has very good chapters on other key aspects of faculty development.

17. Intercultural Resource Corporation. (1993). *A different place* and *Creating community* [Motion pictures]. Yarmouth, ME: Intercultural Press.

These are two companion videos: *A different place* (20 minutes) presents a skit of an ongoing classroom discussion with an American instructor, three American students, and international students—including one each from South Africa, Japan, El Salvador, Russia and China. After the discussion, each of the participants talks to the camera about their struggles in class.

In *Creating community* (15 minutes), experts analyze what happened in the classroom discussion and make recommendations for instructors to increase the probability of creating an inclusive classroom.

18. *Intergroup Relations Center at Arizona State University*. Retrieved June 11, 2004, from http://www.asu.edu/provost/intergroup/geninfomain.html

The Intergroup Relations Center was started in 1997 to promote positive intergroup relations among people on campus and to improve the campus climate. It has grown to be involved in national diversity initiatives. The site includes diversity links for instructors related to pedagogy and curriculum. This is one of the rare resources that acknowledges that with diversity comes conflict and the need to manage that conflict in a positive way.

*19. Jacobson, W.; Borgford-Parnell, J.; Frank, K.; Peck, M.; & Reddick, L. (2002). Operational diversity: Saying what we mean, doing what we say. In D. Lieberman & C. Wehlburg, (Eds.), *To improve the academy, 20.* Bolton, MA: Anker.

This article describes a process that the staff at the University of Washington's Center for Instructional Development and Research went through (probably still on-going) to articulate their beliefs about diversity, turn those beliefs into action, and to assess the outcomes. The authors describe what is a long-term project with multiple strands.

The staff essentially started where most of the diversity research suggests, by examining their own thoughts, feelings, and beliefs. From there, they developed a statement on diversity to make explicit their implicit assumptions that were guiding their practice. This was clearly an iterative process. They also surveyed themselves based on the specific actions described in their diversity statement, contrasting what they *actually do* in their consulting work with faculty to what they think they *should do.*

Through examining the findings from the survey, the staff uncovered areas where they were not as effective as they wanted to be, and, as a result, each person committed to doing specific professional development activities related to diversity.

According to the authors, the effects of this process include staff members' raised awareness of and attention to diversity issues; increased development of materials, workshops and resources on the topic; and "...demonstrate[d] ... possibility of change" (p. 135). By virtue of going through such a process and understanding the complexity of it, this faculty development unit is in a position to collaborate with other departments to help them make such a change.

I think it is a good model for other organizations that have the commitment to undertake a similar culture change.

20. Lutzker, M. (1995). *Multiculturalism in the college curriculum: A handbook of strategies and resources for faculty.* The Greenwood Educators' Reference Collection. Westport, CN: Greenwood Press.

Lutzker is a librarian and has taken the perspective of teachers needing help in developing a more multicultural approach to their courses. (Her definition of "multicultural" appears to include race, ethnicity, nationality, and gender.) In the introduction she describes models of introducing diversity into the curriculum and rebuts frequently cited reasons for not including it into curricula. The book includes two main sections: "Strategies" and "Resources." Under "Strategies," Lutzker outlines ways instructors in any discipline can think about their courses so that they address them in a new way. She asks instructors to think critically about each aspect of their course: Develop reading lists with a critical eye, evaluate the textbook, rearrange the syllabus around broad themes, and redesign student assignments. She alerts instructors to the inherent bias in much language and in certain labels and descriptions, and she highlights the different importance and forms of names in different cultures. Lutzker lists a number of ideas instructors can use to educate themselves and their students about multicultural issues, and she outlines a number of ways to design multicultural student projects, including some that do not require library research. She also addresses the problem of student resistance and how to address it in the classroom.

Under "Resources," Lutzker the librarian is in full evidence: These chapters are essentially annotated bibliographies of encyclopedias, key primary sources, books of historical photographs, catalogs of films and videos, directories, and periodicals. The book was published in 1995, so the Internet resources are not up-to-date. Very useful, however, is her chapter called "Locating Additional Resources: Hints for Searching the Online Catalog" in which she demystifies Library of Congress key words and subject headings. In her appendix she includes a list of publishers and distributors of multicultural books. Finally, she includes a highly personal "selected annotated bibliography" related to multiculturalism in many different disciplines.

21. McCloskey, D. N. (1999). *Crossing: A memoir.* University of Chicago Press.

This book is not about teaching and learning. It is not even about college issues. It is a memoir of an academic, however, a transgendered person. Donald McCloskey was a successful economist with two grown children who, after 30 years of marriage, became Deirdre McCloskey. I was jarred at first reading this book because she has a quirky writing style, and she spoke in two voices (Donald's and Deirdre's) and sometimes a third, Dee's—who was sort of a transitory being once McCloskey decided to make the gender change but had not been through all the operations (facial plastic surgery and electrolysis, rib removal, breast augmentation, voice box operations, and genital change).

McCloskey is very good at explaining women's perspectives because, in a sense, she had to learn them as a grown up. So she has trained to be a good observer. Also she is six feet tall and does not want to be taken for a man in drag, so she feels she must get "it right," so she will not seem campy.

Deirdre is very likable, and the way she describes Donald suggests that he was a sort of macho, not so likeable, in fact an arrogant fellow, with no sense of his "feminine side" as far as I can tell. Deirdre also works hard to be honest, and she seems so pleased to be a woman even though she recognizes how much she has lost by making such a choice (including her marriage and her two children). But, as she says, (I am paraphrasing): I wasn't *unhappy* as Donald. But I am happier as Deirdre. It's not about sex. It's about identity. This book makes you understand that. [For a very different approach to describing her "life in two genders," see Jennifer Finney Boylan's 2003 memoir, *She's not there*, New York: Broadway Books.]

22. McIntosh, P. (1989). White privilege: Unpacking the invisible knapsack. *Peace and Freedom*. July/August, 10-12.

This classic article, reprinted many places, outlines the advantages white people have that non-white people do not have, but that white people tend not to acknowledge, even to themselves.

23. Morey, A. I.; & Kitano, M. K. (Eds.). (1997). *Multicultural course transformation in higher education: A broader truth.* Boston: Allyn & Bacon.

This book differs from Fiol-Matta and Chamberlain's and Friedman et al.'s (see earlier) in that it is more of a textbook. The chapters were written for the book, as opposed to the book being a dissemination of information from projects. However, similarities among the three books are that they all make the point that curriculum transformation is a long-term continuous process that, to be effective, requires supportive organizational change and faculty development. Each book describes models for change and then gives examples of the changed or changing courses within a curriculum.

Morey and Kitano describe a model for course change planning that urges instructors to set explicit multicultural goals for a specific course. Then the book suggests key concepts around which instructors can develop teaching units:

Race, gender, sexuality, and ability as socially constructed concepts

Postmodern challenges to scientific views of objectivity

The politics of representation in language and the media

Tension between community and diversity—do we emphasize differences among groups or …commonalities? (p. 35)

Other chapters address classroom dynamics and the "hidden curriculum" – that is, the maintenance of the status quo – student assessment, strategies for teaching classes with diverse students, creating a good learning climate for students for whom English is not their first language, and chapters on addressing multicultural concerns in various disciplines and levels of college courses.

24. *A multicultural prism: Voices from the field.* [Motion picture]. (1994). Macomb, IL: Western Illinois University.

Experts in the field, primarily professors of Education, discuss the definitions of "multicultural education," describe ways to implement multicultural education on various campuses, and analyze the resistance to such changes in academia. Most useful are the three vignettes (totaling about six minutes playing time out of a total of 38 minutes) relating to multicultural education.

25. *National Consortium of Directors of LGBT Resources in Higher Education.* (2002). Retrieved June 11, 2004, from http://www.lgbtcampus.org/

The site is a comprehensive place for finding out about Lesbian, Gay, Bisexual, and Transgender programs, jobs, organizations, exhibits, and so forth.

26. Ouellett, M. L., & Stanley, C. A. (2004). Fostering diversity in a faculty development organization. In *To improve the academy, 22,* 206-225. Bolton, MA: Anker.

As a follow up piece to their 2000 *To Improve the Academy* article (Read the annotation on Stanley and Ouellett first), Matthew Ouellett and Christine Stanley continue to track Professional and Organizational Development Network in Higher Education's (POD's) progress toward becoming a truly multicultural organization. In particular, they examine historically two key initiatives that POD's Diversity Commission runs: The Travel Grant Program and the Internship Program. Both are designed to attract and retain people from underrepresented groups to POD and to faculty development. Ouellett and Stanley report on an empirical exploration of the two programs. The results suggest both are successful conduits for new members to POD; both build on POD's reputation for networking, openness and informal mentoring; and the programs generate positive outcomes for both participants as individuals and for POD as an organization.

The authors argue that POD has developed over the years into an organization that is on the brink of becoming truly multicultural—that is, that POD "[a]ctively engages in envisioning, planning, and problem solving to find ways to ensure the full inclusion of all" (p. 218). Ouellett and Stanley have been on the forefront over the years pulling and prodding POD to become a multicultural organization. The good news is that they document and celebrate substantial changes POD has made toward that goal.

27. Roberts, H.; Gonzales, J. C.; Harris, O. D.; Huff, D. J.; Johns, A. M.; Lou, R.; & Scott. O. L. (1994). *Teaching from a multicultural perspective. Survival Skills for Scholars*, Vol. 12, Thousand Oaks, CA: Sage.

As all the *Survival Skills for Scholars* volumes aim to be, this book is short and practical. The authors assume the good will and motivation of the reader to want to teach from a multicultural perspective (which seems to be defined here to include race, nationality, ethnicity, class, gender, and sexual orientation). They write from both a personal perspective as well as a research base.

The authors offer activities and processes for improving the learning experiences for all students. Much of what they suggest can be summarized as their advocacy for on-going assessment and self-assessment by instructor and students, within contexts that make sense to all of them. The authors discuss different classroom teaching methods, learning and assessment projects, ways of revising the curriculum, and the needs of linguistically diverse students. The book concludes with a moving chapter on being a mentor to nontraditional students.

28. Sarkisian, E. (1997). *Teaching American students: A guide for international faculty and teaching assistants in colleges and universities.* (Rev. Ed.). Cambridge, MA: Harvard Printing.

This is a short, practical book for international instructors. It gives the reader appropriate information about U.S. college students and higher education expectations in the U.S. It includes concrete advice on making presentations understandable and interesting and on creating opportunities for interaction in the classroom. See Derek Bok Center for companion videotape.

29. Stanley, C. A.; & Ouellett, M. L. (2000). On the path: POD as a multicultural organization. In *to improve the academy, 18,* 38-54. Bolton, MA: Anker.

Christine Stanley and Mathew Ouellett explore the organizational history of the Professional and Organizational Development Network in Higher Education, or POD, as it relates to diversity, particularly through the vehicle of POD's Diversity Commission. Subscribing to the theory of Multicultural Organization Development, they track systematic change efforts to make POD an organization that not only values diversity but also works to combat social injustice and other forms of oppression. Without declaring POD to be at a specific stage of development toward the quest of becoming truly multicultural, they encourage readers of POD's annual journal to move the organization further by taking responsibility for the organizational change effort in concrete ways. They believe that a multicultural POD will be a better organization for all members.

30. Tatum, B. D. (1992). Talking about race, learning about racism: The application of racial identity development theory in the classroom. *Harvard Educational Review, 62*(1), 1-24.

Tatum describes how student resistance to talking about issues of racism in the college classroom can be understood and addressed productively by applying racial identity theory and helping students make sense of their resistance. Identity development theory is also useful as a framework for understanding conflicting behaviors between individuals of different races.

31.Tips for teachers: Teaching in a racially diverse classroom. (1997). Derek Bok Center for Teaching and Learning and the Office of Race Relations and Minority Affairs, Harvard University. Retrieved June 11, 2004, from http://www.fas.harvard.edu/~bok_cen/docs/TFTrace.html

This document includes a useful set of questions for instructors to examine their assumptions about different sensitive race issues. Also, it has suggestions for approaches to classroom discussion and inclusion in the classroom. It describes some specific strategies to manage hot moments.

32. Wah, L. M. (1994). *The color of fear.* [Motion picture], Berkeley, CA, StirFry Seminars & Consulting.

Eight men of different races (AfricanAmerican, Latino, White, and Asian) spend a weekend together to talk about personal issues of race and discrimination. It is a personal and powerful 90 minute program. [See Women's Video Project for a comparable video focused on women.]

33. Warren, L. (2002). Managing Hot Moments in the Classroom. Retrieved August 16, 2005, from http://bokcenter.fas.harvard.edu/docs/hotmoments.html

Warren has written a short, practical article that encourages instructors to keep their cool when a difficult moment happens in class so that students can learn something from the incident.

34. Women's Video Project. (1998). *The way home.* [Motion picture]. Oakland, CA: The World Trust.

Women in eight different "councils" (Indigenous, AfricanAmerican, Arab, Asian, EuropeanAmerican, Jewish, Latina, and Multiracial) discuss their personal issues of race, racism, diversity, homophobia, and oppression. The 92 minute video includes clips of the discussions in the individual councils. In some ways, *The way home* and *The color of fear* (see Wah, Lee Mun) are similar in that they each focuses on a single gender and the participants deal fiercely with these issues; yet in this video, the groups are separated by race and ethnicity, and in *The color of fear*, African Americans, Latinos, Whites and Asians face one another to talk. While *The color of fear* occurred in one weekend, the discussions in *The way home* took place over several months.

Stephanie Nickerson is a freelance faculty development consultant who has worked in the field for many years and taught college for 22 years. She can be reached by mail at 16 West 16th Street, New York, NY 10011, by telephone at (212) 255-3486, and by email at snickers2653@yahoo.com.

Chapter 46

Multicultural Online Resources: What Are They, Where Are They, and Are They Bias Free?

Denise C. Camin

Multicultural education, sometimes referred to as diversity education, is becoming more of a staple in the classroom. Yet teachers at all levels have had little or no training in this field. As a result programs become trite efforts to meet a need without really focusing on planning the best approach with the best materials. Without a clear understanding of the best approaches for choosing materials that meet the needs of their students, educators inevitably spend time on activities that really do not serve their intended purposes.

Originally part of a project for a course on multicultural education on the West Lafayette campus of Purdue University, the resource guide began as a plan during the fall of 2002 to review the *literature* of multicultural online resources with the idea of creating the *perfect multicultural web site of resources for educators*. However, at the beginning of this search for materials, it became evident that a number of multicultural web sites already existed in various formats and were aimed at educators of all levels. Additionally, many of these sites offered resources geared to specialized audiences and provided communication venues for educators to connect. However, despite the wealth of resources and information found, it was not always clear how the materials were chosen, if these resources were indeed bias-free, or if, in reality, they reflected biases of the sites' developers.

To critically evaluate resources required an assessment tool focused not only on multicultural issues but also the special nature of online materials: accessibility, design and ease of use, download times for slower connections, browser differences, and so forth. Dr. Paul Gorski, creator of the Multicultural Pavilion web site, had created such a tool. (See the second section of the resource guide.) Using this tool, faculty and faculty developers can begin to determine the value of resources for their own classes and campuses. One key issue that must be addressed is that of audience needs. While there are some clear-cut guidelines for multicultural resources, the final determination of value will lie with the audience needs. There is no single "best fit" for all groups. Some will need or desire a greater level of interaction and involvement, while others will use the resources as a starting point for beginning a discussion on how best to teach inclusively. Still others will seek higher student involvement in the decision-making process, creating a more learner-centered, problem-solving approach to guide learners through the process of critically evaluating the resources.

To aid this decision making, I've provided some proposed guidelines for both faculty and faculty developers, incorporating the resources of their programs with a few suggestions for ways to begin not only a discussion of teaching inclusively but also a program of support for finding and using resources.

Guidelines for Faculty and Faculty Developers and Trainers

1. *Determine the reasons for including multicultural resources.* For faculty, this means really examining the driving purpose in order to determine the best resources and the best way to use these with students. Is this an individual decision or a university directive?

   Teachers: What do you want to accomplish by incorporating multicultural resources in your teaching? Many teachers revert to teaching as they have been taught, and for multicultural education that often means focusing on a multicultural unit or using multicultural activities during "holidays." Instead, try a more global or thematic approach to the overall course or subject. For example, some of the web sites included in the resource guide for this chapter specifically deal with math. Instead of having a multicultural unit, try incorporating multiculturalism as part of the overall approach. Or focus on the issue of ethics and examine current events with a more multicultural approach, such as issues of voter indifference based on how diverse populations view politics and/or their lack of voice.

   Faculty developers or trainers: What is the desired outcome or goal? Is this an individual faculty issue or a more global need? Is this the result of student concerns, or is it community related? Rather than simply creating workshops and/or offering resources, create a goal and then plan how best to meet it given time constraints and resources. Is funding available for some creative activities? Included in the resource guide is a section on systemic changes currently taking place in many universities. If your needs tend toward a more global outcome, you might use the resources as support or as a guide for drafting a grant for funding.

2. *Determine the audience needs.* Though this seems like a simple task, it often presents problems. Teachers are often accused of planning to teach their ideal rather than their actual student population. If this is the case, for faculty or faculty developers and trainers, there will be problems. One suggestion might be to use the surveys included at some of the sites for ideas on how to design something more specific for your audience needs. By assessing what the audience needs, you will have a better feel for what to include. Rather than guess, survey learners to see what they want and use this survey as a guide in planning your approach.

   Teachers: If your purpose is to create a more inclusive classroom atmosphere and your student population is younger, you might not want to use the Implicit Attitude Tests provided by Harvard University, but you might want to use these as a resource and create a modified activity that works towards the same purpose – a greater awareness of hidden bias – or you might want to introduce these tests as possible starting points in a course centering on ethics or the humanities. For individual instructors, the institutional surveys included at some of the sites in the resource guide could serve as a starting point for a classroom project focused on assessing inclusivity. Rather than offer students an open-ended research project, a theme of multicultural issues could be devised with student groups taking sections and collaborating as a class on a finished "study."

   Faculty developers or trainers: If your learners are faculty, you might use the Implicit Attitude Tests as an ice-breaker to a discussion focused on hidden bias As you will see in the "institutional" section of the resource guide, even though many universities have similar approaches, the individual needs were assessed (usually via survey) before putting a plan into action. This cannot be stressed enough: what works in one setting might not work as well in another. For faculty developers, that means really understanding your audience.

3. *Determine the level of involvement of learners.* Ideally, the more actively involved the learner, the greater change in behavior learning, but how much involvement is necessary? Do learners help plan the activities and take a greater ownership role in learning? Is their only involvement related to the learning process?

   Teachers: While the level of students might determine some of these things, younger students could be more actively involved in making decisions if properly guided. Involvement could center on working with resources for a specific project or on evaluating material. If projects involve family members, it is wise to meet with parents and/or notify them in writing to head off problems or concerns. If the classroom has a diverse climate, students can research their ethnic roots, either specifically or more globally. If the classroom is less diverse, students can assume "roles" and conduct similar research from those standpoints.

Faculty developers or trainers: Will the involvement include taking ideas back to the classroom and adding a multicultural dimension to the classroom? Will it involve a re-envisioning of curricula to determine problems in addressing multicultural needs of a diverse student population? If the idea is to help faculty create an inclusive classroom environment, a workshop focused on awareness might be a start, but a better approach would be a modeling of how to use materials in specific courses. Often faculty are unaware of how multicultural issues can be addressed in courses outside of literature, art, ethics, history, and so forth. An online course will offer greater involvement over a longer period of time and might be a better choice than a one-time workshop.

4. *Determine the level of commitment and the approach.* These two actually do go hand-in-hand. Ideally, embracing diversity would be an ongoing lifestyle or teaching style change, but in reality, this might be too big of an undertaking in the beginning. For example, a teacher or faculty developer might wish to overhaul an entire program based on reviewing some of the resources included in the guide, but realistically such a review might not be possible if the guide is being read two weeks before school begins. Instead, decide what can be done within the current time frame and then plan for future improvements. For example, rather than an information session, the approach could involve ongoing discussions as part of faculty meetings.

Teachers: How much time are you willing to devote to curriculum changes? How committed is your institution to supporting you in your efforts? Use these questions as your guideline for determining what resources you will use and how you will use them. Rather than revising an entire curriculum, focus on a subject or plan for a multicultural awareness activity each week. While incorporating an activity might not be the desired approach, it might be more realistic and manageable. Many institutions offer monetary incentives in the form of grants or faculty involvement in diversity committees, but can you spare the time?

Faculty developers or trainers: Do you have the time and resources to devote to your ideal project? If not, what can you do to raise awareness on a much smaller scale? While it might be desirable to involve all faculty members, maybe the initial program should focus on graduate assistants or new faculty first. Rather than planning a one-day workshop or institute presentation, encourage the departments to support a more on-going forum via a course management system if your institution already uses one.

5. *Determine your knowledge and comfort level.* This seems like a given, but often educators are so enthusiastic they neglect to really think through the project before beginning. Do you have a good feel for the issues affecting cultures other than your own? If not, how do you propose to get that awareness? Maybe initially the resource guide will be used to develop a greater awareness of other cultures and personal hidden biases. Maybe it will serve to connect you to people who can act as resources. Secondly, how will you handle conflict? Inevitably, discussions of sensitive issues create a climate of unease. How do you handle the racial or gender-based slurs that may be encountered in literature or in the news? What do you do when confronted with a volatile classroom situation? Maybe the key is pairing a news story or piece of literature with an informational site, teaching students to look beyond the surface and develop a more empathetic awareness.

Teachers: I have learned to preface activities with disclaimers, letting my students know I sometimes feels uncomfortable as a way of introducing the discussion. While many of the resources seek to promote multicultural awareness, others may open up dialogues that breed discomfort. Educators need to be aware and approach this issue proactively: if you would rather not deal with the feelings brought out by Peggy McIntosh's "White Privilege: Unpacking the Invisible Knapsack" in your introductory freshman course, then do not. Work through potential problems with colleagues of color before introducing this essay in the classroom. I have found it useful to offer choices to students when tackling thought-provoking pieces of literature like Ellison's racially charged "Battle Royal" or those dealing with AIDS like Kushner's "Angels in America" or Dark's "In the Gloaming." Rather than force students (even adults) to read something that makes them uncomfortable, I offer a choice of literature that exposes them to diversity but with varying degrees of discomfort. When the classroom discussions begin, I often find that many students have read all of the material. However, in the spirit of offering students flexibility, instead of requiring the entire class to participate in the Implicit Attitudes Test, you can offer this option as a choice.

Faculty developers or trainers: Many of your goals will reflect those of teachers. The University of Michigan offers Diversity Dialogues as a way of dealing with issues on a global scale. Perhaps your plan could be to create a discussion group, online or via brown bag lunches, to help faculty deal with issues that arise in the classroom. Or maybe your goal is to involve more guest speakers to promote cultural awareness, either formally or informally.

Armed with an awareness of individual purposes, the next step is seeing what resources are available. The following *Annotated Resource Guide of Online Multicultural Resources* was compiled by Denise C. Camin, Associate Professor of English at DeVry University, Tinley Park, IL, and Jerene Kunkler, a graduate student at Purdue University, West Lafayette, IN, when both were students in EDCI 585, Multicultural Education, in the fall of 2002. It was revised during the spring of 2004 to update material and include a section focused on institutions engaged in multicultural and/or diversity systemic change.

This listing is a continual work-in-progress, so it in no way represents an inclusive offering of all the online multicultural resources available. However, it does offer a collection of quality web sites and online multicultural resources to aid educators in their quest for classroom materials.

The resources have been organized into categories and then listed alphabetically for ease of access: Institutions of Higher Learning Engaged in Multicultural Transformation Efforts, Evaluation Tools, Specialty Portals, Web-Based Products, Multicultural Mathematics Resources, and Web Sites. All of the resources are online, though some are fee-based. A few of the specialty portals are included in Frank Bruno's (2000) article, "Bridges on the I-Way: Multicultural Resources Online – Multicultural Portals," and most, though not all, of the mathematics offerings are found in Paul Gorski's (2000) article, "Bridges on the I-Way: Multicultural Resources Online – Multicultural Education and Mathematics on the Internet." (See the References at the end of this guide.) Some of the "diversity" offerings deal with gender and sexuality issues or accessibility in addition to the more traditional definition of multiculturalism.

Institutions of Higher Learning Engaged in Multicultural Transformation Efforts

As a result of an increasing awareness of the need for helping educators better serve their diverse student populations and prepare future educators, a number of institutions have created task forces and/or committees focused on this issue. Many universities are creating administrative positions specifically focused on multicultural initiatives, such as the University of Connecticut, while others are concentrating on a taskforce approach. The following list is by no means inclusive of every institution's efforts to promote diversity; it merely offers a glimpse at the kinds of changes being made. Rather than highlight best practices, it serves to provide ideas for those wanting to make changes in their own settings.

Community, Diversity and Social Justice Academic Affairs Team – University of Massachusetts (http://www.umass.edu/wost/cdsj/)

This program is the result of a study dating back to 1996 and has culminated in a campus-wide effort that involves a group representative of the major stakeholders faculty, students, staff and administrators – divided into five teams to effect "systemic change." Its mission statement points to a concerted effort to create an environment to support a diverse community while preparing students to better function in a multicultural world. One of the key features of this site is the "Academic Affairs Survey of Employee Attitudes and Experiences" and the subsequent report of its findings. While not specifically a model for other institutions, those looking to effect change can gain concrete ideas to use in developing their own tools, goals, and plan of action.

Diversity Action Council (DAC) Portland State University (http://www.president.pdx.edu/Initiatives/diversity/DAChome.phtml)

In keeping with its charge to create a more inclusive university environment, the DAC, like many of the other institutions noted here, includes a diverse population of faculty, students, staff and administrators. The site offers links to information about its activities, newsletter, meeting summaries, presidential initiatives, and action plan. One unique feature of this program is the "Faculty-in-Residence for Diversity," a position charged with supporting faculty in revising curriculum, restructuring classrooms, and developing research initiatives aimed at promoting a more diverse university. This position could also serve as the university's liaison for diversity and designer of the university's Diversity Institute. The beauty of this program is its realization of the need for a more dedicated faculty support system for effecting change.

Diversity Network Duquesne University (http://www.cte.duq.edu/diversitynetwork.html)

A division of the Center for Teaching Excellence, this site offers a more informal approach in the form of a discussion summary based on answering two focus questions in 2001. While the site does not offer additional information about organizational changes resulting from the feedback, it does present ideas for those institutions looking to get started with limited funding. Moreover, educators could use the information to engage students in a research effort focused on examining the issues related to institutional change.

A Framework to Foster Diversity at Penn State (http://www.equity.psu.edu/framework/background.asp)

Another initiative that resulted from students voicing concerns about diversity, Penn State's program is in its second phase: 2004 – 2009. Like many of the other programs included in this resource guide, Penn State focused on specific goals and categories for its plan (seven Challenges) and specific concerns for each. However, unlike other sites that only offer the planning and implementation phases, this one provides a glimpse at the program's midpoint evaluation procedures, the best practices found, and a subsequent report outlining a "coherent, university-wide paradigm for diversity." The site also includes a link to the *Penn State Diversity Newswire,* "updated information [on] University-wide diversity initiatives."

Office of Multicultural Affairs - Virginia Tech (http://www.multicultural.vt.edu)

Virginia Tech's (VT) multicultural initiatives are best summed up in the Diversity Strategic Plan (http://dsp.multicultural.vt.edu/), one of the links offered at the main page of this site. Spanning a period from 2000 – 2005, the plan has five specific goals in addition to a plan for implementation. Much more "polished" looking than many of the other university initiatives, this plan's appeal is its attention to detail: a page categorized by each piece of the plan with links to further detail, findings based on assessments of major stakeholders (further subdivided between undergraduate and graduate students), ties with VT's core values, research studies supporting the necessity for diversity, and tools and resources for implementation. The implementation plan for each of the five major goals includes specific sub-goals and tasks to meet each of these, assignment of tasks to specific stakeholders, measurement guidelines for meeting these goals[?], and a deadline for completion. Another key feature is information from a recent workshop, "Managing Programs that Promote the Newly Adopted," including group discussion topics and the "Standards for Inclusive Policies, Practices and Programs" (April 2004), which are "intended to be broad in concept but flexible in application, providing a framework of expectation but leaving the details to those with the expertise and responsibility for program development and oversight." Among its standards are legal, inclusion, climate, competency, accountability, and student development.

Plan 2008: Educational Quality through Racial and Ethnic Diversity – University of Wisconsin, Eau-Claire (http://www.uwec.edu/chancellor/Diversity/)

This university program of change encompasses all of the campuses in "a comprehensive, system-wide change." Like Virginia Tech's, this plan spans a specific time period and is focused on overall institutional change, although this one includes a note for requiring "departments … to develop long-range curricular and staffing plans" as well as requiring those involved in hiring and recruiting to participate in training programs "once every five years." And like Virginia Tech's, this plan includes specific accountability, outcomes, and time frames for meeting each goal. Two new features are the inclusion of designators for each goal (new, revised, continuing) and information about the cost involved, though for many of the goals have incurred "no new cost." Institutions looking to establish similar programs could use the information found here as a starting point.

Provost's Task Force on Multicultural Curriculum Transformation — Northern Illinois. University (http://www3.niu.edu/mcti/mcti1.htm)

This program's vision method sums up its overall position: "The task force envisions an enriched academic environment at Northern Illinois University where faculty address multicultural perspectives in their teaching and curricula, accommodate the needs of a diverse student population, and engage in activities that promote scholarship of multicultural curricula." Based initially on student concerns, the focus here is on revising the curriculum rather than restructuring the university, though it seems a more aware faculty and diverse multicultural curriculum will act as a catalyst to system wide changes. In addition to its mission statement and history, the site defines multicultural curriculum transformation and offers a plan based on five phases and three central components, all central to educators: increased personal knowledge, amended course content and syllabi, and revised classroom behaviors. An interesting feature of this program is the monetary incentive for faculty via support for multicultural transformation projects.

University of Michigan – Office of the Provost (http://www.provost.umich.edu/reports/tblg/index.html)

As have other institutions, this university has created an administrative position to address academic multicultural initiatives, providing leadership and overseeing implementation of its programs. Among the offerings found at this site is a report from the task force charged with exploring the "Campus Climate for Transgender, Bisexual, Lesbian, and Gay (TBLG) Faculty, Staff, and Students," in response to student concerns in 2003. This report's decidedly research-like approach provides information not only about what was found but also provides recommendations for needed changes. Though not generalizable in the research-sense, this project could provide other institutions with a guideline for proactive evaluation of programs and procedures for inclusion on those campuses.

Multicultural Evaluation Tool

In order to more effectively use this guide, it is important to have criteria for evaluating materials.

A Multicultural Model for Evaluating Educational Web Sites by Paul Gorski

(http://www.edchange.org/multicultural/resources/webeval.html)

Created in December of 1999 and found in the "Lists, Tools, and Fact Sheets" section of the Multicultural Pavilion web site, this evaluative tool offers criteria for evaluating multicultural educational web sites. A mix of both online issues and multicultural needs, Gorski's tool provides a handy reference for educators and/or students, and the heading on the "Lists, Tools, and Fact Sheets" page invites educators to "print, copy, and distribute freely" as long as the name and e-mail of the author is included. Additionally, the site includes a link to the article "which led to the model."

Specialty Portals

Portals are "openings" or "entries" to new worlds: these offer an entry into, or for, ethnic-centered groups.

Asian-American Portals

Asian American Community Links (http://www.janet.org/~ebihara/aacyber_community.html)

An eclectic mix of resources and organizations, this site offers a link to the Asian-American community for the Asian-American community. In addition to cultural and arts information, links are also provided for civil advocacy, health resources, media, and academic or business organizations. Among the media resources are links to periodicals focused on the interests of the Asian-American community, and included in the "online organizations" is a link to the Asian Community Online Network.

The Asian Community Online Network (http://www.acon.org/)

Billed as a resource for "bringing people and organizations together in our communities," this site focuses more on helping Asians and Pacific Islanders who have relocated to the U.S. Among the resources are Outreach, E-Mail Hosting, Jobs, National and Regional E-Mail groups, and so forth. Though not specifically a resource for educators, this site provides links to the Asian-American community, and the regional networks could provide a local connection to aid families as well as possibly provide classroom speakers.

Asia Links: Linking the World to Asia (http://www.asia-links.com/company/dec6_99.htm)

This site, like Click2Asia, focuses on trying to connect diverse groups of Asians by providing a common space with resources to aid Asians as a community rather than as separate entities. Divided into Asia Biz, Asia Insider, and Asia Jobs, this portal's resources focus more on the financial well being of Asians.

Black/African-American Portals

BlackFamilies.com (http://www.blackfamilies.com)

Although this site centers on supporting and creating strong Black families, the offerings range from issues of interest to a general audience to those more related to a scholarly following. There is a "Reference and Education" subsection including information for adult education, preschool, and Kthrough12.

Black Issues in Higher Education (http://www.blackissues.com/)

Introduced as "your portal to diversity," this site offers an array of resources for addressing the needs of the African American community: links to diversity training resources, current and archived issues of its journal of the same name (available only to subscribers), news items, and information about its annual conference. Though less an actual portal and more a web site supporting the publication, it does fit the portal definition in the grid-like link offerings at the top of the page.

BlackVoices.com (http://www.blackvoices.com)

This site includes topical and geographical discussion forums, including 30 "chocolate" cities, those major urban U.S. cities with large African-American populations and a topical Nation of Islam chat group. It also notes that it is "the most visited black site in the world." This site would be a valuable resource for understanding Black culture and for exposing students to the diverseness of this culture.

Resources for African Americans (http://www.blackonomics.com/resources.ihtml)

More focused on economic issues and seemingly more "parent-oriented," this site offers some good resources for families, including a reading room, articles, events, a gallery, and links to other resources online, such as "Little Africa." Like many of the Asian American portals, this one has a purpose related to growing empowerment through economic stability by increasing African American awareness.

Latino Portals

Hispanic Online (–HYPERLINK "http://www.hispaniconline.com/" —http://www.hispaniconline.com/)

One of the three multicultural portals included in Frank Bruno's "Bridges on the I-Way: Multicultural Resources Online (Multicultural Portals)," this resource attempts to provide a "bridge" to Hispanic culture, providing an inclusive offering of everything from educational resources, to economic interests, to political topics, to features of interest to recent immigrants. Though the text of the site is all in English, some of the discussion contributors did use Spanish. In the past, this portal was the Spanish version of America Online (AOL); however, AOL now has a Spanish version its subscribers can access when they log in to their own homepage.

Latino USA (http://www.latinousa.org)

Noted as the best site in October of 1999 according to *Hispanic Magazine*, (per Frank Bruno's "Bridges on the I-Way: Multicultural Resources Online"), this one is focused on news and events of interest to Latinos, and offerings in this site include Real Audio programs from National Public Radio. According to Bruno, these programs focus on stereotypes ("Taco Bell and Latino Stereotypes") and issues of interest ("Today's Latino Youth" and "Latinos in High Tech").

Picosito (http://www.picosito.com)

Another Hispanic portal included in Frank Bruno's "Bridges on the I-Way: Multicultural Resources Online (Multicultural Portals)," this resource is in Bruno's words "more geared to public policy issues and is a little hipper in its graphical displays, with links to the people and publications mentioned." It also includes a link "to 'The Digital Divide and the U.S. Hispanic Population,' a provocative report about Hispanics not having equal access to technology for economic reasons": http://www.benton.org/DigitalBeat/db080699.html.

Portalatino.com (http://www.portalatino.com)

This portal resembles many of those offered for African-Americans and Asian-Americans, though the mix of resources tends more towards current events, music, and entertainment, promoting itself as a "digital platform" or creative link to music industry and audiovisual resources for Latinos. Bright and welcoming, the web site's design reflects colorful Hispanic culture, and although it could be used by non-Hispanics, the entire site is in Spanish.

Native-American Portals

Native Web (http://www.nativeweb.com)

Similar to the other ethnic-centered sites, this one offers the same wide range of resources though the focus is on cultural issues for "indigenous cultures around the world": current events, literature, business and economy, law and legal issues, libraries and collections, and so forth. Unlike the others, this one includes a "Relief Center" for those interested in making donations to the reservations and is slow to load using a dial-up connection, but the wealth of material is worth the wait.

Web-Based Products

American Slavery: A Composite Autobiography (http://www.slavenarratives.com)

This product was noted in Frank Bruno's "A Roundup of CD-ROM and Electronic Products" included in the March 2001 issue of the *Multicultural Review.* Though this product is fee-based ($215 - $900, depending on the use agreement), there is a 30day free trial offered. The site, as noted by Bruno, has an extensive collection of slave narratives ("40-volume collection of firsthand slave narrative [which have] been digitized") in Adobe Acrobat format. Additionally, there are discussion forums: "general interest, genealogists, and educators' groups." Focused on materials for a junior high or older audience, Bruno feels this site is an exceptionally valuable resource for Black Studies programs.

Diversity Your World (http://www.slinfo.com/)

Another product noted in Frank Bruno's "A Roundup of CD-ROM and Electronic Products" included in the March 2001 issue of the *Multicultural Review,* this resource is also fee-based ($495 - $995, depending on the number of users), although there is a two-week free trial. It has a number of valuable resources for secondary and college-age users and includes an extensive database, though perhaps not the most extensive based on diversity. Bruno notes that basic "ethnic" offerings are available, though perhaps not those that are less commonplace, as when he tried searching for "el dia de los muertos" and found nothing.

International Index to Black Periodicals Full-Text (http://iibp.Chadwyck.com)

The most expensive of the fee-based databases included in Frank Bruno's "A Roundup of CD-ROM and Electronic Products" included in the March 2001 issue of the *Multicultural Review* ($2,395 - $3,995, though public library subscriptions are available), this product is geared to a high school or older audience. However, there is nothing noted about a free trial. According to Bruno, this site offers "full text coverage from 1998 for over 25 Black Studies periodicals. ... These journals are international and multidisciplinary in perspective ... concentrate primarily on humanities and social science topics including art, cultural criticism, economics, education, health, history, language, literature, philosophy, politics, popular culture, psychology, religion, science and technology, and sociology."

Multicultural Math and Science Resources

This is a collection provided by Paul Gorski in his article, "Bridges on the I-Way: Multicultural Resources Online – Multicultural Education and Mathematics on the Internet," in the September 2000 issue of the *Multicultural*

Review as well as online in his Multicultural SuperSite sponsored by McGraw Hill, http://www.mhhe.com/socscience/education/multi/sites/math.html. A few resources were also added by the authors of this guide.

In addition to the resources listed below, Gorski's web site includes some gender-related resources like CyberSisters, a "telementoring" web site. (There may be math resources included in some of the other multicultural resources included in the other sections as well, but those listed here focus primarily on math issues.)

Annotated Bibliography of Multicultural Perspectives in Mathematics Education (http://jwilson.coe.uga.edu/DEPT/Multicultural/MEBib94.html)

According to Gorski, this is an "extensive index of books, articles, and other materials related to multicultural education ... divided into three major categories: Theory, Research, and Practice." However, the sources are print-based, and no links are provided.

Ask Dr. Math (http://forum.swarthmore.edu/dr.math/)

This is an interactive site offering a forum for students to find the answers to tough math question from a "team of experts" at Swarthmore, the site's host.

Barrier-Free Education (http://barrier-free.arch.gatech.edu)

This site centers on accessibility for those students with disabilities that interfere with their access to math and science resources. It is offered as a resource from Georgia Tech and includes labs and lessons modified for accessibility.

Biographies of Women Mathematicians (http://www.agnesscott.edu/lriddle/women/women.htm)

The site is a collection of essays written about women mathematicians, which continues to grow as the result of its encouraging submissions. The site can be searched "alphabetically or chronologically."

The Compatibility of Good Mathematics Tasks with Good Multicultural Teaching Strategies (http://mathforum.org/mathed/nctm96/multicultural/grover.html)

This site represents a summary of a presentation at San Diego National Council of Teaching Mathematics, includes a guide to pedagogically sound multicultural approaches to teaching mathematics, lesson plans to help teachers put these ideas into practice (in question format), and a list of resources, though not available online, used by the presenters.

Ethnomathematics (http://www.cs.uidaho.edu/~casey931/seminar/ethno.html)

According to Gorski, "This site, by Nancy Casey of the University of Idaho, explores the meanings and implications of 'ethnomathematics' and related topics."

Integrating Gender and Equity Reform in Math, Science, and Engineering Instruction (http://www.coe.uga.edu/ingear/)

"InGEAR houses a collection of curriculum materials promoting excellence and equity in math, science, and engineering education. The site includes specific teaching strategies, online publications and articles, and a collection of classroom activities that address gender issues" (Gorski, 2000, p.69).

Multicultural Math Fair: Links for Activities (http://forum.swarthmore.edu/alejandre/mathfair/mmflinks.html)

"Another product of Math Forum, this site houses a collection of mathematics lesson plans and classroom activities based around multicultural themes. Several of the lesson plans are in Spanish" (Gorski, 2000, p.69).

Multicultural Math Goals (–HYPERLINK "http://people.clarityconnect.com/webpages/terri/multicultural.html" —http://people.clarityconnect.com/webpages/terri/multicultural.html)

"Terri Husted created this page of resources and frameworks for incorporating multicultural teaching and learning into mathematics education. In addition to offering her own set of goals for math education, she includes book reviews and links to related sites" (Gorski, 2000, p.70).

Multicultural Perspectives in Mathematics Education (http://jwilson.coe.uga.edu/DEPT/Multicultural/MathEd.html

"University of Georgia's Department of Mathematics hosts this resource directory to help educators understand the role of multicultural teaching and learning in mathematics education. The site includes an annotated bibliography, dissertation references, and web links" (Gorski, 2000, p.70).

Profile of Equitable Mathematics and Science Classrooms and Teachers (http://www.col-ed.org/smcnws/equity/profile.html)

"Joy Wallace of the Columbia Education Center developed this set of equity guidelines for math and science classrooms and teachers. Special attention is given to physical environment, curriculum, language, pedagogy, behavior management, and assessment" (Gorski, 2000, p.70).

Teaching Mathematics Effectively and Equitably to Females (http://iume.tc.columbia.edu/eric_archive/mono/ti17.pdf)

Housed in the archives of Columbia's Teacher College, in this monograph offered in PDF format, "Katherine Hanson of the Education Development Center explores classroom climate issues for females in mathematics in this ERIC article" (Gorski, 2000, p.70).

Women in Math Project (http://darkwing.uoregon.edu/~wmnmath/)

"Marie Vitulli of the University of Oregon directs this large collection of resources highlighting women's achievements in mathematics. The site includes a directory of publications, a biographical collection, and related statistics" (Gorski, 2000, p.70).

Wyoming Clearinghouse for Mathematics and Science (http://smtc.uwyo.edu/wcms/Science/Resources/MulticulLinks.asp)

Found during a search for multicultural education resources, this site links to the Eisenhower National Clearinghouse for Mathematics and Science, which includes information about women in science, gender equity, "the faces of African-American scientists" bibliography, and the Consortium for Equity in Standards and Testing.

Web Sites (multicultural and/or intercultural)

A plethora of web sites exist for multicultural education, some focused on specialized ethnicities and others with a broader focus. The important element of any resource, whether it be online or in print, is the relevance for the intended audience. Rather than anoint a few sites as "good" or "excellent," it is far better to provide a guideline for making judgments and then letting faculty and/or faculty developers make these decisions for their own unique audience needs.

Adult Higher Education Alliance AHEA (http://www.ahea.org/index.htm)

Though focused on all issues involving adult higher education, there are a number of links to organizations related to the needs of adult learners as well as articles centered on issues of diversity and multicultural education. Using the site's search function and the term "multicultural education" produced 118 articles including "Multicultural Perspectives in Academic Discourse," "Diversity: Adult Learners and Cultural Perspectives on Learning," "Highly Motivating Instruction for Culturally Diverse Adult Students," and our favorite, "Culturally Proficient Educators: A Cultural Proficiency Model in Professional Education Programs" (http://www.ahea.org/culturally_proficent.htm). Those engaged in teacher education, faculty development and/or institutional change efforts will find this site to be a valuable resource.

African-American Multicultural Resources (http://www.zianet.com/cjcox/edutech4learning/african.html)

This site offers some of the more standard kinds of resources related to African-American history and culture, but it also offers some unique links, such as the one to the "African-American Odyssey: A Quest for Full Citizenship" from the Library of Congress, with its focus on the journey of African-Americans from slavery to an equal role as American citizens, and the "African-American History Challenge," an interactive quiz, which offers teachers a chance to request a class code for "grading" purposes.

American Association of Colleges for Teacher Education – AACTE (http://www.aacte.org/Multicultural/multicultural_edu_resources.htm)

This site offers a number of resources including current projects, a section focused on special study groups, an area centering on issues "about multicultural education," multicultural education resources, and minority recruitment and retention issues. Probably more academic than other offerings, this site focuses on an academic audience and is better suited for post-secondary users and/or educators.

Asian/Eastern Multicultural Resources (http://www.zianet.com/cjcox/edutech4learning/asian.html)

This site provides links to a number of quality sites devoted to Asian and/or Eastern cultures, including a link to the "Asian American Resource Guide" from the University of Southern California, "The Asian Reading Room" from the Library of Congress, "Asian Studies Virtual WWW Library," and so forth. The first resource noted here includes an extensive literature review, audio and video recordings, and links to other online resources.

Asian American Studies Resources (http://sun3.lib.uci.edu/~dtsang/aas2.htm)

Created as an "alternative research" effort of Daniel Tsang (UC Irvine), this site offers a diverse range of resources related to the study of Asian American issues, including but not limited to alternative lifestyles, journals, movement groups, and Asian Canadian resources. The Table of Contents at the beginning of the site allows for quick access to information, though scrolling offers visitors the chance to browse the entire site to get a feel for the range of information.

AskERIC Education Information – Multicultural Education (–HYPERLINK "http://www.eduref.org/" —http://www.eduref.org/)

Because of the closing of the ERIC databases, this resource was relocated. However, it opens to the main resource page. Use the "search" option in the upper right-hand corner and "multicultural education" to access the more than 1300 sources available.

Some of the resources include lesson plans, Internet sites and discussion groups. One interesting feature is the AskERIC Responses, this one focusing on the question of "what information do you have about multicultural education?" While many of the Internet sites are duplicates of many offered already elsewhere in this bibliography, the two discussion groups – MULTC ED and Multicultural (Yahoo discussion group) – are new resources.

Bilingual Education (http://www.csun.edu/~hcedu013/eslbil.html)

Though it might be debatable that a link to a list of resources for bilingual education fits in a list of multicultural resources, the information in this web site offers resources for working with bilingual students and articles supporting the need for bilingual education for supporting a diverse student population.

Center for Research on Education, Diversity and Excellence –CREDE (http://www-rcf.usc.edu/~cmmr/crede.html)

One of the many pieces of the USC site, this page offers a number of resources not previously encountered in other multicultural educational web sites, namely the "standards for effective teaching" and two new resources related to "para-educators" and their role in multiculturalism.

Comisión de Modernización Pedagógica (http://www.pucp.edu.pe/cmp)

The beauty of this site is the authenticity of a resource created by a different culture. However, this one is completely in Spanish. "This web site includes information about the innovations implemented at [the] university regarding teaching, learning, and assessment at the university level. Besides information about many issues related to the learning process it also contains some examples of innovations implemented [in our university]." The authors of the site welcome visitors and invite comments.

Community Arts Network (http://www.communityarts.net/readingroom/resdivlinks.php)

Although this site links to the "Reading Room," the resources are diverse and cover a myriad array of links to other sites, including but not limited to feminist, Arab, Asian, Black, and Latino art resources. These include museum links, periodicals, portals, and research studies.

Curriculum and Instruction 406: Introduction to Multicultural Education (http://www.lib.iastate.edu/commons/ci406/01spr/resources.html)

An actual Iowa State University course web site from Spring 2001, this site offers a comprehensive list of resources though most are available to Iowa State students only. However, the list does provide information about periodicals and indexes that can be found at other libraries, and nearer the end, there is a listing of selected international web resources, a few of which are also mentioned in our listing.

DEET Initiatives: Multicultural Education (http://www.eduweb.vic.gov.au/curriculumatwork/deet/me_index.htm)

This web site is a collection of curriculum resources from the State of Victoria in Australia. There is a link to SOFWeb (http://www.sofweb.vic.edu.au/lem/multi/index.htm), links to topical resources (art, health, technology, and so forth), teacher support materials, and so forth.

Diversity – Ohio University (http://www.ohio.edu/diversity/resource/research.cfm)

While some of the links at this site are duplications of this guide, there are others that have not been found elsewhere, such as the links to "The Affirmative Action and Diversity Project: A Web Page for Research," "Ethnic NewsWatch," "LGBT Resources in Higher Education," and "Teaching Tolerance.Org." Despite the universal appeal of this site, it would probably be most beneficial to those engaged in higher education initiatives and/or professional development.

Dialogue to Action Initiative (http://www.thataway.org/)
This website is a great resource for those who facilitate dialogues on race and other challenging topics. There is a "dialogue leaders'" discussion list (an e-mail listserv), resources and links to other resources, and the opportunity to organize a discussion using the site's resources.

The Diversity Channel (http://www.thediversitychannel.com/)
This is an intriguing site and concept relating to increasing multicultural sensitivity and respect, though the main purpose seems to promote the program offerings. This site could be used for educator institute days to create a greater awareness of diversity issues. The "Diversity Hour" is a forum that allows for an ongoing dialogue with other professionals and can provide answers to questions about multicultural issues, though it seems more related to business than education. It includes a live, moderated webcast, chat rooms focused on a question of the month, and focused listservs (bulletin boards).

Diversity Education Program, UC Davis (http://diversity.ucdavis.edu/)
This site is the home page for the university's program and includes educational activities related to diversity, articles, links to external resources, and a listing of books and videos in addition to the campus resources. Because the educational activities change periodically, educators could use the link as a discussion starter periodically throughout the term.

Diversity Related Links (http://www.ceet.niu.edu/faculty/murali/diverse.htm)
A web site created by a faculty member at Northern Illinois University in DeKalb, IL, this resource is specifically focused on multicultural education resources for higher education. It is simply a list of links, organized by categories and then listed alphabetically. Some of the offerings include a list of minority student organizations, minority career centers, a diversity IQ quiz, "A Synthesis of Scholarship in Multicultural Education," and so forth. Though the author includes a disclaimer regarding quality and "working" links, a few of the UVA links are non-working. I have alerted her to the problem

Diversity Resources Network (http://www.diversitywork.com/)
This is a community of diversity and violence prevention trainers and educators who are committed to social justice. They offer their resources to share with others. According to the site creators, they "are members of

a long-standing community of diversity and violence prevention trainers and educators who are committed to social justice. We offer this site to provide free access to our teaching tools, analysis,exercises, and essays. We hope that you will find them useful in your work. We want this site to promote greater connections among us and to facilitate the sharing of resources."

Diversity RX (http://www.diversityrx.org/)

Primarily focused on creating an awareness of multicultural issues for healthcare providers, this site helps build cultural responsiveness and competency in health care. There is a section on "models and practices," legal issues, policies, networking, and so forth and so forth, as well as links to a "Multicultural Best Practices Report," "Medical Interpretation and Resource Guide," and a database of resources for helping develop "cultural competency."

Diversity Web – An Interactive Resource Hub for Higher Education (http://www.diversityweb.org/)

Provided by the combined efforts of the University of Maryland and the Association of American Colleges and Universities (AACU), this site's focus is providing resources for higher education. Links to *The Diversity Digest* (focused on faculty involvement), "research and trends," recommended resources, a discussion board, information about the listserv (see note below), and. The discussions include a featured topic and town hall chats. One recent discussion focused on whether or not college freshman should be required to take diversity courses. However, the persistent "Macromedia Flash" pop-up can become annoying.

Education World's Teacher Resources: Multicultural Education (http://db.education-world.com/perl/browse?cat_id=6396)

This link offers a list of 112 resources for educators related to the topic of multicultural education, either from the AskERIC Digest or the ERIC database. A sampling of the articles includes titles such as "American Indians in Higher Education: The Community College Experience," "American Indians and Alaska Natives in Higher Education: Research on Participation and Graduation," and "Considerations in Teaching Culturally Diverse Children." and so forth

Elementary Education Resources (http://www.pitt.edu/~poole/eledCountries.html)

While many of the resources included here can be found in other sites listed in this annotated listing, the links to Arab resources online is something unique to this site.

Family Diversity Projects (http://www.familydiv.org/)

Family Diversity Projects uses art as a vehicle for social change. The home page opens to a listing of books devoted to multicultural and diversity issues. For example, two of their traveling exhibits offer portraits of multiracial families and LGBT (Lesbian, Gay, Bisexual, and Transgender) families. The site is more of a support site for family use than for educators, though it provides interesting insights into other lifestyles with a family focus.

Global Diversity @ Work (http://www.diversityatwork.com/)

This site features the work of Trevor Wilson, who makes a strong business case for diversity at work. Periodical surveys are available online focused on diversity issues with the compiled results offered at a later date. There is also a "Virtual Networking" section planned for the near future, a virtual diversity course, links to other resources, and so forth. The search links section is divided topically, and the only problem with the site overall is that a few links are non-functional.

Hispanic and/or Latino Multicultural Resources (http://www.zianet.com/cjcox/edutech4learning/hispanic.html)

This site has numerous links to quality information, including LANIC (Latin American Network Information Center), ENLACE (Engaging Latino Communities for Education), Promoting Academic Achievement of Latino Students (research and journal articles from the ERIC database), OYEME! (searchable database focused on Hispanic issues), and Hispanics Online.

Hope in the Cities (http://www.hopeinthecities.org/)

Hope in the Cities is a national organization in the U.S. that establishes and supports organizations like Oregon Uniting. It is affiliated with an international organization: MRA – Initiatives for Change. Site navigation is via a drop-down menu with links to topics or via the "quick navigation" links.

IECC: Intercultural E-Mail Classroom Connections (http://www.iecc.org/)

This link offers a way to "help teachers link with partners in other cultures and countries." Although it is less a multicultural resource than a way of connecting classrooms across cultures, "IECC is a free teaching.com service to help teachers link with partners in other cultures and countries for email classroom pen-pal and other project exchanges. Since its creation in 1992, IECC has distributed over 28,000 requests for e-mail partnerships."

Implicit Attitude Tests (–HYPERLINK "https://implicit.harvard.edu/implicit/" —https://implicit.harvard.edu/implicit/)

This site relates specifically to issues of diversity. Project Implicit is a current research project to ascertain the science behind the "hidden" meanings found in the actions of people. There are Implicit Attitude (IA) tests that are part of the research project as well as demonstration tests related to one of four countries: Australia, Canada, South Africa, and the United Kingdom. Before being allowed to take the tests, participants are warned that they may learn something disagreeable, which is probably a good thing. The tests include issues related to age, gender, various ethnicities (including Arabs and Muslims), skin tone (light versus dark), weight, religion, sexual orientation, disabilities, and so forth, helping raise diversity awareness and offering an interesting way to begin a discussion of the issues. Though the "tests" propose the idea that there is a way of measuring racial preference, I found the activity to "lead" me to answer incorrectly at times because of a learning curve, or lack of one. However, the tests offer an interesting way to involve students or educators in a discussion of multicultural issues.

Indiana University's Multicultural Education Resource page (http://php.indiana.edu/~smir/mced.htm)

A myriad number of educational multicultural resources, this page is divided into one section focused on educators and another on education students. The student section includes a number of useful links, including "Teacher Talk," the University of Maryland Diversity database, education theories, and education reform. The educator section is just as useful for students, including collaborative activities, syllabi for "intercultural" programs, and so forth. However, a few of the links, including those to the simulations, no longer work.

Institute for Urban and Minority Education (http://iume.tc.columbia.edu/)

Formerly the Eric Clearinghouse on Urban Education, the Institute is now part of the Teachers College at Columbia University. This group's mission is to provide support and resources to schools and others involved in education, as well as to engage in research related issues. The site includes a link to the *Journal of African American History*, Eric Archives, the Institute's own journal – *IUME,* information about current research projects at the Institute and elsewhere, materials for parents and educators, and a search feature for finding additional online resources, either at the Institute or via Google.

International Intercultural Education: Resources for International Projects (http://www.mccneb.edu/intercultural/resources.htm)

A listing of resources including Fulbright Grants, this site offers a wide range of resources including links to professional organizations related to intercultural education, demographic information, census information, exchange rates, information about the "U.S. foreign born population," and a link to "Foreign-Born," a site for foreign-born citizens.

Maricopa Community Colleges (http://www.maricopa.edu/diversity/intl.htm)

This community college system in Arizona offers numerous resources for educators in addition to this section devoted to multicultural resources, international resources, and intercultural issues. One interesting feature is the "student services chart" that provides a glimpse at one school's approach to dealing with the needs of minority students' educational needs.

McGraw Hill's Intro to Education – Valuable Web Resource List (http://www.mhhe.com/socscience/education/intro/resources.html)

Part of a site devoted to "the foundations of education," the site offers numerous resources related to various teaching issues, many focusing on issues of diversity. Although many of the others include resources related to diversity, the main divisions (further subdivided) are "Student Diversity in a Multicultural Society," "Achieving Diversity," and "Equity and Pluralism." However, a few of the links are no longer operable.

The Men's Resource Center of Western Massachusetts – MRC (http://www.mensresourcecenter.org/)

The MRC is a non-profit organization dedicated to exploring male positive, profeminist, gay affirmative, antiracist issues and ideas. It includes links to other resources, including antiviolence information, programs, and publications.

Metropolitan Community College International/Intercultural Education Resources for International Projects (http://www.mccneb.edu/intercultural/resources.htm)

This offering from the Omaha, NE college system, offers some professional resources not available from other sites. Many of the resources focus on Native American issues, possibly a reflection of the population base of the community. There are links to census data, the Stanley Foundation, American Indian Higher Education Consortium, Classroom Connect (K through12 resources) and a site for "foreign-born citizens."

Model Strategies in Bilingual Education: Professional Development (http://www.ed.gov/pubs/ModStrat/index.html)

A slightly dated offering (1995) from the U.S. Department of Education's Office of Bilingual Education and Minority Language Affairs, this comprehensive study offers an in-depth look at, and models for, training teachers to work with bilingual children. The "link" outline offers the choice of reviewing specific sections or reading the study in its entirety.

Multicultural Education and Ethnic Groups: Selected Internet Resources (http://wwwlibrary.csustan.edu/lboyer/multicultural/main.htm)

The site is offered by the California State University's Stanislaus Library and includes numerous links to full-text background articles (a small sample), ethnic culture, the "best multicultural site," clearinghouses, databases, holiday calendars, electronic journals, discussion groups, specific ethnic groups, and so forth.

Multicultural Education Internet Resources (http://www.library.vanderbilt.edu/peabody/books/internet/ktwelve/multicult.html)

Though this listing from Vanderbilt University includes a number of resources already noted elsewhere in our annotated resource list, some of the links are new. For example, there is a link to Culture Quest (Hispanic resources) and another to Multicultural Resources for Children.

Multicultural Education Internet Resource Guide (http://jan.ucc.nau.edu/~jar/Multi.html)

Offered by Dr. Jon Reyhner of Northern Arizona University, this site was updated as of May 11, 2004 and provides over "100 sites" devoted to multicultural education. To further aid users, asterisks have been added to indicate levels of recommendation, though no information is given as to how the resources were evaluated. A note in the beginning offers a brief introduction, and at the end of the page, the author has provided links to other sections focused on specific issues: ESL, Bilingual education, American Indian education, Indigenous language, and so forth. One special feature of this site is the list of links to professional organizations focused on multicultural education (near the end) and the links to journals related to these issues.

Multicultural Education Resources (http://www.udel.edu/sine/educ/multcult.htm)

A page developed as part of an education course, this site offers e-mail connections for teachers interested in linking their classrooms to international classrooms. Though many of the resources listed in this site have been noted elsewhere, the bibliography from the University of Florida, the "Librarians Information Online Network Multicultural Forum," a "Multicultural Book Review Home Page," "A Synthesis of Scholarship in Multicultural Education," and various background articles are new offerings.

Multicultural Pavilion - "Resources and dialogues for students, educators, and activists" (http://curry.edschool.virginia.edu/go/multicultural/)

The award-winning site created by Dr. Paul Gorski in his position with the Curry School of Education at the University of Virginia offers a multitude of resources including discussion forums, activities, a "multicultural e-Rolodex," a "new model for the Digital Divide," songs, movies, and so forth.

Multicultural Perspectives (http://www.leaonline.com/loi/mcp)

Published by Lawrence Erlbaum Associates, Incorporated beginning in 2000, this journal offers a range of articles in its eighteen issues from a variety of perspectives though with a decidedly academic focus. "This publication promotes the philosophy of social justice, equity, and inclusion" and "celebrates cultural and ethnic diversity as a national strength that enriches the fabric of society." Educators could use the articles for professional growth, gaining a greater understanding of multicultural issues, and/or classroom enrichment. A free issue is provided for review, but the journal is available both online and in print by subscription.

Multicultural Resources (http://www.lasalle.edu/mcis/html/resour1.htm)
This site offers a mix of resources including multicultural journals, resources categorized by ethnic groups, and resources for educators. One feature that sets this site apart from others is the "Multiculturalism Higher Education Institutions" section featuring an annotated list of publications, including a few studies focused on perceptions of faculty and students relating to diversity issues.

Multicultural Review (http://www.mcreview.com/)
This online multicultural journal features articles about issues of multicultural education primarily for an audience of educators, though some of the articles could be used to promote classroom discussion. However, only a sampling is provided without subscription.

Multicultural Supersite – sponsored by McGraw-Hill and created by Dr. Paul Gorski (http://www.mhhe.com/socscience/education/multi/)
As its name implies, this is a comprehensive site with numerous links to all things related to multicultural education issues: multicultural supersites, discussion forums, intercultural activities, a multicultural library, promising practices, and so forth.

There are a number of good activities, including case studies, an interesting multicultural quiz, and a discussion forum with three discussion topics: administration, frequently asked questions, and practical approaches.

Multicultural Teaching (http://www.crlt.umich.edu/multiteaching/multiteaching.html))
This site is from the Center for Research on Learning and Teaching at the University of Michigan. There are links to Multicultural Occasional Papers (not specifically explained, these seem written by faculty but not formally published), Teaching Strategies, External Resources, and Annotated Bibliographies, though the listing is not annotated. I love annotated bibliographies so that I can get a sense of a book or article or other resource before I actually track it down, and the teaching strategies section provides educators with some concrete ideas for the improving the climate in their classrooms, as does the occasional paper titled "Creating Inclusive College Classrooms."

Multicultural Web Sites: Diversity and Ethnic Studies
(http://www.public.iastate.edu/~savega/multicul.htm)
Created by Susan A. Vega Garcia, this site includes a number of solid resources for educators at all levels, including a link to *Standards: An*

International Journal of Multicultural Studies and other journals. Although many of the resources are also included in this chapter, many have not been. There are a number of great features to this site, including the "table of contents" list of links at the top of the page, the addition of an alternate lifestyles category (LGBT), and the Library Research Guides. However, for me, the appeal of this site is the brief annotation for each entry, something often missing from other sites.

National Association for Multicultural Education – NAME (http://www.nameorg.org/)

This site offers information focused on the professional organization responsible for the award bestowed on the Multicultural Pavillion, an annual conference, professional publications, position papers, listservs, other resources, and nominations for the upcoming year's award. Some of the resources in the "other" category include information about films, lesson plans, web resources, articles, interviews, journals, newspapers, "equity assistance centers," and a reference library.

Native American Issues (http://www.library.arizona.edu/huerta/personal.html)

The links included in this section of the University of Arizona's library site focus on interviews with Judge Huerta on a number of issues of importance to the Native community, offered as audio clips. There are also links to video clips.

National Education Association (NEA) Multicultural Education Resources (http://www.nea.org/))

To access the multicultural education resources in this database, use the search option found on the home page and the phrase "multicultural education." A recent search yielded approximately 189 results. Primarily articles, some are offered in PDF format, but there are some extra "perks" for online readers, including an "Ask the Expert" section for personal communication and links to some interviews, including one with James Banks on Multicultural Education in print format: http://www.nea.org/neatoday/9809/banks.html. Additionally, the search function found at this site could be used to find more specific information related to multicultural education, such as professional development (10 results).

New Horizons for Learning (http://www.newhorizons.org/)

The site offers links to articles about "transforming education," a link to the *New Horizons for Learning Online Journal,* and a searchable database for resources directly related to multicultural education. A search for "multicultural education" yielded approximately 40 journal articles ranging from "The Scope of Multicultural Education," to "The Handbook of Research in Multicultural Education," to "The Interdisciplinary Project Model: A Workable Response to the Challenges of Multicultural Education in Our Nation's Secondary Schools."

New Horizon for Learning's "Multicultural Children's Literature: Creating and Applying an Evaluation Tool in Response to the Needs of Urban Educators" (http://www.newhorizons.org/strategies/multicultural/higgins.htm)

One of the articles available through the New Horizons for Learning web site, the author, Jennifer Johnson Higgins, provides not only a list of multicultural children's literature that passed the evaluative "test," but also information on the process and reasoning behind the project. The result is a listing of resources to aid educators in bringing a more multicultural literary world into their classrooms.

New Horizons for Learning's Resources for Multicultural Education – Bibliography (http://www.newhorizons.org/strategies/multicultural/biblio_multicultural.htm)

This is an annotated bibliography of print resources focused on equity pedagogy. The sources include items from 1978 – 1999, and the listing has a copyright date of 2002.

Ohio Literacy Resource Center - OLCR (http://literacy.kent.edu/Oasis/Resc/Educ/mcres.html)

The Multicultural Resources section of the LINCS provides a limited offering but one with few duplications from other sites. As do many of the multicultural sites from the Midwest, this site also includes many Native American resources. A nice feature is the annotations providing information about each listing.

Oregon Uniting (http://www.oregonuniting.org/)

Oregon Uniting is a grass roots organization that sponsors Dialogues on Race in Oregon. This source provides a model for one community's approach to addressing the issue of diversity.

Oyate: A Native American Book Store site (http://www.kstrom.net/isk/books/oyate.html)

This site offers a link to the resources available at the bookstore as well as online reviews of many of the books.

Parlo: Language. Culture. Life (http://www.parlo.com/)

This site is from a leader in interactive language learning, and though it may not seem "multicultural," it offers a chance to experience other cultures via language. However, some parts of the site are focused on selling its online language courses.

Poynter Online (http://www.poynter.org/subject.asp?id=5)

Focused more on journalists and the issues that face them (and the idea of promoting the seminars it creates for a profit), the site does offer some interesting articles related to diversity, which could be used as discussion starters for educators.

Resources Center to the Iberoamerican Education Organization (http://www.oei.es/credi.htm)

Another good truly other culture offering, this web page has many documents and information about Education in Latin-American countries. However, as with a few others included in this resource guide, this site is entirely in Spanish.

Robert Jensen's Writings on Racial Privilege (http://uts.cc.utexas.edu/~rjensen/freelance/racearticles.htm)

Robert Jensen, a white journalist at the University of Texas, writes and speaks often about the invisible privilege of being White and male. The web site includes a number of articles written by Jensen as well as a link to his home page.

SOFWeb (http://www.sofweb.vic.edu.au/lem/multi/index.htm)

This section of the site maintained by the State of Victoria, Australia, focuses on multicultural education, although it includes links to resources for ESL (English as a Second Language), LMERC (Language and Multicultural Education Resource Center), and LOTE (Languages Other Than English). There is a link for support information related to September 11, 2001, another about information for the United Nations International Day for Eliminating Racial Discrimination, and support material for educators, including guidelines for the Multicultural Policy for Victorian Schools.

Teaching for Change (http://www.teachingforchange.org/)

Formerly the Network of Educators on the Americas (NEA), this site focuses on resources related to multicultural issues as reforming education. There are links to additional resources for educators including lists of videos and books, resources by subject and topic, and "Behind the Headlines," a section of critical articles related to issues in the news.

Teaching Tolerance (http://www.tolerance.org/)

Teaching Tolerance of the Southern Poverty Law Center is a key resource that continues to provide useful teaching tools and continually updates issues in the media. Tests for hidden biases, tools for taking action against intolerance ("Do Something"), and Tolerance Watch are just a few features of this site. Further subdivisions include information for teachers, parents, teens, and children. Educators can find a variety of uses for this site, including research projects, surveys development and school diversity initiatives.

Through Our Parents' Eyes: Tucson's Diverse Community (http://www.library.arizona.edu/parents/062501_welcome.html)

Another offering of the University of Arizona, this site offers insight into the Native community with respect to culture, education, and links to other sites focused on Native culture. One interesting feature is the link to

"Storytellers: Native American Authors Online."

United Nations Educational, Scientific and Cultural Organization – UNESCO (http://www.unesco.org/)

One of the premier features of this site is the opportunity for visitors to access resources in a number of native languages: French, English, Spanish, Russian, Arabic, and Chinese. In addition to legal information and a calendar of international activities and resources, this site provides information about "what's new" in the area of intercultural education, publications, statistics, projects, events, information services, and so forth. "Mirrors," sites offered to enable access of data more quickly, are also available. One mirror is located in the U.S. (through the University of Nebraska) and the other is in Japan.

University of Southern California's (USC) Center for Multilingual Multicultural Research (http://www.usc.edu/dept/education/CMMR/home.html)

As a result of its focus on research, there is a wealth of academic resources related to multicultural education found at this site. In addition to the impressive attention to issues of diversity, this site offers a glimpse at the research being done related to multiculturalism. Among its many key features are the option of frames or no frames (for those with visual learning problems), the annotated list of research activities, and the grid-like site index following it. Included in the site index is a link to a multilingual electronic discussion (listserv) as well as links to full text articles, professional development, and Supreme Court Decisions (since 1893) related to language issues. Perhaps its most impressive feature is the date of its inception, 1983.

As noted in this excerpt from the main page of the web site, "The Center is an organized research unit at the University of Southern California, facilitating the research collaboration, dissemination and professional development activities of faculty, students, and others across School of Education, university and outside organizational lines. Faculty in the Rossier School of Education developed the USC Center for Multilingual, Multicultural Research in the Spring of 1983, as a result of deliberations of the Dean's Task Force for Bilingual Crosscultural Education. The Center provides a base for those interested in multilingual education, English-as-a second language, and foreign language instruction, multicultural education and related areas; and the opportunity to come together for research and program collaboration. There are four principal activities the Center strives for: (1) research; (2) publications; (3) training; and (4) public service" (USC, 2001).

University of Southern California's Center for Multilingual Multicultural Research – Bilingual/ESL/Multicultural Education Resources (http://www-rcf.usc.edu/~cmmr/BEResources.html)

Another site offered by USC, this one focuses more on resources for educators. An interesting note is the disclaimer at the beginning of the web page noting that the center does not necessarily endorse the material presented and a note inviting submission of sites for inclusion.

References

Bruno, F. A. (2000). Bridges on the I-way: Multicultural resources online – multicultural portals. *Multicultural Review*, *9*, 52-54, 59.

Gorski, P. (2000). Bridges on the I-way: Multicultural resources online – multicultural education and mathematics on the Internet. *Multicultural Review*, *9*, 68-70.

Denise C. Camin is an associate professor of English at DeVry University, Tinsley Park Campus, 18624 West Creek Drive, Tinsley Park, IL, 60477.

Made in the USA
Charleston, SC
17 May 2012